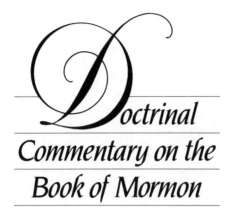

Doctrinal
Commentary on the
Book of Mormon

Volume III—Alma through Helaman

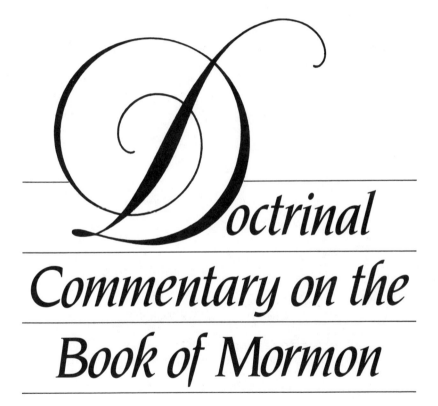

octrinal
Commentary on the
Book of Mormon

Joseph Fielding McConkie
Robert L. Millet

BOOKCRAFT
Salt Lake City, Utah

Library of Congress Catalog Card Number: 87–71701
ISBN 0–88494–807–2

5th Printing, 1996

Printed in the United States of America

Contents

Preface

The Book of Mormon is a pearl of great price. It contains a true story, the saga of a message, and is historically sound and accurate. It is a repository of doctrine, a sacred collection of some of the greatest theology ever assembled into one volume; literally a standard work, a divinely given measure against which we assess truth and error. More than that, it is a pattern for living, an invitation to come unto Christ and a guide for so doing.

Hence it is not enough for one to read the Book of Mormon, though that is a necessary beginning. It is not enough to study and teach from its saving doctrines, though for all Latter-day Saints to do such would lift immeasurably the level of gospel scholarship in the Church. Rather, we must come to *live* the Book of Mormon, to heed the counsel and direction of its writers and compiler, to discover and abide by its precepts. In doing this we draw near to God. The Book of Mormon, then, is not just another treatise on religion; it *is* religion. It is the religion of Jesus Christ, who is its author.

As in the first two volumes in this series, we here confine our commentary to doctrine; we focus almost exclusively upon the principles of the gospel, those precepts which lead men and women to Christ. We depart somewhat from the established format when we discuss Alma 43–62, the chapters on Nephite-Lamanite wars, where a verse-by-verse commentary does not seem especially appropriate or needed. In that section we do not reproduce the Book of Mormon text, but we present a brief essay in which are set forth some of the most salient doctrines and gospel principles related to the chapters concerned.

As before, we recommend that when using the book the reader have in hand the modern editions of the LDS scriptures, so that he or she may take advantage of their footnotes, the Topical Guide, and the other supplementary material they provide.

Though for what follows we as the authors are indebted to many people, we alone are responsible for the commentary; the work is a private endeavor and is not in any way an official publication of either The Church of Jesus Christ of Latter-day Saints or of Brigham Young University. We do, however, sincerely believe the contents of this volume to be true, and we hope that by using it readers will be strengthened in their faith and built up in their commitment to Christ and his restored Church and kingdom.

Acknowledgments

As with the first two volumes of this work, we are appreciative of the encouragement and support of Cory Maxwell, editorial manager of Bookcraft. His patience and his willingness to work around our own complicated schedules has been a key ingredient in bringing this volume to fruition. We are particularly grateful for the wisdom and insight of George Bickerstaff—for his blending his keen editorial skills with a generous portion of Christianity. We thank also Lori Soza, a conscientious and capable secretary, who has worked steadily to prepare the manuscript for publication.

Our wives and children continue to be supportive of our desires to complete what we feel to be an important project. We are indebted to them everlastingly.

Abbreviations

The following abbreviations have been used to simplify references in the text of this work. Publication details on each source cited are listed in the Bibliography.

CR	Conference Report
Commentary	Joseph Fielding McConkie and Robert L. Millet, *Doctrinal Commentary on the Book of Mormon*, 4 vols.
HC	Joseph Smith, *History of The Church of Jesus Christ of Latter-day Saints*, 7 vols.
Hymns	*Hymns of The Church of Jesus Christ of Latter-day Saints*
JD	*Journal of Discourses*, 26 vols.
JST	Joseph Smith Translation of the Bible
Millennial Messiah	Bruce R. McConkie, *The Millennial Messiah*
Mortal Messiah	Bruce R. McConkie, *The Mortal Messiah*, 4 vols.
New Witness	Bruce R. McConkie, *A New Witness for the Articles of Faith*
Promised Messiah	Bruce R. McConkie, *The Promised Messiah*
Teachings	Joseph Smith, *Teachings of the Prophet Joseph Smith*

The Book of

Alma

In the book of Alma we encounter some of the most profound of all the messages of the Nephite-Jaredite record. We watch and listen as a converted Alma and the sons of Mosiah preach the gospel with power and persuasion to both the Nephites and the Lamanites. We reflect and ponder upon the unparalleled witness of Christ and the Atonement set forth by these American Apostles. We read with deep appreciation as Alma and his missionary associates deliver the doctrine of Christ to the apostate Zoramites, thereby leaving behind priceless doctrinal gems of everlasting worth. We sorrow with Alma as he discourses on the doctrines of salvation to an errant son, but we glory in the fact that the declaration of doctrine in the spirit of pure testimony is our surest check on waywardness and immorality. We witness the hand of God in leading his people into defensive war, and we reflect soberly upon the eternal verity that only those who trust in and rely upon the God of the land, Jesus Christ, enjoy his approbation and his favor.

The Evil Ends of Priestcraft

Alma 1:1–15

1. Now it came to pass that in the first year of the reign of the judges over the people of Nephi, from this time forward, king Mosiah having gone the way of all the earth, having warred a good warfare, walking uprightly before God, leaving none to reign in his stead; nevertheless he had established laws, and they were acknowledged by the people; therefore they were obliged to abide by the laws which he had made.

2. And it came to pass that in the first year of the reign of Alma in the judgment-seat, there was a man brought before him to be judged, a man who was large, and was noted for his much strength.

3. And he had gone about among the people, preaching to them that which he termed to be the word of God, bearing down against the church; declaring unto the people that every priest and teacher ought to become popular; and they ought not to labor with their hands, but that they ought to be supported by the people.

4. And he also testified unto the people that all mankind should be saved at the last day, and that they need not fear nor tremble, but that they might lift up their heads and rejoice; for the Lord had created all men, and had also redeemed all men; and, in the end, all men should have eternal life.

5. And it came to pass that he did teach these things so much that many did believe on his words, even so many that they began to support him and give him money.

6. And he began to be lifted up in the pride of his heart, and to wear very costly apparel, yea, and even began to establish a church after the manner of his preaching.

7. And it came to pass as he was going, to preach to those who believed on his word, he met a man who belonged to the church of God, yea, even one of their teachers; and he began to contend with him sharply, that he might lead away the people of the church; but the man withstood him, admonishing him with the words of God.

8. Now the name of the man was Gideon; and it was he who was an instrument in the hands of God in delivering the people of Limhi out of bondage.

9. Now, because Gideon withstood him with the words of God he was wroth with Gideon, and drew his sword and began to smite him. Now Gideon being stricken with many years, therefore he was not able to withstand his blows, therefore he was slain by the sword.

10. And the man who slew him was taken by the people of the church, and was brought before Alma, to be judged according to the crimes which he had committed.

11. And it came to pass that he stood before Alma and pleaded for himself with much boldness.

12. But Alma said unto him: Behold, this is the first time that priestcraft has been introduced among this people. And behold, thou art not only guilty of priestcraft, but hast endeavored to enforce it by the sword; and were priestcraft to be enforced among this people it would prove their entire destruction.

13. And thou hast shed the blood of a righteous man, yea, a man who has done much good among this people; and were we to spare thee his blood would come upon us for vengeance.

14. Therefore thou art condemned to die, according to the law which has been given us by Mosiah, our last king; and it has been acknowledged by this people; therefore this people must abide by the law.

15. And it came to pass that they took him; and his name was Nehor; and they carried him upon the top of the hill Manti, and there he was caused, or rather did acknowledge, between the heavens and the earth, that what he had taught to the people was contrary to the word of God; and there he suffered an ignominious death.

1. Having warred a good warfare] King Mosiah had fought against wickedness and battled Beelzebub all his days. He had been true and faithful to his trust to lead his people in paths of truth and righteousness. He had passed the tests of mortality. His salvation was secure. He was like his colleague on another continent, Paul the Apostle, who said just prior to his death: "I have fought a good fight, I have finished my course, I have kept the faith: henceforth there is laid up for me a crown of righteousness, which the Lord, the righteous judge, shall give me at that day: and not to me only, but unto all them also that love his appearing" (2 Timothy 4:7–8).

1. He had established laws, and they were acknowledged by the people] See Mosiah 29:25.

3. That which he termed to be the word of God] Indeed, what he spoke was not the word of God, but it was what he would have wished the word of God to be. The perverse and the malicious frequently devise their own form of divinity, conjure up their own words of truth, and create their own set of values. They then blaspheme against divine order by stating that their views are heaven-sent and have God's approbation.

3. Bearing down against the church] How often the true Church is the object of ridicule and the target of the fiery darts of the adversary! The Church of Jesus Christ is the custodian of the gospel of Jesus Christ and thus the only place where the ordinances of salvation may be found. When the kingdom of God is established on earth; when the Church has been restored; when the necessary priesthoods and keys and authorities have been bestowed—when these conditions are obtained, mankind will come unto Christ (and thus unto salvation) through the statutes and ordinances of the Church or they will not enjoy the blessings of heaven. Though the Church is but the means to an end (Christ is the end), a person deceives himself who supposes that he can enjoy the benefits and privileges of the gospel in his life without being active and involved in the living Church.

3. Every priest and teacher ought to become popular] Here is priestcraft at its best. Nephi had declared centuries earlier: "Priestcrafts are that men preach and set themselves up for a light unto the world, that they may get gain and praise of the world; but they seek not the welfare of Zion" (2 Nephi 26:29). One possessed of the spirit of priestcraft is eager to gain attention, eager to receive the applause of the crowd, eager for recognition and reward. He or she seeks a following, and does so for all the wrong reasons. He or she preaches—in some cases even preaches the truth—for money or for fame, not for the establishment of Zion.

Such persons are motivated by mammon, driven by desire, impelled by impulse, and prompted by the quest for prominence.

3. They ought not to labor with their hands] See Mosiah 2:14; 27:4–5.

4. Nehor's doctrine would be very popular among many of our own day. He obviously did not believe in a fall, from which mankind required redemption. He advocated some form of humanism, the pernicious belief that men and women have but to fulfill their genetic blueprint in order to be happy, for they are by nature good and noble, having no need for divine assistance. As we will see later in the story, in the main the people of Ammonihah, a perverse lot given over to the profession of Nehor, "repented not of their sins; . . . for they were of the profession of Nehor, and did not believe in the repentance of their sins" (Alma 15:15). Nehor taught the people that they should "lift up their heads," that is, lift up their heads in their wickedness (compare Alma 30:18); he surely preached against guilt and shame and judgment. Like his master, Lucifer, his program propounded the pernicious but popular belief that all mankind would eventually be saved, without righteousness, without faith, without atonement and repentance (see Moses 4:1–4). His doctrine had been foreseen by ancient Nephite prophets. Nephi had warned: "And there shall also be many which shall say: Eat, drink, and be merry; nevertheless, fear God—he will justify in committing a little sin; yea, lie a little, take the advantage of one because of his words, dig a pit for thy neighbor; there is no harm in this; and do all these things, for tomorrow we die; and if it so be that we are guilty, God will beat us with a few stripes, and at last we shall be saved in the kingdom of God" (2 Nephi 28:8).

5. Many did believe on his words] Why would people believe him? How could he seduce so many? Perhaps it was because his system of salvation was so easy, his promise of eternal reward so attractive, his demands so few. He denied prophecy and revelation (see Alma 21:4, 8) and thus found no place for absolute values or absolute truth. Like his counterpart Korihor, his doctrine was "pleasing unto the carnal mind" (Alma 30:53).

6. To wear very costly apparel] Here was an obvious sign of his apostasy, an evidence that his heart was impure. "Costly apparel" is symbolic of submission to the world's standards, an acquiescence to the allurements of appearance.

6. To establish a church after the manner of his preaching] In the true Church, doctrines and beliefs and practices are based not upon the whims and ways of the congregants, or even of its leaders, but rather upon prophecy and revelation, upon truth, upon things as they were and are and are to come (see D&C

93:24). False churches are built upon false principles and false practices. They are more a reflection of ephemeral values and relativistic ritual than of reality.

7–9. Gideon, a noble and faithful servant of God and of the people (see Mosiah 20:17–22; 22:3–9), now weighed down with years, sought to withstand Nehor with the power of the word. And nothing is more abhorrent to the immoral and the perverse than the truth; pure, diamond truth. It cuts the wicked to the core of their beings, and thus they fight it with vicious and often irrational anger (see 1 Nephi 16:1–2; 2 Nephi 9:40; 33:5). Unable to stand up and defend his falsehoods in the face of truth spoken with power and conviction, Nehor sought to silence his accuser.

12. The first time that priestcraft has been introduced] Though Nephi had defined priestcraft and warned of its consequences more than four centuries earlier (see 2 Nephi 26:29), it appears that Nehor was the first in the Nephite society to put it into practice. And in his case he sought to enforce it through a cruel murder.

12. It would prove their entire destruction] A civilization that wastes its strength in the pursuit of either wealth or glory will not stand. A nation that fosters or encourages selfishness, that allows greed and lust to go unchecked, will sink under its own weight. Babylon will fall because its citizenry will come in time to shun and hate and destroy all that oppose them. Zion will arise and shine forth as an ensign to the nations because its municipals seek the interest of their neighbors and do all things with an eye single to the glory of God (D&C 82:19). The only true antidote to priestcraft is charity (see 2 Nephi 26:30–31).

14–15. Nehor had taken a man's life, and according to the laws of God and man his own life was required (see Alma 1:18; 30:10; JST, Genesis 9:12–13; D&C 42:19).

Priestcraft and Persecution Spread

Alma 1:16–24

16. Nevertheless, this did not put an end to the spreading of priestcraft through the land; for there were many who loved the vain things of the world, and they went forth preaching false doctrines; and this they did for the sake of riches and honor.

17. Nevertheless, they durst not lie, if it were known, for fear of the law, for liars were punished; therefore they pretended to preach according to their belief; and now the law could have no power on

any man for his belief.

18. And they durst not steal, for fear of the law, for such were punished; neither durst they rob, nor murder, for he that murdered was punished unto death.

19. But it came to pass that whosoever did not belong to the church of God began to persecute those that did belong to the church of God, and had taken upon them the name of Christ.

20. Yea, they did persecute them, and afflict them with all manner of words, and this because of their humility; because they were not proud in their own eyes, and because they did impart the word of God, one with another, without money and without price.

21. Now there was a strict law among the people of the church, that there should not any man,

belonging to the church, arise and persecute those that did not belong to the church, and that there should be no persecution among themselves.

22. Nevertheless, there were many among them who began to be proud, and began to contend warmly with their adversaries, even unto blows; yea, they would smite one another with their fists.

23. Now this was in the second year of the reign of Alma, and it was a cause of much affliction to the church; yea, it was the cause of much trial with the church.

24. For the hearts of many were hardened, and their names were blotted out, that they were remembered no more among the people of God. And also many withdrew themselves from among them.

16. Many who loved the vain things of the world] Vain things are shallow, hollow, empty, and worthless. They offer glitter and sparkle and pizzazz, but can promise no lasting reward. So many people of this world crave popularity, praise, and public acclaim; such persons never know the security and sacred satisfaction which come from divine approval, nor, ironically, can they appease the inner hunger for celestial sociality, the need for caring friends and loved ones. So many people of this world lust after money and exhaust their strength in their quest for this world's goods; such persons never know the quiet prosperity of the Spirit, the wealth of wisdom that comes from seeking first the kingdom of God, or the riches of eternity that are available to the single-minded disciple (see D&C 6:7; 38:39).

16. Preaching false doctrines . . . for the sake of riches and honor] Occasionally false doctrine is disseminated by the "hopelessly ignorant," those who make but feeble effort to discover and learn the truth. It is also presented and perpetuated by "the proud and self-vaunting ones," those who "read by the lamp of their own conceit." (Joseph F. Smith, *Gospel Doctrine*, p. 373.) And, of course, falsehood is made available by those more interested in filling their coffers than filling a need, those obsessed more with graft than with goodness.

17. Liars were punished] It would be interesting to know exactly how liars were handled among the Nephites. We would suppose that unrepentant liars who held membership in the Church were dealt with in harmony with the principle found in modern revelation. "Thou shalt not lie," the Lord commanded in 1831; "he that lieth and will not repent shall be cast out," that is, cut off from the Church (D&C 42:21). In the end, of course, liars will be thrust down to hell in the postmortal spirit world and will inherit a telestial kingdom in eternity (see 2 Nephi 9:34; D&C 63:17–18; 76:103–6).

17. The law could have no power on any man for his belief] Although one could believe as one pleased, it appears that when one's false teachings were translated into actions that violated the laws of society, such a person was liable to prosecution. See the episode with Korihor in Alma 30:18–21.

19–20. As the night follows the day, so also does ridicule and persecution follow the true Church. Darkness cannot tolerate light, and the prince of darkness certainly has no regard for those who have taken upon themselves the name of the Lord of Light. It is a bitter irony that those who choose to traverse the broad roads of worldliness cannot rest while some others seek to navigate the strait and narrow course to eternal life. Nothing brings greater discomfort to the perverse than to be in the presence of the pure. Nothing alarms and aggravates the haughty and the pompous more than the humble and the contrite. And surely nothing incenses the practitioner of priestcraft more than witnessing the selfless service of one whose eye is single to the glory of God.

21. The Saints of the Most High are called to declare the glad tidings of the gospel. They are not called to malign or attack the faith and religious persuasions of others. Truth stands on its own and does not require the cheap crutch of criticism of alternate systems of belief. In the words of Elder Marvin J. Ashton: "We have no time for contention. We only have time to be about our Father's business." (CR, April 1978, p. 9.) Further, members of the Church of Christ are counseled, "Strengthen your brethren in all your conversation, in all your prayers, in all your exhortations, and in all your doings" (D&C 108:7).

22–24. It is the spirit of pride that motivates some of the Saints to contend warmly with nonmembers, to argue and debate the meaning of scriptures, to fight and quarrel with those of our Father's children who might choose not to affiliate with the true Church. Such a spirit is not of God but is indeed of the devil, who stirs up people to contend one with another (see 3 Nephi 11:28–30). Even though our message to the world is true; even though what we declare will sanctify and save all who accept and follow it; even though the Lord himself is in this work—notwithstanding all this, the Spirit cannot and will not abide with those who seek by argument or heated discussion to establish the truth of spiritual matters. We teach and we testify. We bear witness. We speak with all the sobriety and sincerity we can muster. We plead with our listeners to give heed to our words, to ponder them, and to petition the heavens to ascertain the truth, but we do not contend. Those Church members who do not take the proper course in this regard—who argue endlessly and quarrel tirelessly—these lose the Spirit of God and become an easy prey to the arch-deceiver. Before they are aware, they lose their souls.

The Faithful Begin to Prosper

Alma 1:25–33

25. Now this was a great trial to those that did stand fast in the faith; nevertheless, they were steadfast and immovable in keeping the commandments of God, and they bore with patience the persecution which was heaped upon them.

26. And when the priests left their labor to impart the word of God unto the people, the people also left their labors to hear the word of God. And when the priest had imparted unto them the word of God they all returned again diligently unto their labors; and the priest, not esteeming himself above his hearers, for the preacher was no better than the hearer, neither was the teacher any better than the learner; and thus they were all equal, and they did all labor, every man according to his strength.

27. And they did impart of their substance, every man according to that which he had, to the poor, and the needy, and the sick, and the afflicted; and they did not wear costly apparel, yet they were neat and comely.

28. And thus they did establish the affairs of the church; and thus they began to have continual peace again, notwithstanding all their persecutions.

29. And now, because of the steadiness of the church they began to be exceedingly rich, having abundance of all things whatsoever they stood in need— an abundance of flocks and herds, and fatlings of every kind, and also abundance of grain, and of gold, and of silver, and of precious things, and abundance of silk and fine-twined linen, and all manner of good homely cloth.

30. And thus, in their prosperous circumstances, they did not send away any who were naked, or that were hungry, or that were athirst, or that were sick, or that had not been nourished; and they did not set their hearts upon riches; therefore they were liberal to all, both old and young, both bond and free, both male and female, whether out of the church or in the church, having no respect to persons as to those who stood in need.

31. And thus they did prosper and become far more wealthy than those who did not belong to their church.

32. For those who did not belong to their church did indulge themselves in sorceries, and in idolatry or idleness, and in babblings, and in envyings and strife; wearing costly apparel; being lifted up in the pride of their own eyes; persecuting, lying, thieving, robbing, committing whoredoms, and murdering, and all manner of wickedness; nevertheless, the law was put in force upon all those who did transgress it, inasmuch as it was possible.

33. And it came to pass that by thus exercising the law upon them, every man suffering according to that which he had done, they became more still, and durst not commit any wickedness if it were known; therefore, there was much peace among the people of Nephi until the fifth year of the reign of the judges.

25. A great trial to those that did stand fast in the faith] It is not easy to stand by and watch friends and loved ones, former members of the household of faith, lose the Spirit and eventually forsake the faith. It is painful to observe people as they spiritually self-destruct, but after all efforts to plead and persuade have failed we must allow for individual agency. And we must bear with patience the persecutions and taunts of others.

25. They were steadfast and immovable] Steadfastness is a sign of spiritual maturity, an evidence that one is on the even course that leads to salvation. "To be immovable in righteousness is to be consistent when it comes to matters of values and faith and courage. To be immovable is to have an allegiance to principles that is independent of circumstance and situation. It is to be firm in one's commitment to the truth, steady in one's loyalty to eternal verities." (*Commentary* 2:180.)

26. The people also left their labors to hear the word of God] Edification is a form of spiritual education that is perfected as both speaker and hearer approach the class or sermon with joint preparation. When the speaker seeks the influence of the Spirit and delivers his or her message by that power, and at the same time the listener seeks the Spirit and receives the message by that same sacred influence, both are edified and rejoice together (see D&C 50:13–22).

26. The priest, not esteeming himself above his hearers] In the Lord's Church the members are a congregation of equals; there are no degrees, no academic titles, no worldly attainments that separate members of the group. The gospel has been restored in our day, for example, that every man and woman may speak in the name of God the Lord, even the Savior of the world (see D&C 1:20). The bishop perhaps is a plumber, while his clerk is the vice president of a large corporation. The stake president is a farmer, while his high council is composed of lawyers and physicians and professors.

27. And they did impart of their substance] See Jacob 2:17–19. Oneness in spirit leads eventually to oneness in social relations, oneness in regard to this world's goods and resources. As the people of God labor to acquire the gifts and callings of God, they come to know and experience the fruit of the Spirit (see Galatians 5:22). They come to truly love their neighbors as themselves. The Savior instructed the Latter-day Saints: "And now, verily, verily, I say unto thee, put your trust in that Spirit which leadeth to do good—yea, to do justly, to walk humbly, to judge righteously; and this is my Spirit" (D&C 11:12).

27. They did not wear costly apparel] One of the tell-tale signs of creeping apostasy among the Nephites—and, by extension, that of any civilization—is their obsession with costly apparel. It is noteworthy that the text seldom mentions the beauty or appearance of the clothing, only that it costs much. When form has replaced function to such a degree that a people place a premium upon those things that are the most expensive, then their appreciation for that which matters most is fading rapidly. On the other hand, when a people like the Nephites (at this period in their history) choose to be pleasant in appearance, to be "neat and comely"—not being obsessed with fleeting fashions and fads—then they have established proper priorities and will enjoy the approbation of heaven. "And again, thou shalt not be proud in thy heart," the Lord declared; "let all thy garments be plain, and their beauty the beauty of the work of thine own hands" (D&C 42:40).

28. One of the great lessons in the Book of Mormon is that one can be righteous in the face of gross wickedness. Thus one can stand in holy places and be not moved, can be at peace in a world of turmoil.

29–31. One of the ways in which the Almighty prospers his people is through blessing them with an abundance of this world's goods, with flocks and herds and land and fruits of the field. But this is only one way. The Saints need not be confused or disappointed on this matter. When a people pay their tithing with faithfulness, God may choose to prosper them with money or property, but he may instead open the windows of heaven and pour down revelation, knowledge from on high (see Malachi 3:10). In the days of Nephi and Lehi, sons of Helaman, the Lord prospered the people of his fold through Church growth: "And it came to pass that in this same year there was exceedingly great prosperity in the church, insomuch that there were thousands who did join themselves unto the church and were baptized unto repentance. And so great was the prosperity of the church, and so many the blessings which were poured out upon the people, that even the high priests and the teachers were themselves astonished beyond measure." (Helaman 3:24–25.) The perennial promise in the Book of Mormon is that if the people keep the commandments of God they shall prosper in the land; if they do not keep the commandments, they shall be cut off from his presence (see 1 Nephi 2:20; 2 Nephi 1:20; Alma 36:30; 37:13). The latter expression, the warning, may well define more than any other statement what the Lord means in regard to prosperity: we are prospered when we enjoy his Spirit and feel his presence.

30. They did not send away any] See Mosiah 2:17; 4:16–18; Matthew 25:40.

30. Whether out of the church or in the church] We are human beings, Christians, as well as Latter-day Saints. Our Heavenly Father loves his sons and daughters throughout the earth, no matter what are their religious persuasions. And so must we. Truly there are limits to what we can do, and certainly all things must be done in wisdom and order (see Mosiah 4:27). "And yet, given that there are millions of hungry and naked and destitute souls in the world, how are disciples [of Christ] to live with themselves? How are we to handle the fact that there is only so much we can do, only so many we can assist and still manage to care for our own? . . . If every family contributed regularly to every needy cause, there would be insufficient money for the family to live. If every Christian man or woman gave themselves consistently to every project designed to alleviate suffering, there would be no time to earn a living or care for their own. True disciples pray for discernment and for discretion. They seek to be as generous and giving as is appropriate and practical. . . . Even when we are not in a position to contribute dramatically to the alleviation of hunger in Africa or India, for example, there is still something we can do, something vital for those who aspire to discipleship. We can avoid as we would a plague the tendency to be indifferent, to ignore the problem because it is not in our own backyards. Further, we can teach our families or friends by precept and by example to use wisely the food and other resources we have been blessed to have. Even if we just become aware of suffering and pain, our heightened sensitivity helps us deal more tenderly, more charitably, with sufferers within our own limited reach. At least those are starting points." (Robert L. Millet, *An Eye Single to the Glory of God*, pp. 64–65.)

32. Nephi had taught some five hundred years earlier: "Behold, the Lord esteemeth all flesh in one; [but] he that is righteous is favored of God. . . . And he loveth those who will have him to be their God." (1 Nephi 17:35, 40.) Those who revel in the works of the flesh may profit in regard to the items of exchange in this telestial tenement, but their prosperity is temporary and their joy but for a season (see 3 Nephi 27:11).

Amlici Perpetuates the Profession of Nehor

Alma 2:1–38

1. And it came to pass in the commencement of the fifth year of their reign there began to be a contention among the people; for a certain man, being called Amlici, he being a very cunning man, yea, a wise man as to the wisdom of the world, he being after the order of the man that slew Gideon by the sword, who was executed according to the law—

2. Now this Amlici had, by his cunning, drawn away much people after him; even so much that they began to be very powerful; and they began to endeavor to establish Amlici to be a king over the people.

3. Now this was alarming to the people of the church, and also to all those who had not been drawn away after the persuasions of Amlici; for they knew that according to their law that such things must be established by the voice of the people.

4. Therefore, if it were possible that Amlici should gain the voice of the people, he, being a wicked man, would deprive them of their rights and privileges of the church; for it was his intent to destroy the church of God.

5. And it came to pass that the people assembled themselves together throughout all the land, every man according to his mind, whether it were for or against Amlici, in separate bodies, having

much dispute and wonderful contentions one with another.

6. And thus they did assemble themselves together to cast in their voices concerning the matter; and they were laid before the judges.

7. And it came to pass that the voice of the people came against Amlici, that he was not made king over the people.

8. Now this did cause much joy in the hearts of those who were against him; but Amlici did stir up those who were in his favor to anger against those who were not in his favor.

9. And it came to pass that they gathered themselves together, and did consecrate Amlici to be their king.

10. Now when Amlici was made king over them he commanded them that they should take up arms against their brethren; and this he did that he might subject them to him.

11. Now the people of Amlici were distinguished by the name of Amlici, being called Amlicites; and the remainder were called Nephites, or the people of God.

12. Therefore the people of the Nephites were aware of the intent of the Amlicites, and therefore they did prepare to meet them; yea, they did arm themselves with swords, and with cimeters, and with bows, and with arrows, and

with stones, and with slings, and with all manner of weapons of war, of every kind.

13. And thus they were prepared to meet the Amlicites at the time of their coming. And there were appointed captains, and higher captains, and chief captains, according to their numbers.

14. And it came to pass that Amlici did arm his men with all manner of weapons of war of every kind; and he also appointed rulers and leaders over his people, to lead them to war against their brethren.

15. And it came to pass that the Amlicites came upon the hill Amnihu, which was east of the river Sidon, which ran by the land of Zarahemla, and there they began to make war with the Nephites.

16. Now Alma, being the chief judge and the governor of the people of Nephi, therefore he went up with his people, yea, with his captains, and chief captains, yea, at the head of his armies, against the Amlicites to battle.

17. And they began to slay the Amlicites upon the hill east of Sidon. And the Amlicites did contend with the Nephites with great strength, insomuch that many of the Nephites did fall before the Amlicites.

18. Nevertheless the Lord did strengthen the hand of the Nephites, that they slew the Amlicites with great slaughter, that they began to flee before them.

19. And it came to pass that the Nephites did pursue the Amlicites all that day, and did slay them with much slaughter, insomuch that there were slain of the Amlicites twelve thousand five hundred thirty and two souls; and

there were slain of the Nephites six thousand five hundred sixty and two souls.

20. And it came to pass that when Alma could pursue the Amlicites no longer he caused that his people should pitch their tents in the valley of Gideon, the valley being called after that Gideon who was slain by the hand of Nehor with the sword; and in this valley the Nephites did pitch their tents for the night.

21. And Alma sent spies to follow the remnant of the Amlicites, that he might know of their plans and their plots, whereby he might guard himself against them, that he might preserve his people from being destroyed.

22. Now those whom he had sent out to watch the camp of the Amlicites were called Zeram, and Amnor, and Manti, and Limher; these were they who went out with their men to watch the camp of the Amlicites.

23. And it came to pass that on the morrow they returned into the camp of the Nephites in great haste, being greatly astonished, and struck with much fear, saying:

24. Behold, we followed the camp of the Amlicites, and to our great astonishment, in the land of Minon, above the land of Zarahemla, in the course of the land of Nephi, we saw a numerous host of the Lamanites; and behold, the Amlicites have joined them;

25. And they are upon our brethren in that land; and they are fleeing before them with their flocks, and their wives, and their children, towards our city; and except we make haste they obtain possession of our city, and our fathers, and our wives, and our children be slain.

26. And it came to pass that the people of Nephi took their tents, and departed out of the valley of Gideon towards their city, which was the city of Zarahemla.

27. And behold, as they were crossing the river Sidon, the Lamanites and the Amlicites, being as numerous almost, as it were, as the sands of the sea, came upon them to destroy them.

28. Nevertheless, the Nephites being strengthened by the hand of the Lord, having prayed mightily to him that he would deliver them out of the hands of their enemies, therefore the Lord did hear their cries, and did strengthen them, and the Lamanites and the Amlicites did fall before them.

29. And it came to pass that Alma fought with Amlici with the sword, face to face; and they did contend mightily, one with another.

30. And it came to pass that Alma, being a man of God, being exercised with much faith, cried, saying: O Lord, have mercy and spare my life, that I may be an instrument in thy hands to save and preserve this people.

31. Now when Alma had said these words he contended again with Amlici; and he was strengthened, insomuch that he slew Amlici with the sword.

32. And he also contended with the king of the Lamanites; but the king of the Lamanites fled back from before Alma and sent his guards to contend with Alma.

33. But Alma, with his guards, contended with the guards of the king of the Lamanites until he slew and drove them back.

34. And thus he cleared the ground, or rather the bank, which was on the west of the river Sidon, throwing the bodies of the Lamanites who had been slain into the waters of Sidon, that thereby his people might have room to cross and contend with the Lamanites and the Amlicites on the west side of the river Sidon.

35. And it came to pass that when they had all crossed the river Sidon that the Lamanites and the Amlicites began to flee before them, notwithstanding they were so numerous that they could not be numbered.

36. And they fled before the Nephites towards the wilderness which was west and north, away beyond the borders of the land; and the Nephites did pursue them with their might, and did slay them.

37. Yea, they were met on every hand, and slain and driven, until they were scattered on the west, and on the north, until they had reached the wilderness, which was called Hermounts; and it was that part of the wilderness which was infested by wild and ravenous beasts.

38. And it came to pass that many died in the wilderness of their wounds, and were devoured by those beasts and also the vultures of the air; and their bones have been found, and have been heaped up on the earth.

1–38. The spirit of Nehor lives on. Priestcraft and deceit and murder continue to raise their ugly heads because Amlici, "a very cunning man, yea, a wise man as to the wisdom of the world," applies his craft and thereby gains the support of the wayward or the undiscerning. He defies the canons of both church and state:

he seeks to destroy the church of God and to achieve monarchial power contrary to the voice of the people and the prescribed system of judges. Amlici arms his followers, leads them against the Nephites, and as is consistently the case with dissidents from the true order of worship among the Nephites, joins hands with the Lamanites.

30. O Lord, have mercy and spare my life] These are not the soul cries of one terrified by the possibility of imminent death. Rather, they are the petition of a righteous man, the pleading of one who is on speaking terms with God. Alma's confidence is in his Lord. His life is in order and his prayer is a prayer of faith. His desires are neither selfish nor out of harmony with the divine will.

Men Bring Curses upon Themselves

Alma 3:1–27

1. And it came to pass that the Nephites who were not slain by the weapons of war, after having buried those who had been slain—now the number of the slain were not numbered, because of the greatness of their number—after they had finished burying their dead they all returned to their lands, and to their houses, and their wives, and their children.

2. Now many women and children had been slain with the sword, and also many of their flocks and their herds; and also many of their fields of grain were destroyed, for they were trodden down by the hosts of men.

3. And now as many of the Lamanites and the Amlicites who had been slain upon the bank of the river Sidon were cast into the waters of Sidon; and behold their bones are in the depths of the sea, and they are many.

4. And the Amlicites were distinguished from the Nephites, for they had marked themselves with red in their foreheads after the manner of the Lamanites; never-theless they had not shorn their heads like unto the Lamanites.

5. Now the heads of the Lamanites were shorn; and they were naked, save it were skin which was girded about their loins, and also their armor, which was girded about them, and their bows, and their arrows, and their stones, and their slings, and so forth.

6. And the skins of the Lamanites were dark, according to the mark which was set upon their fathers, which was a curse upon them because of their transgression and their rebellion against their brethren, who consisted of Nephi, Jacob, and Joseph, and Sam, who were just and holy men.

7. And their brethren sought to destroy them, therefore they were cursed; and the Lord God set a mark upon them, yea, upon Laman and Lemuel, and also the sons of Ishmael, and Ishmaelitish women.

8. And this was done that their seed might be distinguished from

the seed of their brethren, that thereby the Lord God might preserve his people, that they might not mix and believe in incorrect traditions which would prove their destruction.

9. And it came to pass that whosoever did mingle his seed with that of the Lamanites did bring the same curse upon his seed.

10. Therefore, whosoever suffered himself to be led away by the Lamanites was called under that head, and there was a mark set upon him.

11. And it came to pass that whosoever would not believe in the tradition of the Lamanites, but believed those records which were brought out of the land of Jerusalem, and also in the tradition of their fathers, which were correct, who believed in the commandments of God and kept them, were called the Nephites, or the people of Nephi, from that time forth—

12. And it is they who have kept the records which are true of their people, and also of the people of the Lamanites.

13. Now we will return again to the Amlicites, for they also had a mark set upon them; yea, they set the mark upon themselves, yea, even a mark of red upon their foreheads.

14. Thus the word of God is fulfilled, for these are the words which he said to Nephi: Behold, the Lamanites have I cursed, and I will set a mark on them that they and their seed may be separated from thee and thy seed, from this time henceforth and forever, except they repent of their wickedness and turn to me that I may have mercy upon them.

15. And again: I will set a mark upon him that mingleth his seed with thy brethren, that they may be cursed also.

16. And again: I will set a mark upon him that fighteth against thee and thy seed.

17. And again, I say he that departeth from thee shall no more be called thy seed; and I will bless thee, and whomsoever shall be called thy seed, henceforth and forever; and these were the promises of the Lord unto Nephi and to his seed.

18. Now the Amlicites knew not that they were fulfilling the words of God when they began to mark themselves in their foreheads; nevertheless they had come out in open rebellion against God; therefore it was expedient that the curse should fall upon them.

19. Now I would that ye should see that they brought upon themselves the curse; and even so doth every man that is cursed bring upon himself his own condemnation.

20. Now it came to pass that not many days after the battle which was fought in the land of Zarahemla, by the Lamanites and the Amlicites, that there was another army of the Lamanites came in upon the people of Nephi, in the same place where the first army met the Amlicites.

21. And it came to pass that there was an army sent to drive them out of their land.

22. Now Alma himself being afflicted with a wound did not go up to battle at this time against the Lamanites;

23. But he sent up a numerous army against them; and they went up and slew many of the Lamanites, and drove the remainder of them out of the borders of their land.

24. And then they returned again and began to establish peace in the land, being troubled no more for a time with their enemies.

25. Now all these things were done, yea, all these wars and contentions were commenced and ended in the fifth year of the reign of the judges.

26. And in one year were thousands and tens of thousands of souls sent to the eternal world, that they might reap their rewards according to their works, whether they were good or whether they were bad, to reap eternal happiness or eternal misery, according to the spirit which they listed to obey, whether it be a good spirit or a bad one.

27. For every man receiveth wages of him whom he listeth to obey, and this according to the words of the spirit of prophecy; therefore let it be according to the truth. And thus endeth the fifth year of the reign of the judges.

6–9. Because of their disobedience and their refusal to follow the counsel and direction of the prophets, a curse had come upon the Lamanites. The mark of that curse was a dark skin, whereby they might be known and distinguished so that the Nephites might not mix with them and assume their way of life (see 1 Nephi 2:23; 2 Nephi 5:21–24).

10. Was called under that head] After a period of time in Book of Mormon history, lineal descent becomes virtually irrelevant. Basically, Nephites are those who give heed to the prophets, and Lamanites are those who refuse to do so.

13. There should be no confusion here. God set the mark of the dark skin upon the Lamanites, while the people of Amlici marked themselves with red.

19. They brought upon themselves the curse] "Just as obedience and righteousness bring blessings, so wickedness and rebellion result in cursings. . . . Cursings are the opposite of blessings, and the greater the opportunity given a people to earn blessings, the more severe will be the cursings heaped upon them, if they do not measure up and gain the proffered rewards." (Bruce R. McConkie, *Mormon Doctrine*, p. 175.) Essentially we bring the cursings of God upon ourselves whenever we fail to qualify for the blessings—the protecting power of the Almighty and the guidance and direction of his Spirit.

26. The eternal world] That is, tens of thousands were ushered into that eternal world we know as the postmortal spirit world, there to undergo a "partial judgment," a temporary consignment to paradise on the one hand or hell or outer darkness on the other (see Alma 34:34; 40:11–15; 48:23).

27. Wages of him whom he listeth to obey] See Alma 5:42. All people will eventually be justly dealt with and receive a reward commensurate with their faithfulness. They will inhabit a place hereafter which has been prepared by their Master, a world and a kingdom suited to the deeds done in the body and the desires of the heart. The righteous receive from the Lord Jesus the blessing of eternal life. The wicked receive little of what they were promised in life by their benighted master, for "the devil will not support his children at the last day, but doth speedily drag them down to hell" (Alma 30:60). Peter taught that "of whom a man is overcome, of the same is he brought in bondage" (2 Peter 2:19). Paul likewise explained that "to whom ye yield yourselves servants to obey, his servants ye are to whom ye obey; whether of sin unto death, or of obedience unto righteousness" (Romans 6:16).

Divine Judgments Awaken Us to a Remembrance of Our Duty

Alma 4:1–5

1. Now it came to pass in the sixth year of the reign of the judges over the people of Nephi, there were no contentions nor wars in the land of Zarahemla;

2. But the people were afflicted, yea, greatly afflicted for the loss of their brethren, and also for the loss of their flocks and herds, and also for the loss of their fields of grain, which were trodden under foot and destroyed by the Lamanites.

3. And so great were their afflictions that every soul had cause to mourn; and they believed that it was the judgments of God sent upon them because of their wickedness and their abominations; therefore they were awakened to a remembrance of their duty.

4. And they began to establish the church more fully; yea, and many were baptized in the waters of Sidon and were joined to the church of God; yea, they were baptized by the hand of Alma, who had been consecrated the high priest over the people of the church, by the hand of his father Alma.

5. And it came to pass in the seventh year of the reign of the judges there were about three thousand five hundred souls that united themselves to the church of God and were baptized. And thus ended the seventh year of the reign of the judges over the people of Nephi; and there was continual peace in all that time.

3. It is normal and natural when things go wrong to begin to search for causes, to begin to look carefully at one's attitudes and behaviors to ascertain whether one has offended God. If a person is sincere in his searchings, if he asks God to reveal his weakness, if he is indeed open enough to ask, "What lack I yet?" the Lord can awaken him to a remembrance of his duty. That is, the Spirit of Jesus Christ can bring to remembrance commitments, covenants, and divine counsel, thereby placing in vivid relief the ideal and the real in our lives. If we are teachable, divine judgments can remind us rapidly of the ephemeral nature of this mortal sphere, of man's powerlessness before the Infinite, and of the necessity of an unconditional surrender to the will of God in order to gain the victory here and thereby qualify for eternal rewards hereafter.

4–5. To establish the church more fully] On the one hand, the church began to be established more fully in the hearts and minds of the members; on the other, it began to have an influence on those not of the faith, such that in one year 3,500 persons came unto Christ through repentance and baptism. Though the record says that the converts were "baptized by the hand of Alma," we would suppose that many of these were baptized by other legal administrators under Alma's direction, by virtue of the keys of the priesthood he held as president of the Church or presiding high priest.

4. By the hand of his father Alma] See Mosiah 29:42.

Pride Prevents Progress of the Church

Alma 4:6–12

6. And it came to pass in the eighth year of the reign of the judges, that the people of the church began to wax proud, because of their exceeding riches, and their fine silks, and their fine-twined linen, and because of their many flocks and herds, and their gold and their silver, and all manner of precious things, which they had obtained by their industry; and in all these things were they lifted up in the pride of their eyes, for they began to wear very costly apparel.

7. Now this was the cause of much affliction to Alma, yea, and to many of the people whom Alma had consecrated to be teachers, and priests, and elders over the church; yea, many of them were sorely grieved for the wickedness which they saw had begun to be among their people.

8. For they saw and beheld with great sorrow that the people of the church began to be lifted up in the pride of their eyes, and to set their hearts upon riches and upon the vain things of the world, that they began to be scornful, one towards another, and they began to persecute those that did not believe according to their own will and pleasure.

9. And thus, in this eighth year of the reign of the judges, there began to be great contentions

among the people of the church; yea, there were envyings, and strife, and malice, and persecutions, and pride, even to exceed the pride of those who did not belong to the church of God.

10. And thus ended the eighth year of the reign of the judges; and the wickedness of the church was a great stumbling-block to those who did not belong to the church; and thus the church began to fail in its progress.

11. And it came to pass in the commencement of the ninth year, Alma saw the wickedness of the church, and he saw also that the example of the church began to lead those who were unbelievers on from one piece of iniquity to another, thus bringing on the destruction of the people.

12. Yea, he saw great inequality among the people, some lifting themselves up with their pride, despising others, turning their backs upon the needy and the naked and those who were hungry, and those who were athirst, and those who were sick and afflicted.

6–12. In describing the reasons for the fall of the Nephite nation, Mormon got to the heart of the matter. "Behold," he wrote to his son Moroni, "the pride of this nation, or the people of the Nephites, hath proven their destruction except they should repent" (Moroni 8:27). Of course, they did not repent. And they fell. It was of this fall that the Lord spoke in a modern revelation. "And if ye seek the riches which it is the will of the Father to give unto you, ye shall be the richest of all people, for ye shall have the riches of eternity; and it must needs be that the riches of the earth are mine to give; but *beware of pride, lest ye become as the Nephites of old*" (D&C 38:39, italics added). President Ezra Taft Benson called pride "the universal sin, the great vice." Further, he said, pride is "the great stumbling block to Zion."

"The central feature of pride," President Benson explained, "is enmity—enmity toward God and enmity toward our fellowmen. *Enmity* means 'hatred toward, hostility to, or a state of opposition.' It is the power by which Satan wishes to reign over us. Pride is essentially competitive in nature. We pit our will against God's." In addition, "the proud make every man their adversary by pitting their intellects, opinions, works, wealth, talents, or any other worldly measuring device against others." President Benson warned: "God will have a humble people. Either we can choose to be humble or we can be compelled to be humble." (CR, April 1989, pp. 3–7.)

6. Very costly apparel] See Alma 1:6, 27.

7. The cause of much affliction to Alma] There are few things more painful to Church leaders than to witness the spiritual demise of their flock, to see their people focused inordinately upon vain things. It is the cause of sleepless nights and much pleading in prayer, for these servants know full well that their congregants cannot find happiness in trusting in the ways and whims of this world.

7. Teachers, and priests] See 2 Nephi 5:26; Jacob 1:17–18; Alma 45:22. Because there were no Levites in the colony of Lehi (the Nephites and the Mulekites were of the lineage of Joseph and Judah, respectively), we assume that there was no Aaronic Priesthood among the Nephites, at least until the coming of Jesus to the Americas. The words *priests* and *teachers* thus appear to be descriptive of their ministerial duties in the higher priesthood rather than referring to offices in the Aaronic Priesthood. (See Joseph Fielding Smith, *Doctrines of Salvation* 3:87; *Promised Messiah*, p. 427; *New Witness*, p. 311.)

8. They began to be scornful, one towards another] C. S. Lewis wrote: "Pride gets no pleasure out of having something, only out of having more of it than the next man" (*Mere Christianity*, p. 109). When a person spends all of his time looking over—comparing and contrasting himself with others—rather than looking up to Christ, he will soon grieve the Spirit of Christ and thus alienate the very power by which relationships are sweetened and sustained. Rather than being filled with love, he is filled with suspicion or resentment. Resentment tends to lead eventually to persecution.

9. If any people in all the wide world have reason to be humble—to know whence their blessings come and in whom they must trust for salvation—it is the Saints. In fact, one who is afflicted severely with pride is not, in the truest sense, a Saint. It is thus ironic and tragic that pride should exist among those who know better, among those called out of the world into the marvelous light of Christ (see 1 Peter 2:9).

10–12. Whenever Christians fail to live up to their covenants, whenever those called to be pure in heart are instead as salt which has been tainted through mixture and contamination, whenever those commissioned to be the light of the world do no more than provide a faint flicker to a darkened world—when these conditions obtain, the Church has failed in fulfilling its mission to make a difference for good. Whenever members of the Church begin to proselyte others to partake of their sins and thereby share their guilt, to that extent the Church becomes a hindrance, a stumbling block to those who so desperately need its righteous influence.

The Power of Pure Testimony

Alma 4:13–20

13. Now this was a great cause for lamentations among the people, while others were abasing themselves, succoring those who stood in need of their succor, such as imparting their substance to the poor and the needy, feeding the hungry, and suffering all manner of afflictions, for Christ's sake, who should come according to the spirit of prophecy;

14. Looking forward to that day, thus retaining a remission of their sins; being filled with great joy because of the resurrection of the dead, according to the will and power and deliverance of Jesus Christ from the bands of death.

15. And now it came to pass that Alma, having seen the afflictions of the humble followers of God, and the persecutions which were heaped upon them by the remainder of his people, and seeing all their inequality, began to be very sorrowful; nevertheless the Spirit of the Lord did not fail him.

16. And he selected a wise man who was among the elders of the church, and gave him power according to the voice of the people, that he might have power to enact laws according to the laws which had been given, and to put them in force according to the wickedness and the crimes of the people.

17. Now this man's name was Nephihah, and he was appointed chief judge; and he sat in the judgment-seat to judge and to govern the people.

18. Now Alma did not grant unto him the office of being high priest over the church, but he retained the office of high priest unto himself; but he delivered the judgment-seat unto Nephihah.

19. And this he did that he himself might go forth among his people, or among the people of Nephi, that he might preach the word of God unto them, to stir them up in remembrance of their duty, and that he might pull down, by the word of God, all the pride and craftiness and all the contentions which were among his people, seeing no way that he might reclaim them save it were in bearing down in pure testimony against them.

20. And thus in the commencement of the ninth year of the reign of the judges over the people of Nephi, Alma delivered up the judgment-seat to Nephihah, and confined himself wholly to the high priesthood of the holy order of God, to the testimony of the word, according to the spirit of revelation and prophecy.

13. While others were abasing themselves] One need not submit to either the blatant evil of the perverse or the subtle persuasions of the sly. Indeed, the Book of Mormon is a powerful witness of the fact that one can live a life of fidelity and devotion in the midst of pride and priestcraft and greed and persecution. So it was that while some who claimed membership in the true

Church in Alma's day were untrue to their trust and reveled in their pride, others of the household of faith stood firm and steadfast. They abased themselves, that is, they acknowledged that their prosperity was a gift from the Almighty and not simply a product of their own industry; further, they acknowledged their need for divine assistance and realized their absolute nothingness without the Lord. They were personal witnesses of the fact that in all eternity no person can come unto God except he or she put off the carnal and fallen state and partake of the cleansing powers of the blood of Christ. (Compare Mosiah 4:1–2.)

14. Retaining a remission of their sins] See *Commentary* 2:161–62.

14. Great joy because of the resurrection of the dead] Mortal life may be a challenge, but immortality is assured through the atonement and resurrection of Christ the Lord. We may be beaten and bruised and battered on every hand by the vicissitudes of life, but we can glory in the assurance that life goes on hereafter and that for the faithful a refined and regenerated sociality will exist everlastingly. Like Job, we can exult in the sweet realization that body and spirit will be reunited (see Job 19:25–27), inseparably joined in the glorious resurrection.

15. The Spirit of the Lord did not fail him] "Living in troubled and sinful times may lead some to despair. Others may conclude that little can be done to reform a reprobate world and may thereafter feel bitterness and animosity toward those who bring a stench and a stain upon humanity. Those Saints who seek the influence of the Comforter will, however, take a different course: they will come to view the world as the Lord does." (Joseph Fielding McConkie and Robert L. Millet, *The Holy Ghost*, p. 80.) The Comforter will bring perspective. He will bring peace. He will bring rest in a turbulent world.

16–18. The plight of the Church seemed to dictate to Alma that he needed to focus his efforts and his strength where they could be of greatest benefit—on the spiritual well-being of society. Inasmuch as the Nephite society was governed by the voice of the people, it appears that Alma made to the people a recommendation for his replacement and then sought their voice in the matter. They sustained Nephihah as the second governor or chief judge, while Alma continued and intensified his priestly labors.

19. Preach the word of God] There is power in the word of God, a supernal power that can transform human souls and rivet men's hearts upon eternal verities. Preaching the word is prerequisite to the formation of faith. Joseph Smith, paraphrasing the Apostle Paul, said: "Faith comes by hearing the word of God, through the testimony of the servants of God; that testimony is always attended by the spirit of prophecy and revelation" (*Teachings*, p. 148; compare Romans 10:17). The word is sharp and powerful, like a two-edged sword, dividing truth from error, substance from vanity, sham and pretense from reality. Later in our story Mormon will write, in regard to Alma and his companions' approach to the apostate Zoramites: "And now, as the preaching of the word had a great tendency to lead the people to do that which was just—yea, it had had more powerful effect upon the minds of the people than the sword, or anything else, which had happened unto them—therefore Alma thought it was expedient that they should try the virtue of the word of God" (Alma 31:5).

19. Stir them up in remembrance of their duty] The gospel is preached and testimony is borne to the Saints in order to stir the memory, refocus the heart on covenants and commitments, and rededicate the mind to a life of service and obedience. The Spirit—conveyed through the inspired servants of the Lord—brings things to remembrance (John 14:26), particularly things of lasting worth, things that matter.

19. Bearing down in pure testimony] "The teacher's divine commission has been clearly articulated by the scriptures and by living prophets. He or she is to teach the gospel of Jesus Christ. It is to be taught out of the standard works and from the words of the living oracles. It is to be taught by the power of the Holy Ghost. It is to be applied to the life situations of the listeners, thus 'likening the scriptures' unto the Saints. Finally, and as the capstone of the teaching enterprise, the teacher is to bear witness, by the power of the Holy Ghost, that what has been taught is true. Faith is developed and commitment is built as a result of testimony, pure and solid testimony.

"The Holy Ghost is the converter. The gospel teacher has much to do in the preparation of the lesson, the search of the scriptures, the declaration of the truth; but the Holy Ghost is the converter. And the gospel teacher must never forget this. He or she must never seek to usurp the role of the Spirit nor upstage him whose influence results in renewal and righteousness. The person who bears pure testimony never seeks for cheap substitutes for the Spirit. He never relies upon methodologies which might confuse sentimentality with spirituality, emotional display with edification. His witness is more than story, and his testimony is more than an expression of gratitude. He tries the virtue of the word of God (Alma 31:5), trusts in the power of the scriptures and the words of the prophets to penetrate to the heart of his listeners, and bears witness of his message with sincerity and with soberness." (Joseph Fielding McConkie and Robert L. Millet, *The Holy Ghost*, pp. 119–20.)

Mormon explains that Alma determined to bear down in pure testimony against the people. His expressions were not motivated by anger or spite, nor directed against the people in the spirit of condemnation. Rather, his heart—motivated by the pure love of Christ—was bent upon saving their souls. He loved them and simply could not stand by and allow them to destroy themselves.

Alma and His Followers Delivered
by the Power of the Word

Alma 5:1–9

1. Now it came to pass that Alma began to deliver the word of God unto the people, first in the land of Zarahemla, and from thence throughout all the land.

2. And these are the words which he spake to the people in the church which was established in the city of Zarahemla, according to his own record, saying:

3. I, Alma, having been consecrated by my father, Alma, to be a high priest over the church of God, he having power and authority from God to do these things, behold, I say unto you that he began to establish a church in the land which was in the borders of Nephi; yea, the land which was called the land of Mormon; yea, and he did baptize his brethren in the waters of Mormon.

4. And behold, I say unto you, they were delivered out of the hands of the people of king Noah, by the mercy and power of God.

5. And behold, after that, they were brought into bondage by the hands of the Lamanites in the wilderness; yea, I say unto you, they were in captivity, and again the Lord did deliver them out of bondage by the power of his word; and we were brought into this land, and here we began to establish the church of God throughout this land also.

6. And now behold, I say unto you, my brethren, you that belong to this church, have you sufficiently retained in remembrance the captivity of your fathers? Yea, and have you sufficiently retained in remembrance his mercy and long-suffering towards them? And moreover, have ye sufficiently retained in remembrance that he has delivered their souls from hell?

7. Behold, he changed their hearts; yea, he awakened them out of a deep sleep, and they awoke unto God. Behold, they were in the midst of darkness; nevertheless, their souls were illuminated by the light of the everlasting word; yea, they were encircled about by the bands of death, and the chains of hell, and an everlasting destruction did await them.

8. And now I ask of you, my brethren, were they destroyed? Behold, I say unto you, Nay, they were not.

9. And again I ask, were the bands of death broken, and the chains of hell which encircled

them about, were they loosed? I
say unto you, Yea, they were
loosed, and their souls did expand,

and they did sing redeeming love.
And I say unto you that they are
saved.

1–9. History is the collective memorial of a people; its lessons
are most poignant and should be written in our hearts and souls.
It is a reservoir of wisdom from which we need to drink deeply
and frequently. It is in the past that we find direction for the
present and the future. The annals of the faithful inevitably give
us reason for gratitude and humility, out of which grow a
renewed sense of obligation.

1. Deliver the word of God] Introducing the ministry of the
Savior, Matthew recorded that Jesus "went about all Galilee,
teaching in their synagogues, and *preaching the gospel of the
kingdom,* and healing all manner of sickness and all manner of
disease among the people" (Matthew 4:23, italics added). Such is
everlastingly the pattern among the Lord's prophets. They are
ambassadors of the Word of God, teachers of eternal principles,
witnesses of the verities of heaven, with no claim on mortal men
for their power, authority, or message.

2. According to his own record] Mormon here indicates
that he is about to quote from the record of Alma.

3. Consecrated . . . a high priest over the church of God]
One does not properly preach save he has been properly called.
Here Alma establishes that such is the case with him. He has been
"consecrated" by his father, meaning that he has been properly
called and set apart to his holy office according to the pattern of
the priesthood, which is the same in all ages. He holds the office
of high priest and is the presiding officer in the Church. (See
Commentary 1:269.) Elder Bruce R. McConkie has written: "God's
chief representative on earth, the one who holds the highest spiritual position in his kingdom in any age, is called *the high priest.*
This special designation of the chief spiritual officer of the Church
has reference to the administrative position which he holds rather
than to the office to which he is ordained in the priesthood."
(*Mormon Doctrine,* pp. 355–56.)

7. How does one describe the process of redemption or second
birth? Alma uses such imagery as a changed heart, a soul awaken-
ing out of a deep sleep, and the prisoner of darkness being freed to
stand in the light. His illustrations are apt. See *Commentary*
2:168–76.

9. Sing redeeming love] "Praise ye the Lord: for it is good to
sing praises unto our God; for it is pleasant; and praise is comely"
(Psalm 147:1). Surely all within the household of faith ought to

acknowledge the greatness of their God in songs of praise. "For my soul delighteth in the song of the heart; yea, the song of the righteous is a prayer unto me, and it shall be answered with a blessing upon their heads. Wherefore, lift up thy heart and rejoice, and cleave unto the covenants which thou hast made." (D&C 25:12–13.) Songs of praise to our God help sanctify and cleanse our souls. Inspired music lifts the soul, teaches the gospel, and builds and sustains our faith. The Lord's people sing the song of redeeming love when they break forth in anthems of praise and gratitude to the Almighty and when they affirm by testimony the greatness and goodness of God (see 2 Nephi 9:8, 10, 13, 17, 19–20; see also Robert L. Millet and Joseph Fielding McConkie, *In His Holy Name*, pp. 95–98).

9. They are saved] To be saved is to be freed from the effects of Adam's fall, to overcome death and hell, to know a fulness of joy; it is to inherit eternal life. Ours is a lost and fallen world in which the soul is temporarily imprisoned. Salvation, in the full and complete sense, is to be redeemed or freed from the pains and sorrows of mortality and to rejoice in the glories of eternal splendor. "Salvation is for a man to be saved from all his enemies; for until a man can triumph over death, he is not saved. A knowledge of the priesthood alone will do this." (*Teachings*, p. 305; see also pp. 297, 301.) One can obtain the promise of salvation in this life, but one must pass through death and resurrection to receive complete salvation. Salvation, or exaltation, comes to the faithful in the life beyond.

The Conditions of Salvation

Alma 5:10–13

10. And now I ask of you on what conditions are they saved? Yea, what grounds had they to hope for salvation? What is the cause of their being loosed from the bands of death, yea, and also the chains of hell?

11. Behold, I can tell you—did not my father Alma believe in the words which were delivered by the mouth of Abinadi? And was he not a holy prophet? Did he not speak the words of God, and my father Alma believe them?

12. And according to his faith there was a mighty change wrought in his heart. Behold I say unto you that this is all true.

13. And behold, he preached the word unto your fathers, and a mighty change was also wrought in their hearts, and they humbled themselves and put their trust in the true and living God. And behold, they were faithful until the end; therefore they were saved.

11–13. What are the conditions of salvation? Specifically, people must believe the word (v. 11); experience the mighty change, the new birth (v. 12); humble themselves and put their trust in God (v. 13); and remain steadfast and faithful to the end of their mortal lives (v. 13).

11. The crowning evidence that Abinadi was a prophet rests in the fact that he preached the word of God. It is generally supposed that a prophet must foretell the future; this is not necessarily so. The primary responsibility of a prophet is to be a teacher of the word of God and to bear personal witness of Christ (Revelation 19:10). As necessary and appropriate, prophets may prophesy future events. Such prophecies, however, are of little or no value independent of the inspired declaration of the truths of salvation. Indeed, faith comes by hearing the heaven-sent word as taught by the servants of God, which testimony is always accompanied by the spirit of prophecy and revelation (see Romans 10:17; *Teachings*, p. 148).

Characteristics of Spiritual Birth

Alma 5:14–31

14. And now behold, I ask of you, my brethren of the church, have ye spiritually been born of God? Have ye received his image in your countenances? Have ye experienced this mighty change in your hearts?

15. Do ye exercise faith in the redemption of him who created you? Do you look forward with an eye of faith, and view this mortal body raised in immortality, and this corruption raised in incorruption, to stand before God to be judged according to the deeds which have been done in the mortal body?

16. I say unto you, can you imagine to yourselves that ye hear the voice of the Lord, saying unto you, in that day: Come unto me ye blessed, for behold, your works have been the works of righteousness upon the face of the earth?

17. Or do ye imagine to yourselves that ye can lie unto the Lord in that day, and say—Lord, our works have been righteous works upon the face of the earth—and that he will save you?

18. Or otherwise, can ye imagine yourselves brought before the tribunal of God with your souls filled with guilt and remorse, having a remembrance of all your guilt, yea, a perfect remembrance of all your wickedness, yea, a remembrance that ye have set at defiance the commandments of God?

19. I say unto you, can ye look up to God at that day with a pure heart and clean hands? I say unto you, can you look up, having the image of God engraven upon your countenances?

20. I say unto you, can ye think of being saved when you have

yielded yourselves to become subjects to the devil?

21. I say unto you, ye will know at that day that ye cannot be saved; for there can no man be saved except his garments are washed white; yea, his garments must be purified until they are cleansed from all stain, through the blood of him of whom it has been spoken by our fathers, who should come to redeem his people from their sins.

22. And now I ask of you, my brethren, how will any of you feel, if ye shall stand before the bar of God, having your garments stained with blood and all manner of filthiness? Behold, what will these things testify against you?

23. Behold will they not testify that ye are murderers, yea, and also that ye are guilty of all manner of wickedness?

24. Behold, my brethren, do ye suppose that such an one can have a place to sit down in the kingdom of God, with Abraham, with Isaac, and with Jacob, and also all the holy prophets, whose garments are cleansed and are spotless, pure and white?

25. I say unto you, Nay; except ye make our Creator a liar from the beginning, or suppose that he is a liar from the beginning, ye cannot suppose that such can have place in the kingdom of heaven; but they shall be cast out for they are the children of the kingdom of the devil.

26. And now behold, I say unto you, my brethren, if ye have experienced a change of heart, and if ye have felt to sing the song of redeeming love, I would ask, can ye feel so now?

27. Have ye walked, keeping yourselves blameless before God? Could ye say, if ye were called to die at this time, within yourselves, that ye have been sufficiently humble? That your garments have been cleansed and made white through the blood of Christ, who will come to redeem his people from their sins?

28. Behold, are ye stripped of pride? I say unto you, if ye are not ye are not prepared to meet God. Behold ye must prepare quickly; for the kingdom of heaven is soon at hand, and such an one hath not eternal life.

29. Behold, I say, is there one among you who is not stripped of envy? I say unto you that such an one is not prepared; and I would that he should prepare quickly, for the hour is close at hand, and he knoweth not when the time shall come; for such an one is not found guiltless.

30. And again I say unto you, is there one among you that doth make a mock of his brother, or that heapeth upon him persecutions?

31. Wo unto such an one, for he is not prepared, and the time is at hand that he must repent or he cannot be saved!

14. His image in your countenances] One measure of the new birth is the appearance of the new man. Paul described the process of salvation as obtaining "the mind of Christ" (1 Corinthians 2:16); that is, learning to think as Christ thinks, believe as he believes, feel as he feels, and do as he would do. Peter described the same thing as partaking of "the divine nature" (2 Peter

1:4), meaning that we must acquire the attributes of godliness. Joseph Smith explained: "The Savior most clearly show[ed] unto us the nature of salvation, and what he proposed unto the human family when he proposed to save them—that he proposed to make them like unto himself, and he was like the Father, the great prototype of all saved beings; and for any portion of the human family to be assimilated into their likeness is to be saved; and to be unlike them is to be destroyed; and on this hinge turns the door of salvation" (*Lectures on Faith* 7:16). As a child learns by imitating and emulating parents and those older than himself, so we learn godliness by imitating others who have set an example in righteousness, especially Jesus Christ. Alma appropriately describes this process of becoming Christlike as receiving the image of Christ in our countenances.

14. Mighty change in your hearts] The heart can be a symbol for the entire soul, the source of life and power in all that we do. To experience a "mighty change" in our hearts is to gain a full and complete commitment to the gospel cause. It is to be filled with spiritual vigor. It is to have a soul consecrated to the upbuilding of the kingdom. See *Commentary* 2:168–76.

15. Exercise faith in the redemption] To exercise faith in the redemption of Christ is to have perfect confidence that in Christ is found the power to remit sins, heal souls, raise the dead, and triumph in all that is right and good. It is to trust the simplicity of gospel answers; it is to seek the sanction of heaven on all that one does.

15. An eye of faith] To have an eye of faith is to be believing. It is to see the hand of God in all things. It is the confidence that all things will work together for our good if we walk uprightly and are true to our covenants. (See Mormon 9:27; D&C 90:24.)

17. How foolish and dark the mind that supposes a person can lie to God, hide his sins, and excuse and cleanse his soul with words of fulsome praise. Why would anyone reverence a God so easily deceived by fools? And of what pleasure would a heaven be that was filled with such beings?

18. Souls filled with guilt and remorse] Addressing himself to those who suppose that they can enter the kingdom of heaven unworthily, Moroni said: "Behold, I say unto you that ye would be more miserable to dwell with a holy and just God, under a consciousness of your filthiness before him, than ye would to dwell with the damned souls in hell. For behold, when ye shall be brought to see your nakedness before God, and also the glory of God, and the holiness of Jesus Christ, it will kindle a flame of unquenchable fire upon you." (Mormon 9:4–5.)

18. A perfect remembrance of all your wickedness] Jacob

testified that we will have a "perfect knowledge of all our guilt, and our uncleanness, and our nakedness," when we stand before the judgment bar (2 Nephi 9:14; see *Commentary* 1:243). There can be no justice in the judgment unless the eyes of God are all-seeing. Repentance alone has the power to edit from the book of life the account of unworthy deeds.

19. A pure heart and clean hands] "Who shall ascend into the hill of the Lord? or who shall stand in his holy place?" the ancient psalmist asked. And in response he wrote: "He that hath clean hands, and a pure heart; who hath not lifted up his soul unto vanity, nor sworn deceitfully. He shall receive the blessing from the Lord, and righteousness from the God of his salvation." (Psalm 24:3–5.) Elder Dallin H. Oaks has written: "If we do righteous acts and refrain from evil acts, we have clean hands. If we act for the right motives and if we refrain from forbidden desires and attitudes, we have pure hearts." (*Pure in Heart*, p. 1.)

19. Image of God engraven upon your countenances] See commentary on verse 14.

20–21. Those who have labored in opposition to the kingdom of God can hardly expect an honored place in that kingdom.

21–22. No principle was better understood among the ancient Saints than that no unclean thing could enter the presence of the Lord. Thus the imagery common to the scriptures is to depict the Saints of God, those living righteous lives, as wearing "robes of righteousness" (2 Nephi 9:14; Revelation 19:8), or "garments of salvation" (Isaiah 61:10). This imagery is closely associated with the temple, which is the earthly representation of the divine presence, or our sought-after heavenly abode. In the temple we are taught, primarily with symbolic representation, how we return to the presence of God. (See D&C 109:80.)

The garments of salvation are also a symbol of divine protection. Nephi sought such a blessing in this language: "O Lord, wilt thou encircle me around in the robe of thy righteousness! O Lord, wilt thou make a way for mine escape before mine enemies! Wilt thou make my path straight before me! Wilt thou not place a stumbling block in my way—but that thou wouldst clear my way before me, and hedge not up my way, but the ways of mine enemy." (2 Nephi 4:33.)

22. Garments stained with blood] A soul spoiled by the effects of sin. See 2 Nephi 9:44; Jacob 1:19; 2:2.

23. Ye are murderers] Reference is not being made to the taking of life but rather to the destruction of souls, the killing of spiritual sensitivities (compare Alma 36:14).

24. Salvation has little or nothing to do with offices or callings; it is not dependent upon prominence in the earthly kingdom.

Rather, salvation is the result of living in such a manner that our "garments [i.e., our souls] are cleansed and are spotless, pure and white." All who do this are entitled to sit down with people such as Abraham, Isaac, and Jacob and to obtain the same eternal blessings and rewards as they receive. (See Alma 7:25.)

25. To suppose that the unclean (those who have disdained works of righteousness) can enter the kingdom of heaven is not only to suppose that mercy can rob justice but is also to make God a liar. The idea not only denies the nature of God but also destroys the nature of the celestial world. It would make heaven but an endless extension of earth life in which good and evil would continue their war with each other.

26. Benjamin instructed his people: "As ye have come to the knowledge of the glory of God, . . . and have tasted of his love, and have received a remission of your sins, which causeth such exceedingly great joy in your souls, even so I would that ye should remember, and always retain in remembrance, the greatness of God, and your own nothingness, and his goodness and long-suffering towards you, unworthy creatures, and humble yourselves even in the depths of humility, calling on the name of the Lord daily, and standing steadfastly in the faith of that which is to come. . . . [for] if ye do this ye shall always rejoice, and be filled with the love of God, and always retain a remission of your sins; and ye shall grow in the knowledge of the glory of him that created you, or in the knowledge of that which is just and true." (Mosiah 4:11–12.)

26. Can ye feel so now?] This is a call to keep our witness and our experience with the Spirit current and up to date. Though it is important to develop and maintain reservoirs of faith—repositories of memories and experiences and encounters with the divine which have built and strengthened testimony—we must be ever on guard against spiritual lethargy, against coasting upon our memories, against living only in the past. We cannot afford to pause and homestead on spiritual plateaus. Our task is to move on, to progress.

27. Keeping yourselves blameless before God] There is a power in living "blameless" that cannot otherwise be known. "Beloved, if our heart condemn us not," wrote the Apostle John, "then have we confidence toward God. And whatsoever we ask, we receive of him, because we keep his commandments, and do those things that are pleasing in his sight." (1 John 3:21–22). In like manner Joseph Smith taught that if we will "let virtue garnish" our thoughts unceasingly our confidence will "wax strong in the presence of God" and heavenly knowledge will distill upon our souls as the dews from heaven (see D&C 121:45). The Saints of God are acknowledged to be blameless by the only truly blameless one, the Redeemer. This designation they receive not because they never erred, but because of their trust in him and their willingness to keep his commandments and to give themselves in service to his people (see D&C 4:2; 84:61).

27. Garments . . . cleansed] To have garments that are cleansed is to have souls that are sanctified; it is to have cleansed the temple of our body, making of it a fit abode for the Spirit of the Lord.

27. Redeem his people from their sins] Sin is ever the enemy of salvation. Christ did not come to redeem people "in their sins, but to redeem them from their sins" (Helaman 5:10; compare Alma 11:37). Salvation is like entrance into the temple; all are invited to enter and receive its blessings, but none can do so unless they are striving to keep themselves from sin.

28. Pride] "As spoken of in the revelations, *pride* is the opposite of humility. It is inordinate self-esteem arising because of one's position, achievements, or possessions. It has the effect of centering a person's heart on the things of the world rather than the things of the Spirit. (1 John 2:15–17.) As humility, which is an attribute of godliness possessed by true saints, leads to salvation, so pride, which is of the devil, leads to damnation (2 Nephi 28:15). 'God resisteth the proud, but giveth grace unto the humble' (James 4:6; 1 Peter 5:5)." (Bruce R. McConkie, *Mormon Doctrine*, p. 593).

28. The kingdom of heaven is soon at hand] In one sense this meant to the Nephites that Christ, the King of all the earth, would come into mortality (see v. 50; Alma 7:9; 10:20). In another sense it means that each of us, as we face the time of death, must reckon with ourselves in regard to the commandments of God. That is, we know not the day nor the hour in which our experience in mortality will end. Be it a few years or many (as mortals count them), the time spent on earth will seem all too short. The phrase is not being used in this text with the same meaning given to it by the Baptist, who declared, "Repent ye: for the kingdom of heaven is at hand" (Matthew 3:2; see also 4:17; 10:7). John's reference was to the reestablishment of the Church of Jesus Christ among those of the nation of Israel. See commentary on verses 50–51.

29. Stripped of envy] The antidote to virtually every spiritual ill is charity. When the people of the Lord's fold are filled with his pure love, they seek to build up one another, take joy in the accomplishments or acquisitions of one another, and feel no desire to have more than they need. Some of the most serious sins known to mankind, such as murder and adultery, are generally due to pride and envy and covetousness.

30. Mock of his brother] There is something very un-

Christian about poking fun at another. It is an unholy practice to
make a man an offender for a word, to delight in the faults or
weaknesses of another, or to laugh at or scorn the unfortunate.
Such things are alien to the Spirit of God, and those who continue
in them will come short of the glory of God.

All Are Called to Work Righteousness and Be Saved

Alma 5:32–37

32. Yea, even wo unto all ye
workers of iniquity; repent,
repent, for the Lord God hath
spoken it!

33. Behold, he sendeth an invitation unto all men, for the arms
of mercy are extended towards
them, and he saith: Repent, and I
will receive you.

34. Yea, he saith: Come unto me
and ye shall partake of the fruit of
the tree of life; yea, ye shall eat
and drink of the bread and the
waters of life freely;

35. Yea, come unto me and
bring forth works of righteousness,
and ye shall not be hewn down

and cast into the fire—

36. For behold, the time is at
hand that whosoever bringeth
forth not good fruit, or whosoever
doeth not the works of righteousness, the same have cause to wail
and mourn.

37. O ye workers of iniquity; ye
that are puffed up in the vain
things of the world, ye that have
professed to have known the ways
of righteousness nevertheless have
gone astray, as sheep having no
shepherd, notwithstanding a shepherd hath called after you and is
still calling after you, but ye will
not hearken unto his voice!

33. He sendeth an invitation unto all men] From Adam to
the last person to be born on this mortal earth, none will be left
without the opportunity to hear the gospel of salvation. True,
many will depart this life without having had that chance; yet in
the providence of a just God that opportunity will be offered them
in the world of spirits before the day of judgment and resurrection. To all such the gospel will be taught as it would have been
taught them on earth. Those in the world of spirits who, if they
had had the opportunity, would have accepted the gospel in mortality and lived its principles with integrity will do so there, and
no blessings given to the righteous will be lost to them (see D&C
137). Any theology that fails to attest to this principle is unworthy
of a just and loving God.

The testimony of the prophets of all ages is that God has invited "all to come unto him and partake of his goodness; and he
denieth none that come unto him, black and white, bond and

free, male and female; and he remembereth the heathen; and all are alike unto God, both Jew and Gentile" (2 Nephi 26:33; see *Commentary* 1:311–12). All who have inherited death by Adam's fall can have the promise of salvation through Christ's atonement.

33. The arms of mercy] The "arm of mercy" (3 Nephi 9:14) is a metaphor carrying essentially the same meaning as the promise that Christ would have "healing in his wings" (Malachi 4:2); that is, having broken the bands of death and conquered all the limitations of mortality, Christ is now in a position to extend those same blessings to all who will come unto him.

34. The fruit of the tree of life] In the allegory of Eden, Christ is the tree of life, and to partake of that fruit is to partake of the cleansing powers of Christ and to receive the blessings of his Spirit (see *Commentary* 1:75–76). In his bread-of-life sermon given at Capernaum, Christ declared: "Verily, verily, I say unto you, He that believeth on me hath everlasting life. I am that bread of life. Your fathers did eat manna in the wilderness, and are dead. This is the bread which cometh down from heaven, that a man may eat thereof, and not die." (John 6:47–50.) In a broader sense, the entirety of the gospel is the fruit we obtain from Christ, who is the source of eternal life.

34. The bread and the waters of life] Again, the idea clothed in the metaphor is that of the flesh and blood of Christ (see John 6:53–56).

35. Bring forth works of righteousness] If the seed is from the tree of life, it will bring forth fruit like that of its parent tree. Indeed, "every seed bringeth forth unto its own likeness" (Alma 32:31). Those who have truly chosen to follow Christ will bring forth fruits worthy of Christ. Once individuals have been born again, once the Spirit of the Lord has begun to bring about the mighty change, once they have become new creatures in Christ, Christ begins to live in them (see Galatians 2:20). That is, their works become his works; they are motivated and given meaning and substance and effect by him, through the power of his Spirit.

37. Professed to have known the ways of righteousness] Like a fire that gives no warmth, the profession of faith without the attending actions purges no sins and merits no place in the heavenly kingdom. The Lord hates sham and hypocrisy, and his wrath is easily kindled against such: "Behold, vengeance cometh speedily upon the inhabitants of the earth, a day of wrath, a day of burning, a day of desolation, of weeping, of mourning, and of lamentation; and as a whirlwind it shall come upon all the face of the earth, saith the Lord. And upon my house shall it begin, and from my house shall it go forth, saith the Lord; first among those among you, saith the Lord, who have professed to know my name and have not known me, and have blasphemed against me in the midst of my house, saith the Lord." (D&C 112:24–26; compare 41:1; 50:4; 56:1; 1 Peter 4:17–18.)

Salvation Through the Name of Christ

Alma 5:38–42

38. Behold, I say unto you, that the good shepherd doth call you; yea, and in his own name he doth call you, which is the name of Christ; and if ye will not hearken unto the voice of the good shepherd, to the name by which ye are called, behold, ye are not the sheep of the good shepherd.

39. And now if ye are not the sheep of the good shepherd, of what fold are ye? Behold, I say unto you, that the devil is your shepherd, and ye are of his fold; and now, who can deny this? Behold, I say unto you, whosoever denieth this is a liar and a child of the devil.

40. For I say unto you that whatsoever is good cometh from God, and whatsoever is evil cometh from the devil.

41. Therefore, if a man bringeth forth good works he hearkeneth unto the voice of the good shepherd, and he doth follow him; but whosoever bringeth forth evil works, the same becometh a child of the devil, for he hearkeneth unto his voice, and doth follow him.

42. And whosoever doeth this must receive his wages of him; therefore, for his wages he receiveth death, as to things pertaining unto righteousness, being dead unto all good works.

38. The good shepherd] Perhaps no messianic designation was better known among the ancients than that of the good shepherd (see Psalm 23; Isaiah 40:10–11; Ezekiel 34:2; see also John 10:14).

38. In his own name he doth call you] "Behold, Jesus Christ is the name which is given of the Father, and there is none other name given whereby man can be saved; wherefore, all men must take upon them the name which is given of the Father, for in that name shall they be called at the last day; wherefore, if they know not the name by which they are called, they cannot have place in the kingdom of my Father" (D&C 18:23–25).

Entrance into the kingdom of heaven requires that we take upon ourselves the name of Christ. Salvation is found in no other name (see Mosiah 5:9–10; Acts 4:12). The significance of this proclamation is worthy of careful consideration. How is it that the power of salvation is vested in a name? Be it remembered that

Christ in his mortal ministry was careful to establish the fact that he came in his "Father's name" (John 5:43), that all his works were done in the name of the Father (see John 10:25), and that he sought to glorify the name of the Father in all he did (see John 12:28). Thus the Son assumed the name and power of his Father, and through the name and by that divine investiture he extended the promise of salvation to all who would take upon themselves his name as he had taken upon himself the name of his Father. Such is the system of salvation.

The idea that blessings come through a name finds expression in society. It has been the custom of fathers in all ages, and we suppose among virtually all peoples, to place their name upon their posterity. As the crown of womanhood is in granting life, so the crown of manhood is the conferring upon one's posterity the family name. Often, ceremony and ritual are associated with a father placing his name—indeed, his most prized possession—upon the newborn. In the giving of a name, the father declares the child to be his, making him or her a rightful heir of all that he possesses. The children, in return, are taught to love and respect their parents and to so live as to bring honor to the name that has been given them as a sacred trust. The rebellious child can be disinherited, in which case he forfeits all blessings associated with the bearing of the family name.

Such is the order and pattern of heaven. God, the eternal Father, placed his name upon Jesus of Nazareth, his only begotten in the flesh, and by so doing testified that the Galilean was his own Son, that the love and protection of heaven would be with him. Christ, a rightful heir to the dominion, power, and glory of his Father, was empowered to act in the divine name. In turn, the Savior invites all his earthly brothers and sisters to return to that heavenly family of which they were once a part, to take again the family name, and become heirs of the blessings associated with it. Thus salvation centers in our accepting Christ as our Savior, being born again into the family of the Father through the waters of baptism, and living worthy of all the ordinances of the house of the Lord wherein we are endowed with the powers of heaven. Those rejecting such, like the rebellious children in the families of men, will be disinherited from the royal family of heaven and left to seek citizenship in some other kingdom.

39. We march with the army of Israel or the army of Satan. There is no middle ground. We accept Jesus as the Christ and follow him or we do not. There is no compromise in that great war that began in heaven. If we have not chosen to follow Christ we have chosen to follow another, and there is none other to follow save it be the devil.

39. A child of the devil] Just as we can take upon us the name of Christ and become the sons and daughters of God and heirs to his kingdom, so we can choose to take upon us the name of the adversary and become heirs of his kingdom. Thus Cain, through his rebellion, took upon himself the name Perdition (see Moses 5:24), as will others who, like Cain, received the fulness of gospel truth and then chose to deny it and war against it (D&C 76:31–33). Just as the people of Zion are eventually sealed to Christ (Mosiah 5:15), so the municipals of Babylon who deny and defy the truth shall eventually be sealed to Beelzebub (2 Nephi 9:46; Alma 34:35; Helaman 13:32).

To the supposedly religious of his day who rejected him, Christ said: "Ye are of your father the devil, and the lusts of your father ye will do. He was a murderer from the beginning, and abode not in the truth, because there is no truth in him. When he speaketh a lie, he speaketh of his own: for he is a liar, and the father of it." (John 8:44.) "Remember," Abinadi said, "that he that persists in his own carnal nature, and goes on in the ways of sin and rebellion against God, remaineth in his fallen state and the devil hath all power over him. Therefore he is as though there was no redemption made, being an enemy to God." (Mosiah 16:5.) In the Old World, such were called the sons of Belial (Deuteronomy 13:13; Judges 19:22; 20:13; 1 Samuel 10:27).

40. See Omni 1:25; commentary on Moroni 7:16–17.

42. Being dead unto all good works] That is, they are spiritually dead, inert to righteousness and the ways of the righteous. Good works are essential to salvation. To merely believe in God and Christ makes us no better than the devils; if they did not have a sure knowledge of the Eternal Father and his Only Begotten Son they would have no need to war against them.

The Power of the Law of Witnesses

Alma 5:43–49

43. And now, my brethren, I would that ye should hear me, for I speak in the energy of my soul; for behold, I have spoken unto you plainly that ye cannot err, or have spoken according to the commandments of God.

44. For I am called to speak after this manner, according to the holy order of God, which is in Christ Jesus; yea, I am commanded to stand and testify unto this people the things which have been spoken by our fathers concerning the things which are to come.

45. And this is not all. Do ye not suppose that I know of these

things myself? Behold, I testify unto you that I do know that these things whereof I have spoken are true. And how do ye suppose that I know of their surety?

46. Behold, I say unto you they are made known unto me by the Holy Spirit of God. Behold, I have fasted and prayed many days that I might know these things of myself. And now I do know of myself that they are true; for the Lord God hath made them manifest unto me by his Holy Spirit; and this is the spirit of revelation which is in me.

47. And moreover, I say unto you that it has thus been revealed unto me, that the words which have been spoken by our fathers are true, even so according to the spirit of prophecy which is in me, which is also by the manifestation of the Spirit of God.

48. I say unto you, that I know of myself that whatsoever I shall say unto you, concerning that which is to come, is true; and I say unto you, that I know that Jesus Christ shall come, yea, the Son, the Only Begotten of the Father, full of grace, and mercy, and truth. And behold, it is he that cometh to take away the sins of the world, yea, the sins of every man who steadfastly believeth on his name.

49. And now I say unto you that this is the order after which I am called, yea, to preach unto my beloved brethren, yea, and every one that dwelleth in the land; yea, to preach unto all, both old and young, both bond and free; yea, I say unto you the aged, and also the middle aged, and the rising generation; yea, to cry unto them that they must repent and be born again.

43. Spoken . . . plainly that ye cannot err] Similarly, Nephi testified that he had "spoken plainly" and that his brothers could not misunderstand that which he had taught; thus his words would "stand as a testimony" against them. His teachings, he said, were "sufficient to teach any man the right way; for the right way is to believe in Christ and deny him not; for by denying him ye also deny the prophets and the law" (2 Nephi 25:28). A modern prophet, President Harold B. Lee, frequently challenged those who teach the gospel to do so in such a manner that their students would not only understand what they had been taught but also could not *misunderstand* the principles taught.

44. The holy order of God] The "holiest order of God" is the Melchizedek Priesthood (see D&C 84:18–19). Before the day of Melchizedek, this priesthood was called *"the Holy Priesthood, after the Order of the Son of God"* (D&C 107:3). Melchizedek, we are told, "having been approved of God, . . . was ordained an high priest after *the order of the covenant* which God made with Enoch, it being after *the order of the Son of God*; which order came, not by man, nor the will of man; neither by father nor mother; neither by beginning of days nor end of years; but of God; and it was delivered unto men by the calling of his own voice, according to his own will, unto as many as believed on his name" (JST, Genesis 14:27–29; italics added).

It is marvelously significant that the word *order* constitutes part of the proper name of the priesthood. The Lord's house is a house of order, and all that is done in it must be done in proper and orderly fashion. Such words as *ordain* and *ordinance*, which are associated with the governing of the Church, are rooted in the word *order*. The holy order of God is the priesthood. It is the priesthood received by the young elder, the priesthood associated with the new and everlasting covenant of marriage, and the fulness of priesthood bestowed upon those ordained kings and priests of the Most High God (see *Teachings*, p. 322).

The theme of the verses that follow is that, of necessity, there must be authority that controls and governs the manner in which the gospel is taught. That system is announced anew in a modern revelation which declares that those "preaching the word" are to do so "saying none other things than that which the prophets and apostles have written, and that which is taught them by the Comforter through the prayer of faith" (D&C 52:9). Thus as we teach from the scriptures we partake of their spirit, the spirit of revelation, and our minds are enlightened, and we are then able to expound, expand, and apply the message of heaven to the circumstances and situation of those we are teaching. The scriptures are the seedbed for revelation.

The classic illustration of this principle for our day came by way of instruction to three of the early missionaries of the Church. "My servant, Orson Hyde," the revelation begins, "was called by his ordination to proclaim the everlasting gospel, by the Spirit of the living God, from people to people, and from land to land, in the congregations of the wicked, in their synagogues, reasoning with and expounding all scriptures unto them. And, behold, and lo, this is an ensample unto all those who were ordained unto this priesthood, whose mission is appointed unto them to go forth—

"And this is the ensample unto them, that they shall speak as they are moved upon by the Holy Ghost. And whatsoever they shall speak when moved upon by the Holy Ghost shall be scripture, shall be the will of the Lord, shall be the mind of the Lord, shall be the word of the Lord, shall be the voice of the Lord, and the power of God unto salvation.

"Behold, this is the promise of the Lord unto you, O ye my servants. Wherefore, be of good cheer, and do not fear, for I the Lord am with you, and will stand by you; and ye shall bear record of me, even Jesus Christ, that I am the Son of the living God, that I was, that I am, and that I am to come. This is the word of the

Lord unto you, my servant Orson Hyde, and also unto my servant Luke Johnson, and unto my servant Lyman Johnson, and unto my servant William E. McLellin, and unto all the faithful elders of my church—

"Go ye into all the world, preach the gospel to every creature, acting in the authority which I have given you, baptizing in the name of the Father, and of the Son, and of the Holy Ghost." (D&C 68:1–8.)

The revelation is most instructive; in it we see again the divine order—the gospel is to be taught from the scriptures and by the Spirit. When it is taught in that manner, additional revelation readily comes to expound and explain the revelations previously given. This is the reason why there cannot be a closed canon. As long as the Elders of Israel have the spirit of revelation, that spirit by which the scriptures are given, we will find the canon of scripture forever growing. It is in this spirit that Elder Boyd K. Packer referred to the Doctrine and Covenants as "the book that will never be closed" (CR, April 1990, p. 47). We also note in the revelation just cited that this is the system by which the gospel is to be taught among all peoples of the earth, whether righteous or wicked.

Affirming that Alma taught after this order, the record says: "And Alma went and began to declare the word of God unto the church which was established in the valley of Gideon, according to the revelation of the truth of the word which had been spoken by his fathers, and according to the spirit of prophecy which was in him, according to the testimony of Jesus Christ, the Son of God, who should come to redeem his people from their sins, and the holy order by which he was called" (Alma 6:8).

44. The things . . . spoken by our fathers] The reference is to the scriptures as they were had among the Nephites.

45–48. A knowledge of the scriptures alone does not make one a competent witness of the verity of gospel principles. A witness from the Spirit can stand independent of all else. The testimony of the scriptures is always to be sustained by a living testimony—the manifestation of the Spirit to the one declaring the scriptures. "The crowning, convincing, converting power of gospel teaching," wrote Elder Bruce R. McConkie, "is manifest when an inspired teacher says, 'I know by the power of the Holy Ghost, by the revelations of the Holy Spirit to my soul, that the doctrines I have taught are true.' This divine seal of approval makes the spoken word binding upon the hearers. . . . It should be added that when the Lord's servants preach in power, by the promptings of the Holy Spirit, the Lord adds his own witness to the truth of their words. That witness comes in the form of signs and gifts and miracles. Such are always found when the preached word, given in power, is believed by hearers with open hearts." (*Promised Messiah*, pp. 516–17.)

48. Steadfastly believeth] See *Commentary* 1:301–2; see also 2 Nephi 31:20; *Commentary* 2:162.

49. This is the order after which I am called] See commentary on verse 44.

49. To preach unto all] The system by which salvation comes is the same for all people—it is not negotiable. It matters not whether they be old or young, bond or free, rich or poor, learned or unschooled; each must believe the same truths, tread the same path, and comply with the same terms.

The Kingdom of Heaven Is Soon at Hand

Alma 5:50–51

50. Yea, thus saith the Spirit: Repent, all ye ends of the earth, for the kingdom of heaven is soon at hand; yea, the Son of God cometh in his glory, in his might, majesty, power, and dominion. Yea, my beloved brethren, I say unto you, that the Spirit saith: Behold the glory of the King of all the earth; and also the King of heaven shall very soon shine forth among all the children of men.

51. And also the Spirit saith unto me, yea, crieth unto me with a mighty voice, saying: Go forth and say unto this people—Repent, for except ye repent ye can in nowise inherit the kingdom of heaven.

50. The kingdom of heaven is soon at hand] The ultimate fulfillment of these prophetic words is the establishment of the millennial kingdom, that time when Christ will come in glory, might, majesty, power, and dominion to rule and reign as Lord of lords and King of kings. In a limited sense, however, the kingdom of God would come when Jesus would come to earth in fourscore years' time. In another sense the coming of the heavenly kingdom is equally close for men of all ages. This is so because those who live well, those who choose to repent and honor their God and his Christ—irrespective of when they lived or how long they lived— will obtain citizenship in the heavenly kingdom hereafter. They are prepared, at the time of death, to meet their Maker and enjoy association with the faithful of ages past. Those who spurn the truth and reject the prophets, on the other hand, enter into hell at the time of death and are confronted by the reality of their sins. It is for them as though they had lived to behold the great and dreadful day of the Second Coming of the Lord in glory. (See Bruce R. McConkie, *Doctrinal New Testament Commentary* 1:674–75.)

"I will reveal myself from heaven with power and great glory, with all the hosts thereof, and dwell in righteousness with men on earth a thousand years, and the wicked shall not stand," the Savior declared (D&C 29:11). Describing the Second Coming, Isaiah said: "The moon shall be confounded, and the sun ashamed, when the Lord of hosts shall reign in mount Zion, and in Jerusalem, and before his ancients gloriously" (Isaiah 24:23). It is the destiny of the righteous of all ages, as the Revelator declared, to live and reign "with Christ a thousand years" (Revelation 20:4; see also Revelation 5:10; JST, Revelation 2:26–27).

Acceptance of Christ Is Evidenced in Works of Righteousness

Alma 5:52–56

52. And again I say unto you, the Spirit saith: Behold, the ax is laid at the root of the tree; therefore every tree that bringeth not forth good fruit shall be hewn down and cast into the fire, yea, a fire which cannot be consumed, even an unquenchable fire. Behold, and remember, the Holy One hath spoken it.

53. And now my beloved brethren, I say unto you, can ye withstand these sayings; yea, can ye lay aside these things, and trample the Holy One under your feet; yea, can ye be puffed up in the pride of your hearts; yea, will ye still persist in the wearing of costly apparel and setting your hearts upon the vain things of the world, upon your riches?

54. Yea, will ye persist in supposing that ye are better one than another; yea, will ye persist in the persecution of your brethren, who humble themselves and do walk after the holy order of God, wherewith they have been brought into this church, having been sanctified by the Holy Spirit, and they do bring forth works which are meet for repentance—

55. Yea, and will you persist in turning your backs upon the poor, and the needy, and in withholding your substance from them?

56. And finally, all ye that will persist in your wickedness, I say unto you that these are they who shall be hewn down and cast into the fire except they speedily repent.

52. Alma's declaration was not just that the wicked shall be destroyed but that all who failed to bring forth works of righteousness will be as the tree hewn down and cast into the fire (compare Matthew 3:10; Luke 3:9; D&C 97:7). As there is no neutrality where the kingdom of God is concerned, so no lack of commitment is acceptable where right and proper works are needed. The Apostle Paul, teaching this same principle, charged the meridian Saints to "work out [their] own salvation with fear and trembling" (Philippians 2:12).

52. An unquenchable fire] Only the sons of perdition are damned forever in outer darkness. All other divine punishment and suffering—even that denominated as endless and eternal—will terminate at the time of the second resurrection (see D&C 19:6–12). Those who will eventually inherit the telestial kingdom suffer and repent in hell after death. The Prophet Joseph Smith observed: "A man is his own tormenter and his own condemner. Hence the saying, They shall go into the lake that burns with fire and brimstone. The torment of disappointment in the mind of man is as exquisite as a lake burning with fire and brimstone. I say, so is the torment of man." (*Teachings*, p. 357.)

53. As with the preceding verse, no reference is made to overt acts or wicked deeds. The warning is sounded to those whose hearts are set upon the things of the world, those whose attention centers in satiating their own appetites. Whether it be in the form of stylish fashions, excessive leisure, or some other diversion is of no moment; what is important is that service to both God and man has not been rendered. (See also D&C 121:34–36.)

54. The gospel of man is to "outdo" others, while the gospel of Christ is to "do for" others. The works of righteousness sanctify the soul and evidence true repentance. (See also D&C 84:33–34.)

55. That spirit which fosters inequality and selfishness is contrary to the law of the gospel and offensive to the Spirit of the Lord (see *Commentary* 2:164–67).

Names of the Righteous Written in the Book of Life

Alma 5:57–62

57. And now I say unto you, all you that are desirous to follow the voice of the good shepherd, come ye out from the wicked, and be ye separate, and touch not their unclean things; and behold, their names shall be blotted out, that the names of the wicked shall not be numbered among the names of the righteous, that the word of God may be fulfilled, which saith:

The names of the wicked shall not be mingled with the names of my people;
58. For the names of the righteous shall be written in the book of life, and unto them will I grant an inheritance at my right hand. And now, my brethren, what have ye to say against this? I say unto you, if ye speak against it, it matters not, for the word of

God must be fulfilled.

59. For what shepherd is there among you having many sheep doth not watch over them, that the wolves enter not and devour his flock? And behold, if a wolf enter his flock doth he not drive him out? Yea, and at the last, if he can, he will destroy him.

60. And now I say unto you that the good shepherd doth call after you; and if you will hearken unto his voice he will bring you into his fold, and ye are his sheep; and he commandeth you that ye suffer no ravenous wolf to enter among you, that ye may not be destroyed.

61. And now I, Alma, do command you in the language of him who hath commanded me, that ye observe to do the words which I have spoken unto you.

62. I speak by way of command unto you that belong to the church; and unto those who do not belong to the church I speak by way of invitation, saying: Come and be baptized unto repentance, that ye also may be partakers of the fruit of the tree of life.

57. Touch not their unclean things] Sin is born in the touching stage. Of the tree of life Adam and Eve were commanded, "Ye shall not eat of it, neither shall ye touch it, lest ye die" (Genesis 3:3). As with our first parents, so with us—we cannot partake of forbidden fruits save we first touch them. To refuse to touch is the fence of safety. Many a bitter tear has been shed by those who thought it cute to flirt with sin or nibble at that which is forbidden.

57. Their names shall be blotted out] See *Commentary* 2:301.

58. Names of the righteous . . . written in the book of life] "The *book of life,* or *Lamb's book of Life,* is the record kept in heaven which contains the names of the faithful and an account of their righteous covenants and deeds. (D&C 128:6–7; Psalm 69:28; Revelation 3:5; 21:27.) The book of life is the book containing the names of those who shall inherit eternal life; it is the book of eternal life. (Daniel 12:1–4; Hebrews 12:23; D&C 76:68; 132:19.) It is 'the book of the names of the sanctified, even them of the celestial world.' (D&C 88:2.) Names of faithful saints are recorded in the book of life while they are yet in mortality. (Luke 10:20; Philippians 4:3; *Teachings,* p. 9.) But those names are blotted out in the event of wickedness. (Revelation 13:8; 17:8; 22:19.)" (Bruce R. McConkie, *Mormon Doctrine,* p. 97.)

60. Suffer no ravenous wolf to enter among you] The honest and sincere truth-seeker is always welcome in the congregation of the Saints. During his visit among the Nephites, for instance, Christ commanded them to meet together often and added, "Ye shall not forbid any man from coming unto you when ye shall meet together, but suffer them that they may come unto you and forbid them not; but ye shall pray for them, and shall not cast them out; and if it so be that they come unto you oft ye shall pray for them unto the Father, in my name" (3 Nephi 18:22–23). Such a commandment does not suppose that we would welcome a wolf among us. We have no obligation to provide the devil with a platform to promote falsehood and advocate sin, nor can we tolerate the desires of evil and conspiring men who seek to prey upon the Saints.

62. Be partakers of the fruit of the tree of life] Christ is the tree of life. To be a partaker of the fruit of the tree of life is to feast upon the principles of salvation as taught and revealed by him. See *Commentary* 1:75–77.

Order Required in the Things of God

Alma 6:1–8

1. And now it came to pass that after Alma had made an end of speaking unto the people of the church, which was established in the city of Zarahemla, he ordained priests and elders, by laying on his hands according to the order of God, to preside and watch over the church.

2. And it came to pass that whosoever did not belong to the church who repented of their sins were baptized unto repentance, and were received into the church.

3. And it also came to pass that whosoever did belong to the church that did not repent of their wickedness and humble themselves before God—I mean those who were lifted up in the pride of their hearts—the same were rejected, and their names were blotted out, that their names were not numbered among those of the righteous.

4. And thus they began to establish the order of the church in the city of Zarahemla.

5. Now I would that ye should understand that the word of God was liberal unto all, that none were deprived of the privilege of assembling themselves together to hear the word of God.

6. Nevertheless the children of God were commanded that they should gather themselves together oft, and join in fasting and mighty prayer in behalf of the welfare of the souls of those who knew not God.

7. And now it came to pass that when Alma had made these regulations he departed from them, yea, from the church which was in the city of Zarahemla, and went over upon the east of the river Sidon, into the valley of Gideon, there having been a city built, which was called the city of Gideon, which was in the valley that was called Gideon, being called after the man who was slain by the hand of Nehor with the sword.

8. And Alma went and began to declare the word of God unto the church which was established in the valley of Gideon, according to the revelation of the truth of the word which had been spoken by his fathers, and according to the spirit of prophecy which was in him, according to the testimony of

Jesus Christ, the Son of God, who should come to redeem his people from their sins, and the holy order by which he was called. And thus it is written. Amen.

1. Ordained . . . by laying on his hands] Ordination—that is, the formal ritual by which the priesthood, its offices, or the rights of presidency are conferred—must be done by the laying on of hands. Such is the order of heaven. The laying on of hands constitutes a visual and documentable event whereby the authority of the priesthood can be traced back to the Lord from whence it comes. The hands laid upon the head of the recipient of the ordination are a symbolic representation of the hands of the Lord (see D&C 36:2).

1. The order of God] This reference is to the priesthood, or the "holy order of God," as Alma refers to it earlier (see Alma 5:43–49).

3. Names were blotted out] See *Commentary* 2:301.

4. Order of the church] The order of the Church is maintained and manifest through ordinances and ordinations. One does not capriciously lay claim to authority or priesthood office, nor can one receive the ordinances of salvation without properly complying with commandments and appropriate procedures governing their performance.

5. The word of God was liberal unto all] In teaching the gospel there is to be no distinction between the rich and the poor. The word of God is to be freely and generously given to all, regardless of social standing. "For if there come unto your assembly a man with a gold ring, in goodly apparel, and there come in also a poor man in vile raiment; and ye have respect to him that weareth the gay clothing, and say unto him, Sit thou here in a good place; and say to the poor, Stand thou there, or sit here under my footstool: are ye not then partial in yourselves, and are become judges of evil thoughts?" (James 2:2–4.)

6. The children of God] The phrase is appropriate in both a literal and a figurative sense. Because both Adam and Eve rightfully claim God as their Father, and because we descend from them, we are spoken of in the scriptures as the "children of God" (Moses 6:8). In this instance, however, reference is to baptized members of the Church, those who by covenant have been born again and thereby received into the family of Jesus Christ (see Mosiah 5:1–7).

6. Gather themselves together oft] It has ever been the command of the Lord that his people "[meet] together oft both to pray and to hear the word of the Lord" (4 Nephi 1:12). Moroni wrote: "And the church did meet together oft, to fast and to pray, and to speak one with another concerning the welfare of their souls" (Moroni 6:5).

8. The holy order by which he was called] See Alma 4:20; 5:44.

Alma Perceives That the People of Gideon Are More Faithful

Alma 7:1–6

1. Behold my beloved brethren, seeing that I have been permitted to come unto you, therefore I attempt to address you in my language; yea, by my own mouth, seeing that it is the first time that I have spoken unto you by the words of my mouth, I having been wholly confined to the judgment-seat, having had much business that I could not come unto you.

2. And even I could not have come now at this time were it not that the judgment-seat hath been given to another, to reign in my stead; and the Lord in much mercy hath granted that I should come unto you.

3. And behold, I have come having great hopes and much desire that I should find that ye had humbled yourselves before God, and that ye had continued in the supplicating of his grace, that I should find that ye were blameless before him, that I should find that ye were not in the awful dilemma that our brethren were in at Zarahemla.

4. But blessed be the name of God, that he hath given me to know, yea, hath given unto me the exceedingly great joy of knowing that they are established again in the way of his righteousness.

5. And I trust, according to the Spirit of God which is in me, that I shall also have joy over you; nevertheless I do not desire that my joy over you should come by the cause of so much afflictions and sorrow which I have had for the brethren at Zarahemla, for behold, my joy cometh over them after wading through much affliction and sorrow.

6. But behold, I trust that ye are not in a state of so much unbelief as were your brethren; I trust that ye are not lifted up in the pride of your hearts; yea, I trust that ye have not set your hearts upon riches and the vain things of the world; yea, I trust that you do not worship idols, but that ye do worship the true and living God, and that ye look forward for the remission of your sins, with an everlasting faith, which is to come.

1–2. These verses imply that Alma has had little or no opportunity to speak personally to this group before. His references to speaking "in my language" and "by my own mouth" indicate that as the chief judge or governor, as well as the president or presiding high priest of the Church, he had either sent his words by messengers or had his directives or sermons delivered to all parts of the land by his servants.

2. The judgment-seat hath been given to another] See Alma 4:15–20.

3. Continued in the supplicating of his grace] That is, Alma's desire is that the people of Gideon have maintained their trust in and reliance upon the mercy and grace of the divine Redeemer. The power by which individuals are cleansed and purified from sin at baptism—the atoning power of Christ the Lord, given as a free gift—is the same power by which individuals retain a remission of sins from day to day after baptism (see Mosiah 4:11–12, 26).

4–5. Alma discerns by the power of the Spirit that the people in this city are more spiritually prepared to receive the word than were those in Zarahemla. No doubt the light of spiritual receptivity, the animating power of goodness and humility, shone in the faces of some of the congregants.

Jesus Christ: The Fundamental Verity

Alma 7:7–16

7. For behold, I say unto you there be many things to come; and behold, there is one thing which is of more importance than they all—for behold, the time is not far distant that the Redeemer liveth and cometh among his people.

8. Behold, I do not say that he will come among us at the time of his dwelling in his mortal tabernacle; for behold, the Spirit hath not said unto me that this should be the case. Now as to this thing I do not know; but this much I do know, that the Lord God hath power to do all things which are according to his word.

9. But behold, the Spirit hath said this much unto me, saying: Cry unto this people, saying— Repent ye, and prepare the way of the Lord, and walk in his paths, which are straight; for behold, the

kingdom of heaven is at hand, and the Son of God cometh upon the face of the earth.

10. And behold, he shall be born of Mary, at Jerusalem which is the land of our forefathers, she being a virgin, a precious and chosen vessel, who shall be overshadowed and conceive by the power of the Holy Ghost, and bring forth a son, yea, even the Son of God.

11. And he shall go forth, suffering pains and afflictions and temptations of every kind; and this that the word might be fulfilled which saith he will take upon him the pains and the sicknesses of his people.

12. And he will take upon him death, that he may loose the bands of death which bind his people; and he will take upon him their infirmities, that his bowels may be

filled with mercy, according to the flesh, that he may know according to the flesh how to succor his people according to their infirmities.

13. Now the Spirit knoweth all things; nevertheless the Son of God suffereth according to the flesh that he might take upon him the sins of his people, that he might blot out their transgressions according to the power of his deliverance; and now behold, this is the testimony which is in me.

14. Now I say unto you that ye must repent, and be born again; for the Spirit saith if ye are not born again ye cannot inherit the kingdom of heaven; therefore come and be baptized unto repentance, that ye may be washed from your sins, that ye may have faith on the Lamb of God, who taketh away the sins of the world, who is mighty to save and to cleanse from all unrighteousness.

15. Yea, I say unto you come and fear not, and lay aside every sin, which easily doth beset you, which doth bind you down to destruction, yea, come and go forth, and show unto your God that ye are willing to repent of your sins and enter into a covenant with him to keep his commandments, and witness it unto him this day by going into the waters of baptism.

16. And whosoever doeth this, and keepeth the commandments of God from thenceforth, the same will remember that I say unto him, yea, he will remember that I have said unto him, he shall have eternal life, according to the testimony of the Holy Spirit, which testifieth in me.

7. One thing which is of more importance] Joseph Smith taught that "the fundamental principles of our religion are the testimony of the Apostles and Prophets, concerning Jesus Christ, that He died, was buried, and rose again the third day, and ascended into heaven; and all other things which pertain to our religion are only appendages to it" (*Teachings*, p. 121). All doctrines and principles and practices have meaning—are of efficacy, virtue, or force —only to the degree that they are rooted in and anchored to the atonement of Jesus Christ. In the words of Elder Boyd K. Packer: "Truth, glorious truth, proclaims there is . . . a Mediator. . . . Through Him mercy can be fully extended to each of us without offending the eternal law of justice. This truth is the very root of Christian doctrine. You may know much about the gospel as it branches out from there, but if you only know the branches and those branches do not touch that root, if they have been cut free from that truth, there will be no life nor substance nor redemption in them." (CR, April 1977, p. 80.)

8. For some reason, Alma is unclear as to exactly when the Savior will appear in the Americas. Earlier prophets taught specifically that Jesus would come among the Nephites after his death and resurrection (see 1 Nephi 12:4–6; 2 Nephi 26:1).

9. The kingdom of heaven is at hand] See Alma 5:28, 50; 10:20.

10. He shall be born of Mary] See *Commentary* 1:78; Mosiah 3:8.

10. At Jerusalem] These words have spawned a host of heckles and sneers directed at the Book of Mormon. Persons of a skeptical and cynical spirit ask: "Didn't Joseph Smith know that Jesus was born of Mary *in Bethlehem*?" We answer: Yes, he was born *in* Bethlehem, but he was also born *at* Jerusalem, meaning that Bethlehem, the smaller community, was within the environs of Jerusalem, the larger city. In our day it would be as if someone from Sandy or even Provo, Utah, had said to one somewhat unfamiliar with the Wasatch Front, "I am from Salt Lake City." (See *A Sure Foundation*, pp. 3–4.)

10. Who shall be overshadowed and conceive by the power of the Holy Ghost] Jesus was the son of Mary, a mortal woman. And he was the son of Elohim, the Eternal Father. He was not the son of the Holy Ghost, as some have supposed from the New Testament account (Matthew 1:18). "If [the New Testament passage] is interpreted to mean that the Holy Ghost is the Father of our Lord," Elder Bruce R. McConkie has written, "we can only say the record has come down to us in a corrupted form, for the Holy Spirit and the Father are two separate personages. But providentially there are parallel passages that clarify and expand upon the paternity of Him whom Mary bore." These passages are, of course, in the Book of Mormon, particularly here in Alma 7. Continuing, Elder McConkie stated: "Jesus, thus, is the Son of God, not of the Holy Ghost, and properly speaking Mary was with child 'by the power of the Holy Ghost,' rather than 'of the Holy Ghost,' and she was, of course, 'overshadowed' by the Holy Spirit, in a way incomprehensible to us, when the miraculous conception took place." (*Promised Messiah*, pp. 463–64; see also *Mortal Messiah* 1:314–15.)

11–12. These verses are most important. They point up the vital verity that our Lord's suffering and atonement were more extensive and expansive than we are wont to suppose. His suffering and pain throughout his life (how he should "go forth"), as well as his supreme agony in Gethsemane—all of this was necessary, not alone to pay the price for sin but also to allow our empathic exemplar to feel with and for his people. His passion helped to perfect his empathy and his ability to succor those of us who so desperately need understanding and affection and divine assistance. Elder Neal A. Maxwell has taught this principle beautifully: "Can we, even in the depths of disease, tell Him anything at all about suffering? In ways we cannot comprehend, our sicknesses and infirmities were borne by Him even before they were borne by us. The very weight of our combined sins caused Him to descend below all. We have never been, nor will we be, in depths such as He has known. Thus His atonement made perfect His empathy and His mercy and His capacity to succor us, for which we can be everlastingly grateful as He tutors us in our trials." (*Even As I Am*, p. 116.)

11. Temptations of every kind] The Apostle Paul taught: "For verily [Christ] took not on him the nature of angels; but he took on him the seed of Abraham. Wherefore in all things it behooved him to be made like unto his brethren, that he might be a merciful and faithful high priest in things pertaining to God, to make reconciliation for the sins of the people. For in that he himself hath suffered being tempted, he is able to succor them that are tempted." Further: "For we have not an high priest which cannot be touched with the feeling of our infirmities; but was in all points tempted like as we are, yet without sin." (Hebrews 2:16–18; 4:15.)

12. He will take upon him death] That is, he will submit to death, surrender his own mortal life to the greater plan of happiness which requires his suffering and death and subsequent rise from the tomb. Jesus did not have to die, meaning that his nature was such—as the Son of Man of Holiness, thus possessing the powers of immortality—that he could have lived forever. Had he not given up the ghost of his own free will he could have spurned the powers of earth and remained alive. His was a voluntary offering. "Therefore doth my Father love me, because I lay down my life, that I might take it again. No man taketh it from me, but I lay it down of myself. I have power to lay it down, and I have power to take it again." (John 10:17–18.)

12. That he may loose the bands of death which bind his people] Only through submitting to death could our Lord then meet and conquer this universal foe, the one thing that every mortal has in common with every other mortal. "For behold, he surely must die that salvation may come; yea, it behooveth him and becometh expedient that he dieth, to bring to pass the resurrection of the dead" (Helaman 14:15). "For as in Adam all die, even so in Christ shall all be made alive" (1 Corinthians 15:22).

12. How to succor his people] "Behold, and hearken, . . . saith the Lord your God, even Jesus Christ, your advocate, who knoweth the weakness of man and how to succor them who are tempted" (D&C 62:1).

13. Now the Spirit knoweth all things] There were some things associated with mortal life—physical testing and trial and pain and harassment and estrangement and embarrassment—that the Lord Jehovah needed to experience firsthand. And so he came to earth. He came to suffer according to the flesh. The great God of the ancients condescended to walk among men that he might work out his own salvation and also make the same available to those who received his word and trusted in his redeeming grace. Though it is true that the Spirit knows all things, the God of mercy needed to experience infirmity, weakness, and sickness personally in order to identify with and comfort his people, and often to deliver them from such things.

13. That he might take upon him the sins of his people] In a way that we cannot comprehend, Jesus of Nazareth assumed the burden and consequence of the sins of all mankind. "The immediate consequence of sin is withdrawal of the Spirit (see Alma 34:35). It may be that such a withdrawal from an individual is what leads to feelings of guilt and pain and emptiness. Jesus Christ, in taking upon him the effects of the sins of all mankind, was thus exposed to the awful (and to Jesus, unusual) withdrawal of that Spirit which had been his constant companion from the beginning." (Robert L. Millet, *Life in Christ*, p. 68.) President Brigham Young explained: "The Father withdrew His Spirit from His Son, at the time he was to be crucified. . . . At the very moment, at the hour when the crisis came for him to offer up his life, the Father withdrew Himself, withdrew His Spirit. . . . That is what made him sweat blood. If he had had the power of God upon him, he would not have sweat blood." (*JD* 3:206.)

14. Ye must repent, and be born again] See *Commentary* 2:168–76.

14. That ye may be washed from your sins] The scriptures seldom speak of having our sins "washed away" in the waters of baptism (see Acts 22:16; D&C 39:10), though the Saints frequently use this expression to teach the purpose of baptism. Perhaps the more useful analogy is that which attests to the Holy Ghost as the agent, the medium by which sins and dross are burned out of the human soul as though by fire, thus giving rise to the phrase "baptism by fire." Sins are remitted not in the waters of baptism, as we say casually, but rather as we receive the cleansing and sanctifying influence of the Spirit in our lives. See 2 Nephi 31:17; 3 Nephi 12:2; Moroni 6:4; *Teachings*, p. 314; *New Witness*, pp. 239, 290.

14. Who is mighty to save] See 2 Nephi 31:19.

15. Baptism is an ordinance of profound symbolism. In the purest sense, we are baptized to witness our willingness to accept Christ, to take upon us his name, and to commit ourselves to receive his atonement. We go down into the watery grave as a token and a remembrance of our Master's descent into the tomb of death. We come forth, as did he, unto a newness of life: his a resurrected immortality, ours a sanctified mortality. Having been "planted . . . in the likeness of his death," we are thereby "in the likeness of his resurrection" (Romans 6:3–5).

15. Lay aside every sin] Alma is not counselling the people to put away their sins one at a time, a bit here and a bit there. This is the world's approach. It may sound commendable, but it is terrestrial at best. To be born again is to have our natures changed, not always immediately but certainly in process of time. To lay aside every sin is to rid oneself of all sin and the desire for it; to put off all sinfulness; to confess and forsake sin; and to rely on the merits and mercies of the Holy Messiah.

16. See 2 Nephi 31:19–20; Mosiah 18:8–10.

Alma's Commendation and Final Charge to the People of Gideon

Alma 7:17–27

17. And now my beloved brethren, do you believe these things? Behold, I say unto you, yea, I know that ye believe them; and the way that I know that ye believe them is by the manifestation of the Spirit which is in me. And now because your faith is strong concerning that, yea, concerning the things which I have spoken, great is my joy.

18. For as I said unto you from the beginning, that I had much desire that ye were not in the state of dilemma like your brethren, even so I have found that my desires have been gratified.

19. For I perceive that ye are in the paths of righteousness; I perceive that ye are in the path which leads to the kingdom of God; yea, I perceive that ye are making his paths straight.

20. I perceive that it has been made known unto you, by the testimony of his word, that he cannot walk in crooked paths; neither doth he vary from that which he hath said; neither hath he a shadow of turning from the right to the left, or from that which is right to that which is wrong; therefore, his course is one eternal round.

21. And he doth not dwell in unholy temples; neither can filthiness or anything which is unclean be received into the kingdom of God; therefore I say unto you the time shall come, yea, and it shall be at the last day, that he who is filthy shall remain in his filthiness.

22. And now my beloved brethren, I have said these things unto you that I might awaken you to a sense of your duty to God, that ye may walk blameless before him, that ye may walk after the holy order of God, after which ye have been received.

23. And now I would that ye should be humble, and be submis-

sive and gentle; easy to be entreated; full of patience and long-
suffering; being temperate in all
things; being diligent in keeping
the commandments of God at all
times; asking for whatsoever
things ye stand in need, both spiritual and temporal; always returning thanks unto God for whatsoever things ye do receive.

24. And see that ye have faith,
hope, and charity, and then ye
will always abound in good works.

25. And may the Lord bless you,
and keep your garments spotless,
that ye may at last be brought to
sit down with Abraham, Isaac, and
Jacob, and the holy prophets who
have been ever since the world
began, having your garments

spotless even as their garments are
spotless, in the kingdom of heaven
to go no more out.

26. And now my beloved
brethren, I have spoken these
words unto you according to the
Spirit which testifieth in me; and
my soul doth exceedingly rejoice,
because of the exceeding diligence
and heed which ye have given
unto my word.

27. And now, may the peace of
God rest upon you, and upon your
houses and lands, and upon your
flocks and herds, and all that you
possess, your women and your
children, according to your faith
and good works, from this time
forth and forever. And thus I have
spoken. Amen.

17. See commentary on verses 4–5.

19. Ye are in the paths of righteousness] They are not
perfect but are striving, through their allegiance to and trust in
Christ, to become such. Like the people to whom Paul wrote, their
salvation is nearer than when they initially believed the truth (see
Romans 13:11). They are on track. Their course is approved of
God.

19. Ye are making his paths straight] Righteousness prepares the way of the Lord; it builds faith, strengthens resolve,
heightens commitment, and prepares the heart for the establishment of Zion.

20. Our Lord is absolutely dependable and everlastingly constant. His truths are eternal, his ways and doings are forever the
same, and his purposes unfailing. Though the principle on which
the government of heaven is conducted is revelation suited to the
circumstances in which the children of the kingdom are placed
(see *Teachings*, p. 256), God's ways are never capricious, never
variable. On him we may rely with unshaken confidence. See 1
Nephi 10:19; Alma 37:12; D&C 3:2.

21. He doth not dwell in unholy temples] That is, his
Spirit cannot abide with those who have violated their covenants
or broken the commandments and remain unrepentant. See 1
Corinthians 3:17; 6:19; Mosiah 2:37; Alma 34:36; 3 Nephi 27:19.

21. He who is filthy shall remain in his filthiness] This is
speaking of the ultimate in filthiness, the pinnacle of unholiness,

the sons of perdition. These are they who deny and defy, vessels of wrath, poisoned cisterns, people who stare at the light of the Son and yet shun him. See also Mormon 9:14; D&C 88:35, 102.

22. After the holy order of God] See commentary on Alma 5:44.

23–24. Alma is counseling the people of Gideon to live worthy of the companionship of the Spirit, that they might enjoy the "fruit of the Spirit" (Galatians 5:22). Humility, gentleness, patience, long-suffering—these virtues come by and through the power of the Holy Ghost; they begin to flow from a regenerated heart. See *Commentary* 2:163.

25. To sit down with Abraham, Isaac, and Jacob] To us, to "sit down" with these ancient worthies is to qualify for their company, to be confident and at ease in their presence, and to receive exaltation and godhood, for that is the condition and state of these patriarchs (see D&C 132:37).

27. May the peace of God rest upon you] "Peace I leave with you," the Savior said, "my peace I give unto you: not as the world giveth, give I unto you. Let not your heart be troubled, neither let it be afraid." (John 14:27.) "And the peace of God, which passeth all understanding, shall keep your hearts and minds through Christ Jesus" (Philippians 4:7; see also Romans 5:1; Colossians 3:15).

Alma Has Success in Melek

Alma 8:1–6

1. And now it came to pass that Alma returned from the land of Gideon, after having taught the people of Gideon many things which cannot be written, having established the order of the church, according as he had before done in the land of Zarahemla, yea, he returned to his own house at Zarahemla to rest himself from the labors which he had performed.

2. And thus ended the ninth year of the reign of the judges over the people of Nephi.

3. And it came to pass in the commencement of the tenth year of the reign of the judges over the people of Nephi, that Alma departed from thence and took his journey over into the land of Melek, on the west of the river Sidon, on the west by the borders of the wilderness.

4. And he began to teach the people in the land of Melek according to the holy order of God, by which he had been called; and he began to teach the people throughout all the land of Melek.

5. And it came to pass that the people came to him throughout all the borders of the land which was by the wilderness side. And they were baptized throughout all the land;

6. So that when he had finished his work at Melek he departed thence, and traveled three days' journey on the north of the land of Melek; and he came to a city which was called Ammonihah.

1. The order of the church] It is difficult to determine exactly how the Church was organized among the Nephites. Because the Book of Mormon is a Christ-centered record, the writers did not choose to detail the organization of the Church, except to mention a few of its officers and to lay stress upon its function.

2–6. No doubt there were many cities and villages in which Alma preached and of which we have little or no record. Mormon, our writer-editor, was striving to preserve those lessons and precepts which would be of everlasting worth to future readers. In some cases, therefore, he did not seem to feel the need to repeat a concept or a lesson or a teaching experience over and over again. Rather, he provided one strong illustration (such as Alma's discourse at Zarahemla) to make his point. In this case, because the people of Melek responded positively and receptively to his gospel message, Mormon reserved the space on the plates for something else: there was a negative lesson to be learned from the people in Ammonihah.

Alma Struggles to Teach the Wicked in Ammonihah

Alma 8:7–18

7. Now it was the custom of the people of Nephi to call their lands, and their cities, and their villages, yea, even all their small villages, after the name of him who first possessed them; and thus it was with the land of Ammonihah.

8. And it came to pass that when Alma had come to the city of Ammonihah he began to preach the word of God unto them.

9. Now Satan had gotten great hold upon the hearts of the people of the city of Ammonihah; therefore they would not hearken unto the words of Alma.

10. Nevertheless Alma labored much in the spirit, wrestling with God in mighty prayer, that he would pour out his Spirit upon the people who were in the city; that he would also grant that he might baptize them unto repentance.

11. Nevertheless, they hardened their hearts, saying unto him: Behold, we know that thou art Alma; and we know that thou art high priest over the church which thou hast established in many parts of the land, according to your tradition; and we are not of thy church, and we do not believe in such foolish traditions.

12. And now we know that because we are not of thy church we know that thou hast no power

over us; and thou hast delivered up the judgment-seat unto Nephihah; therefore thou art not the chief judge over us.

13. Now when the people had said this, and withstood all his words, and reviled him, and spit upon him, and caused that he should be cast out of their city, he departed thence and took his journey towards the city which was called Aaron.

14. And it came to pass that while he was journeying thither, being weighed down with sorrow, wading through much tribulation and anguish of soul, because of the wickedness of the people who were in the city of Ammonihah, it came to pass while Alma was thus weighed down with sorrow, behold an angel of the Lord appeared unto him, saying:

15. Blessed art thou, Alma; therefore, lift up thy head and rejoice, for thou hast great cause to rejoice; for thou hast been faithful in keeping the commandments of God from the time which thou receivedst thy first message from him. Behold, I am he that delivered it unto you.

16. And behold, I am sent to command thee that thou return to the city of Ammonihah, and preach again unto the people of the city; yea, preach unto them. Yea, say unto them, except they repent the Lord God will destroy them.

17. For behold, they do study at this time that they may destroy the liberty of thy people, (for thus saith the Lord) which is contrary to the statutes, and judgments, and commandments which he has given unto his people.

18. Now it came to pass that after Alma had received his message from the angel of the Lord he returned speedily to the land of Ammonihah. And he entered the city by another way, yea, by the way which is on the south of the city of Ammonihah.

7. Compare 1 Nephi 2:8–10. Because the Book of Mormon is an abridgment, we lack access to many of the details of the Nephite history, particularly details which Mormon did not feel contributed to the most valuable lessons.

9. "The Spirit [meaning the Light of Christ] enlighteneth every man through the world, that hearkeneth to the voice of the Spirit. And every one that hearkeneth to the voice of the Spirit cometh unto God, even the Father. And the Father teacheth him of the covenant"—the gospel covenant. "And the whole world lieth in sin, and groaneth under darkness and under the bondage of sin. And by this you may know they are under the bondage of sin, because they come not unto me." (D&C 84:46–50.) That is, because they receive not the message of the gospel as preached by his anointed servants.

10. Alma labored much in the spirit, wrestling with God in mighty prayer] Alma knew that something unusual would need to take place if the hardened inhabitants of Ammonihah were to be touched by his message. He therefore pleaded with anxiety and with all the energy of his heart for an endowment and an outpouring of divine grace, such as would soften hearts and magnify his poor words to such extent that souls might be won. Alma's experience is a marvelous example of a pertinent but often painful reality—that the righteousness and personal power of the preacher is only one factor in the conversion of a people. The listeners must open their hearts, be willing to acknowledge and confess their weaknesses, and ponder and pray about what is spoken. Alma labored with all the faith he could muster. But faith is built upon evidence, and in this case (as in the case with Mormon in Mormon 3:12 or with Jesus in Mark 6:1–5) the intransigence of the Ammonihahites precluded the miracle of conversion at that time.

11–12. Where righteousness reigned in a Nephite society the people were allowed to worship or believe as they chose, as long as their behavior stayed within legal bounds (see Alma 1:17; 30:7).

14. Being weighed down with sorrow] There are few pains as poignant to the righteous servant of God as that which comes through being prevented from sharing the truths of the gospel. Alma has known the instability of a double-minded life, has felt the pangs of conscience which follow in the wake of sin not repented of, has lived through the achings and agonies of unrealized potential. He also knows the gladness of remitted sin, the unspeakable joy of restoration to righteousness, the peace of partaking of Christ's redeeming love. He knows the power and majesty of the Almighty to deliver one from bitter darkness into the marvelous light of Christ. He has been born again and desires the same for all people.

15. Thou hast great cause to rejoice; for thou hast been faithful] An angel sent from the courts of glory—the same angel who had struck down the wayward and wandering Alma and the sons of Mosiah about two decades earlier (see Mosiah 27, Alma 36)—had returned to offer consolation and comfort and counsel. His initial message was one of assurance, the quiet but powerful acknowledgment that Alma had been faithful, that his offering was acceptable before God. A peace of soul comes to the obedient and the faithful that is unknown to the flighty and the inconsistent, an inner awareness that God is pleased with their efforts. Such feelings may come in spite of results, in spite of "success" or lack of it, at least as measured by worldly standards. One who labors with fidelity and devotion, seeking diligently to lead others to baptism, is successful in the Lord's eyes.

16. There are many reasons why we in the true Church send out missionaries. First and foremost is to make the blessings of the gospel—the covenants and saving ordinances in particular—available to all of our Heavenly Father's children. Second, the labor of selfless service associated with missionary work builds a saintly character and a stability of soul in the missionary that proves an invaluable asset to the kingdom of God. Third, we preach the gospel as a way of warning the nations of that which is to come. "Behold, I sent you out to testify and warn the people, and it becometh every man who hath been warned to warn his neighbor. Therefore, they are left without excuse, and their sins are upon their own heads." (D&C 88:81–82.) Further: "Let your preaching be the warning voice, every man to his neighbor, in mildness and in meekness" (D&C 38:41). Alma was to return to Ammonihah to lift a warning voice, to declare with words of soberness that a speedy and certain destruction awaited the people there if they did not repent.

18. He returned speedily] Although the idea of returning to the city of Ammonihah, to the abuse and scorn which he knew awaited him there, must have been an unpleasant one, Alma was obedient to the words and will of the Lord as delivered by the angel. He hurried to do what he had been called to do.

Amulek Is Prepared to Receive Alma

Alma 8:19–32

19. And as he entered the city he was an hungered, and he said to a man: Will ye give to an humble servant of God something to eat?

20. And the man said unto him: I am a Nephite, and I know that thou art a holy prophet of God, for thou art the man whom an angel said in a vision: Thou shalt receive. Therefore, go with me into my house and I will impart unto thee of my food; and I know that thou wilt be a blessing unto me and my house.

21. And it came to pass that the man received him into his house; and the man was called Amulek; and he brought forth bread and meat and set before Alma.

22. And it came to pass that Alma ate bread and was filled; and he blessed Amulek and his house, and he gave thanks unto God.

23. And after he had eaten and was filled he said unto Amulek: I am Alma, and am the high priest over the church of God throughout the land.

24. And behold, I have been called to preach the word of God among all this people, according to the spirit of revelation and prophecy; and I was in this land and they would not receive me, but they cast me out and I was about to set my back towards this land forever.

25. But behold, I have been commanded that I should turn

again and prophesy unto this people, yea, and to testify against them concerning their iniquities.

26. And now, Amulek, because thou hast fed me and taken me in, thou art blessed; for I was an hungered, for I had fasted many days.

27. And Alma tarried many days with Amulek before he began to preach unto the people.

28. And it came to pass that the people did wax more gross in their iniquities.

29. And the word came to Alma, saying: Go; and also say unto my servant Amulek, go forth and prophesy unto this people, saying—Repent ye, for thus saith the Lord, except ye repent I will visit this people in mine anger; yea, and I will not turn my fierce anger away.

30. And Alma went forth, and also Amulek, among the people, to declare the words of God unto them; and they were filled with the Holy Ghost.

31. And they had power given unto them, insomuch that they could not be confined in dungeons; neither was it possible that any man could slay them; nevertheless they did not exercise their power until they were bound in bands and cast into prison. Now, this was done that the Lord might show forth his power in them.

32. And it came to pass that they went forth and began to preach and to prophesy unto the people, according to the spirit and power which the Lord had given them.

19–27. This incident dramatizes how the Lord prepares the way for his servants. It highlights how divine providence orchestrates the scheme of things in such a way as to accomplish the greatest good. Before Alma had even returned to town, an angel had appeared to Amulek with specific instructions as to how he was to meet and care for Alma.

20. Thou wilt be a blessing unto me and my house] It is indeed a privilege to house and care for the servants of the Lord. Their presence and personal power proves an unspeakable blessing to the home in which they reside temporarily. Mormon's account indicates that "Alma tarried many days with Amulek before he began to preach unto the people" (verse 27). One can but imagine what a remarkable experience it must have been to be tutored and prepared by Alma and by angels (see Alma 10:10). Amulek's home, during this brief season, would have served as a most unusual missionary training center.

30. They were filled with the Holy Ghost] That is, they enjoyed the gifts and powers of the Spirit in their ministry: discernment, prophecy, revelation, knowledge, wisdom, the ministry of angels, charity, and many others. Having been sanctified from sin, they had their hearts and mouths filled with holiness and with heavenly power. They spoke what was given them from above. Their words enjoyed the justifying and sustaining power of God.

31. Mormon here speaks of their experiences retrospectively. See Alma 14:17–29.

Alma Warns the People of Ammonihah

Alma 9:1–34

1. And again, I, Alma, having been commanded of God that I should take Amulek and go forth and preach again unto this people, or the people who were in the city of Ammonihah, it came to pass as I began to preach unto them, they began to contend with me, saying:

2. Who art thou? Suppose ye that we shall believe the testimony of one man, although he should preach unto us that the earth should pass away?

3. Now they understood not the words which they spake; for they knew not that the earth should pass away.

4. And they said also: We will not believe thy words if thou shouldst prophesy that this great city should be destroyed in one day.

5. Now they knew not that God could do such marvelous works, for they were a hard-hearted and a stiffnecked people.

6. And they said: Who is God, that sendeth no more authority than one man among this people, to declare unto them the truth of such great and marvelous things?

7. And they stood forth to lay their hands on me; but behold, they did not. And I stood with boldness to declare unto them, yea, I did boldly testify unto them, saying:

8. Behold, O ye wicked and perverse generation, how have ye forgotten the tradition of your fathers; yea, how soon ye have forgotten the commandments of God.

9. Do ye not remember that our father, Lehi, was brought out of Jerusalem by the hand of God? Do ye not remember that they were all led by him through the wilderness?

10. And have ye forgotten so soon how many times he delivered our fathers out of the hands of their enemies, and preserved them from being destroyed, even by the hands of their own brethren?

11. Yea, and if it had not been for his matchless power, and his mercy, and his long-suffering towards us, we should unavoidably have been cut off from the face of the earth long before this period of time, and perhaps been consigned to a state of endless misery and woe.

12. Behold, now I say unto you that he commandeth you to repent; and except ye repent, ye can in nowise inherit the kingdom of God. But behold, this is not all—he has commanded you to repent, or he will utterly destroy you from off the face of the earth; yea, he will visit you in his anger, and in his fierce anger he will not turn away.

13. Behold, do ye not remember the words which he spake unto Lehi, saying that: Inasmuch as ye shall keep my commandments, ye shall prosper in the land? And again it is said that: Inasmuch as

ye will not keep my commandments ye shall be cut off from the
presence of the Lord.

14. Now I would that ye should
remember, that inasmuch as the
Lamanites have not kept the commandments of God, they have
been cut off from the presence of
the Lord. Now we see that the
word of the Lord has been verified
in this thing, and the Lamanites
have been cut off from his presence, from the beginning of their
transgressions in the land.

15. Nevertheless I say unto you,
that it shall be more tolerable for
them in the day of judgment than
for you, if ye remain in your sins,
yea, and even more tolerable for
them in this life than for you,
except ye repent.

16. For there are many promises
which are extended to the
Lamanites; for it is because of the
traditions of their fathers that
caused them to remain in their
state of ignorance; therefore the
Lord will be merciful unto them
and prolong their existence in the
land.

17. And at some period of time
they will be brought to believe in
his word, and to know of the
incorrectness of the traditions of
their fathers; and many of them
will be saved, for the Lord will be
merciful unto all who call on his
name.

18. But behold, I say unto you
that if ye persist in your wickedness that your days shall not be
prolonged in the land, for the
Lamanites shall be sent upon you;
and if ye repent not they shall
come in a time when you know
not, and ye shall be visited with
utter destruction; and it shall be
according to the fierce anger of the
Lord.

19. For he will not suffer you

that ye shall live in your iniquities,
to destroy his people. I say unto
you, Nay; he would rather suffer
that the Lamanites might destroy
all his people who are called the
people of Nephi, if it were possible
that they could fall into sins and
transgressions, after having had so
much light and so much knowledge given unto them of the Lord
their God;

20. Yea, after having been such
a highly favored people of the
Lord; yea, after having been
favored above every other nation,
kindred, tongue, or people; after
having had all things made known
unto them, according to their
desires, and their faith, and
prayers, of that which has been,
and which is, and which is to
come;

21. Having been visited by the
Spirit of God; having conversed
with angels, and having been
spoken unto by the voice of the
Lord; and having the spirit of
prophecy, and the spirit of revelation, and also many gifts, the gift
of speaking with tongues, and the
gift of preaching, and the gift of
the Holy Ghost, and the gift of
translation;

22. Yea, and after having been
delivered of God out of the land of
Jerusalem, by the hand of the
Lord; having been saved from
famine, and from sickness, and all
manner of diseases of every kind;
and they having waxed strong in
battle, that they might not be
destroyed; having been brought
out of bondage time after time,
and having been kept and preserved until now; and they have
been prospered until they are rich
in all manner of things—

23. And now behold I say unto
you, that if this people, who have
received so many blessings from

the hand of the Lord, should transgress contrary to the light and knowledge which they do have, I say unto you that if this be the case, that if they should fall into transgression, it would be far more tolerable for the Lamanites than for them.

24. For behold, the promises of the Lord are extended to the Lamanites, but they are not unto you if ye transgress; for has not the Lord expressly promised and firmly decreed, that if ye will rebel against him that ye shall utterly be destroyed from off the face of the earth?

25. And now for this cause, that ye may not be destroyed, the Lord has sent his angel to visit many of his people, declaring unto them that they must go forth and cry mightily unto this people, saying: Repent ye, for the kingdom of heaven is nigh at hand;

26. And not many days hence the Son of God shall come in his glory; and his glory shall be the glory of the Only Begotten of the Father, full of grace, equity, and truth, full of patience, mercy, and long-suffering, quick to hear the cries of his people and to answer their prayers.

27. And behold, he cometh to redeem those who will be baptized unto repentance, through faith on his name.

28. Therefore, prepare ye the way of the Lord, for the time is at hand that all men shall reap a reward of their works, according to that which they have been—if

they have been righteous they shall reap the salvation of their souls, according to the power and deliverance of Jesus Christ; and if they have been evil they shall reap the damnation of their souls, according to the power and captivation of the devil.

29. Now behold, this is the voice of the angel, crying unto the people.

30. And now, my beloved brethren, for ye are my brethren, and ye ought to be beloved, and ye ought to bring forth works which are meet for repentance, seeing that your hearts have been grossly hardened against the word of God, and seeing that ye are a lost and a fallen people.

31. Now it came to pass that when I, Alma, had spoken these words, behold, the people were wroth with me because I said unto them that they were a hardhearted and a stiffnecked people.

32. And also because I said unto them that they were a lost and a fallen people they were angry with me, and sought to lay their hands upon me, that they might cast me into prison.

33. But it came to pass that the Lord did not suffer them that they should take me at that time and cast me into prison.

34. And it came to pass that Amulek went and stood forth, and began to preach unto them also. And now the words of Amulek are not all written, nevertheless a part of his words are written in this book.

1–34. Mormon seems to be quoting here from Alma's own account of his encounter with the people of Ammonihah, an account which presumably was written some time after the preaching. Regarding the Lord's often assisting his servants to remember what has happened, see *Commentary* 2:249.

2. The testimony of one man] Truly, in the mouth of two or three witnesses shall every word be established (see 2 Corinthians 13:1). Alma responds to this criticism (also voiced in verse 6) by inviting Amulek to share his testimony in what we have now as chapters 10–11.

2. The earth should pass away] The contenders do not realize here that they are speaking the truth, speaking of the time yet future when there shall be a new heaven and a new earth, first at the time of the Second Coming (initiation of the Millennium) when the earth will be terrestrialized, and again at the end of the earth, after the thousand years, when the earth will become the fit abode of those who inherit celestial glory.

6. Who is God . . . ?] Compare these words with those of King Noah. See *Commentary* 2:204.

7–14. Here Alma pleads with his people to remember, to recall that God is able to deliver his people from destruction. He cites examples from their nation's past to illustrate that Jehovah's hand is ever ready to assist his people if they will reach out to him.

15–17. The promises of the Lord to the Lamanites are sure and certain. Because their sins were so often a result of incorrect tradition (as opposed to the Nephites, who sinned against great light), God will be merciful to them. See Helaman 7:24; 15:11–12.

17. They will be brought to believe] From the record of Enos on the small plates of Nephi we read the following: "And it came to pass that after I had prayed and labored with all diligence, the Lord said unto me: I will grant unto thee according to thy desires, because of thy faith. And now behold, this was the desire which I desired from him—that if it should so be, that my people, the Nephites, should fall into transgression, and by any means be destroyed, and the Lamanites should not be destroyed, that the Lord God would preserve a record of my people, the Nephites; even if it so be by the power of his holy arm, that it might be brought forth at some future day unto the Lamanites, that, perhaps, they might be brought unto salvation." (Enos 1:12–13.)

18. The fulfillment of this prophecy is recorded in Alma 16:1–3 and 25:1–2.

19–24. To sin against light—to walk in paths of wickedness when one has been enlightened by the Spirit, has enjoyed its gifts, and has been heir to the promises of the Almighty—is to place oneself in a precarious position. It represents the height of ingratitude. Truly, "he who sins against the greater light shall receive the greater condemnation" (D&C 82:3; Luke 12:48; see also Alma 24:30).

26. The Son of God shall come in his glory] See commentary on Alma 7:7.

26. The glory of the Only Begotten of the Father] Jesus Christ enjoyed the glory and power of the Eternal Father while in mortality because he was the Only Begotten Son of the Father in the flesh, because he inherited the powers of the Father from that exalted Sire.

26. Full of grace, equity, and truth] Our Lord possesses all of the godly attributes and virtues in their perfection. There is no knowledge which he does not possess, no tenderness, no charity, no patience, no mercy and long-suffering that are not naturally a part of his perfect being (see *Lectures on Faith*).

26. To answer their prayers] "Proper prayers are made to the Father, in the name of the Son, by the power of the Holy Ghost. The Father answers prayers, but he does it through the Son, into whose hands he has committed all things." (Bruce R. McConkie, *Promised Messiah*, p. 557; see also p. 335; *Mortal Messiah* 4:74.)

27. To redeem those who will be baptized] That is, those who will take his name upon themselves, those who accept and wish to apply to their lives his atoning sacrifice, those who wish to evidence their belief by participating symbolically in the death and burial and resurrection of the Holy One (see Romans 6:3–5; Alma 7:14–15).

28. All men shall reap a reward of their works] All men shall stand before God to be judged according to that which they have done or failed to do. The law of justice—either to bless or condemn—will then be put into full effect.

28. The salvation of their souls] See commentary on Alma 11:40.

29. This is the voice of the angel] It appears that Alma has been quoting or paraphrasing the words of the angel delivered to him, presumably at the time of their preparation in Amulek's home (see Alma 10:10).

30. Ye are my brethren, and ye ought to be beloved] They are his brethren and sisters in the sense that they are children of God and descendants of Lehi, just as he is. They are not beloved in the sense of being bound together in that brotherly and sisterly love known only to the faithful Saints.

30. Works which are meet for repentance] Works which are equal to, worthy of, evidence of one's repentance. That is, Alma exhorts the people to repent of their sins so that the works of righteousness will flow from their regenerated hearts.

30. Ye are a lost and a fallen people] People remain forever lost and fallen until they come unto Christ through forsaking their sins and putting off the natural man. Lehi taught that "all mankind were in a lost and in a fallen state, and ever would be save they should rely on this Redeemer" (1 Nephi 10:6; see also Mosiah 3:19; 16:3–5; Alma 12:22; 42:6–12).

Amulek Delivers a Confirming Witness

Alma 10:1–11

1. Now these are the words which Amulek preached unto the people who were in the land of Ammonihah, saying:

2. I am Amulek; I am the son of Giddonah, who was the son of Ishmael, who was a descendant of Aminadi; and it was the same Aminadi who interpreted the writing which was upon the wall of the temple, which was written by the finger of God.

3. And Aminadi was a descendant of Nephi, who was the son of Lehi, who came out of the land of Jerusalem, who was a descendant of Manasseh, who was the son of Joseph who was sold into Egypt by the hands of his brethren.

4. And behold, I am also a man of no small reputation among all those who know me; yea, and behold, I have many kindreds and friends, and I have also acquired much riches by the hand of my industry.

5. Nevertheless, after all this, I never have known much of the ways of the Lord, and his mysteries and marvelous power. I said I never had known much of these things; but behold, I mistake, for I have seen much of his mysteries and his marvelous power; yea, even in the preservation of the lives of this people.

6. Nevertheless, I did harden my heart, for I was called many times and I would not hear; therefore I knew concerning these things, yet I would not know; therefore I went on rebelling against God, in the wickedness of my heart, even until the fourth day of this seventh month, which is in the tenth year of the reign of the judges.

7. As I was journeying to see a very near kindred, behold an angel of the Lord appeared unto me and said: Amulek, return to thine own house, for thou shalt feed a prophet of the Lord; yea, a holy man, who is a chosen man of God; for he has fasted many days because of the sins of this people, and he is an hungered, and thou shalt receive him into thy house and feed him, and he shall bless thee and thy house; and the blessing of the Lord shall rest upon thee and thy house.

8. And it came to pass that I obeyed the voice of the angel, and returned towards my house. And as I was going thither I found the man whom the angel said unto me: Thou shalt receive into thy house—and behold it was this same man who has been speaking unto you concerning the things of God.

9. And the angel said unto me he is a holy man; wherefore I know he is a holy man because it was said by an angel of God.

10. And again, I know that the things whereof he hath testified are true; for behold I say unto you, that as the Lord liveth, even so has he sent his angel to make these things manifest unto me; and this he has done while this Alma hath dwelt at my house.

11. For behold, he hath blessed mine house, he hath blessed me, and my women, and my children, and my father and my kinsfolk; yea, even all my kindred hath he blessed, and the blessing of the Lord hath rested upon us according to the words which he spake.

2–3. This brief mention of Aminadi interpreting the writing on the wall of the temple should not be confused with the episode recorded in Daniel 5:13–28. Aminadi was a Nephite. We know nothing of this story beyond what Amulek here states. We assume that the account, which must have been fascinating, is contained on the large plates of Nephi.

3. Lehi . . . was a descendant of Manasseh] We know from earlier sources in our present Book of Mormon that Lehi was a descendant of Joseph of old (1 Nephi 5:14; 6:2; 2 Nephi 3:4), but it is from the 116 manuscript pages that became lost, that had been translated from Mormon's abridgment of the book of Lehi, that we learn specifics. Elder Erastus Snow explained in 1882: "The Prophet Joseph informed us that the record of Lehi was contained on the 116 pages that were first translated and subsequently stolen, and of which an abridgment is given us in the first Book of Nephi, which is the record of Nephi individually, *he himself being of the lineage of Manasseh; but that Ishmael was of the lineage of Ephraim,* and that his sons married into Lehi's family, and Lehi's sons married Ishmael's daughters" (*JD* 23:184, italics added).

4. Amulek was well known in the community and well-to-do. This is his way of saying: "I'm not exactly a nobody. You would do well to take my words seriously."

5–6. One assumes that Amulek had not been a bad man. He seems to have been a member of the Church in that day, one who had witnessed the miraculous, had heard the truth preached numerous times and seen God's hand working, but had not opened himself to the realm of divine experience. "And now, behold, I say unto you. . . . thou hast rejected me many times because of pride and the cares of the world." (D&C 39:7, 9.)

6. I was called . . . and I would not hear; therefore I knew . . . yet I would not know] The voice of the Lord calls to us regularly. It is not wickedness or carnality alone which keep us from feeling and hearing the word; it is preoccupation. We need not be guilty of gross sin to be unready for the impressions of the Spirit; we need only have our minds and hearts focused upon other things, to be so involved in the thick of thin things that we are not taking the time to ponder or meditate upon matters of substance. Excessive labor in secondary causes leads to a lessening of spiritual opportunities. President Ezra Taft Benson told the following story, which highlights the need for being attentive and open to heavenly guidance:

"Bishop John Wells, a former member of the Presiding Bishopric, was a great detail man and was responsible for many Church reports. President David O. McKay and President Harold

B. Lee used to relate an experience from his life that is instructive to all of us.

"A son of Bishop and Sister Wells was killed in a railroad accident in Emigration Canyon, east of Salt Lake City. He was run over by a freight car. Sister Wells could not be consoled. She received no comfort during the funeral and continued her mourning after her son was laid to rest. Bishop Wells feared for her health, as she was in a state of deep anguish.

"One day, soon after the funeral, Sister Wells was lying on her bed in a state of mourning. The son appeared to her and said, 'Mother, do not mourn, do not cry. I am all right.' He then related to her how the accident took place. Apparently there had been some question—even suspicion—about the accident, because the young man was an experienced railroad man. But he told his mother that it was clearly an accident.

"He told her that as soon as he realized that he was in another sphere, he had tried to reach his father but could not. His father was so busy with the details of his office and work that he could not respond to the promptings. Therefore, the son had come to his mother. He then said, 'Tell Father that all is well with me, and I want you not to mourn anymore.'

"President McKay used this experience to teach that we must always be responsive to the whisperings of the Spirit. These promptings come most often when we are not under the pressure of appointments and when we are not caught up in the worries of day-to-day life." (*Come unto Christ*, p. 18.)

6. I went on rebelling against God, in the wickedness of my heart] That is, Amulek continued to live and function beneath his spiritual privileges, to exist in twilight when he could have been basking in the glory of the noonday Son.

10. I know that the things whereof he hath testified are true] It is not enough for us to bear witness, in a general way, that the gospel is true. We do not perfect our witness and we do not enjoy the fruits of pure testimony until we are able to bear witness that what we have taught is the truth. If a person has delivered an address on the law of tithing, it is appropriate and right for him to bear specific witness at the conclusion of the talk that tithing is a true principle and that the things he has said are verily true. And so on with regard to faith and repentance and atonement and rebirth and chastity and myriad other topics: we teach and then we testify.

10. As the Lord liveth] Amulek here swears with an oath that the teachings of Alma are true. This was the most serious, the most sacred manner of expression available at the time. See *Commentary* 1:39–40.

11. Indeed, the blessing of gospel living had come to Amulek's home. There is, however, a cost to discipleship, sometimes a high cost, even occasionally the loss of family association. See commentary on Alma 15:16.

Ammonihah Lawyers Seek to Ensnare Amulek

Alma 10:12–32

12. And now, when Amulek had spoken these words the people began to be astonished, seeing there was more than one witness who testified of the things whereof they were accused, and also of the things which were to come, according to the spirit of prophecy which was in them.

13. Nevertheless, there were some among them who thought to question them, that by their cunning devices they might catch them in their words, that they might find witness against them, that they might deliver them to their judges that they might be judged according to the law, and that they might be slain or cast into prison, according to the crime which they could make appear or witness against them.

14. Now it was those men who sought to destroy them, who were lawyers, who were hired or appointed by the people to administer the law at their times of trials, or at the trials of the crimes of the people before the judges.

15. Now these lawyers were learned in all the arts and cunning of the people; and this was to enable them that they might be skilful in their profession.

16. And it came to pass that they began to question Amulek, that thereby they might make him cross his words, or contradict the words which he should speak.

17. Now they knew not that Amulek could know of their designs. But it came to pass as they began to question him, he perceived their thoughts, and he said unto them: O ye wicked and perverse generation, ye lawyers and hypocrites, for ye are laying the foundation of the devil; for ye are laying traps and snares to catch the holy ones of God.

18. Ye are laying plans to pervert the ways of the righteous, and to bring down the wrath of God upon your heads, even to the utter destruction of this people.

19. Yea, well did Mosiah say, who was our last king, when he was about to deliver up the kingdom, having no one to confer it upon, causing that this people should be governed by their own voices—yea, well did he say that if the time should come that the voice of this people should choose iniquity, that is, if the time should come that this people should fall into transgression, they would be ripe for destruction.

20. And now I say unto you that well doth the Lord judge of your iniquities; well doth he cry unto this people, by the voice of his angels: Repent ye, repent, for the kingdom of heaven is at hand.

21. Yea, well doth he cry, by the voice of his angels that: I will come down among my people, with equity and justice in my

hands.

22. Yea, and I say unto you that if it were not for the prayers of the righteous, who are now in the land, that ye would even now be visited with utter destruction; yet it would not be by flood, as were the people in the days of Noah, but it would be by famine, and by pestilence, and the sword.

23. But it is by the prayers of the righteous that ye are spared; now therefore, if ye will cast out the righteous from among you then will not the Lord stay his hand; but in his fierce anger he will come out against you; then ye shall be smitten by famine, and by pestilence, and by the sword; and the time is soon at hand except ye repent.

24. And now it came to pass that the people were more angry with Amulek, and they cried out, saying: This man doth revile against our laws which are just, and our wise lawyers whom we have selected.

25. But Amulek stretched forth his hand, and cried the mightier unto them, saying: O ye wicked and perverse generation, why hath Satan got such great hold upon your hearts? Why will ye yield yourselves unto him that he may have power over you, to blind your eyes, that ye will not understand the words which are spoken, according to their truth?

26. For behold, have I testified against your law? Ye do not understand; ye say that I have spoken against your law; but I have not, but I have spoken in favor of your law, to your condemnation.

27. And now behold, I say unto you, that the foundation of the destruction of this people is beginning to be laid by the unrighteousness of your lawyers and your judges.

28. And now it came to pass that when Amulek had spoken these words the people cried out against him, saying: Now we know that this man is a child of the devil, for he hath lied unto us; for he hath spoken against our law. And now he says that he has not spoken against it.

29. And again, he has reviled against our lawyers, and our judges.

30. And it came to pass that the lawyers put it into their hearts that they should remember these things against him.

31. And there was one among them whose name was Zeezrom. Now he was the foremost to accuse Amulek and Alma, he being one of the most expert among them, having much business to do among the people.

32. Now the object of these lawyers was to get gain; and they got gain according to their employ.

12–32. One of the signs of moral decay, of apostasy and corruption within a society, is an emphasis on technicalities of law. This comes about when, in order to advance their cause, people seek to play the letter against the spirit of the law and in effect to legalize chicanery. Among the pure in heart God's laws are etched on the soul; they are found written in the countenances and inscribed on the inward parts. Among the perverse, however, law is a means of accomplishing the manipulation of others. Both anciently and in our own day, lawyers who seek to uphold the law, who strive to bring the lawless to account, who earnestly endeavor to protect the rights of all—these perform a valuable and appreciated service in society. On the other hand, when lawyers undertake to generate business for themselves by encouraging litigation in instances when patience and long-suffering would be more appropriate; when they cover up the truth; when their manipulations result in the guilty not being brought to justice, thereby penalizing and punishing the innocent; and when they employ the witchery of words or the sophistry of speech to deceive the unwary or the trusting—when they do such things they have become pawns in the hand of the father of all lies. They have sold their souls. Amulek stated the matter simply: "The foundation of the destruction of this people is beginning to be laid by the unrighteousness of your lawyers and your judges" (verse 27).

17. Amulek, possessed of the Spirit of God and thus the gift of discernment, saw through the sham and hypocrisy of the lawyers' approach. He knew their hearts and condemned their deeds.

19. See Mosiah 29:27.

20. The kingdom of heaven is at hand] See Alma 5:28; 7:9.

22–23. See Helaman 13:12.

23. In his fierce anger] "Prepare ye, prepare ye for that which is to come, for the Lord is nigh; and the anger of the Lord is kindled, and his sword is bathed in heaven, and it shall fall upon the inhabitants of the earth" (D&C 1:12–13; see also 56:1).

Nephite Judges Paid According to Their Labor

Alma 11:1–19

1. Now it was in the law of Mosiah that every man who was a judge of the law, or those who were appointed to be judges, should receive wages according to the time which they labored to judge those who were brought before them to be judged.

2. Now if a man owed another, and he would not pay that which he did owe, he was complained of to the judge; and the judge executed authority, and sent forth officers that the man should be brought before him; and he judged the man according to the law and the evidences which were brought against him, and thus the man was compelled to pay that which he owed, or be stripped, or be cast out from among the people as a thief and a robber.

3. And the judge received for his wages according to his time—a senine of gold for a day, or a senum of silver, which is equal to a senine of gold; and this is according to the law which was given.

4. Now these are the names of

the different pieces of their gold, and of their silver, according to their value. And the names are given by the Nephites, for they did not reckon after the manner of the Jews who were at Jerusalem; neither did they measure after the manner of the Jews; but they altered their reckoning and their measure, according to the minds and the circumstances of the people, in every generation, until the reign of the judges, they having been established by king Mosiah.

5. Now the reckoning is thus—a senine of gold, a seon of gold, a shum of gold, and a limnah of gold.

6. A senum of silver, an amnor of silver, an ezrom of silver, and an onti of silver.

7. A senum of silver was equal to a senine of gold, and either for a measure of barley, and also for a measure of every kind of grain.

8. Now the amount of a seon of gold was twice the value of a senine.

9. And a shum of gold was twice the value of a seon.

10. And a limnah of gold was the value of them all.

11. And an amnor of silver was as great as two senums.

12. And an ezrom of silver was as great as four senums.

13. And an onti was as great as them all.

14. Now this is the value of the lesser numbers of their reckoning—

15. A shiblon is half of a senum; therefore, a shiblon for half a measure of barley.

16. And a shiblum is a half of a shiblon.

17. And a leah is the half of a shiblum.

18. Now this is their number, according to their reckoning.

19. Now an antion of gold is equal to three shiblons.

1–3. At a later time, in responding to Korihor's accusation that the leaders of the Nephites glutted themselves on the labors of their people, Alma said: "Thou knowest that we do not glut ourselves upon the labors of this people; for behold I have labored even from the commencement of the reign of the judges until now, with mine own hands for my support, notwithstanding my many travels round about the land to declare the word of God unto my people. And notwithstanding the many labors which I have performed in the church, I have never received so much as even one senine for my labor; neither has any of my brethren, *save it were in the judgment-seat: and then we have received only according to law for our time.*" (Alma 30:32–33, italics added.)

4–19. These verses seem to describe not a group of Nephite coins but rather a system of weights and measures by which to establish various degrees of monetary worth. It appears that at the time of the establishment of the reign of the judges by King Mosiah, a standardized system of weights and measures was put into effect throughout the land of the Nephites.

Amulek Teaches the Fatherhood and Sonship of Christ

Alma 11:20–39

20. Now, it was for the sole purpose to get gain, because they received their wages according to their employ, therefore, they did stir up the people to riotings, and all manner of disturbances and wickedness, that they might have more employ, that they might get money according to the suits which were brought before them; therefore they did stir up the people against Alma and Amulek.

21. And this Zeezrom began to question Amulek, saying: Will ye answer me a few questions which I shall ask you? Now Zeezrom was a man who was expert in the devices of the devil, that he might destroy that which was good; therefore, he said unto Amulek: Will ye answer the questions which I shall put unto you?

22. And Amulek said unto him: Yea, if it be according to the Spirit of the Lord, which is in me; for I shall say nothing which is contrary to the Spirit of the Lord. And Zeezrom said unto him: Behold, here are six onties of silver, and all these will I give thee if thou wilt deny the existence of a Supreme Being.

23. Now Amulek said: O thou child of hell, why tempt ye me? Knowest thou that the righteous yieldeth to no such temptations?

24. Believest thou that there is no God? I say unto you, Nay, thou knowest that there is a God, but thou lovest that lucre more than him.

25. And now thou hast lied before God unto me. Thou saidst unto me—Behold these six onties, which are of great worth, I will give unto thee—when thou hadst it in thy heart to retain them from me; and it was only thy desire that I should deny the true and living God, that thou mightest have cause to destroy me. And now behold, for this great evil thou shalt have thy reward.

26. And Zeezrom said unto him: Thou sayest there is a true and living God?

27. And Amulek said: Yea, there is a true and living God.

28. Now Zeezrom said: Is there more than one God?

29. And he answered, No.

30. Now Zeezrom said unto him again: How knowest thou these things?

31. And he said: An angel hath made them known unto me.

32. And Zeezrom said again: Who is he that shall come? Is it the Son of God?

33. And he said unto him, Yea.

34. And Zeezrom said again: Shall he save his people in their sins? And Amulek answered and said unto him: I say unto you he shall not, for it is impossible for him to deny his word.

35. Now Zeezrom said unto the people: See that ye remember these things; for he said there is but one God; yet he saith that the Son of God shall come, but he shall not save his people—as though he had authority to command God.

36. Now Amulek saith again unto him: Behold thou hast lied, for thou sayest that I spake as though I had authority to command God because I said he shall not save his people in their sins.

37. And I say unto you again that he cannot save them in their sins; for I cannot deny his word,

and he hath said that no unclean thing can inherit the kingdom of heaven; therefore, how can ye be saved, except ye inherit the kingdom of heaven? Therefore, ye cannot be saved in your sins.

38. Now Zeezrom saith again unto him: Is the Son of God the very Eternal Father?

39. And Amulek said unto him: Yea, he is the very Eternal Father of heaven and of earth, and all things which in them are; he is the beginning and the end, the first and the last;

20. See commentary on Alma 10:12–32.

21. Zeezrom] See Alma 10:31.

22. Yea, if it be according to the Spirit of the Lord] Those called to speak and act in the name of the Lord are careful in their ministry. They have no private agenda, no favorite doctrines, no special lessons they seek to put forward according to the whim of the moment. Rather, they strive earnestly to be in tune with that Spirit which teaches and shows a person what he or she must do at all times. They speak the words of Christ, meaning that they speak by the power of the Holy Ghost and thereby make known only that which the Lord would have made known (see 2 Nephi 32:3–5). Thus they answer only the questions that seem appropriate at the time, and deliver that "portion of the word" (Alma 12:9–11; D&C 71:1) which is needful for the edification of those they serve.

23. When the disciple of Christ has his eye single to the glory of God—focused upon his Redeemer, the cause of the kingdom, and the glories to be obtained hereafter—he cannot have his attention turned by the fleeting enticements of this fallen world.

24. Thou knowest that there is a God] Amulek has discerned the soul and the intents of Zeezrom. Compare Jacob 7:14; Alma 30:42.

24. Thou lovest that lucre more than him] Of the sons and daughters of Adam and Eve who gave heed to the words of Satan, the scripture says, "they loved Satan more than God" (Moses 5:13). It is not necessarily true that they did not feel a love for God. They may have. But they loved Satan more. And so it is with money, that "filthy lucre" of which the scriptures speak (see Titus 1:11). It isn't that some members of the faith do not love God. They probably do. They just love this world's goods more.

26–33. This is a discussion—a question-and-answer session— that could be difficult to follow. Zeezrom, in his eagerness to trap Amulek in his own words, asks whether there is more than one God. Amulek answers that there is not. Amulek is, of course, speaking entirely of the Savior, of the Lord Jehovah; he is not making reference to our Father in Heaven or to the Godhead. That same Jehovah had spoken anciently to Isaiah: "I, even I, am the Lord; and beside me there is no saviour" (Isaiah 43:11). Zeezrom then asks whether it is the *Son* of God who will come as the Messiah, to which Amulek answers simply, "Yea." From the crafty lawyer's perspective at this point it would appear that Amulek is contradicting himself. But in fact the Nephite missionary is delivering a profound truth: Jesus Christ is both God and Son of God. Is there only one God? Yes, there is only one God who shall come to take away the sins of the world and ransom fallen men and women from the temporal and spiritual death brought into the world by the fall of Adam. That God is also the Son of God, the Son of Man, meaning the Son of the Man of Holiness (see Moses 6:57).

31. See Alma 10:10.

34–37. Even the Omnipotent One, the Lord Jehovah, cannot save his people *in* their sins. He came on a search-and-rescue mission to save people *from* their sins. But no one, not the least and lowliest of mankind or the mightiest Apostle and prophet, can be saved in sin. Such is the divine decree. Speaking of the Amulek-Zeezrom encounter, Nephi later said: "For he said unto him that the Lord surely should come to redeem his people, but that he should not come to redeem them in their sins, but to redeem them from their sins. And he hath power given unto him from the Father to redeem them from their sins because of repentance." (Helaman 5:10–11.)

37. No unclean thing can inherit the kingdom of heaven] See 1 Nephi 15:34; 3 Nephi 27:19–20.

38–39. Jesus Christ is "the Son of God, the Father of heaven and earth, the Creator of all things from the beginning" (Mosiah 3:8). He is Father and he is Son, depending upon which of his roles and functions we are viewing at the time. For a detailed discussion of the ministry of Christ as the Father and the Son, see *Commentary* 2:225–30. In short, Amulek is declaring that Christ is the God who should come (verse 27), that he is the Son of God (verse 33), and that he is the Father of heaven and earth (verse 39).

Salvation or Eternal Life Is Available Through Christ

Alma 11:40

40. And he shall come into the world to redeem his people; and he shall take upon him the transgressions of those who believe on his name; and these are they that shall have eternal life, and salvation cometh to none else.

40. "*Salvation* is eternal life. It is life in the highest heaven, life among the Gods and the angels. The word *salvation* means exactly the same thing as eternal life, but simply lays stress upon one's saved condition, his state being one of deliverance from death and sin through the atoning sacrifice of Jesus Christ. *Exaltation* is another word with which we have come to identify the glories of the celestial kingdom; exaltation has the same meaning as eternal life; it has the same meaning as salvation. To be saved is to be exalted, the latter term simply laying stress upon the elevated and ennobled status of one who so qualifies to dwell with and be part of the Church of the Firstborn, the Church of the Exalted." (Robert L. Millet and Joseph Fielding McConkie, *The Life Beyond*, p. 134.)

Elder Bruce R. McConkie has written: "We are ofttimes prone to create artificial distinctions, to say that salvation means one thing and exaltation another, to suppose that salvation means to be resurrected, but that exaltation or eternal life is something in addition thereto. It is true that there are some passages of scripture that use salvation in a special and limited sense in order to give an overall perspective of the plan of salvation that we would not otherwise have. (2 Nephi 9:1–27; D&C 76:40–49; 132:15–17.) These passages show the difference between general or universal salvation that consists of coming forth from the grave in immortality, and specific or individual salvation that consists of an inheritance in the celestial kingdom. . . .

"Since it is the prophetic purpose to lead men to full salvation in the highest heaven of the celestial world, when they speak and write about salvation, almost without exception, they mean eternal life or exaltation. They use the terms *salvation, exaltation,* and *eternal life* as synonyms, as words that mean exactly the same thing without any difference, distinction, or variance whatever." (*Promised Messiah*, p. 129.)

40. He shall take upon him the transgressions of those who believe on his name] This is an important principle which must be viewed properly in order to avoid confusion. There are persons who teach that Christ suffered only for those who will repent. This is false. It is incorrect. The Lord suffered for every soul, "yea, the pains of every living creature, both men, women, and children, who belong to the family of Adam" (2 Nephi 9:21; see also D&C 18:11; 19:16). His suffering and atonement are efficacious, however, only for those who repent and come unto him. Thus to refuse to repent is to mock his pain and shun his sufferings. It is, in the words of Paul, to do "despite unto the spirit of grace" (Hebrews 10:29).

Jesus Christ Breaks the Bands of Death

Alma 11:41–46

41. Therefore the wicked remain as though there had been no redemption made, except it be the loosing of the bands of death; for behold, the day cometh that all shall rise from the dead and stand before God, and be judged according to their works.

42. Now, there is a death which is called a temporal death; and the death of Christ shall loose the bands of this temporal death, that all shall be raised from this temporal death.

43. The spirit and the body shall be reunited again in its perfect form; both limb and joint shall be restored to its proper frame, even as we now are at this time; and we shall be brought to stand before God, knowing even as we know now, and have a bright recollection of all our guilt.

44. Now, this restoration shall come to all, both old and young, both bond and free, both male and female, both the wicked and the righteous; and even there shall not so much as a hair of their heads be lost; but every thing shall be restored to its perfect frame, as it is now, or in the body, and shall be brought and be arraigned before the bar of Christ the Son, and God the Father, and the Holy Spirit, which is one Eternal God, to be judged according to their works, whether they be good or whether they be evil.

45. Now, behold, I have spoken unto you concerning the death of the mortal body, and also concerning the resurrection of the mortal body. I say unto you that this mortal body is raised to an immortal body, that is from death, even from the first death unto life, that they can die no more; their spirits uniting with their bodies, never to be divided; thus the whole becoming spiritual and immortal, that they can no more see corruption.

46. Now, when Amulek had finished these words the people began again to be astonished, and also Zeezrom began to tremble. And thus ended the words of Amulek, or this is all that I have written.

41–46. All men and women who have taken a physical body will be redeemed in the sense that they will be resurrected and in the sense that they will thereafter stand before God to be judged. There is no exception. Resurrection is a free gift. All shall be quickened and made alive (see 1 Corinthians 15:21–22). Moroni wrote: "And because of the redemption of man, which came by Jesus Christ, they are brought back into the presence of the Lord; yea, this is wherein all men are redeemed, because the death of Christ bringeth to pass the resurrection, which bringeth to pass a redemption from an endless sleep" (Mormon 9:13).

43. Joseph Smith the Prophet taught: "As concerning the resurrection, I will merely say that all men will come from the grave as they lie down, whether old or young; there will not be 'added unto their stature one cubit,' neither taken from it; all will be raised by the power of God, having spirit in their bodies, and not blood." (*Teachings*, pp. 199–200.) President Joseph F. Smith further explained: "The body will come forth as it is laid to rest, for there is no growth or development in the grave. As it is laid down, so will it arise, and changes to perfection will come by the law of restitution. But the spirit will continue to expand and develop, and the body, after the resurrection will develop to the full stature of man." (*Improvement Era*, June 1904; cited in *Teachings*, p. 200, n. 4.) By way of clarification, his son, Joseph Fielding Smith, observed: "President Smith was in full accord with Amulek and Alma. He taught that the body will be restored as stated in Alma 11:42–45 and 40:22–23. While he expresses the thought that the body will come forth as it was laid down, he also expresses the thought that it will take time to adjust the body from the condition of imperfections. This, of course, is reasonable, but at the same time the length of time to make these adjustments will *not* cover any appreciable extent of time. President Smith never intended to convey the thought that it would require weeks or months of time in order for the defects to be removed. These changes will come naturally, of course, but *almost instantly*." (*Doctrines of Salvation* 2:293–94.)

A modern revelation declares: "They who are of a celestial spirit shall receive the same body which was a natural body; even ye shall receive your bodies, and your glory shall be that glory by which your bodies are quickened" (D&C 88:28). The Prophet also stated: "There is no fundamental principle belonging to a human system that ever goes into another in this world or in the world to come; I care not what the theories of men are. We have the testimony that God will raise us up, and he has the power to do it. If any one supposes that any part of our bodies, that is, the fundamental parts thereof, ever goes into another body, he is mistaken." (*HC* 5:339.)

43. A bright recollection of all our guilt] See *Commentary* 1:243.

44. The bar of Christ the Son, and God the Father, and the Holy Spirit, which is one Eternal God] The scriptures teach that the Father has committed all judgment unto the Son (John 5:22) and that the keeper of the gate of judgment is Christ, the Holy One of Israel, that he employs no servant there (2 Nephi 9:41). Are we then judged by Christ or by the members of the Godhead? Paul wrote, speaking of the Savior, that "in him dwelleth all the fulness of the Godhead bodily" (Colossians 2:9).

That is to say, in Christ is to be found the justice and judgment and mercy and grace and power of the other members of the eternal Presidency. He is the embodiment of their mind, will, and power. What he says or does is what they would have said or done under similar circumstances. Thus this passage means simply that "Christ's judicial decisions are those of the other two members of the Godhead because all three are perfectly united as one." (*Promised Messiah,* pp. 215–16.) We are judged by Jesus Christ, who is the representation of the Father and of the Holy Ghost. See *Commentary* 1:243–44.

The same principle holds in regard to being baptized in the name of Christ. People are baptized in the name of Christ as they are baptized in the name of the Father, and of the Son, and of the Holy Ghost (see 3 Nephi 11:23–25).

45. They can die no more] Any teaching which supposes that persons can pass through death to life everlasting and then back through death again is false. What is true of our Lord is true of all of us: "Knowing that Christ being raised from the dead dieth no more; death hath no more dominion over him. For in that he died, he died unto sin once: but in that he liveth, he liveth unto God." (Romans 6:9–10.)

45. Their spirits uniting with their bodies, never to be divided] See D&C 93:33; 138:17.

45. The whole becoming spiritual] This may appear at first a strange use of the word *spiritual.* The resurrected body is physical, tangible, substantial. And yet it is spiritual, meaning immortal, not subject to death. In describing the physical body, Paul wrote to the Corinthians: "It is sown [planted in the grave] in corruption; it is raised [in the resurrection] in incorruption: it is sown in dishonour; it is raised in glory: it is sown in weakness; it is raised in power: *it is sown a natural body; it is raised a spiritual body*" (1 Corinthians 15:42–44, italics added). Similarly, in a modern revelation the Lord stated that "the earth abideth the law of a celestial kingdom, for it filleth the measure of its creation, and transgresseth not the law—wherefore, it shall be sanctified; yea, notwithstanding it shall die, it shall be quickened again, and shall abide the power by which it is quickened, and the righteous shall inherit it. For notwithstanding they [the righteous] die, *they also shall rise again, a spiritual body.*" (D&C 88:25–27, italics added.)

46. Zeezrom began to tremble] See Alma 12:7.

Alma Denounces Zeezrom's Nefarious Plan

Alma 12:1–8

1. Now Alma, seeing that the words of Amulek had silenced Zeezrom, for he beheld that Amulek had caught him in his lying and deceiving to destroy him, and seeing that he began to tremble under a consciousness of his guilt, he opened his mouth and began to speak unto him, and to establish the words of Amulek, and to explain things beyond, or to unfold the scriptures beyond that which Amulek had done.

2. Now the words that Alma spake unto Zeezrom were heard by the people round about; for the multitude was great, and he spake on this wise:

3. Now Zeezrom, seeing that thou hast been taken in thy lying and craftiness, for thou hast not lied unto men only but thou hast lied unto God; for behold, he knows all thy thoughts, and thou seest that thy thoughts are made known unto us by his Spirit;

4. And thou seest that we know that thy plan was a very subtle plan, as to the subtlety of the devil, for to lie and to deceive this people that thou mightest set them against us, to revile us and to cast us out—

5. Now this was a plan of thine adversary, and he hath exercised his power in thee. Now I would that ye should remember that what I say unto thee I say unto all.

6. And behold I say unto you all that this was a snare of the adversary, which he has laid to catch this people, that he might bring you into subjection unto him, that he might encircle you about with his chains, that he might chain you down to everlasting destruction, according to the power of his captivity.

7. Now when Alma had spoken these words, Zeezrom began to tremble more exceedingly, for he was convinced more and more of the power of God; and he was also convinced that Alma and Amulek had a knowledge of him, for he was convinced that they knew the thoughts and intents of his heart; for power was given unto them that they might know of these things according to the spirit of prophecy.

8. And Zeezrom began to inquire of them diligently, that he might know more concerning the kingdom of God. And he said unto Alma: What does this mean which Amulek hath spoken concerning the resurrection of the dead, that all shall rise from the dead, both the just and the unjust, and are brought to stand before God to be judged according to their works?

1–8. Amulek's words, spoken by the power of the Holy Spirit, penetrated the hardened heart of Zeezrom. The crafty lawyer was exposed by two men who knew, through the gift of discernment and the spirit of prophecy (see verse 7), that Zeezrom was sinning against light and thus lying to them and to others.

1. He began to tremble under a consciousness of his guilt] See verse 7; see also commentary on Alma 15:3.

1. To establish the words of Amulek] That is, Alma began to bear a similar witness, to teach the same truths, to confirm the former's words.

3. Thou hast lied unto God] To Ananias—who, in company with his wife, Sapphira, chose to keep back a part of the proceeds from the sale of their property when expected to consecrate their all—the Apostle Peter said: "Why hath Satan filled thine heart to lie to the Holy Ghost, and to keep back part of the price of the land? Whiles it remained, was it not thine own? and after it was sold, was it not in thine own power? why hast thou conceived this thing in thine heart? *thou has not lied unto men, but unto God."* (Acts 5:3–4, italics added.)

3. He knows all thy thoughts] "There is none else save God that knowest thy thoughts and the intents of thy heart" (D&C 6:16). See also Alma 18:32.

5. He hath exercised his power in thee] Satan need not do all his own dirty work. He moves upon, tempts, inspires, and possesses others to cause them to think and act in ways that seek to halt or hinder the plan of righteousness. However, as Joseph Smith taught, "The devil has no power over us only as we permit him" (*Teachings*, p. 181).

6. That he might encircle you about with his chains] See Alma 5:7–10; 12:9–11.

8. We see in this verse an example of the marvelous transformation that can begin to take place because of the power of the word. Zeezrom, only a short time before, had asked baiting, trapping questions. Now that he is confronted by the power of God and having his sins laid open to view, his queries begin to change, to reflect a type of sincere inquiry after the truth. In the language of the scripture, he has been born again to see the kingdom of God (see John 3:3; *Teachings*, p. 328). He asks concerning Amulek's words on the resurrection of the dead (see Alma 11:41–44), a matter which is strange, unfathomable, and indeed mysterious to those who spurn the ways of God.

The Mysteries of God Unfolded to Those Who Seek

Alma 12:9–11

9. And now Alma began to expound these things unto him, saying: It is given unto many to know the mysteries of God; nevertheless they are laid under a strict command that they shall not impart only according to the portion of his word which he doth grant unto the children of men, according to the heed and diligence which they give unto him.

10. And therefore, he that will harden his heart, the same receiveth the lesser portion of the word; and he that will not harden his heart, to him is given the greater portion of the word, until it is given unto him to know the mysteries of God until he know them in full.

11. And they that will harden their hearts, to them is given the lesser portion of the word until they know nothing concerning his mysteries; and then they are taken captive by the devil, and led by his will down to destruction. Now this is what is meant by the chains of hell.

9–11. It is a remarkable thing how two people can be seated beside one another, hear exactly the same message preached, and come away with two different conclusions regarding the import of the declaration. To one listener the presentation is as the gibberish of alien tongues; to another, as manna from heaven. To one listener the messenger is seen as weak and unpolished, the pronouncement as unimportant and unnecessary; to the second, the messenger seems to be fired with the power of Almighty God and his sermon deep and profound. Indeed, to some it is given to know the mysteries of God and to see the power of God resting upon his servants, simply because they are prepared to so receive, because they are open to truth. In regard to what the scriptures call the "mystery of godliness," Elder Bruce R. McConkie has written: "To those devoid of spiritual understanding, it is as though the inspired authors had set out, deliberately and with earnest intent, to sow the seeds of darkness and misunderstanding as to the God or Gods who live and abide and are. . . . At least to the spiritually sick and to the spiritually dead, who seek God through reason and the intellect alone, the scriptures appear to be a compilation of confusion and contradiction. And it was not intended to be otherwise, for salvation is of the Spirit and comes only to those who are spiritually alive and well, those who come to know God, not by reason and the intellect alone, but through the spirit of prophecy and revelation." *(Promised Messiah,* p. 113.)

What is a mystery to one man may not be a mystery to another; it is simply a matter of preparation, readiness, and receptivity. To the world and the worldly the doctrines of faith, repentance, and rebirth are mysteries. To the recent convert the doctrine of atonement may be a mystery. To the experienced and seasoned Saint the matter of a plurality of gods and of man becoming as God may be mysteries. To the people of Zarahcmla the noble King Benjamin said: "I have not commanded you to come up hither to trifle with the words which I shall speak, but that you should hearken unto me, and open your ears that ye may hear, and your hearts that ye may understand, and your minds that the mysteries of God may be unfolded to your view" (Mosiah 2:9). Benjamin then went on to speak of divine indebtedness, of putting off the natural man through the atonement of Christ, and of serving one another as a means of retaining a remission of sins from day to day. These are sacred and solemn matters, to be sure. They are mysteries to the world and to those who live outside the realm of the divine influence.

9. Those charged with proclaiming the gospel message are to be sensitive to the Spirit, discerning enough to recognize that "portion of [God's] word" suited to those being taught. Full-time missionaries, for example, are given a specific commission to teach that portion of the word necessary to introduce sincere investigators to the message of the Restoration. They are not commissioned to teach doctrines that could be more easily understood and appreciated after baptism and the reception of the Holy Ghost. Their specific assignment is to "declare glad tidings," the tidings that the Lord has spoken anew in our day through modern prophets (see D&C 19:29; 31:3–4), and to proclaim that the truthfulness of the message may be tested through the Book of Mormon. We are to teach those outside the Church how to get into the Church and thereafter allow the Holy Ghost to teach the fulness of the gospel (D&C 39:6; see also 71:1).

And thus it is that the Latter-day Saints are possessors and stewards over sacred matters, holy things, which "are not lawful for man to utter" (D&C 76:115; see also 2 Corinthians 12:4). Some experiences are ineffable, so transcendently glorious that they defy human expression or description. Of these things it is not *possible* for man to speak. Some truths and experiences "are not lawful for man to utter" in the sense that it is not *permitted* or appropriate to speak of them, except as led and directed by the Holy Spirit. Some special things are to be kept within the household of faith, among those who believe (see Moses 1:42; 4:32). "Remember that that which cometh from above is sacred, and must be spoken with care, and by constraint of the Spirit; and in this there is no condemnation" (D&C 63:64).

Just as it would be unwise and dangerous to feed strong meat to infants, so also it is unwise and dangerous to provide deeper doctrines or sacred ordinances for public display (see JST, Matthew 7:9–11; see also Matthew 13:10–13; 1 Corinthians 3:1–2; D&C 19:21–22). Too frequently those who encounter these things prematurely are unable to digest them properly and ultimately turn with bitterness against the very source of truth. In short, it matters a great deal not only *what* people are taught, but also *when* they are taught it.

9. The mysteries of God] The specific reference is to the resurrection of the dead, the inseparable union of body and spirit.

10. The lesser portion of the word] Those who cry out, "I have enough"; those who refuse to learn more; those who are content to exist at their present level of light and truth, who say essentially, "Thus far and no further"—these shall live and die in ignorance of the mysteries of God and shall thereby subject themselves to the chains of hell. God is gracious: He provides for us that which we are willing—and thus able—to receive.

10. Until he know them in full] This fulness, of course, cannot come to pass in this life; it is only in and after the resurrection that we can come to know all things, even as God knows them.

Man to Be Judged by His Words, His Works, and His Thoughts

Alma 12:12–18

12. And Amulek hath spoken plainly concerning death, and being raised from this mortality to a state of immortality, and being brought before the bar of God, to be judged according to our works.

13. Then if our hearts have been hardened, yea, if we have hardened our hearts against the word, insomuch that it has not been found in us, then will our state be awful, for then we shall be condemned.

14. For our words will condemn us, yea, all our works will condemn us; we shall not be found spotless; and our thoughts will also condemn us; and in this awful state we shall not dare to look up to our God; and we would fain be glad if we could command the rocks and the mountains to fall upon us to hide us from his presence.

15. But this cannot be; we must come forth and stand before him in his glory, and in his power, and in his might, majesty, and dominion, and acknowledge to our everlasting shame that all his judgments are just; that he is just in all his works, and that he is merciful unto the children of men, and that he has all power to save every man that believeth on his name and bringeth forth fruit meet for repentance.

16. And now behold, I say unto you then cometh a death, even a second death, which is a spiritual death; then is a time that whoso ever dieth in his sins, as to a temporal death, shall also die a spiritual death; yea, he shall die as to things pertaining unto righteousness.

17. Then is the time when their torments shall be as a lake of fire and brimstone, whose flame ascendeth up forever and ever; and then is the time that they shall be chained down to an everlasting destruction, according to the power and captivity of Satan, he having subjected them according to his will.

18. Then, I say unto you, they shall be as though there had been no redemption made, for they cannot be redeemed according to God's justice; and they cannot die, seeing there is no more corruption.

13. Then we shall be condemned] See Alma 32:38–40.

14. Our words, our works, and our thoughts are but illustrations, evidences of what we really are or have become. Those who seek with all their hearts to come unto Christ and be perfected in him; who desire earnestly to forsake sin and sinfulness; who yearn, who hunger and thirst after righteousness—these shall in time have their hearts changed, transformed by the unspeakable gift of the Holy Ghost. They speak "not as other men" (JST, Matthew 3:25). They perform the works of righteousness, not alone because such is required of them but also because they desire to do so, because it is the right thing to do. Their thoughts are upon good things, upon noble things, uplifting things, because their eye is single to the glory of God. They are not perfect, for they still err occasionally in judgment, speak or work or think what they should not. But their desires are to be like and with God, and they therefore repent speedily (D&C 109:21) and return without let or hindrance to the path of peace.

14. If we could command the rocks and the mountains to fall upon us] Like Alma, who desired at the apogee of his agony to become extinct (Alma 36:15), the wicked would rather face anything but their God. (See also Mormon 9:1–5; Hosea 10:8; Luke 23:30.) Such, however, will not be possible.

15. Acknowledge . . . that all his judgments are just] In the Day of Judgment, following the resurrection, there will be no disputing as to one's goodness or one's eternal station. In that day when we shall see as we are seen and know as we are known, every person shall be confronted with what he or she has become. No facade. No pretense. No sham. We shall face up to truth, diamond truth, truth which will be sharper than a two-edged sword.

16. A second death, which is a spiritual death] See commentary on Helaman 14:16–18.

17. Their torments shall be as a lake of fire and brimstone] The suffering to which the wicked are subjected takes place in the postmortal spirit world. This is hell, both a place and a state of mind. Concerning hell as a state of mind, Joseph Smith explained: "A man is his own tormenter and his own condemner. Hence the saying, They shall go into the lake that burns with fire and brimstone. The torment of disappointment in the mind of man is as exquisite as a lake burning with fire and brimstone." (*Teachings*, p. 357.)

17–18. For all except the sons of perdition this suffering is eternal only in the sense that it is God's suffering and he is eternal (see D&C 19:4–12). It will come to an end at the time of the second resurrection (at the end of the Millennium). The sons of perdition, those who have known the power and goodness of God and who then deny and defy that power, shall indeed suffer in outer darkness forever. For those who reject the gospel and sneer at its saving power, it is as though there had been no redemption made, as though Christ had never come into the world, as though there had been a Fall but no hope for deliverance from it.

A Probationary State Provided for Man

Alma 12:19–27

19. Now it came to pass that when Alma had made an end of speaking these words, the people began to be more astonished;

20. But there was one Antionah, who was a chief ruler among them, came forth and said unto him: What is this that thou hast said, that man should rise from the dead and be changed from this mortal to an immortal state, that the soul can never die?

21. What does the scripture mean, which saith that God placed cherubim and a flaming sword on the east of the garden of Eden, lest our first parents should enter and partake of the fruit of the tree of life, and live forever? And thus we see that there was no possible chance that they should live forever.

22. Now Alma said unto him: This is the thing which I was about to explain. Now we see that Adam did fall by the partaking of the forbidden fruit, according to the word of God; and thus we see, that by his fall, all mankind became a lost and fallen people.

23. And now behold, I say unto you that if it had been possible for Adam to have partaken of the fruit of the tree of life at that time, there would have been no death, and the word would have been void, making God a liar, for he said: If thou eat thou shalt surely die.

24. And we see that death comes upon mankind, yea, the death which has been spoken of by Amulek, which is the temporal death; nevertheless there was a space granted unto man in which he might repent; therefore this life became a probationary state; a time to prepare to meet God; a time to prepare for that endless state which has been spoken of by us, which is after the resurrection of the dead.

25. Now, if it had not been for the plan of redemption, which was laid from the foundation of the world, there could have been no resurrection of the dead; but there was a plan of redemption laid, which shall bring to pass the resurrection of the dead, of which has been spoken.

26. And now behold, if it were possible that our first parents could have gone forth and partaken of the tree of life they would have been forever miserable, having no preparatory state; and thus the plan of redemption would have been frustrated, and the word of God would have been void, taking none effect.

27. But behold, it was not so; but it was appointed unto men that they must die; and after death, they must come to judgment, even that same judgment of which we have spoken, which is the end.

20–21. Antionah's query is actually a valid one: If, according to the earliest scriptural accounts, God prevented Adam and Eve in Eden from partaking of the fruit of the tree of life (and thereby prevented them from living in mortality forever), why would Alma and Amulek speak of the gospel plan as a means whereby men and women could live forever through Christ? Alma, of course, will explain that God did not desire our first parents to live forever in their fallen (unredeemed) condition, but rather made known a plan whereby they could be made ready, after a life of mortality, to enter through Christ into resurrected immortality.

22. By his fall, all mankind became a lost and fallen people] This is a hard doctrine, one from which too many Latter-day Saints tend to flee. It is the doctrine that Lehi taught (see 1 Nephi 10:4–6), that Benjamin declared (see Mosiah 3:18–19), that Abinadi made known (see Mosiah 16:1–3), that the Brother of Jared professed (see Ether 3:2). It is the burden of scripture, particularly the Book of Mormon. Adam fell. His posterity fell with him, in the sense that all mankind—no one excepted—became, through conception (see Moses 6:55), subject to a fallen nature, a nature which must be put off through sincere repentance unto Christ. Though we are not heir to an "original sin"—a taint that many Christians think entailed upon the posterity of Adam and Eve as a result of their disobedience—we are subject to the Fall and thereby in dire need of redemption. In fact, the Fall and the Atonement are a package deal, a joint doctrine; there is no place in the Book of Mormon where the atonement of Christ is taught wherein the fall of Adam is not also taught or implied. If there had been no fall, there would have been no need for atonement. This is true on an individual as well as a cosmic basis.

23. Mortal or physical death was absolutely necessary in order for the plan of God to be put into effect. As Jacob declared, "Death hath passed upon all men, to fulfill the merciful plan of the great Creator" (2 Nephi 9:6). Death is the final stage of life.

23. The word would have been void, making God a liar] Compare Alma 42:5; see also Moses 3:17.

24. This life became a probationary state] In mortality we are on probation. We are here to be tried, tested, and proved in all things, to see whether we will be obedient to that which the Lord commands us to do. See Abraham 3:25; 2 Nephi 2:21; Alma 42:4.

24. A time to prepare to meet God] See Alma 34:32. In this life we seek to so live that the Holy Ghost, who is the representative and messenger of the Father and the Son, can abide with us. Through that Spirit we come to gain the mind of Christ (see 1 Corinthians 2:16)—to think and feel and act as the Father and the Son would under similar circumstances. Through that Spirit we are justified—pronounced innocent from sin, exonerated from fault and declared free from stain; sanctified—cleansed and purified, made holy and free from the effects of sin; and sealed—tied and bound everlastingly into the family of God. The Holy Ghost prepares us to see and enter the kingdom of God, and then in process of time makes of us Saints, sanctified souls prepared to be with and like our Eternal Sire.

24. That endless state] This is a reference to life hereafter, life in the kingdoms of glory, life beyond the resurrection.

25. The plan of redemption, which was laid from the foundation of the world] The plan of salvation, that which we know as the gospel of Jesus Christ, is in reality the plan of the Father, the gospel of God. It was preached and its terms and conditions—including the Creation, the Fall, and the Atonement—were known and put into effect before the world was made. See Mosiah 4:6; 15:19; 18:13.

26. If Adam and Eve had been permitted to partake of the fruit of the tree of life before living out their mortal lives, they would have been taken into immortality without the experience—the pains, the struggles, the opportunities to overcome, the posterity, and thus the joys—of this life. They would have been damned in their progress. And the rest of us would have known no progress; we would have remained forever as unembodied spirits.

Obedience to the Commandments Brings Men into the Rest of the Lord

Alma 12:28–37

28. And after God had appointed that these things should come unto man, behold, then he saw that it was expedient that man should know concerning the things whereof he had appointed unto them;

29. Therefore he sent angels to converse with them, who caused men to behold of his glory.

30. And they began from that time forth to call on his name; therefore God conversed with men, and made known unto them the plan of redemption, which had been prepared from the foundation of the world; and this he made known unto them according to their faith and repentance and their holy works.

31. Wherefore, he gave commandments unto men, they having first transgressed the first commandments as to things which were temporal, and becoming as Gods, knowing good from evil, placing themselves in a state to act, or being placed in a state to act according to their wills and pleasures, whether to do evil or to do good—

32. Therefore God gave unto

them commandments, after having made known unto them the plan of redemption, that they should not do evil, the penalty thereof being a second death, which was an everlasting death as to things pertaining unto righteousness; for on such the plan of redemption could have no power, for the works of justice could not be destroyed, according to the supreme goodness of God.

33. But God did call on men, in the name of his Son, (this being the plan of redemption which was laid) saying: If ye will repent, and harden not your hearts, then will I have mercy upon you, through mine Only Begotten Son;

34. Therefore, whosoever repenteth, and hardeneth not his heart, he shall have claim on mercy through mine Only Begotten Son, unto a remission of his sins; and these shall enter into my rest.

35. And whosoever will harden his heart and will do iniquity,

behold, I swear in my wrath that he shall not enter into my rest.

36. And now, my brethren, behold I say unto you, that if ye will harden your hearts ye shall not enter into the rest of the Lord; therefore your iniquity provoketh him that he sendeth down his wrath upon you as in the first provocation, yea, according to his word in the last provocation as well as the first, to the everlasting destruction of your souls; therefore, according to his word, unto the last death, as well as the first.

37. And now, my brethren, seeing we know these things, and they are true, let us repent, and harden not our hearts, that we provoke not the Lord our God to pull down his wrath upon us in these his second commandments which he has given unto us; but let us enter into the rest of God, which is prepared according to his word.

29. He sent angels to converse with men] See Moses 5:6; D&C 29:42.

30. God conversed with men] "And thus the Gospel began to be preached, from the beginning, being declared by holy angels sent forth from the presence of God, and by his own voice, and by the gift of the Holy Ghost" (Moses 5:58).

31. They having first transgressed the first commandments] Adam and Eve partook of the forbidden fruit and were thus unable to remain in the Garden of Eden.

31. Becoming as Gods, knowing good from evil] See Moses 4:11.

31. Placing themselves in a state to act] Agency is largely a product of knowledge and understanding. Adam and Eve, in their paradisiacal condition, were naively innocent and thus unable to serve as responsible moral agents. Having partaken of the fruit of the tree of knowledge of good and evil, having gained an understanding of good and evil, having broadened their scope of the plan of salvation, they were now in a position to act instead of simply being acted upon (see 2 Nephi 2:13).

33. See Moses 5:8.

34. He shall have claim on mercy] "And now, the plan of mercy could not be brought about except an atonement should be made; therefore God himself atoneth for the sins of the world, to bring about the plan of mercy, to appease the demands of justice, that God might be a perfect, just God, and a merciful God also" (Alma 42:15). "Wherefore, my beloved brethren, have miracles ceased because Christ hath ascended into heaven, and hath sat down on the right hand of God, to claim of the Father his rights of mercy which he hath upon the children of men?" (Moroni 7:27.)

34. These shall enter into my rest] From the scriptures and the prophets come several definitions of entering the rest of God. A person enters the rest of God whenever he gains a witness of the divinity of the work of the Lord, when he comes to that quiet but powerful assurance that God's hand is guiding the prophets and Apostles who preside over his Church and kingdom. It is a settled conviction of the truth, a peace that steadies one in a time of trouble and confusion (see Moroni 7:3; Joseph F. Smith, *Gospel Doctrine*, pp. 58, 126). A person enters into the rest of God when he enters into the personal presence of the Lord (see JST, Exodus 34:2) or encounters the fulness of the glory of God (D&C 84:24). The rest of God is also that which one enters when one has lived a faithful life and is received into paradise in the postmortal spirit world (see Alma 40:12; 60:13). In the ultimate sense, to enter the rest of the Lord is to enter into what some scriptures call the Church of the Firstborn, the Church of the exalted, that organization beyond the veil whose membership is composed of those who have received the promise of eternal life (see D&C 76:54, 67, 94; 88:5; Hebrews 12:22–23).

36. If ye will harden your hearts ye shall not enter into the rest of the Lord] Those who enter the rest of the Lord come to know the mysteries of God. Those who harden their hearts and thus close their minds to additional light and truth shall not go where God and Christ are; they shall not enter into the rest of the Lord (see verses 11, 13).

36. The first provocation] This is a reference to the refusal of the ancient Israelites, under Moses, to receive the further light and knowledge which the Lawgiver sought to give them, including the fulness of the blessings of the priesthood and thus the privilege of coming into the divine presence. "And this greater priesthood administereth the gospel and holdeth the key of the mysteries of the kingdom, even the key of the knowledge of God. Therefore, in the ordinances thereof, the power of godliness is manifest. And without the ordinances thereof, and the authority of the priesthood, the power of godliness is not manifest unto men in the flesh; for without this"—the power of godliness—"no man can see the face of God, even the Father, and live. Now this

Moses plainly taught to the children of Israel in the wilderness, and sought diligently to sanctify his people that they might behold the face of God; but they hardened their hearts and could not endure his presence; therefore, the Lord in his wrath, for his anger was kindled against them, swore that they should not enter into his rest while in the wilderness, which rest is the fulness of his glory." (D&C 84:19–24; see also JST, Exodus 34:1–2; JST, Deuteronomy 10:1–2; Psalm 95:11; Hebrews 3:11.)

36. The everlasting destruction of your souls] See *Commentary* 1:189.

Requisites for Holding the Holy Priesthood

Alma 13:1–9

1. And again, my brethren, I would cite your minds forward to the time when the Lord God gave these commandments unto his children; and I would that ye should remember that the Lord God ordained priests, after his holy order, which was after the order of his Son, to teach these things unto the people.

2. And those priests were ordained after the order of his Son, in a manner that thereby the people might know in what manner to look forward to his Son for redemption.

3. And this is the manner after which they were ordained—being called and prepared from the foundation of the world according to the foreknowledge of God, on account of their exceeding faith and good works; in the first place being left to choose good or evil; therefore they having chosen good, and exercising exceedingly great faith, are called with a holy calling, yea, with that holy calling which was prepared with, and according to, a preparatory redemption for such.

4. And thus they have been called to this holy calling on account of their faith, while others would reject the Spirit of God on account of the hardness of their hearts and blindness of their minds, while, if it had not been for this they might have had as great privilege as their brethren.

5. Or in fine, in the first place they were on the same standing with their brethren; thus this holy calling being prepared from the foundation of the world for such as would not harden their hearts, being in and through the atonement of the Only Begotten Son, who was prepared—

6. And thus being called by this holy calling, and ordained unto the high priesthood of the holy order of God, to teach his commandments unto the children of men, that they also might enter into his rest—

7. This high priesthood being after the order of his Son, which order was from the foundation of the world; or in other words, being without beginning of days or end of years, being prepared from eternity to all eternity, according to his foreknowledge of all

things—
8. Now they were ordained after this manner—being called with a holy calling, and ordained with a holy ordinance, and taking upon them the high priesthood of the holy order, which calling, and ordinance, and high priesthood, is

without beginning or end—
9. Thus they become high priests forever, after the order of the Son, the Only Begotten of the Father, who is without beginning of days or end of years, who is full of grace, equity, and truth. And thus it is. Amen.

1–9. In these verses Alma details requisites for holding the holy priesthood, that priesthood known to our dispensation as the higher priesthood or Melchizedek Priesthood. All that he says is equally descriptive of the manner in which the priesthood was or is always conferred, whether in the pre-earth life or in mortality, the system of its conferral being one and the same in both cases. Thus these verses can be profitably studied from either point of view. In the commentary that follows, the foreordination to the priesthood in pre-earth life is emphasized.

1. I would cite your minds forward . . . that ye should remember] That is, I would call your attention to an earlier time, even to the very beginning, "when the Lord God" gave these commandments "unto his children." In a similar vein Moses challenged the children of Israel to "remember the days of old," to "consider the years of many generations." Ask your fathers, Moses was saying, or your elders, for they will remember that such things were once taught (see Deuteronomy 32:7).

1. His holy order . . . the order of his Son] "There are, in the church, two priesthoods, namely, the Melchizedek and Aaronic, including the Levitical Priesthood. Why the first is called the Melchizedek Priesthood is because Melchizedek was such a great high priest. Before his day it was called *the Holy Priesthood, after the Order of the Son of God*. But out of respect or reverence to the name of the Supreme Being, to avoid the too frequent repetition of his name, they, the church, in ancient days, called that priesthood after Melchizedek, or the Melchizedek Priesthood." (D&C 107:1–4.) The Book of Mormon designates what in this dispensation we have been instructed to call the Melchizedek Priesthood as "the holy order," "the holy order of God," "the order of his Son," or in some instances just "the order."

2. Christ is the great high priest (Hebrews 3:1), and all who were ordained to the priestly office in ancient days were thought of as types or prophecies of him. The priests referred to in this verse are those commissioned to teach the gospel from the time of Adam to the time of Moses (see Alma 12:29–37; 13:1). This is a continuation of the discourse commenced in the previous chapter.

2. After the order of his Son] The holy priesthood is administered to the children of men according to different orders. As Joseph Smith taught, "All priesthood is Melchizedek, but there are different portions or degrees of it" (*Teachings*, p. 180). The preparatory gospel (law of Moses) operates under that order we know as Aaronic. The fulness of the everlasting gospel operates under different orders. The Church operates under an ecclesiastical order of offices, quorums, and councils. In our day one enters into the patriarchal order in holy temples through entering into the new and everlasting covenant of marriage (see D&C 131:1–4; Bruce R. McConkie, CR, October 1977, p. 50). In addition, one enters into the holy order of God through proving worthy of all the blessings of the temple, through eventually receiving what the scriptures call the fulness of the priesthood. President Ezra Taft Benson thus explained: "To enter into the order of the Son of God is the equivalent today of entering into the fulness of the Melchizedek Priesthood, which is only received in the house of the Lord" (*Ensign*, August 1985, p. 8).

3. Called and prepared from the foundation of the world] As in the Grand Council in Heaven Christ was called and ordained to his earthly ministry, so were all who minister in his name first called in heavenly councils, where they too were ordained to the labors that would be theirs in mortality (see *Teachings*, p. 365). None were called to offices for which they had not been properly prepared. In teaching this principle, Alma's reference is to men like Adam, Enoch, Noah, Abraham, Isaac, Jacob, and many other faithful priesthood holders of the earth's early history. Modern revelation uses as illustrations Joseph and Hyrum Smith, Brigham Young, John Taylor, and Wilford Woodruff. These, we are told, were "among the noble and great ones who were chosen in the beginning to be rulers in the Church of God. Even before they were born, *they, with many others, received their first lessons in the world of spirits and were prepared to come forth in the due time of the Lord to labor in his vineyard for the salvation of the souls of men."* (D&C 138:53–56, italics added.)

3. Exceeding faith and good works] Those designated in heavenly councils as "noble and great" had proven themselves even in the pre-earth estate. To suppose that in our spirit existence prior to mortal birth we walked exclusively by sight, never having to exercise faith, is to misunderstand the purpose of that existence as a training ground for mortality. Those born into this life with the gift of faith merited that blessing, for we are told that there is a law "irrevocably decreed in heaven before the foundations of this world, upon which all blessings are predicated" (D&C 130:20). Good works were also requisite for such high and holy foreordinations. Surely there is no better preparation for exercising faith and doing good works in the second estate than actually exercising faith and doing good works in the first.

3. The first place] Our first estate (see Abraham 3:26; Jude 1:6), that period from the time of spirit birth to our entrance into mortality.

3. Being left to choose good or evil] This phrase affirms the existence of good, evil, and agency in our first estate. The scriptural declaration that God gave us agency in that estate (see Moses 4:3) also attests to the existence of good and evil, for without these agency would have been a needless gift.

3. Called with a holy calling] The reference is to foreordinations to the higher priesthood. Paul referred to the Melchizedek Priesthood as "the heavenly calling" (Hebrews 3:1). See commentary on verse 6.

3. A preparatory redemption for such] All doctrines, ordinances, and powers associated with the gospel of Jesus Christ assume force and meaning only in and through Christ's atoning sacrifice. Such was the plan prepared before the foundation of the earth. Men are called to receive the priesthood to assist in the redemption of souls. They are called to preach and make available what Paul described as the "ministry of reconciliation" (2 Corinthians 5:18). They are called to bless lives—to lighten burdens, to strengthen the feeble knees and lift up the hands that hang down—just as their Master, the great high priest, is called upon to do. The priesthood bearers before and after Christ are thus involved in the work of his ministry. Their work is preparatory. They, like the preeminent forerunner, John the Baptist, prepare the way of the Lord. Those prophets and priests who labored before the meridian of time sought to prepare mankind for the coming of the Redeemer. In the words of Elder Bruce R. McConkie: "They could preach redemption; they could foretell its coming; but their work was preparatory only. Redemption itself would come through the ministry of Him of whom they were but types and shadows." (*Promised Messiah,* p. 451.) Those who have lived since that time seek to instruct and warn and exhort mankind—all in preparation for his second advent, that final redemption of the earth and its inhabitants.

4. We would suppose that in our pre-earth existence all persons had the opportunity to exercise faith and involved themselves in works of righteousness. Those so doing obtained a birthright to the blessings of the priesthood as Abraham's seed. Before the day of judgment, that opportunity will again be extended, and again it will become the privilege of those men exercising faith and doing works of righteousness to have the priesthood conferred upon them.

4. Hardness of their hearts and blindness of their minds]
The voice of the Spirit speaks to us in our hearts and minds (see
D&C 8:2). Gospel understanding can be neither heartless nor
mindless. Neither feeling nor intellect, standing alone, is sufficient
to bring the understanding and faith essential to salvation. Thus in
the pre-earth life those who rejected the fulness of gospel blessings did it as it is done in mortality, that is, by ignoring the feelings
of their hearts and by closing the windows of their minds to light
and truth.

5. It would appear from this verse that the spirits of all men
were created with equal capacity and opportunity to obtain the
fulness of heaven's blessings; yet some, long before they were
born into mortality, closed their eyes and hardened their hearts to
the plan of redemption.

5. Who was prepared] We are told that it was necessary for
the earthly Christ to advance from grace to grace until he received
the fulness of his Father (see D&C 93:11–14). In so doing he was
but following the path and pattern of his pre-earth existence. See
commentary on verse 3.

6. Being called] We do not vie for office or position in the
kingdom of God. All who serve, all who hold the priesthood or
any ecclesiastical office, must be called of God (see Articles of
Faith 1:5). There are no self-ordinations.

6. Holy calling] That Alma referred to the priesthood as a
"holy calling" is most appropriate and descriptive. "The rights of
the priesthood are inseparably connected with the powers of
heaven," Joseph Smith said, and "the powers of heaven cannot be
controlled nor handled only upon the principles of righteousness."
Thus the Prophet declared that the scepter of the priesthood must
be "an unchanging scepter of righteousness and truth." (D&C
121:36, 46.)

6. Ordained] Invested with authority by the laying on of
hands by one who has authority (see D&C 42:11).

6. The high priesthood of the holy order of God] There
are two meanings of the title high priest. First, high priest is one of
the ordained offices in the Melchizedek Priesthood. Second,
"God's chief representative on earth, the one who holds the
highest spiritual position in his kingdom in any age, is called *the
high priest.* This special designation of the chief spiritual officer of
the Church has reference to the administrative position which he
holds rather than to the office to which he is ordained in the
priesthood." (Bruce R. McConkie, *Mormon Doctrine,* pp. 355–56.)

6. To teach his commandments] Joseph Smith taught: "The
duty of a High Priest is to administer in spiritual and holy things,
and to hold communion with God. . . . And again, it is the High

Priests' duty to be better qualified to teach principles and doctrines, than the Elders." (*Teachings*, p. 21.) Thus the primary charge of the high priest—indeed, the primary responsibility of all who hold the higher priesthood—is teaching the doctrines of salvation. A revelation of our day states that the "greater priesthood administereth the gospel and holdeth the key of the mysteries of the kingdom, even the key of the knowledge of God" (D&C 84:19). The Melchizedek Priesthood, Joseph Smith taught, "is the channel through which all knowledge, doctrine, the plan of salvation and every important matter is revealed from heaven" (*Teachings*, pp. 166–67).

6. His rest] See commentary on Alma 12:34.

7. This high priesthood being after the order of his Son] Christ is the pattern, the standard, the example in all things. In heavenly councils he was called and ordained to his earthly ministry on account of his exceedingly great faith and good works in that first estate. He complied fully with the discipline and order of that heavenly kingdom. All who held the priesthood before the day of his mortal ministry were to be types and shadows of what he would be and do as he labored in mortality. Their ordination and ministry were to be living prophecies of his own. In like manner, all who have been called to the holy priesthood since the day of his coming in the flesh are to serve as he served, imitating his example in all that they do; they are to be living witnesses of what he was.

7. Without beginning of days or end of years] This phrase, commonly associated with descriptions of the Melchizedek Priesthood (see Hebrews 7:3; D&C 84:17), is intended to dramatize its endless duration. The priesthood, like Christ, is from eternity past to eternity future. It existed before days were numbered upon this earth, and will continue throughout the endless expanses of eternity. From the earliest of times it was understood that the holy order came "not by man, nor the will of man; neither by father nor mother; neither by beginning of days nor end of years; but of God; and it was delivered unto men by the calling of his own voice, according to his own will, unto as many as believed on his name" (JST, Genesis 14:28–29).

8–9. The declaration of the preceding verses is now summarized. To hold the priesthood one must be called of God (it is not a matter of self-choice); righteousness is a prerequisite to its conferral; and it must be conveyed according to the order of the Church (i.e., by the laying on of hands). Thus, all who receive the priesthood must receive it in the same manner as Christ received it and are to be types or witnesses of him, sharing a power which is as endless as God himself.

To Obtain Salvation Men Must Honor the Priesthood

Alma 13:10–13

10. Now, as I said concerning the holy order, or this high priesthood, there were many who were ordained and became high priests of God; and it was on account of their exceeding faith and repentance, and their righteousness before God, they choosing to repent and work righteousness rather than to perish;

11. Therefore they were called after this holy order, and were sanctified, and their garments were washed white through the blood of the Lamb.

12. Now they, after being sanctified by the Holy Ghost, having their garments made white, being pure and spotless before God, could not look upon sin save it were with abhorrence; and there were many, exceedingly great many, who were made pure and entered into the rest of the Lord their God.

13. And now, my brethren, I would that ye should humble yourselves before God, and bring forth fruit meet for repentance, that ye may also enter into that rest.

10–11. Alma, speaking more than a hundred years before the ministry of Christ, observed that many had exercised "exceeding faith," repented of their sins, and lived righteously. These, he said, were ordained to the "holy order," were sanctified and washed their garments white through the blood of the Lamb. Those magnifying their callings in the priesthood in our day have been promised that by so doing they too "are sanctified by the Spirit unto the renewing of their bodies" (D&C 84:33). By the magnifying of our callings, that is, by serving faithfully where and as as we are called to serve, we sanctify ourselves. Sanctification is the process of becoming clean, pure, and spotless before the Lord. That process involves faithful service, which in turn is essential to the remission of sins and the refining of our souls.

Applying this principle, James wrote that "if any of you do err from the truth, and one convert him; let him know, that he which converteth the sinner from the error of his way shall save a soul from death, and shall hide a multitude of sins" (James 5:19–20). James's point is that the sins being hidden are those of the minister, not just those of the one being ministered to. Commenting on this verse, Elder Bruce R. McConkie has written: "By reclaiming an erring brother, we save both him and ourselves. Our sins are hidden (remitted) because we ministered for the salvation and blessing of another member of the kingdom. In principle this special reward for Christ's ministers applies also to those who preach the gospel and bring souls into the kingdom. The minister is rewarded with salvation and, of necessity, in the process, is freed from his own sins." (*Doctrinal New Testament Commentary* 3:279.)

The whole concept of priesthood revolves around this doctrine. Men are entrusted with the priesthood so that they may serve and bless others. Through faithfulness in this divine investiture of authority they sanctify their own souls, that they lay up the blessings of heaven in store, that they perish not, but bring salvation to their own souls (see D&C 4:1–4).

11. Garments were washed white] See commentary on Alma 5:22–23.

12. The Holy Ghost is a sanctifier. The sanctified soul is one that has been baptized of water and of the Spirit. The Spirit baptism is frequently referred to in holy writ as the baptism of fire and the Holy Ghost (see Matthew 3:11; Luke 3:16; 2 Nephi 31:13–14; 3 Nephi 11:35; 12:1–2; Mormon 7:10; D&C 20:41; 33:11; 39:6). It is the work of the Holy Ghost to burn out of the repentant soul the dross or iniquity, carnality, sensuality, and evil in any form. The persons thus cleansed become new creatures of the Holy Ghost (see Mosiah 27:24–26). They are born again.

"The baptism of fire is not something in addition to the receipt of the Holy Ghost; rather, it is the actual enjoyment of the gift which is offered by the laying on of hands at the time of baptism. 'Remission of sins,' the Lord says, comes 'by baptism and by fire, yea, even the Holy Ghost.' (D&C 19:31; 2 Nephi 31:17.) Those who receive the baptism of fire are 'filled as if with fire' (Helaman 5:45)."

"*Sanctification* is a state of saintliness, a state attained only by conformity to the laws and ordinances of the gospel. The plan of salvation is the system and means provided whereby men may sanctify their souls and thereby become worthy of a celestial inheritance." (Bruce R. McConkie, *Mormon Doctrine*, pp. 73, 675.)

12. There were many, exceedingly great many] When the righteous in paradise—those assured of a glorious resurrection—assembled to greet the Christ during his short ministry among them, they constituted an "innumerable company" (see D&C 138:12). The number of the faithful Saints who lived from the time of Adam to the time when Christ visited the world of the spirits appears to have been appreciably greater than we have generally supposed. Though it is true that the gate is strait and the way of holiness is narrow, the "few there be that find it" (Matthew 7:14), presumably a relative expression, may well total, in real terms, a large number of our Father's children who will go on to exaltation in the highest heaven. There is no ceiling on the number of saved beings; God desires to save all who will be saved.

13. Bring forth fruit meet for repentance] Neither the profession of faith nor the confession of sin supplants the need for works of righteousness. As the tree is known by its fruits, so the repentant soul is known by its deeds. See commentary on Alma 34:30.

Melchizedek: A Type of Christ

Alma 13:14–19

14. Yea, humble yourselves even as the people in the days of Melchizedek, who was also a high priest after this same order which I have spoken, who also took upon him the high priesthood forever.

15. And it was this same Melchizedek to whom Abraham paid tithes; yea, even our father Abraham paid tithes of one–tenth part of all he possessed.

16. Now these ordinances were given after this manner, that thereby the people might look forward on the Son of God, it being a type of his order, or it being his order, and this that they might look forward to him for a remission of their sins, that they might enter into the rest of the Lord.

17. Now this Melchizedek was a king over the land of Salem; and his people had waxed strong in iniquity and abomination; yea, they had all gone astray; they were full of all manner of wickedness;

18. But Melchizedek having exercised mighty faith, and received the office of the high priesthood according to the holy order of God, did preach repentance unto his people. And behold, they did repent; and Melchizedek did establish peace in the land in his days; therefore he was called the prince of peace, for he was the king of Salem; and he did reign under his father.

19. Now, there were many before him, and also there were many afterwards, but none were greater; therefore, of him they have more particularly made mention.

14. Melchizedek] Melchizedek is an enigma to those whose knowledge of him is confined to the Bible. In that record he rather mysteriously crosses the path of Abraham, who unhesitatingly recognizes him as a being of superior spiritual rank. Abraham pays tithes to him and receives from him what appears to be like the sacrament. Melchizedek then disappears from the scene as suddenly as he had appeared (Genesis 14:18–20; see especially the JST). He remains lost to the sacred chronicle for a thousand years, at which point a psalmic reference describes him as a type for the coming of the Messiah (see Psalm 110:4). Again a thousand years pass without mention of him until Paul, writing to the Hebrews, argues that the Melchizedek Priesthood is superior to the Aaronic, and that the gospel the Savior brought is superior to the Mosaic system (see Hebrews 7). Indeed, so great is the mystery that has come to surround the man Melchizedek that some have supposed him to have been born without parents (see Hebrews 7:3).

Though the present verses contain the only references to Melchizedek in the Book of Mormon, we can be confident that the plates of brass provided Alma with appreciably more information than our Bible contains. From the Joseph Smith Translation we learn, and suppose Alma to have known, that Melchizedek was a man of faith who wrought righteousness and who even, as a child, "stopped the mouths of lions, and quenched the violence of fire." He was "approved of God" and was ordained a high priest after the order of the Son of God. Through the teaching of the gospel he obtained peace in Salem and thus merited the title Prince of peace. He and his people then "wrought righteousness, and obtained heaven," meaning that they were caught up like Enoch and his people and obtained the promise that they would return with them during the millennial day. Thus he was also "called the king of heaven by his people, or, in other words, the King of peace." (See JST, Genesis 14:26–40.)

It was revealed to Joseph Smith that Abraham received the priesthood from Melchizedek (see D&C 84:14). Depicting that event, Joseph Smith recounted: "Abraham says to Melchizedek, I believe all that thou hast taught me concerning the priesthood and the coming of the Son of Man; so Melchizedek ordained Abraham and sent him away. Abraham rejoiced, saying, Now I have a priesthood." (*Teachings*, pp. 322–23.) Joseph Smith also learned by revelation that it was because Melchizedek was such a great high priest—that is, because he so closely emulated Christ—that the priesthood was named after him among the ancient Saints (see D&C 107:1–4). How appropriate that Alma should say of Melchizedek that "none were greater"! (Alma 13:19.)

14. After this same order] The priesthood held by the Nephites traced itself back to the Old World. The requisites, discipline, and order were one and the same. As with all gospel principles, to understand them in one age is to know and understand them in all ages. In the days of Adam it was promised that the "same Priesthood, which was in the beginning, shall be in the end of the world also" (Moses 6:7). Thus we can say that all mankind may be saved by obedience to the laws and ordinances of the gospel, and that those laws and ordinances and the priesthood by which they must be administered are everlastingly the same.

14. Took upon him the high priesthood forever] The language is that of the Psalmist who recounted the promise of the Father to the Son. "The Lord hath sworn, and will not repent, Thou art a priest for ever after the order of Melchizedek" (Psalm 110:4). Wrote Elder Bruce R. McConkie: "God swore an oath that Christ should be a priest forever; that is, though our Lord had possessed the priesthood in pre-existence, he would receive it anew in mortality and would have it forever—in time and in eternity. And this sets the pattern for all who become sons of God and joint—heirs with Christ" (*Doctrinal New Testament Commentary* 3:173).

15. From the Joseph Smith Translation we learn that Melchizedek was the keeper of God's storehouse and that God had appointed him to receive tithes for the poor. "Wherefore, Abram paid unto him tithes of all that he had, of all the riches which he possessed, which God had given him more than that which he had need" (JST, Genesis 14:37–39).

16. These ordinances . . . being a type of his order] All gospel ordinances are teaching devices, all testify of Christ and of our need to be one with him. Alma's illustration of this verity is the priesthood. The manner in which a man was called, ordained, and served in God's name typified the call, ordination, and service of God's own Son. See commentary on verse 7.

17–19. In these verses Alma establishes Melchizedek as a type for Christ, noting the following parallels: First, like Christ, he was a king. The very name of this great high priest—*Melchi-zedek*, "king of righteousness" or, perhaps more correctly, "my king is righteousness"—affirms and testifies of the goodness and power of the coming Messiah. Righteousness is also a name-title of Christ (see Moses 7:45). As Melchizedek ruled his kingdom in righteousness, so Christ will eventually rule and reign upon this earth, doing so with the unchanging scepter of righteousness and truth, possessing an everlasting dominion without compulsory means (see D&C 121:46).

Second, Melchizedek ruled over the city of Salem (a name which means "peace"). In like manner, Christ will reinstitute the glory of David's day when nought is known but peace among the Lord's people. Third, both Melchizedek and Christ were known as the "great high priest." In Old Testament times the primary duty of the priest was to offer sacrifice at the altar and to act as mediator between God and men. It was by virtue of the priestly functions that the nations of Israel were reconciled to their God.

"Through the ministrations of the priesthood the people of Israel were instructed in the doctrine of sin and its expiation, in forgiveness and worship. In short, the priest was the indispensable source of religious knowledge for the people, and the channel through which spiritual life was communicated." (*International Standard Bible Encyclopedia* 4:2439.)

Fourth, both were men of "mighty faith" who taught "repentance" to their people. Of Melchizedek we read, "his people wrought righteousness, and obtained heaven" (JST, Genesis 14:34). And of course the same will be true of all who sustain Christ and his teachings in righteousness. Fifth, both bore the title Prince of Peace, being teachers of that gospel by which peace and joy come. Sixth, of Melchizedek we read, "and he did reign under his father," as does Christ, who professes no authority save that of his Father (see John 5:30). Seventh, though there were many prophets before Melchizedek and many after him, Alma described the king of Salem by saying "none were greater." Thus this great prophet, priest, and king stood as a classic type of the Promised Messiah, of whom it is true not only that none were greater, but also that none have been as great.

All Interpret Scripture at Their Own Peril

Alma 13:20

20. Now I need not rehearse the matter; what I have said may suffice. Behold, the scriptures are before you; if ye will wrest them it shall be to your own destruction.

20. Wrest them . . . to your own destruction] From the time the first copy of the Book of Mormon was published, all who come into possession of its sacred truths must accept or reject them at the peril of their eternal lives. We cannot reject the mind, the will, the word of the Lord and at the same time make legitimate claim to accepting him. As it is with the Book of Mormon, so it is with all scripture, be it ancient or modern; we cannot with impunity close our hearts and minds to that which the Lord has said or to that which he will yet say. Some profess to accept the voice of heaven, but only after having distorted its purpose to suit their own. Peter, like Alma, warned that the spiritually untutored and unstable who wrest—that is, twist or distort—the scriptures do so to their own destruction (see 2 Peter 3:16).

Common practices among those who abuse and wrest scripture include: (1) designating the literal as figurative and the figurative as literal; (2) stretching a text beyond what it meant, this to justify actions that assuredly the text did not intend; (3) squeezing a text so tightly that no appropriate applications can be made from it; (4) granting some obscure passage the power and authority to overturn the plain meaning of a host of other texts; and (5) picking and choosing from holy writ that which suits their fancy, while reading all else with a blind eye.

Angels Announce Christ's Birth to the
Righteous of All Nations

Alma 13:21–26

21. And now it came to pass that when Alma had said these words unto them, he stretched forth his hand unto them and cried with a mighty voice, saying: Now is the time to repent, for the day of salvation draweth nigh;

22. Yea, and the voice of the Lord, by the mouth of angels, doth declare it unto all nations; yea, doth declare it, that they may have glad tidings of great joy; yea, and he doth sound these glad tidings among all his people, yea, even to them that are scattered abroad upon the face of the earth; wherefore they have come unto us.

23. And they are made known unto us in plain terms, that we may understand, that we cannot err; and this because of our being wanderers in a strange land; therefore, we are thus highly favored, for we have these glad tidings declared unto us in all parts of our vineyard.

24. For behold, angels are declaring it unto many at this time in our land; and this is for the purpose of preparing the hearts of the children of men to receive his word at the time of his coming in his glory.

25. And now we only wait to hear the joyful news declared unto us by the mouth of angels, of his coming; for the time cometh, we know not how soon. Would to God that it might be in my day; but let it be sooner or later, in it I will rejoice.

26. And it shall be made known unto just and holy men, by the mouth of angels, at the time of his coming, that the words of our fathers may be fulfilled, according to that which they have spoken concerning him, which was according to the spirit of prophecy which was in them.

21. The day of salvation] In one sense, reference is to the day of the Savior's birth. In another sense, to say that "the day of salvation draweth nigh" is to lay stress upon the importance of preparing in this life for death, that "night of darkness wherein there can be no labor performed" (Alma 34:33; compare JST, Luke 12:41–44).

22. As Christ was Savior to all the world, so the announcement of his birth was made to "all nations," to "all his people." Indeed, it had been written anciently: "He shall come, as it is written in the book of the prophets, to take away the sins of the world, and to bring salvation unto the heathen nations, to gather together those who are lost, who are of the sheepfold of Israel; yea, even the dispersed and afflicted; and also to prepare the way, and make possible the preaching of the gospel unto the Gentiles; and to be a light unto all who sit in darkness, unto the uttermost parts of the earth; to bring to pass the resurrection from the dead, and to ascend up on high, to dwell on the right hand of the Father" (JST, Luke 3:5–7).

22. The voice of the Lord, by the mouth of angels] The proclamation of angels is one of the means by which the gospel is preached. Of the Adamic dispensation the scriptures attest: "And thus the Gospel began to be preached, from the beginning, being declared by holy angels sent forth from the presence of God, and by his own voice, and by the gift of the Holy Ghost" (Moses 5:58; compare D&C 20:35). Angels—seen and unseen—witness to the "chosen vessels" about the divine Sonship of the Lord Jesus, and these in turn bear witness to "the residue of men" (Moroni 7:31–32). Indeed, "Whether by mine own voice or by the voice of my servants, it is the same" (D&C 1:38).

24. Angels are declaring it unto many] God, who declares himself to all nations, will eventually declare himself to all within those nations. All are entitled to the witness of heaven, especially and particularly as it relates to the testimony of Christ, and many receive that witness by the ministration of angels, for such is their gift (Moroni 10:14).

25. One wonders whether the choir that heralded the birth of Christ to the shepherds of Bethlehem might also have borne their angelic witness in heavenly strains of music to congregations of the faithful wherever they were found throughout the world.

26. Just and holy men] The revelations of heaven are vouchsafed to those worthy of them. One wonders whether certain shepherds who saw and heard this heaven-sent message in the Old World were not among those "just and holy men" spoken of. Surely they were lifetime witnesses of this marvelous event. Luke testifies that "they made known abroad the saying which was told them concerning this child" (Luke 2:17).

Alma Seals His Sermon with Testimony

Alma 13:27–31

27. And now, my brethren, I wish from the inmost part of my heart, yea, with great anxiety even unto pain, that ye would hearken unto my words, and cast off your sins, and not procrastinate the day of your repentance;

28. But that ye would humble yourselves before the Lord, and call on his holy name, and watch and pray continually, that ye may not be tempted above that which ye can bear, and thus be led by the Holy Spirit, becoming humble, meek, submissive, patient, full of love and all long–suffering;

29. Having faith on the Lord; having a hope that ye shall receive eternal life; having the love of God always in your hearts, that ye may be lifted up at the last day and enter into his rest.

30. And may the Lord grant unto you repentance, that ye may not bring down his wrath upon you, that ye may not be bound down by the chains of hell, that ye may not suffer the second death.

31. And Alma spake many more words unto the people, which are not written in this book.

27–30. As Alma concludes his preachment he follows the pattern of the prophets and seals with testimony that which he has taught. His has been the voice of warning, a call to repentance, an appeal to live worthy of the Holy Spirit, an entreaty to his listeners to have faith in Christ and the hope of eternal life. His emphasis is on the need for humility, watchfulness, and constant prayer; his stress is on meekness, submissiveness, patience, love, and long-suffering, combined to dispel any idea that salvation is available for anything less than the labor of a lifetime. To be born again is generally a process, not an event.

27. Not procrastinate the day of your repentance] See commentary on Alma 34:33.

28. Too often people have taken license with the following words of Paul the Apostle: "There hath no temptation taken you but such as is common to man: but God is faithful, who will not suffer you to be tempted above that ye are able; but will with the temptation also make a way to escape, that ye may be able to bear it" (1 Corinthians 10:13). They have falsely supposed that they could hurl themselves into the path of sin, enter into forbidden territory, or wander briefly from that road which is strait and narrow—and then be divinely delivered from spiritual destruction. Such people are deceived. They have bought into another of Satan's lies. Unless they repent, they will lose their souls. We cannot repeatedly tempt God and expect him to keep us from the effects of our shortsightedness. Rather, as Alma here teaches, we must be vigilant, ever watchful, careful and cautious so as not to slip into sin. The promise of the Almighty is that there is no situation out of which God cannot deliver us and no temptation that he cannot empower us against—if we are seeking with all our heart to avoid the taints of the world, if we are striving to navigate the gospel path with fidelity and devotion.

29. Having delivered one of the most doctrinally profound sermons in all of holy writ, having pointed toward the sacred promises which are available to those who seek the face of the Lord with singlemindedness, having spoken of the mysteries of the kingdom, Alma now comes back to the basics and focuses upon those matters which are foundational and fundamental to sainthood. It is noteworthy that Alma should suggest that the way to enter the rest of the Lord, here and hereafter, is to seek the Spirit and seek those precious gifts—faith, hope, and charity—which bring peace in this world and eternal glory in the world to come.

30. May the Lord grant unto you repentance] See Alma 34:14–15; Acts 5:29–31; 11:18; 2 Timothy 2:23–25. "The return to the path of purity and peace through repentance is not simply a grand work which man must perform on his own. . . . Rather, repentance is granted and available as a free gift to man through the Atonement; through the grace and goodness of Jesus Christ, men and women are not only entitled to repent but also are enabled to do so." In short, "Since God grants repentance, it cannot be viewed as a human work alone." (Robert L. Millet, *By Grace Are We Saved*, p. 34.)

30. Second death] See Alma 12:32; *Commentary* 2:30–31.

Alma and Amulek Falsely Accused

Alma 14:1–5

1. And it came to pass after he had made an end of speaking unto the people many of them did believe on his words, and began to repent, and to search the scriptures.

2. But the more part of them were desirous that they might destroy Alma and Amulek; for they were angry with Alma, because of the plainness of his words unto Zeezrom; and they also said that Amulek had lied unto them, and had reviled against their law and also against their lawyers and judges.

3. And they were also angry with Alma and Amulek; and because they had testified so plainly against their wickedness, they sought to put them away privily.

4. But it came to pass that they did not; but they took them and

bound them with strong cords, and took them before the chief judge of the land.

5. And the people went forth and witnessed against them—testifying that they had reviled against the law, and their lawyers and judges of the land, and also of all the people that were in the land; and also testified that there was but one God, and that he should send his Son among the people, but he should not save them; and many such things did the people testify against Alma and Amulek. Now this was done before the chief judge of the land.

1–5. When the servants of falsehood contend with the servants of truth, each side must fight with its own weapons. The servants of light cannot use falsehoods to advance their cause, nor can the servants of the prince of darkness use truth—though they may appear to do so. Truth without light, truth without virtue, truth without goodness, truth without mercy, truth without righteousness, truth without holiness—this is truth without honesty. Like the dusk of day, it is harbinger of the darkness to come.

Zeezrom Rejected for Recanting Falsehoods

Alma 14:6–7

6. And it came to pass that Zeezrom was astonished at the words which had been spoken; and he also knew concerning the blindness of the minds, which he had caused among the people by his lying words; and his soul began to be harrowed up under a consciousness of his own guilt; yea, he began to be encircled about by the pains of hell.

7. And it came to pass that he began to cry unto the people, saying: Behold, I am guilty, and these men are spotless before God. And he began to plead for them from that time forth; but they reviled him, saying: Art thou also possessed with the devil? And they spit upon him, and cast him out from among them, and also all those who believed in the words which had been spoken by Alma and Amulek; and they cast them out, and sent men to cast stones at them.

6–7. Knowing that he has employed "lying words," Zeezrom's conscience is stung by the doctrines taught and the testimony borne. His effort to right the matter by defending Alma and Amulek, however, is rewarded in the same spirit in which previously he sought to abuse and confound them. Might we say that Satan is no respecter of persons—that he will turn with equal wrath upon one and all who oppose him.

Those Causing Others to Suffer Will Be Justly Recompensed

Alma 14:8–11

8. And they brought their wives and children together, and whosoever believed or had been taught to believe in the word of God they caused that they should be cast into the fire; and they also brought forth their records which contained the holy scriptures, and cast them into the fire also, that they might be burned and destroyed by fire.

9. And it came to pass that they took Alma and Amulek, and carried them forth to the place of martyrdom, that they might witness the destruction of those who were consumed by fire.

10. And when Amulek saw the pains of the women and children who were consuming in the fire, he also was pained; and he said unto Alma: How can we witness this awful scene? Therefore let us stretch forth our hands, and exercise the power of God which is in us, and save them from the flames.

11. But Alma said unto him: The Spirit constraineth me that I must not stretch forth mine hand; for behold the Lord receiveth them up unto himself, in glory; and he doth suffer that they may do this thing, or that the people may do this thing unto them, according to the hardness of their hearts, that the judgments which he shall exercise upon them in his wrath may be just; and the blood of the innocent shall stand as a witness against them, yea, and cry mightily against them at the last day.

8–11. God is not the author of evil, yet within limits and bounds he allows it to exist. This is done so that the righteous might merit the fulness of his glory and that the wicked, the workers of evil, might in like fashion merit the fulness of his wrath. Suffering sanctifies the souls of the faithful. The inflicting of that suffering soils all that is decent and makes the perpetrator a fit companion to the devil, to merit as *he* has merited and to be rewarded as *he* will be rewarded. Mocking and scourging, bonds and imprisonment, flight and refuge, destitution and torment have been the common lot of Saints in all ages. Yet that God who is not unmindful of the sparrow that falls has witnessed it all—he "having provided some better things for them through their sufferings, for without sufferings they could not be made perfect" (JST, Hebrews 11:40).

8. They . . . brought forth their records] This is one of the evidences in the Book of Mormon that many (if not most) of the believers had scriptural records. Though there may have been only one set of metal plates (such as the brass plates), surely hundreds and thousands of other sets of records, copies—less durable but more accessible—could be found among the descendants of Lehi. See Jacob 7:23; Alma 33:2; Helaman 3:13; 3 Nephi 5:9.

A Blessing of Protection Rests upon the Lord's Servants

Alma 14:12–13

12. Now Amulek said unto Alma: Behold, perhaps they will burn us also.
13. And Alma said: Be it accord-ing to the will of the Lord. But, behold, our work is not finished; therefore they burn us not.

13. Our work is not finished; therefore they burn us not] It will be remembered that Abinadi told the wicked priests of King Noah's court that they were without the power to slay him until he had delivered his message (see Mosiah 13:7). This is the principle that Alma is teaching Amulek. When the Lord gives a servant a mission, that person is expected to have full confidence that he will enjoy the protection of heaven in the accomplishment of that which he has been called to do. See *Commentary* 1:208–9; 2:213.

The Spirit of Mockery

Alma 14:14–22

14. Now it came to pass that when the bodies of those who had been cast into the fire were consumed, and also the records which were cast in with them, the chief judge of the land came and stood before Alma and Amulek, as they were bound; and he smote them with his hand upon their cheeks, and said unto them: After what ye have seen, will ye preach again unto this people, that they shall be cast into a lake of fire and brimstone?

15. Behold, ye see that ye had not power to save those who had been cast into the fire; neither has God saved them because they were of thy faith. And the judge smote them again upon their cheeks, and asked: What say ye for yourselves?

16. Now this judge was after the order and faith of Nehor, who slew Gideon.

17. And it came to pass that Alma and Amulek answered him nothing; and he smote them again, and delivered them to the officers to be cast into prison.

18. And when they had been cast into prison three days, there came many lawyers, and judges, and priests, and teachers, who were of the profession of Nehor; and they came in unto the prison to see them, and they questioned them about many words; but they answered them nothing.

19. And it came to pass that the judge stood before them, and said: Why do ye not answer the words of this people? Know ye not that I have power to deliver you up unto the flames? And he commanded them to speak; but they answered nothing.

20. And it came to pass that they departed and went their ways, but came again on the

morrow; and the judge also smote them again on their cheeks. And many came forth also, and smote them, saying: Will ye stand again and judge this people, and condemn our law? If ye have such great power why do ye not deliver yourselves?

21. And many such things did they say unto them, gnashing their teeth upon them, and spitting upon them, and saying: How shall we look when we are damned?

22. And many such things, yea, all manner of such things did they say unto them; and thus they did mock them for many days. And they did withhold food from them that they might hunger, and water that they might thirst; and they also did take from them their clothes that they were naked; and thus they were bound with strong cords, and confined in prison.

14–22. As men filled with the Spirit of God have conducted themselves with decorum and dignity in all ages and among all people with whom they have labored, so those filled with the spirit of the devil have manifested the same ugliness of spirit whenever they have appeared on the scene. How similar these devils incarnate were to those who mocked the Christ! He too was smitten upon the cheek, gnashed at, and spat upon. He too was artfully questioned by unscrupulous and double-tongued lawyers and priests. He too chose to remain silent rather than dignify their cunning inquisition with answers. And he too was taunted for not having the power to save himself from the agonies of the cross.

Well might we say that the Savior and those that come in his name have received like treatment in all ages. One paragraph from the experiences of the Prophet Joseph Smith will illustrate the point: "The constable who served this second warrant upon me had no sooner arrested me than he began to abuse and insult me; and so unfeeling was he with me, that although I had been kept all the day in court without anything to eat since the morning, yet he hurried me off to Broome county, a distance of about fifteen miles, before he allowed me any kind of food whatever. He took me to a tavern, and gathered in a number of men, who used every means to abuse, ridicule and insult me. They spit upon me, pointed their fingers at me, saying, 'Prophesy, prophesy!' and thus did they imitate those who crucified the Savior of mankind, not knowing what they did." (*HC* 1:91.)

16. The order and faith of Nehor] Nehor was a large, powerful, and persuasive man who organized a church in the first year of the reign of the judges. His church was founded on the doctrine of universal salvation. He held that all were to be saved; none were to be lost, and none were to fear for that which they had done. He also introduced the idea of a ministry built upon the principles of priestcraft. The teachers of liberal doctrine expect liberal support. See Alma 1:1–15.

Mockers Destroyed and Alma and Amulek Delivered

Alma 14:23–29

23. And it came to pass after they had thus suffered for many days, (and it was on the twelfth day, in the tenth month, in the tenth year of the reign of the judges over the people of Nephi) that the chief judge over the land of Ammonihah and many of their teachers and their lawyers went in unto the prison where Alma and Amulek were bound with cords.

24. And the chief judge stood before them, and smote them again, and said unto them: If ye have the power of God deliver yourselves from these bands, and then we will believe that the Lord will destroy this people according to your words.

25. And it came to pass that they all went forth and smote them, saying the same words, even until the last; and when the last had spoken unto them the power of God was upon Alma and Amulek, and they rose and stood upon their feet.

26. And Alma cried, saying: How long shall we suffer these great afflictions, O Lord? O Lord, give us strength according to our faith which is in Christ, even unto deliverance. And they broke the cords with which they were bound; and when the people saw this, they began to flee, for the fear of destruction had come upon them.

27. And it came to pass that so great was their fear that they fell to the earth, and did not obtain the outer door of the prison; and the earth shook mightily, and the walls of the prison were rent in twain, so that they fell to the earth; and the chief judge, and the lawyers, and priests, and teachers, who smote upon Alma and Amulek, were slain by the fall thereof.

28. And Alma and Amulek came forth out of the prison, and they were not hurt; for the Lord had granted unto them power, according to their faith which was in Christ. And they straightway came forth out of the prison; and they were loosed from their bands; and the prison had fallen to the earth, and every soul within the walls thereof, save it were Alma and Amulek, was slain; and they straightway came forth into the city.

29. Now the people having heard a great noise came running together by multitudes to know the cause of it; and when they saw Alma and Amulek coming forth out of the prison, and the walls thereof had fallen to the earth, they were struck with great fear, and fled from the presence of Alma and Amulek even as a goat fleeth with her young from two lions; and thus they did flee from the presence of Alma and Amulek.

23. The land of Ammonihah] Reference is to the country immediately surrounding the city of the same name. It lay between the river Sidon and the ocean and was situated in the same region as the cities of Melek, Noah, and Aaron, though the exact location cannot be determined. It was inhabited almost exclusively by the followers of Nehor and was notorious for the wickedness of its inhabitants. The destruction of its chief judge was but a type of the destruction that shortly awaited all the inhabitants of the city (see Alma 16), and, for that matter, that eventually awaits all who drink of the same cup.

24. If ye have the power of God] These words of the chief judge immediately bring to mind the language of his master in his attempts to entice the Savior to the improper use of heaven's powers. "If thou be the Son of God," he taunted, "command that these stones be made bread." And again, "If thou be the Son of God, cast thyself down" from this pinnacle and the angels will "bear thee up." (See Matthew 4:3–6.)

24. Then we will believe] Of one thing we have perfect assurance—the last thing wanted by those who demand signs is signs; the last thing wanted by those who demand evidence is evidence. A world of signs and evidences would not soften their hearts. The leaders of the Jews sought signs, and Christ gave them signs sufficient to convince any people, yet they rejected him (see 2 Nephi 10:4).

25. We note with interest that the junior devils can but echo the words of their master. There is no evidence of freedom of thought among the legions of hell.

26. How long shall we suffer these afflictions . . . ?] See a similar plea from Joseph Smith in D&C 121:1–6.

27. The taunting request for a manifestation of power by the chief judge and his minions is now honored.

Spiritual Sickness and Physical Sickness May Be Related

Alma 15:1–12

1. And it came to pass that Alma and Amulek were commanded to depart out of that city; and they departed, and came out even into the land of Sidom; and behold, there they found all the people who had departed out of the land of Ammonihah, who had been cast out and stoned, because they believed in the words of Alma.

2. And they related unto them all that had happened unto their wives and children, and also concerning themselves, and of their power of deliverance.

3. And also Zeezrom lay sick at Sidom, with a burning fever, which was caused by the great tribulations of his mind on account of his wickedness, for he supposed that Alma and Amulek were no more; and he supposed that they had been slain because of his iniquity. And this great sin, and his many other sins, did

harrow up his mind until it did become exceedingly sore, having no deliverance; therefore he began to be scorched with a burning heat.

4. Now, when he heard that Alma and Amulek were in the land of Sidom, his heart began to take courage; and he sent a message immediately unto them, desiring them to come unto him.

5. And it came to pass that they went immediately, obeying the message which he had sent unto them; and they went in unto the house unto Zeezrom; and they found him upon his bed, sick, being very low with a burning fever; and his mind also was exceedingly sore because of his iniquities; and when he saw them he stretched forth his hand, and besought them that they would heal him.

6. And it came to pass that Alma said unto him, taking him by the hand: Believest thou in the power of Christ unto salvation?

7. And he answered and said: Yea, I believe all the words that thou hast taught.

8. And Alma said: If thou believest in the redemption of Christ thou canst be healed.

9. And he said: Yea, I believe according to thy words.

10. And then Alma cried unto the Lord, saying: O Lord our God, have mercy on this man, and heal him according to his faith which is in Christ.

11. And when Alma had said these words, Zeezrom leaped upon his feet, and began to walk; and this was done to the great astonishment of all the people; and the knowledge of this went forth throughout all the land of Sidom.

12. And Alma baptized Zeezrom unto the Lord; and he began from that time forth to preach unto the people.

1–12. In the preceding chapter the chief judge of the city of Ammonihah, with many of its leading teachers and lawyers (all, we assume, of the persuasion and profession of Nehor), taunted Alma and Amulek to give them a manifestation of the power of their priesthood, which resulted in the tormentors' destruction. Now Zeezrom, presumably unaware of events in Ammonihah after his expulsion, in the depths of humility and the extremity of his soul, petitions Alma and Amulek for the blessing of that priesthood unto a restoration of health and a forgiveness of sins. Because of his faith in Christ, his requests are granted unto his everlasting benefit. Though the cast changes, the story is universal. The great cities of men (the Ammonihahs) war against God and are destroyed, while some few of their number (the Zeezroms) humble themselves and reach forth their hand to God and his servants and are saved with an everlasting salvation.

3. Zeezrom lay sick . . . with a burning fever] The Savior taught that there is not necessarily a tie between sin and natural disaster, that a person's being persecuted or plagued or constantly pummelled with calamity and tragedy is no reason to suppose that he or she is guilty of transgression against God or his laws (see

Luke 13:1–5; John 9:1–3). Joseph Smith explained: "It is a false idea that the Saints will escape all the judgments, whilst the wicked suffer; for all flesh is subject to suffer, and 'the righteous shall hardly escape;' still many of the Saints will escape, for the just shall live by faith; yet many of the righteous shall fall a prey to disease, to pestilence, etc., by reason of the weakness of the flesh, and yet be saved in the Kingdom of God. So that it is an unhallowed principle to say that such and such have transgressed because they have been preyed upon by disease or death, for all flesh is subject to death; and the Savior has said, 'Judge not, lest ye be judged.'" (*Teachings*, pp. 162–63.)

At the same time it is important to note that some physical ailments have their roots in spiritual maladies. The Apostle Paul spoke of the consequences of partaking unworthily of the sacrament of the Lord's Supper: "For as often as ye eat this bread, and drink this cup," he wrote, "ye do shew [proclaim, announce] the Lord's death till he come. Wherefore whosoever shall eat this bread, and drink this cup of the Lord, unworthily, shall be guilty of the body and blood of the Lord. But let a man examine himself, and so let him eat of that bread and drink of that cup. For *he that eateth and drinketh unworthily, eateth and drinketh damnation to himself, not discerning the Lord's body. For this cause many are weak and sickly among you and many sleep.*" (1 Corinthians 11:26–30, italics added.) The tentacles of guilt descend to the depth of the human heart to do immeasurable damage to the soul.

The physical and the spiritual are inseparably connected. We cannot do despite to the spiritual without at the same time damaging the physical. When a person sins against light—when he or she wantonly goes at cross purposes to the ways of the Lord and sets at naught honor and decency and conscience and principles—that person does damage to the soul, of which the physical body is an integral part. When Jesus of Nazareth commanded the infirm of body to rise up, and further declared, "Thy sins be forgiven thee," his enemies accused him of blasphemy. The Master asked simply: "Does it require more power to forgive sins than to make the sick rise up and walk?" (JST, Luke 5:23; see also JST, Matthew 9:5.) That is to say, the same power by which death is rebuked or ailments are cured is able to rebuke the evil one and cure a sin-sick soul. In like manner, if one has the faith to be healed physically, he has the faith by which that cleansing and healing power can work a spiritual miracle and purify him from the stains of sin. (See James 5:15; Bruce R. McConkie, *Doctrinal New Testament Commentary* 3:275.)

6. Believest thou in the power of Christ unto salvation?] Our faith always and forever must be in the Son of God, and, through him, in the Eternal Father. We never place our trust absolutely in man, even a good man. Zeezrom's faith needed to be in Christ the Lord, not in Alma, not even in the power Alma possessed. The power unto life and salvation is in Christ, the Person.

10. Alma cried unto the Lord] We would assume that we are given but a glimpse of the whole story here. Surely Alma did more on this occasion than offer a sincere prayer; we would suppose that he laid his hands on the head of Zeezrom and (assisted by Amulek) in behalf of this faithful person exercised the powers of the priesthood he held.

Alma Establishes the Church in Sidom

Alma 15:13–19

13. And Alma established a church in the land of Sidom, and consecrated priests and teachers in the land, to baptize unto the Lord whosoever were desirous to be baptized.

14. And it came to pass that they were many; for they did flock in from all the region round about Sidom, and were baptized.

15. But as to the people that were in the land of Ammonihah, they yet remained a hard-hearted and a stiffnecked people; and they repented not of their sins, ascribing all the power of Alma and Amulek to the devil; for they were of the profession of Nehor, and did not believe in the repentance of their sins.

16. And it came to pass that Alma and Amulek, Amulek having forsaken all his gold, and silver, and his precious things, which were in the land of Ammonihah, for the word of God,

he being rejected by those who were once his friends and also by his father and his kindred;

17. Therefore, after Alma having established the church at Sidom, seeing a great check, yea, seeing that the people were checked as to the pride of their hearts, and began to humble themselves before God, and began to assemble themselves together at their sanctuaries to worship God before the altar, watching and praying continually, that they might be delivered from Satan, and from death, and from destruction—

18. Now as I said, Alma having seen all these things, therefore he took Amulek and came over to the land of Zarahemla, and took him to his own house, and did administer unto him in his tribulations, and strengthened him in the Lord.

19. And thus ended the tenth year of the reign of the judges over the people of Nephi.

13. Consecrated priests and teachers] In our day we would say "ordained priests and teachers." Literally, to consecrate is to "set apart," or to "make holy." We note that both the priests and the teachers were given the authority to baptize. As we have discussed earlier in this work, so far as we know there was no Aaronic Priesthood among the Nephites (because there were no Levites), at least until the coming of the resurrected Lord to them in the meridian of time. Thus priests and teachers among the Nephites held the Melchizedek Priesthood, and the words *priests* and *teachers* describe their ministerial duties, not the offices to which they were ordained. (See *Commentary* 1:31, 225.)

15. Of the profession of Nehor] See Alma 14:16.

16. Here we learn of one of the sad but ever-present realities of membership in Christ's Church: there is a price to be paid. "The word of truth is as sharp and powerful as a two-edged sword. It is no respecter of persons, nor does its cutting power stop short of tender and dear relations. . . . Surely no one wants families to be forever, joined and united, more than Jesus. No one wants father and mother, brother and sister, parents and children—families—to be close and at peace more than the Christ. And yet the Lord . . . highlights a less than pleasant point—that gospel living costs something, even occasionally the loss of family and friends. It may well result in division and variance." (Robert L. Millett, *An Eye Single to the Glory of God*, p. 86.)

18. Strengthened him in the Lord] That is, Alma schooled and encouraged him in the principles of the gospel and made available that strength and perspective that come from the Comforter.

Destruction Comes to the Wicked

Alma 16:1–12

1. And it came to pass in the eleventh year of the reign of the judges over the people of Nephi, on the fifth day of the second month, there having been much peace in the land of Zarahemla, there having been no wars nor contentions for a certain number of years, even until the fifth day of the second month in the eleventh year, there was a cry of war heard throughout the land.

2. For behold, the armies of the Lamanites had come in upon the wilderness side, into the borders of the land, even into the city of Ammonihah, and began to slay the people and destroy the city.

3. And now it came to pass, before the Nephites could raise a sufficient army to drive them out of the land, they had destroyed the people who were in the city of Ammonihah, and also some around the borders of Noah, and taken others captive into the wilderness.

4. Now it came to pass that the Nephites were desirous to obtain those who had been carried away captive into the wilderness.

5. Therefore, he that had been appointed chief captain over the armies of the Nephites, (and his

name was Zoram, and he had two sons, Lehi and Aha)—now Zoram and his two sons, knowing that Alma was high priest over the church, and having heard that he had the spirit of prophecy, therefore they went unto him and desired of him to know whither the Lord would that they should go into the wilderness in search of their brethren, who had been taken captive by the Lamanites.

6. And it came to pass that Alma inquired of the Lord concerning the matter. And Alma returned and said unto them: Behold, the Lamanites will cross the river Sidon in the south wilderness, away up beyond the borders of the land of Manti. And behold there shall ye meet them, on the east of the river Sidon, and there the Lord will deliver unto thee thy brethren who have been taken captive by the Lamanites.

7. And it came to pass that Zoram and his sons crossed over the river Sidon, with their armies, and marched away beyond the borders of Manti into the south wilderness, which was on the east side of the river Sidon.

8. And they came upon the armies of the Lamanites, and the Lamanites were scattered and driven into the wilderness; and they took their brethren who had been taken captive by the Lamanites, and there was not one

soul of them had been lost that were taken captive. And they were brought by their brethren to possess their own lands.

9. And thus ended the eleventh year of the judges, the Lamanites having been driven out of the land, and the people of Ammonihah were destroyed; yea, every living soul of the Ammonihahites was destroyed, and also their great city, which they said God could not destroy, because of its greatness.

10. But behold, in one day it was left desolate; and the carcasses were mangled by dogs and wild beasts of the wilderness.

11. Nevertheless, after many days their dead bodies were heaped up upon the face of the earth, and they were covered with a shallow covering. And now so great was the scent thereof that the people did not go in to possess the land of Ammonihah for many years. And it was called Desolation of Nehors; for they were of the profession of Nehor, who were slain; and their lands remained desolate.

12. And the Lamanites did not come again to war against the Nephites until the fourteenth year of the reign of the judges over the people of Nephi. And thus for three years did the people of Nephi have continual peace in all the land.

1–3. We learn later in the story that the Lamanites are angry with the Nephites because of those converted Lamanites, the Anti-Nephi-Lehies, who were slain because of their oath of peace (see Alma 24:17–30; 25:1–2).

5–6. God has promised to lead his people in battle when their cause is just, and many a prophet has stood at the head of the army of Israel. It was also the practice of the leaders of his people in ancient times to obtain the blessing and direction of heaven prior to going to war. In harmony with that tradition, Zoram seeks to learn from Alma (who he knows has the spirit of prophecy) where the Lamanites have taken their Nephite captives in the wilderness. His inquiry is rewarded as the Lord reveals that information to Alma.

5. Zoram] Zoram was a righteous, God-fearing man, appointed chief captain of the Nephite armies. He sought to rescue those taken prisoner by the Lamanite army that had destroyed the city of Ammonihah and also taken captives from around the borders of Noah. He should not be confused with the apostate by the same name who founded the sect known as the Zoramites (see Alma 30:59; 31).

10. In one day it was left desolate] See the prophecy in Alma 9:4, 18.

11. Desolation of Nehors] The desolation of the city of Ammonihah is an important part of the message of the Book of Mormon. Ammonihah and Nehor are symbols—history as prophecy. Ammonihah and Nehor were to the nation of the Nephites what the Book of Mormon is to us—a warning voice! They were types casting shadows upon the cities of Zarahemla, Moroni, Moronihah, Gilgal, Onihah, Mocum, Jerusalem, Gadiandi, Gadiomnah, Jacob, Gimgimno, Jacobugath, Laman, Josh, Gad, and Kishkumen, all of which, like Nehor, had the blood of the prophets and the Saints upon their hands, and all of which were destroyed before the coming of Christ to the Nephites in the meridian dispensation (see 3 Nephi 8, 9).

How perfect the type—Ammonihah, a city pretending religion, a religion perfectly tolerant of any action save it be the preaching of the gospel of repentance! To preach repentance, to testify of Christ, to speak of the necessity of good works—these were sins too grievous to be borne. Their effect was to unite in wrath and bitterness the diversified factions within the congregations of this ever-tolerant religion. These missionaries of righteousness must be mocked, ridiculed, beaten, and imprisoned. Their adherents must be stoned, driven from the community, or burned at the stake. Such were the seeds they planted and such was the harvest they reaped in the desolation of Nehors. We are left to wonder to what extent Ammonihah is a prophetic foreshadowing of that which the scriptures denominate as the "desolation of abomination" (D&C 84:114, 117; 88:85), events that will precede and attend the coming of our Lord and Master that will bring again that peace once known to the faithful of the Nephite nation.

The Land of Zarahemla Prepared for the Coming of Christ

Alma 16:13–21

13. And Alma and Amulek went forth preaching repentance to the people in their temples, and in their sanctuaries, and also in their synagogues, which were built after the manner of the Jews.

14. And as many as would hear their words, unto them they did impart the word of God, without any respect of persons, continually.

15. And thus did Alma and Amulek go forth, and also many more who had been chosen for the work, to preach the word throughout all the land. And the establishment of the church became general throughout the land, in all the region round about, among all the people of the Nephites.

16. And there was no inequality among them; the Lord did pour out his Spirit on all the face of the land to prepare the minds of the children of men, or to prepare their hearts to receive the word which should be taught among them at the time of his coming—

17. That they might not be hardened against the word, that they might not be unbelieving, and go on to destruction, but that they might receive the word with joy, and as a branch be grafted into the true vine, that they might enter into the rest of the Lord their God.

18. Now those priests who did go forth among the people did preach against all lyings, and deceivings, and envyings, and strifes, and malice, and revilings, and stealing, robbing, plundering, murdering, committing adultery, and all manner of lasciviousness, crying that these things ought not so to be—

19. Holding forth things which must shortly come; yea, holding forth the coming of the Son of God, his sufferings and death, and also the resurrection of the dead.

20. And many of the people did inquire concerning the place where the Son of God should come; and they were taught that he would appear unto them after his resurrection; and this the people did hear with great joy and gladness.

21. And now after the church had been established throughout all the land—having got the victory over the devil, and the word of God being preached in its purity in all the land, and the Lord pouring out his blessings upon the people—thus ended the fourteenth year of the reign of the judges over the people of Nephi.

13. Temples . . . sanctuaries . . . synagogues] The passage is most instructive relative to the nature of worship in both the New World and the Old during the Old Testament time period. From it we learn that the places of worship among the ancients were temples, sanctuaries, and synagogues. The reference to temples in the plural is of special interest because virtually all non-Mormon sources insist that for Israel there was to be but one temple, and that in Jerusalem. We have no interest in reviewing scholarly arguments, but simply observe that such an idea was not shared by the family of Lehi, who were in the Americas only a relatively short time before they began building a temple (see 2 Nephi 5:16). There are several Book of Mormon references to temples (see Jacob 1:17; 2:2, 11; Mosiah 1:18; Alma 10:2; 23:2; 3 Nephi 11:1).

Further, the view generally reflected in non-Latter-day Saint publications is that the synagogue (i.e., "gathering-place") did not come into being until the Babylonian exile. Since the exiles had no access to the temple, it is thought that the synagogue developed as its substitute. We would simply respond that the need to gather together for instruction in the principles of the gospel traces itself to the days of Adam. Nor would we expect to see it acknowledged in Bible commentary that sanctuaries existed apart from the temple as places of worship, yet the Book of Mormon refers to them as such, identifying them as places to worship "God before the altar" (Alma 15:17). Commentators reluctantly admit, however, that in pre-Mosaic times laymen freely offered sacrifices at altars of earth or stone. Nor did Moses put an end to such a practice, but simply sought to regulate it and avoid abuse (see Exodus 20:24–26; Deuteronomy 16:21).

Formal worship among the Nephites before the coming of Christ appears to have been carried out in instructional meetings in the synagogue under the direction of ordained teachers; ritual offerings at the altar of sacrifice, either at the temple or at sanctuaries, under the direction of those holding the office of priest; and the same essential system of temple worship known in the Old World. When large congregations met together for instruction, it was at either the sanctuary or the temple.

14. Without any respect of persons] "For the Lord your God is God of gods, and Lord of lords, a great God, a mighty, and a terrible, which regardeth not persons, nor taketh reward" (Deuteronomy 10:17). See also Alma 1:30; Romans 2:11; James 2:1–9.

15. Under the direction of Alma a sizeable missionary force went forth preaching "the word," meaning that they testified of Christ and taught the principles of his gospel.

16–17. As there was a spirit that went forth to prepare the way before the appearance of Christ to the Nephites, so there is a spirit that must go forth to prepare the way before his final return. "I will pour out my spirit upon all flesh; and your sons and your daughters shall prophesy, your old men shall dream dreams, your young men shall see visions: and also upon the servants and upon the handmaids in those days will I pour out my spirit. And I will shew wonders in the heavens and in the earth, blood, and fire, and pillars of smoke. The sun shall be turned into darkness, and the moon into blood, before the great and the terrible day of the Lord come." (Joel 2:28–31.) And again: "Hearken and hear, O ye inhabitants of the earth. Listen, ye elders of my church together, and hear the voice of the Lord; for he calleth upon all men, and he commandeth all men everywhere to repent. For behold, the Lord God hath sent forth the angel crying through the midst of heaven, saying: Prepare ye the way of the Lord, and make his paths straight, for the hour of his coming is nigh." (D&C 133:16–17.) Even before the first missionaries of this dispensation went forth, the Lord declared, "The field is white already to harvest" (D&C 4:4), which we would interpret to mean that the hearts and minds of many have been prepared for this day and this hour. The seed of the gospel will take root and will grow into the mighty oak of the millennial day.

16. No inequality among them] Faith blesses the life of the learned and the unlearned alike; repentance and baptism wash away the impoverished man's sins with the same ease that they cleanse the soul of the wealthy, while the Holy Ghost brings the same light and understanding to both. The principles and blessings of the gospel know no rank or station; they are uninfluenced by age or gender; they reach out with equal love and warmth to all.

17. A branch . . . grafted into the true vine] "I AM the true vine, and my Father is the husbandman," Christ declared. "I am the vine, ye are the branches: He that abideth in me, and I in him, the same bringeth forth much fruit: for without me ye can do nothing. If a man abide not in me, he is cast forth as a branch, and is withered; and men gather them, and cast them into the fire, and they are burned." (John 15:1, 5.) One is grafted into the true branch when he or she comes to the knowledge of the true Messiah and accepts his gospel. See 1 Nephi 10:14; 15:12–15; also *Commentary* 1:118.

17. Enter into the rest of the Lord] See Alma 12:34–37; compare D&C 84:24.

18. All vices of the flesh, all the seeds of carnality, all that is impure or unclean must be done away, for all such hinder the pure flow of intelligence from God to man. Having escaped the corruption that is in the world, we are then, by diligence, to obtain faith and add to our faith virtue, "and to virtue knowledge; and to knowledge temperance; and to temperance patience; and to patience godliness; and to godliness brotherly kindness; and to brotherly kindness charity. For if these things be in you, and abound, they make you that ye shall neither be barren nor unfruitful in the knowledge of our Lord Jesus Christ." (2 Peter 1:5–8.) That is, we are, through Christ, to replace the "works of the flesh" with the "fruit of the Spirit" (Galatians 5:19–25).

19. While the nation of the Jews looked for a messiah who would come as a conquering hero, a triumphant king, the Nephite Saints understood that he must first descend below all things, be stricken, smitten, and afflicted; that he must first come as servant to all, and suffer all things even unto death; that he must be the firstfruits of them that slept and would extend the blessings of resurrection to all.

19. Holding forth] That is, believing in, looking forward to, anticipating anxiously.

20. He would appear unto them] The present generation would pass away before the appearance of Christ. Yet the promise was "unto them"—meaning their nation, family, and kindred. Perhaps as an angelic host they too would be permitted to enjoy that unparalleled experience.

Obtaining the Spirit of Prophecy and Revelation

Alma 17:1–5

1. And now it came to pass that as Alma was journeying from the land of Gideon southward, away to the land of Manti, behold, to his astonishment, he met with the sons of Mosiah journeying towards the land of Zarahemla.

2. Now these sons of Mosiah were with Alma at the time the angel first appeared unto him; therefore Alma did rejoice exceedingly to see his brethren; and what added more to his joy, they were still his brethren in the Lord; yea, and they had waxed strong in the knowledge of the truth; for they were men of a sound understanding and they had searched the scriptures diligently, that they might know the word of God.

3. But this is not all; they had given themselves to much prayer, and fasting; therefore they had the spirit of prophecy, and the spirit of revelation, and when they taught, they taught with power and authority of God.

4. And they had been teaching the word of God for the space of fourteen years among the Lamanites, having had much success in bringing many to the knowledge of the truth; yea, by the power of their words many were brought before the altar of God, to call on his name and confess their sins before him.

5. Now these are the circumstances which attended them in their journeyings, for they had many afflictions; they did suffer much, both in body and in mind, such as hunger, thirst and fatigue, and also much labor in the spirit.

1. Ammon was leading the people of Anti-Nephi-Lehi to Zarahemla when he met Alma, his brother in the gospel (see Alma 27).

2. There is a love, a brotherhood or sisterhood, a bond shared by those who labor in the Lord's service that surpasses all other feelings of comradery. Such are the emotions experienced in this unexpected missionary reunion. Alma and the sons of Mosiah parted company fourteen years before with little to offer the Lord but willing hearts and youthful exuberance. They now meet as men of seasoned faith, men of sound understanding—an understanding that comes only by an earnest desire for the word of the Lord, coupled with faithful service in his name.

2. The angel first appeared unto him] It will be remembered that Alma and the sons of Mosiah were rebellious in their youth and went about seeking to destroy the Church. As they were doing so, an angel of the Lord appeared, warning them that their efforts to destroy the Church would lead to their own destruction (see Mosiah 27:11–17; Alma 36:6–9). The reference here to the angel "first" appearing to Alma suggests another visit or visits by the same angel. Indeed, this was the case. While Alma, the missionary, lamented over the wickedness of the people of Ammonihah, the same angel appeared to console him and to commend him for his faithful labors (see Alma 8:14–15).

2. Men of a sound understanding] These had "waxed strong in the knowledge of the truth." They were possessed of that knowledge, that understanding, that wisdom which is given from above. Though they had searched the scriptures diligently, the grasp of principles, of saving verities, had come through revelation, through divine teaching.

3. They had given themselves to much prayer, and fasting] Their pleadings were earnest. Their requests to God were sincere. They demonstrated this through fasting. Fasting is a principle of power. As one fasts and as the body grows weaker, one becomes ever more aware of the need for physical and spiritual sustenance, for those things which both strengthen the body and enliven the soul. Fasting leads to a consciousness of victory over self, victory over the flesh, victory over the appetites, and thus to that quiet confidence which we know as spirituality.

3. The spirit of prophecy, and the spirit of revelation] All saving truths are manifest and must be learned by the spirit of revelation. In turn, they are to be taught by the spirit of prophecy. In many ways the spirit of revelation is the spirit of prophecy. The spirit of revelation is that spirit which manifests things to the hearts and souls of men. It is the spirit that enlightens the mind of both the spokesman and the listener. It is the spirit by which all gospel truths must be learned. When the teacher or preacher of the word so attunes himself with the Spirit of the Lord that what he says and does is what the Lord would say and do in the same circumstance, he has obtained the spirit of revelation and of prophecy. Most generally, the spirit of prophecy is the spirit of forth-telling rather than the spirit of foretelling. It is by the spirit of prophecy that the scriptures are properly interpreted and appropriately applied in a given situation. To have the spirit of prophecy is to preach by the power of the Holy Ghost; it is to speak "with the tongue of angels," to speak "the words of Christ" (2 Nephi 32:2–3), to declare the mind, will, voice, and word of the Lord. The manifestation of future events may be associated with either spirit, but the unfolding of the past is generally associated with the spirit of revelation.

3. They taught with power and authority] "I call upon the weak things of the world," the Lord declared, "those who are unlearned and despised, to thrash the nations by the power of my Spirit" (D&C 35:13). For the gospel comes not "in word only," as Paul testified, "but also in power, and in the Holy Ghost, and in much assurance" (1 Thessalonians 1:5). Those called to teach the word of God are to "declare faithfully the commandments and the revelations," doing so "with power and authority" (D&C 28:3). They are to "diminish not a word" (Jeremiah 26:2), neither adding to nor taking from the heaven-sent message. Thus, when the messenger has been properly called and prepared, the Lord's promise is: "You shall have my Spirit and my word, yea, the power of God unto the convincing of men" (D&C 11:21).

4. Many were brought before the altar of God] The altar was a place of prayer and confession to God, a place of sacrifice, a place of covenant, a place of the divine presence. "An altar of earth thou shalt make unto me," the Lord told Israel in the days of Moses, "and shalt sacrifice thereon thy burnt offerings, and thy peace offerings, thy sheep, and thine oxen: in all places where I record my name I will come unto thee, and I will bless thee" (Exodus 20:24).

5. Much labor in the spirit] Spiritual strength and stability is not the child of ease. The soul that has borne no burdens knows no strength.

Mosiah's Sons Preach the Word of God to the Lamanites

Alma 17:6–17

6. Now these were their journeyings: Having taken leave of their father, Mosiah, in the first year of the judges; having refused the kingdom which their father was desirous to confer upon them, and also this was the minds of the people;

7. Nevertheless they departed out of the land of Zarahemla, and took their swords, and their spears, and their bows, and their arrows, and their slings; and this they did that they might provide food for themselves while in the wilderness.

8. And thus they departed into the wilderness with their numbers which they had selected, to go up to the land of Nephi, to preach the word of God unto the Lamanites.

9. And it came to pass that they journeyed many days in the wilderness, and they fasted much and prayed much that the Lord would grant unto them a portion of his Spirit to go with them, and abide with them, that they might be an instrument in the hands of God to bring, if it were possible, their brethren, the Lamanites, to the knowledge of the truth, to the knowledge of the baseness of the traditions of their fathers, which were not correct.

10. And it came to pass that the Lord did visit them with his Spirit, and said unto them: Be comforted. And they were comforted.

11. And the Lord said unto them also: Go forth among the Lamanites, thy brethren, and establish my word; yet ye shall be patient in long-suffering and afflictions, that ye may show forth good examples unto them in me, and I will make an instrument of thee in my hands unto the salvation of many souls.

12. And it came to pass that the hearts of the sons of Mosiah, and also those who were with them, took courage to go forth unto the Lamanites to declare unto them the word of God.

13. And it came to pass when they had arrived in the borders of the land of the Lamanites, that they separated themselves and departed one from another, trusting in the Lord that they should meet again at the close of their harvest; for they supposed that great was the work which they had undertaken.

14. And assuredly it was great, for they had undertaken to preach the word of God to a wild and a hardened and a ferocious people; a people who delighted in murdering the Nephites, and robbing and plundering them; and their hearts were set upon riches, or upon gold and silver, and precious stones; yet they sought to obtain these things by murdering and plundering, that they might not labor for them with their own hands.

15. Thus they were a very indolent people, many of whom did worship idols, and the curse of God had fallen upon them because of the traditions of their fathers; notwithstanding the promises of the Lord were extended unto them on the conditions of repentance.

16. Therefore, this was the cause for which the sons of Mosiah had undertaken the work, that perhaps they might bring them unto repentance; that perhaps they might bring them to know of the plan of redemption.

17. Therefore they separated themselves one from another, and went forth among them, every man alone, according to the word and power of God which was given unto him.

8. Their numbers which they had selected] See Mosiah 28:1; Alma 16:15.

8. To preach the word of God] The principles of faith, repentance, and baptism are as essential to a lasting world peace as they are to an eternal repose. Within the story of the Book of Mormon, Lamanite conversion to the gospel always brought with it a reconciliation of all difficulties between the Nephites and the Lamanites.

9. Portion of his Spirit] This Book of Mormon phrase (see also Alma 18:35; 24:8) simply refers to the influence and power of the Holy Ghost.

9. An instrument in the hands of God] At the conference in which he was sustained as the tenth president of the Church, President Joseph Fielding Smith said: "I desire to say that no man of himself can lead this church. It is the Church of the Lord Jesus Christ; he is at the head. The Church bears his name, has his priesthood, administers his gospel, preaches his doctrine, and does his work.

"He chooses men and calls them to be instruments in his hands to accomplish his purposes, and he guides and directs them in their labors. But men are only instruments in the Lord's hands, and the honor and glory for all that his servants accomplish is and should be ascribed unto him forever.

"If this were the work of a man, it would fail, but it is the work of the Lord, and he does not fail. And we have the assurance that if we keep the commandments and are valiant in the testimony of Jesus and are true to every trust, the Lord will guide and direct us and his church in the paths of righteousness, for the accomplishment of all his purposes." (CR, April 1970, p. 113.)

9. Traditions . . . which were not correct] Righteous traditions are the sanctuary of memory. They preserve purpose and meaning. They protect the sacred and virtuous. They hallow strength, courage, and honor. They bind generations in a common cause. They have been a source of inspiration and direction to countless souls. By contrast, evil and false traditions have filled the world with confusion and have become "the very mainspring of all corruption," causing the earth to groan under the weight of their iniquity. They are "an iron yoke," a "strong band," the "very handcuffs, and chains, and shackles, and fetters of hell" (D&C 123:7–8). They are a system whereby depravity, corruption, and darkness of all forms are and have been passed from generation to generation. False traditions blind the eyes and minds of otherwise good and well-intentioned people. It may be that more people have rejected the restored gospel—or, having accepted it, have subsequently refused the counsel of living prophets—because of the effects of false traditions than for any other reason.

10. Where the Spirit of the Lord is, the spirit of peace, comfort, and assurance is found. This heaven-sent Spirit brings with it a sense of confidence; it lifts and encourages. The Spirit of the Lord is wholly incompatible with such spirits as despondency or despair.

11. The charge to the missionaries is to establish the "word" of the Lord among the Lamanites. Salvation will come to these their wayward brothers only by compliance with the same principles by which it has come to the Nephites. There is but one standard, and all must rise to it. Nevertheless, the Lord is more patient with some than with others. The standard will not and cannot change, but because of their spiritually impoverished condition the Lord will allow the Lamanites more time to grow up to that standard. The missionaries must learn patience and long-suffering with their contacts and must bear persecution and hardship in that same spirit.

15. Traditions of their fathers] See commentary on verse 9.

15. The promises of the Lord] See Alma 9:16–17.

16. The plan of redemption] This is the very plan announced by the Father in the Grand Council of heaven. It is the plan embraced by the Savior when he said, "Father, thy will be done" (Moses 4:2), the plan sustained by those who kept their first estate, the plan fought against by Lucifer and his minions and opposed by all who advocate salvation based upon doctrines or teachings foreign to the plan of righteousness.

Ammon Armed with the Power of God

Alma 17:18–39

18. Now Ammon being the chief among them, or rather he did administer unto them, and he departed from them, after having blessed them according to their several stations, having imparted the word of God unto them, or administered unto them before his departure; and thus they took their several journeys throughout the land.

19. And Ammon went to the land of Ishmael, the land being called after the sons of Ishmael, who also became Lamanites.

20. And as Ammon entered the land of Ishmael, the Lamanites took him and bound him, as was their custom to bind all the Nephites who fell into their hands, and carry them before the king; and thus it was left to the pleasure of the king to slay them, or to retain them in captivity, or to cast them into prison, or to cast them out of his land, according to his will and pleasure.

21. And thus Ammon was carried before the king who was over the land of Ishmael; and his name was Lamoni; and he was a descendant of Ishmael.

22. And the king inquired of Ammon if it were his desire to dwell in the land among the Lamanites, or among his people.

23. And Ammon said unto him: Yea, I desire to dwell among this people for a time; yea, and perhaps until the day I die.

24. And it came to pass that king Lamoni was much pleased with Ammon, and caused that his bands should be loosed; and he would that Ammon should take one of his daughters to wife.

25. But Ammon said unto him: Nay, but I will be thy servant. Therefore Ammon became a servant to king Lamoni. And it came to pass that he was set among other servants to watch the flocks of Lamoni, according to the custom of the Lamanites.

26. And after he had been in the service of the king three days, as he was with the Lamanitish servants going forth with their flocks to the place of water, which was called the water of Sebus, and all the Lamanites drive their flocks hither, that they may have water—

27. Therefore, as Ammon and the servants of the king were driving forth their flocks to this place of water, behold, a certain number of the Lamanites, who had been with their flocks to water, stood and scattered the flocks of Ammon and the servants of the king, and they scattered them insomuch that they fled many ways.

28. Now the servants of the king began to murmur, saying: Now the king will slay us, as he has our brethren because their flocks were scattered by the wickedness of these men. And they began to weep exceedingly, saying: Behold, our flocks are scattered already.

29. Now they wept because of the fear of being slain. Now when Ammon saw this his heart was swollen within him with joy; for, said he, I will show forth my power unto these my fellow-servants, or the power which is in me, in restoring these flocks unto the king, that I may win the hearts of these my fellow-servants, that I may lead them to believe in my words.

30. And now, these were the thoughts of Ammon, when he saw the afflictions of those whom he termed to be his brethren.

31. And it came to pass that he flattered them by his words, saying: My brethren, be of good cheer and let us go in search of the flocks, and we will gather them together and bring them back unto the place of water; and thus we will preserve the flocks unto the king and he will not slay us.

32. And it came to pass that they went in search of the flocks, and they did follow Ammon, and they rushed forth with much swiftness and did head the flocks of the king, and did gather them together again to the place of water.

33. And those men again stood to scatter their flocks; but Ammon said unto his brethren: Encircle the flocks round about that they flee not; and I go and contend with these men who do scatter our flocks.

34. Therefore, they did as Ammon commanded them, and he went forth and stood to contend with those who stood by the waters of Sebus; and they were in number not a few.

35. Therefore they did not fear Ammon, for they supposed that one of their men could slay him according to their pleasure, for they knew not that the Lord had promised Mosiah that he would deliver his sons out of their hands; neither did they know anything concerning the Lord; therefore they delighted in the destruction of their brethren; and for this cause they stood to scatter the

flocks of the king.

36. But Ammon stood forth and began to cast stones at them with his sling; yea, with mighty power he did sling stones amongst them; and thus he slew a certain number of them insomuch that they began to be astonished at his power; nevertheless they were angry because of the slain of their brethren, and they were determined that he should fall; therefore, seeing that they could not hit him with their stones, they came forth with clubs to slay him.

37. But behold, every man that lifted his club to smite Ammon, he smote off their arms with his sword; for he did withstand their blows by smiting their arms with the edge of his sword, insomuch that they began to be astonished,

and began to flee before him; yea, and they were not few in number; and he caused them to flee by the strength of his arm.

38. Now six of them had fallen by the sling, but he slew none save it were their leader with his sword; and he smote off as many of their arms as were lifted against him, and they were not a few.

39. And when he had driven them afar off, he returned and they watered their flocks and returned them to the pasture of the king, and then went in unto the king, bearing the arms which had been smitten off by the sword of Ammon, of those who sought to slay him; and they were carried in unto the king for a testimony of the things which they had done.

18–39. This is one of the often-told and loved stories of the Book of Mormon. It is a vivid dramatization of the attributes needed to be a successful missionary or servant of the Lord. In it Ammon becomes a messiah figure—humble servant, good shepherd, hope to the distraught, protector and defender of the king's flock. Those who scatter the king's sheep are properly rewarded; those who raise their arms with sword in hand have them cut off. Ammon, whose power was heaven-sent, sought no honor for himself save it were that of teaching the doctrines of his Father to King Lamoni and his people.

22–23. Here we see one of the primary characteristics of a successful missionary: a love of the people and a love for the land in which the missionaries serve. For all we know, Ammon may have left behind wife and children, at least friends and acquaintances. He left the comfort and peace and predictability of the known for a new life—fourteen years—life among the unknown, among a people who had been enemies to the Nephites for generations. But Ammon was focused, dedicated, his eye single to the glory of God. He had put his hand to the plough and had no inclination to look back (see Luke 9:62). He had been born of the Spirit and in that condition he was "desirous that salvation should be declared to every creature, for [he] could not bear that any human soul should perish; yea, even the very thoughts that any soul should endure endless torment did cause [him] to quake and tremble" (see Mosiah 28:3).

25. I will be thy servant] The ambassadors of the Lord Jesus are called upon to do that which their Master does best—love and serve. Selfless service sanctifies both giver and receiver.

29. The servants of the Lord pray and petition the heavens for teaching moments, for those special occasions when the power and goodness of God and his word can be manifest. The spirit of readiness and receptivity must be had by those outside the faith before the message of truth can be delivered and accepted.

The Lamanites Believe Ammon to Be the Great Spirit

Alma 18:1–7

1. And it came to pass that king Lamoni caused that his servants should stand forth and testify to all the things which they had seen concerning the matter.

2. And when they had all testified to the things which they had seen, and he had learned of the faithfulness of Ammon in preserving his flocks, and also of his great power in contending against those who sought to slay him, he was astonished exceedingly, and said: Surely, this is more than a man. Behold, is not this the Great Spirit who doth send such great punishments upon this people, because of their murders?

3. And they answered the king, and said: Whether he be the Great Spirit or a man, we know not; but this much we do know, that he cannot be slain by the enemies of the king; neither can they scatter the king's flocks when he is with us, because of his expertness and great strength; therefore, we know that he is a friend to the king. And now, O king, we do not believe that a man has such great power, for we know he cannot be slain.

4. And now, when the king heard these words, he said unto them: Now I know that it is the Great Spirit; and he has come down at this time to preserve your lives, that I might not slay you as I did your brethren. Now this is the Great Spirit of whom our fathers have spoken.

5. Now this was the tradition of Lamoni, which he had received from his father, that there was a Great Spirit. Notwithstanding they believed in a Great Spirit, they supposed that whatsoever they did was right; nevertheless, Lamoni began to fear exceedingly, with fear lest he had done wrong in slaying his servants;

6. For he had slain many of them because their brethren had scattered their flocks at the place of water; and thus, because they had had their flocks scattered they were slain.

7. Now it was the practice of these Lamanites to stand by the waters of Sebus to scatter the flocks of the people, that thereby they might drive away many that were scattered unto their own land, it being a practice of plunder among them.

1–7. Because of the apostasy of their fathers, the knowledge of God and the great plan of redemption had been totally lost to

Lamoni and his people. By tradition they held that there was a Great Spirit, one apparently in the form and likeness of a man, who knew all things and had the power to bring great evil upon them. There is no hint in the text that this Great Spirit was involved in the granting of blessings or the giving of commandments. No divine code to regulate behavior appears to have existed among the Lamanites, ("they supposed that whatsoever they did was right"). We would assume that the Lamanites involved themselves in various rituals designed to appease this Spirit, whom they obviously feared.

King Lamoni Believes Ammon's Words

Alma 18:8–23

8. And it came to pass that king Lamoni inquired of his servants, saying: Where is this man that has such great power?

9. And they said unto him: Behold, he is feeding thy horses. Now the king had commanded his servants, previous to the time of the watering of their flocks, that they should prepare his horses and chariots, and conduct him forth to the land of Nephi; for there had been a great feast appointed at the land of Nephi, by the father of Lamoni, who was king over all the land.

10. Now when king Lamoni heard that Ammon was preparing his horses and his chariots he was more astonished, because of the faithfulness of Ammon, saying: Surely there has not been any servant among all my servants that has been so faithful as this man; for even he doth remember all my commandments to execute them.

11. Now I surely know that this is the Great Spirit, and I would desire him that he come in unto me, but I durst not.

12. And it came to pass that when Ammon had made ready the horses and the chariots for the king and his servants, he went in unto the king, and he saw that the countenance of the king was changed; therefore he was about to return out of his presence.

13. And one of the king's servants said unto him, Rabbanah, which is, being interpreted, powerful or great king, considering their kings to be powerful; and thus he said unto him: Rabbanah, the king desireth thee to stay.

14. Therefore Ammon turned himself unto the king, and said unto him: What wilt thou that I should do for thee, O king? And the king answered him not for the space of an hour, according to their time, for he knew not what he should say unto him.

15. And it came to pass that Ammon said unto him again: What desirest thou of me? But the king answered him not.

16. And it came to pass that Ammon, being filled with the Spirit of God, therefore he perceived the thoughts of the king.

And he said unto him: Is it because thou hast heard that I defended thy servants and thy flocks, and slew seven of their brethren with the sling and with the sword, and smote off the arms of others, in order to defend thy flocks and thy servants; behold, is it this that causeth thy marvelings?

17. I say unto you, what is it, that thy marvelings are so great? Behold, I am a man, and am thy servant; therefore, whatsoever thou desirest which is right, that will I do.

18. Now when the king had heard these words, he marveled again, for he beheld that Ammon could discern his thoughts; but notwithstanding this, king Lamoni did open his mouth, and said unto him: Who art thou? Art thou that Great Spirit, who knows all things?

19. Ammon answered and said unto him: I am not.

20. And the king said: How knowest thou the thoughts of my heart? Thou mayest speak boldly, and tell me concerning these things; and also tell me by what power ye slew and smote off the arms of my brethren that scattered my flocks—

21. And now, if thou wilt tell me concerning these things, whatsoever thou desirest I will give unto thee; and if it were needed, I would guard thee with my armies; but I know that thou art more powerful than all they; nevertheless, whatsoever thou desirest of me I will grant it unto thee.

22. Now Ammon being wise, yet harmless, he said unto Lamoni: Wilt thou hearken unto my words, if I tell thee by what power I do these things? And this is the thing that I desire of thee.

23. And the king answered him, and said: Yea, I will believe all thy words. And thus he was caught with guile.

8–23. Knowing that he would have had no chance to receive a respectful hearing from Lamoni when he first came into his land, Ammon had agreed to be his servant. This pleased the king and created the opportunity for Ammon to manifest the power of his God in defense of Lamoni's shepherds and flocks. The miracle of strength and power of protection granted him created the opportunity for him to teach King Lamoni the gospel. This is similar to the pattern followed by Christ in his ministry. He too came as the humble servant, performing miracles to bless the common people and create the opportunity to be heard by them.

16. He perceived the thoughts of the king] In the ultimate sense, only God knows the thoughts and intents of the children of men (see verse 32; D&C 6:16). On occasion, however, he does grant to his chosen servants the discerning and revelatory powers needed to know the motives and dispositions of those they teach or confront (see Jacob 7:14; Alma 11:24; 30:42).

23. He was caught with guile] His questions and inquiry were all a part of Ammon's plan or strategy.

Ammon Teaches the Creation, the Fall, and the Atonement

Alma 18:24–43

24. And Ammon began to speak unto him with boldness, and said unto him: Believest thou that there is a God?

25. And he answered, and said unto him: I do not know what that meaneth.

26. And then Ammon said: Believest thou that there is a Great Spirit?

27. And he said, Yea.

28. And Ammon said: This is God. And Ammon said unto him again: Believest thou that this Great Spirit, who is God, created all things which are in heaven and in the earth?

29. And he said: Yea, I believe that he created all things which are in the earth; but I do not know the heavens.

30. And Ammon said unto him: The heavens is a place where God dwells and all his holy angels.

31. And king Lamoni said: Is it above the earth?

32. And Ammon said: Yea, and he looketh down upon all the children of men; and he knows all the thoughts and intents of the heart; for by his hand were they all created from the beginning.

33. And king Lamoni said: I believe all these things which thou hast spoken. Art thou sent from God?

34. Ammon said unto him: I am a man; and man in the beginning was created after the image of God, and I am called by his Holy Spirit to teach these things unto this people, that they may be brought to a knowledge of that which is just and true;

35. And a portion of that Spirit dwelleth in me, which giveth me knowledge, and also power according to my faith and desires which are in God.

36. Now when Ammon had said these words, he began at the creation of the world, and also the creation of Adam, and told him all the things concerning the fall of man, and rehearsed and laid before him the records and the holy scriptures of the people, which had been spoken by the prophets, even down to the time that their father, Lehi, left Jerusalem.

37. And he also rehearsed unto them (for it was unto the king and to his servants) all the journeyings of their fathers in the wilderness, and all their sufferings with hunger and thirst, and their travail, and so forth.

38. And he also rehearsed unto them concerning the rebellions of Laman and Lemuel, and the sons of Ishmael, yea, all their rebellions did he relate unto them; and he expounded unto them all the records and scriptures from the time that Lehi left Jerusalem down to the present time.

39. But this is not all; for he expounded unto them the plan of redemption, which was prepared from the foundation of the world; and he also made known unto them concerning the coming of Christ, and all the works of the Lord did he make known unto them.

40. And it came to pass that after he had said all these things, and expounded them to the king, that the king believed all his words.

41. And he began to cry unto

the Lord, saying: O Lord, have mercy; according to thy abundant mercy which thou hast had upon the people of Nephi, have upon me, and my people.

42. And now, when he had said this, he fell unto the earth, as if he were dead.

43. And it came to pass that his servants took him and carried him in unto his wife, and laid him upon a bed; and he lay as if he were dead for the space of two days and two nights; and his wife, and his sons, and his daughters mourned over him, after the manner of the Lamanites, greatly lamenting his loss.

24–43. What do you teach a person who has no knowledge of God or the gospel and yet has consented to listen and believe? Where do you start? What principles do you emphasize? The way in which Ammon taught King Lamoni constitutes a classic response to such questions. Ammon taught him what we have come to know as the three pillars of eternity—the Creation, the Fall, and the Atonement. These three doctrines, which are inseparably associated one with the other, constitute the foundation upon which all other gospel principles must rest. Indeed, any principle that cannot comfortably rest on the foundation of these doctrines (or be tied to it) has no place in the teachings in God's kingdom. To testify that Jesus of Nazareth is our Savior raises the question (particularly to one such as Lamoni), From what do we need to be saved? The answer, of course, is the fall of Adam. This in turn raises the question, From what did Adam fall? The answer is the paradisiacal state in which all things were originally created. Thus the Creation becomes parent to the Fall, and the Fall parent to the Atonement.

Ammon began his instruction to Lamoni as the scriptures begin their instruction to all of us, that is, by rehearsing the story of the Creation in order that the Lamanite king might know the power of God and know that God is the creator of all things both in heaven and on earth. Ammon recounted the story of Adam's creation, with the testimony that the first of all men was made in the image and likeness of God his Father. Then—and all this is in the order and pattern of the scriptures—Ammon unfolded the doctrine of the Fall: the story of how Adam and Eve introduced corruption and death into their previously paradisiacal state so that they might fill the measure of their creation, having posterity and becoming subject to death. "Adam fell," Lehi said, "that men might be; and men are, that they might have joy" (2 Nephi 2:25). The Fall, in turn, created the need for a Redeemer, one who could free Adam, Eve, and all their posterity from the effects of their fallen state and make it possible for them to return to that God who gave them life. Thus God "created Adam, and by Adam came the fall of man. And because of the fall of man came Jesus Christ,

even the Father and the Son; and because of Jesus Christ came
the redemption of man." (Mormon 9:12.) Such, Ammon testified,
was the "plan of redemption, which was prepared from the foundation of the world" (v. 39). And "the king believed all his words"
(v. 40).

24. With boldness] Those who teach by the power of the
Holy Ghost teach with boldness, or, as the Apostle Paul stated,
with "much assurance" (1 Thessalonians 1:5). Timidity or uncertainty are not companions of the Spirit. The servants of the Lord
are taught to speak forth the words of truth with boldness,
without being overbearing (see Alma 38:12).

26–28. Some have been critical of Ammon's response to
Lamoni, knowing that God is a corporeal being and, thus, more
than just "a Great Spirit." In fact, Ammon's statement is techni-
cally correct. The God of the Old Testament was Jehovah, who
had not as yet obtained a body of flesh and bones.

**28. Created all things which are in heaven and in the
earth]** Speaking to the Nephites, the resurrected Christ declared:
"I am Jesus Christ the Son of God. I created the heavens and the
earth, and all things that in them are. I was with the Father from
the beginning. I am in the Father, and the Father in me; and in
me hath the Father glorified his name." (3 Nephi 9:15; see also
D&C 93:9–10.)

32. He knows all the thoughts and intents of the heart]
If God were unable to read the thoughts and desires of our hearts,
he would also be unable to judge our actions. The very nature of
Godhood requires that he has a perfect knowledge of our
thoughts and the intent of our hearts. The assurance of the scriptures is that the judgment of God will combine works and desires
as one (see Alma 29:5; 41:3; D&C 18:38; 137:9).

34. Just and true] That which is "just" is that which is
"right." Thus the justified are those who have done that which is
right and proper in the eyes of God, or whose lives have been
made right through the mediation of a greater power. That which
is "true" is that which is "faithful" or "trustworthy." To be brought
to a knowledge of that which is "just and true" is to come to that
knowledge which marks a straight course, one which can be followed with full confidence and trust.

35. A portion of that Spirit dwelleth in me] See commentary on Alma 17:9.

35. Which giveth me knowledge] The Spirit is and must be
the source of that knowledge which is eternal. Since "the
Comforter knoweth all things" (D&C 42:17; compare Moses 6:61),
all true religion is revealed religion.

35. And also power] We know God only to the extent that
we have become like him. It follows that as we increase in the

knowledge of God, the power that we have through faith increases also.

39. Plan of redemption] See commentary on Alma 17:16.

Trances As a Source of Divine Revelation

Alma 19:1–17

1. And it came to pass that after two days and two nights they were about to take his body and lay it in a sepulchre, which they had made for the purpose of burying their dead.

2. Now the queen having heard of the fame of Ammon, therefore she sent and desired that he should come in unto her.

3. And it came to pass that Ammon did as he was commanded, and went in unto the queen, and desired to know what she would that he should do.

4. And she said unto him: The servants of my husband have made it known unto me that thou art a prophet of a holy God, and that thou hast power to do many mighty works in his name;

5. Therefore, if this is the case, I would that ye should go in and see my husband, for he has been laid upon his bed for the space of two days and two nights; and some say that he is not dead, but others say that he is dead and that he stinketh, and that he ought to be placed in the sepulchre; but as for myself, to me he doth not stink.

6. Now, this was what Ammon desired, for he knew that king Lamoni was under the power of God; he knew that the dark veil of unbelief was being cast away from his mind, and the light which did light up his mind, which was the light of the glory of God, which was a marvelous light of his goodness—yea, this light had infused such joy into his soul, the cloud of darkness having been dispelled, and that the light of everlasting life was lit up in his soul, yea, he knew that this had overcome his natural frame, and he was carried away in God—

7. Therefore, what the queen desired of him was his only desire. Therefore, he went in to see the king according as the queen had desired him; and he saw the king, and he knew that he was not dead.

8. And he said unto the queen: He is not dead, but he sleepeth in God, and on the morrow he shall rise again; therefore bury him not.

9. And Ammon said unto her: Believest thou this? And she said unto him: I have had no witness save thy word, and the word of our servants; nevertheless I believe that it shall be according as thou hast said.

10. And Ammon said unto her: Blessed art thou because of thy exceeding faith; I say unto thee, woman, there has not been such great faith among all the people of the Nephites.

11. And it came to pass that she watched over the bed of her husband, from that time even until that time on the morrow which Ammon had appointed that he should rise.

12. And it came to pass that he arose, according to the words of Ammon; and as he arose, he

stretched forth his hand unto the woman, and said: Blessed be the name of God, and blessed art thou.

13. For as sure as thou livest, behold, I have seen my Redeemer; and he shall come forth, and be born of a woman, and he shall redeem all mankind who believe on his name. Now, when he had said these words, his heart was swollen within him, and he sunk again with joy; and the queen also sunk down, being overpowered by the Spirit.

14. Now Ammon seeing the Spirit of the Lord poured out according to his prayers upon the Lamanites, his brethren, who had been the cause of so much mourning among the Nephites, or among all the people of God because of their iniquities and their traditions, he fell upon his knees, and began to pour out his soul in prayer and thanksgiving to God for what he had done for his brethren; and he was also overpowered with joy; and thus they all three had sunk to the earth.

15. Now, when the servants of the king had seen that they had fallen, they also began to cry unto God, for the fear of the Lord had come upon them also, for it was they who had stood before the king and testified unto him concerning the great power of Ammon.

16. And it came to pass that they did call on the name of the Lord, in their might, even until they had all fallen to the earth, save it were one of the Lamanitish women, whose name was Abish, she having been converted unto the Lord for many years, on account of a remarkable vision of her father—

17. Thus, having been converted to the Lord, and never having made it known, therefore, when she saw that all the servants of Lamoni had fallen to the earth, and also her mistress, the queen, and the king, and Ammon lay prostrate upon the earth, she knew that it was the power of God; and supposing that this opportunity, by making known unto the people what had happened among them, that by beholding this scene it would cause them to believe in the power of God, therefore she ran forth from house to house, making it known unto the people.

1–17. Having heard of Ammon's message, Lamoni "fell unto the earth, as if he were dead" (Alma 18:42), in which state he remained for three days. His condition was so like death that his servants insisted that his body was in a state of decay, that it stank, and that it ought to be buried. The queen refused, believing her husband to still be alive. She sent for Ammon, having been told that he was "a prophet of a holy God." "He is not dead," Ammon assured her "but he sleepeth in God"; and he said her husband would arise on the morrow (that being the third day). Lamoni came forth as promised, and as he did so he praised God and testified that he had seen the Redeemer. He then prophesied that the Savior would be born of a woman and would redeem from among all mankind those who would believe on his name.

At this point both he and the queen were "overpowered by

the Spirit" and fell into a trance together. In like manner Ammon was also "overpowered with joy," and thus "all three had sunk to the earth"; whereupon the servants of Lamoni, those who had previously been witnesses of Ammon's power, commenced praying in the name of the Lord, doing so with such power and faith that each of them in turn fell into the similar trance. Thus all in the court of the king had fallen into a trance save one woman by the name of Abish, who had previously been converted. She commenced going from house to house telling the people of these marvelous things God had done.

This remarkable story sheds considerable light on a number of biblical texts. In both the Old and New Testaments we have instances in which the bodily functions of prophets were suspended as part of a revelatory experience. Indeed, such a state was recognized as a vehicle for receiving revelation. The first of such stories involved Balaam, who, "falling into a trance," had "his eyes open[ed]" that he might see "the vision of the Almighty" (Numbers 24:4, 16). The second involved King Saul and his search for David. Having been told that David was at Ramah, Saul "sent a party of men to seize him. When they saw the company of prophets in rapture, with Samuel standing at their head, the Spirit of God came upon them and they fell into prophetic rapture. When this was reported to Saul he sent another party. These also fell into a rapture, and when he sent more men a third time, they did the same. Saul himself then set out for Ramah and came to the great cistern in Secu. He asked where Samuel and David were and was told that they were at Naioth in Ramah. On his way there the Spirit of God came upon him too and he went on, in a rapture as he went, till he came to Naioth in Ramah. There he too stripped off his clothes and like the rest fell into a rapture before Samuel and lay down naked all that day and all that night. That is why men say, 'Is Saul also among the prophets?'" (New English Bible, 1 Samuel 19:20–24.)

We read of Ezekiel being transported by the Spirit to Tell-abib, near the river Chebar, where he apparently remained in a trance for seven days. At the end of that period the word of the Lord came to him. (See Ezekiel 3:14–17.) (The appropriate word to describe his state seems most difficult to find. For instance, the King James Version renders it "astonished"; the New English Bible, "dumbfounded"; the Jersualem Bible, "stunned"; the Moffat, "overwhelmed.") The "hand of the Lord" falls on him, and he sees the "visions of God," hears the voice of the Almighty, is "lifted up between the earth and the heaven," and passes from the river of Chebar to the Lord's house in Jerusalem (Ezekiel 8:1–3).

In the context of the New Testament we read that Peter "fell into a trance, and saw the heaven opened," whereupon the revelation of matchless importance was given which extended the blessings of the gospel to Gentiles as well as to Jews (see Acts 10:10–11; see also 11:5). And it is significant that Paul, the great missionary to the Gentiles, received his call to that labor in a similar state. "While I prayed in the temple," he testified, "I was in a trance; and saw [the Lord] saying unto me, Make haste, and get thee quickly out of Jerusalem: for they will not receive thy testimony concerning me. . . . And he said unto me, Depart: for I will send thee far hence unto the Gentiles." (Acts 22:17, 21.) Paul's writings suggest that he had other experiences of like nature. "I will come to visions and revelations of the Lord," he said. "I knew a man in Christ above fourteen years ago, (whether in the body, I cannot tell; or whether out of the body, I cannot tell: God knoweth;) such an one caught up to the third heaven. And I knew such a man, (whether in the body, or out of the body, I cannot tell: God knoweth;) how that he was caught up into paradise, and heard unspeakable words, which it is not lawful for a man to utter." (2 Corinthians 12:1–4.)

From what we can deduce from scriptural writ, it appears that a trance is a state in which the body and its functions become quiescent in order that the full powers of the Spirit may be centered on the revelations of heaven. Freed from the fetters of a mortal body, man's spirit can be ushered into the divine presence; it can hear what otherwise could not be heard and see what otherwise could not be seen—even the visions of eternity and even the Almighty himself. Yet the trance, like all other spiritual experiences, is subject to counterfeiting. Such counterfeits were common, for instance, to the frontier camp meetings of the United States. The trance might be likened to another medium of revelation, namely that of the gift of tongues, which was also commonly mimicked at the camp meetings and in many other settings. None would question tongues as a legitimate gift of heaven, and likewise there is no question that the gift of tongues has been and is often counterfeited.

Though a trance is not sufficient proof of true religion, it certainly does not militate against it, as the Bible, both Old and New Testaments, and the Book of Mormon attest. It is of interest that the false prophet Shemaiah wrote to the priest Zephaniah, charging him to keep the temple a house of order by putting the mad prophets in prison and in stocks. His reference to mad prophets is understood to have been directed to those prophets who claimed authority through some ecstasy or trance. His purpose in so doing was to have the prophet Jeremiah imprisoned, it being well known that Jeremiah made claim to such experiences. (See Jeremiah 29:26–27.)

The story of Ammon and Lamoni affirms religious trances as a legitimate revelatory device. Lamoni, as already noted, came forth from his trance testifying that he had seen the Redeemer and then prophesied relative to the Savior's birth and the necessity of all mankind believing on his name. The testimony of his servants was that while they were in this state of physical insensibility, angels instructed them in the principles of salvation and their obligation to live righteously. Indeed, they experienced a change of heart and no longer had a desire to do evil. Such is the state in which the power of God overcomes the "natural frame" and one is "carried away in God." The test of the legitimacy of the religious trance, like that of tongues, is the efficacy of its purpose. Its genuineness must be ascertained by the same standards that determine the verity of revelation in all other forms—that is, by the asking of such questions as: Does it teach faith in Christ, repentance, sacrifice, obedience to the laws and ordinances of the gospel, and loyalty to the Lord's current and constituted Church and his anointed servants?

4. A holy God] Man of Holiness is the name of our Heavenly Father (Moses 6:57). His house, law, words, ordinances, messengers, promises, priesthood, and Spirit are all spoken of as being holy, as is and must be any and all things that emanate from him. That is, they must be perfect in righteousness (see D&C 67:9). Thus no worship that is improper, impure, unclean, or unholy is acceptable to him.

4. In his name] See verse 13.

6. This account of what King Lamoni experienced is an apt description of the conversion process, a process universal to all who choose the light of the gospel in preference to the darkness of unbelief so common to the world.

6. The dark veil of unbelief] Darkness and unbelief are inseparable companions. Thus the Saints of all ages have been commanded to learn the truths of the gospel that they might chase darkness from among them (see D&C 50:25). Indeed, the "world groaneth under sin and darkness even now," the Lord declared. And of the Latter-day Saints he said: "Your minds in times past have been darkened because of unbelief, and because you have treated lightly the things you have received," having specific reference to the Book of Mormon and other revelations of the Restoration. (See D&C 84:53–57.)

6. The light which did light up his mind] The terms *light* and *truth* are used interchangeably in the scriptures. God is light. God is truth. Truth shines (D&C 88:7); truth sanctifies (John 17:17); truth abideth and hath no end (D&C 88:66); light and truth forsake that which is evil (D&C 93:37).

6. Infused such joy into his soul] The message of salvation is aptly described as "glad tidings of great joy" (Mosiah 3:3; Alma 13:22). True principles, properly understood, always enlighten and lift.

8. He sleepeth in God] That is, he is in a trance. See discussion on verses 1–17.

12. Blessed be the name of God] To praise God is one thing; to praise *the name* of God is another. God's name is a symbol of his essence, power, and authority. To praise his name is to do more than acknowledge the verity of his existence; it is to assert that salvation comes only in and through his holy name. It is to attest that no proper prayer can be offered save it be offered in his name; it is to acknowledge that all gospel ordinances must be performed by the authority of his name; it is to profess that the gospel cannot be taught save it is taught in his name, that miracles, healings, prophecies—indeed, "all things"—must be properly done in the sacred name of Christ if they are to be recognized and upheld in the heavens. (See D&C 46:31; Robert L. Millet and Joseph Fielding McConkie, *In His Holy Name*, chapters 1, 5–6.)

13. Awaking from the trance into which he had fallen, having been overpowered by the Spirit, Lamoni testifies that he has seen the Redeemer and prophetically announces his birth by a mortal woman and his redemptive ministry. The power of Lamoni's testimony has the same effect on his wife as Ammon's words had had upon him. Together Lamoni and his queen fall into a trance wherein the revelations of heaven will be manifest to them.

Ammon's Life Preserved

Alma 19:18–24

18. And they began to assemble themselves together unto the house of the king. And there came a multitude, and to their astonishment, they beheld the king, and the queen, and their servants prostrate upon the earth, and they all lay there as though they were dead; and they also saw Ammon, and behold, he was a Nephite.

19. And now the people began to murmur among themselves; some saying that it was a great evil that had come upon them, or upon the king and his house, because he had suffered that the Nephite should remain in the land.

20. But others rebuked them, saying: The king hath brought this evil upon his house, because he slew his servants who had had their flocks scattered at the waters of Sebus.

21. And they were also rebuked by those men who had stood at the waters of Sebus and scattered the flocks which belonged to the king, for they were angry with Ammon because of the number which he had slain of their brethren at the waters of Sebus,

while defending the flocks of the king.

22. Now, one of them, whose brother had been slain with the sword of Ammon, being exceedingly angry with Ammon, drew his sword and went forth that he might let it fall upon Ammon, to slay him; and as he lifted the sword to smite him, behold, he fell dead.

23. Now we see that Ammon could not be slain, for the Lord had said unto Mosiah, his father: I will spare him, and it shall be unto him according to thy faith—therefore, Mosiah trusted him unto the Lord.

24. And it came to pass that when the multitude beheld that the man had fallen dead, who lifted the sword to slay Ammon, fear came upon them all, and they durst not put forth their hands to touch him or any of those who had fallen; and they began to marvel again among themselves what could be the cause of this great power, or what all these things could mean.

18. All lay there as though they were dead] It appears that the suspension of normal body functions is so complete that there is no observable difference between this state of spiritual repose and that of death.

22–23. It is within the power of that God who gave us life to lengthen or shorten our sojourn in mortality. The righteous are not taken before their time. As the Lord revealed to Joseph the Seer: "Thy days are known, and thy years shall not be numbered less; therefore, fear not what man can do, for God shall be with you forever and ever" (D&C 122:9).

Those in Trances Awake and Commence Teaching the Gospel

Alma 19:25–36

25. And it came to pass that there were many among them who said that Ammon was the Great Spirit, and others said he was sent by the Great Spirit;

26. But others rebuked them all, saying that he was a monster, who had been sent from the Nephites to torment them.

27. And there were some who said that Ammon was sent by the Great Spirit to afflict them because of their iniquities; and that it was the Great Spirit that had always attended the Nephites, who had ever delivered them out of their hands; and they said that it was this Great Spirit who had destroyed so many of their brethren, the Lamanites.

28. And thus the contention began to be exceedingly sharp among them. And while they were thus contending, the woman servant who had caused the multitude to be gathered together came, and when she saw the contention which was among the multitude

she was exceedingly sorrowful, even unto tears.

29. And it came to pass that she went and took the queen by the hand, that perhaps she might raise her from the ground; and as soon as she touched her hand she arose and stood upon her feet, and cried with a loud voice, saying: O blessed Jesus, who has saved me from an awful hell! O blessed God, have mercy on this people!

30. And when she had said this, she clasped her hands, being filled with joy, speaking many words which were not understood; and when she had done this, she took the king, Lamoni, by the hand, and behold he arose and stood upon his feet.

31. And he, immediately, seeing the contention among his people, went forth and began to rebuke them, and to teach them the words which he had heard from the mouth of Ammon; and as many as heard his words believed, and were converted unto the Lord.

32. But there were many among them who would not hear his words; therefore they went their way.

33. And it came to pass that when Ammon arose he also administered unto them, and also did all the servants of Lamoni; and they did all declare unto the people the selfsame thing—that their hearts had been changed; that they had no more desire to do evil.

34. And behold, many did declare unto the people that they had seen angels and had conversed with them; and thus they had told them things of God, and of his righteousness.

35. And it came to pass that there were many that did believe in their words; and as many as did believe were baptized; and they became a righteous people, and they did establish a church among them.

36. And thus the work of the Lord did commence among the Lamanites; thus the Lord did begin to pour out his Spirit upon them; and we see that his arm is extended to all people who will repent and believe on his name.

25–26. It is obvious from this account that many perceive the doings and handiwork of God and understand his ways; others are absolutely oblivious to what is divine and can neither recognize nor believe a heavenly manifestation.

29. As with her husband, the queen comes forth from her trance testifying of Christ and his redemptive labor.

29. O blessed God] That is, praise, magnify, or extol the virtues of our God, who is Jesus Christ! "Bless the Lord [Jehovah], O my soul," wrote the Psalmist. "O Lord [Jehovah] my God, thou art very great; thou art clothed with honour and majesty" (Psalm 104:1).

30. It would appear that the queen is speaking in tongues. It is difficult to tell whether she is preaching in the language of God, the Adamic (see Moses 6:5–6), or simply speaking with the tongue of angels, that is, speaking the words of Christ by the power of the Holy Ghost (see 2 Nephi 32:2–3).

33–34. All who had been consumed by the power of God and carried away in a trance now come forth teaching and testifying of the same principles. There is no division among them. Their message is of the necessity of accepting Christ, the doctrine of revelation, and repenting and working works of righteousness.

33. They had no more desire to do evil] Those whose hearts have been turned to God have their values turned to righteousness. After King Benjamin had delivered an inspired address, after his people had been converted, had experienced a "mighty change" by "the Spirit of the Lord Omnipotent," they had "no more disposition to do evil, but to do good continually" (Mosiah 5:2; compare Alma 13:12; 1 John 3:9). Of his own conversion, President Joseph F. Smith said: "The feeling that came upon me was that of pure peace, of love and of light. I felt in my soul that if I had sinned—and surely I was not without sin—that it had been forgiven me; that I was indeed cleansed from sin; my heart was touched, and I felt that I would not injure the smallest insect beneath my feet. *I felt as if I wanted to do good everywhere to everybody and to everything. I felt a newness of life, a newness of desire to do that which was right. There was not one particle of desire for evil left in my soul.*" (*Gospel Doctrine*, p. 96, italics added.)

34. They had seen angels] Angels have a significant mission. They preach the gospel. They bear witness of Christ and his gospel to the "chosen vessels," that the chosen vessels may then bear witness to the residue of the people (see Moroni 7:31–32).

36. Believe on his name] See verse 12.

The Lord Sends Ammon to Middoni to Deliver His Imprisoned Brethren

Alma 20:1–7

1. And it came to pass that when they had established a church in that land, that king Lamoni desired that Ammon should go with him to the land of Nephi, that he might show him unto his father.

2. And the voice of the Lord came to Ammon, saying: Thou shalt not go up to the land of Nephi, for behold, the king will seek thy life; but thou shalt go to the land of Middoni; for behold, thy brother Aaron, and also Muloki and Ammah are in prison.

3. Now it came to pass that when Ammon had heard this, he said unto Lamoni: Behold, my brother and brethren are in prison at Middoni, and I go that I may deliver them.

4. Now Lamoni said unto Ammon: I know, in the strength of the Lord thou canst do all things. But behold, I will go with thee to the land of Middoni; for

the king of the land of Middoni, whose name is Antiomno, is a friend unto me; therefore I go to the land of Middoni, that I may flatter the king of the land, and he will cast thy brethren out of prison. Now Lamoni said unto him: Who told thee that thy brethren were in prison?

5. And Ammon said unto him: No one hath told me, save it be God; and he said unto me—Go and deliver thy brethren, for they are in prison in the land of Middoni.

6. Now when Lamoni had heard this he caused that his servants should make ready his horses and his chariots.

7. And he said unto Ammon: Come, I will go with thee down to the land of Middoni, and there I will plead with the king that he will cast thy brethren out of prison.

2. The voice of the Lord directs Ammon not to go to the land of Nephi, as Lamoni had requested, for Lamoni's father would seek his life; rather, he was to go to the land of Middoni to seek the deliverance of his brother Aaron and also Muloki and Ammah, who were in prison. We note with interest that the revelation advises him of the predicament of his brethren and charges him to rectify the situation, yet it gives no suggestion as to how that might be accomplished. Nevertheless Ammon proceeds without questions or doubts on what would appear to a daunting task. Well might he have said, as did Nephi before him, "I was led by the Spirit, not knowing beforehand the things which I should do" (1 Nephi 4:6).

4. In the strength of the Lord thou canst do all things] As the Apostle Paul declared, "If God be for us, who can be against us?" (Romans 8:31.) How singular it is that Lamoni, who a few days before thought Ammon to be more than a man, now realizes that his strength rests in the God of heaven! We are reminded of the admonition given the youthful Joseph Smith: "For although a man may have many revelations, and have power to do many mighty works, yet if he boasts in his own strength, and sets at naught the counsels of God, and follows after the dictates of his own will and carnal desires, he must fall and incur the vengeance of a just God upon him" (D&C 3:4).

Lamoni's Father Seeks to Kill Ammon

Alma 20:8–20

8. And it came to pass that as Ammon and Lamoni were journeying thither, they met the father of Lamoni, who was king over all the land.

9. And behold, the father of

Lamoni said unto him: Why did ye not come to the feast on that great day when I made a feast unto my sons, and unto my people?

10. And he also said: Whither art thou going with this Nephite, who is one of the children of a liar?

11. And it came to pass that Lamoni rehearsed unto him whither he was going, for he feared to offend him.

12. And he also told him all the cause of his tarrying in his own kingdom, that he did not go unto his father to the feast which he had prepared.

13. And now when Lamoni had rehearsed unto him all these things, behold, to his astonishment, his father was angry with him, and said: Lamoni, thou art going to deliver these Nephites, who are sons of a liar. Behold, he robbed our fathers; and now his children are also come amongst us that they may, by their cunning and their lyings, deceive us, that they again may rob us of our property.

14. Now the father of Lamoni commanded him that he should slay Ammon with the sword. And he also commanded him that he should not go to the land of Middoni, but that he should return with him to the land of Ishmael.

15. But Lamoni said unto him: I will not slay Ammon, neither will I return to the land of Ishmael, but I go to the land of Middoni that I may release the brethren of Ammon, for I know that they are just men and holy prophets of the true God.

16. Now when his father had heard these words, he was angry with him, and he drew his sword that he might smite him to the earth.

17. But Ammon stood forth and said unto him: Behold, thou shalt not slay thy son; nevertheless, it were better that he should fall than thee, for behold, he has repented of his sins; but if thou shouldst fall at this time, in thine anger, thy soul could not be saved.

18. And again, it is expedient that thou shouldst forbear; for if thou shouldst slay thy son, he being an innocent man, his blood would cry from the ground to the Lord his God, for vengeance to come upon thee; and perhaps thou wouldst lose thy soul.

19. Now when Ammon had said these words unto him, he answered him, saying: I know that if I should slay my son, that I should shed innocent blood; for it is thou that hast sought to destroy him.

20. And he stretched forth his hand to slay Ammon. But Ammon withstood his blows, and also smote his arm that he could not use it.

10. One of the children of a liar] For generations the Lamanites retained a deep hatred toward the Nephites See 2 Nephi 5:14; Jacob 7:24; Enos 1:20; Mosiah 10:17.

15. Just men and holy prophets of the true God] This is a remarkable expression of testimony on the part of Lamoni. Of men he has never met, he confidently testifies that they are "just men," which is to say that they keep covenants with exactness and honor; they are "holy prophets," which is to say that they are men of genuine sanctity and righteousness; and theirs is the "true God," which is to denounce all other forms of worship as spurious and devoid of the power to save or bless.

17. Thy soul could not be saved] Ammon's statement implies that the king would have been guilty of murder. Joseph Smith taught that one guilty of murder, "one that sheds innocent blood, cannot have forgiveness" (*Teachings*, p. 339). Such a one would be guilty of the unforgivable sin, one for which the atonement of Christ cannot bring remission of sins. For a more detailed treatment see commentary on Alma 39:6.

18. His blood would cry from the ground . . . for vengeance] In holy writ blood is often used to represent life or the soul of man (see Leviticus 17:11). "The voice of thy brother's blood crieth unto me from the ground," the Lord told Cain (Genesis 4:10). Similarly, "the cry of the blood of the saints shall ascend up to God from the ground" against those who slew them (2 Nephi 26:3). Indeed, their souls implore the Lord of Sabaoth, the Lord of Hosts, to avenge their blood (see Revelation 6:10). The promise is that "the Lord cometh out of his place to punish the inhabitants of the earth for their iniquity: the earth also shall disclose her blood, and shall no more cover her slain" (Isaiah 26:21). See *Commentary* 1:333–34.

Ammon Rescues His Brethren

Alma 20:21–30

21. Now when the king saw that Ammon could slay him, he began to plead with Ammon that he would spare his life.

22. But Ammon raised his sword, and said unto him: Behold, I will smite thee except thou wilt grant unto me that my brethren may be cast out of prison.

23. Now the king, fearing he should lose his life, said: If thou wilt spare me I will grant unto thee whatsoever thou wilt ask, even to half of the kingdom.

24. Now when Ammon saw that he had wrought upon the old king according to his desire, he said unto him: If thou wilt grant that my brethren may be cast out of prison, and also that Lamoni may retain his kingdom, and that ye be not displeased with him, but grant that he may do according to his own desires in whatsoever thing he thinketh, then will I spare thee; otherwise I will smite thee to the earth.

25. Now when Ammon had said these words, the king began to rejoice because of his life.

26. And when he saw that Ammon had no desire to destroy him, and when he also saw the great love he had for his son

Lamoni, he was astonished exceedingly, and said: Because this is all that thou hast desired, that I would release thy brethren, and suffer that my son Lamoni should retain his kingdom, behold, I will grant unto you that my son may retain his kingdom from this time and forever; and I will govern him no more—

27. And I will also grant unto thee that thy brethren may be cast out of prison, and thou and thy brethren may come unto me, in my kingdom; for I shall greatly desire to see thee. For the king was greatly astonished at the words which he had spoken, and also at the words which had been spoken by his son Lamoni, therefore he was desirous to learn them.

28. And it came to pass that Ammon and Lamoni proceeded on their journey towards the land of Middoni. And Lamoni found favor in the eyes of the king of the land; therefore the brethren of Ammon were brought forth out of prison.

29. And when Ammon did meet them he was exceedingly sorrowful, for behold they were naked, and their skins were worn exceedingly because of being bound with strong cords. And they also had suffered hunger, thirst, and all kinds of afflictions; nevertheless they were patient in all their sufferings.

30. And, as it happened, it was their lot to have fallen into the hands of a more hardened and a more stiffnecked people; therefore they would not hearken unto their words, and they had cast them out, and had smitten them, and had driven them from house to house, and from place to place, even until they had arrived in the land of Middoni; and there they were taken and cast into prison, and bound with strong cords, and kept in prison for many days, and were delivered by Lamoni and Ammon.

26–27. As selfless service created the opportunity for Ammon to teach the gospel to Lamoni, so Ammon's selfless concern for Lamoni and for his own brethren without any interest in earthly honors or wealth now creates the opportunity for him and his brethren to teach the gospel to Lamoni's father. Ammon was a powerful preacher of righteousness whose example of love and commitment spoke with effect and eloquence equal to that of his words.

29. They were patient in all their sufferings] The sons of Mosiah and their missionary brethren had their hearts riveted on the things of God's kingdom; they loved truth and righteousness more than their own lives. Perspective breeds and perpetuates patience. Because they could see and feel things from God's point of view, they were willing to wait upon the promises of the Lord with all patience and faith.

30. A more hardened and . . . stiffnecked people] That is, they had fallen into the hands of the Amalekites and the

Amulonites (see Alma 21:1–4). We know that Amulon was one of the wicked priests of Noah (Mosiah 23:32). The present text is silent as to the identity of Amaleki.

Characteristics of False Religions

Alma 21:1–10

1. Now when Ammon and his brethren separated themselves in the borders of the land of the Lamanites, behold Aaron took his journey towards the land which was called by the Lamanites, Jerusalem, calling it after the land of their fathers' nativity; and it was away joining the borders of Mormon.

2. Now the Lamanites and the Amalekites and the people of Amulon had built a great city, which was called Jerusalem.

3. Now the Lamanites of themselves were sufficiently hardened, but the Amalekites and the Amulonites were still harder; therefore they did cause the Lamanites that they should harden their hearts, that they should wax strong in wickedness and their abominations.

4. And it came to pass that Aaron came to the city of Jerusalem, and first began to preach to the Amalekites. And he began to preach to them in their synagogues, for they had built synagogues after the order of the Nehors; for many of the Amalekites and the Amulonites were after the order of the Nehors.

5. Therefore, as Aaron entered into one of their synagogues to preach unto the people, and as he was speaking unto them, behold there arose an Amalekite and began to contend with him,

saying: What is that thou hast testified? Hast thou seen an angel? Why do not angels appear unto us? Behold are not this people as good as thy people?

6. Thou also sayest, except we repent we shall perish. How knowest thou the thought and intent of our hearts? How knowest thou that we have cause to repent? How knowest thou that we are not a righteous people? Behold, we have built sanctuaries, and we do assemble ourselves together to worship God. We do believe that God will save all men.

7. Now Aaron said unto him: Believest thou that the Son of God shall come to redeem mankind from their sins?

8. And the man said unto him: We do not believe that thou knowest any such thing. We do not believe in these foolish traditions. We do not believe that thou knowest of things to come, neither do we believe that thy fathers and also that our fathers did know concerning the things which they spake, of that which is to come.

9. Now Aaron began to open the scriptures unto them concerning the coming of Christ, and also concerning the resurrection of the dead, and that there could be no redemption for mankind save it were through the death and sufferings of Christ, and the atonement of his blood.

10. And it came to pass as he began to expound these things unto them they were angry with him, and began to mock him; and they would not hear the words which he spake.

2. Amalekites] A sect of Nephite apostates, the greater part of whom were after the order of Nehor (see verse 4; 24:28–29; also see commentary on Alma 14:16). They affiliated themselves with the Lamanites and aided in the building of the Lamanite city Jerusalem. As is so often the case with apostates, they possessed an unmeasured hatred for that which they had betrayed. Again and again we see that those who leave the faith can never really leave the faith alone. The Lamanite generals placed those of their number in command positions in their armies because of their intense hatred of their former brethren and because of their more wicked and murderous dispositions (see Alma 43:6).

2. The people of Amulon] Amulon was one of the most prominent and degraded priests of King Noah. He undoubtedly aided in the martyrdom of Abinadi. When King Noah was burned to death by his enraged subjects, Amulon, with his fellow priests, fled into the wilderness. There they hid themselves for an extended period, eventually capturing some Lamanite maidens and taking them to wife. The children they had deserted, displeased with their fathers' conduct, later renounced that parentage and "took upon themselves the name of Nephi" (see Mosiah 25:12).

Meanwhile the former priests commenced to cultivate what they called the land of Amulon. When discovered by the Lamanites, with the wives they had kidnapped, they pleaded for mercy and were spared. Amulon and his group then joined the Lamanites, and soon after that the Lamanite king made Amulon the ruler of the lands of Amulon and Helam. It was by virtue of this appointment that Amulon and his group became the overseers of the people of Alma, who were eventually freed from their brutality by the providence of God. These former priests instructed the Lamanites in the learning of the Nephites.

Thus the Amulonites were Nephites on their fathers' side and Lamanites on their mothers'. Their education was that of the Nephites, and many of them became followers of Nehor. Scattered throughout the lands of Amulon, Helam, and Jerusalem, they assumed a leading role as opponents of Ammon and his missionary brethren. None of their number repented and accepted the gospel. Rather, they became leaders in the persecutions carried on against the suffering people of Anti-Nephi-Lehi and, with the Amalekites, made martyrs of many of those Saints.

2. A great city, which was called Jerusalem] This was a

Lamanite city, built within the borders of the land of Nephi. Nephite apostates—the Amulonites and Amalekites—aided in its construction. Its inhabitants always warred against those sent to it with the message of salvation. It is listed among those cities destroyed at the time of Christ's death. "Waters have I caused to come up in the stead thereof," the Lord said, "to hide their wickedness and abominations from before my face, that the blood of the prophets and the saints shall not come up any more unto me against them" (3 Nephi 9:7).

3. The masters of wickedness are frequently those who have once known the paths of virtue and truth and then have turned against them. As the Lamanites placed Amalekites and Zoramites at the head of their armies because of their unmatched hatred against the Nephites (see Alma 43:6), so the prince of darkness places at the head of his legions, to war against the church and kingdom of God on earth, those who have once known the purity of gospel truths.

4. Synagogues after the order of the Nehors] The Amalekites and the Amulonites had not eschewed all religion but rather had embraced one that justified their iniquities and fed their hatred and wrath for those who preached the doctrine of Christ. It was held in the order of Nehor that all ought to have the right to do as they pleased—if what they pleased was that which pleased those of the persuasion of Nehor.

5. Why do not angels appear unto us?] In harmony with the order of heaven, angels appear unto "just and holy men" (see Alma 13:26; D&C 67:10–13). The Savior's teaching as recorded in Luke 16:29–31 is relevant here. Clearly, those who will not hear the word of God as preached by one such as Aaron will not hear it if preached by one who has come back from the dead. The issue is the message, not the messenger.

6. God will save all men] Such was the doctrine espoused by Lucifer in the Grand Council of heaven and popularized by Nehor among the descendants of Lehi. We are left to wonder why the Amalekites and the Amulonites thought it necessary to build synagogues and sanctuaries and assemble to worship in them when salvation, according to their theology, was as easily obtained without their doing so. We note with interest that false religious ideologies that hold that ritual and form are unnecessary and are as a general rule meticulous about the "form of godliness." It is also our experience that those ideologies that pride themselves in their ecumenical attitudes and open-mindedness are the first to close ranks in angry wrath against the true servants of the Lord and the message of salvation.

7. The Son of God shall come to redeem mankind from their sins] See commentary on Alma 33.

8. We do not believe that thou knowest of things to come] As we shall soon see with Korihor the anti-Christ, those who oppose the truth and fight the Lord and his servants often falsely and absurdly generalize beyond their own experience: because they do not know, they assume no one else does. Because they are past feeling, they presume that no one else can and does feel. It is thus characteristic of false religion to deny the principle of revelation, to demand a closed canon and heavens that are sealed. It is equally characteristic for them to refuse to see, hear, feel, or taste the things of the Spirit—they are aptly described as being spiritually dead. (See also commentary on Alma 30:13, 15, 28.)

9–10. The form of worship among the Amalekites and the Amulonites obviously embraced a selective use of the scriptures from which Aaron now quotes. He teaches the same principles taught by Ammon to Lamoni—that we could not be redeemed from the effects of the Fall save it were through the death and suffering of Christ and the atonement of his blood. (See commentary on Alma 34:9–16.)

10. They were angry with him] The wicked take the truth to be hard. They are angry with words of truth and righteousness. See 1 Nephi 16:1–2; 2 Nephi 1:26; 9:40; 33:5.

The Faith of the Lord's Servants Is Rewarded

Alma 21:11–23

11. Therefore, when he saw that they would not hear his words, he departed out of their synagogue, and came over to a village which was called Ani-Anti, and there he found Muloki preaching the word unto them; and also Ammah and his brethren. And they contended with many about the word.

12. And it came to pass that they saw that the people would harden their hearts, therefore they departed and came over into the land of Middoni. And they did preach the word unto many, and few believed on the words which they taught.

13. Nevertheless, Aaron and a certain number of his brethren were taken and cast into prison, and the remainder of them fled out of the land of Middoni unto the regions round about.

14. And those who were cast into prison suffered many things, and they were delivered by the hand of Lamoni and Ammon, and they were fed and clothed.

15. And they went forth again to declare the word, and thus they

were delivered for the first time out of prison; and thus they had suffered.

16. And they went forth whithersoever they were led by the Spirit of the Lord, preaching the word of God in every synagogue of the Amalekites, or in every assembly of the Lamanites where they could be admitted.

17. And it came to pass that the Lord began to bless them, insomuch that they brought many to the knowledge of the truth; yea, they did convince many of their sins, and of the traditions of their fathers, which were not correct.

18. And it came to pass that Ammon and Lamoni returned from the land of Middoni to the land of Ishmael, which was the land of their inheritance.

19. And king Lamoni would not suffer that Ammon should serve him, or be his servant.

20. But he caused that there should be synagogues built in the land of Ishmael; and he caused that his people, or the people who were under his reign, should assemble themselves together.

21. And he did rejoice over them, and he did teach them many things. And he did also declare unto them that they were a people who were under him, and that they were a free people, that they were free from the oppressions of the king, his father; for that his father had granted unto him that he might reign over the people who were in the land of Ishmael, and in all the land round about.

22. And he also declared unto them that they might have the liberty of worshiping the Lord their God according to their desires, in whatsoever place they were in, if it were in the land which was under the reign of king Lamoni.

23. And Ammon did preach unto the people of king Lamoni; and it came to pass that he did teach them all things concerning things pertaining to righteousness. And he did exhort them daily, with all diligence; and they gave heed unto his word, and they were zealous for keeping the commandments of God.

16. They were led by the Spirit of the Lord] These courageous and faithful missionaries depended on the Spirit of the Lord to give direction as to where they should go and what they ought to preach. To the early missionaries of this dispensation the Lord said: "Neither take ye thought beforehand what ye shall say; but treasure up in your minds continually the words of life, and it shall be given you in the very hour that portion that shall be meted unto every man" (D&C 84:85).

17. For these Lamanite converts to embrace the message of the gospel required them to acknowledge both personal sins and the fact that the traditions of their fathers had been born of wickedness and darkness. Those having the spiritual integrity to do so undoubtedly faced considerable opposition and persecution from family and from the society of which they were a part.

22. Liberty of worshiping] It is characteristic of true religion to grant liberty of worship to all—"let them worship how, where, or what they may" (Articles of Faith 1:11).

23. All things . . . pertaining to righteousness] The whole system of salvation is one in which we advance from grace to grace until we receive a fulness of understanding and a fulness of the blessings of heaven (see D&C 93:13–20).

Aaron Teaches the Gospel to Lamoni's Father

Alma 22:1–14

1. Now, as Ammon was thus teaching the people of Lamoni continually, we will return to the account of Aaron and his brethren; for after he departed from the land of Middoni he was led by the Spirit to the land of Nephi, even to the house of the king which was over all the land save it were the land of Ishmael; and he was the father of Lamoni.

2. And it came to pass that he went in unto him into the king's palace, with his brethren, and bowed himself before the king, and said unto him: Behold, O king, we are the brethren of Ammon, whom thou hast delivered out of prison.

3. And now, O king, if thou wilt spare our lives, we will be thy servants. And the king said unto them: Arise, for I will grant unto you your lives, and I will not suffer that ye shall be my servants; but I will insist that ye shall administer unto me; for I have been somewhat troubled in mind because of the generosity and the greatness of the words of thy brother Ammon; and I desire to know the cause why he has not come up out of Middoni with thee.

4. And Aaron said unto the king: Behold, the Spirit of the Lord has called him another way; he

has gone to the land of Ishmael, to teach the people of Lamoni.

5. Now the king said unto them: What is this that ye have said concerning the Spirit of the Lord? Behold, this is the thing which doth trouble me.

6. And also, what is this that Ammon said—If ye will repent ye shall be saved, and if ye will not repent, ye shall be cast off at the last day?

7. And Aaron answered him and said unto him: Believest thou that there is a God? And the king said: I know that the Amalekites say that there is a God, and I have granted unto them that they should build sanctuaries, that they may assemble themselves together to worship him. And if now thou sayest there is a God, behold I will believe.

8. And now when Aaron heard this, his heart began to rejoice, and he said: Behold, assuredly as thou livest, O king, there is a God.

9. And the king said: Is God that Great Spirit that brought our fathers out of the land of Jerusalem?

10. And Aaron said unto him: Yea, he is that Great Spirit, and he created all things both in heaven and in earth. Believest thou this?

11. And he said: Yea, I believe that the Great Spirit created all

things, and I desire that ye should tell me concerning all these things, and I will believe thy words.

12. And it came to pass that when Aaron saw that the king would believe his words, he began from the creation of Adam, reading the scriptures unto the king—how God created man after his own image, and that God gave him commandments, and that because of transgression, man had fallen.

13. And Aaron did expound unto him the scriptures from the creation of Adam, laying the fall of man before him, and their carnal state and also the plan of redemption, which was prepared from the foundation of the world, through Christ, for all whosoever would believe on his name.

14. And since man had fallen he could not merit anything of himself; but the sufferings and death of Christ atone for their sins, through faith and repentance, and so forth; and that he breaketh the bands of death, that the grave shall have no victory, and that the sting of death should be swallowed up in the hopes of glory; and Aaron did expound all these things unto the king.

1. The Lord has a plan, a scheme, a system for the presentation of the gospel and the salvation of his sons and daughters. Those who seek to be in tune with the Infinite have the glorious privilege of participating in that plan, of being a vital part in the blessing of mankind. One day we shall see how very much the Lord was involved in the affairs of the people on this earth, how masterfully and marvelously he has orchestrated the doings and feelings of his children in order to bring about the greatest blessing to the greatest number.

3. We will be thy servants] See commentary on Alma 17:25.

3. Administer unto me] To give, teach, or instruct.

6. Ye shall be saved] See commentary on Alma 5:9.

6. At the last day] A euphemism for the Day of Judgment.

7. The father of Lamoni is here being born again to see the kingdom of God (see *Teachings*, p. 328). He feels the Spirit, is touched and moved by its influence, and now comes to trust in and believe the words of the Nephite spokesmen (compare Alma 18:23).

8. These are touching and tender words. They are the testimony of one of the greatest missionaries in the history of the world. Aaron knows. He knows. He does not just *hope* there is a God, nor does he derive his witness from the physical evidences (though many) that point toward the reasonableness of a belief in a God. He knows because he has seen and felt and heard. He has experienced the Spirit of the Lord and can therefore speak with power and authority from God.

10–14. The account of the conversion of Lamoni's father at the hands of Aaron is virtually a repeat of the story of Ammon's teaching and converting Lamoni (see Alma 18:28–36). He first testifies that "the Great Spirit" is God, the creator of all things both in heaven and on earth. He reads from the scriptures the account of

Adam's creation in the image and likeness of God and explains how the earth and all things upon it became corruptible, or mortal, by virtue of Adam's fall. Death and the grave would have ruled supreme save a plan of redemption had been provided, a plan which gave the sure promise that God's own Son would take upon himself mortal flesh, and that through his suffering and death he would atone for Adam's fall. Christ's atoning sacrifice would break the bands of physical death and grant mankind the hope of eternal glory if they would take upon themselves the sacred name of their Redeemer.

12. Reading the scriptures] Aaron—and, we would assume, the other Nephite missionaries—had copies of the scriptures which were used for the teaching of the gospel. See also Mosiah 13:11.

13. Here we have it again—the three pillars of eternity: the Creation, the Fall, and the Atonement. One cannot appreciate the need for Christ unless and until he knows that there was a Fall; that the Fall brought corruption and death; and that the Fall opened the way for men and women to become carnal, sensual, and devilish by nature. Simply stated, one does not crave water until he knows he needs water.

13. The plan of redemption . . . prepared from the foundation of the world] The gospel of God the Father (Romans 1:1; 15:16), known also as the gospel of Jesus Christ, was the plan of salvation taught and declared by the Eternal Father in the premortal world.

13. Believe on his name] See commentary on Alma 19:12.

14. Since man had fallen he could not merit anything of himself] Herein is one of the great messages in all eternity, but one that unfortunately is little understood even by many who are of the household of faith. We will not be saved in the highest heaven because we earn our way there. We will not be crowned with glory and eternal lives because we "worked out our salvation" by ourselves. It is as heretical to believe that we are exalted by works as it is to teach that we are saved by grace alone. As important as our works are in evidencing our acceptance of and commitment to Christ the Lord—works such as receiving the ordinances of salvation, performing deeds of kindness and acts of Christian charity, and enduring faithfully to the end—our works will not and cannot save us. It is impossible for any human being to do enough good deeds in this mortal sphere to qualify for life in the celestial kingdom. No, ultimately we are saved not by our works but by his works—the Lord's.

"Wherefore," Lehi said to his son Jacob, "I know that thou art redeemed, *because of the righteousness of thy Redeemer*" (2 Nephi 2:3, italics added). That is to say, before the Father, the Lord Jesus intercedes for us on the basis of *his* works. "Listen to him who is the advocate with the Father," the Savior urges in a modern revelation, "who is pleading your cause before him—saying: Father, *behold the sufferings and death of him who did no sin, in whom thou wast well pleased; behold the blood of thy Son which was shed, the blood of him whom thou gavest that thyself might be glorified.*" What an unusual defense! What an unnatural scene! What a glorious message! The Mediator pleads our cause on the basis of his works—his atonement. What, then, is our role? "Wherefore, Father," he continues, "spare these my brethren *that believe on my name,* that they may come unto me and have everlasting life." (D&C 45:3–5, italics added.)

Truly there is a power in Christ, "power not only to create the worlds and divide the seas but also to still the storms of the human heart, to heal the pain of scarred and beaten souls. We must learn to trust in him more, in the arm of flesh less. We must learn to rely on him more, and on man-made solutions less. We must learn to surrender our burdens to him more. We must learn and work to our limits and then be willing to seek that grace or enabling power which will make up the difference, that sacred power which indeed makes all the difference!" (Robert L. Millet, *Life in Christ,* p. 108.) Truly Nephi taught this priceless and precious message when he reminded us that "it is by grace that we are saved, after all we can do" (2 Nephi 25:23). After—meaning not "following or subsequent to" but rather "above and beyond"—after all we can do, it will be finally by the condescension and mercy and grace of the Holy One of Israel that we become like him, vessels fit to live with him who bought us with his blood.

14. The grave shall have no victory] Aaron is presumably quoting Isaiah (Isaiah 25:8), just as Abinadi (Mosiah 16:7) and Paul (1 Corinthians 15:55) did in regard to Christ's victory over the grave.

Obtaining the Hope of Eternal Life

Alma 22:15–18

15. And it came to pass that after Aaron had expounded these things unto him, the king said: What shall I do that I may have this eternal life of which thou hast spoken? Yea, what shall I do that I may be born of God, having this wicked spirit rooted out of my breast, and receive his Spirit, that I may be filled with joy, that I may not be cast off at the last day? Behold, said he, I will give up all that I possess, yea, I will forsake my kingdom, that I may receive

this great joy.

16. But Aaron said unto him: If thou desirest this thing, if thou wilt bow down before God, yea, if thou wilt repent of all thy sins, and will bow down before God, and call on his name in faith, believing that ye shall receive, then shalt thou receive the hope which thou desirest.

17. And it came to pass that when Aaron had said these words, the king did bow down before the Lord, upon his knees; yea, even he did prostrate himself upon the earth, and cried mightily, saying:

18. O God, Aaron hath told me that there is a God; and if there is a God, and if thou art God, wilt thou make thyself known unto me, and I will give away all my sins to know thee, and that I may be raised from the dead, and be saved at the last day. And now when the king had said these words, he was struck as if he were dead.

15. What shall I do that I may have . . . eternal life . . . ?] From Adam's day to ours, and from ours to that time when the last of the human family draws a breath on this mortal sphere, this is the grand question of all existence: What must we do to obtain eternal life? Such was the question addressed by the rich young ruler to the Master. "Keep the commandments," was the Savior's answer. "Which?" came the rejoinder. Christ reviewed the ten commandments of Sinai. "The young man saith unto him: All these things have I kept from my youth up: what lack I yet? Jesus said unto him, If thou wilt be perfect, go and sell that thou hast, and give to the poor, and thou shalt have treasure in heaven: and come and follow me. But when the young man heard that saying, he went away sorrowful: for he had great possessions." (Matthew 19:16–22.)

We are left to suppose that the inquiring rich man had assumed he would receive direction to conform to some ritualistic requirement of the Mosaic system. He did not understand that the Lord requires the whole soul and that those who gain salvation do so by their willingness to lay all of their energy, talent, and means upon the altar of God. How much more perfect the desires of Lamoni's father, whose power and fortune would undoubtedly have far exceeded his Old World counterpart. "I will give up all that I possess," he said, "yea, I will forsake my kingdom, that I may receive this great joy." Such is the pattern: we obtain the kingdom of heaven by forsaking the kingdoms of earth.

16. Bow down before God] How often had the king's servants bowed before him in expression of respect and honor? Now it is for the king to acknowledge that same homage to another king, one infinitely greater than himself.

16. The hope which thou desirest] The hope of eternal life is born of faith and repentance. It matters not whether we be rich or poor, educated or ignorant, old or young; the system of salvation is the same for all peoples in all ages. That hope begins by pulling the weeds of sin, that the seeds of faith may be planted and have room to grow.

18. I will give away all my sins to know thee] Such is the perfect and fair price exacted of all who truly desire to know God. It is much more difficult an offering to make than one of silver and gold. It is an affirmation of the eternal verity that no unclean thing can enter his presence. It places the promise of eternal life in the reach of all. It excuses nothing and rewards all that has been right and good.

18. Be saved at the last day] The notion that one can be saved by the expression of belief in the midst of one's mortal probation vulgarizes all other gospel principles. It negates the need for repentance, suspends the necessity of the ordinances of salvation, denies the principle of advancement from grace to grace, excuses the need for continued gospel study, and shields us from the sanctifying influence of righteous works. The voice of the Lord may speak rendering the promise that one's calling and election is sure, but even then the promise is contingent upon continued righteousness and faithful service in the Lord's vineyard. True it is, as herein stated, that one is saved only "at the last day."

18. Struck as if he were dead] See discussion on trances, commentary on Alma 19:1–17.

Lamoni's Father Teaches His Own Household

Alma 22:19–26

19. And it came to pass that his servants ran and told the queen all that had happened unto the king. And she came in unto the king; and when she saw him lay as if he were dead, and also Aaron and his brethren standing as though they had been the cause of his fall, she was angry with them, and commanded that her servants, or the servants of the king, should take them and slay them.

20. Now the servants had seen the cause of the king's fall, therefore they durst not lay their hands on Aaron and his brethren; and they pled with the queen saying:

Why commandest thou that we should slay these men, when behold one of them is mightier than us all? Therefore we shall fall before them.

21. Now when the queen saw the fear of the servants she also began to fear exceedingly, lest there should some evil come upon her. And she commanded her servants that they should go and call the people, that they might slay Aaron and his brethren.

22. Now when Aaron saw the determination of the queen, he, also knowing the hardness of the hearts of the people, feared lest

that a multitude should assemble themselves together, and there should be a great contention and a disturbance among them; therefore he put forth his hand and raised the king from the earth, and said unto him: Stand. And he stood upon his feet, receiving his strength.

23. Now this was done in the presence of the queen and many of the servants. And when they saw it they greatly marveled, and began to fear. And the king stood forth, and began to minister unto them. And he did minister unto them, insomuch that his whole household were converted unto the Lord.

24. Now there was a multitude gathered together because of the commandment of the queen, and there began to be great murmurings among them because of Aaron and his brethren.

25. But the king stood forth among them and administered unto them. And they were pacified towards Aaron and those who were with him.

26. And it came to pass that when the king saw that the people were pacified, he caused that Aaron and his brethren should stand forth in the midst of the multitude, and that they should preach the word unto them.

23. Rejoicing in the knowledge that he has obtained, the king administers those same principles to his household. Those people too are converted. It is characteristic of those who are truly converted to seek to share the fruit of the tree of life with family and other loved ones (see 1 Nephi 8:12; Enos 1:9).

26. Preach the word] The power of conversion is in the "word," that is, in "preaching the gospel of the kingdom." Such was the example of the Savior, and such is the witness of virtually all scripture (see Matthew 4:23; Luke 20:1). Too often, those called to "preach the word" choose instead to be spiritual cheerleaders or to moralize on ethical principles. As well intended as such efforts may be, they lack the power of conversion.

Boundaries Between the Nephites and the Lamanites Described

Alma 22:27–35

27. And it came to pass that the king sent a proclamation throughout all the land, amongst all his people who were in all his land, who were in all the regions round about, which was bordering even to the sea, on the east and on the

west, and which was divided from the land of Zarahemla by a narrow strip of wilderness, which ran from the sea east even to the sea west, and round about on the borders of the seashore, and the borders of the wilderness which was on the north by the land of Zarahemla, through the borders of Manti, by the head of the river Sidon, running from the east towards the west—and thus were the Lamanites and the Nephites divided.

28. Now, the more idle part of the Lamanites lived in the wilderness, and dwelt in tents; and they were spread through the wilderness on the west, in the land of Nephi; yea, and also on the west of the land of Zarahemla, in the borders by the seashore, and on the west in the land of Nephi, in the place of their fathers' first inheritance, and thus bordering along by the seashore.

29. And also there were many Lamanites on the east by the seashore, whither the Nephites had driven them. And thus the Nephites were nearly surrounded by the Lamanites; nevertheless the Nephites had taken possession of all the northern parts of the land bordering on the wilderness, at the head of the river Sidon, from the east to the west, round about on the wilderness side; on the north, even until they came to the land which they called Bountiful.

30. And it bordered upon the land which they called Desolation, it being so far northward that it came into the land which had been peopled and been destroyed, of whose bones we have spoken, which was discovered by the people of Zarahemla, it being the place of their first landing.

31. And they came from there up into the south wilderness. Thus the land on the northward was called Desolation, and the land on the southward was called Bountiful, it being the wilderness which is filled with all manner of wild animals of every kind, a part of which had come from the land northward for food.

32. And now, it was only the distance of a day and a half's journey for a Nephite, on the line Bountiful and the land Desolation, from the east to the west sea; and thus the land of Nephi and the land of Zarahemla were nearly surrounded by water, there being a small neck of land between the land northward and the land southward.

33. And it came to pass that the Nephites had inhabited the land Bountiful, even from the east unto the west sea, and thus the Nephites in their wisdom, with their guards and their armies, had hemmed in the Lamanites on the south, that thereby they should have no more possession on the north, that they might not overrun the land northward.

34. Therefore the Lamanites could have no more possessions only in the land of Nephi, and the wilderness round about. Now this was wisdom in the Nephites—as the Lamanites were an enemy to them, they would not suffer their afflictions on every hand, and also that they might have a country whither they might flee, according to their desires.

35. And now I, after having said this, return again to the account of Ammon and Aaron, Omner and Himni, and their brethren.

Freedom of Worship Granted the Lamanites

Alma 23:1–4

1. Behold, now it came to pass that the king of the Lamanites sent a proclamation among all his people, that they should not lay their hands on Ammon, or Aaron, or Omner, or Himni, nor either of their brethren who should go forth preaching the word of God, in whatsoever place they should be, in any part of their land.

2. Yea, he sent a decree among them, that they should not lay their hands on them to bind them, or to cast them into prison; neither should they spit upon them, nor smite them, nor cast them out of their synagogues, nor scourge them; neither should they cast stones at them, but that they should have free access to their houses, and also their temples, and their sanctuaries.

3. And thus they might go forth and preach the word according to their desires, for the king had been converted unto the Lord, and all his household; therefore he sent his proclamation throughout the land unto his people, that the word of God might have no obstruction, but that it might go forth throughout all the land, that his people might be convinced concerning the wicked traditions of their fathers, and that they might be convinced that they were all brethren, and that they ought not to murder, nor to plunder, nor to steal, nor to commit adultery, nor to commit any manner of wickedness.

4. And now it came to pass that when the king had sent forth this proclamation, that Aaron and his brethren went forth from city to city, and from one house of worship to another, establishing churches, and consecrating priests and teachers throughout the land among the Lamanites, to preach and to teach the word of God among them; and thus they began to have great success.

1. Preaching the word of God] See commentary on Alma 22:26.

2. Synagogues . . . temples . . . sanctuaries] See commentary on Alma 16:13.

3. The king . . . converted . . . and all his household] See Alma 22:23.

4. Establishing churches] They set about organizing congregations so that the gospel might be taught and the ordinances of salvation performed. The Church of Jesus Christ administers the gospel; It is the service agency by which the ordinances of salvation and the teachings and revelations of the Master are made available, in an organized and systematic manner, to the people of the covenant.

4. Consecrating priests and teachers] See commentary on Alma 15:13.

Lamanite Converts Seek Peace

Alma 23:5–18

5. And thousands were brought to the knowledge of the Lord, yea, thousands were brought to believe in the traditions of the Nephites; and they were taught the records and prophecies which were handed down even to the present time.

6. And as sure as the Lord liveth, so sure as many as believed, or as many as were brought to the knowledge of the truth, through the preaching of Ammon and his brethren, according to the spirit of revelation and of prophecy, and the power of God working miracles in them—yea, I say unto you, as the Lord liveth, as many of the Lamanites as believed in their preaching, and were converted unto the Lord, never did fall away.

7. For they became a righteous people; they did lay down the weapons of their rebellion, that they did not fight against God any more, neither against any of their brethren.

8. Now, these are they who were converted unto the Lord:

9. The people of the Lamanites who were in the land of Ishmael;

10. And also of the people of the Lamanites who were in the land of Middoni;

11. And also of the people of the Lamanites who were in the city of Nephi;

12. And also of the people of the Lamanites who were in the land of Shilom, and who were in the land of Shemlon, and in the city of Lemuel, and in the city of Shimnilom.

13. And these are the names of the cities of the Lamanites which were converted unto the Lord; and these are they that laid down the weapons of their rebellion, yea, all their weapons of war; and they were all Lamanites.

14. And the Amalekites were not converted, save only one; neither were any of the Amulonites; but they did harden their hearts, and also the hearts of the Lamanites in that part of the land wheresoever they dwelt, yea, and all their villages and all their cities.

15. Therefore, we have named all the cities of the Lamanites in which they did repent and come to the knowledge of the truth, and were converted.

16. And now it came to pass that the king and those who were converted were desirous that they might have a name, that thereby they might be distinguished from their brethren; therefore the king consulted with Aaron and many of their priests, concerning the name that they should take upon them, that they might be distinguished.

17. And it came to pass that they called their names Anti-Nephi-Lehies; and they were called by this name and were no more called Lamanites.

18. And they began to be a very industrious people; yea, and they were friendly with the Nephites; therefore, they did open a correspondence with them, and the curse of God did no more follow them.

6. The power of God working miracles in them] To mend

a broken limb, to rid a body of disease, to raise the dead—all these are miracles indeed, yet miracles of a lesser order than the miracles of cleansing a soul from sin, breathing the breath of spiritual life into the soul previously dead to the things of the Spirit, planting faith where there had been no faith, evoking righteousness where there had been none. Such are the great miracles that the gospel works upon people's hearts and souls.

6. And were converted unto the Lord, never did fall away] Two things are worthy of note here, namely, the nature of the preaching done by the sons of Mosiah and the depth of the conversions. These two aspects of conversion are inextricably tied. These missionaries did not trifle with the Lamanites; they did not entertain them or seek by sophistry or by manipulation to bring people into the Church. They preached the gospel. They preached creation, fall, and atonement. They preached faith, repentance, and rebirth. They preached Christ. That is, their message was substantive and sacred, and it was presented by the power of the Holy Ghost. Thus the listeners were converted to Christ, not to the missionaries or the other members of the Church, as pleasant and sincere and dedicated as those might be. They were converted to Christ, and thus their testimonies and their lives were built upon the only sure foundation (see Helaman 5:12).

7. They did lay down the weapons of their rebellion] Their hearts had been changed and they thereafter enjoyed that peace of spirit which eventually manifests itself in social relations.

16–17. It is a natural and wholesome desire, common to people of all ages, to bear a name of honor. Such a name becomes a source of identity, strength, and encouragement.

17. They called their names Anti-Nephi-Lehies] It is not clear exactly why they called themselves Anti-Nephi-Lehies. Viewing the word *anti* as meaning "opposed to" or "against," perhaps their action symbolizes a desire to dissolve barriers between Nephites and Lamanites and thus establish peace; their name could in this sense represent their opposition to a Nephite-Lamanite distinction. That is, they wanted neither Nephites nor Lamanites, nor "any manner of -ites" (4 Nephi 1:17).

Another possibility suggests itself. *Webster's Dictionary* of 1828 indicates that the word *anti* means "like" or "mirror image of." In that case *anti-Christ* would mean not just opposed to Christ but also deceptively similar to Christ, and perhaps the name Anti-Nephi-Lehies would symbolize their desire to be as Nephi and Lehi of old, that is, that they might remember the goodness and faithfulness of their first Nephite prophet leaders (see Helaman 5:6).

18. Industrious people] Idleness is incompatible with the spirit of the gospel. The Lord's people have always been an industrious people, eager to improve their lot in life, eager to improve and develop the earth and take advantage of the blessings of this life.

18. The curse of God did no more follow them] That is, they had their sins remitted, had their souls reoriented toward the things of God, and began to enjoy rich outpourings of his Spirit. It may be also that the mark of the curse, the dark skin (2 Nephi 5:21), was removed from them. "And it came to pass that those Lamanites who had united with the Nephites were numbered among the Nephites; and their curse was taken from them, and their skin became white like unto the Nephites; and their young men and their daughters became exceedingly fair, and they were numbered among the Nephites, and were called Nephites" (3 Nephi 2:14–16).

Wickedness Cannot Tolerate Righteousness

Alma 24:1–4

1. And it came to pass that the Amalekites and the Amulonites and the Lamanites who were in the land of Amulon, and also in the land of Helam, and who were in the land of Jerusalem, and in fine, in all the land round about, who had not been converted and had not taken upon them the name of Anti-Nephi-Lehi, were stirred up by the Amalekites and by the Amulonites to anger against their brethren.

2. And their hatred became exceedingly sore against them, even insomuch that they began to rebel against their king, insomuch that they would not that he should be their king; therefore, they took up arms against the people of Anti-Nephi-Lehi.

3. Now the king conferred the kingdom upon his son, and he called his name Anti-Nephi-Lehi.

4. And the king died in that selfsame year that the Lamanites began to make preparations for war against the people of God.

1–4. Those who chose to war against the Anti-Nephi-Lehies had lost no freedoms by the conversion of their brethren; they had forfeited no rights. Wickedness hates righteousness and must, by its nature, war against it. See verses 28–30.

The Converted Lamanites Rejoice In Christ

Alma 24:5–10

5. Now when Ammon and his brethren and all those who had come up with him saw the preparations of the Lamanites to destroy their brethren, they came forth to the land of Midian, and there Ammon met all his brethren; and from thence they came to the land of Ishmael that they might hold a council with Lamoni and also with his brother Anti-Nephi-Lehi, what they should do to defend themselves against the Lamanites.

6. Now there was not one soul among all the people who had been converted unto the Lord that would take up arms against their brethren; nay, they would not even make any preparations for war; yea, and also their king commanded them that they should not.

7. Now, these are the words which he said unto the people concerning the matter: I thank my God, my beloved people, that our great God has in goodness sent these our brethren, the Nephites, unto us to preach unto us, and to convince us of the traditions of our wicked fathers.

8. And behold, I thank my great God that he has given us a portion of his Spirit to soften our hearts, that we have opened a correspondence with these brethren, the Nephites.

9. And behold, I also thank my God, that by opening this correspondence we have been convinced of our sins, and of the many murders which we have committed.

10. And I also thank my God, yea, my great God, that he hath granted unto us that we might repent of these things, and also that he hath forgiven us of those our many sins and murders which we have committed, and taken away the guilt from our hearts, through the merits of his Son.

6–10. We can think of no more perfect illustration of the "mighty change of heart" spoken of by Alma than that illustrated by these converted Lamanites, who now refuse to take up arms against those who would slay them (see Alma 5:12–14). Theirs is an uncompromising confidence in the promises of God and a love for their brethren (who have now declared themselves their enemies) that exceeds their love for their own mortal lives.

10. Forgiven . . . our . . . murders] Because of the false traditions of their fathers, before their conversion these Lamanites had taken life in unrighteous wars. Though such needless killing is a sin of the gravest magnitude, it is not the same as the willful and premeditated taking of life that, in the United States system of jurisprudence, is called first-degree murder; or that is spoken of in the scriptures as being "sin unto death" (1 John 5:16–17), meaning that its perpetrators cannot, even through repentance, obtain a glory greater than that of the telestial kingdom in the worlds to come. (See D&C 42:79; Revelation 22:15; also 3 Nephi 30:2.)

10. Taken away the guilt . . . through the merits of his Son] Because of the atonement of Christ, the truly repentant have not only the burden of sin lifted from them but also the burden of guilt. Through the Atonement we become yoked to Christ; he thereby shares our burden.

The Anti-Nephi-Lehies Covenant Not to Take Up the Sword

Alma 24:11–19

11. And now behold, my brethren, since it has been all that we could do, (as we were the most lost of all mankind) to repent of all our sins and the many murders which we have committed, and to get God to take them away from our hearts, for it was all we could do to repent sufficiently before God that he would take away our stain—

12. Now, my best beloved brethren, since God hath taken away our stains, and our swords have become bright, then let us stain our swords no more with the blood of our brethren.

13. Behold, I say unto you, Nay, let us retain our swords that they be not stained with the blood of our brethren; for perhaps, if we should stain our swords again they can no more be washed bright through the blood of the Son of our great God, which shall be shed for the atonement of our sins.

14. And the great God has had mercy on us, and made these things known unto us that we might not perish; yea, and he has made these things known unto us beforehand, because he loveth our souls as well as he loveth our children; therefore, in his mercy he doth visit us by his angels, that the plan of salvation might be made known unto us as well as unto future generations.

15. Oh, how merciful is our God! And now behold, since it has been as much as we could do to get our stains taken away from us, and our swords are made bright, let us hide them away that they may be kept bright, as a testimony to our God at the last day, or at the day that we shall be brought to stand before him to be judged, that we have not stained our swords in the blood of our brethren since he imparted his word unto us and has made us clean thereby.

16. And now, my brethren, if our brethren seek to destroy us, behold, we will hide away our swords, yea, even we will bury them deep in the earth, that they may be kept bright, as a testimony that we have never used them, at the last day; and if our brethren destroy us, behold, we shall go to our God and shall be saved.

17. And now it came to pass that when the king had made an end of these sayings, and all the people were assembled together, they took their swords, and all the

weapons which were used for the shedding of man's blood, and they did bury them up deep in the earth.

18. And this they did, it being in their view a testimony to God, and also to men, that they never would use weapons again for the shedding of man's blood; and this they did, vouching and covenanting with God, that rather than shed the blood of their brethren they would give up their own lives; and rather than take away from a brother they would give unto him; and rather than spend their days in idleness they would labor abundantly with their hands.

19. And thus we see that, when these Lamanites were brought to believe and to know the truth, they were firm, and would suffer even unto death rather than commit sin; and thus we see that they buried their weapons of peace, or they buried the weapons of war, for peace.

11. Many murders] See commentary on verse 10.

12. Best beloved brethren] Though the "mighty change of heart" experienced by Anti-Nephi-Lehi, the king of the Lamanites, has brought him a love for his enemies that is greater than his concern for his own life, he still has an even greater love for his own brethren who have chosen to love and honor God.

13. Though it is true that the actual event of atonement lay in the future, from the days of Adam men and women of faith called upon the Father in the name of the Son; pleaded for forgiveness by virtue of the precious blood that would be spilled in the meridian of time; and knew the joy of their redemption through the merits and mercy of the Holy Messiah.

14. He has made these things known unto us beforehand] See Alma 39:17–19.

14. Visit us by his angels] A natural attendant to the kind of faith these converted Lamanites had would be the ministry of angels. Anti-Nephi-Lehi specifically states that the angels came to teach them the gospel or plan of salvation.

15. His word . . . made us clean] Truth sanctifies the soul (see John 17:17–19). To know the truth, to live the truth, to teach the truth—each has a sanctifying power upon our souls. Conversely, there can be no cleansing of the soul in ignorance, no exalting of the soul without our living the principles of exaltation, and no expansion of the soul in the refusal to share the light granted us.

16. We shall go to our God and shall be saved] Indeed, salvation consists of our returning to abide in the presence of that God who gave us life.

19. They buried the weapons of war, for peace] This inspired covenant of the Anti-Nephi-Lehies to bury their weapons and never again shed man's blood with them was rewarded with great blessings, notwithstanding, as we shall read, one thousand and five of their number were later slain by the Lamanites. Some have attempted to extrapolate from this instance that this is the course—a course of conscientious objection—that ought to be followed by those of the household of faith in all instances in which their lives and liberties are threatened by evil forces. But the larger context of this instance does not justify such an idea. As the story yet unfolds, it will be necessary for the Anti-Nephi-Lehies to abandon their lands and move in a body to that land of Jershon, where they can be protected by the Nephites (see Alma 27:20–24). It will also be necessary for their sons, who have not entered into the covenant that the Anti-Nephi-Lehies have made, to take up arms "to protect the Nephites and themselves from bondage" (see Alma 53:16–17).

Eventually, men and women must learn the lesson of the ages, a lesson stressed by Mormon just prior to his death, a message he could offer with over a thousand years of Nephite perspective before him: "Know ye," he said to the future remnants of Israel, "that ye must lay down your weapons of war, and delight no more in the shedding of blood, and take them not again, save it be that God shall command you" (Mormon 7:4).

Many Converted Through the Righteous Resolve of the Anti-Nephi-Lehies

Alma 24:20–27

20. And it came to pass that their brethren, the Lamanites, made preparations for war, and came up to the land of Nephi for the purpose of destroying the king, and to place another in his stead, and also of destroying the people of Anti-Nephi-Lehi out of the land.

21. Now when the people saw that they were coming against them they went out to meet them, and prostrated themselves before them to the earth, and began to call on the name of the Lord; and thus they were in this attitude when the Lamanites began to fall upon them, and began to slay them with the sword.

22. And thus without meeting any resistance, they did slay a thousand and five of them; and we know that they are blessed, for they have gone to dwell with their God.

23. Now when the Lamanites saw that their brethren would not flee from the sword, neither would they turn aside to the right hand or to the left, but that they would lie down and perish, and praised God even in the very act of perishing under the sword—

24. Now when the Lamanites saw this they did forbear from slaying them; and there were many whose hearts had swollen in them for those of their brethren who had fallen under the sword, for they repented of the things

which they had done.

25. And it came to pass that they threw down their weapons of war, and they would not take them again, for they were stung for the murders which they had committed; and they came down even as their brethren, relying upon the mercies of those whose arms were lifted to slay them.

26. And it came to pass that the people of God were joined that day by more than the number who had been slain; and those who had been slain were righteous people, therefore we have no reason to doubt but what they were saved.

27. And there was not a wicked man slain among them; but there were more than a thousand brought to the knowledge of the truth; thus we see that the Lord worketh in many ways to the salvation of his people.

26. When righteous people die, we have no reason to doubt but that they are saved. That is, they are heirs of the celestial kingdom. When the righteous (those true to their gospel covenants) pass from this life to the next, they "are received into a state of happiness, which is called paradise, a state of rest, a state of peace, where they shall rest from all their troubles and from all care, and sorrow" (Alma 40:12). Since they have kept their second estate, the eternal promise is that they "shall have glory added upon their heads for ever and ever" (Abraham 3:26). Given, then, that there is no apostasy in paradise, all who obtain that station have the sure promise of celestial glory in the day of resurrection.

Our Most Bitter Enemies Are Those Who Were Once Numbered Among Us

Alma 24:28–30

28. Now the greatest number of those of the Lamanites who slew so many of their brethren were Amalekites and Amulonites, the greatest number of whom were after the order of the Nehors.

29. Now, among those who joined the people of the Lord, there were none who were Amalekites or Amulonites, or who were of the order of Nehor, but they were actual descendants of Laman and Lemuel.

30. And thus we can plainly discern, that after a people have been once enlightened by the Spirit of God, and have had great knowledge of things pertaining to righteousness, and then have fallen away into sin and transgression, they become more hardened, and thus their state becomes worse than though they had never known these things.

28. Amalekites or Amulonites] See commentary on Alma 21:1–4.

30. Daniel Tyler records a conversation that he and Isaac Behunnin had with the Prophet Joseph Smith about the trials and persecutions to which the Prophet had been subject. As they talked, the Prophet observed that his greatest difficulties came at the hands of those who had once tasted of the things of the Spirit and then turned against them. To this, Elder Behunnin remarked: "If I should leave this Church, I would not do as those men have done; I would go to some remote place where Mormonism had never been heard of, settle down, and no one would ever learn that I knew anything about it."

Joseph Smith replied: "Brother Behunnin, you don't know what you would do. No doubt these men once thought as you do. Before you joined this Church you stood on neutral ground. When the gospel was preached, good and evil were set before you. You could choose either or neither. There were two opposite masters inviting you to serve them. When you joined this Church you enlisted to serve God. When you did that you left the neutral ground, and you never can get back on to it. Should you forsake the Master you enlisted to serve, it will be by the instigation of the evil one, and you will follow his dictation and be his servant." (*Juvenile Instructor*, vol. xxvii, 1892, p. 491.)

The rule for all ages seems to be that the most bitter enemies the prophets and kingdom of God will have are those who once embraced the faith and later were filled with an evil spirit and left. How strange it is that people leave the churches of the world by the hundreds of thousands every year to embrace the restored gospel with no feelings of bitterness toward those churches they have left! Yet when people leave the Church of Jesus Christ, frequently they cannot leave it alone, but must wear out their lives in bitter attacks against it. As Joseph Smith attested, there is no neutrality where the Church and kingdom of God are concerned. (See Joseph Fielding McConkie and Robert L. Millet, *Sustaining and Defending the Faith*, chapter 1.)

Joseph Smith stated in 1834: "From apostates the faithful have received the severest persecutions. Judas was rebuked and immediately betrayed his Lord into the hands of His enemies, because Satan entered into him. There is a superior intelligence bestowed upon such as obey the Gospel with full purpose of heart, which, if sinned against, the apostate is left naked and destitute of the Spirit of God, and he is, in truth, nigh unto cursing, and his end is to be burned. When once that light which was in them is taken from them, they become as much darkened as they were previously enlightened, and then, no marvel, if all their power should be enlisted against the truth, and they, Judas like, seek the destruction of those who were their greatest benefactors. What nearer friend on earth, or in heaven, had Judas than the Savior? And his first object was to destroy Him." (*Teachings*, p. 67.)

Repentant Lamanites Martyred by the Seed of Amulon

Alma 25:1–7

1. And behold, now it came to pass that those Lamanites were more angry because they had slain their brethren; therefore they swore vengeance upon the Nephites; and they did no more attempt to slay the people of Anti-Nephi-Lehi at that time.

2. But they took their armies and went over into the borders of the land of Zarahemla, and fell upon the people who were in the land of Ammonihah, and destroyed them.

3. And after that, they had many battles with the Nephites, in the which they were driven and slain.

4. And among the Lamanites who were slain were almost all the seed of Amulon and his brethren, who were the priests of Noah, and they were slain by the hands of the Nephites;

5. And the remainder, having fled into the east wilderness, and having usurped the power and authority over the Lamanites, caused that many of the Lamanites should perish by fire because of their belief—

6. For many of them, after having suffered much loss and so many afflictions, began to be stirred up in remembrance of the words which Aaron and his brethren had preached to them in their land; therefore they began to disbelieve the traditions of their fathers, and to believe in the Lord, and that he gave great power unto the Nephites; and thus there were many of them converted in the wilderness.

7. And it came to pass that those rulers who were the remnant of the children of Amulon caused that they should be put to death, yea, all those that believed in these things.

2. The land of Ammonihah] The city of Ammonihah and "every living soul of the Ammonihahites" were destroyed because they martyred the Saints and persecuted the prophets (see Alma 16:9).

5–7. It became obvious to some among the Lamanites that the power of God was with the Nephites. As they lamented their afflictions, they were reminded of the words Aaron and his brethren had spoken to them and realized that the traditions of their fathers were lies and vanity. Such thinking would have been regarded as traitorous by the children of Amulon, who, in the dark spirit of their father, caused that the Lamanites who had started to believe in the Lord should be burned to death. In so doing, the seed of Amulon was fulfilling the prophecy of Abinadi who, while he was being scorched by the flames that took his life, cried out saying: "Behold, even as ye have done unto me, so shall it come to pass that thy seed shall cause that many shall suffer the pains that I do suffer, even the pains of death by fire; and this because they believe in the salvation of the Lord their God" (Mosiah 17:15).

Abinadi's Prophecy of God's Vengeance Fulfilled

Alma 25:8–12

8. Now this martyrdom caused that many of their brethren should be stirred up to anger; and there began to be contention in the wilderness; and the Lamanites began to hunt the seed of Amulon and his brethren and began to slay them; and they fled into the east wilderness.

9. And behold they are hunted at this day by the Lamanites. Thus the words of Abinadi were brought to pass, which he said concerning the seed of the priests who caused that he should suffer death by fire.

10. For he said unto them: What ye shall do unto me shall be a type of things to come.

11. And now Abinadi was the first that suffered death by fire because of his belief in God; now this is what he meant, that many should suffer death by fire, according as he had suffered.

12. And he said unto the priests of Noah that their seed should cause many to be put to death, in the like manner as he was, and that they should be scattered abroad and slain, even as a sheep having no shepherd is driven and slain by wild beasts; and now behold, these words were verified, for they were driven by the Lamanites, and they were hunted, and they were smitten.

8–12. "And it will come to pass that ye shall be afflicted with all manner of diseases because of your iniquities," Abinadi prophesied to Noah and his priests. "Yea, and ye shall be smitten on every hand, and shall be driven and scattered to and fro, even as a wild flock is driven by wild and ferocious beasts. And in that day ye shall be hunted, and ye shall be taken by the hand of your enemies, and then ye shall suffer, as I suffer, the pains of death by fire. Thus God executeth vengeance upon those that destroy his people." (Mosiah 17:16–19.)

10. See Mosiah 13:10.

Seeing the Power of God upon the Nephites
Leads Many Lamanites to Repent

Alma 25:13–17

13. And it came to pass that when the Lamanites saw that they could not overpower the Nephites they returned again to their own land; and many of them came over to dwell in the land of Ishmael and the land of Nephi, and did join themselves to the people of God, who were the people of Anti-Nephi-Lehi.

14. And they did also bury their weapons of war, according as their brethren had, and they began to be a righteous people; and they did walk in the ways of the Lord, and did observe to keep his commandments and his statutes.

15. Yea, and they did keep the law of Moses; for it was expedient that they should keep the law of Moses as yet, for it was not all fulfilled. But notwithstanding the law of Moses, they did look forward to the coming of Christ, considering that the law of Moses was a type of his coming, and believing that they must keep those outward performances until the time that he should be revealed unto them.

16. Now they did not suppose that salvation came by the law of Moses; but the law of Moses did serve to strengthen their faith in Christ; and thus they did retain a hope through faith, unto eternal salvation, relying upon the spirit of prophecy, which spake of those things to come.

17. And now behold, Ammon, and Aaron, and Omner, and Himni, and their brethren did rejoice exceedingly, for the success which they had had among the Lamanites, seeing that the Lord had granted unto them according to their prayers, and that he had also verified his word unto them in every particular.

13–17. It is a genuine conversion to Christ of which we read, not a military surrender. These reborn disciples joined the Anti-Nephi-Lehies in burying their weapons of war, in walking in the ways of the Lord, in observance of the law of Moses with all its ritual, and in understanding of its purpose as a type for the coming of Christ. Theirs was not a conversion of convenience but, rather, one representing a total commitment to Christ.

15–16. Abinadi had explained to the priests of Noah: "And now ye have said that salvation cometh by the law of Moses. I say unto you that it is expedient that ye should keep the law of Moses as yet; but I say unto you, that the time shall come when it shall no more be expedient to keep the law of Moses. And moreover, I say unto you, that salvation doth not come by the law alone; and were it not for the atonement, which God himself shall make for the sins and iniquities of his people, that they must unavoidably perish, notwithstanding the law of Moses." (Mosiah 13:27–28; see also 2 Nephi 25:30; Alma 34:13–14.)

Ammon Rejoices over the Lamanite Conversions

Alma 26:1–9

1. And now, these are the words of Ammon to his brethren, which say thus: My brothers and my brethren, behold I say unto you, how great reason have we to rejoice; for could we have supposed when we started from the land of Zarahemla that God would have granted unto us such great blessings?

2. And now, I ask, what great blessings has he bestowed upon us? Can ye tell?

3. Behold, I answer for you; for our brethren, the Lamanites, were in darkness, yea, even in the darkest abyss, but behold, how many of them are brought to behold the marvelous light of God! And this is the blessing which hath been bestowed upon us, that we have been made instruments in the hands of God to bring about this great work.

4. Behold, thousands of them do rejoice, and have been brought into the fold of God.

5. Behold, the field was ripe, and blessed are ye, for ye did thrust in the sickle, and did reap with your might, yea, all the day long did ye labor; and behold the number of your sheaves! And they shall be gathered into the garners, that they are not wasted.

6. Yea, they shall not be beaten down by the storm at the last day; yea, neither shall they be harrowed up by the whirlwinds; but when the storm cometh they shall be gathered together in their place, that the storm cannot penetrate to them; yea, neither shall they be driven with fierce winds whithersoever the enemy listeth to carry them.

7. But behold, they are in the hands of the Lord of the harvest, and they are his; and he will raise them up at the last day.

8. Blessed be the name of our God; let us sing to his praise, yea, let us give thanks to his holy name, for he doth work righteousness forever.

9. For if we had not come up out of the land of Zarahemla, these our dearly beloved brethren, who have so dearly beloved us, would still have been racked with hatred against us, yea, and they would also have been strangers to God.

1. We started from the land of Zarahemla] See Alma 17:6–11.

3. Instruments in the hands of God] See commentary on Alma 17:9.

4. Thousands of them do rejoice] Gospel principles, properly understood, cause the hearts and souls of men to rejoice. It is prophesied that when the lost sheep of Israel return to the fold of God in the last days, they will do so "with songs and everlasting joy upon their heads," that in their conversion they will experience "joy and gladness," and that "sorrow and sighing" shall flee from them (see Isaiah 35:10). Even in the pre-existence when the plan of salvation was announced, "the morning stars sang together, and all the sons of God shouted for joy" (Job 38:7).

5. See D&C 4:4.

6–7. These are they who have entered into the "rest of the Lord," meaning that they enjoy peace, assurance, and confidence amidst all the storms of life. Having built upon the rock of revelation, they have a personal assurance of the verity of the gospel; and having clothed themselves in the robes of righteousness, they are protected from the fiery darts of the adversary.

7. He will raise them up at the last day] That is, he will raise them at the last day in the resurrection of the just (see JST, John 6:54).

8. Let us sing to his praise] Music and song have been an important part of the worship of the Saints in all gospel dispensations. The praise of God has ascended to the heavens through the sweet sounds of the harpist and the thundering majesty of great choirs. While but one can speak at a time in worship services, all can unite in hymns or anthems of praise to our God. Whereas the individual shout of adulation may be deemed indecorous, to raise our voices in harmonious strains of praise exalts the soul and makes the heavens echo with our testimony of his mercy and goodness.

As the term is used in this passage, however, Ammon feels the need to sing praises to God in the same sense that one sings the song of redeeming love (see Alma 5:26). We sing to the praise of the Almighty as we keep his commandments, as we express gratitude in prayer, as we acknowledge his hand in all things. In this spirit Elder Bruce R. McConkie offered the following psalm of praise:

> Praise ye the Lord:
> Praise him for his goodness;
> Praise him for his grace;
> Exalt his name and seek his face—
> O praise ye the Lord.
>
> Blessed is the Lord:
> Bless him for his mercy;
> Bless him for his love;
> Exalt his name and seek his face—
> O blessed is the Lord.
>
> Praise ye the Lord:
> Praise him who all things did create;
> Praise him who all things did redeem;

Exalt his name and seek his face—
O praise ye the Lord.

Seek ye the Lord:
Seek him who rules on high;
Seek him whose will we know;
Exalt his name and seek his face—
O seek ye the Lord.
(CR, October 1973, p. 57.)

8. Work righteousness forever] The working of righteousness is everlastingly the labor of God. Salvation involves our learning to labor as he labors.

In the Strength of God We Can Do All Things

Alma 26:10–16

10. And it came to pass that when Ammon had said these words, his brother Aaron rebuked him, saying: Ammon, I fear that thy joy doth carry thee away unto boasting.

11. But Ammon said unto him: I do not boast in my own strength, nor in my own wisdom; but behold, my joy is full, yea, my heart is brim with joy, and I will rejoice in my God.

12. Yea, I know that I am nothing; as to my strength I am weak; therefore I will not boast of myself, but I will boast of my God, for in his strength I can do all things; yea, behold, many mighty miracles we have wrought in this land, for which we will praise his name forever.

13. Behold, how many thousands of our brethren has he loosed from the pains of hell; and they are brought to sing redeeming love, and this because of the power of his word which is in us, therefore have we not great reason to rejoice?

14. Yea, we have reason to praise him forever, for he is the Most High God, and has loosed our brethren from the chains of hell.

15. Yea, they were encircled about with everlasting darkness and destruction; but behold, he has brought them into his everlasting light, yea, into everlasting salvation; and they are encircled about with the matchless bounty of his love; yea, and we have been instruments in his hands of doing this great and marvelous work.

16. Therefore, let us glory, yea, we will glory in the Lord; yea, we will rejoice, for our joy is full; yea, we will praise our God forever. Behold, who can glory too much in the Lord? Yea, who can say too much of his great power, and of his mercy, and of his long-suffering towards the children of men? Behold, I say unto you, I cannot say the smallest part which I feel.

10. Aaron's concern is a valid one. We must always be on the alert to avoid boasting about our accomplishments, even if (perhaps especially if) the accomplishments are in the spiritual realm. Few persons are able to keep an eye single to the glory of God to such an extent that they look to God and acknowledge his hand in all things.

11. My joy is full] In the ultimate sense one cannot have fulness of joy in this life but only in and after the resurrection (see D&C 93:33–34). There is a joy, however, which comes to those who share the message of the gospel, a joy which transcends earthly pleasures (see D&C 18:14–16).

12. "I call upon the weak things of the world," the Lord announced in our dispensation, "those who are unlearned and despised, to thrash the nations by the power of my Spirit; and their arm shall be my arm, and I will be their shield and their buckler; and I will gird up their loins, and they shall fight manfully for me; and their enemies shall be under their feet; and I will let fall the sword in their behalf, and by the fire of mine indignation will I preserve them" (D&C 35:13–14).

12. I know that I am nothing] "Man is nothing," Moses declared after having viewed the expanses of eternity and after learning of the majesty and power of God (see Moses 1:10). Yet when the power of God is placed upon us, an endowment that—assuming worthiness on our part—is rightfully ours as his offspring, we can do all things in his name. In short, man is nothing without divine intervention.

12. In his strength I can do all things] Paul wrote: "I can do all things through Christ which strengtheneth me" (Philippians 4:13; compare 1 Nephi 17:3, 50).

13. From the pains of hell] They are loosed from the pains of hell, here and hereafter. Many suffer hell on earth in the sense that they are smitten by conscience, tormented by a damned soul that cannot find happiness in sin. Of necessity, those who die under the bondage of sin are consigned hereafter to that portion of the spirit world referred to in the Book of Mormon as hell, where they must pay for their sins. Here "there shall be weeping, and wailing, and gnashing of teeth, and this because of their own iniquity, being led captive by the will of the devil" (Alma 40:13). Thus, as Ammon states, this great host of Lamanite converts have escaped the "pains of hell," as do all who repent, are baptized, and continue in faith. See commentary on Alma 42:12–14.

13. To sing redeeming love] See commentary on Alma 5:9, 26.

13. The power of his word which is in us] There is a power in the word of God, a power that dispels darkness and brings light, a power that supplants uncertainty and brings assurance, a power that uproots heartache, gloom, and despair, and brings in their stead peace, rejoicing, and gladness.

14. The Most High God] The Father, author, and creator, of all things.

16. I cannot say the smallest part which I feel] About some sacred matters we are forbidden to speak. It would not be proper to discuss them. Others simply cannot be spoken because of the limitations of human language. Spiritual experiences— events and feelings—often transcend the temporal and therefore defy description and preclude expression.

The Sons of Mosiah Redeemed

Alma 26:17–20

17. Who could have supposed that our God would have been so merciful as to have snatched us from our awful, sinful, and polluted state?

18. Behold, we went forth even in wrath, with mighty threatenings to destroy his church.

19. Oh then, why did he not consign us to an awful destruction, yea, why did he not let the sword of his justice fall upon us, and doom us to eternal despair?

20. Oh, my soul, almost as it were, fleeth at the thought. Behold, he did not exercise his justice upon us, but in his great mercy hath brought us over that everlasting gulf of death and misery, even to the salvation of our souls.

18. See Mosiah 27:10; Alma 36:6.

19. The sword of his justice] If God be God, he must be just; and justice demands that the Lord of Hosts take up his sword against those who war against him and desire to destroy his kingdom. Isaiah spoke of his "sword bathed in heaven" (meaning either "anointed," or "drunk to its fill") with which he will come down upon the world in judgment (Isaiah 34:5; see also D&C 1:13; *The Interpreter's Bible* 5:356).

20. That everlasting gulf of death and misery] Only the mercy of a God could conquer the effects of death and the misery of sin. Such is the effect of the atoning sacrifice of Christ. It extends to everyone the blessing of resurrection, the endless union of body and spirit; and to the faithful it grants the promise of exaltation.

The Natural Man Cannot Know the Things of God

Alma 26:21–22

21. And now behold, my brethren, what natural man is there that knoweth these things? I say unto you, there is none that knoweth these things, save it be the penitent.

22. Yea, he that repenteth and exerciseth faith, and bringeth forth good works, and prayeth continually without ceasing—unto such it is given to know the mysteries of God; yea, unto such it shall be given to reveal things which never have been revealed; yea, and it shall be given unto such to bring thousands of souls to repentance, even as it has been given unto us to bring these our brethren to repentance.

21. "The natural man receiveth not the things of the Spirit of God: for they are foolishness unto him: neither can he know them, because they are spiritually discerned" (1 Corinthians 2:14).

22. King Benjamin declared the natural man to be an enemy to God (see Mosiah 3:19). Ammon here describes the natural man as the man who is without repentance, faith, good works, and constant prayer. A person ceases to be a natural man when the Holy Ghost becomes his companion. The natural man is the man devoid of the spirit of prophecy and revelation. The man of God, as contrasted with the natural man, has the promise that he may know things that are not generally known and that he may be an instrument for righteousness in the hands of God to bring many unto repentance. The promise is not appended to a priesthood office or to a particular calling. Indeed, the promise is not limited to men. It extends to every faithful member of the Church (see also D&C 76:5–10).

22. The mysteries of God] See Alma 12:9–11.

Success Promised to Those Who Bear Afflictions Well

Alma 26:23–34

23. Now do ye remember, my brethren, that we said unto our brethren in the land of Zarahemla, we go up to the land of Nephi, to preach unto our brethren, the Lamanites, and they laughed us to scorn?

24. For they said unto us: Do ye suppose that ye can bring the Lamanites to the knowledge of the truth? Do ye suppose that ye can convince the Lamanites of the incorrectness of the traditions of their fathers, as stiffnecked a people as they are; whose hearts delight in the shedding of blood;

whose days have been spent in the grossest iniquity; whose ways have been the ways of a transgressor from the beginning? Now my brethren, ye remember that this was their language.

25. And moreover they did say: Let us take up arms against them, that we destroy them and their iniquity out of the land, lest they overrun us and destroy us.

26. But behold, my beloved brethren, we came into the wilderness not with the intent to destroy our brethren, but with the intent that perhaps we might save some few of their souls.

27. Now when our hearts were depressed, and we were about to turn back, behold, the Lord comforted us, and said: Go amongst thy brethren, the Lamanites, and bear with patience thine afflictions, and I will give unto you success.

28. And now behold, we have come, and been forth amongst them; and we have been patient in our sufferings, and we have suffered every privation; yea, we have traveled from house to house, relying upon the mercies of the world—not upon the mercies of the world alone but upon the mercies of God.

29. And we have entered into their houses and taught them, and we have taught them in their streets; yea, and we have taught them upon their hills; and we have also entered into their temples and their synagogues and taught them; and we have been cast out, and mocked, and spit upon, and smote upon our cheeks; and we have been stoned, and taken and bound with strong cords, and cast into prison; and through the power and wisdom of God we have been delivered again.

30. And we have suffered all manner of afflictions, and all this, that perhaps we might be the means of saving some soul; and we supposed that our joy would be full if perhaps we could be the means of saving some.

31. Now behold, we can look forth and see the fruits of our labors; and are they few? I say unto you, Nay, they are many; yea, and we can witness of their sincerity, because of their love towards their brethren and also towards us.

32. For behold, they had rather sacrifice their lives than even to take the life of their enemy; and they have buried their weapons of war deep in the earth, because of their love towards their brethren.

33. And now behold I say unto you, has there been so great love in all the land? Behold, I say unto you, Nay, there has not, even among the Nephites.

34. For behold, they would take up arms against their brethren; they would not suffer themselves to be slain. But behold how many of these have laid down their lives; and we know that they have gone to their God, because of their love and of their hatred to sin.

23–26. It is an interesting reversal of positions to have their fellow Nephites laugh the sons of Mosiah to scorn because of their righteous desires, when those now scorning had a short time before been subject to the others' faithless tauntings. It is also interesting to learn that there were some among the Nephites who felt that the sword was the proper solution to their problems with the Lamanites. It is obvious that it took both greater faith and greater courage to do missionary work among them than it took to go to battle against them. Nevertheless it is the purpose of the Lord whenever possible to save, not to destroy, the wayward nations of the earth.

27–31. The Lord had previously promised the sons of Mosiah and those who went with them that if they would go among the Lamanites and faithfully declare his word, being patient in long-suffering and afflictions, they would be the means whereby many souls would receive the blessings of salvation (see Alma 17:11).

30. See D&C 18:15–16.

The Power, Wisdom, and Understanding of God

Alma 26:35

35. Now have we not reason to rejoice? Yea, I say unto you, there never were men that had so great reason to rejoice as we, since the world began; yea, and my joy is carried away, even unto boasting in my God; for he has all power, all wisdom, and all understanding; he comprehendeth all things, and he is a merciful Being, even unto salvation, to those who will repent and believe on his name.

35. He has all power] God has all power. There is no righteous deed or work that he cannot do. There are no laws that he did not ordain (D&C 88:37–38, 42). Joseph Smith said it thus: "Unless God had power over all things, and was able by his power to control all things, and thereby deliver his creatures who put their trust in him from the power of all beings that might seek their destruction, whether in heaven, on earth, or in hell, men could not be saved" (*Lectures on Faith* 4:12).

35. All wisdom] God has all wisdom. Wisdom is a gift of God (D&C 46:17). Indeed, there is no wisdom save it has come from God. Wisdom embraces the wise application of knowledge and an understanding of that which is in one's eternal best interest. Wisdom comes as a person applies his heart to understanding (Mosiah 12:27).

35. All understanding] "Great is our Lord, and of great power: his understanding is infinite" (Psalm 147:5).

35. He comprehendeth all things] "He comprehendeth all things, and all things are before him, and all things are round about him; and he is above all things, and in all things, and is through all things, and is round about all things; and all things are by him, and of him, even God, forever and ever" (D&C 88:41).

35. A merciful Being . . . to those who will repent] Alma taught that "whosoever repenteth shall find mercy; and he that findeth mercy and endureth to the end the same shall be saved" (Alma 32:13). Thus, in the full and complete sense, to obtain the mercy of the Lord is to obtain salvation. In a similar sense, the Lord said: "I, the Lord, am merciful and gracious unto those who fear me, and delight to honor those who serve me in righteousness and in truth unto the end" (D&C 76:5).

"Mercy is not showered promiscuously upon mankind," wrote Elder Bruce R. McConkie, "except in the general sense that it is manifest in the creation and peopling of the earth and in the granting of immortality to all men as a free gift" (*Mormon Doctrine*, p. 484). Rather, mercy is granted (because of the grace, love, and condescension of God), as it is with all blessings, to those who comply with the law upon which its receipt is predicated (see D&C 130:20–21). That law is the law of righteousness: *those who sow righteousness reap mercy* (see Hosea 10:12). There is no promise of mercy to the wicked; rather, as stated in the Ten Commandments, the Lord promises to show mercy unto thousands of them that love him and keep his commandments (see Exodus 20:6; Daniel 9:4; D&C 70:18).

God Is Mindful of Every People

Alma 26:36–37

36. Now if this is boasting, even so will I boast; for this is my life and my light, my joy and my salvation, and my redemption from everlasting wo. Yea, blessed is the name of my God, who has been mindful of this people, who are a branch of the tree of Israel, and has been lost from its body in a strange land; yea, I say, blessed be the name of my God, who has been mindful of us, wanderers in a strange land.

37. Now my brethren, we see that God is mindful of every people, whatsoever land they may be in; yea, he numbereth his people, and his bowels of mercy are over all the earth. Now this is my joy, and my great thanksgiving; yea, and I will give thanks unto my God forever. Amen.

36. A branch of the tree of Israel . . . lost from its body] Reference is to the Lamanites, who lost the knowledge of their rightful inheritance through wickedness and rebellion. This is the same sense in which the tribes of Israel are lost in our day—not in the sense that they are hidden in some unknown place trying to find their way back, but rather that they have become temporarily lost as to their identity and thus as to their place in the Master's fold. They await the shepherds he sends to search them out from among the nations of the earth.

37. God is mindful of every people] The God of whom Ammon bore witness was not a local god with bounded powers and limited interests. His love was not confined to some small fragment of the earth's population, neither was his power to bless or to save rationed among a favored few. There are none to whom the gospel will not go, whether it be in this life or in the next. There are none who cannot obtain the assurance of salvation through obedience to the laws and ordinances of the gospel. There are none for whom the atonement of Christ does not bring an everlasting restoration of body and spirit, none who through worthiness cannot obtain all that the Father has. A theology that promised less would be unworthy of our allegiance, unworthy of our God.

The Amalekites Seek to Destroy All Who Worship in Truth

Alma 27:1–3

1. Now it came to pass that when those Lamanites who had gone to war against the Nephites had found, after their many struggles to destroy them, that it was in vain to seek their destruction, they returned again to the land of Nephi.

2. And it came to pass that the Amalekites, because of their loss, were exceedingly angry. And when they saw that they could not seek revenge from the Nephites, they began to stir up the people in anger against their brethren, the people of Anti-Nephi-Lehi; therefore they began again to destroy them.

3. Now this people again refused to take their arms, and they suffered themselves to be slain according to the desires of their enemies.

1–2. The Amalekites, who personify the spirit of apostasy—having once partaken of the fruit of the tree of life and then turned against it—now devote the whole energy of their souls to fighting God. Since they can find no success in war with the Nephites, they turn on their brethren the Anti-Nephi-Lehies, seeking their destruction. All who have embraced light and truth are, of necessity, their enemies.

1. It was in vain to seek their destruction] As long as the Nephite nation was worthy of the protection of the Lord, it was vain for any people or nation to seek its destruction. This is inherent in the concept of a covenant people being granted a promised land. The land is the symbol of the covenant they have made. As long as they honor their covenants, they retain the promise of protection. In the violation of their covenants they forfeit the right to divine protection and no longer have claim upon the land. See 2 Nephi 1:7.

3. See Alma 24:6.

Ammon Leads the People of Anti-Nephi-Lehi to Safety

Alma 27:4–14

4. Now when Ammon and his brethren saw this work of destruction among those whom they so dearly beloved, and among those who had so dearly beloved them—for they were treated as though they were angels sent from God to save them from everlasting destruction—therefore, when Ammon and his brethren saw this great work of destruction, they were moved with compassion, and they said unto the king:

5. Let us gather together this people of the Lord, and let us go down to the land of Zarahemla to our brethren the Nephites, and flee out of the hands of our enemies, that we be not destroyed.

6. But the king said unto them: Behold, the Nephites will destroy us, because of the many murders and sins we have committed against them.

7. And Ammon said: I will go and inquire of the Lord, and if he say unto us, go down unto our brethren, will ye go?

8. And the king said unto him: Yea, if the Lord saith unto us go, we will go down unto our brethren, and we will be their slaves until we repair unto them the many murders and sins which we have committed against them.

9. But Ammon said unto him: It is against the law of our brethren, which was established by my father, that there should be any slaves among them; therefore let us go down and rely upon the mercies of our brethren.

10. But the king said unto him: Inquire of the Lord, and if he saith unto us go, we will go; otherwise we will perish in the land.

11. And it came to pass that Ammon went and inquired of the Lord, and the Lord said unto him:

12. Get this people out of this land, that they perish not; for Satan has great hold on the hearts of the Amalekites, who do stir up the Lamanites to anger against their brethren to slay them; therefore get thee out of this land; and blessed are this people in this generation, for I will preserve them.

13. And now it came to pass that Ammon went and told the king all the words which the Lord had said unto him.

14. And they gathered together all their people, yea, all the people of the Lord, and did gather together all their flocks and herds, and departed out of the land, and came into the wilderness which divided the land of Nephi from the land of Zarahemla, and came over near the borders of the land.

4–14. Ammon, as the prophet-leader of this people, having in a spiritual sense led them to God, now leads them to a temporal salvation, a land of safety. In so doing he becomes a rather remarkable type for the Messiah, who will also first offer the doctrines of the kingdom and eventually lead all who have embraced those doctrines to a place of safety. Similarly, as we are about to read, these people will be given Ammon's name (see verse 26), even as all the faithful must be given the name of our Lord and Master.

   4. Treated as though they were angels sent from God] An angel is a messenger from the Lord. The Hebrew word *malak*, for instance, means "messenger," "representative," or "angel." In the context of the Old Testament it is used in reference to both human and spirit messengers. For that matter, those who come in the name of the Savior ought to be accorded the same respect that would be granted the Master. This was the spirit in which those in Galatia received the Apostle Paul. Of that reception he wrote: "My temptation which was in my flesh ye despised not, nor rejected; but received me as an angel of God, even as Christ Jesus" (Galatians 4:14).

   5. People of the Lord] These converted Lamanites are now properly referred to as "people of the Lord" and, as such, are entitled to the same blessings of protection enjoyed by the nation of the Nephites. See verse 12.

   9. King Mosiah had taught the people: "I desire that this land be a land of liberty, and every man may enjoy his rights and privileges alike, so long as the Lord sees fit that we may live and inherit the land, yea, even as long as any of our posterity remains upon the face of the land" (Mosiah 29:32). In modern revelation the Savior declared simply that "it is not right that any man should be in bondage one to another" (D&C 101:79).

   12. Satan has great hold on the hearts of the Amalekites] See commentary on Alma 21:1–4.

Nephites Give Anti-Nephi-Lehies the Land of Jershon

Alma 27:15–25

15. And it came to pass that Ammon said unto them: Behold, I and my brethren will go forth into the land of Zarahemla, and ye shall remain here until we return; and we will try the hearts of our brethren, whether they will that ye shall come into their land.

16. And it came to pass that as Ammon was going forth into the land, that he and his brethren met Alma, over in the place of which has been spoken; and behold, this was a joyful meeting.

17. Now the joy of Ammon was so great even that he was full; yea,

he was swallowed up in the joy of his God, even to the exhausting of his strength; and he fell again to the earth.

18. Now was not this exceeding joy? Behold, this is joy which none receiveth save it be the truly penitent and humble seeker of happiness.

19. Now the joy of Alma in meeting his brethren was truly great, and also the joy of Aaron, of Omner, and Himni; but behold their joy was not that to exceed their strength.

20. And now it came to pass that Alma conducted his brethren back to the land of Zarahemla; even to his own house. And they went and told the chief judge all the things that had happened unto them in the land of Nephi, among their brethren, the Lamanites.

21. And it came to pass that the chief judge sent a proclamation throughout all the land, desiring the voice of the people concerning the admitting their brethren, who were the people of Anti-Nephi-Lehi.

22. And it came to pass that the voice of the people came, saying: Behold, we will give up the land of Jershon, which is on the east by the sea, which joins the land Bountiful, which is on the south of the land Bountiful; and this land Jershon is the land which we will give unto our brethren for an inheritance.

23. And behold, we will set our armies between the land Jershon and the land Nephi, that we may protect our brethren in the land Jershon; and this we do for our brethren, on account of their fear to take up arms against their brethren lest they should commit sin; and this their great fear came because of their sore repentance which they had, on account of their many murders and their awful wickedness.

24. And now behold, this will we do unto our brethren, that they may inherit the land Jershon; and we will guard them from their enemies with our armies, on condition that they will give us a portion of their substance to assist us that we may maintain our armies.

25. Now, it came to pass that when Ammon had heard this, he returned to the people of Anti-Nephi-Lehi, and also Alma with him, into the wilderness, where they had pitched their tents, and made known unto them all these things. And Alma also related unto them his conversion, with Ammon and Aaron, and his brethren.

16. See Alma 17:1.

17–19. A fulness of joy is found only among resurrected, exalted beings (D&C 93:33). Indeed, exaltation consists in gaining a fulness of joy; it is to enter into the "joy of the Lord" (D&C 51:19). In mortality men experience joy only in righteousness—that is, in obedience to the laws and ordinances of the gospel—the gospel being the "glad tidings of great joy." Joy is characteristic of the presence of the Holy Ghost, from whom it comes. It is experienced only when the Spirit is present, and that most acutely in the manifestation that our sins have been remitted, in the knowledge that our path is pleasing to and approved by God, and in our helping others find the way to light and salvation (see Mosiah 4:3; D&C 18:13).

The reunion between Alma and Ammon was attended by a marvelous outpouring of the Spirit, with the attendant feelings of rejoicing. These feelings were so powerful in Ammon's case that they exhausted his strength, causing him to fall to the earth in a manner similar to what had taken place at Lamoni's conversion (see Alma 19:12–14).

25. Alma . . . related unto them his conversion] Like Paul, Alma's apostolic colleague who also related his conversion frequently (see Acts 9, 22, 26), Alma bears witness of the transformation from spiritual death to life that can come through the mediation and mercy of Jesus Christ. Alma's restitution for sin consisted in a life of dedication and service, a life which itself testified of the miracle of forgiveness and the marvelous life to be found in Jesus the Redeemer.

Anti-Nephi-Lehies Called the People of Ammon

Alma 27:26

26. And it came to pass that it did cause great joy among them. And they went down into the land of Jershon, and took possession of the land of Jershon; and they were called by the Nephites the people of Ammon; therefore they were distinguished by that name ever after.

26. They were called . . . the people of Ammon] Upon settling in the land of Jershon, the Lamanite converts—or the people of Anti-Nephi-Lehi, as they had chosen to call themselves (see Alma 24:1)—became designated by their Nephite neighbors as Ammonites, or the people of Ammon. Thus this nation within a nation was named after the chief missionary who had labored among them and who now became their presiding high priest (see Alma 30:20).

It seems most fitting that this people be known as Ammonites, given that Ammon, like them, had once been unholy and unruly, and yet when converted had become a man of powerful faith and courage.

The Ammonites Are Highly Favored of the Lord

Alma 27:27–30

27. And they were among the people of Nephi, and also numbered among the people who were of the church of God. And they were also distinguished for their zeal towards God, and also towards men; for they were perfectly honest and upright in all things; and they were firm in the faith of Christ, even unto the end.

28. And they did look upon shedding the blood of their brethren with the greatest abhorrence; and they never could be prevailed upon to take up arms against their brethren; and they never did look upon death with any degree of terror, for their hope and views of Christ and the resurrection; therefore, death was swallowed up to them by the victory of Christ over it.

29. Therefore, they would suffer death in the most aggravating and distressing manner which could be inflicted by their brethren, before they would take the sword or cimeter to smite them.

30. And thus they were a zealous and beloved people, a highly favored people of the Lord.

27–30. See Alma 23:6; 24:19. "He that is righteous is favored of God" (1 Nephi 17:35). Such was the case with the people of Ammon—a people "perfectly honest and upright in all things," a people "firm in the faith of Christ," a people who looked upon their past sins with abhorrence, a people who because of their abiding faith in the atonement of Christ and the power of the resurrection did not fear death. Surely the heavens rejoiced over them, and the righteous of all generations ought to emulate them.

28. Never did look upon death with any degree of terror] It is a contradiction to profess saving faith and yet to cling tenaciously to life and be terrified by death. If our faith does not reach beyond the shadow of death, we are, as Paul said, "of all men most miserable" (1 Corinthians 15:19). "Those that die in me," the Lord promised, "shall not taste of death, for it shall be sweet unto them" (D&C 42:46). "Precious in the sight of the Lord is the death of his saints" (Psalm 116:15).

28. Death was swallowed up] See Isaiah 25:8; 1 Corinthians 15:54.

30. They were a zealous and beloved people] Some people "have a zeal of God, but not according to knowledge" (Romans 10:2). That is, their zeal—excitement, enthusiasm, eagerness—is not refined by the wisdom and judgment that must accompany righteous actions. Others, like the people of Ammon, had a zeal for righteousness, but a zeal that was tempered by common sense and by the quiet peace which whispers that the Lord is pleased.

Tremendous Battle Brings Great Mournings

Alma 28:1–14

1. And now it came to pass that after the people of Ammon were established in the land of Jershon, and a church also established in the land of Jershon, and the armies of the Nephites were set round about the land of Jershon, yea, in all the borders round about the land of Zarahemla; behold the armies of the Lamanites had followed their brethren into the wilderness.

2. And thus there was a tremendous battle; yea, even such an one as never had been known among all the people in the land from the time Lehi left Jerusalem; yea, and tens of thousands of the Lamanites were slain and scattered abroad.

3. Yea, and also there was a tremendous slaughter among the people of Nephi; nevertheless, the Lamanites were driven and scattered, and the people of Nephi returned again to their land.

4. And now this was a time that there was a great mourning and lamentation heard throughout all the land, among all the people of Nephi—

5. Yea, the cry of widows mourning for their husbands, and also of fathers mourning for their sons, and the daughter for the brother, yea, the brother for the father; and thus the cry of mourning was heard among all of them, mourning for their kindred who had been slain.

6. And now surely this was a sorrowful day; yea, a time of solemnity, and a time of much fasting and prayer.

7. And thus endeth the fifteenth year of the reign of the judges over the people of Nephi;

8. And this is the account of Ammon and his brethren, their journeyings in the land of Nephi, their sufferings in the land, their sorrows, and their afflictions, and their incomprehensible joy, and the reception and safety of the brethren in the land of Jershon. And now may the Lord, the Redeemer of all men, bless their souls forever.

9. And this is the account of the wars and contentions among the Nephites, and also the wars between the Nephites and the Lamanites; and the fifteenth year of the reign of the judges is ended.

10. And from the first year to the fifteenth has brought to pass the destruction of many thousand lives; yea, it has brought to pass an awful scene of bloodshed.

11. And the bodies of many thousands are laid low in the earth, while the bodies of many thousands are moldering in heaps upon the face of the earth; yea, and many thousands are mourning for the loss of their kindred, because they have reason to fear, according to the promises of the Lord, that they are consigned to a state of endless wo.

12. While many thousands of others truly mourn for the loss of their kindred, yet they rejoice and exult in the hope, and even know, according to the promises of the Lord, that they are raised to dwell at the right hand of God, in a state of never-ending happiness.

13. And thus we see how great the inequality of man is because of sin and transgression, and the power of the devil, which comes

by the cunning plans which he hath devised to ensnare the hearts of men.

14. And thus we see the great call of diligence of men to labor in the vineyards of the Lord; and thus we see the great reason of sorrow, and also of rejoicing— sorrow because of death and destruction among men, and joy because of the light of Christ unto life.

1. Church . . . established] The Lord's house being a house of order, whatever organization is necessary to teach and administer the ordinances of the gospel has, from the days of Adam, always been established among the Lord's people. Among all peoples and in all dispensations the Saints have met together to edify and instruct one another.

6. A time of much fasting and prayer] Fasting was commonly associated with times of grief or sorrow among the ancients. The Psalmist indicated sympathy with his adversaries' sickness by fasting (see Psalm 35:13). Old Testament texts suggest that there was a mourning fast in behalf of the dead (see 1 Samuel 31:13; 2 Samuel 1:12). David, for instance, demonstrated his grief at Abner's death by fasting (see 2 Samuel 3:35). It appears that such a fast was preserved as a funeral custom among the Nephites (see Alma 30:2).

8. Sorrows . . . afflictions . . . incomprehensible joy] This strange but common threesome capsulizes not only the missionary experiences of the sons of Mosiah but also the experience of countless other missionaries and Apostles of the Lord as they have gone forth to the nations and peoples of the earth. Indeed, the Son of Man himself was "a man of sorrows, and acquainted with grief" (Isaiah 53:3–4; Mosiah 14:3–4). Yet notwithstanding the difficulties associated with laboring in the Lord's cause, we are assured that "eye hath not seen, nor ear heard, neither have entered into the heart of man, the things which God hath prepared for them that love him" (1 Corinthians 2:9).

11–12. To those of our day, the Lord has given what has properly been called the law of the mourner. It is stated thus: "Thou shalt live together in love, insomuch that thou shalt weep for the loss of them that die, and more especially for those that have not hope of a glorious resurrection. And it shall come to pass that those that die in me shall not taste of death, for it shall be sweet unto them; and they that die not in me, wo unto them, for their death is bitter." (D&C 42:45–47.)

11. A state of endless wo] "Now this is the state of the souls of the wicked, yea, in darkness, and a state of awful, fearful looking for the fiery indignation of the wrath of God upon them; thus they remain in this state . . . until the time of their resurrection" (Alma 40:14). From modern revelation we learn that the expression "endless wo" does not mean that the intended punishment is of endless duration, but rather that it is God's punishment, and God is endless; therefore he has chosen to call that punishment that comes from him by this name, or endless. This is done to make the warning more express, "that it might work upon the hearts of the children of men" in the hope that it will dissuade them from sin. (See D&C 19:4–13.)

12. A state of never-ending happiness] The righteous will know happiness in paradise, in the resurrection, and throughout the endless ages of eternity. It is their right to sit down in the kingdom of heaven with their righteous progenitors "to go no more out" (Alma 7:25).

13. How great the inequality of man] That is to say, men and women establish inequality because of their choices—they either open themselves to the happiness and joy of the blessings of God or they block the blessings of that healing and lifting influence which is within reach of all.

14. The great call of diligence] That is, there is a great call to diligent service in the labors of our Master. Each and every one of us is to serve with all his heart, might, mind, and strength (see D&C 4:2).

14. Joy because of the light of Christ unto life] "Ye are a chosen generation, a royal priesthood, an holy nation, a peculiar [purchased] people; that ye should shew forth the praises of him who hath called you out of darkness into his marvelous light" (1 Peter 2:9).

Alma's Desire to Teach with the Voice of an Angel

Alma 29:1–3

1. O that I were an angel, and could have the wish of mine heart, that I might go forth and speak with the trump of God, with a voice to shake the earth, and cry repentance unto every people!

2. Yea, I would declare unto every soul, as with the voice of thunder, repentance and the plan of redemption, that they should repent and come unto our God, that there might not be more sorrow upon all the face of the earth.

3. But behold, I am a man, and do sin in my wish; for I ought to be content with the things which the Lord hath allotted unto me.

1–3. In this beautiful and spirit-filled expression, Alma wishes for the voice of an angel and the spiritual power to declare the message of salvation to every people upon the face of the earth. Perhaps he desires to affect the world for good just as the angel who appeared to him and the sons of Mosiah had dramatically affected the course of events in Nephite history. He then chides himself, saying, "I do sin in my wish," and concludes that he ought to be content with the office and call the Lord has given him. In the verses that follow he declares that the Lord grants to all men according to their desires (verses 4 and 5). What, then, of his desire to raise the warning voice among all nations? Ought it not be noted that, through the going forth of the Book of Mormon, Alma does indeed speak with the eloquence of an angel to those of every nation, kindred, and tongue! Ought it not be noted also that there was no sin in his desire to declare the gospel to the peoples of the earth, and that people by the tens of thousands, yes, by the tens of millions, will yet hear this voice as the voice of an angel echoing through the ages to touch their hearts and direct their course. The earth has known few teachers the equal of Alma the Younger.

1. O that I were an angel] We observe again that an "angel" is a messenger of God and that Alma is, indeed, such a messenger (see commentary on Alma 27:4). We are also reminded of the words of Nephi, wherein he said that angels speak by the power of the Holy Ghost, and that upon receiving the Holy Ghost one could speak with the tongue of angels (2 Nephi 32:2–3). Angels do not have a priesthood beyond that held by mortals, nor do they have a gospel that differs in any way from that known by those in the flesh. It is our right to speak with the same clarity, the same power, and the same assurance known to angels in declaring the gospel. And as to those to whom the gospel is declared, it will make no difference to the heavenly tribunal if they rejected the message of a mortal or an immortal messenger, for the message and its power to cleanse sin and bring salvation are the same.

2. Plan of redemption] That plan announced in heaven whereby salvation could come to all men through the atonement of Christ and obedience to the laws and ordinances of his gospel.

2. That there might not be more sorrow] How sweet it is to imagine the condition of mankind should all of the earth's inhabitants choose to live gospel standards! The peace, prosperity, and blessings that would follow would be sufficient to attest to the verity of the gospel plan. It is beyond the capacity of the mortal mind to concoct a more perfect Utopia.

3. I ought to be content] Each of us must, through the influence and comfort of the Holy Spirit, come to understand and appreciate and value his or her own assignment, learn to magnify it, and thereby experience the accompanying joy which follows in the wake of faithful service. It has been wisely said that in the Lord's service it matters not *where* we serve but *how*.

God Grants unto Men According to Their Desires

Alma 29:4–7

4. I ought not to harrow up in my desires, the firm decree of a just God, for I know that he granteth unto men according to their desire, whether it be unto death or unto life; yea, I know that he allotteth unto men, yea, decreeth unto them decrees which are unalterable, according to their wills, whether they be unto salvation or unto destruction.

5. Yea, and I know that good and evil have come before all men; he that knoweth not good from evil is blameless; but he that knoweth good and evil, to him it is given according to his desires, whether he desireth good or evil, life or death, joy or remorse of conscience.

6. Now, seeing that I know these things, why should I desire more than to perform the work to which I have been called?

7. Why should I desire that I were an angel, that I could speak unto all the ends of the earth?

4–5. Agency is the gift of heaven. It is only in and through the proper exercise of this gift that men and women can obtain exaltation, that they can willingly serve God and become like him. As with all of heaven's gifts, its power to exalt is matched by an equal power to condemn when abused or misused. Agency is fruit plucked from the tree of life. In it are seeds which, if properly planted, nurtured, and pruned, will bear the fruits of salvation; but if allowed to grow wild, they will produce the gall of bitterness and eventual destruction. Agency is our glory or our condemnation (see D&C 93:31–32).

4. A just God] God possesses the attribute of justice in its perfection. "Without the idea of the existence of the attribute justice in the Deity," Joseph Smith declared, "men could not have confidence sufficient to place themselves under his guidance and direction; for they would be filled with fear and doubt lest the judge of all the earth would not do right, and thus fear or doubt, existing in the mind, would preclude the possibility of the exercise of faith in him for life and salvation" (*Lectures on Faith* 4:13).

5. He that knoweth not good from evil is blameless] Accountability is something we grow into. That is, children "begin to become accountable." We do so by learning to distinguish between opposites, so that we might clearly choose between good and evil. The precious child born without the ability to so distinguish stands blameless before the Lord. See D&C 29:46–50.

5. He that knoweth good and evil, to him it is given according to his desires] Given the necessary time, both the righteous and the unrighteous desires of our hearts will find a way to express themselves. This is a simple manifestation of the verity that desires govern our choices and choices take us where we really want to go. It is also inherent in the plan of salvation that judgment involve a perfect blend of works and desires (see Alma 41:3; D&C 18:38; 137:9). Thus, if we really wanted to do something—be it good or evil—but were unable to do it because of circumstances beyond our control, short of our repenting, a just God will reward or punish us as if we had actually done it.

"The laws of God can reward a righteous desire or attitude because an omniscient God can determine it," Elder Dallin H. Oaks has written. "If a person does not perform a particular commandment because he is genuinely unable to do so, but truly would if he could, our Heavenly Father will know this and will reward that person accordingly.

"Upon the same principle, evil thoughts or desires are sinful under the laws of God even though not translated into the actions that would make them punishable under the laws of man. Similarly, if a person performs a seemingly righteous act but does so for the wrong reasons, such as to achieve a selfish purpose, his *hands* may be clean but his *heart* is not 'pure.' His act will not be counted for righteousness." (Dallin H. Oaks, *Pure in Heart*, pp. 12–13.)

God Grants Nations As Much Light As They Will Receive

Alma 29:8

> 8. For behold, the Lord doth grant unto all nations, of their own nation and tongue, to teach his word, yea, in wisdom, all that he seeth fit that they should have; therefore we see that the Lord doth counsel in wisdom, according to that which is just and true.

8. As the treasures of heaven are rationed to men according to the preparation they have made, so it is with nations. They too receive of heaven's light as they have prepared themselves for it and as they are worthy to receive it. Thus, as some people have been favored of God and greatly blessed, conversely some nations and some people have chosen to be hard of heart and to walk in darkness.

God is merciful and gracious. He bestows upon individuals and nations that degree of eternal light which they are equipped and prepared to receive. He is the Father and God of all men and women of all ages and all cultures, and his love for them is as great as it is for the Christian nations or the Latter-day Saints. It is a doctrine of the true Church that the Almighty has granted portions of his light to such notables as Socrates, Confucius, Buddha, the Reformers, and to many, many others, in order that whole nations might be lifted to higher standards of living. Ultimately, of course, there is only one standard—the gospel standard; and God will provide an opportunity for every soul to receive the fulness of the everlasting gospel either in this world or in the world to come. (See First Presidency Message, 15 February 1978; see also Joseph F. Smith, *Gospel Doctrine*, p. 31.)

Prophetically we have been told that the restored gospel must go to those of every nation, kindred, tongue, and people (Revelation 14:6–7). A revelation to Joseph Smith adds that the message of the Restoration must go to all nations in their own language (D&C 90:11). Alma's declaration suggests that not only must it go to all nations in their own language, but that it must also be declared by their own people. That is, the gospel must yet be taught in Russia by Russian elders, in China by Chinese elders, and so forth throughout the nations of the earth. Such a view is in harmony with Nephi's vision of the last days in which he saw congregations of the Saints "upon all the face of the earth" before the return of Christ (see 1 Nephi 14:12–14).

Alma Rejoices over Those Who Have Repented

Alma 29:9–10

9. I know that which the Lord hath commanded me, and I glory in it. I do not glory of myself, but I glory in that which the Lord hath commanded me; yea, and this is my glory, that perhaps I may be an instrument in the hands of God to bring some soul to repentance; and this is my joy.

10. And behold, when I see many of my brethren truly penitent, and coming to the Lord their God, then is my soul filled with joy; then do I remember what the Lord has done for me, yea, even that he hath heard my prayer; yea, then do I remember his merciful arm which he extended towards me.

9–10. Peace and joy are the wages of those who labor in the Lord's vineyard. As Alma rejoices over those whom he has been instrumental in bringing back into the fold, we are reminded of the manner in which his own father rejoiced when his then wayward son was struck down by the angel of the Lord. When Alma the Younger's companions found that he could neither speak nor move they carried him to his father and related to the latter all that had happened. Strange though it may have seemed, the elder Alma's heart was filled with joy and praise when he looked upon the body of his much-loved son, for he knew it was God's power that had brought about his son's condition and that his long-continued prayers had been answered. In his joy he gathered the people to witness this mighty manifestation of the goodness and might of the Lord. Unitedly they fasted and prayed for the stricken youth. For two days they continued their supplications, at the end of which time the young Alma stood upon his feet and declared: "I have repented of my sins, and have been redeemed of the Lord; behold I am born of the Spirit" (Mosiah 27:24). Scriptural writ contains no more lofty and dramatic language than that which he used to describe the anguish and suffering associated with his repentance and the "exquisite and sweet" joy that he experienced in his redemption (Alma 36:21).

Alma Remembers the Captivity of His Fathers

Alma 29:11–12

11. Yea, and I also remember the captivity of my fathers; for I surely do know that the Lord did deliver them out of bondage, and by this did establish his church; yea, the Lord God, the God of Abraham, the God of Isaac, and the God of Jacob, did deliver them out of bondage.

12. Yea, I have always remembered the captivity of my fathers; and that same God who delivered them out of the hands of the Egyptians did deliver them out of bondage.

11–12. When the angel of the Lord appeared to the wayward Alma and his companions, he specifically charged Alma to remember the captivity of his fathers in the lands of Helam and Nephi and the manner in which the Lord had delivered them (see Mosiah 27:16). Alma was true to that charge and apparently made frequent reference to it in his preaching. He came to see the Lord's deliverance of the repentant nation as a type for the deliverance of all who have labored under the bondage of sin and sought redemption through Christ. See also Alma 5:5–6; 36:2.

12. I have always remembered] Memory is a powerful motivator to righteousness. The repentant sinner need only remember the agony and suffering through which he once passed on the road to spiritual recovery. The prosperous man need only remember an earlier life when food and clothing and shelter were more difficult to obtain. And a free people need only reflect seriously upon a time when the living God miraculously delivered them or their ancestors from bondage.

Alma Rejoices in the Success of the Lord's Work

Alma 29:13–17

13. Yea, and that same God did establish his church among them; yea, and that same God hath called me by a holy calling, to preach the word unto this people, and hath given me much success, in the which my joy is full.

14. But I do not joy in my own success alone, but my joy is more full because of the success of my brethren, who have been up to the land of Nephi.

15. Behold, they have labored exceedingly, and have brought forth much fruit; and how great shall be their reward!

16. Now, when I think of the success of these my brethren my soul is carried away, even to the separation of it from the body, as it were, so great is my joy.

17. And now may God grant unto these, my brethren, that they may sit down in the kingdom of God; yea, and also all those who are the fruit of their labors that they may go no more out, but that they may praise him forever. And may God grant that it may be done according to my words, even as I have spoken. Amen.

13–17. Alma was called of God to declare repentance among the Nephites, while Ammon and his brothers and other missionaries chose to declare the same truths among the Lamanites. Each of these men magnified his calling and, in so doing, sanctified his own soul and found cause for great rejoicing in the success of his fellow servants. Each was entitled to know the fulness of the joy of the Lord.

13. Called . . . by a holy calling] See commentary on Alma 5:3.

15. They . . . have brought forth much fruit] Indeed, there had been a bountiful harvest of souls. Many thousands had come unto Christ through the ordinances of salvation and were now on that road which leads to eternal life.

16. See commentary on Alma 27:17–19.

17. That they may go no more out] That is: "May they, through God's help, stay faithful and forever intact in the fold of the Good Shepherd. May they never wander from the strait and narrow path." Mortality is a probationary estate in which even the sanctified are warned to take heed lest they fall (see D&C 20:34). Those who in death obtain paradise, or the rest of the Lord, are no longer in a probationary estate. For the faithful, the day of probation ends at the time of death. Satan can no longer have any power over them. (See Robert L. Millet and Joseph Fielding McConkie, *The Life Beyond*, pp. 140–41.)

Keeping the Commandments Brings Peace

Alma 30:1–5

1. Behold, now it came to pass that after the people of Ammon were established in the land of Jershon, yea, and also after the Lamanites were driven out of the land, and their dead were buried by the people of the land—
2. Now their dead were not numbered because of the greatness of their numbers; neither were the dead of the Nephites numbered—but it came to pass after they had buried their dead, and also after the days of fasting, and mourning, and prayer, (and it was in the sixteenth year of the reign of the judges over the people of Nephi) there began to be continual peace throughout all the land.
3. Yea, and the people did observe to keep the commandments of the Lord; and they were strict in observing the ordinances of God, according to the law of Moses; for they were taught to keep the law of Moses until it should be fulfilled.
4. And thus the people did have no disturbance in all the sixteenth year of the reign of the judges over the people of Nephi.
5. And it came to pass that in the commencement of the seventeenth year of the reign of the judges, there was continual peace.

1–5. Whenever a people live the gospel, whenever they live in harmony with the statutes and ordinances God has given them, whenever they follow the light of their consciences and subscribe to the rules and standards established for those of the household of faith, they come to know the peace of the Spirit. Keeping the commandments brings the quiet assurance that one's course in life is pleasing in the sight of God, a consciousness of victory over self which we know as spirituality. "Learn of me, and listen to my words; walk in the meekness of my Spirit, and you shall have peace in me" (D&C 19:23).

Men's Beliefs Protected by Law

Alma 30:6–11

6. But it came to pass in the latter end of the seventeenth year, there came a man into the land of Zarahemla, and he was Anti-Christ, for he began to preach unto the people against the prophecies which had been spoken by the prophets, concerning the coming of Christ.

7. Now there was no law against a man's belief; for it was strictly contrary to the commands of God that there should be a law which should bring men on to unequal grounds.

8. For thus saith the scripture: Choose ye this day, whom ye will serve.

9. Now if a man desired to serve God, it was his privilege; or rather, if he believed in God it was his privilege to serve him; but if he did not believe in him there was no law to punish him.

10. But if he murdered he was punished unto death; and if he robbed he was also punished; and if he stole he was also punished; and if he committed adultery he was also punished; yea, for all this wickedness they were punished.

11. For there was a law that men should be judged according to their crimes. Nevertheless, there was no law against a man's belief; therefore, a man was punished only for the crimes which he had done; therefore all men were on equal grounds.

6. Here we find an interesting definition of an anti-Christ: one who defies and denies the prophecies concerning the coming of Christ. This definition would, of course, pertain primarily to those who lived before the meridian of time. In our day we would speak of an anti-Christ as one who denies the divine birth of Jesus; who downplays the significance of his teachings; who claims that Jesus' sufferings, death, and resurrection have no significance for mankind. Many in this dispensation have been seduced into the damnable heresy that Jesus was merely a good man, a brilliant speaker, and a loving and tender example of mercy and forgiveness—these things alone. The restored gospel—especially as made known through the Book of Mormon—testifies that Jesus Christ was and is divine, that he is God.

7. There was no law against a man's belief] See commentary on Alma 1:17.

7. A law which should bring men on to unequal grounds] That is, the Lord and his servants had forbidden discrimination according to belief. The Lord desires that all his children in all ages accept the gospel and affiliate themselves with his true Church. He will not bring this to pass, however, through pressure or unrighteous dominion of any kind. The Nephite society, though theocratic in nature, did not require nonmembers of the Church to accept purely gospel laws (except as those pertained to behavior and life in society), nor did it make it disadvantageous in society to remain outside the faith.

8. See Moses 6:33; Joshua 24:15.

10. Laws of justice, equity, and reparation, a vital part of Israelite social and religious life, were perpetuated among the Nephites.

10. If he murdered he was punished unto death] Capital punishment was in effect among the Nephites. It was the law in ancient Israel and was carried to the New World by this group of Hebrews. See JST, Genesis 9:12–13; Alma 1:14, 18; D&C 42:19.

The Diabolical Doctrines of an Anti-Christ

Alma 30:12–18

12. And this Anti-Christ, whose name was Korihor, (and the law could have no hold upon him) began to preach unto the people that there should be no Christ. And after this manner did he preach, saying:

13. O ye that are bound down under a foolish and a vain hope, why do ye yoke yourselves with such foolish things? Why do ye look for a Christ? For no man can know of anything which is to come.

14. Behold, these things which ye call prophecies, which ye say are handed down by holy prophets, behold, they are foolish traditions of your fathers.

15. How do ye know of their surety? Behold, ye cannot know of things which ye do not see; therefore ye cannot know that there shall be a Christ.

16. Ye look forward and say that ye see a remission of your sins. But behold, it is the effect of a

frenzied mind; and this derangement of your minds comes because of the traditions of your fathers, which lead you away into a belief of things which are not so.

17. And many more such things did he say unto them, telling them that there could be no atonement made for the sins of men, but every man fared in this life according to the management of the creature; therefore every man prospered according to his genius, and that every man conquered according to his strength; and whatsoever a man did was no crime.

18. And thus he did preach unto them, leading away the hearts of many, causing them to lift up their heads in their wickedness, yea, leading away many women, and also men, to commit whoredoms—telling them that when a man was dead, that was the end thereof.

13–18. The Book of Mormon is everlastingly relevant. It is at once timeless and timely. President Ezra Taft Benson has taught us repeatedly that the Book of Mormon was written for our day. He writes: "The Nephites never had the book; neither did the Lamanites of ancient times. It was meant for us. Mormon wrote near the end of the Nephite civilization. Under the inspiration of God, who sees all things from the beginning, he abridged centuries of records, choosing the stories, speeches, and events that would be most helpful to us. Each of the major writers of the Book of Mormon testified that he wrote for future generations [see 2 Nephi 25:21; Jacob 1:3; Enos 1:15–16; Jarom 1:2; Mormon 7:1; Mormon 8:34–35; 9:30]. . . . If they saw our day, and chose those things which would be of greatest worth to us, is not that how we should study the Book of Mormon? We should constantly ask ourselves, 'Why did the Lord inspire Mormon (or Moroni or Alma) to include that in his record? What lesson can I learn from that to help me live in this day and age?'" (*A Witness and a Warning*, pp. 19–20.)

President Benson has further explained: "The Book of Mormon brings men to Christ through two basic means. First, it tells in a plain manner of Christ and His gospel. It testifies of His divinity and of the necessity for a Redeemer and the need of our putting trust in Him. It bears witness of the Fall and the Atonement and the first principles of the gospel, including our need of a broken heart and a contrite spirit and a spiritual rebirth. It proclaims we must endure to the end in righteousness and live the moral life of a Saint.

"Second, the Book of Mormon exposes the enemies of Christ. It confounds false doctrines and lays down contention. (See 2 Nephi 3:12.) It fortifies the humble followers of Christ against the evil designs, strategies, and doctrines of the devil in our day. The type of apostates in the Book of Mormon is similar to the type we have today. God, with his infinite foreknowledge, so molded the Book of Mormon that we might see the error and know how to combat false educational, political, religious, and philosophical concepts of our time." (*A Witness and a Warning*, p. 3.)

13. Bound down under a foolish and a vain hope] Here Korihor seeks to make the believers self-conscious for holding forth a belief in that which is to come, in the unseen, in that which mortal ear has not heard. He plays upon their sense of security by suggesting that they are bound down, yoked, by their acceptance of specific religious beliefs and practices. Few things are more threatening to a people than to suggest that they are blindly obedient or, worse yet, that they are slaves to their religious way of life. The natural man is prone to lash out with: "No. I am not a slave. I can do as I please. Just watch this . . ." Korihor, like his modern counterparts, offers to liberate us from what he thinks of as our naive worldview, to set us free from ourselves. On the other hand, the wisest among us—those who find satisfaction in serving God, in keeping his commandments, those whose system of values and feelings of personal worth derive from sources vertical rather than horizontal—say: "I obey because I choose to do so. I do these things because they are what I truly want to do. I am free to choose, and this is what I choose to do."

13. No man can know of anything which is to come] This is a denial of prophecy, a denial of any knowledge beyond that which we have at the present moment. Anti-Christs, always natural men, consider things of the Spirit to be foolish (see 1 Corinthians 2:11–14). Their tightly controlled epistemological system does not permit the discussion (and certainly not the acceptance) of such things as spirit or revelation or inspiration.

15. Ye cannot know of things which ye do not see] This position is a radical form of empiricism, a pure naturalism. To state it in another way: "If I cannot see it, it does not exist. I can only deal with that which is seen or felt or heard by the physical senses." From the world's perspective, seeing is believing. From the gospel perspective, believing is seeing.

16. It is the effect of a frenzied mind] This is another way of saying that those who feel some need for redemption from sin are deluded, "deranged" in mind, and irrationally concerned with matters which need not trouble them.

17. For Korihor there was no need for an atonement, simply because there was nothing from which man needed redemption.

17. Every man fared in this life according to the management of the creature] Korihor was a secular humanist, as was Nehor, his predecessor (see commentary on Alma 1:4). He believed that if success came it was because the individual had earned it. If progress was made it was because of hard work, consistent effort, and fulfillment of one's goals. The humanist focuses upon man: Man is the measure; all things rotate around man; man is the center of the universe; man has the power to solve his own problems, the power to make himself happy, the power to do anything he sets his mind to. Humanism points toward man's genius, toward man's strength, toward man's works and accomplishments. It is an anti-Christian philosophy and is thus false, devilish, and destructive. It draws man's attention away from the one source which could bring liberation from this world's woes and give satisfaction and happiness in the world to come. It deflects one's vision away from Christ and away from that grace or enabling power which comes from him.

17. Whatsoever a man did was no crime] We can now see why Korihor taught that there should be no Christ. From his point of view there was no need for a Christ, inasmuch as there was no sin. This is a form of ethical relativism, a statement that there are no absolute truths and thus no absolute values, no rights and wrongs. One can appreciate why Korihor's doctrine was so well received by the worldly people in Zarahemla.

18. Lift up their heads in their wickedness] That is, he encouraged them to feel pride in their actions, to feel no shame in their sins. See Alma 1:4.

18. When a man was dead, that was the end] What we believe certainly affects what we do. That is, our behavior follows directly on the heels of our beliefs. If one believes that all life ends at death, that there is no continuation of the spirit following our mortal demise, then one might as well grab for all the excitement he can while he is still breathing. It is not surprising, therefore, that nihilism, a denial of immortality, should in many cases lead to a life of immorality.

The Nephites Confront Korihor

Alma 30:19–29

19. Now this man went over to the land of Jershon also, to preach these things among the people of Ammon, who were once the people of the Lamanites.

20. But behold they were more wise than many of the Nephites; for they took him, and bound him, and carried him before Ammon, who was a high priest over that people.

21. And it came to pass that he caused that he should be carried out of the land. And he came over into the land of Gideon, and began to preach unto them also; and here he did not have much success, for he was taken and bound and carried before the high priest, and also the chief judge over the land.

22. And it came to pass that the high priest said unto him: Why do ye go about perverting the ways of the Lord? Why do ye teach this people that there shall be no

Christ, to interrupt their rejoicings? Why do ye speak against all the prophecies of the holy prophets?

23. Now the high priest's name was Giddonah. And Korihor said unto him: Because I do not teach the foolish traditions of your fathers, and because I do not teach this people to bind themselves down under the foolish ordinances and performances which are laid down by ancient priests, to usurp power and authority over them, to keep them in ignorance, that they may not lift up their heads, but be brought down according to thy words.

24. Ye say that this people is a free people. Behold, I say they are in bondage. Ye say that those ancient prophecies are true. Behold, I say that ye do not know that they are true.

25. Ye say that this people is a guilty and a fallen people, because

of the transgression of a parent. Behold, I say that a child is not guilty because of its parents.

26. And ye also say that Christ shall come. But behold, I say that ye do not know that there shall be a Christ. And ye say also that he shall be slain for the sins of the world—

27. And thus ye lead away this people after the foolish traditions of your fathers, and according to your own desires; and ye keep them down, even as it were in bondage, that ye may glut yourselves with the labors of their hands, that they durst not look up with boldness, and that they durst not enjoy their rights and privileges.

28. Yea, they durst not make use of that which is their own lest they should offend their priests, who do yoke them according to their desires, and have brought them to believe, by their traditions and their dreams and their whims and their visions and their pretended mysteries, that they should, if they did not do according to their words, offend some unknown being, who they say is God—a being who never has been seen or known, who never was nor ever will be.

29. Now when the high priest and the chief judge saw the hardness of his heart, yea, when they saw that he would revile even against God, they would not make any reply to his words; but they caused that he should be bound; and they delivered him up into the hands of the officers, and sent him to the land of Zarahemla, that he might be brought before Alma, and the chief judge who was governor over all the land.

19–29. Again, we would presume that the reason why Korihor was apprehended was that he had encouraged (through his preaching) the kinds of actions which were unlawful in Nephite society. Korihor was inspired by the demonic and spoke with great confidence and audacity before Ammon and Giddonah. Eventually he was brought before Alma, who met his challenges with the power of God.

23. Here Korihor challenges the institution and the authority of the priesthood by bringing charges of priestcraft and unrighteous dominion against the priests of the Church.

24. I say they are in bondage] See commentary on verse 13.

24. Ye do not know that they are true] "The doubter errs grossly through generalizing beyond his own experiences. What he has not experienced, no one else can. Because *he* does not know, no one knows; because he cannot feel, surely no one has felt; because he is lacking in evidence concerning the coming of a Christ, unquestionably the evidence amassed by every believing soul is either insufficient or naively misinterpreted. Those who dare not believe dare not allow others to believe." (*Commentary* 2:86.)

25. This is subtle. It is a carefully contrived argument which plays upon a truth to put forward a falsehood. To be sure, all mankind are fallen creatures as a result of the transgression of our first parents in Eden. The Lord, however, atoned for the "original guilt" (Moses 6:54) associated with that specific act of transgression. A child is indeed not guilty because of its parents (see Articles of Faith 1:2), but the child does inherit a fallen or mortal nature through conception, a nature which must be renovated through the cleansing powers of the blood of Christ.

26. Ye do not know] See commentary on verse 24.

27–28. One whose motives are malevolent cannot conceive of benevolence, of motives that are pure. Korihor had a secret agenda, a quest for power and riches and fame, and he therefore assumed the same of others.

28. God . . . never has been seen or known] See commentary on verse 24.

Faith Comes by Hearkening, Not by Signs

Alma 30:30–60

30. And it came to pass that when he was brought before Alma and the chief judge, he did go on in the same manner as he did in the land of Gideon; yea, he went on to blaspheme.

31. And he did rise up in great swelling words before Alma, and did revile against the priests and teachers, accusing them of leading away the people after the silly traditions of their fathers, for the sake of glutting on the labors of the people.

32. Now Alma said unto him: Thou knowest that we do not glut ourselves upon the labors of this people; for behold I have labored even from the commencement of the reign of the judges until now, with mine own hands for my support, notwithstanding my many travels round about the land to declare the word of God unto my people.

33. And notwithstanding the many labors which I have performed in the church, I have never received so much as even one senine for my labor; neither has any of my brethren, save it were in the judgment-seat; and then we have received only according to law for our time.

34. And now, if we do not receive anything for our labors in the church, what doth it profit us to labor in the church save it were to declare the truth, that we may have rejoicings in the joy of our brethren?

35. Then why sayest thou that we preach unto this people to get gain, when thou, of thyself, knowest that we receive no gain? And now, believest thou that we deceive this people, that causes such joy in their hearts?

36. And Korihor answered him, Yea.

37. And then Alma said unto him: Believest thou that there is a God?

38. And he answered, Nay.

39. Now Alma said unto him: Will ye deny again that there is a

God, and also deny the Christ? For
behold, I say unto you, I know
there is a God, and also that Christ
shall come.

40. And now what evidence
have ye that there is no God, or
that Christ cometh not? I say unto
you that ye have none, save it be
your word only.

41. But, behold, I have all things
as a testimony that these things
are true; and ye also have all
things as a testimony unto you
that they are true; and will ye
deny them? Believest thou that
these things are true?

42. Behold, I know that thou
believest, but thou art possessed
with a lying spirit, and ye have put
off the Spirit of God that it may
have no place in you; but the devil
has power over you, and he doth
carry you about, working devices
that he may destroy the children
of God.

43. And now Korihor said unto
Alma: If thou wilt show me a sign,
that I may be convinced that there
is a God, yea, show unto me that
he hath power, and then will I be
convinced of the truth of thy
words.

44. But Alma said unto him:
Thou hast had signs enough; will
ye tempt your God? Will ye say,
Show unto me a sign, when ye
have the testimony of all these thy
brethren, and also all the holy
prophets? The scriptures are laid
before thee, yea, and all things
denote there is a God; yea, even
the earth, and all things that are
upon the face of it, yea, and its
motion, yea, and also all the
planets which move in their
regular form do witness that there
is a Supreme Creator.

45. And yet do ye go about,
leading away the hearts of this
people, testifying unto them there

is no God? And yet will ye deny
against all these witnesses? And
he said: Yea, I will deny, except ye
shall show me a sign.

46. And now it came to pass
that Alma said unto him: Behold, I
am grieved because of the hardness of your heart, yea, that ye
will still resist the spirit of the
truth, that thy soul may be
destroyed.

47. But behold, it is better that
thy soul should be lost than that
thou shouldst be the means of
bringing many souls down to
destruction, by thy lying and by
thy flattering words; therefore if
thou shalt deny again, behold God
shall smite thee, that thou shalt
become dumb, that thou shalt
never open thy mouth any more,
that thou shalt not deceive this
people any more.

48. Now Korihor said unto him:
I do not deny the existence of a
God, but I do not believe that
there is a God; and I say also, that
ye do not know that there is a
God; and except ye show me a
sign, I will not believe.

49. Now Alma said unto him:
This will I give unto thee for a
sign, that thou shalt be struck
dumb, according to my words; and
I say, that in the name of God, ye
shall be struck dumb, that ye shall
no more have utterance.

50. Now when Alma had said
these words, Korihor was struck
dumb, that he could not have
utterance, according to the words
of Alma.

51. And now when the chief
judge saw this, he put forth his
hand and wrote unto Korihor,
saying: Art thou convinced of the
power of God? In whom did ye
desire that Alma should show
forth his sign? Would ye that he
should afflict others, to show unto

thee a sign? Behold, he has showed unto you a sign; and now will ye dispute more?

52. And Korihor put forth his hand and wrote, saying: I know that I am dumb, for I cannot speak; and I know that nothing save it were the power of God could bring this upon me; yea, and I always knew that there was a God.

53. But behold, the devil hath deceived me; for he appeared unto me in the form of an angel, and said unto me: Go and reclaim this people, for they have all gone astray after an unknown God. And he said unto me: There is no God; yea, and he taught me that which I should say. And I have taught his words; and I taught them because they were pleasing unto the carnal mind; and I taught them, even until I had much success, insomuch that I verily believed that they were true; and for this cause I withstood the truth, even until I have brought this great curse upon me.

54. Now when he had said this, he besought that Alma should pray unto God, that the curse might be taken from him.

55. But Alma said unto him: If this curse should be taken from thee thou wouldst again lead away the hearts of this people; therefore, it shall be unto thee even as the Lord will.

56. And it came to pass that the curse was not taken off of Korihor;

but he was cast out, and went about from house to house begging for his food.

57. Now the knowledge of what had happened unto Korihor was immediately published throughout all the land; yea, the proclamation was sent forth by the chief judge to all the people in the land, declaring unto those who had believed in the words of Korihor that they must speedily repent, lest the same judgments would come unto them.

58. And it came to pass that they were all convinced of the wickedness of Korihor; therefore they were all converted again unto the Lord; and this put an end to the iniquity after the manner of Korihor. And Korihor did go about from house to house, begging food for his support.

59. And it came to pass that as he went forth among the people, yea, among a people who had separated themselves from the Nephites and called themselves Zoramites, being led by a man whose name was Zoram—and as he went forth amongst them, behold, he was run upon and trodden down, even until he was dead.

60. And thus we see the end of him who perverteth the ways of the Lord; and thus we see that the devil will not support his children at the last day, but doth speedily drag them down to hell.

---

30. He went on to blaspheme] "Blasphemy consists in either or both of the following: 1. Speaking irreverently, evilly, abusively, or scurrilously against God or sacred things; or 2. Speaking profanely or falsely about Deity.

"Among a great host of impious and sacrilegious speaking that constitute blasphemy are such things as: Taking the name of God in vain; evil-speaking about the Lord's anointed; belittling sacred temple ordinances, or patriarchal blessings, or sacramental administrations; claiming unwarranted divine authority; and promulgating with profane piety a false system of salvation." (Bruce R. McConkie, *Mormon Doctrine*, p. 90; see also Robert L. Millet and Joseph Fielding McConkie, *In His Holy Name*, chapter 8.)

32–33. See Alma 11:1.

34. See commentary on verses 27–28.

39. I know there is a God, and also that Christ shall come] Alma here demonstrates the one thing that the believer can and should do in the face of opposition and challenge: bear fervent witness and leave the rest to God. Alma knows and he knows that he knows, and that is all that matters. He feels neither threatened nor overly troubled by an unbeliever, except as the unbeliever imposes his skepticism upon the innocent and the unwary.

40–41. "We ask, have the united efforts of all the Korihors the world has ever known successfully proved that there is no God? Have they proved that Jesus was not the Christ, the promised Messiah? Where is the man that can refute the testimony of those humble shepherds who heard the heavenly host sing, and who found the infant child wrapped in swaddling clothes, lying in a manger? Who is it that can come forth and refute the testimony of the wise men who followed the star and paid homage to the Christ child? Who is it that can discredit the testimony of John that the heavens were opened to him and that he heard a voice saying, 'This is my beloved Son?'

"Can the combined wisdom of the ages refute the reality of the resurrection? How can anyone prove that Christ did not break the bands of death? . . . And what of the testimony of Joseph Smith and Sidney Rigdon that the heavens were opened to them. . . . What evidence does one present to an unbiased jury to prove that on a beautiful spring morning in the year of 1820 the heavens were not opened, that the Father and the Son did not appear to the youthful Joseph Smith? How does one disprove the testimony of a prophet? . . .

"We accept the feelings of the Spirit or we reject them, but we do not argue them. The Sadducees and Pharisees taunted Jesus for proof, yet when it was presented in overwhelming abundance they continued to disbelieve. Be assured that when such people seek proof, that proof is the last thing in the world that they really want. As to the Korihors, we need not assume the burden of proof that is rightly theirs. If they assert we are without a God, without prophets, and without revelation, it is for them to prove it. We await that proof as have the Saints of God from the days of

Adam." (Joseph Fielding McConkie and Robert L. Millet, *Sustaining and Defending the Faith,* pp. 92–94.)

41. I have all things as a testimony] To those who hearken to the voice of the Spirit, who open their hearts to things as they really are, all things bear witness that there is a God. Alma will enumerate some of these things (see verse 44).

42. I know that thou believest] See verse 52; Jacob 7:14; Alma 11:24.

42. Thou art possessed with a lying spirit] Korihor was possessed with the motives, the thoughts, the feelings of the father of lies.

42. Ye have put off the Spirit of God that it may have no place in you] Amulek will later explain to the Zoramites: "If ye have procrastinated the day of your repentance even until death, behold, ye have become subjected to the spirit of the devil, and he doth seal you his; therefore, the Spirit of the Lord hath withdrawn from you, and hath no place in you, and the devil hath all power over you" (Alma 34:35).

43. If thou wilt show me a sign] Korihor is banking on the prevalence of an important principle—that generally speaking God does not give signs to the unfaithful. Anti-Christs know this. They know, as does their master, that signs follow faith, that the heavens seldom if ever vouchsafe the miraculous and the wondrous in behalf of the unbelieving. And thus when no sign is given they feel they have evidence for their own position. Unfortunately for this strategy, as in the cases of Sherem (see Jacob 7), an exception is made; a sign is granted, a condemnatory sign. For a discussion of the perilous end of sign-seekers see *Commentary* 2:87–89.

44. Alma delineates the different ways in which God has manifest himself to the people of the earth, means whereby Korihor and people like him might come to believe in him. They serve as signs, as evidences that he exists. They include: (1) the testimony of Alma and his companions; (2) the testimony of the holy prophets; (3) the word of God as found in scripture; and (4) the testimony of the cosmos, the assurance from nature's design and perfect organization that there is an all-wise and all-powerful creator. See Helaman 8:24; D&C 88:45–47.

47. It is better that thy soul should be lost] Compare 1 Nephi 4:13.

48. It appears that when faced with the possibility of physical harm Korihor moves rapidly from bitter atheism to elusive agnosticism.

49–51. It would appear that Korihor, like Zacharias, the father of John the Baptist (see Luke 1:20, 62–63), was struck *deaf* and dumb, inasmuch as the people had to write to Korihor in order to communicate with him. A modern revelation explains the principle that condemned Korihor: "Faith cometh not by signs, but signs follow those that believe. Yea, signs come by faith, not by the will of men, nor as they please, but by the will of God. Yea, signs come by faith, unto mighty works, for without faith no man pleaseth God; and with whom God is angry he is not well pleased; wherefore, *unto such he showeth no signs, only in wrath unto their condemnation.*" (D&C 63:9–11, italics added.)

51. Would ye that he should afflict others . . . ?] Elder George A. Smith related the following remarkable story: "When The Church of Jesus Christ of Latter-day Saints was first founded, you could see persons rise up and ask, 'What sign will you show us that we may be able to believe?' I recollect a Campbellite preacher who came to Joseph Smith, I think his name was Hayden. He came in and made himself known to Joseph, and said that he had come a considerable distance to be convinced of the truth. 'Why,' said he, 'Mr. Smith, I want to know the truth, and when I am convinced, I will spend all my talents and time in defending and spreading the doctrines of your religion, and I will give you to understand that to convince me is equivalent to convincing all my society, amounting to several hundreds.' Well, Joseph commenced laying before him the coming forth of the work, and the first principles of the Gospel, when Mr. Hayden exclaimed, 'O this is not the evidence I want, the evidence that I wish to have is a notable miracle; I want to see some powerful manifestation of the power of God, I want to see a notable miracle performed; and if you perform such a one, then I will believe with all my heart and soul, and will exert all my power and all my extensive influence to convince others; and if you will not perform a miracle of this kind, then I am your worst and bitterest enemy.' 'Well,' said Joseph, 'what will you have done? Will you be struck blind, or dumb? Will you be paralyzed, or will you have one hand withered? Take your choice, choose which you please, and in the name of the Lord Jesus Christ it shall be done.' 'That is not the kind of miracle I want,' said the preacher. 'Then, sir,' replied Joseph, 'I can perform none; I am not going to bring any trouble upon any body else, sir, to convince you.'" (*JD* 2:326.)

52. I always knew that there was a God] See verse 42. In his heart, in the deepest recesses of his soul, and in spite of his rebellion against light and truth, Korihor—like so many who profane the name and works of the Almighty—knew there was a God.

53. He appeared unto me in the form of an angel] Satan is one who "transformeth himself nigh unto an angel of light" (2 Nephi 9:9; see also 2 Corinthians 11:14). Elder Bruce R. McConkie has written: "Lucifer does not come personally to every false prophet, as he did to Korihor, any more than the Lord comes personally to every true prophet, as he did to Joseph Smith. Such an appearance—either of God on the one hand or of Satan on the other—is, however, the end result of full devotion to the respective causes involved. In each instance an earthly representative, by obedience to the laws that are ordained, may see the face of the master he serves." (*Millennial Messiah*, p. 72.)

53. There is no God] It is not uncommon to find such inconsistencies in the teachings of the perverse. Here we see that Korihor receives his commission from an angel, who then declares that there is no God. Whence, then, came the angel?

53. He taught me that which I should say] Just as the servants of Jehovah who prove worthy have it given to them what they should say (see Helaman 5:18; 13:3; D&C 84:85; 100:5–6), so Satan whispers to his servants that which he would want said.

53. I taught them because they were pleasing unto the carnal mind] Finally we come face to face with the facts: Korihor wrested the scriptures, twisted the truth, and proclaimed a hedonistic and nihilistic way of life in order to appeal to those who sought religious license for their perversion. Indeed, as the Savior taught, a wicked and adulterous generation seeks signs but refuses to hearken to the voice of the Spirit (Matthew 12:39; see also *Teachings,* pp. 157, 278).

53. Until . . . I verily believed that they were true] We only need speak falsehood for a short time before we begin to believe and practice falsehood. We only need to fabricate slightly over time before it begins to be difficult to remember what the truth really is. In the case of Korihor, as his conscience began to be seared by the proclamation of that which degrades and destroys, presumably his value system and his way of life began to shift in order to be consistent with his beliefs.

54–56. This is not the action of an unkind or unmerciful person. Alma refuses to plead with the Lord for the curse to be taken away because he knows, by the spirit of prophecy and revelation, that should Korihor be released from his affliction he will continue in the work of rebellion against the plan and purposes of God.

57–58. One man had perished and many were spared the perils of dwindling in unbelief (see 1 Nephi 4:13). As in the case of Ananias and Sapphira in the New Testament (see Acts 5:11) and of Sherem in the Book of Mormon (see Jacob 7:21–23), the painful reality of the power of God provided a marvelous object lesson that turned the people to the truth and focused them upon the doctrine of Christ.

59. What a poignant and pathetic way to be introduced to the

Zoramites! Korihor, wandering from house to house for support, is trampled down and killed by this group of Nephite dissenters.

60. Here we have one of the most potent of Mormon's precepts, a classic illustration of the "and thus we see" lessons provided by the inspired prophet-writers.

60. The end of him who perverteth the ways of the Lord] The lesson of Korihor is important, not because it is typical of what happens in this life to all anti-Christs but because it illustrates what happens eventually to all such persons. In hell, after death, as well as in eternity, they are silenced as regards dragging others down by the declaration of degrading doctrine. And, like salt that has lost its savor, they are forever cast out of the divine presence.

60. The devil will not support his children at the last day] One who in Faustian fashion sells his soul to Satan need not expect in times of difficulty any sense of fraternal or familial attachment, any type of protection or support from the arch-deceiver. He who knows no love knows no family. He who was willing to promise salvation before the world was made will have no power to raise his own out of perdition. He is not one to be trusted. Indeed, he "rewardeth [his subjects] no good thing" (Alma 34:39).

Alma Encounters the Apostate Zoramites

Alma 31:1–7

1. Now it came to pass that after the end of Korihor, Alma having received tidings that the Zoramites were perverting the ways of the Lord, and that Zoram, who was their leader, was leading the hearts of the people to bow down to dumb idols, his heart again began to sicken because of the iniquity of the people.

2. For it was the cause of great sorrow to Alma to know of iniquity among his people; therefore his heart was exceedingly sorrowful because of the separation of the Zoramites from the Nephites.

3. Now the Zoramites had gathered themselves together in a land which they called Antionum, which was east of the land of Zarahemla, which lay nearly bordering upon the seashore, which was south of the land of Jershon, which also bordered upon the wilderness south, which wilderness was full of the Lamanites.

4. Now the Nephites greatly feared that the Zoramites would enter into a correspondence with the Lamanites, and that it would be the means of great loss on the part of the Nephites.

5. And now, as the preaching of the word had a great tendency to lead the people to do that which was just—yea, it had had more powerful effect upon the minds of the people than the

sword, or anything else, which had happened unto them—therefore Alma thought it was expedient that they should try the virtue of the word of God.

6. Therefore he took Ammon, and Aaron, and Omner; and Himni he did leave in the church in Zarahemla; but the former three he took with him, and also Amulek and Zeezrom, who were at Melek; and he also took two of his sons.

7. Now the eldest of his sons he took not with him, and his name was Helaman; but the names of those whom he took with him were Shiblon and Corianton; and these are the names of those who went with him among the Zoramites, to preach unto them the word.

1. Leading the hearts of the people to bow down to dumb idols] There is no mention in the text of specific gods to which the Zoramites had devoted themselves, except that the people were lifted up in pride through their virtual worship of gold, silver, and fine goods (verses 24–25). We are guilty of idolatry whenever the object of our adoration, our devotion, or the ardent desires of our hearts is anything other than the true and living God. Whenever a people have strayed from the ordinances of God and broken the everlasting covenant, it is not long before they become idolatrous: "They seek not the Lord to establish his righteousness, but every man walketh in his own way, and after the image of his own god, whose image is in the likeness of the world, and whose substance is that of an idol, which waxeth old and shall perish in Babylon, even Babylon the great, which shall fall" (D&C 1:15–16; compare Isaiah 65:2).

1. His heart again began to sicken] There are few things more painful to one who knows—who has tasted of the goodness and known of the love and power of the Almighty—than to witness the carelessness and waywardness of those who wander in the morass of evil. Those who have been partakers of the divine nature are sickened by the sins of their day and pained for those who revel in their sins.

2. See *Commentary* 2:311.

4. Indeed, the Nephites' worst fears in this regard were eventually realized. See Alma 35:10; 43:4.

5. Who can measure the power of the word of God as delivered directly by him, as declared by angels, as contained in scriptures, or as spoken by the power of the Holy Ghost? Here Alma declares that the word is the most powerful instrument for change known to mortal man—stronger than intellectual persuasion or military might. The word heals the wounded soul (see Jacob 2:8), nourishes that soul (see Moroni 6:4), cuts through falsehood and leads one to Christ (see Helaman 3:27–30), is the foundation for faith (see Alma 5:5–13; Romans 10:17; *Teachings*, p. 148), and results in firmness and steadfastness in the faith (see Helaman 15:7–8). "True doctrine, understood," Elder Boyd K. Packer has taught, "changes attitudes and behavior. The study of the doctrines of the gospel will improve behavior quicker than a study of behavior will improve behavior." (CR, October 1986, p. 20.)

5. They should try the virtue of the word of God] That is, Alma felt that he and his missionary associates should trust the Lord, trust in and rely on the powers of heaven, experiment upon the promises of God regarding the power of his word—all this in order to work a mighty change in the hearts of those to whom they were called to preach.

The Errors of the Zoramites Described

Alma 31:8–23

8. Now the Zoramites were dissenters from the Nephites; therefore they had had the word of God preached unto them.

9. But they had fallen into great errors, for they would not observe to keep the commandments of God, and his statutes, according to the law of Moses.

10. Neither would they observe the performances of the church, to continue in prayer and supplication to God daily, that they might not enter into temptation.

11. Yea, in fine, they did pervert the ways of the Lord in very many instances; therefore, for this cause, Alma and his brethren went into the land to preach the word unto them.

12. Now, when they had come into the land, behold, to their astonishment they found that the Zoramites had built synagogues, and that they did gather themselves together on one day of the week, which day they did call the day of the Lord; and they did worship after a manner which Alma and his brethren had never beheld;

13. For they had a place built up in the center of their synagogue, a place for standing, which was high above the head; and the top thereof would only admit one person.

14. Therefore, whosoever desired to worship must go forth and stand upon the top thereof, and stretch forth his hands towards heaven, and cry with a loud voice, saying:

15. Holy, holy God; we believe that thou art God, and we believe that thou art holy, and that thou wast a spirit, and that thou art a spirit, and that thou wilt be a spirit forever.

16. Holy God, we believe that thou hast separated us from our brethren; and we do not believe in the tradition of our brethren, which was handed down to them by the childishness of their fathers; but we believe that thou hast elected us to be thy holy children; and also thou hast made it known unto us that there shall be no Christ.

17. But thou art the same yesterday, today, and forever; and

thou hast elected us that we shall be saved, whilst all around us are elected to be cast by thy wrath down to hell; for the which holiness, O God, we thank thee; and we also thank thee that thou hast elected us, that we may not be led away after the foolish traditions of our brethren, which doth bind them down to a belief of Christ, which doth lead their hearts to wander far from thee, our God.

18. And again we thank thee, O God, that we are a chosen and a holy people. Amen.

19. Now it came to pass that after Alma and his brethren and his sons had heard these prayers, they were astonished beyond all measure.

20. For behold, every man did go forth and offer up these same prayers.

21. Now the place was called by them Rameumptom, which, being interpreted, is the holy stand.

22. Now, from this stand they did offer up, every man, the selfsame prayer unto God, thanking their God that they were chosen of him, and that he did not lead them away after the tradition of their brethren, and that their hearts were not stolen away to believe in things to come, which they knew nothing about.

23. Now, after the people had all offered up thanks after this manner, they returned to their homes, never speaking of their God again until they had assembled themselves together again to the holy stand, to offer up thanks after their manner.

8. The Zoramites were dissenters from the Nephites] How often it is the case that those who were once enlightened, those who once had known the sweet joy of membership in the Lord's kingdom, become the bitterest enemies of faith (see Alma 24:30). Sinning against light always leads to grosser darkness.

9. Until the time of the Lord's atoning sacrifice was made in the flesh, faithfulness to that portion of the law of Moses prescribed by the prophets was prerequisite to divine approbation. Elder Bruce R. McConkie has written: "We cannot always tell . . . whether specific sacrificial rites performed in Israel were part of the Mosaic system or whether they were the same ordinances performed by Adam and Abraham as part of the gospel law itself. Further, it appears that some of the ritualistic performances varied from time to time, according to the special needs of the people and the changing circumstances in which they found themselves. Even the Book of Mormon does not help us in these respects. We know the Nephites offered sacrifices and kept the law of Moses. *Since they held the Melchizedek Priesthood and there were no Levites among them, we suppose their sacrifices were those that antedated the ministry of Moses and that, since they had the fulness of the gospel itself, they kept the law of Moses in the sense that they conformed to its myriad moral principles and its endless ethical restrictions.* We suppose this would be one of the reasons why Nephi was able to say, 'The law hath become dead unto us.' (2 Nephi 25:25.) *There is, at least, no intimation in the Book of Mormon that the Nephites offered the daily sacrifices required by the law or that they held the various feasts that were part of the religious life of their Old World kinsmen." (Promised Messiah,* p. 427, italics added.) See also *Commentary* 1:296–97; 2:34–35, 210.

10. The Zoramites had forsaken the counsel and teachings of the true Church as well as of the law of Moses.

11. They did pervert the ways of the Lord] Abinadi had chastised the priests of Noah as follows: "I say unto you, wo be unto you for perverting the ways of the Lord! For if ye understand these things ye have not taught them; therefore, ye have perverted the ways of the Lord." (Mosiah 12:26.)

12–18. The manner of worship of the Zoramites, as well as their perverse doctrinal orientation, is most interesting. Their worship was quite simple: on one day of the week (denominated the "day of the Lord") the people would gather at their own synagogues, ascend one by one the Rameumptom or holy stand, and uniformly utter a prepared prayer. They seemed to be possessed with a belief in what we would call predestination, or unconditional election of individuals to eternal life. They viewed themselves as the elect, the chosen and holy ones, while all others were doomed to suffer the wrath of God in hell.

12. They did gather themselves together on one day of the week] See commentary on verse 23.

15. Thou wilt be a spirit forever] Here we gain a subtle insight into the doctrinal stance of the Zoramites: they were anti-Christs. To say that the God to whom they addressed themselves—presumably Jehovah—would be a spirit forever was the same as saying that "there shall be no Christ" (verse 16). That is, they denied the condescension of the great God, the incarnation, the divine sonship of Christ.

16. Thou hast made it known unto us] Whether the Zoramites had deceived themselves into believing that God had indeed spoken to them, or whether Satan or one of his demons had appeared or spoken in the name of God, is unknown and immaterial, for the result was the same.

22. Their hearts were not stolen away to believe in things to come] Perhaps this is an indication that the Zoramites, like most anti-Christs, denied the spirit of prophecy (see Jacob 7:7; Alma 21:8; 30:13).

23. In our day the Lord has counseled regarding Sabbath worship: "That thou mayest more fully keep thyself unspotted from the world, thou shalt go to the house of prayer and offer up thy sacraments upon my holy day; for verily this is a day appointed unto you to rest from your labors, and to pay thy devotions unto the Most High; *nevertheless thy vows shall be offered up in righteousness on all days and at all times"* (D&C 59:9–11, italics added).

Alma's Prayer in Behalf of the Zoramites

Alma 31:24–38

24. Now when Alma saw this his heart was grieved; for he saw that they were a wicked and a perverse people; yea, he saw that their hearts were set upon gold, and upon silver, and upon all manner of fine goods.

25. Yea, and he also saw that their hearts were lifted up unto great boasting, in their pride.

26. And he lifted up his voice to heaven, and cried, saying: O, how long, O Lord, wilt thou suffer that thy servants shall dwell here below in the flesh, to behold such gross wickedness among the children of men?

27. Behold, O God, they cry unto thee, and yet their hearts are swallowed up in their pride. Behold, O God, they cry unto thee with their mouths, while they are puffed up, even to greatness, with the vain things of the world.

28. Behold, O my God, their costly apparel, and their ringlets, and their bracelets, and their ornaments of gold, and all their precious things which they are ornamented with; and behold, their hearts are set upon them, and yet they cry unto thee and say—We thank thee, O God, for we are a chosen people unto thee, while others shall perish.

29. Yea, and they say that thou hast made it known unto them that there shall be no Christ.

30. O Lord God, how long wilt thou suffer that such wickedness and infidelity shall be among this people? O Lord, wilt thou give me strength, that I may bear with mine infirmities. For I am infirm, and such wickedness among this people doth pain my soul.

31. O Lord, my heart is exceedingly sorrowful; wilt thou comfort my soul in Christ. O Lord, wilt thou grant unto me that I may have strength, that I may suffer with patience these afflictions which shall come upon me, because of the iniquity of this people.

32. O Lord, wilt thou comfort my soul, and give unto me success, and also my fellow laborers who are with me—yea, Ammon, and Aaron, and Omner, and also Amulek and Zeezrom, and also my two sons—yea, even all these wilt thou comfort, O Lord. Yea, wilt thou comfort their souls in Christ.

33. Wilt thou grant unto them that they may have strength, that they may bear their afflictions which shall come upon them because of the iniquities of this people.

34. O Lord, wilt thou grant unto us that we may have success in bringing them again unto thee in Christ.

35. Behold, O Lord, their souls

are precious, and many of them are our brethren; therefore, give unto us, O Lord, power and wisdom that we may bring these, our brethren, again unto thee.

36. Now it came to pass that when Alma had said these words, that he clapped his hands upon all them who were with him. And behold, as he clapped his hands upon them, they were filled with the Holy Spirit.

37. And after that they did separate themselves one from another,

taking no thought for themselves what they should eat, or what they should drink, or what they should put on.

38. And the Lord provided for them that they should hunger not, neither should they thirst; yea, and he also gave them strength, that they should suffer no manner of afflictions, save it were swallowed up in the joy of Christ. Now this was according to the prayer of Alma; and this because he prayed in faith.

24–35. This is a remarkable prayer, a heartfelt petition. It is an honest expression of a righteous man, a declaration of his utter disgust with the sins of these people, an inquiry as to how long God would allow such perversion to prevail, and a plea for strength in bearing up under his burdens. It also demonstrates how the Lord through the Spirit can transform the human heart, can turn a person around in his thinking, can bestow love where disdain once was, can cause one to change from denunciation and fierce judgment to tender mercy and compassion. At first Alma is sickened by their sins. Then he pleads for strength. Alma asks for "comfort in Christ." We notice that his prayer then continues as follows: "O Lord, wilt thou grant unto us that we may have success in bringing them again unto thee in Christ. Behold, O Lord, their souls are precious, and many of them are our brethren; therefore, give unto us, O Lord, power and wisdom that we may bring these, our brethren, again unto thee." (Verses 34–35.)

31. Wilt thou comfort my soul in Christ] Comfort comes in and through Christ. It comes to us through the mediation of the Comforter, the Holy Ghost. The Spirit heals our souls, provides divine perspective, and points our minds toward those things which matter most. It is the Comforter who teaches us "the peaceable things of the kingdom" (D&C 36:2; 39:5–6), the "peaceable things of immortal glory" (Moses 6:61).

35. Their souls are precious] "In a modern revelation the Lord explained that 'the worth of souls is great in the sight of God' (D&C 18:10). Latter-day Saints are fond of quoting this verse and then skipping down the scriptural page to those verses that speak further of the joy that comes from bringing the blessings of the gospel into the lives of many. The question might be asked: *Why* is the worth of souls great? . . . We might respond that as children of the Man of Holiness we have marvelous possibilities. As sons and daughters of God, we are possessed (although now in rudimentary form) of the attributes of godliness. The Lord provides an additional answer from scripture: 'For, behold, the Lord your Redeemer suffered death in the flesh; wherefore he suffered the pain of all men, that all men might repent and come unto him. And he hath risen again from the dead, that he might bring all men unto him, on conditions of repentance. And how great is his joy in the soul that repenteth! Wherefore, you are called to cry repentance unto this people.' (D&C 18:11–14.) Simply stated, the soul is of infinite worth. We are not our own. We have been bought with an infinite price (1 Corinthians 6:19–20), even with 'the precious blood of Christ, as of a lamb without blemish and without spot' (1 Peter 1:19)." (Robert L. Millet, *An Eye Single to the Glory of God*, pp. 34–35.) "Souls are as precious in the sight of God as they ever were," the Prophet Joseph affirmed; "and the Elders were never called to drive any down to hell, but to persuade and invite all men everywhere to repent, that they may become the heirs of salvation" (*Teachings*, p. 77; see also D&C 109:43).

36. He clapped his hands upon all them who were with him] Presumably this means that Alma laid his hands upon their heads and either set them apart to their assignments or else bestowed a special blessing upon them before they were to face a difficult challenge. In any case, thereafter "they were filled with the Holy Spirit."

37. "Any man that shall go and preach this gospel of the kingdom, and fail not to continue faithful in all things, shall not be weary in mind, neither darkened, neither in body, limb, nor joint; and a hair of his head shall not fall to the ground unnoticed. And they shall not go hungry, neither athirst. Therefore, take ye no thought for the morrow, for what ye shall eat, or what ye shall drink, or wherewithal ye shall be clothed. . . . Neither take ye thought beforehand what ye shall say; but treasure up in your minds continually the words of life, and it shall be given you in the very hour that portion that shall be meted unto every man." (D&C 84:80–81, 85; see also Matthew 6:25–34; 3 Nephi 13:25–34.)

38. This because he prayed in faith] James, the brother of our Lord, knew much of the power of prayer. He wrote: "If any of you lack wisdom, let him ask of God, that giveth to all men liberally, and upbraideth not; and it shall be given him. But let him ask in faith, nothing wavering." (James 1:5–6.) Further: "Pray one for another, that ye may be healed. The effectual fervent prayer of a righteous man availeth much." (James 5:16.)

The Poor Are Often the Most Responsive to the Gospel Message

Alma 32:1–3

1. And it came to pass that they did go forth, and began to preach the word of God unto the people, entering into their synagogues, and into their houses; yea, and even they did preach the word in their streets.

2. And it came to pass that after much labor among them, they began to have success among the poor class of people; for behold, they were cast out of the synagogues because of the coarseness of their apparel—

3. Therefore they were not permitted to enter into their synagogues to worship God, being esteemed as filthiness; therefore they were poor; yea, they were esteemed by their brethren as dross; therefore they were poor as to things of the world; and also they were poor in heart.

1–3. Typically, when the gospel message goes to a nation or city the first willing to hear and accept it are those of the lower social classes. Humility of circumstances and humility of spirit are often found in company together. Writing to the Corinthian Saints, the Apostle Paul observed: "Not many wise men after the flesh, not many mighty, not many noble, are called; but God hath chosen the foolish things of the world to confound the wise; and God hath chosen the weak things of the world to confound the things which are mighty; and base things of the world, and things which are despised, hath God chosen, yea, and things which are not, to bring to nought things that are: that no flesh should glory in his presence" (1 Corinthians 1:26–29).

Celsus, the second-century philosopher, is often quoted in descriptions of the infant Christian church. The basic material of his description—the general social level of the converts—is much like Paul's, but the spirit is sharply different. Christians, he held, "do not even want to give or to receive a reason for what they believe, and use such expressions as 'Do not ask questions; just believe' and 'Thy faith will save thee.' . . . Their injunctions are like this: 'Let no one educated, no one wise, no one sensible draw near. For anyone stupid, anyone uneducated, anyone who is a child, let him come boldly.' By the fact that they themselves admit that these people are worthy of their God, they show that they want and are able to convince only the foolish, dishonourable, and stupid, and only slaves, women, and little children. . . . In private houses also we see wool-workers, cobblers, laundry workers, and the most bucolic and illiterate yokels, who would not dare to say anything at all in front of their elders and more intelligent masters." (Origen, in *Contra Celsum* 1:9; 3:44.)

These descriptions given by Paul and Celsus aptly profile the typical Christian convert as seen by believer and unbeliever respectively in the period associated with the New Testament. The most striking thing about such expressions is that they are remarkably similar to the kind of thing we have so often read about the early converts to Mormonism. Nor does the similarity stop there, for it has been echoed by thousands of missionaries who have been the first to open various cities and regions to the teaching of the gospel; in so doing, they have found that the well-to-do, those resting comfortably in their own self-sufficiency, have little or no interest in their message, while those whose conditions are appreciably more humble are often more willing to listen.

3. Dross] The scum thrown off in the smelting process.

Humility Is Essential to Obtaining Gospel Understanding

Alma 32:4–16

4. Now, as Alma was teaching and speaking unto the people upon the hill Onidah, there came a great multitude unto him, who were those of whom we have been speaking, of whom were poor in heart, because of their poverty as to the things of the world.

5. And they came unto Alma; and the one who was the foremost among them said unto him: Behold, what shall these my brethren do, for they are despised of all men because of their poverty, yea, and more especially by our priests; for they have cast us out of our synagogues which we have labored abundantly to build with our own hands; and they have cast us out because of our exceeding poverty; and we have no place to worship our God; and behold, what shall we do?

6. And now when Alma heard this, he turned him about, his face immediately towards him, and he beheld with great joy; for he beheld that their afflictions had truly humbled them, and that they were in a preparation to hear the word.

7. Therefore he did say no more to the other multitude; but he stretched forth his hand, and cried unto those whom he beheld, who were truly penitent, and said unto them:

8. I behold that ye are lowly in heart; and if so, blessed are ye.

9. Behold thy brother hath said, What shall we do?—for we are cast out of our synagogues, that we cannot worship our God.

10. Behold I say unto you, do ye suppose that ye cannot worship God save it be in your synagogues only?

11. Moreover, I would ask, do ye suppose that ye must not worship God only once in a week?

12. I say unto you, it is well that ye are cast out of your synagogues, that ye may be humble, and that ye may learn wisdom; for it is necessary that ye should learn wisdom; for it is because that ye are cast out, that ye are despised of your brethren because of your exceeding poverty, that ye are brought to a lowliness of heart; for ye are necessarily brought to be humble.

13. And now, because ye are compelled to be humble blessed are ye; for a man sometimes, if he is compelled to be humble, seeketh repentance; and now surely, whosoever repenteth shall find mercy; and he that findeth mercy and endureth to the end the same shall be saved.

14. And now, as I said unto you, that because ye were compelled to be humble ye were blessed, do ye not suppose that they are more blessed who truly humble themselves because of the word?

15. Yea, he that truly humbleth himself, and repenteth of his sins, and endureth to the end, the same shall be blessed—yea, much more blessed than they who are compelled to be humble because of their exceeding poverty.

16. Therefore, blessed are they who humble themselves without being compelled to be humble; or rather, in other words, blessed is he that believeth in the word of God, and is baptized without stubbornness of heart, yea, without being brought to know the word, or even compelled to know, before they will believe.

4. Poor in heart] Such are the "poor in spirit" spoken of by Christ in the Beatitudes. The invitation to all such is the same as that given here by Alma, that is, to come to Christ and be enriched by the fulness of gospel blessings. See verse 8 and also 3 Nephi 12:3.

6. It has been wisely observed that a blessing is anything that brings us nearer to God. Thus our afflictions often become our greatest blessings. It is in our extremities that most often we meet God, not in our comfort. Thus any time conditions come to pass— even what at the time might be construed as tragic or unfortunate conditions—that lead us toward the truth or contribute to our eventual well-being, we have indeed been blessed.

6. A preparation to hear the word] In order to receive or accept the word of truth, a person must be prepared to hear it. That preparation may come through enforced humility, as is the case with the poor Zoramites, or it may come voluntarily as one's heart yearns for the fulfillment or peace of mind that can follow an introduction to God-given truth.

10. Pure worship, though enhanced by mood and atmosphere, is in reality a matter of the heart. Individuals worship God Almighty in spirit and in truth as they humble themselves before him, as they seek to know and abide by his will, as they ponder upon the glory in the wonders and beauty of his creations. "Deity is worshiped in prayer, song, sermon, and testimony; by the making of covenants, offering of sacrifices, performance of ordinances, and the participation in religious rituals and ceremonies; he is worshiped by man's act of believing divine truths, by his being converted to them in their fulness; he may be worshiped in thought, word, and deed. But the most perfect of all worship comes from those who first believe the gospel, who then participate in its outward forms, and who finally keep the standards of personal righteousness that appertain to it." (Bruce R. McConkie, *Mormon Doctrine*, p. 849.) We also worship Christ the Lord through emulation, through imitation, through seeking to be like him: through serving others and growing in spiritual graces until that perfect day when we are endowed by him with the fulness of the glory of the Father (see D&C 93:12–20).

12. That ye may learn wisdom] The wisdom learned by the poorer segment of the Zoramites was that they were not at all self-sufficient, that they could not save themselves, that happiness here and eternal reward hereafter could come only through the mediation and mercy of Jesus Christ.

13. Whosoever repenteth shall find mercy] To suppose that mercy is granted unconditionally is to deny God the attribute of justice and to suppose that the wicked and rebellious are rewarded and blessed equally with the faithful. It is axiomatic that recipients of his grace and mercy will be saved in the kingdom of heaven. See commentary on Alma 26:35.

14–16. It is the gift of faith freely rendered that brings forth the richest of heaven's blessings. "Blessed are ye if ye shall believe in me and be baptized, after that ye have seen me and know that I am," the resurrected Christ told those assembled at the temple in Bountiful. "And again, more blessed are they who shall believe in your words because that ye shall testify that ye have seen me, and that ye know that I am. Yea, blessed are they who shall believe in your words and come down into the depths of humility and be baptized, for they shall be visited with fire and with the Holy Ghost, and shall receive a remission of their sins." (3 Nephi 12:1–2.)

16. Blessed is he that believeth . . . without stubbornness of heart] There are no blessings to be had in resisting the impressions of the Spirit. Surveys among converts to the Church indicate that the great majority of them knew the message of the Restoration to be true upon first hearing it. It is also generally true that those who respond most readily to the message of the missionaries continue after baptism to grow in the things of the Spirit more rapidly, and sink their spiritual roots deeper, than those who confused intellect and independence of thought with stubbornness of heart.

Faith Precedes the Miracle

Alma 32:17–20

17. Yea, there are many who do say: If thou wilt show unto us a sign from heaven, then we shall know of a surety; then we shall believe.

18. Now I ask, is this faith? Behold, I say unto you, Nay; for if a man knoweth a thing he hath no cause to believe, for he knoweth it.

19. And now, how much more cursed is he that knoweth the will of God and doeth it not, than he that only believeth, or only hath cause to believe, and falleth into transgression?

20. Now of this thing ye must judge. Behold, I say unto you, that it is on the one hand even as it is on the other; and it shall be unto every man according to his work.

17–20. Of his missionary experiences, Paul said: "For the Jews require a sign, and the Greeks seek after wisdom; but we preach Christ crucified, unto the Jews a stumblingblock, and unto the Greeks foolishness; but unto them which are called, both Jews and Greeks, Christ the power of God, and the wisdom of God" (1 Corinthians 1:22–24). "There never was a people in the universe more difficult to be persuaded of the truth than the Jews: and had not their religion been incontestably proved by the most striking and indubitable miracles, they never would have received it. This slowness of heart to believe, added to their fear of being deceived, induced them to require *miracles* to attest to every thing that professed to come from God. They were a wicked and adulterous generation, continually seeking signs, and never saying, It is enough." The particular sign they sought above all others was a Messiah in the form of a conquering king or military hero, and thus they rejected the lowly Jesus of Nazareth.

The Greeks, in like manner, "could not believe that proclaiming supreme happiness through a man that was crucified at Judea as a malefactor could ever comport with reason and common sense; for both the *matter* and *manner* of the preaching were opposite to every notion they had formed of what was dignified and philosophic. . . . Thus Christ crucified was to the Jews a stumbling block, and to the Greeks foolishness." (*Clarke's New Testament Commentary* 2:195.)

Such are the difficulties of sign seekers: first, they are without the wisdom to know what signs ought to be trusted and what witness they ought to seek; second, they falsely suppose that signs will bring faith and spiritual security, whereas the order of heaven is that signs *follow* those that believe. "Yea, signs come by faith, not by the will of men, nor as they please, but by the will of God. Yea, signs come by faith, unto mighty works, for without faith no man pleaseth God; and with whom God is angry he is not well pleased; wherefore, unto such he showeth no signs, only in wrath unto their condemnation." (D&C 63:10–11.)

Faith Cannot Be Exercised in Untruths

Alma 32:21

21. And now as I said concerning faith—faith is not to have a perfect knowledge of things; therefore if ye have faith ye hope for things which are not seen, which are true.

21. Faith is not to have a perfect knowledge] Faith and perfect knowledge are not incompatible, else how would God, whose knowledge is perfect, possess the attribute of faith? (See Hebrews 11:3.) Alma is defining faith from the viewpoint of mortality, not the vantage point of the eternities. In our present world, faith serves as an assurance of the existence of the unseen. By contrast, in the *Lectures on Faith* Joseph Smith spoke of faith in its unlimited sense. Faith, he declared, is "the principle by which Jehovah works, and through which he exercises power over all temporal as well as eternal things. Take this principle or attribute—for it is an attribute—from the Deity, and he would cease to exist." (*Lectures on Faith* 1:16.) Among exalted beings, "Faith, then, is the first great governing principle which has power, dominion, and authority over all things; by it they exist, by it they are upheld, by it they are changed, or by it they remain, agreeable to the will of God. Without it there is no power, and without power there could be no creation nor existence!" (*Lectures on Faith* 1:24; see also 2:2.)

Faith is a process, a divine process built upon knowledge and understanding of eternal verities as well as upon personal righteousness. One may possess a slight amount of faith—having but little understanding of the principles of the gospel and living but a portion of the gospel law; or one may possess that quality and kind of faith which Joseph Smith called "faith unto life and salvation." We must remember that Alma is speaking to a people with little or no faith. They must be instructed simply and plainly, must build their knowledge and witness of truth slowly but surely. They do not know of the Christ, of the necessity for the ordinances, or of the gifts and graces which are the companions of the Saints.

They must be nurtured slowly. For them, faith and knowledge are almost at opposite ends of a continuum.

On the other hand, to those who already possess enough faith to have come out of the world, to have believed in the Lord Jesus and accepted the words of his anointed servants—to such the process of faith is grander and more expansive. These come to understand the nature and kind of being that God is, and in so doing they come to appreciate that faith is a principle of power which characterizes the work of God. God has all knowledge. God has all faith. By virtue of his omniscience and his omnipotence he commands that things come to pass. By virtue of his perfect faith, this virtue and principle of power, he has absolute confidence that his word will be fulfilled and his command realized. "In the eternal sense," Elder Bruce R. McConkie has written, "because faith is the power of God himself, it embraces within its fold a knowledge of all things. This measure of faith, the faith by which the worlds are and were created and which sustains and upholds all things, is found only among resurrected persons. It is the faith of saved beings. But mortals are in process, through faith, of gaining eternal salvation. Their faith is based on a knowledge of the truth, within the meaning of Alma's statement that 'faith is not to have a perfect knowledge of things,' but that men have faith when they 'hope for things which are not seen, which are true.' In this sense faith is both preceded and supplanted by knowledge, and when any person gains a perfect knowledge on any given matter, then, as pertaining to that thing, he has faith no longer; or, rather, his faith is dormant; it has been supplanted by pure knowledge." (New Witness, pp. 209–10.)

According to Joseph Smith, faith is built upon knowledge of three things: (1) the idea of the existence of God; (2) a correct idea of his character, perfections, and attributes; and (3) an actual knowledge that the course in life one is pursuing is according to God's will (see Lectures on Faith 3:2–5). The first two prerequisites for faith in God have to do with a knowledge of God. They may be had through studying and searching and pondering the word of the Lord and the testimonies of those who have known him. The third prerequisite has to do with ourselves. A person may have the assurance from the Lord that he is on course only if he is indeed on course! There exists in the souls of the faithful a constant yearning to improve, to repent, to bring their lives into harmony with the heavens. There also exists in those souls a quiet confidence born of the Spirit, a consciousness of increasing victory over self, a subtle but certain assurance and peace that the Lord is pleased. Such a knowledge, such a victory, comes only through an unconditional surrender to the will of the Master, only through a willingness to sacrifice all things for the kingdom's sake (see D&C 97:8; *Lectures on Faith* 6:7).

21. Which are true] Alma defines faith as the "hope for things which are not seen" and adds the very important qualification "which are true." Faith cannot successfully be exercised in falsehoods or untruths. Gods of wood and stone, gods created by the hands of men, cannot dispense the blessings of heaven. Nor is such power found in gods created in the minds of men and crafted by the witchery of words. Sincerity is commendable. Zeal is to be appreciated. But saving faith can be exercised only in that which is true. Some would like to suppose that these gods born of men share in heaven's powers if worshipped with sufficient sincerity or pursued with zeal. Such is not the case. Miscalculated longitudes and latitudes, though coupled with sincerity and zeal, will not bring to the safety of its home port the ship lost at sea.

Joshua charged the children of Israel to "fear the Lord, and serve him in sincerity and in truth" (Joshua 24:14). One can hardly imagine his having directed the Lord's hosts to "fear the Lord, and serve him in sincerity and error," or to serve him in "truth and hypocrisy." The formula for heaven's blessings is, and ever must be, that we worship in sincerity and in truth. Thus the Lord's people in the last days have been charged to serve him "in righteousness and in truth unto the end" (D&C 76:5). Illustrating this doctrine, Joseph Smith taught that is was through faith in the atoning sacrifice of Christ that Abel offered an animal sacrifice that was acceptable to God. "Cain," however, "offered of the fruit of the ground, and was not accepted, because he could not do it in faith, he could have no faith, or could not exercise faith contrary to the plan of heaven," which required the ritual to be a type of the shedding of Christ's blood, the Prophet declared. (*Teachings*, p. 58.)

President N. Eldon Tanner explained: "The scriptures give us evidence of the reality and personality of God and his Son, Jesus Christ. In order to believe in God it is necessary for us to understand his nature and attributes. Our faith in him must be based on true principles. Faith will avail us nothing if it is based on a false premise. For example, some of the early American colonists in dealing with the Indians gave them gunpowder to plant with the promise that they could raise a crop of gunpowder. In explicit faith the Indians planted the gunpowder, but of course they harvested nothing from their efforts because their faith was based on falsehood." (CR, April 1978, p. 20.)

There is another facet to faith which is often misunderstood. Faith is not the power of positive thinking. One does not have faith simply because he is positive or optimistic. Faith is based on the truth, the truth as God knows it, the truth as a manifestation of the will and pleasure of the Lord. We do need to be positive, for there is no virtue in being long-faced and dreary. But faith is another matter entirely. If a priesthood bearer is called upon to heal a dying man, for example, he does not command the sick one to rise from his bed of affliction in the name of faith, when that "faith" is no more than wishful thinking or hope that the man will live. "Working by faith is not the mere speaking of a few well-chosen words," Elder McConkie wrote. "Anyone with the power of speech could have commanded the rotting corpse of Lazarus to come forth, but only one whose power was greater than death could bring life again to the brother of Mary and Martha. Nor is working by faith merely a mental desire, however strong, that some eventuality shall occur. There may be those whose mental powers and thought processes are greater than any of the saints, but only persons who are in tune with the Infinite can exercise the spiritual forces and powers that come from him.

"Those who work by faith must first have faith; no one can use a power that he does not possess, and the faith or power must be gained by obedience to those laws upon which its receipt is predicated. . . . And then—when the day is at hand and the hour has arrived for the miracle to be wrought—then they must be in tune with the Holy Spirit of God. He who is the Author of faith, he whose power faith is, he whose works are the embodiment of justice and judgment and wisdom and all good things, even he must approve the use of his power in the case at hand. Faith cannot be exercised contrary to the order of heaven or contrary to the will and purposes of him whose power it is. Men work by faith when they are in tune with the Spirit and when what they seek to do by mental exertion and by the spoken word is the mind and will of the Lord." (*New Witness,* pp. 191–92.)

God Is Merciful unto Those Who Believe on His Name

Alma 32:22

22. And now, behold, I say unto you, and I would that ye should remember, that God is merciful unto all who believe on his name; therefore he desireth, in the first place, that ye should believe, yea, even on his word.

22. "Belief, humble belief, is the foundation of all righteousness and the beginning of spiritual progression," wrote Elder Bruce R. McConkie. "It goes before good works, opens the door to an eternal store of heavenly truth, and charts the course to eternal life." With but few exceptions, *belief* is used in holy writ as a synonym for *faith*. Belief in Christ brings salvation. Failure to believe in Christ brings damnation. False systems of religious belief close the doors of heaven, while belief in principles of truth opens those doors. "It is one thing to believe God is a personal being in whose image man is made, as the scriptures attest, and quite another to believe he is a spirit nothingness that fills the immensity of space, as the creeds of Christendom aver. What men believe is the governing force in their lives. If they truly believe the truth, they will be saved in the kingdom of God; if they truly believe a lie, they will fail to gain this high reward.

"Salvation comes to those who believe the gospel of the Lord Jesus Christ. Rejection of his gospel closes the door to salvation. Men believe his gospel, are seeking to believe, or do not believe; and if they do not, they must of necessity believe something else. Men do not and cannot live in a vacuum; they believe one thing or another. Disbelief in the gospel consists of belief in other things that do not lead to salvation. . . .

"Thus God's holy word calls for a belief in Christ that is infinite and eternal. It is not a mere lip-service declaration that he is the Savior nor a mere confessing with idle lips that he is Lord of all. To believe in Christ in the sense of gaining eternal life is to believe his words and accept his messengers. It is to honor his prophets and take counsel from his apostles. It is to have 'the mind of Christ' (1 Corinthians 2:16), to believe what he believes, and to say what he would say in all situations. It is to abide in the truth and keep the commandments. It is to enjoy the gifts of the Spirit, to work the works of righteousness, and to perform miracles as he did." (*New Witness,* pp. 21–24.) It is to believe in his name, to take that name upon us, and to have full confidence in the promises associated with our so doing.

Angels Minister to Women, and Little Children Are Given Revelations

Alma 32:23

23. And now, he imparteth his word by angels unto men, yea, not only men but women also. Now this is not all; little children do have words given unto them many times, which confound the wise and the learned.

23. Who can receive revelation? Who can enjoy the ministry of angels? Who can dream dreams or see visions? Who is entitled to know the mysteries of the kingdom? Can we not reason that if God has spoken to so much as one of his children, and that he is a just and impartial God, he then must be willing, on the same terms, to speak to each and all of his offspring? It is a strange notion that God has the power of creation but not the power of communication. Indeed, as all true prophets have testified of Christ so they have testified "that the voice of the Lord is unto all men" (D&C 1:2). Could it be supposed that a wise and loving father would speak to his sons and not his daughters? That he would speak to the older children but not the younger? Are we to suppose that there is some power that binds his tongue and constrains the feelings of his heart? What parent's heart could endure the thought of giving birth to children to whom he or she could not speak? Is it not reasonable to suppose that there is no more sublime joy known to exalted beings than that of guiding the path of their own children?

Alma Likens Obtaining Faith to Nourishing a Good Seed

Alma 32:24–43

24. And now, my beloved brethren, as ye have desired to know of me what ye shall do because ye are afflicted and cast out—now I do not desire that ye should suppose that I mean to judge you only according to that which is true—

25. For I do not mean that ye all of you have been compelled to humble yourselves; for I verily believe that there are some among you who would humble themselves, let them be in whatsoever circumstances they might.

26. Now, as I said concerning faith—that it was not a perfect knowledge—even so it is with my words. Ye cannot know of their surety at first, unto perfection, any more than faith is a perfect knowledge.

27. But behold, if ye will awake and arouse your faculties, even to an experiment upon my words, and exercise a particle of faith, yea, even if ye can no more than desire to believe, let this desire work in you, even until ye believe in a manner that ye can give place for a portion of my words.

28. Now, we will compare the word unto a seed. Now, if ye give place, that a seed may be planted in your heart, behold, if it be a true seed, or a good seed, if ye do not cast it out by your unbelief, that ye will resist the Spirit of the Lord, behold, it will begin to swell within your breasts; and when you feel these swelling motions, ye will begin to say within yourselves—It must needs be that this is a good seed, or that the word is good, for it beginneth to enlarge my soul; yea, it beginneth to enlighten my understanding, yea, it beginneth to be delicious to me.

29. Now behold, would not this increase your faith? I say unto

you, Yea; nevertheless it hath not grown up to a perfect knowledge.

30. But behold, as the seed swelleth, and sprouteth, and beginneth to grow, then you must needs say that the seed is good; for behold it swelleth, and sprouteth, and beginneth to grow. And now, behold, will not this strengthen your faith? Yea, it will strengthen your faith: for ye will say I know that this is a good seed; for behold it sprouteth and beginneth to grow.

31. And now, behold, are ye sure that this is a good seed? I say unto you, Yea; for every seed bringeth forth unto its own likeness.

32. Therefore, if a seed groweth it is good, but if it groweth not, behold it is not good, therefore it is cast away.

33. And now, behold, because ye have tried the experiment, and planted the seed, and it swelleth and sprouteth, and beginneth to grow, ye must needs know that the seed is good.

34. And now, behold, is your knowledge perfect? Yea, your knowledge is perfect in that thing, and your faith is dormant; and this because you know, for ye know that the word hath swelled your souls, and ye also know that it hath sprouted up, that your understanding doth begin to be enlightened, and your mind doth begin to expand.

35. O then, is not this real? I say unto you, Yea, because it is light; and whatsoever is light, is good, because it is discernible, therefore ye must know that it is good; and now behold, after ye have tasted this light is your knowledge perfect?

36. Behold I say unto you, Nay; neither must ye lay aside your faith, for ye have only exercised your faith to plant the seed that ye might try the experiment to know if the seed was good.

37. And behold, as the tree beginneth to grow, ye will say: Let us nourish it with great care, that it may get root, that it may grow up, and bring forth fruit unto us. And now behold, if ye nourish it with much care it will get root, and grow up, and bring forth fruit.

38. But if ye neglect the tree, and take no thought for its nourishment, behold it will not get any root; and when the heat of the sun cometh and scorcheth it, because it hath no root it withers away, and ye pluck it up and cast it out.

39. Now, this is not because the seed was not good, neither is it because the fruit thereof would not be desirable; but it is because your ground is barren, and ye will not nourish the tree, therefore ye cannot have the fruit thereof.

40. And thus, if ye will not nourish the word, looking forward with an eye of faith to the fruit thereof, ye can never pluck of the fruit of the tree of life.

41. But if ye will nourish the word, yea, nourish the tree as it beginneth to grow, by your faith with great diligence, and with patience, looking forward to the fruit thereof, it shall take root; and behold it shall be a tree springing up unto everlasting life.

42. And because of your diligence and your faith and your patience with the word in nourishing it, that it may take root in you, behold, by and by ye shall pluck the fruit thereof, which is most precious, which is sweet above all that is sweet, and which is white above all that is white, yea, and pure above all that is pure; and ye shall feast upon this

fruit even until ye are filled, that ye hunger not, neither shall ye thirst.
43. Then, my brethren, ye shall reap the rewards of your faith, and your diligence, and patience, and long-suffering, waiting for the tree to bring forth fruit unto you.

26. Ye cannot know of their surety at first] There are no shortcuts to a testimony of the gospel. We cannot fully understand principles that we have not lived. "If any man will do his will," the Savior declared, "he shall know of the doctrine, whether it be of God, or whether I speak of myself" (John 7:17).

An understanding of the principles of salvation does not come in an instant. The idea is demeaning to the principles involved. Joseph Smith did not come out of the Sacred Grove knowing all that was necessary for his salvation. He, like Christ, found it necessary to advance from grace to grace. To suppose that at some sort of a religious revival we can obtain all the knowledge necessary to be saved vulgarizes true religion. The divine injunction, the Prophet Joseph Smith taught, is that we seek learning "even by study, and also by faith." This that we might "grow up" in the knowledge of God and that we might "receive a fulness of the Holy Ghost." (D&C 109:14–15.) Similarly, Paul admonished us to "grow up into [Christ] in all things" (Ephesians 4:15). "The things of God," said the Prophet, "are of deep import; and time, and experience, and careful and ponderous and solemn thoughts can only find them out" (*Teachings*, p. 137).

27. Arouse your faculties] Centuries earlier, Jacob had written: "O my brethren, hearken unto my words; arouse the faculties of your souls; shake yourselves that ye may awake from the slumber of death; and loose yourselves from the pains of hell that ye may not become angels to the devil" (Jacob 3:11). "In the midst of a fallen world, a world prone to degradation and spiritual decay, it is often necessary for men and women to be jolted from their carnal security and brought to the frightening realization that they are working at cross purposes to God; that they are going contrary to their own inner spiritual nature; and that they are on a collision course with misery and destruction. Such an arousal from the deep sleep of spiritual death often comes through the powerful testimony of one of the Lord's legal administrators, a witness and warning which are attended by the spirit of prophecy and revelation." (*Commentary* 2:29.)

27. An experiment upon my words] The quest for truth is essentially an experiment upon the words of Christ. The experimenter is encouraged to "prove all things; hold fast that which is good" (1 Thessalonians 5:21). We do then know (see Ether 12:6; John 7:17; compare Malachi 3:10).

27. No more than desire to believe] This is the beginning, the introduction to true faith. Alma asks the Zoramites to desire to believe, to hope that perhaps what he is saying is true. One who approaches his or her study and experiment upon the Book of Mormon and the gospel with a neutral attitude may miss the mark and miss the opportunity to know. There must be an openness to the possibility that the gospel message is true. There must be a deliberate suspension of disbelief.

27. Give place for a portion of my words] "We consider that God has created man with a mind capable of instruction," taught the Prophet Joseph Smith, "and a faculty which may be enlarged in proportion to the heed and diligence given to the light communicated from heaven to the intellect; and that the nearer man approaches perfection, the clearer are his views, and the greater his enjoyments, till he has overcome the evils of his life and lost every desire for sin; and like the ancients, arrives at that point of faith where he is wrapped in the power and glory of his Maker and is caught up to dwell with Him. But we consider that this is a station to which no man ever arrived in a moment: he must have been instructed in the government and laws of that kingdom by proper degrees, until his mind is capable in some measure of comprehending the propriety, justice, equality, and consistency of the same." (*Teachings,* p. 51.)

"It is the will of the heavens that all men receive truth according to their ability to decipher and digest eternal verities. . . . This concept demonstrates both divine wisdom and mercy. Men ought not to receive more than they are ready to receive; the Lord would never want to drown one in the living waters!" (Joseph Fielding McConkie and Robert L. Millet, *Sustaining and Defending the Faith,* p. 99; see also Alma 12:9–11; D&C 19:29, 31; 71:1.)

28. A true seed] A true seed, or correct principle, is one in which faith can be exercised. It is one which, if properly understood and nourished, will grow and bring forth good fruit in its season. In this case, the seed is not some vague philosophical abstraction; rather, the seed is something very specific. It is the word of truth concerning the coming of Christ (see Alma 33:22–23; 34:4–5). The proposition or principle Alma is challenging them to consider, asking them to pray about, encouraging them to experience, pertains to Christ Jesus.

28. Ye will resist the Spirit of the Lord] "There are many that harden their hearts against the Holy Spirit, that it hath no place in them; wherefore, they cast many things away which are written and esteem them as things of naught" (2 Nephi 33:2).

28. Feel these swelling motions] This is the beginning of testimony. Truth is felt. We know and recognize it by a feeling within our souls. Joseph Smith wrote: "I was one day reading the Epistle of James, first chapter and fifth verse, which reads: If any of you lack wisdom, let him ask of God, that giveth to all men liberally, and upbraideth not; and it shall be given him. Never did any passage of scripture come with more power to the heart of man than this did at this time to mine. It seemed to enter with great force into every feeling of my heart." (Joseph Smith—History 1:12.) Explaining to Oliver Cowdery why his efforts at translation had been unsuccessful, the Lord said, "I will cause that your bosom shall burn within you; therefore, you shall feel that it is right" (D&C 9:8). Conversely, the Savior warned the meridian disciples against those who would not "understand with their heart" (Matthew 13:15); Nephi spoke of his rebellious brothers as being "past feeling" (1 Nephi 17:45); and Paul described those given up to uncleanness and greed as "having the understanding darkened," as being blind of heart, and as "being past feeling" (Ephesians 4:18–19).

28. It beginneth to enlarge my soul] Alma repeatedly emphasizes that obtaining spiritual maturity is a process. That which is of God enlarges the soul, while that which is of the adversary quietly "cheateth" souls "and leadeth them away carefully down to hell" (2 Nephi 28:21).

28. It beginneth to enlighten my understanding] "And that which doth not edify is not of God, and is darkness. That which is of God is light; and he that receiveth light, and continueth in God, receiveth more light; and that light groweth brighter and brighter until the perfect day." (D&C 50:23–24.)

28. It beginneth to be delicious to me] Describing the fruit of the tree of life, Lehi said, "it filled my soul with exceedingly great joy; wherefore, I began to be desirous that my family should partake of it also; for I knew that it was desirable above all other fruit" (1 Nephi 8:12). Lucy Mack Smith records a similar vision granted her husband, Joseph Smith Sr. Finding that the fruit of the tree was "delicious beyond description," he also determined that he could not eat it alone. He gathered his family to the tree and invited them to eat. "The more we ate," he said, "the more we seemed to desire, until we even got down upon our knees and scooped it up, eating it by double handfuls." (*History of Joseph Smith by His Mother Lucy Mack Smith,* pp. 49–50.)

29. We need not be so vain as to suppose that because we have a testimony, because we have had spiritual experiences of one sort or another, we have a perfect or even an adequate knowledge of the gospel.

30–31. As temporal seeds produce after their own kind, so it is with spiritual seeds. Each produces that which is in its own image and likeness. The seeds of faith produce faith, the seeds of righteousness produce righteousness, virtue produces virtue, and so on. Conversely, meanness produces meanness, hatred produces hatred, as vanity, impurity, hypocrisy, and all other seeds germinated in darkness and sin produce after their own kind. Those who accept the challenge to experiment upon the proposition that Jesus is the Christ do more than read and pray about him; they seek to do those things he has commanded us to do. They do his will. Then they come to know. Further, those who do the works of Christ begin to receive the fruits of Christ and acquire the nature of Christ, since every good seed brings forth fruit after its own likeness (see Moroni 7:13–16). To acknowledge, in this case, that the seed is good is to acknowledge that Jesus is the Christ, that his Church is true, and that his power and authority are held by his anointed servants.

32–33. That which causes the soul to grow is good and of God. Seeds that do not have that effect are to be cast away. All good seeds, that is, all good doctrine, will share characteristics in common with all other good doctrine—they will lift the soul, enlighten the mind, bring a sense of peace and joy, encourage, inspire, motivate to faithfulness, create a desire for a greater knowledge of the things of God, and attract other good seeds.

34. Your faith is dormant] See commentary on verse 21.

34. Your mind doth begin to expand] The gospel does not just stretch the heart and the soul of its adherents; it expands their minds. Sainthood cannot be found in ignorance. True religion could hardly be mindless. Indeed, the religion of heaven must embrace an endowment to the intellect.

35. Is not this real] Spiritual experience is real. Spiritual things are known. They cannot be explained away by reference to the physical senses and the meager means of measuring those senses. Indeed, things of the Spirit descend to the core of being and can be known with greater certitude than things of the physical world.

35. Because it is light] The light of the gospel quickens the understanding and enlightens the eye. "And if your eye be single to my glory," the Lord said, "your whole bodies shall be filled with light, and there shall be no darkness in you; and that body which is filled with light comprehendeth all things" (D&C 88:67).

35. Because it is discernible] The gospel of Jesus Christ is not a mystery. It is discernible. An understanding of it is within the capacity of all who are expected to live it. None need be dependent for their salvation on the scholarship, understanding, or spiritual gifts and powers of others.

35. Tasted this light] In the midst of a great doctrinal discourse, Joseph Smith said: "This is good doctrine. It tastes good. I can taste the principles of eternal life, and so can you. They are given to me by the revelations of Jesus Christ; and I know that when I tell you these words of eternal life as they are given to me, you taste them, and I know that you believe them. You say honey is sweet, and so do I. I can also taste the spirit of eternal life. I know it is good; and when I tell you of these things which were given me by inspiration of the Holy Spirit, you are bound to receive them as sweet, and rejoice more and more." (*Teachings*, p. 355.)

37–43. The spirit has the same need for nourishment as the physical body. Spiritual health requires the same attention to diet as does its physical counterpart. Many are sick or, to all intents and purposes, dead in the realm of spiritual things because their spirits have known no diet other than the mundane, the impure, the unholy. Others are spiritually anemic, having only nibbled at eternal truths and preferring to stuff their bellies with spiritual junk food. Still others, who have feasted upon the meat of the gospel, lack spiritual strength because they have not exercised or used the spiritual gifts that have been given them.

Spiritual strength, testimony, faith—none are the product of a moment; all must be nurtured, each comes quietly, almost imperceptibly. Impatience is characteristic of the spiritually immature. A mistake common to the spiritually inexperienced is the establishing of deadlines for the Lord. This is done by determining that they will submit themselves to a given ritual of spiritual activities for a specified period, by which time the Lord is to have manifest himself or his will to the prescribed degree. This would be something akin to a parent giving a child a goal to grow a given number of inches in a prescribed period, promising rewards if they succeed and punishments should they fail. A good seed properly nourished will bring forth a rich harvest, but the season of harvest is of the Lord's choosing—it will come "in his own time, and in his own way, and according to his own will" (D&C 88:68).

38. "Some [seeds] fell upon stony places, where they had not much earth: and forthwith they sprung up, because they had no deepness of earth: And when the sun was up, they were scorched; and because they had no root, they withered away" (Matthew 13:5–6).

40. Eye of faith] The faithful look forward with an eye of faith to that which is to come, as contrasted with an eye of skepticism, doubt, or unbelief. We see now with an eye of faith. One day the pure in heart shall truly behold with their eyes that which they viewed in mortality with an eye of faith (see Ether 12:19).

42. If we so live that we nourish the seed—seek to strengthen our witness and knowledge of Christ—all the days of our lives, there will come a time when we shall see as we are seen and know as we are known. We shall partake of the tree of life in the ultimate sense, that is, partake of the glory of the celestial kingdom; we shall drink of the waters of life and eat the hidden manna in exaltation evermore.

Zenos Renders Thanks to the Son of God

Alma 33:1–11

1. Now after Alma had spoken these words, they sent forth unto him desiring to know whether they should believe in one God, that they might obtain this fruit of which he had spoken, or how they should plant the seed, or the word of which he had spoken, which he said must be planted in their hearts; or in what manner they should begin to exercise their faith.

2. And Alma said unto them: Behold, ye have said that ye could not worship your God because ye are cast out of your synagogues. But behold, I say unto you, if ye suppose that ye cannot worship God, ye do greatly err, and ye ought to search the scriptures; if ye suppose that they have taught you this, ye do not understand them.

3. Do ye remember to have read what Zenos, the prophet of old, has said concerning prayer or worship?

4. For he said: Thou art merciful, O God, for thou hast heard my prayer, even when I was in the wilderness; yea, thou wast merciful when I prayed concerning those who were mine enemies, and thou didst turn them to me.

5. Yea, O God, and thou wast merciful unto me when I did cry unto thee in my field; when I did cry unto thee in my prayer, and thou didst hear me.

6. And again, O God, when I did turn to my house thou didst hear me in my prayer.

7. And when I did turn unto my closet, O Lord, and prayed unto thee, thou didst hear me.

8. Yea, thou art merciful unto thy children when they cry unto thee, to be heard of thee and not of men, and thou wilt hear them.

9. Yea, O God, thou hast been merciful unto me, and heard my cries in the midst of thy congregations.

10. Yea, and thou hast also heard me when I have been cast out and have been despised by mine enemies; yea, thou didst hear my cries, and wast angry with mine enemies, and thou didst visit them in thine anger with speedy destruction.

11. And thou didst hear me because of mine afflictions and my sincerity; and it is because of thy Son that thou hast been thus merciful unto me, therefore I will cry unto thee in all mine afflictions, for in thee is my joy; for thou hast turned thy judgments away from me, because of thy Son.

1. See commentary on verses 22–23.
2. Ye ought to search the scriptures] To these Zoramites,

displaced from their places of worship because of their poverty, Alma gave the charge to "search the scriptures." This implies that even the poor in that society had access to holy writ and the ability to read and understand it.

3–11. From these verses written by Zenos in the form of a prayer, literally a psalm of thanksgiving, we obtain a sketch of his prophetic activities. Because of his witness of the Redeemer, Zenos was put to death by his enemies (see Helaman 8:19). Alma quotes the psalm because it illustrates the propriety of praying in whatever circumstance one finds oneself, be it wilderness, fields, home, or closet. In so doing, he places special emphasis on the mercy extended to men through the atonement of the Son of God.

3. Zenos, the prophet of old] See *Commentary* 1:147.

4. Thou didst turn them to me] It is by the power of charity, the pure love of Christ—a love sought and then bestowed upon the seeker—that disputing parties can be reconciled and differences resolved. "The effectual fervent prayer of a righteous man availeth much" (James 5:16), and it is through this means that enemies are forged into friends, warring nations into cooperative bodies.

8. To be heard of thee and not of men] "Our prayers are to God, not to men. Our yearnings for divine assistance are addressed to the Man of Holiness, not to unholy and finite men and women. . . . The esteem and approbation of the present world cannot bestow those silent but certain honors that will come in the Savior's due time to the pure in heart." (Robert L. Millet, *An Eye Single to the Glory of God,* p. 58; see also commentary on 3 Nephi 13:1–8, 16–18.)

11. Thou didst hear me because of mine afflictions and my sincerity] How often afflictions lead some to sincerity! When our souls have been stretched; when our bodies or our hearts have been racked with pain and frustration; when our present hopes have been dashed; when there is no place to go but to God for comfort—at such a time our words more truly reflect and mirror the soul's sincere desire.

11. It is because of thy Son that thou hast been thus merciful unto me] Zenos, Zenock, Ezias, and Neum—prophets on the brass plates whose words are not in our Bible—had the gospel in its purity and preached with that same purity. Their messages are gospel-centered and Christ-centered. Their understanding of God and the Godhead is like our own: they believed in God the Eternal Father, in his Son Jesus Christ the Redeemer, and in the Holy Ghost. They worshipped and prayed to the Father in the name of the Son. And they sought and preached forgiveness of sin through the condescension and mediation of that sinless Son of Man.

Ancient Prophets Prophesied of the Messiah As God's Son

Alma 33:12–21

12. And now Alma said unto them: Do ye believe those scriptures which have been written by them of old?

13. Behold, if ye do, ye must believe what Zenos said; for, behold he said: Thou hast turned away thy judgments because of thy Son.

14. Now behold, my brethren, I would ask if ye have read the scriptures? If ye have, how can ye disbelieve on the Son of God?

15. For it is not written that Zenos alone spake of these things, but Zenock also spake of these things—

16. For behold, he said: Thou art angry, O Lord, with this people, because they will not understand thy mercies which thou hast bestowed upon them because of thy Son.

17. And now, my brethren, ye see that a second prophet of old has testified of the Son of God, and because the people would not understand his words they stoned him to death.

18. But behold, this is not all; these are not the only ones who have spoken concerning the Son of God.

19. Behold, he was spoken of by Moses; yea, and behold a type was raised up in the wilderness, that whosoever would look upon it might live. And many did look and live.

20. But few understood the meaning of those things, and this because of the hardness of their hearts. But there were many who were so hardened that they would not look, therefore they perished. Now the reason they would not look is because they did not believe that it would heal them.

21. O my brethren, if ye could be healed by merely casting about your eyes that ye might be healed, would ye not behold quickly, or would ye rather harden your hearts in unbelief, and be slothful, that ye would not cast about your eyes, that ye might perish?

12–21. No doctrine is more fundamental to true Christianity than that of the divine sonship of Christ. Nor has any doctrine been subject to more perversion and sophistry in the creeds of men than the relationship of the Son to the Father. On this matter the Old Testament is virtually silent, and the New Testament, without the aid of modern revelation, may be confusing. In the Old Testament there are many references to Christ's birth, ministry, death, and resurrection, but few plain statements that he would be begotten of the Eternal Father and thus be his literal offspring. In the midst of a passage that is clearly Messianic, the Lord says of the seed of David: "I will be his father, and he shall be my son" (2 Samuel 7:14). In the second Psalm we read of the Lord attesting: "Thou art my Son; this day have I begotten thee" (Psalm 2:7). It is, however, to the Book of Mormon that we turn to be taught this doctrine in plainness. In the present instance Alma quotes both Zenos and Zenock as teaching that the mercy of God is to be manifest through his Son.

We are also reminded that some six hundred years before the earthly advent of Jesus Christ, Nephi saw in vision his mother, Mary, bearing the divine child in her arms, and heard the angel declare him to be "the Son of the Eternal Father" (see 1 Nephi 11:13–21). Prophesying of the Savior's birth, Alma the Younger described Mary as "a precious and chosen vessel, who shall be overshadowed and conceive by the power of the Holy Ghost, and bring forth a son, yea, even the Son of God" (Alma 7:10). Similarly, King Benjamin told his people that the "Lord Omnipotent" would come down from heaven and take upon himself a "tabernacle of clay." "He shall be called Jesus Christ," he said, "the Son of God, the Father of heaven and earth, the Creator of all things from the beginning; and his mother shall be called Mary." (Mosiah 3:5–8.)

17. They stoned him to death] Zenock, like his prophetic colleague, Zenos, was put to death for his witness of the Redeemer. The doctrine of Christ speaks peace to the penitent but arouses the antagonism and anger of the unclean.

19. He was spoken of by Moses] Indeed, he was spoken of by all the holy prophets (see Jacob 4:4; 7:11; Mosiah 13:33; 3 Nephi 20:24; Acts 10:43).

19. A type was raised up in the wilderness] The brazen serpent held up by Moses was a type or shadow of Christ (see Numbers 21:5–9; John 3:14–15). Many who were bitten by serpents died, but those who looked to the brazen serpent were healed. In like manner those who look to Christ, after they have been poisoned by sin and waywardness promoted by the serpent, are freed from sin and live the abundant life. Some among the ancient Israelites, however, just like many in our day, refused to look to Christ, either because of the simpleness of the way (see 1 Nephi 17:41; Alma 37:46) or from disbelief (Alma 33:20).

The Divine Sonship of Christ Is the Seed from Which All Faith Must Grow

Alma 33:22–23

22. If so, wo shall come upon you; but if not so, then cast about your eyes and begin to believe in the Son of God, that he will come to redeem his people, and that he shall suffer and die to atone for their sins; and that he shall rise again from the dead, which shall bring to pass the resurrection, that all men shall stand before him, to

be judged at the last and judgment day, according to their works.

23. And now, my brethren, I desire that ye shall plant this word in your hearts, and as it beginneth to swell even so nourish it by your faith. And behold, it will become a tree, springing up in you unto everlasting life. And then may God grant unto you that your burdens may be light, through the joy of his Son. And even all this can ye do if ye will. Amen.

22–23. The beginning of Alma 33 records that those to whom Alma had delivered his marvelous discourse about planting the seed of faith and attempting an experiment upon the word inquired of him how they should plant the seed or the word of which he had spoken. Alma responded by quoting the thanksgiving psalm of Zenos, a passage from Zenock, and the story of Moses' raising a snake upon a pole and inviting those afflicted by poisonous snakes to look upon it. Having done this, Alma testified that salvation comes only by "belief in the Son of God." That is, salvation comes only to those who embrace the doctrine that Christ is literally God's son.

Alma then attests that all other doctrines of salvation grow out of the doctrine of Christ's divine sonship. He cites the doctrines of atonement, resurrection, and judgment as natural appendages to the doctrine of divine sonship. If Christ is literally the Son of the Eternal Father, he can work out an infinite and eternal atonement, he can lay down his life and take it up again, and by so doing he can lay claim to the right to sit in judgment upon all for whom he made that everlasting sacrifice. If, on the other hand, he is not the son of a mortal woman and an eternal and glorified Man, he is without the ability to take up his life again (for mortals have no such power). Thus there is no faith unto salvation save that faith which centers in Christ as God's son.

22. He shall suffer and die to atone for their sins] Jacob expounded the doctrine of Christ as follows: "And he cometh into the world that he may save all men if they will hearken unto his voice; for behold, he suffereth the pains of all men, yea, the pains of every living creature, both men, women, and children, who belong to the family of Adam. And he suffereth this that the resurrection might pass upon all men, that all might stand before him at the great and judgment day." (2 Nephi 9:21–22; compare Mosiah 3:7; D&C 18:11; 19:16.)

23. That your burdens may be light] Our burdens become light as we shed them through the atonement of Christ, as we yoke ourselves everlastingly to him who bore the greatest burden of all. The Master said: "Come unto me, all ye that labour and are heavy laden, and I will give you rest. Take my yoke upon you, and learn of me; for I am meek and lowly in heart: and ye shall find rest unto your souls. For my yoke is easy, and my burden is light." (Matthew 11:28–30.)

"The Lord's yoke, his strengthening tie and lifeline to us, is customized—suited perfectly and precisely to those who in sincerity seek to follow him. Discipleship is personal, not competitive. Rather, he who knows the hearts and minds of men and women chooses the challenges and orchestrates the opportunities that will result in optimal learning and maximal development. . . .

"There is no weight in life greater than the burden of sin. The Master beckons us to unburden ourselves of the taints of a telestial world and adorn ourselves with the robes of righteousness. He invites us to shed the superficial, discard the ephemeral and the transient, and eschew the cheap and the gaudy." (Robert L Millet, *An Eye Single to the Glory of God*, p. 18.)

23. All this can ye do if ye will] Agency was a central issue in the first estate, the matter over which the war in heaven was fought. God wants all of his children to return to him, but not through coercion or unrighteous dominion. Theirs is the choice.

> Know this, that ev'ry soul is free
> To choose his life and what he'll be;
> For this eternal truth is giv'n:
> That God will force no man to heav'n.
>
> He'll call, persuade, direct aright,
> And bless with wisdom, love, and light,
> In nameless ways be good and kind,
> But never force the human mind.
>
> Freedom and reason make us men;
> Take these away, what are we then?
> Mere animals, and just as well
> The beasts may think of heav'n or hell.
>
> May we no more our pow'rs abuse,
> But ways of truth and goodness choose;
> Our God is pleased when we improve
> His grace and seek his perfect love.
> (*Hymns*, no. 240.)

Amulek Affirms That the Word Is in Christ

Alma 34:1–8

1. And now it came to pass that after Alma had spoken these words unto them he sat down upon the ground, and Amulek arose and began to teach them, saying:

2. My brethren, I think that it is impossible that ye should be ignorant of the things which have been spoken concerning the coming of Christ, who is taught by us to be the Son of God; yea, I know that these things were taught unto you bountifully before your dissension from among us.

3. And as ye have desired of my beloved brother that he should make known unto you what ye should do, because of your afflictions; and he hath spoken somewhat unto you to prepare your minds; yea, and he hath exhorted you unto faith and to patience—

4. Yea, even that ye would have so much faith as even to plant the word in your hearts, that ye may try the experiment of its goodness.

5. And we have beheld that the great question which is in your minds is whether the word be in the Son of God, or whether there shall be no Christ.

6. And ye also beheld that my brother has proved unto you, in many instances, that the word is in Christ unto salvation.

7. My brother has called upon the words of Zenos, that redemption cometh through the Son of God, and also upon the words of Zenock; and also he has appealed unto Moses, to prove that these things are true.

8. And now, behold, I will testify unto you of myself that these things are true. Behold, I say unto you, that I do know that Christ shall come among the children of men, to take upon him the transgressions of his people, and that he shall atone for the sins of the world; for the Lord God hath spoken it.

2. See Alma 31:8.

3. He hath exhorted you unto faith and to patience] Alma's discourse on faith (Alma 32) is a classic: it sets forth the terms and conditions by which faith in Christ is developed. It focuses upon how one who is lacking in faith may, through the divine experiment, grow from desire to belief, through a hope that there is and shall be a Christ, to that point at which that person's faith is perfect and he or she is able eventually to partake of the fruit of the tree of life. Alma's plea with the Zoramites is to be patient with that which they do not know at present, to wait upon the Lord, to trust in his infinite and eternal purposes.

4–5. To plant the word in their hearts was to let the idea—the concept that Jesus is the Christ and that he shall come into the world—rest in their minds and hearts, and then to ponder, pray, and thus test its truthfulness. See Alma 32:28; 33:23.

6–7. Alma spoke according to that order and consistent pattern of those called to testify of the truth: he first preached the word, then drew upon the testimonies of the prophets and seers who had preceded him (in this case, Zenos, Zenock, and Moses), and then bore his own witness.

8. See commentary on Alma 5:45.

Jesus Christ Offers an Infinite and Eternal Sacrifice

Alma 34:9–14

9. For it is expedient that an atonement should be made; for according to the great plan of the Eternal God there must be an atonement made, or else all mankind must unavoidably perish; yea, all are hardened; yea, all are fallen and are lost, and must perish except it be through the atonement which it is expedient should be made.

10. For it is expedient that there should be a great and last sacrifice; yea, not a sacrifice of man, neither of beast, neither of any manner of fowl; for it shall not be a human sacrifice; but it must be an infinite and eternal sacrifice.

11. Now there is not any man that can sacrifice his own blood which will atone for the sins of another. Now, if a man murdereth, behold will our law, which is just, take the life of his brother? I say unto you, Nay.

12. But the law requireth the life of him who hath murdered; therefore there can be nothing which is short of an infinite atonement which will suffice for the sins of the world.

13. Therefore, it is expedient that there should be a great and last sacrifice, and then shall there be, or it is expedient there should be, a stop to the shedding of blood; then shall the law of Moses be fulfilled; yea, it shall be all fulfilled, every jot and tittle, and none shall have passed away.

14. And behold, this is the whole meaning of the law, every whit pointing to that great and last sacrifice; and that great and last sacrifice will be the Son of God, yea, infinite and eternal.

9. It is expedient that an atonement should be made]
The Atonement was not simply a nice thing, a sweet offering of a gentle and kind man; it was and is absolutely necessary. Though Christ's atonement was a voluntary offering, though he suffered and laid down his life of his own free will, what he did needed to be done; all eternity hung in the balance until it was an accomplished reality. Had there been no atonement, no amount of goodness, no amount of caring and concern, no amount of human strength could have made up the difference. We are forever indebted to him who bought us with his blood.

9. All are hardened; yea, all are fallen and are lost]

Because of the fall of Adam and Eve, all the children of men inherit the conditions of mortality, including a fallen nature. They are oblivious to things of righteousness, are hardened and insensitive to matters spiritual, are lost and alienated from the family of God. "Adam fell," Elder Bruce R. McConkie has written. "We know that this fall came because of transgression, and that Adam broke the law of God, became mortal, and was thus subject to sin and disease and all the ills of mortality. We know that the effects of his fall passed upon all his posterity; all inherited a fallen state, a state of mortality, a state in which spiritual and temporal death prevail. In this state all men sin. All are lost. All are fallen. All are cut off from the presence of God. . . . Such a way of life is inherent in this mortal existence." Further: "Spiritual death passes upon all men when they become accountable for their sins. Being thus subject to sin they die spiritually; they die as pertaining to the things of the Spirit; they die as pertaining to the things of righteousness; they are cast out of the presence of God. It is of such men that the scriptures speak when they say that the natural man is an enemy to God." (*Promised Messiah,* pp. 244, 350.)

10–14. Because of the importance of the doctrinal concept contained herein, it seems appropriate to quote from an earlier volume of this commentary. "The atonement of Jesus Christ is infinite and eternal. First, it is infinite in the sense that it is timeless—embracing past, present, and future. Our Savior is the Lamb 'slain from the foundation of the world' (Revelation 13:8), and the effects of his atonement reach back to Eden and forward to the Millennium's end. Adam and Eve were taught to call upon God in the name of the Son for a remission of their sins, by virtue of an atonement which would be worked out some four thousand years hence (Moses 5:8). Enoch saw and bore witness some three thousand years before the events of Gethsemane and Calvary: 'The Righteous is lifted up, and the Lamb is slain from the foundation of the world' (Moses 7:47). Jesus Christ offered himself a ransom for sin in one singular moment in earth's history, so 'that as many as would believe and be baptized in his holy name, and endure in faith to the end, should be saved—not only those who believed after he came in the meridian of time, in the flesh, but all those from the beginning, even as many as were before he came, who believed in the words of the holy prophets . . . , as well as those who should come after, who should believe in the gifts and callings of God by the Holy Ghost, which beareth record of the Father and of the Son' (D&C 20:25–27; cf. Alma 39:17–19). Those who lived before the meridian of time were taught to repent and believe in the name of the Holy One, 'to look forward unto the Messiah, and believe in him to come as though he already was' (Jarom 1:11).

"Second, the atonement of Jesus Christ is infinite in the sense that it conquers the most universal reality in mortal existence—death. The earth and every plant and animal upon it—all forms of life—are subject to death through the Fall. The light of the Atonement must shine upon all who were previously shadowed by the effects of the Fall. An infinite atonement must bring life to all that is subject to death.

"Third, the Atonement is infinite in that it encompasses all the worlds Christ created. Jesus Christ, as Jehovah, advanced and progressed in the premortal existence to the point at which he, under the direction of Elohim, became the creator of countless worlds (Moses 1:33; 7:30) and became known as the Lord Omnipotent. In speaking of those orbs formed by the Lord Jehovah, God said to Moses: 'And by *the word of my power*, have I created them, *which is mine Only Begotten Son*, who is full of grace and truth. And worlds without number have I created; and I also created them for mine own purpose; and by the Son I created them, which is mine Only Begotten.' And then, in discussing the role of the Son in the redemption and glorification of these worlds (their 'passing away'), the divine word continued: 'But only an account of this earth, and the inhabitants thereof, give I unto you. For behold, there are *many worlds that have passed away by the word of my power*. And there are many that now stand, and innumerable are they unto man; but all things are numbered unto me, for they are mine and I know them.' (Moses 1:32–33, 35.) Likewise, in the Vision of the Glories, the Lord explained that by Christ, 'and through him, and of him, the worlds are and were created, and the inhabitants thereof are begotten sons and daughters unto God' (D&C 76:24; cf. vv. 40–42). In 1843 Joseph Smith prepared a poetic version of the Vision; the verses associated with the above passage read as follows:

And I heard a great voice, bearing record from heav'n,
'He's the Saviour, and only begotten of God—
By him, of him, and through him, the worlds were all made,
Even all that careen in the heavens so broad,

'Whose inhabitants too, from the first to the last,
Are sav'd by the very same Saviour of ours;
And, of course, are begotten God's daughters and sons,
By the very same truths and the very same pow'rs.'
(*Times and Seasons* 4:82–83.)

"Fourth, the atonement of Jesus Christ is infinite because Christ himself is an infinite being. From his mother, Mary—a mortal woman—he inherited mortality, the capacity to die. On the other hand, he inherited from his Father, the Almighty Elohim, immortality, the power to live forever. The suffering and sacrifice in Gethsemane and on Golgotha were undertaken by a being who was greater than man, one possessing the powers of a God. This was no human sacrifice, not even simply an act of a wise and all-loving teacher. It was more, infinitely more, than an example of submission or a model of humanitarianism. He did for us what no other being could do. Yes, it is true that 'there was no other good enough to pay the price of sin. He only could unlock the gate of heav'n and let us in.' ('There Is a Green Hill Far Away,' *Hymns*, no. 194.) But it is equally true that what Jesus of Nazareth accomplished in and through the awful atonement is beyond human comprehension; it is the work of an infinite personage." (*Commentary* 1:236–38, italics in original.)

10. A great and last sacrifice] Christ's atonement was great and last in terms of its spiritual significance, its impact, its time-lessness and eternal and everlasting relevance, not necessarily in terms of its chronology. John the Baptist, as a part of his prayer of ordination upon the heads of Joseph Smith and Oliver Cowdery, explained that the Aaronic Priesthood "shall never be taken again from the earth, *until the sons of Levi do offer again an offering unto the Lord in righteousness*" (D&C 13). According to Oliver Cowdery, the Baptist said: "Upon you my fellow-servants, in the name of Messiah, I confer this Priesthood and this authority, which shall remain upon earth, *that the sons of Levi may yet offer an offering unto the Lord in righteousness!*" (*Messenger and Advocate*, vol. 1 [October 1834], pp. 14–16, italics added; cited in 1981 ed. of the Pearl of Great Price, p. 59.) Likewise, a modern revelation speaks of the sons of Moses and the sons of Aaron offering an acceptable sacrifice in the temple to be erected in Independence, Jackson County, Missouri (see D&C 84:31).

Joseph Smith taught: "The offering of sacrifice has ever been connected and forms a part of the duties of the Priesthood. It began with the Priesthood, and will be continued until after the coming of Christ. . . . *These sacrifices, as well as every ordinance belonging to the Priesthood, will, when the Temple of the Lord shall be built, and the sons of Levi be purified, be fully restored and attended to in all their powers, ramifications, and blessings.* This ever did and ever will exist when the powers of the Melchizedek Priesthood are sufficiently manifest; else how can the restitution of all things spoken of by the Holy Prophets be brought to pass? It is not to be understood that the law of Moses will be established again with all its rites and variety of ceremonies; this has never been spoken of by the prophets; but *those things which existed prior to Moses' day, namely, sacrifice, will be continued.* It may be asked by some, what necessity for sacrifice, since the Great Sacrifice was offered? In answer to which, if repentance, baptism, and faith existed prior to the days of Christ, what necessity for them since that time?" (*Teachings*, pp. 172–73, italics added.) It may be that such a sacrifice, as a part of the restitution of all things, will be instituted one final time to point toward the great and last sacrifice of Jesus the Lamb (see Joseph Fielding Smith, *Doctrines of Salvation* 3:94; Bruce R. McConkie, *Mortal Messiah* 1:128).

10. Not a sacrifice of man, . . . it shall not be a human sacrifice] As we have observed Jesus Christ was more than man, more than human. He was God, and thus his sacrifice was infinite in the sense that it was not limited by what puny man can do.

11. That is, no mortal man can do such a thing. But Jesus Christ, the Son of Man of Holiness (Moses 6:57), was empowered through conception to accomplish his foreordained task.

13. A stop to the shedding of blood] When the resurrected Lord appeared to the Nephites, he told them: "I am the light and the life of the world. I am Alpha and Omega, the beginning and the end. And ye shall offer up unto me no more the shedding of blood. . . . And ye shall offer for a sacrifice unto me a broken heart and a contrite spirit." (3 Nephi 9:18–20.) In our day that same Lord has commanded: "Thou shalt offer a sacrifice unto the Lord thy God in righteousness, even that of a broken heart and a contrite spirit" (D&C 59:8; compare Psalm 51:17; Isaiah 66:2; 2 Nephi 2:7).

14. The law of Moses was as one grand prophecy of Christ, inasmuch as it testified of the salvation to be obtained in and through his atoning blood. Jesus was the fulfillment of that prophecy.

14. Every whit pointing to that great and last sacrifice] "Everything connected with the lesser law pointed to the higher law, or in other words it pointed to Christ and his gospel. Each Mosaic performance was so arranged and so set up that it was a type and a shadow of what was to be. Their sacrifices were performed in similitude of the coming sacrifice of their Messiah; the rituals out of which they gained forgiveness of sins were tokens of what was to be in the life of Him whose atonement made forgiveness possible; their every act, every ordinance, every performance—all that they did—pointed the hearts and minds of believing worshippers forward to Jesus Christ and him crucified. All this was understood by those among them who were faithful and true; the rebellious and slothful were like their modern counterparts, unbelieving, nonconforming, unsaved." (Bruce R. McConkie, *Promised Messiah*, p. 416.)

14. The Son of God, yea, infinite and eternal] As we noted earlier, the atonement was infinite because Christ was an infinite being.

Mercy Satisfies Justice Through the Atonement

Alma 34:15–16

15. And thus he shall bring salvation to all those who shall believe on his name; this being the intent of this last sacrifice, to bring about the bowels of mercy, which overpowereth justice, and bringeth about means unto men that they may have faith unto repentance.

16. And thus mercy can satisfy the demands of justice, and encircles them in the arms of safety, while he that exercises no faith unto repentance is exposed to the whole law of the demands of justice; therefore only unto him that has faith unto repentance is brought about the great and eternal plan of redemption.

15. He shall bring salvation] That is, he shall make eternal life or exaltation available to those who believe and obey. See commentary on Alma 11:40.

15. To bring about the bowels of mercy, which overpowereth justice] See commentary on Alma 12:34; 42:15.

15. Bringeth about means unto men . . . unto repentance] That is, through the merits and mercy and grace of the Holy Messiah, a means, a way, a path is provided whereby man can forsake sin and a sinful nature, come unto Christ, and be perfected in him.

16. Justice may be satisfied in two ways: (1) keeping the law perfectly; or (2) suffering the effects of a broken law. Christ satisfied the demands of justice in both of these ways; he kept the law perfectly for himself and suffered in the Garden of Eden and on the cross for and in behalf of those of us who repent. Those who refuse to repent are exposed to the "whole law of the demands of justice," that is, they must face without divine aid the consequences of wilful sin. They therefore lose the opportunity for that rehabilitative redemption which can only come through Christ's enabling power. Bruce C. Hafen has provided the following thoughtful insight: "I once wondered if those who refuse to repent but who then satisfy the law of justice by paying for their own sins are then worthy to enter the celestial kingdom. The answer is no. The entrance requirements for celestial life are simply higher than merely satisfying the law of justice. For that reason, paying for our sins will not bear the same fruit as repenting of our sins. Justice is a law of balance and order and it must be satisfied, either through our payment or his. But if we decline the Savior's invitation to let him carry our sins, and then satisfy justice by ourselves, we will not yet have experienced the complete rehabilitation that can occur through a combination of divine assistance and genuine repentance. Working together, those forces have the power permanently to change our hearts and our lives, preparing us for celestial life." (*The Broken Heart*, pp. 7–8.)

Zoramites Are Encouraged to Pray Always

Alma 34:17–29

17. Therefore may God grant unto you, my brethren, that ye may begin to exercise your faith unto repentance, that ye begin to call upon his holy name, that he would have mercy upon you;

18. Yea, cry unto him for mercy; for he is mighty to save.

19. Yea, humble yourselves, and continue in prayer unto him.

20. Cry unto him when ye are in your fields, yea, over all your flocks.

21. Cry unto him in your houses, yea, over all your household, both morning, mid-day, and evening.

22. Yea, cry unto him against the power of your enemies.

23. Yea, cry unto him against the devil, who is an enemy to all righteousness.

24. Cry unto him over the crops of your fields, that ye may prosper in them.

25. Cry over the flocks of your fields, that they may increase.

26. But this is not all; ye must pour out your souls in your closets, and your secret places, and in your wilderness.

27. Yea, and when you do not cry unto the Lord, let your hearts be full, drawn out in prayer unto him continually for your welfare, and also for the welfare of those who are around you.

28. And now behold, my beloved brethren, I say unto you, do not suppose that this is all; for after ye have done all these things, if ye turn away the needy, and the naked, and visit not the sick and afflicted, and impart of your substance, if ye have, to those who stand in need—I say unto you, if ye do not any of these things, behold, your prayer is vain, and availeth you nothing, and ye are as hypocrites who do deny the faith.

29. Therefore, if ye do not remember to be charitable, ye are as dross, which the refiners do cast out, (it being of no worth) and is trodden under foot of men.

20–26. Amulek may well be paraphrasing the message of the ancient prophet Zenos, quoted earlier by Alma (see Alma 33:3–11). Zenos taught that the disposition or attitude of the supplicant was far more important than the location of the prayer— that the great God could hear and would certainly respond to sincere prayers offered in all phases and places of one's existence. We learn from this potent prophetic counsel that the people of God are perfectly justified in petitioning the Most High for divine assistance in regard to their flocks, herds, and fields, meaning (more generally) their temporal welfare. As long as the Saints follow the injunction to seek first the kingdom of God and seek prosperity in order to do good (see Jacob 2:17–19), they are within the bounds of propriety when they pray in faith for the necessities of life, to have sufficient for their needs and circumstances.

21. Few things are of greater import—and thus few things deserve more pleading prayer—than the family. Parents and children who pray morning and night for one another, for their health and strength and protection, for their spiritual well-being and growth, will generally find their hearts turning toward home more frequently and will usually seek an eternal family unit with greater diligence.

22. Power over one's enemies need not entail the destruction of one's enemies. Rather, it might take the form of having enemies miraculously transformed into friends. "Thou wast merciful," Zenos declared to God, "when I prayed concerning those who were mine enemies, and *thou didst turn them to me*" (Alma 33:4, italics added).

23. Cry unto him against the devil] Our constant prayer to our Father in Heaven should be for power to resist the enticements and temptations of Satan, strength to dispel him from our lives.

26. It is not enough to pray for our families or our crops or our business. It is not enough to pray for power over Lucifer. We must also plead with the Lord in silent and secret prayer in behalf of our own souls, that the cleansing powers of the Spirit may make of us new creatures, new creatures in Christ. We must pray for the gifts and guidance of the Spirit, for the inspiration of heaven to accompany us in our daily walk and talk.

27. The Saints of the Most High have a constant prayer in their hearts, a perpetual yearning for the things of God. It is not that they are expected to be uttering prayers beneath their breath every minute of the day, for such could rapidly turn to a meaningless and empty ritual. Rather, in addition to regular prayers in our minds, we are asked to think wholesome thoughts and ponder on worthwhile matters. "Whatsoever things are true, whatsoever things are honest, whatsoever things are just, whatsoever things are pure, whatsoever things are lovely, whatsoever things are of good report; if there be any virtue, and if there be any praise, think on these things" (Philippians 4:8). The Lord has thus commanded us to "let the solemnities of eternity rest upon your minds" (D&C 43:34). Compare Alma 37:36–37; Proverbs 3:5–6.

28–29. We are under obligation in some cases to help to bring about the answers to our prayers. It is not enough to pray that God will alleviate the suffering of the hungry, clothe the naked, lift up the hands that hang down, or strengthen the feeble knees; where possible we must extend ourselves in Christian service to the needy and less fortunate if we expect to enjoy the peaceful assurance that the Lord is pleased with our offerings. Truly, "charity preventeth a multitude of sins" (JST, 1 Peter 4:8).

28. Ye are as hypocrites who do deny the faith] That is, you are acting in ways unbecoming a member of the Lord's household; you have not put on Christ and thus are not involved in Christlike activities.

29. See commentary on Moroni 7:44–48.

Now Is the Day of Our Salvation

Alma 34:30–36

30. And now, my brethren, I would that, after ye have received so many witnesses, seeing that the holy scriptures testify of these things, ye come forth and bring fruit unto repentance.

31. Yea, I would that ye would come forth and harden not your hearts any longer; for behold, now is the time and the day of your salvation; and therefore, if ye will repent and harden not your hearts, immediately shall the great plan of redemption be brought about unto you.

32. For behold, this life is the time for men to prepare to meet God; yea, behold the day of this life is the day for men to perform their labors.

33. And now, as I said unto you before, as ye have had so many witnesses, therefore, I beseech of you that ye do not procrastinate the day of your repentance until the end; for after this day of life, which is given us to prepare for eternity, behold, if we do not improve our time while in this life, then cometh the night of darkness wherein there can be no labor performed.

34. Ye cannot say, when ye are brought to that awful crisis, that I will repent, that I will return to my God. Nay, ye cannot say this; for that same spirit which doth possess your bodies at the time that ye go out of this life, that same spirit will have power to possess your body in that eternal world.

35. For behold, if ye have procrastinated the day of your repentance even until death, behold, ye have become subjected to the spirit of the devil, and he doth seal you his; therefore, the Spirit of the Lord hath withdrawn from you, and hath no place in you, and the devil hath all power over you; and this is the final state of the wicked.

36. And this I know, because the Lord hath said he dwelleth not in unholy temples, but in the hearts of the righteous doth he dwell; yea, and he has also said that the righteous shall sit down in his kingdom, to go no more out; but their garments should be made white through the blood of the Lamb.

31. Now is the time and the day of your salvation] In a general sense, Amulek is stating that mortality is the time given us to prepare for life with God. In a narrower sense, he may be suggesting that the Zoramites should take advantage of the moment, grab for the opportunity at the present to search out and secure the truth, for time and circumstance will quickly rob them of subsequent opportunities.

31. Immediately shall the great plan of redemption be brought about unto you] People do not need to wait until some distant day in order to enjoy the fruits of gospel living. In fact, the true Saints enjoy heaven on earth. Indeed, if we will quickly humble ourselves, call upon the Lord in mighty prayer in behalf of our souls, and submit ourselves to the divine will, we can participate directly and immediately in the blessings of the plan of salvation.

32. The day of this life] Here the word *day* seems to refer to a period of time. Thus Amulek is saying, in essence, "The period of time in this mortal existence is the time granted us to perform our labors."

33. Ye do not procrastinate the day of your repentance] Indeed, procrastination is the thief of eternal life. As a person puts off his repentance until later, he learns to his dismay that the power to change is inversely proportional to the power of habit: the greater the strength of habit, the lesser the strength to change.

33. If we do not improve our time while in this life] This is an unusual phrase, for we generally do not speak of "improving" our time. We might say, "If we do not make effective use of our time . . ." or "If we do not improve ourselves during this period of time, then it will be too late." Jacob warned against wasting "the days of [our] probation" (2 Nephi 9:27), while Samuel the Lamanite warned against procrastinating the time of our repentance until it is "everlastingly too late" (Helaman 13:38). See also 2 Corinthians 6:1–2.

33. Then cometh the night of darkness] If we are not careful, if we do not prepare properly, if we do not focus upon things that matter most, we shall eventually come, unprepared, face to face with death. While the sun shines we are expected to walk in the light and perform labors appropriate to the light, for sooner than we think we shall be called upon to pass through that veil which separates the embodied from the disembodied. The spirit world, called here the "night of darkness" (compare Alma 41:7), is a place wherein righteous works are to be continued, not begun.

33. There can be no labor performed] It is not to be understood from this verse that no labors are performed in the postmortal spirit world after physical death. The Church of the Lamb is organized there, the gospel is preached there to millions, and thus the work of the Lord goes forward on both sides of the veil. If, however, a person has enjoyed the privileges of gospel understanding but chooses in this life to deny or defy that light, to reject the truth and avoid the works of righteousness when he knows better, it becomes extremely difficult for him to turn around, to change directions at the time of death.

Elder Melvin J. Ballard explained that until a person "learns to overcome the flesh, his temper, his tongue, his disposition to indulge in the things God has forbidden, he cannot come into the celestial kingdom of God—he must overcome either in this life or in the life to come. But this life is the time in which men are to repent. Do not let any of us imagine that we can go down to the grave not having overcome the corruptions of the flesh and then lose in the grave all our sins and evil tendencies. They will be with us. They will be with the spirit when separated from the body. . . . The spirit only can repent and change, and then the battle has to go forward with the flesh afterwards. It is much easier to overcome and serve the Lord when both flesh and spirit are combined as one. . . . Every man and woman who is putting off until the next life the task of correcting and overcoming the weakness of the flesh are sentencing themselves to years of bondage, for no man or woman will come forth in the resurrection until they have completed their work, until they have overcome, until they have done as much as they can do." ("The Three Degrees of Glory," sermon delivered in Ogden, Utah, on 22 September 1922.)

34. That awful crisis] The crisis of being unprepared to meet one's Maker.

34. That same spirit which doth possess your bodies] Amulek is here making use of the word *spirit* to refer to one's disposition, attitude, proclivity, spiritual direction. Men and women will not have an immediate reversal of attitude at the time of death. If they have desired evil things; if they have sold their souls for attention and applause and acclaim; if they have craved carnal pleasures alone—if their lives have followed this course, they need not expect to inherit spirituality in the world to come. This is in harmony with what Alma will later call the doctrine of restoration (see Alma 41). In the words of Jacob: "Wo unto all those who die in their sins; for they shall return to God, and behold his face, and remain in their sins" (2 Nephi 9:38). In a positive vein, if a person leaves this life loving the Lord, questing for the Spirit, striving for truth and light, he will continue in that same direction in the world of spirits among persons of like disposition. He will go on to gain eternal life.

34. That eternal world] This is a specific reference to the spirit world and not to life in the kingdoms of glory. As we have seen already (see Elder Ballard's words in commentary on verse 33), all persons will repent. The only questions are where and under what circumstances they will repent and thus what degree of glory they will obtain. There are no murderers and liars and whoremongers in the telestial kingdom, only repentant murderers, liars, and whoremongers. See Alma 3:26; 48:23.

35. He doth seal you his] See commentary on Helaman 13:32, 38. Compare also 2 Nephi 9:46.

35. The Spirit of the Lord hath withdrawn from you] One of the immediate consequences of sin is the withdrawal of the Holy Spirit, a withdrawal which leads to feelings of guilt and pain and emptiness (compare D&C 19:20). Moroni taught that "despair cometh because of iniquity" (Moroni 10:22). When one is void of holiness he opens himself to the influence of the unholy.

35. This is the final state of the wicked] Telestial persons shall, as we have noted above, eventually repent of their sins, and thus being subject to Satan is not exactly their final state: they shall inherit a kingdom of glory. This verse seems to apply more directly to the sons of perdition, those who have lost all desire and disposition to repent, who have gone beyond the point of no return, who shall be resurrected but to a kingdom of no glory. Such is their final state.

36. The righteous shall sit down in his kingdom, to go no more out] They have returned to their heavenly home after a long and arduous sojourn in mortality. They shall advance and progress everlastingly, shall grow from grace to grace and from exaltation to exaltation, and shall reside in the family of the Gods forevermore.

36. Their garments should be made white] "These are they who are just men made perfect through Jesus the mediator of the new covenant, who wrought out this perfect atonement through the shedding of his own blood" (D&C 76:69).

Victory over Sin Is Won Through Vigilance

Alma 34:37–41

37. And now, my beloved brethren, I desire that ye should remember these things, and that ye should work out your salvation with fear before God, and that ye should no more deny the coming of Christ;

38. That ye contend no more against the Holy Ghost, but that ye receive it, and take upon you

the name of Christ; that ye humble yourselves even to the dust, and worship God, in whatsoever place ye may be in, in spirit and in truth; and that ye live in thanksgiving daily, for the many mercies and blessings which he doth bestow upon you.

39. Yea, and I also exhort you, my brethren, that ye be watchful unto prayer continually, that ye may not be led away by the temptations of the devil, that he may not overpower you, that ye may not become his subjects at the last day; for behold, he rewardeth you no good thing.

40. And now my beloved brethren, I would exhort you to have patience, and that ye bear with all manner of afflictions; that ye do not revile against those who do cast you out because of your exceeding poverty, lest ye become sinners like unto them;

41. But that ye have patience, and bear with those afflictions, with a firm hope that ye shall one day rest from all your afflictions.

37. Work out your salvation] In the strictest sense, no one can work out his own salvation. No person can create himself, resurrect himself, ransom himself from sin, or cleanse his own heart from the taints of the world. These are the actions of a God, of an infinite being. We can seek and ask and petition and supplicate. We can apply his blood, take his name, accept his enabling power, and acquire his nature, but we cannot save ourselves. The Saints of God seek above all things for the sanctifying powers of the Spirit in their lives. Through this process they have their hearts changed, and by means of that Spirit they are motivated to righteous works, the works of God. In that sense, Christ has begun to live in them (see Galatians 2:20). Thus Paul implored: "Wherefore, my beloved, as ye have always obeyed, not as in my presence only, but now much more in my absence, work out your own salvation with fear and trembling." And now note the Apostle's words: "*For it is God which worketh in you* both to will and to do of his good pleasure." (Philippians 2:12–13, italics added.)

38. That ye contend no more against the Holy Ghost] "Quench not the Spirit" (1 Thessalonians 5:19), Paul pleaded. "Will ye reject the words of the prophets . . . and quench the Holy Spirit," Jacob asked, "and make a mock of the great plan of redemption, which hath been laid for you? Know ye not that if ye will do these things, that the power of the redemption and the resurrection, which is in Christ, will bring you to stand with shame and awful guilt before the bar of God?" (Jacob 6:8–9.)

38. Humble yourselves even to the dust] See Mosiah 4:1–3; Helaman 12:7–8.

38. That ye live in thanksgiving daily] "Thou shalt thank the Lord thy God in all things. . . . And in nothing doth man offend God, or against none is his wrath kindled, save those who

confess not his hand in all things, and obey not his commandments." (D&C 59:7, 21.)

39. Be watchful unto prayer continually] See Alma 13:28.

39. He rewardeth you no good thing] See Alma 30:60.

Alma's Converts Expelled by the Zoramites

Alma 35:1–14

1. Now it came to pass that after Amulek had made an end of these words, they withdrew themselves from the multitude and came over into the land of Jershon.

2. Yea, and the rest of the brethren, after they had preached the word unto the Zoramites, also came over into the land of Jershon.

3. And it came to pass that after the more popular part of the Zoramites had consulted together concerning the words which had been preached unto them, they were angry because of the word, for it did destroy their craft; therefore they would not hearken unto the words.

4. And they sent and gathered together throughout all the land all the people, and consulted with them concerning the words which had been spoken.

5. Now their rulers and their priests and their teachers did not let the people know concerning their desires; therefore they found out privily the minds of all the people.

6. And it came to pass that after they had found out the minds of all the people, those who were in favor of the words which had been spoken by Alma and his brethren were cast out of the land; and they were many; and they came over also into the land of Jershon.

7. And it came to pass that Alma and his brethren did minister unto them.

8. Now the people of the Zoramites were angry with the people of Ammon who were in Jershon, and the chief ruler of the Zoramites, being a very wicked man, sent over unto the people of Ammon desiring them that they should cast out of their land all those who came over from them into their land.

9. And he breathed out many threatenings against them. And now the people of Ammon did not fear their words; therefore they did not cast them out, but they did receive all the poor of the Zoramites that came over unto them; and they did nourish them, and did clothe them, and did give unto them lands for their inheritance; and they did administer unto them according to their wants.

10. Now this did stir up the Zoramites to anger against the people of Ammon, and they began to mix with the Lamanites and to stir them up also to anger against them.

11. And thus the Zoramites and the Lamanites began to make preparations for war against the people of Ammon, and also against the Nephites.

12. And thus ended the seventeenth year of the reign of the judges over the people of Nephi.

13. And the people of Ammon departed out of the land of Jershon, and came over into the land of Melek, and gave place in the land of Jershon for the armies of the Nephites, that they might contend with the armies of the Lamanites and the armies of the Zoramites; and thus commenced a war betwixt the Lamanites and the Nephites, in the eighteenth year of the reign of the judges; and an account shall be given of their wars hereafter.

14. And Alma, and Ammon, and their brethren, and also the two sons of Alma returned to the land of Zarahemla, after having been instruments in the hands of God of bringing many of the Zoramites to repentance; and as many as were brought to repentance were driven out of their land; but they have lands for their inheritance in the land of Jershon, and they have taken up arms to defend themselves, and their wives, and children, and their lands.

1–14. As we have seen repeatedly in the Book of Mormon, wickedness can have no fellowship with righteousness. The rebellious have no stomach for those who submit to God's will. Frequently, those who shun the light do all they can to expel from their midst and even destroy the children of light. The wicked Zoramites—whose eyes and hearts have been turned aside by their idolatries, their worldly treasures—here move to rid themselves of the poorer element of the society who had opened themselves to the power of the word preached by Alma and Amulek. As with the experience of Paul, their apostolic colleague on another continent, their proclamation of the truth destroys the craft of those who prey upon the innocent and unwary (see Acts 19:25). But the Lord is merciful and is eager to deliver his chosen people (see 1 Nephi 1:20), and provision is made by the people of Ammon to protect the lives of and give succor to the new converts to Christianity.

9. They did administer unto them according to their wants] "And now," King Benjamin had declared, "for the sake of . . . retaining a remission of your sins from day to day, that ye may walk guiltless before God—I would that ye should impart of your substance to the poor . . . both spiritually and temporally, according to their wants" (Mosiah 4:26; see also 18:29; D&C 51:3). A modern revelation affirms: "And you are to be equal, or in other words, you are to have equal claims on the properties [in the storehouse], for the benefit of managing the concerns of your stewardships, every man according to his wants and his needs, inasmuch as his wants are just" (D&C 82:17).

10. See Alma 31:4; 43:4.

The Need for Righteous Counsel in a Day of Turmoil

Alma 35:15–16

15. Now Alma, being grieved for the iniquity of his people, yea for the wars, and the bloodsheds, and the contentions which were among them; and having been to declare the word, or sent to declare the word, among all the people in every city; and seeing that the hearts of the people began to wax hard, and that they began to be offended because of the strictness of the word, his heart was exceedingly sorrowful.

16. Therefore, he caused that his sons should be gathered together, that he might give unto them every one his charge, separately, concerning the things pertaining unto righteousness. And we have an account of his commandments, which he gave unto them according to his own record.

15–16. "The Book of Mormon, which is the most correct book on earth, demonstrates that the major responsibility for teaching our [children] the great plan of the Eternal Father—the Fall, rebirth, Atonement, Resurrection, Judgment, eternal life—rests with fathers. It should be done individually as well as in the family. It should be preached and discussed so our children will know the commandments. It should be done from their youth up—and often.

"May we teach our children as the exemplary Book of Mormon fathers taught their sons. And may they, like Nephi, listen and obey, knowing that because of those teachings they too were born of goodly parents." (Ezra Taft Benson, *A Witness and a Warning*, pp. 71–72.)

God Sustains Those Who Trust Him

Alma 36:1–3

1. My son, give ear to my words; for I swear unto you, that inasmuch as ye shall keep the commandments of God ye shall prosper in the land.

2. I would that ye should do as I have done, in remembering the captivity of our fathers; for they were in bondage, and none could deliver them except it was the God of Abraham, and the God of Isaac, and the God of Jacob; and he surely did deliver them in their afflictions.

3. And now, O my son Helaman, behold, thou art in thy youth, and therefore, I beseech of thee that thou wilt hear my words and learn of me; for I do know that whosoever shall put their trust in God shall be supported in their trials, and their troubles, and their afflictions, and shall be lifted up at the last day.

1. This command and statement of blessing had been among the Nephites from the beginning (see 1 Nephi 2:20–21; 2 Nephi 1:20; Alma 37:13).

1. Ye shall prosper in the land] Prosperity may come in the form of financial reward or the goods of the land. It may, however, come in other ways, such as God opening the windows of heaven and pouring down knowledge upon the heads of his people (see Malachi 3:10; D&C 121:26, 33); bestowing his Spirit or his presence upon individuals or nations (see 2 Nephi 1:20); or strengthening the missionary effort so that thousands and tens of thousands of our Father's other children come unto Christ through his Church and kingdom (see Helaman 3:24–25).

2. See Alma 5:6.

3. Trust in God] "Trust in the Lord with all thine heart; and lean not unto thine own understanding. In all thy ways acknowledge him, and he shall direct thy paths." (Proverbs 3:5–6.) We are required to trust in God with our whole heart. God requires absolute obedience and surrender in every realm of our lives before he will direct our paths. Indeed, we best honor ourselves by first honoring God. To trust God is to acknowledge his wisdom and his goodness, to acknowledge that he knows what is best for us and that he will bring his purposes to pass in his own time, and in his own way, and according to his own will.

3. Shall be supported in their trials] Alma could attest to this principle by personal experience. See verse 27.

3. Shall be lifted up at the last day] That is, he shall be raised in the resurrection in immortality and go on to receive eternal life (see 3 Nephi 27:14–15; JST, John 6:54).

An Angel of God Declares Repentance to Alma

Alma 36:4–11

4. And I would not that ye think that I know of myself—not of the temporal but of the spiritual, not of the carnal mind but of God.

5. Now, behold, I say unto you, if I had not been born of God I should not have known these things; but God has, by the mouth of his holy angel, made these things known unto me, not of any worthiness of myself.

6. For I went about with the sons of Mosiah, seeking to destroy the church of God; but behold, God sent his holy angel to stop us by the way.

7. And behold, he spake unto us, as it were the voice of thunder, and the whole earth did tremble beneath our feet; and we all fell to the earth, for the fear of the Lord came upon us.

8. But behold, the voice said

unto me: Arise. And I arose and stood up, and beheld the angel.

9. And he said unto me: If thou wilt of thyself be destroyed, seek no more to destroy the church of God.

10. And it came to pass that I fell to the earth; and it was for the space of three days and three nights that I could not open my mouth, neither had I the use of my limbs.

11. And the angel spake more things unto me, which were heard by my brethren, but I did not hear them; for when I heard the words—If thou wilt be destroyed of thyself, seek no more to destroy the church of God—I was struck with such great fear and amazement lest perhaps I should be destroyed, that I fell to the earth and I did hear no more.

4. Not of the carnal mind but of God] The carnal mind is the mind which is born of the flesh or of the world, as contrasted with Paul's charge that the Saints obtain the "mind of Christ" (1 Corinthians 2:16). "For my thoughts are not your thoughts, neither are your ways my ways, saith the Lord. For as the heavens are higher than the earth, so are my ways higher than your ways and my thoughts than your thoughts." (Isaiah 55:8–9.) Alma is able to bear witness of these truths because they have been made known to him by the Holy Spirit.

5. Born of God] See *Commentary* 2:168–76, 303–9.

5. Not of any worthiness of myself] Alma rightly observed, as did the Apostle Paul many years later, that his marvelous conversion, which commenced at the hands of a heavenly being, was not the result of his own worthiness. To what, then, do these formerly misguided souls owe the good fortune of their salvation?

Paul, in an eloquent testimony, responds to this seeming irregularity in the order of heaven in this language: "Who [meaning God] hath saved us [himself, Timothy, and by implication many others], and called us with an holy calling, not according to our works, but according to his own purpose and grace, which was given us in Christ Jesus *before the world began*" (2 Timothy 1:9, italics added; compare Galatians 1:14–16). For a discussion as to why not all are accorded a call to repentance in similar fashion see *Commentary* 2:304–5.

9. If thou wilt of thyself be destroyed] "This is not a threat on Alma's mortal life but a solemn warning relative to the eternal welfare of his soul" (*Commentary* 2:306).

10. For three days and three nights Alma was consigned to the darkness of hell, where, as we shall read in the verses that follow, he suffered to the uttermost farthing for his sins. When we read Alma's declaration that he had been "born of God" (verses 5 and 26), it is imperative that we understand that his new birth was not occasioned by the manifestation of an angel but rather through his suffering for his sins and his willing acceptance of Christ.

Suffering Is a Necessary Part of Obtaining a Remission of Sins

Alma 36:12–16

12. But I was racked with eternal torment, for my soul was harrowed up to the greatest degree and racked with all my sins.

13. Yea, I did remember all my sins and iniquities, for which I was tormented with the pains of hell; yea, I saw that I had rebelled against my God, and that I had not kept his holy commandments.

14. Yea, and I had murdered many of his children, or rather led them away unto destruction; yea, and in fine so great had been my iniquities, that the very thought of coming into the presence of my God did rack my soul with inexpressible horror.

15. Oh, thought I, that I could be banished and become extinct both soul and body, that I might not be brought to stand in the presence of my God, to be judged of my deeds.

16. And now, for three days and for three nights was I racked, even with the pains of a damned soul.

12. Racked] Strained to the utmost.

12. Eternal torment] Eternal not in duration but in nature, for it comes from that God who is Eternal (see D&C 19:6–12).

13. I did remember all my sins] Each violation of the divine law must be accounted for. In the day of judgment, the wicked will have "a perfect knowledge" of all their guilt, and their uncleanness, and their nakedness, while the righteous will have a "perfect knowledge of their enjoyment, and their righteousness, being clothed with purity, yea, even with the robe of righteousness" (2 Nephi 9:14). Even when we repent in this life in the sincerity of our hearts, the remembrance of the sin remains, though in time the agony and the sense of personal disappointment leave us.

14–15. There is no greater pain than the shame of sin. Alma describes thus the moment of judgment for the unrepentant sinner: "In this awful state we shall not dare to look up to our God; and we would fain be glad if we could command the rocks and the mountains to fall upon us to hide us from his presence" (Alma 12:14). "Do ye suppose that ye could be happy to dwell with that holy Being," asked Moroni, "when your souls are racked with a consciousness of guilt that ye have ever abused his laws? Behold, I say unto you that ye would be more miserable to dwell with a holy and just God, under a consciousness of your filthiness

before him, than ye would to dwell with the damned souls in hell.
For behold, when ye shall be brought to see your nakedness
before God, and also the glory of God, and the holiness of Jesus
Christ, it will kindle a flame of unquenchable fire upon you."
(Mormon 9:3–5.) On the other hand, the difference between
Alma before and after his conversion is worth noting. Having
been cleansed of his sins, and in vision seeing "God sitting upon
his throne, surrounded with numberless concourses of angels . . .
[his] soul did long to be there" (Alma 36:22).

14. I had murdered many of his children] This is graphic
language. As one who has been born of God, as one who senses
the significance of this mortal sphere and thus the worth of souls,
Alma knows how frighteningly awful it is to lead souls astray
from the path of peace. "None but fools will trifle with the souls of
men," Joseph Smith said (*Teachings*, p. 137). "Fear not them
which kill the body," Jesus taught, "but are not able to kill the
soul: but rather fear him which is able to destroy both soul and
body in hell" (Matthew 10:28).

Christ Has Power to Bear Our Sins

Alma 36:17–19

17. And it came to pass that as I
was thus racked with torment,
while I was harrowed up by the
memory of my many sins, behold,
I remembered also to have heard
my father prophesy unto the
people concerning the coming of
one Jesus Christ, a Son of God, to
atone for the sins of the world.

18. Now, as my mind caught
hold upon this thought, I cried

within my heart: O Jesus, thou
Son of God, have mercy on me,
who am in the gall of bitterness,
and am encircled about by the
everlasting chains of death.

19. And now, behold, when I
thought this, I could remember
my pains no more; yea, I was harrowed up by the memory of my
sins no more.

17–19. Alma's experience dramatically illustrates the power
that is in Christ to bear our sins, to lift the burden of sin from the
souls of those who have been properly cleansed by their own suffering, granting them a newness of life.

18. Gall of bitterness] See *Commentary* 2.308.

19. True repentance requires that we surrender the memory of
the sin, not in the sense that we are without the knowledge that
we once transgressed but rather in the sense that we have laid
down the burden, that our confidence might now wax strong in
the presence of the Lord (see 2 Nephi 10:20). If Alma was without

any memory whatsoever of his sin, he could not have given this recitation to Helaman. We must retain sufficient memory of the pain to avoid a repetition of the suffering. Still, as we grow in the things of the Spirit, that which is forgiven is to be forgotten. It is not true repentance when we cling to a sensuous memory in whose mental replaying we find delight. "Behold, he who has repented of his sins, the same is forgiven, and I, the Lord, remember them no more. By this ye may know if a man repenteth of his sins—behold, he will confess them and forsake them." (D&C 58:42–43.)

The Repentant Experience Great Joy

Alma 36:20–21

20. And oh, what joy, and what marvelous light I did behold; yea, my soul was filled with joy as exceeding as was my pain!
21. Yea, I say unto you, my son, that there could be nothing so exquisite and so bitter as were my pains. Yea, and again I say unto you, my son, that on the other hand, there can be nothing so exquisite and sweet as was my joy.

20. What joy, and what marvelous light] Joy and light are companions of the Spirit and ever stand opposite the misery and darkness associated with sin and the evil one.

20. Joy as exceeding as was my pain] There is no anguish or pain associated with suffering for sin that is not more than matched by the joy that comes from having done so. True repentance is always attended by a spirit of rejoicing (see Mosiah 4:3). Indeed, when we seek a remission of sins even the angels in heaven rejoice over us (see D&C 62:3).

21. So exquisite] Meaning acute, extreme, consummate, exact, complete.

21. There could be nothing . . . so bitter as were my pains] The violation of God's law requires punishment. In so saying we but echo the testimony of Lehi and Alma, who both reasoned that unless a penalty followed the breaking of divine law, the law would be nothing more than the figment of someone's imagination. (See 2 Nephi 2:10–13; Alma 42:16–18.) Modern revelation assures us that this is the case, declaring that the unrepentant must suffer even as Christ suffered. "Which suffering caused myself, even God, the greatest of all, to tremble because of pain, and to bleed at every pore, and to suffer both body and spirit—and would that I might not drink the bitter cup, and shrink" (D&C 19:18).

What, then, of those who accept Jesus as the Christ and allow his infinite and eternal sacrifice to stand in the stead of the suffering just described? Are such excused from all suffering? Contrary to much in the Christian world tradition, the answer is no. True repentance, which centers in faith in Christ and his atoning sacrifice, still requires sufficient suffering on the part of those desiring to repent to make them one in mind and soul with the Savior. The blessings of salvation, though freely given, cannot be wholly undeserved. In all things we must unite our best effort with him who sacrificed all. The testimony of holy writ is that without suffering there is no repentance.

Alma Testifies That He Has Been Born of God

Alma 36:22–23

22. Yea, methought I saw, even as our father Lehi saw, God sitting upon his throne, surrounded with numberless concourses of angels, in the attitude of singing and praising their God; yea, and my soul did long to be there.

23. But behold, my limbs did receive their strength again, and I stood upon my feet, and did manifest unto the people that I had been born of God.

22. Methought I saw] Nephi describes a similar vision his father, Lehi, had had, saying, "he thought he saw God" (1 Nephi 1:8). The pattern is one of moderation and temperance, of modesty in speech. The stories are told without embellishment.

22. Numberless concourses of angels] See *Commentary* 1:26.

23. I had been born of God] Alma's conversion story, the account of his being "born of God," is a scriptural classic. In it we find the elements that ought to characterize every conversion or rebirth. The story dramatically illustrates the following principles:

1. The effectual prayer of the righteous avails much (see James 5:16). The appearance of the angel to Alma came not because of his worthiness but because of that of his parents, who prayed for his conversion with all their heart and soul, and also in response to the united prayers of the congregation of Saints. "And again, the angel said: Behold, the Lord hath heard the prayers of his people, and also the prayers of his servant, Alma, who is thy father; for he has prayed with much faith concerning thee that thou mightest be brought to the knowledge of the truth; therefore, for this purpose have I come to convince thee of the power and authority of God, that the prayers of his servants might be answered according to their faith" (Mosiah 27:14).

2. The violation of the laws of God brings suffering. The

Atonement does not negate the necessity of godly sorrow or godly suffering in the process of cleansing the soul. Pain is a purifying agent. The miracle of healing the sin–laden soul rests with God, yet that miracle is rarely manifest in such a manner as to disallow all suffering.

The word *suffer* carries two distinct meanings: "to allow," as in "suffer the little children to come unto me," and "to feel pain." Both meanings are joined in the origin of the word that means "to bear." *Bear* itself means both "to carry" and "to bear up" or "endure." When a woman bears a child, she carries it in her womb until the time of birth, then in pain she brings the child into the world, and yet her labor and pain bring with it a bonding and love between mother and infant. Spiritual birth follows a like pattern in that it too involves a labor of pain which brings a bonding of love.

3. Marvelous joy is associated with repentance. In it we remove the burden of sin, replacing it with companionship of the Holy Spirit. Repentance is like coming home after a long absence; it is a reunion of love and glad memories.

4. There is a power in Christ to bear the burden of our sins. We can no more remit our own sins than we can give birth to ourselves, resurrect ourselves, or create a place for ourselves in the celestial kingdom. Truly, we are saved by the grace of our God after all we can do (see 2 Nephi 25:23).

5. There is a zeal and devotion that attends true repentance. "I have labored without ceasing," Alma said (verse 24). Paul, Alma's Old World counterpart, said it in this way: "But by the grace of God I am what I am: and his grace which was bestowed upon me was not in vain; but I labored more abundantly than they all: yet not I, but the grace of God which was with me" (1 Corinthians 15:10).

We would err if we supposed that to be born again requires a conversion experience as dramatic as Alma's. It does not. Alma's story is preserved in the scriptures because it is unusual and powerful. For virtually everyone in Alma's day and ours, the process of being born again is quiet and unobtrusive, yet all conversion experiences ought to contain certain elements in common. "We must be cautious," President Ezra Taft Benson has warned, "as we discuss these remarkable examples. Though they are real and powerful, they are the exception more than the rule. For every Paul, for every Enos, and for every King Lamoni, there are hundreds and thousands of people who find the process of repentance much more subtle, much more imperceptible. Day by day they move closer to the Lord, little realizing they are building a godlike life." ("A Mighty Change of Heart," *Ensign*, October 1989, p. 5.)

Devotion and Zeal Attend True Repentance

Alma 36:24-26

24. Yea, and from that time even until now, I have labored without ceasing, that I might bring souls unto repentance; that I might bring them to taste of the exceeding joy of which I did taste; that they might also be born of God, and be filled with the Holy Ghost.

25. Yea, and now behold, O my son, the Lord doth give me exceedingly great joy in the fruit of my labors;

26. For because of the word which he has imparted unto me, behold, many have been born of God, and have tasted as I have tasted, and have seen eye to eye as I have seen; therefore they do know of these things of which I have spoken, as I do know; and the knowledge which I have is of God.

24. I have labored without ceasing] Herein is Alma's restitution for sin. Many in the Christian world who claim a spiritual rebirth appear to have adopted a new religious vocabulary and yet have made no other changes in their lives. The evidence of Alma's new birth was a new life—a life of devotion and service to God.

24. Be filled with the Holy Ghost] "Those who have put off the natural man—what Paul called the 'works of the flesh'—begin to enjoy what he called the 'fruit of the Spirit,' namely, 'love, joy, peace, longsuffering, gentleness, goodness, faith, meekness, temperance'; they begin to 'walk in the Spirit.' (Galatians 5:19–25.) As Benjamin explained, such persons are humble and submissive, eager to know and carry out the will of the Savior, eager to have their own wishes swallowed up in the higher will of God. The Spirit of God sanctifies—it cleanses and purges filth and dross out of the human soul as though by fire. The Spirit does far more, however, than remove uncleanness. It also fills. It fills one with a holy element, with a sacred presence that motivates the person to a godly walk and goodly works. These persons do not necessarily plan out how they will perform the works of righteousness; they do not plot and design which deeds and what actions are to be done in every situation. Rather, they embody righteousness. They are goodness. In their lives, works are seldom a means to some end; good works flow from a regenerate heart and evidence their commitment to Christ. Yes, these persons do have agency. Indeed, they are freer than free, because they have given themselves up to the Lord and his purposes. They choose to do good, but their choices are motivated by the Spirit of the Lord." (Robert L. Millet, *Life in Christ*, pp. 98–99.)

24. Taste of the exceeding joy] See commentary on Alma 32:35.

26. Seen eye to eye as I have seen] Joseph Smith declared: "We don't ask any people to throw away any good they have got; we only ask them to come and get more. What if all the world should embrace this Gospel? They would then see eye to eye, and the blessings of God would be poured out upon the people, which is the desire of my whole soul." (*Teachings*, p. 275.)

The Faithful Are Tried and Blessed

Alma 36:27–30

27. And I have been supported under trials and troubles of every kind, yea, and in all manner of afflictions; yea, God has delivered me from prison, and from bonds, and from death; yea, and I do put my trust in him, and he will still deliver me.

28. And I know that he will raise me up at the last day, to dwell with him in glory; yea, and I will praise him forever, for he has brought our fathers out of Egypt, and he has swallowed up the Egyptians in the Red Sea; and he led them by his power into the promised land; yea, and he has delivered them out of bondage and captivity from time to time.

29. Yea, and he has also brought our fathers out of the land of Jerusalem; and he has also, by his everlasting power, delivered them out of bondage and captivity, from time to time even down to the present day; and I have always retained in remembrance their captivity; yea, and ye also ought to retain in remembrance, as I have done, their captivity.

30. But behold, my son, this is not all; for ye ought to know as I do know, that inasmuch as ye shall keep the commandments of God ye shall prosper in the land; and ye ought to know also, that inasmuch as ye will not keep the commandments of God ye shall be cut off from his presence. Now this is according to his word.

27. We note with interest that Alma praises God for rescuing him from circumstances that he would not have been in had he not been on the Lord's errand in the first place. We find it difficult to imagine that one can be fully devoted to the kingdom of God and at the same time enjoy a life of undisturbed peace and tranquility. One can hardly expect to faithfully serve the Lord without offending the devil and his minions. The spirits deemed worthy to meet the Savior when he made his visit to the spirit world are described as those who had suffered tribulation in his name and yet had remained firm in the faith. (See D&C 138:13–14.) We suppose that it will be much the same when he returns again.

28–29. The angel who declared repentance to Alma instructed him never to forget the captivity of his fathers and the Lord's goodness in delivering them (see Mosiah 27:16). Alma was true to that instruction and frequently returned to that theme in his discourses. This message was particularly poignant for him because, as we have read, he too had been redeemed from bondage by the power of God. As with nations, so with individuals—the transgression of either leads to destruction or bondage and immense suffering.

Scriptures Enlarge the Memory of the People

Alma 37:1–12

1. And now, my son Helaman, I command you that ye take the records which have been entrusted with me;

2. And I also command you that ye keep a record of this people, according as I have done, upon the plates of Nephi, and keep all these things sacred which I have kept, even as I have kept them; for it is for a wise purpose that they are kept.

3. And these plates of brass, which contain these engravings, which have the records of the holy scriptures upon them, which have the genealogy of our forefathers, even from the beginning—

4. Behold, it has been prophesied by our fathers, that they should be kept and handed down from one generation to another, and be kept and preserved by the hand of the Lord until they should go forth unto every nation, kindred, tongue, and people, that they shall know of the mysteries contained thereon.

5. And now behold, if they are kept they must retain their brightness; yea, and they will retain their brightness; yea, and also shall all the plates which do contain that which is holy writ.

6. Now ye may suppose that this is foolishness in me; but behold I say unto you, that by small and simple things are great things brought to pass; and small means in many instances doth confound the wise.

7. And the Lord God doth work by means to bring about his great and eternal purposes; and by very small means the Lord doth confound the wise and bringeth about the salvation of many souls.

8. And now, it has hitherto been wisdom in God that these things should be preserved; for behold, they have enlarged the memory of this people, yea, and convinced many of the error of their ways, and brought them to the knowledge of their God unto the salvation of their souls.

9. Yea, I say unto you, were it not for these things that these records do contain, which are on these plates, Ammon and his brethren could not have convinced so many thousands of the Lamanites of the incorrect tradition of their fathers; yea, these records and their words brought them unto repentance; that is, they brought them to the knowledge of the Lord their God, and to rejoice in Jesus Christ their Redeemer.

10. And who knoweth but what they will be the means of bringing

many thousands of them, yea, and also many thousands of our stiffnecked brethren, the Nephites, who are now hardening their hearts in sin and iniquities, to the knowledge of their Redeemer?

11. Now these mysteries are not yet fully made known unto me;

therefore I shall forbear.

12. And it may suffice if I only say they are preserved for a wise purpose, which purpose is known unto God; for he doth counsel in wisdom over all his works, and his paths are straight, and his course is one eternal round.

1. Nephihah, Alma's successor in the judgment seat, refused to assume responsibility for the sacred records (see Alma 50:38).

2. Helaman is here charged to take responsibility (care and writing) for the large plates of Nephi. His record on the large plates begins at Alma 45.

2. It is for a wise purpose that they are kept] Many of the Nephite prophet-record keepers sensed the significance of their task, but they were not always aware of the particulars of how the records would eventually be used. See Enos 1:13; Words of Mormon 1:7; Alma 37:12, 14, 18.

3–4. The brass plates play a vital role in the Book of Mormon. Nephi killed a man to obtain them, evidencing the importance of intellectual and spiritual literacy to the perpetuation of a civilization (see 1 Nephi 4:13, 18; Omni 1:17). They contained the five books of Moses; the prophecies of many of the Israelite prophets, down to and including Jeremiah; and a genealogy of Lehi and his family (1 Nephi 5). In addition the brass plates were a more extensive scriptural record than the Bible as we know it (see 1 Nephi 13:23). We learn from Benjamin that at least some (or possibly all) of the brass plates were written in Egyptian (see Mosiah 1:4). They were the scriptures of the Nephites, and we suppose that multiple copies were made by the Nephites in order that all the people might have access to the written word of the Lord.

4. See a similar prophecy by Lehi in 1 Nephi 5:18, though Lehi's oracle is somewhat more limited than Alma's: Lehi indicates that the brass plates shall eventually go forth to every nation, kindred, tongue, and people who are of his (Lehi's) seed. How is it that the brass plates shall go forth to all people and nations? First of all, at least a portion of this sacred record shall go to all the world through the dissemination of the Book of Mormon. Its messages from Zenos, Zenock, Neum, and Ezias, as well as the clarifying and expanding contributions (upon what we call biblical matters) shall come to be known and treasured as the Latter-day Saints flood the earth with the Book of Mormon. Eventually, however, this prophecy shall be fulfilled in a day yet future, presumably the Millennium, when the brass plates are delivered to

the Saints and when God raises up, through his appointed chan-
nels, a prophet, seer, and revelator, who will also be a translator
(see Bruce R. McConkie, "The Doctrinal Restoration," in *The
Joseph Smith Translation: The Restoration of Plain and Precious Truths,*
p. 16). Then the contents of this remarkable volume will be
unfolded to all mankind.

5. If they are kept they must retain their brightness] This
may well have a dual meaning. In a practical sense, as long as the
brass plates (and all the plates, for that matter) are properly cared
for, they will not soil or tarnish; they will retain their brightness
and will prove a blessing to all who read them. In another sense,
as long as the brass plates are retained—preserved, valued, cher-
ished as the scriptural gems they are—they will always keep their
brightness, meaning their centrality, their significance, their
importance in the minds and hearts of the people.

**6. By small and simple things are great things brought
to pass]** See 1 Nephi 16:29; D&C 64:33. "We observe vast, sweep-
ing world events," Elder M. Russell Ballard remarked; "however,
we must remember that the purposes of the Lord in our personal
lives generally are fulfilled through the small and simple things,
and not the momentous and spectacular" (*Ensign*, May 1990, p.
6). We must remember that "the lengthy trek to Zion is accomplished one step at a time. Just as we do not generally bound into
the celestial kingdom after only a brief mortal experience and
testing, so also we do not qualify to be called a disciple of Christ
by monumental moves alone. . . . Well might we ask: If the
Prophet Joseph had asked me to journey to Missouri, would I
have gone? If the Lord had called me to serve as an Apostle,
would I have accepted? If I were asked to tend the children or
grandchildren of the members of the First Presidency, would I
hesitate? If I had been bidden to attend the School of the
Prophets, would I take along my scriptures, study and prepare
ahead of time, and attend regularly? If my call to serve as a home
or visiting teacher had come to me through an open vision, would
I accept? Would I be faithful?" (Robert L. Millet, *An Eye Single to
the Glory of God*, pp. 73, 76.)

"You can put it down in your little black book," Elder Boyd K.
Packer has warned us, "that *if you will not be loyal in the small things,
you will not be loyal in the large things.* If you will not respond to the
so-called insignificant or menial tasks which need to be performed
in the Church and Kingdom, there will be no opportunity for
service in the so-called greater challenges. A man who says he will
sustain the President of the Church or the General Authorities,
but cannot sustain his own bishop, is deceiving himself. The man
who will not sustain the bishop of his ward and the president of
his stake will not sustain the President of the Church." ("Follow

the Brethren," *BYU Speeches of the Year,* 1965, pp. 4–5, italics added.) President Joseph F. Smith observed, "To do well those things which God ordained to be the common lot of all mankind, is the truest greatness" (*Gospel Doctrine,* pp. 285–86).

8. Scriptures "enlarge the memory" in the sense that they remind us of our duty to God and man, of our obligation to cling to goodness and eschew evil. They enlarge the memory to the degree that they bring to remembrance the covenants we have entered into to serve God and keep his commandments. They convince many of the error of their ways as they quicken the spiritual sensitivities and heighten commitment; also, as they hold forth the truth—absolute truth and absolute standards of right and wrong. This verse reminds us of Paul's counsel to Timothy: "All scripture given by inspiration of God is profitable for doctrine, for reproof, for correction, for instruction in righteousness: that the man of God may be perfect, thoroughly furnished unto all good works" (JST, 2 Timothy 3:16–17).

9. Were it not for these things] Compare Mosiah 1:4–5.

9. Ammon and his brethren could not have convinced so many] Ammon and his brethren taught from the scriptures. They bore witness of the truth and sustained their testimonies through the power of holy writ.

11. These mysteries] That is, Alma has not been granted a specific vision of the future so as to tell of the impact of the brass plates, the scriptures, on generation upon generation of his people.

12. He doth counsel in wisdom over all his works] God knows what is best. All things—past, present, and future—are ever before him, and he works with and among the children of men in wisdom and in order to bring to pass his eternal purposes.

12. His paths are straight] "The works, and the designs, and the purposes of God cannot be frustrated, neither can they come to naught. For God doth not walk in crooked paths, neither doth he turn to the right hand nor to the left, neither doth he vary from that which he hath said, therefore his paths are straight, and his course is one eternal round." (D&C 3:1–2; compare 1 Nephi 10:19; Alma 7:20.)

The Commandments of the Lord Are Strict

Alma 37:13–20

13. O remember, remember, my son Helaman, how strict are the commandments of God. And he said: If ye will keep my commandments ye shall prosper in the land—but if ye keep not his commandments ye shall be cut off from his presence.

14. And now remember, my son, that God has entrusted you with these things, which are sacred, which he has kept sacred, and also which he will keep and preserve for a wise purpose in him, that he may show forth his power unto future generations.

15. And now behold, I tell you by the spirit of prophecy, that if ye transgress the commandments of God, behold, these things which are sacred shall be taken away from you by the power of God, and ye shall be delivered up unto Satan, that he may sift you as chaff before the wind.

16. But if ye keep the commandments of God, and do with these things which are sacred according to that which the Lord doth command you, (for you must appeal unto the Lord for all things whatsoever ye must do with them) behold, no power of earth or hell can take them from you, for God is powerful to the fulfilling of all his words.

17. For he will fulfil all his promises which he shall make unto you, for he has fulfilled his promises which he has made unto our fathers.

18. For he promised unto them that he would preserve these things for a wise purpose in him, that he might show forth his power unto future generations.

19. And now behold, one purpose hath he fulfilled, even to the restoration of many thousands of the Lamanites to the knowledge of the truth; and he hath shown forth his power in them, and he will also still show forth his power in them unto future generations; therefore they shall be preserved.

20. Therefore I command you, my son Helaman, that ye be diligent in fulfilling all my words, and that ye be diligent in keeping the commandments of God as they are written.

13. Remember . . . how strict are the commandments of God] The word *strict* here does not seem to imply difficulty so much as straightness or narrowness. To walk in the strict ways of the Lord is to stay on course, to navigate the straight and narrow path with care and caution.

13. If ye will keep my commandments ye shall prosper in the land] See 1 Nephi 1:20; Alma 36:1, 30.

15. To Joseph Smith, who had temporarily lost the favor of God by losing the 116 pages of Book of Mormon manuscript, the Lord said: "Remember, remember that it is not the work of God that is frustrated, but the work of men; for although a man may have many revelations, and have power to do many mighty works, yet if he boasts in his own strength, and sets at naught the counsels of God, and follows after the dictates of his own will and carnal desires, he must fall and incur the vengeance of a just God upon him" (D&C 3:3–4).

15. Ye shall be delivered up unto Satan] That is, "You shall lose access to the Spirit of the Lord, shall be left alone to deal with Satan and his minions. You shall be in Lucifer's power."

15. He may sift you as chaff before the wind] Satan will seek to separate us from God and the things of goodness; he will throw us to the four winds, leaving us helpless and defenseless in a lone and dreary world.

16. Helaman is here counseled as to the power of fervent prayer. If he will seek the Almighty in prayer as to the care and upkeep of the records, if he will petition the heavens for direction and deliverance from evil, there is no power—whether men or demons—that can remove them from his hands. God has all power.

17–18. See Enos 1:12–13.

Lessons About the Jaredite Secret Combinations to Be Taught with Caution

Alma 37:21–31

21. And now, I will speak unto you concerning those twenty-four plates, that ye keep them, that the mysteries and the works of darkness, and their secret works, or the secret works of those people who have been destroyed, may be made manifest unto this people; yea, all their murders, and robbings, and their plunderings, and all their wickedness and abominations, may be made manifest unto this people; yea, and that ye preserve these interpreters.

22. For behold, the Lord saw that his people began to work in darkness, yea, work secret murders and abominations; therefore the Lord said, if they did not repent they should be destroyed from off the face of the earth.

23. And the Lord said: I will prepare unto my servant Gazelem, a stone, which shall shine forth in darkness unto light, that I may discover unto my people who serve me, that I may discover unto them the works of their brethren, yea, their secret works, their works of darkness, and their wickedness and abomi-

nations.

24. And now, my son, these interpreters were prepared that the word of God might be fulfilled, which he spake, saying:

25. I will bring forth out of darkness unto light all their secret works and their abominations; and except they repent I will destroy them from off the face of the earth; and I will bring to light all their secrets and abominations, unto every nation that shall hereafter possess the land.

26. And now, my son, we see that they did not repent; therefore they have been destroyed, and thus far the word of God has been fulfilled; yea, their secret abominations have been brought out of darkness and made known unto us.

27. And now, my son, I command you that ye retain all their oaths, and their covenants, and their agreements in their secret abominations; yea, and all their signs and their wonders ye shall keep from this people, that they know them not, lest peradventure they should fall into

darkness also and be destroyed.

28. For behold, there is a curse upon all this land, that destruction shall come upon all those workers of darkness, according to the power of God, when they are fully ripe; therefore I desire that this people might not be destroyed.

29. Therefore ye shall keep these secret plans of their oaths and their covenants from this people, and only their wickedness and their murders and their abominations shall ye make known unto them; and ye shall teach them to abhor such wickedness and abominations and murders; and ye shall also teach them that these people were destroyed on account of their wickedness and abominations and their murders.

30. For behold, they murdered all the prophets of the Lord who came among them to declare unto them concerning their iniquities; and the blood of those whom they murdered did cry unto the Lord their God for vengeance upon those who were their murderers; and thus the judgments of God did come upon these workers of darkness and secret combinations.

31. Yea, and cursed be the land forever and ever unto those workers of darkness and secret combinations, even unto destruction, except they repent before they are fully ripe.

21. Those twenty-four plates] This refers to the Jaredite record, discovered by an expedition from the people of Limhi as they traveled from the land of Nephi in search of Zarahemla. They became lost in the wilderness, missed Zarahemla, and discovered instead what came to be known as Desolation, the site of the final Jaredite wars. There they discovered bones, weapons, and the twenty-four gold plates which had been buried in such a way as to be discovered in the due time of the Lord. These plates were compiled and prepared by Ether, translated originally by King Mosiah, and abridged by Moroni (see Mosiah 8:9; 21:27; 28:10–19; Ether 1:1–2).

21. That the mysteries and the works of darkness . . . may be made manifest] There were certain things Alma wanted exposed and taught and certain things he did not want made known. Alma wanted those things made known that illustrated the lesson of the ages—that whatsoever nation upholds secret combinations to get power and gain shall be destroyed in the due time of the Lord (see Ether 8:20–22). He wanted his people to know of the secret murders, of their plunderings and other wicked dealings, in order that the Nephites might have sufficient understanding to discern and eradicate these practices when they surfaced among them. He asked specifically that Helaman retain in his possession (for safe keeping) the mechanics of the works of wickedness—the secret oaths and covenants, "their agreements in their secret abominations" (verses 27, 29)—in order that such things not get out and be propagated among the Nephites. Although Helaman was true to his charge, secret combinations emerged among the Nephites through an independent revelation from Satan to man (see Helaman 6:25–28).

21. Ye preserve these interpreters] The interpreters included with the Jaredite record, the two stones placed with the sealed record by the brother of Jared (see Ether 3:22–23). These two stones were delivered centuries later to Joseph Smith (see D&C 17:1).

23. I will prepare unto my servant Gazelem, a stone] This may well be a play on words. Is Gazelem the seer stone or the servant? It is difficult to tell from the passage and depends very much on the placement of a comma in the sentence. Perhaps it could refer to both. It is interesting to note that when Jesus called Simon Peter to the ministry he said: "Thou art Simon the son of Jona: thou shalt be called Cephas, which is, by interpretation, a seer, or a stone" (JST, John 1:42). Though this name or title of Gazelem may be used in regard to any seer who utilizes seer stones, it seems in this instance to be a direct reference to Joseph Smith the Prophet.

23. That I may discover . . . their secret works, their works of darkness] Here the word *discover* seems to mean "reveal." The Lord makes available seeric abilities and implements so that his servants may know of the evil abroad in the land among the ungodly. Early in the history of the restored Church the Lord explained to Oliver Cowdery that the gift of revelation had been bestowed upon him for a purpose: "Blessed art thou, for it [the gift of revelation] shall deliver you out of the hands of your enemies, when, if it were not so, they would slay you and bring your soul to destruction" (D&C 8:4).

24–25. Alma is quoting here from a scriptural source unknown and unavailable to us.

26. The Jaredites did not repent, did not heed the counsel of the prophets among them, and were destroyed. The Nephites came to know of their destruction in fulfillment of the prophecy that secret abominations will eventually be made known to the faithful through the seers and revelators.

28. There is a curse upon all this land] The wickedness and wars and desolation of the Jaredites—a people swept off the land by a just God—had essentially left a curse on the land, at least a solemn warning that all who followed a similar course should reap a similar fate (see Ether 2:8–10).

28. When they are fully ripe] When they have reached the apogee of their wickedness, when they have peaked in their perversion, when they, like over-ripe fruit on a tree, are blown to the ground to rot.

30. They murdered all the prophets of the Lord] See, for example, Ether 11.

31. Before they are fully ripe] See Ether 8:22.

Counsel with the Lord in All Things

Alma 37:32–37

32. And now, my son, remember the words which I have spoken unto you; trust not those secret plans unto this people, but teach them an everlasting hatred against sin and iniquity.

33. Preach unto them repentance, and faith on the Lord Jesus Christ; teach them to humble themselves and to be meek and lowly in heart; teach them to withstand every temptation of the devil, with their faith on the Lord Jesus Christ.

34. Teach them to never be weary of good works, but to be meek and lowly in heart; for such shall find rest to their souls.

35. O, remember, my son, and learn wisdom in thy youth; yea, learn in thy youth to keep the commandments of God.

36. Yea, and cry unto God for all thy support; yea, let all thy doings be unto the Lord, and whithersoever thou goest let it be in the Lord; yea, let all thy thoughts be directed unto the Lord; yea, let the affections of thy heart be placed upon the Lord forever.

37. Counsel with the Lord in all thy doings, and he will direct thee for good; yea, when thou liest down at night lie down unto the Lord, that he may watch over you in your sleep; and when thou risest in the morning let thy heart be full of thanks unto God; and if ye do these things, ye shall be lifted up at the last day.

32. Teach them an everlasting hatred against sin and iniquity] The sanctified have lost their disposition for sin (Mosiah 5:2), and the carnal pastimes of the world are more than abhorrent to them (Alma 13:12). It is not enough to teach the people of God about the gift of repentance; we must teach the awful consequences of transgression and must, to be sure, teach them to hate sin. Though we exult in the ransoming power of the Holy One of Israel, though we delight in and sing praises to the name of the Mediator of all men, though we glory in the reconciliation with the Father which is made available through the sinless Son of Man, yet prevention is far, far better than redemption.

33. Preach unto them repentance, and faith on the Lord Jesus Christ] We are to assist our children, and all people who will listen to our message, by declaring the fundamental doctrines of the gospel. There is power in the first principles.

33. To withstand every temptation of the devil, with

their faith on the Lord Jesus Christ] We do not come to resist evil and forsake wickedness through merely gritting our teeth and exercising constant willpower. To be sure, we must do all in our power to hold tightly to the iron rod, but the power to overcome is in and through Jesus Christ. To have faith in Jesus Christ is to trust in him and rely on his holy arm. It is to acknowledge our weakness, our mortality, our frailty, our utter inability to withstand temptations and conquer sin on our own.

34. Dead works, works motivated solely by goals and excellence programs and achievement patterns, eventually deaden the soul and weary the will. The Saints of the Most High are called out of the world and encouraged to forsake the dead letter of ritualistic religion; they are counseled to acquire the Spirit, jettison the works of the flesh, and put on Christ. As they do so, Christ begins, through his Spirit, to live in them, to prompt and guide and motivate them to good works, to his works. Those who live in Christ seldom become weary of good works, at least of those good works which flow from a regenerate heart. Truly the meek and lowly of heart, those who have surrendered their will and acknowledged Christ as Lord of their lives—these find peace and rest here and qualify for that ultimate rest hereafter.

35. Surely the wisest course to follow—a course which when followed from one's youth brings joy and happiness—is to keep the commandments of God. In doing so one comes to be on speaking terms with God.

36–37. This is a call to have one's eye single to the glory of God, a call to seek first the kingdom of God, to do things the way the Lord would want them done. It is to ask oneself regularly, "What would Jesus do?" It is to ask the Lord regularly, "What wilt thou have me to do?" More important, however, it is to be open to the impressions of the soul and the inspiration of the moment, to be guided by that sacred influence which is of Christ, that Spirit which will tell and show us all things that we should do (see 2 Nephi 32:3, 5). Life is a mission and not a career, and he who called and sent us forth to serve should be intimately involved in directing and supervising our personal ministries.

37. Counsel with the Lord in all thy doings] "Trust in the Lord with all thine heart; and lean not unto thine own understanding. In all thy ways acknowledge him, and he shall direct thy paths." (Proverbs 3:5–6.)

The Liahona: A Type of Christ and His Word

Alma 37:38–47

38. And now, my son, I have somewhat to say concerning the thing which our fathers call a ball, or director—or our fathers called it Liahona, which is, being interpreted, a compass; and the Lord prepared it.

39. And behold, there cannot any man work after the manner of so curious a workmanship. And behold, it was prepared to show unto our fathers the course which they should travel in the wilderness.

40. And it did work for them according to their faith in God; therefore, if they had faith to believe that God could cause that those spindles should point the way they should go, behold, it was done; therefore they had this miracle, and also many other miracles wrought by the power of God, day by day.

41. Nevertheless, because those miracles were worked by small means it did show unto them marvelous works. They were slothful, and forgot to exercise their faith and diligence and then those marvelous works ceased, and they did not progress in their journey;

42. Therefore, they tarried in the wilderness, or did not travel a direct course, and were afflicted with hunger and thirst, because of their transgressions.

43. And now, my son, I would

that ye should understand that these things are not without a shadow; for as our fathers were slothful to give heed to this compass (now these things were temporal) they did not prosper; even so it is with things which are spiritual.

44. For behold, it is as easy to give heed to the word of Christ, which will point to you a straight course to eternal bliss, as it was for our fathers to give heed to this compass, which would point unto them a straight course to the promised land.

45. And now I say, is there not a type in this thing? For just as surely as this director did bring our fathers, by following its course, to the promised land, shall the words of Christ, if we follow their course, carry us beyond this vale of sorrow into a far better land of promise.

46. O my son, do not let us be slothful because of the easiness of the way; for so was it with our fathers; for so was it prepared for them, that if they would look they might live; even so it is with us. The way is prepared, and if we will look we may live forever.

47. And now, my son, see that ye take care of these sacred things, yea, see that ye look to God and live. Go unto this people and declare the word, and be sober. My son, farewell.

38. Our fathers called it] Nephi, on the small plates, does not give its name in his description of the ball or director (see 1 Nephi 16).

38. Liahona] Some have suggested that the word means something like "Jehovah is light."

38. The Lord prepared it] See verses 39, 44. Nephi wrote: "And I, Nephi, had also brought the records which were engraven upon the plates of brass; and also the ball, or compass, which was *prepared for my father by the hand of the Lord,* according to that which is written" (2 Nephi 5:12, italics added; compare Mosiah 1:16).

40. And it did work for them according to their faith in God] Indeed, when the Nephites kept the commandments of God, when they followed the direction of their prophet leaders, the Liahona led them toward the promised land. Thus the Liahona was a symbol of their faithfulness, a visible evidence of their standing before God.

43–45. Alma here explains that the Liahona was a type, a shadow, a symbol of Jesus Christ and his word. When a people are faithful, then the words of Christ—given principally through the spirit of prophecy and revelation—lead them forward, like a compass, toward their goal of exaltation and eternal life. Just as the Liahona pointed the Nephites toward the promised land, so can the words of Christ "lead the man of Christ in a strait and narrow course across that everlasting gulf of misery which is prepared to engulf the wicked—and land their souls, yea, their immortal souls, at the right hand of God in the kingdom of heaven, to sit down with Abraham, and Isaac, and with Jacob, and with all our holy fathers, to go no more out" (Helaman 3:29–30).

43. These things are not without a shadow] This is a rather awkward way of saying, "These events have symbolic meaning." A shadow is not the object itself but rather a reflection, an evidence of the nearness of the object. Types or shadows—like animal sacrifice, the brazen serpent, or the Liahona—are not Christ himself, but a reflection of Christ, a representation of the Redeemer. "All things have their likeness," Jehovah explained to father Adam, "and all things are created and made to bear record of me, both things which are temporal, and things which are spiritual; things which are in the heavens above, and things which are on the earth, and things which are in the earth, and things which are under the earth, both above and beneath: all things bear record of me" (Moses 6:63).

44. It is as easy] Is it difficult to live the gospel, to be a Saint, to give heed to the word of Christ? "His way, the gospel way, is easy for those who pursue it with singlemindedness. It is more difficult for those who embark on the Christian cause with hesitation or reservation. Those who have charted their course and pointed themselves toward the abundant life in Christ have their challenges, their difficulties, like anyone else. They meet these roadblocks, however, with courage and perspective, with a quiet confidence borne of the Spirit. Such individuals have no difficulty living the gospel. It is not hard. It is not burdensome." (Robert L. Millet, *An Eye Single to the Glory of God*, p. 4.) Living the gospel and giving heed to the word of Christ are only difficult as we seek to hold on to the trappings of Babylon and pay attention to the enticements of its municipals.

46. It is human nature, especially in our modern day, to complicate things, to look beyond the mark, whereas often the answers to life's most vexing problems are simple and straightforward. And we frequently fail to see things as they really are because of our tendency toward abstraction. This is not a modern phenomenon. We remember that Nephi referred to a similar incident in ancient Israel's history, the occasion when a murmuring band of Hebrews were bitten by fiery, flying serpents (see Numbers 21:69). In order to be healed, the afflicted persons had but to look to a brazen serpent Moses had set up on a pole (symbolic, of course, of the Savior—see John 3:14). "The labor which they had to perform was to look; and because of the simpleness of the way, or the easiness of it, there were many who perished" (1 Nephi 17:41).

47. Look to God and live] Just as Peter needed to keep his eyes on the Son of God in order to walk on the surface of the water of the Sea of Galilee (Matthew 14:22–32), just as Peter summoned the lame man at the Gate Beautiful with the words, "Look on us" (Acts 3:4), even so does our Master invite us to look to him, to fix our gaze and fasten our hearts and souls upon him. Dedicated discipleship entails looking straight ahead to our Lord and Savior, giving little or no heed to the divergent and demanding voices of the world. Jesus pleads: "Look unto me in every thought; doubt not, fear not" (D&C 6:36). As we look to him and to him only we come to enjoy that abundant life which he brought (see John 10:10).

47. Be sober] The gospel message is a voice of gladness, a declaration of good news, a proclamation of peace. It has been delivered to make of us a happy people. But we are also under obligation to take seriously the manner in which the message is presented. Souls are at stake. We are taught to "trifle not with sacred things" (D&C 6:12).

The Unworthy Will Be Cut Off from the Presence of God

Alma 38:1–7

1. My son, give ear to my words, for I say unto you, even as I said unto Helaman, that inasmuch as ye shall keep the commandments of God ye shall prosper in the land; and inasmuch as ye will not keep the commandments of God ye shall be cut off from his presence.

2. And now, my son, I trust that I shall have great joy in you, because of your steadiness and your faithfulness unto God; for as you have commenced in your youth to look to the Lord your God, even so I hope that you will continue in keeping his commandments; for blessed is he that endureth to the end.

3. I say unto you, my son, that I have had great joy in thee already, because of thy faithfulness and thy diligence, and thy patience and thy long-suffering among the people of the Zoramites.

4. For I know that thou wast in bonds; yea, and I also know that thou wast stoned for the word's sake; and thou didst bear all these things with patience because the Lord was with thee; and now thou knowest that the Lord did deliver thee.

5. And now my son, Shiblon, I would that ye should remember, that as much as ye shall put your trust in God even so much ye shall be delivered out of your trials, and your troubles, and your afflictions, and ye shall be lifted up at the last day.

6. Now, my son, I would not that ye should think that I know these things of myself, but it is the Spirit of God which is in me which maketh these things known unto me; for if I had not been born of God I should not have known these things.

7. But behold, the Lord in his great mercy sent his angel to declare unto me that I must stop the work of destruction among his people; yea, and I have seen an angel face to face, and he spake with me, and his voice was as thunder, and it shook the whole earth.

1. Even as I said unto Helaman] See Alma 36:1–3.

1. Cut off from his presence] God seeks no compromise with evil or darkness—they are accorded no amnesty, given no pardons, and claim no place in his eternal kingdom. If mercy should snub justice and allow certain favored sins or sinners place in the heavenly realm, it would no longer be a fit place for the presence of God. Should mercy be granted dominion over justice, heaven would cease to be heaven and God's word would come to naught. Thus, Christ declared that "no unclean thing can enter into his [the Father's] kingdom; therefore nothing entereth into his rest save it be those who have washed their garments in my blood, because of their faith, and the repentance of all their sins, and their faithfulness unto the end" (3 Nephi 27:19).

2. Steadiness and . . . faithfulness unto God] Steadiness bespeaks spiritual balance and constancy of course. It aptly describes those who are well rooted in the principles of the gospel and who are dependable in fulfilling assignments. It is a manifestation of spiritual maturity and is independent of office or calling.

2. Endureth to the end] There is no retirement in the realm of spiritual things. It would be as foolish to suppose that we could cease to eat as it would be to suppose that we no longer needed to nourish our spirits or keep our covenants. See commentary on 1 Nephi 13:37.

3–4. The labor is its own reward, and Shiblon has been greatly blessed because of his efforts to bless others.

5. See commentary on Alma 36:3.

6. There is a knowledge of the heart and soul possessed only by those who have the Holy Ghost as their teacher. To such is granted "wisdom and great treasures of knowledge, even hidden treasures" (D&C 89:19).

Salvation Is Found Only in Christ

Alma 38:8–9

8. And it came to pass that I was three days and three nights in the most bitter pain and anguish of soul; and never, until I did cry out unto the Lord Jesus Christ for mercy, did I receive a remission of my sins. But behold, I did cry unto him and I did find peace to my soul.

9. And now, my son, I have told you this that ye may learn wisdom, that ye may learn of me that there is no other way or means whereby man can be saved, only in and through Christ. Behold, he is the life and the light of the world. Behold, he is the word of truth and righteousness.

8. See Alma 36:18–19.

9. No other way or means whereby man can be saved] None have said it better than Paul: "One Lord, one faith, one baptism" (Ephesians 4:5). See also 2 Nephi 25:20; Mosiah 4:8; Alma 21:9; Acts 4:12.

9. The life and the light of the world] "The light which shineth, which giveth you light, is through [Christ] who enlighteneth your eyes, which is the same light that quickeneth your understandings," the light that "giveth life to all things" and is the "law by which all things are governed." Without the light that comes from Christ (and this is true in both a physical and a spiritual sense), the earth would know no life. Christ is the source of that light which comes from the sun, moon, and stars, as he is the source of the light of truth, and through his atoning sacrifice he became the source of resurrection and eternal life. See D&C 88:6–13.

9. He is the word of truth and righteousness] As *life* and *light* are name titles for Christ, so are *word, truth,* and *righteous.* "And his name is called The Word of God," wrote John the Revelator (Revelation 19:13). Of himself the Savior said, "I am . . . the truth" (John 14:6), and Enoch described him as the "Righteous" (Moses 7:45, 47).

Salvation requires a perfect relationship between truth and righteousness. Surely there can be no salvation in ignorance and sin.

Counsel for Gospel Teachers

Alma 38:10–15

10. And now, as ye have begun to teach the word even so I would that ye should continue to teach; and I would that ye would be diligent and temperate in all things.

11. See that ye are not lifted up unto pride; yea, see that ye do not boast in your own wisdom, nor of your much strength.

12. Use boldness, but not overbearance; and also see that ye bridle all your passions, that ye may be filled with love; see that ye refrain from idleness.

13. Do not pray as the Zoramites do, for ye have seen that they pray to be heard of men, and to be praised for their wisdom.

14. Do not say: O God, I thank thee that we are better than our brethren; but rather say: O Lord, forgive my unworthiness, and remember my brethren in mercy—yea, acknowledge your unworthiness before God at all times.

15. And may the Lord bless your soul, and receive you at the last day into his kingdom, to sit down in peace. Now go, my son, and teach the word unto this people. Be sober. My son, farewell.

10. Temperate in all things] The temperance spoken of here is that of restraint and moderation, particularly in that which we say and teach. For example, it is unwise to use stories, quotations, or information that we cannot verify. Temperance is especially important if the story is of a sensational nature or involves someone of high standing in the Church. Wise teachers will confine themselves to that which they understand, or that for which they are reliable witnesses. Exaggerations, stretching of the truth, and embellished stories and quotations bring no dignity to the gospel or to the teacher. Indeed, such practices are offensive to the Spirit.

11. "He that speaketh of himself seeketh his own glory: but he that seeketh his glory that sent him, the same is true, and no unrighteousness is in him" (John 7:18).

12. Use boldness, but not overbearance] Those who teach by the Spirit teach with confidence, for the Spirit does not lack confidence. They teach, as did the Master, as one having authority, and not as the scribes (see Matthew 7:29). Yet they teach with kindness, love, patience, and understanding. Their purpose is to teach, not impress; to edify, not overwhelm.

12. Bridle all your passions] Passions are to be bridled in order that one may be filled with love. Passions, in the sense that we most often use the word—excessive emotion of a negative sort—are antagonistic to patience, kindness, and virtue.

12. Refrain from idleness] "Cease to be idle; cease to be unclean; cease to find fault one with another; cease to sleep longer than is needful; retire to thy bed early, that ye may not be weary; arise early, that your bodies and your minds may be invigorated" (D&C 88:124).

13–14. See Alma 31:13–23.

14. Acknowledge your unworthiness before God] Though there are those sins which of necessity must be confessed to the appropriate ecclesiastical officer, the instruction to Shiblon, a man of righteousness, falls in the category of petty faults with which the judges in Israel need not be troubled. Forgiveness may need to be sought from the offended party, and always from God, to whom all that is unrighteous or improper is an offense.

Alma Explains Why Corianton Fell into Transgression

Alma 39:1–4

1. And now, my son, I have somewhat more to say unto thee than what I said unto thy brother; for behold, have ye not observed the steadiness of thy brother, his faithfulness, and his diligence in keeping the commandments of God? Behold, has he not set a good example for thee?

2. For thou didst not give so much heed unto my words as did thy brother, among the people of the Zoramites. Now this is what I have against thee; thou didst go on unto boasting in thy strength and thy wisdom.

3. And this is not all, my son. Thou didst do that which was grievous unto me; for thou didst forsake the ministry, and did go over into the land of Siron, among the borders of the Lamanites, after the harlot Isabel.

4. Yea, she did steal away the hearts of many; but this was no excuse for thee, my son. Thou shouldst have tended to the ministry wherewith thou wast entrusted.

1. The steadiness of thy brother] This seems to be a specific reference to Shiblon, although Helaman was also a noble example.

2. Now this is what I have against thee] Alma begins here to set forth what might be termed a "formula for a fall," a foolproof set of guidelines which if followed will result in sin and sorrow. In other words, he describes the sinful pattern into which Corianton unwarily fell victim.

2. Boasting in thy strength and thy wisdom] It is not that Corianton went throughout the streets of Antionum (among the Zoramites) bragging about himself and extolling his virtues. Instead, what he appears to have done is to assume that he possessed strength and wisdom of his own, independent of that strength and wisdom which come from God. In the parlance of our day, Corianton said, "I can handle it!" Unwilling to trust in the power and ways of the Omnipotent One, Corianton was left to his own resources. He thought he knew better. He felt confident he had the willpower to deal with any eventuality. He fell.

3. Thou didst forsake the ministry] Next, Corianton left his duty station. He was not where he should have been. Likewise, members of the Church who fail to attend their meetings, who choose to absent themselves from occasions to which they have by duty and assignment committed themselves, are walking on thin ice. They have forsaken their ministry.

3. After the harlot Isabel] Third, Corianton associated himself with the wrong types of persons. In the Lord's work, especially in the case of full-time missionaries, there are certain locations and certain people that are off-limits, taboo, forbidden. We are not to flirt with temptation, not to deliberately approach the line of sin to see how close we can come without falling into overt transgression. Rather, we are to stay as far away from sin as we can. "There are two influences in the world today," said President George Albert Smith, "and have been from the beginning. One is an influence that is constructive, that radiates happiness and builds character. The other influence is one that destroys, turns men into demons, tears down and discourages. We are all susceptible to both. . . .

"My grandfather [George A. Smith] used to say to his family, 'There is a line of demarkation, well defined, between the Lord's territory and the devil's. If you will stay on the Lord's side of the line you will be under his influence and will have no desire to do wrong; but if you cross to the devil's side of the line one inch, you are in the tempter's power, and if he is successful, you will not be able to think or even reason properly, because you will have lost the Spirit of the Lord.'

"When I have been tempted sometimes to do a certain thing, I have asked myself, 'Which side of the line am I on?' If I determined to be on the safe side, the Lord's side, I would do the right thing every time. So when temptation comes, think prayerfully about your problem, and the influence of the Spirit of the Lord will enable you to decide wisely. There is safety for us only on the Lord's side of the line.

"If you want to be happy," President Smith concluded, "remember, that all happiness worthy of the name is on the Lord's side of the line and all sorrow and disappointment is on the devil's side of the line." (*Sharing the Gospel with Others*, pp. 42–43.)

4. This was no excuse for thee] Fourth, Corianton yielded to pressure from others, or at least he took comfort in knowing that others had indulged in immorality with Isabel. What others may choose to do in regard to temptation is absolutely irrelevant to us as followers of Christ; we work out our own salvation and can neither be blessed nor condemned for what other mortals choose to do. There is neither safety nor security in following a crowd to do evil.

The Three Most Serious Sins

Alma 39:5–6

5. Know ye not, my son, that these things are an abomination in the sight of the Lord; yea, most abominable above all sins save it be the shedding of innocent blood or denying the Holy Ghost?

6. For behold, if ye deny the Holy Ghost when it once has had place in you, and ye know that ye deny it, behold, this is a sin which is unpardonable; yea, and whosoever murdereth against the light and knowledge of God, it is not easy for him to obtain forgiveness; yea, I say unto you, my son, that it is not easy for him to obtain a forgiveness.

5–6. Sexual immorality is here identified as the third most serious sin, exceeded in seriousness only by the sin against the Holy Ghost and murder. When persons tamper with the procreative power they tamper with the sources of human life, with that which is at the heart and core of the plan of salvation. President Joseph F. Smith taught: "No more loathsome cancer disfigures the body and soul of society today than the frightful affliction of sexual sin. It vitiates the very fountains of life, and bequeaths its foul effects to the yet unborn as a legacy of death." (*Improvement Era*, vol. 20, p. 739.)

President Smith also declared: "We desire with holy zeal to

emphasize the enormity of sexual sins. Though often regarded as insignificant by those not knowing the will of God, they are in his eyes an abomination; and if we are to remain his favored people, they must be shunned as the gates of hell. The evil results of these sins are so patent in vice, crime, misery and disease that it would appear that all, young and old, must perceive and sense them. They are destroying the world. If we are to be preserved we must abhor them, shun them, not practice the least of them, for they weaken and enervate, they kill man spiritually, they make him unfit for the company of the righteous and the presence of God." (*Gospel Doctrine*, pp. 275–76.) As to the effects of immorality upon families, see *Commentary* 2:23–24.

Murder, the unlawful killing of another human being with malice aforethought, is the second most serious sin. It is an abomination in the sight of God because it, like unchastity, involves the unlawful tampering with human life. It is a "sin unto death" (see 1 John 5:16–17), an offense which is called the *unforgivable* sin. Joseph Smith taught: "A murderer, for instance, one that sheds innocent blood, cannot have forgiveness" (*Teachings*, p. 339). It is unforgivable in the sense that it is not covered by the atonement of Jesus Christ; the guilty person will suffer for his or her own sin. "The call to repentance and baptism which includes murderers (3 Nephi 30) has reference to those who took life while engaged in unrighteous wars, as did the Lamanites, because they were compelled to do so, and not because they in their hearts sought the blood of their fellow men. On the other hand, the Jews on whose hands the blood of Christ was found were not invited to repent and be baptized (Acts 3:19–21)." (Bruce R. McConkie, *Mormon Doctrine*, p. 520; see also *Teachings*, pp. 188, 339.)

"Satan is called Perdition, meaning he is the author of ruination and the father of lies. Those who bask in the light of heaven and come to know God, and who then sin against that light and come to fight the faith of their fathers with a viciousness and a vengeance known only to the ungodly—these become the *sons of perdition*. Their sin is blasphemy, contempt for and defiance against the Holy Ghost and his witness." (Joseph Fielding McConkie and Robert L. Millet, *The Holy Ghost*, pp. 144–45.) One who sins against the Holy Ghost—who has the heavens opened and comes to know God, and then denies that witness, turns sour to the sweet light of the gospel, and becomes an enemy and apostate to the cause of truth—that person is guilty of denying the Holy Ghost, the most serious sin in all eternity, an offense which shall not be forgiven in this world nor in the world to come. This crime is called the *unpardonable* sin. It is unpardonable in the sense that it is not covered or pardoned by the atonement of Christ, nor may any amount of the guilty person's suffering here or hereafter atone for or pardon the pernicious deed and make up for the misery and suffering to the Saints which inevitably follow in its wake. (For further information on this most serious offense against God and man, see JST, Matthew 12:26–27; Hebrews 6:4–6; 10:29; D&C 76:30–38; 132:27; *Teachings,* pp. 24, 67, 156, 357–58; see also McConkie and Millet, *The Holy Ghost,* pp. 143–48.)

Corianton Counseled to Repent

Alma 39:7–14

7. And now, my son, I would to God that ye had not been guilty of so great a crime. I would not dwell upon your crimes, to harrow up your soul, if it were not for your good.

8. But behold, ye cannot hide your crimes from God; and except ye repent they will stand as a testimony against you at the last day.

9. Now my son, I would that ye should repent and forsake your sins, and go no more after the lusts of your eyes, but cross yourself in all these things; for except ye do this ye can in nowise inherit the kingdom of God. Oh, remember, and take it upon you, and cross yourself in these things.

10. And I command you to take it upon you to counsel with your elder brothers in your undertakings; for behold, thou art in thy youth, and ye stand in need to be nourished by your brothers. And give heed to their counsel.

11. Suffer not yourself to be led away by any vain or foolish thing; suffer not the devil to lead away your heart again after those wicked harlots. Behold, O my son, how great iniquity ye brought upon the Zoramites; for when they saw your conduct they would not believe in my words.

12. And now the Spirit of the Lord doth say unto me: Command thy children to do good, lest they lead away the hearts of many people to destruction; therefore I command you, my son, in the fear of God, that ye refrain from your iniquities;

13. That ye turn to the Lord with all your mind, might, and strength; that ye lead away the hearts of no more to do wickedly; but rather return unto them, and acknowledge your faults and that wrong which ye have done.

14. Seek not after riches nor the vain things of this world; for behold, you cannot carry them with you.

7. Even the most loving of spiritual leaders, those whose hearts are filled with tender mercy and compassion for the persons to whom they minister, must occasionally speak the word of God with sobriety and sternness. They must sound the warning voice. They must call sinners to repentance. They are too kind, too considerate, to do otherwise.

9. The lusts of your eyes] One whose eyes are not focused on Christ may find his eyes—meaning his mind or heart—lusting after the things of this transient world.

9. Cross yourself in all these things] This is an unusual phrase, one not found elsewhere in scripture. To cross oneself may mean to go against one's carnal or sinful nature, to resist the pull of the fallen man. In this way it is similar to the Savior's invitation to "take up [our] cross." Matthew records: "Then said Jesus unto his disciples, If any man will come after me, let him deny himself, and take up his cross, and follow me. And now for a man to take up his cross, is to deny himself all ungodliness, and every worldly lust, and keep my commandments." (JST, Matthew 16:25–26; see also 3 Nephi 12:29–30.)

10. Counsel with your elder brothers] It is not always the case that age leads to wisdom, but it is generally so when persons over the years have chosen to live the gospel and align themselves with the will of heaven. Righteous living, mixed with mortal experience and challenges, leads to a type of wisdom that the world cannot understand. Corianton is counseled to consult with and take advice from his older brothers—Helaman and Shiblon— who have to that date been true and faithful to their trusts.

10. Ye stand in need to be nourished] Indeed, what Corianton needed most was to be strengthened in the faith, built up in his knowledge of saving doctrines, "nourished by the good word of God" (Jacob 6:7; compare Moroni 6:4).

11. There are few things that move the Church of God along more effectively than the power of example. People begin to see the good works in the lives of the Saints and seek thereafter to glorify their Father in heaven through a serious investigation of the gospel message (Matthew 5:16; 3 Nephi 12:16). On the other hand, nothing hurts the cause of truth more than to have a member of the Church, particularly one engaged in ministerial service, violate his covenants and fall short of that fidelity expected by God, the Church, and those outside the faith. In the latter case the wickedness of the Church member becomes, as it were, a great stumbling block to those outside the fold (see Alma 4:10).

12. Command thy children to do good] See Alma 35:15–16; compare 1 Samuel 3:13. As pertaining to the requirement of parents to teach and prepare their little children, the revelation attests: "And again, inasmuch as parents have children in Zion, or in any of her stakes which are organized, that teach them not to understand the doctrine of repentance, faith in Christ the Son of the living God, and of baptism and the gift of the Holy Ghost by the laying on of the hands, when eight years old, the sin be upon the heads of the parents" (D&C 68:25; compare 29:48).

13. Return unto them, and acknowledge your faults] This, for Corianton, was a form of restitution, his effort to make amends for that which he had done to injure the cause of Christianity among the Zoramites.

14. The Savior taught in Galilee: "Wherefore, seek not the things of this world but seek ye first to build up the kingdom of God, and to establish his righteousness, and all these things [the things necessary to live in this world] shall be added unto you" (JST, Matthew 6:38). "Seek not for riches but for wisdom," that same Lord said in our day, "and behold, the mysteries of God shall be unfolded unto you, and then shall you be made rich. Behold, he that hath eternal life is rich." (D&C 6:7; compare 38:39; Jacob 2:17–19; see also *Commentary* 2:15–18.)

14. You cannot carry them with you] There are few things that pass with us from this sphere of activity into the life beyond. Our knowledge, character, attributes, testimony, and relationships with others are among the few things we are allowed to take with us. Some things—primarily earthly things like wealth, fame, or position in the social strata—simply do not make it through celestial customs.

The Atonement of Christ Is Retroactive in Scope

Alma 39:15–19

15. And now, my son, I would say somewhat unto you concerning the coming of Christ. Behold, I say unto you, that it is he that surely shall come to take away the sins of the world; yea, he cometh to declare glad tidings of salvation unto his people.

16. And now, my son, this was the ministry unto which ye were called, to declare these glad tidings unto this people, to prepare their minds; or rather that salvation might come unto them, that they may prepare the minds of their children to hear the word at the time of his coming.

17. And now I will ease your mind somewhat on this subject. Behold, you marvel why these things should be known so long beforehand. Behold, I say unto you, is not a soul at this time as precious unto God as a soul will be at the time of his coming?

18. Is it not as necessary that the plan of redemption should be made known unto this people as well as unto their children?

19. Is it not as easy at this time for the Lord to send his angel to declare these glad tidings unto us as unto our children, or as after the time of his coming?

15–19. "Messianic prophecies—testimonies and testaments of the Redeemer delivered by inspired men and women before the meridian of time—focused the attention and heightened the expectations of the people of God upon the central act in all eternity—the atonement of Jesus Christ. For the faithful, for those who accepted the Messianic message and conformed their lives to the teachings of Jehovah and his prophets—for such persons it was as though the act of atonement, the events in Gethsemane and on Calvary, were moments of the past. As the effects of the Atonement reach to eternity future, so do they reach endlessly to the past: from the days of Adam every gospel ordinance that was performed and every ounce of faith exercised centered in the efficacy and virtue of an atonement, an act of infinite grace that would not come for up to four thousand years. For the obedient, prophecy was as history." (*Commentary* 2:109.) God loves all men and women of all ages. His greatest act of love—the gift of his Only Begotten Son—was not a gift limited to those select persons who lived at the time of and subsequent to the mortal ministry of Jesus of Nazareth. Rather, the great and last sacrifice, though limited in time to a specific moment in earth's history, stretches in its effects from before the world was through the millennial era.

16. This was the ministry unto which ye were called] Preeminent above all other messages proclaimed by the servants of the Lord is this: Jesus Christ and him crucified. The gospel of Jesus Christ is the glad tidings, the good news that deliverance from death and sin is available through the mediation and atonement of Jesus Christ (see 3 Nephi 27:13–14; D&C 76:40–42).

The Mystery of the Resurrection

Alma 40:1–5

1. Now my son, here is somewhat more I would say unto thee; for I perceive that thy mind is worried concerning the resurrection of the dead.

2. Behold, I say unto you, that there is no resurrection—or, I would say, in other words, that this mortal does not put on immortality, this corruption does not put on incorruption—until after the coming of Christ.

3. Behold, he bringeth to pass the resurrection of the dead. But behold, my son, the resurrection is not yet. Now, I unfold unto you a mystery; nevertheless, there are many mysteries which are kept, that no one knoweth them save God himself. But I show unto you one thing which I have inquired diligently of God that I might know that is concerning the resurrection.

4. Behold, there is a time appointed that all shall come forth from the dead. Now when this time cometh no one knows; but God knoweth the time which is appointed.

5. Now, whether there shall be one time, or a second time, or a third time, that men shall come forth from the dead, it mattereth not; for God knoweth all these things; and it sufficeth me to know that this is the case—that there is a time appointed that all shall rise from the dead.

1. As we shall notice, Corianton's problem was at least partially a doctrinal one (see Alma 41:1; 42:1).

2. Christ was the first fruits of the resurrection, the first fruits of them that slept (see 1 Corinthians 15:20). There was no resurrection from the dead, no raising of the body, no inseparable union of body and spirit, until the Lord of Life took death captive and placed all enemies under his feet. Death was the last enemy (see 1 Corinthians 15:25–26). Though individuals were forgiven of sin and reborn into the family of Jesus Christ long ages before his atoning sacrifice was a historical reality, there was no resurrection from the dead on this earth until his own. His rise from the Arimathean's tomb initiated what we call the first resurrection. That first resurrection will resume when he returns in glory and will continue throughout the Millennium. During that time all the dead who have qualified for either a celestial or a terrestrial inheritance will come forth. After the end of the thousand years the second or last resurrection will take place—the resurrection of those who inherit a telestial glory, as well as those who inherit a kingdom of no glory, the sons of perdition.

2. This mortal does not put on immortality] That is, this physical body, subject to death, does not become immortal—no longer subject to death—until after Christ rises from the grave.

2. This corruption does not put on incorruption] That is, this physical body, subject to disease and decay, does not become incorrupt—no longer subject to those conditions—until after Christ rises from the grave.

3. I unfold unto you a mystery] To the world and to the worldly the resurrection is a mystery. In fact, even to those of the household of faith it is incomprehensible and inexplicable. How is it that a dead body can return to life, join with the immortal spirit, and acquire godlike glory and power in the process? It is beyond mortal mind to fathom such a thing. But the Spirit whispers and experience teaches that such is true and real. In response to Zeezrom's question about the resurrection, Alma said: "It is given unto many to know the mysteries of God" (Alma 12:8–9; compare 1 Corinthians 15:51).

3. There are many mysteries which are kept, that no one knoweth them save God himself] Indeed, one of these concerns the particulars of the resurrection—for example, how it is accomplished.

4–5. We are unable to know from the text how much Alma understood regarding the doctrine of resurrection. He spends most of his time with Corianton discussing the spirit world—the state of the soul between death and resurrection. He does not speak in detail of the different resurrections, not even as much as Abinadi had done in his discourse to Alma's father and the other priests of Noah (see Mosiah 15–16). One thing he is certain of: all who have received physical bodies shall rise from the dead.

The State of the Soul Between Death and Resurrection

Alma 40:6–15

6. Now there must needs be a space betwixt the time of death and the time of the resurrection.

7. And now I would inquire what becometh of the souls of men from this time of death to the time appointed for the resurrection?

8. Now whether there is more than one time appointed for men to rise it mattereth not; for all do not die at once, and this mattereth not; all is as one day with God, and time only is measured unto men.

9. Therefore, there is a time appointed unto men that they shall rise from the dead; and there is a space between the time of death and the resurrection. And now, concerning this space of time, what becometh of the souls of men is the thing which I have inquired diligently of the Lord to know; and this is the thing of which I do know.

10. And when the time cometh when all shall rise, then shall they know that God knoweth all the times which are appointed unto man.

11. Now, concerning the state of the soul between death and the resurrection—Behold, it has been made known unto me by an angel, that the spirits of all men, as soon as they are departed from this mortal body, yea, the spirits of all men, whether they be good or evil, are taken home to that God who gave them life.

12. And then shall it come to pass, that the spirits of those who are righteous are received into a state of happiness, which is called paradise, a state of rest, a state of peace, where they shall rest from all their troubles and from all care, and sorrow.

13. And then shall it come to pass, that the spirits of the wicked, yea, who are evil—for behold, they have no part nor portion of the Spirit of the Lord; for behold, they chose evil works rather than good; therefore the spirit of the devil did enter into them, and take possession of their house—and these shall be cast out into outer darkness; there shall be weeping, and wailing, and gnashing of teeth, and this because of their own iniquity, being led captive by the will of the devil.

14. Now this is the state of the souls of the wicked, yea, in darkness, and a state of awful, fearful looking for the fiery indignation of the wrath of God upon them; thus they remain in this state, as

well as the righteous in paradise, until the time of their resurrection.

15. Now, there are some that have understood that this state of happiness and this state of misery of the soul, before the resurrec-

tion, was a first resurrection. Yea, I admit it may be termed a resurrection, the raising of the spirit or the soul and their consignation to happiness or misery, according to the words which have been spoken.

6–15. "Might we ask with Alma: What becomes of man—the eternal spirit—at the time of death? Does it remain forever in a grave of darkness? Or does it continue to exist, and if so, does it retain its individuality? Does the spirit return immediately to the divine presence? And what of the world of spirits—where is it and what of its nature? . . . All such questions and many more are answered with clarity by the revelations of the Restoration, from which we learn of this afterworld, this life beyond the grave." (Robert L. Millet and Joseph Fielding McConkie, *The Life Beyond*, p. 13.)

7. The souls of men] The strictest scriptural definition for *soul* is the union of body and spirit (see 2 Nephi 9:13; D&C 88:15). More commonly, however, the word *soul* refers to the spirit of man, either in its unembodied state (see Abraham 3:23) or its disembodied state (see Alma 40:7, 9, 11, 14, 15, 17, 18, 19, 21, 23).

8. Time only is measured unto men] We are told in the scriptures that in the worlds to come "there shall be time no longer" (see D&C 84:100; 88:110). This refers to mortal time, to temporality, to the temporary nature of things. There will always be chronological time, in the sense that one event precedes or follows another event in time. This scripture is referring to mortality.

11. The spirits of all men . . . are taken home to that God who gave them life] Alma's language is similar to that of the Preacher in Ecclesiastes: "Then shall the dust return to the earth as it was: and the spirit shall return unto God who gave it" (Ecclesiastes 12:7). Both of these scriptural writers are speaking in broadest terms, and their statements should not be interpreted to mean that the spirit, at the time of death, goes into the immediate presence of the Lord. President Brigham Young explained that to speak of the spirit returning to the God who gave it means that "when the spirits leave their bodies they are in the presence of our Father and God" in the sense that they "are prepared to see, hear and understand spiritual things" (*JD* 3:368). To go into the "presence of God" is not necessarily to be "placed within a few yards or rods, or within a short distance of his person" (Orson Pratt, *JD* 16:365). President George Q. Cannon explained: "Alma, when he says that 'the spirits of all men, as soon as they are departed from this mortal body, . . . are taken home to that God who gave them life,' has the idea, doubtless, in his mind that our God is omnipresent—not in His own personality but through His minister, the Holy Spirit. He does not intend to convey the idea that they are immediately ushered into the personal presence of God. He evidently uses that phrase in a qualified sense." (*Gospel Truth*, p. 58.) "As for my going into the immediate presence of God when I die," President Heber C. Kimball observed, "I do not expect it, but I expect to go into the world of spirits and associate with my brethren, and preach the Gospel in the spiritual world, and prepare myself in every necessary way to receive my body again, and then enter through the wall into the celestial world" (*JD* 3:112–13).

12. Paradise is the abode of the righteous in the world of spirits (see 2 Nephi 9:13; Alma 60:13; Moroni 10:34), a "state of happiness," a place hereafter where the spirits of the faithful "expand in wisdom, where they have respite from all their troubles, and where care and sorrow do not annoy" (Joseph F. Smith, *Gospel Doctrine*, p. 448). Those things which burdened the obedient—the worldly cares and struggles, the vicissitudes of life—are shed with the physical body. Paradise is a place where the spirit is free to think and act with a renewed capacity and with the vigor and enthusiasm that characterized one in one's prime. Though a person does not rest per se from the work associated with the spread of the gospel, at the same time he is delivered from those cares and worries so prevalent in a fallen world and a corrupt body.

One of the most misunderstood biblical passages in Christian history has to do with this word *paradise*. To the thief on the cross Jesus said: "Verily I say unto thee, To day shalt thou be with me in paradise" (Luke 23:39–43). This account has spawned a host of incorrect perceptions of doctrine, which in turn have resulted in questionable practices on the part of Christians over the centuries, not the least of which is a type of "death-bed repentance," a notion that one can postpone his confession and repentance until the time just before death. Though we must never de-emphasize or denigrate the value of sincere repentance, no matter how late in one's earthly experience (see Matthew 20:1–16)—for the word of the Lord is clear that "he that repents and does the commandments of the Lord shall be forgiven" (D&C 1:32)—confession and repentance coerced by the threat of death hardly prepare one's soul for a place hereafter among the sanctified.

In discoursing upon the subject, the Prophet Joseph Smith observed: "I will say something about the spirits in prison. There has been much said by modern divines about the words of Jesus (when on the cross) to the thief, saying, 'This day shalt thou be with me in paradise.' King James' translators make it out to say paradise. But what is paradise? It is a modern word: it does not answer at all to the original word that Jesus made use of. . . . There is nothing in the original word in Greek from which this was taken that signifies paradise; but it was—*This day thou shalt be with me in the world of spirits.*" In confirming these truths, the Prophet said: "Hades, the Greek or Sheol, the Hebrew, these two significations mean a world of spirits. Hades, Sheol, paradise, spirits in prison, are all one: it is a world of spirits." (*Teachings*, pp. 309, 310, italics added.) Not discounting in any way, therefore, any feelings of contrition that may have existed in the heart of the thief on the cross, Parley P. Pratt thus explained that this man went into the world of spirits "in a state of ignorance, and sin, being uncultivated, unimproved, and unprepared for salvation. He went there to be taught, and to complete that repentance, which in a dying moment he commenced on earth." (*JD* 1:9.)

13–14. In a broad sense, the whole of the spirit world—paradise and hell—is a "spirit prison," inasmuch as the spirits there, even the righteous, look upon the long absence of their spirits from their bodies as a bondage (see D&C 45:17; 138:50; see also 138:15, 16, 18). "I know it is a startling idea," President Brigham Young stated, "to say that the Prophet [Joseph Smith] and the persecutor of the Prophet, all go to prison together. . . . But they have not got their bodies yet, consequently they are in prison." (*JD* 3:95; compare Moses 7:55–57.) It is in this sense that Christ went and preached to the spirits in prison (see 1 Peter 3:18–20; 4:6). President Joseph F. Smith beheld in vision that the Savior went not in person to preach to the wicked in the postmortal spirit world, but rather that he organized his missionary force in that realm and commissioned the righteous to preach the gospel to the spirits who were in darkness and under the bondage of sin (see D&C 138:20–22, 29–32). Christ went to the spirits in prison in the sense that he went to the spirit world.

Outer darkness, or hell, is made up of those who in mortality spurned the ways of righteousness, those who defied the word of truth, those who chose to walk in their own paths or in paths of disobedience. Joseph Smith pointed out, "The great misery of departed spirits in the world of spirits, where they go after death, is to know that they come short of the glory that others enjoy and that they might have enjoyed themselves, and they are their own accusers" (*Teachings*, pp. 310–11; compare p. 358). Thus hell or outer darkness is both a *place*—a part of the world of spirits where suffering and sorrow and appropriate preparation go on—and a *state*—a condition of the mind associated with remorseful realization.

The righteous, those who have received the ordinances of salvation and proven faithful to the attendant covenants, go into paradise at the time of their physical death. It would appear that all others, including the good and noble men and women of the earth who died without a knowledge of the gospel, enter into hell, outer darkness, or what is sometimes called (in a narrower sense than above—see Bruce R. McConkie, *Mormon Doctrine*, p. 755) spirit prison. This second division is not simply a place of suffering, but also a place of preparation and learning. Joseph Smith taught concerning the necessity of ordinances for entrance into paradise: "Every man that has been baptized and belongs to the kingdom has a right to be baptized for those who have gone before; and a*s soon as the law of the Gospel is obeyed here [the gospel ordinance] by their friends who act as proxy for them, the Lord has administrators there to set them free"* (*Teachings*, p. 367, italics added; see also D&C 138:58; Joseph Fielding Smith, *Doctrines of Salvation* 2:158, 230).

Elder Bruce R. McConkie has written: "Before Christ bridged the gulf between paradise and hell—so that the righteous could mingle with the wicked and preach them the gospel—the wicked in hell were confined to locations which precluded them from contact with the righteous in paradise. . . . Now that the righteous spirits in paradise have been commissioned to carry the message of salvation to the wicked spirits in hell, there is a certain amount of mingling together of the good and bad spirits. Repentance opens the prison doors to the spirits in hell; it enables those bound with the chains of hell to free themselves from darkness, unbelief, ignorance, and sin. As rapidly as they can overcome these obstacles—gain light, believe truth, acquire intelligence, cast off sin, and break the chains of hell—they can leave the hell that imprisons them and dwell with the righteous in the peace of paradise." (*Mormon Doctrine*, p. 755.)

13. And take possession of their house] For the parable Jesus taught in this regard see Matthew 12:43–45.

14. Compare Hebrews 10:26–27.

15. There are at least a couple of ways to try to understand Alma's remarks in this verse. In one sense, Alma may be referring to the "rise" of the righteous spirit to paradise in the same sense that the body rises in the resurrection. If so, it is an odd use of the word *resurrection*. Second, since the doctrines of resurrection and judgment are so inextricably intertwined, since they are always taught together, Alma may be referring to the departure of the spirits into the spirit world at death—and particularly the division of those spirits into paradise and outer darkness—as a type of *first judgment*. This is in fact what President Joseph F. Smith called a "partial judgment" that takes place at the time of death. "Death is not the end," he taught. "When we, sorrowing, lay away our loved ones in the grave, we have an assurance based upon the life, words and resurrection of Christ, that we shall again meet and shake hands and associate with them in a better life, where sorrow and trouble are ended, and where there is to be no more parting.

"This knowledge is one of the greatest incentives that we have to live right in this life, to pass through mortality, doing and feeling and accomplishing good. The spirits of all men, as soon as they depart from this mortal body, whether they are good or evil, we are told in the Book of Mormon, are taken home to that God who gave them life, where *there is a separation, a partial judgment*, and the spirits of those who are righteous are received into a state of happiness which is called paradise. . . . The wicked, on the contrary, have no part nor portion in the Spirit of the Lord, and they are cast into outer darkness, being led captive, because of their own iniquity, by the evil one." (*Gospel Doctrine*, p. 448, italics added; see also p. 449.)

Alma Discourses on the Resurrection

Alma 40:16–26

16. And behold, again it hath been spoken, that there is a first resurrection, a resurrection of all those who have been, or who are, or who shall be, down to the resurrection of Christ from the dead.

17. Now, we do not suppose that this first resurrection, which is spoken of in this manner, can be the resurrection of the souls and their consignation to happiness or misery. Ye cannot suppose that this is what it meaneth.

18. Behold, I say unto you, Nay; but it meaneth the reuniting of the soul with the body, of those from the days of Adam down to the resurrection of Christ.

19. Now, whether the souls and the bodies of those of whom has been spoken shall all be reunited at once, the wicked as well as the righteous, I do not say; let it

suffice; that I say that they all come forth; or in other words, their resurrection cometh to pass before the resurrection of those who die after the resurrection of Christ.

20. Now, my son, I do not say that their resurrection cometh at the resurrection of Christ; but behold, I give it as my opinion, that the souls and the bodies are reunited, of the righteous, at the resurrection of Christ, and his ascension into heaven.

21. But whether it be at his resurrection or after, I do not say; but this much I say, that there is a space between death and the resurrection of the body, and a state of the soul in happiness or in misery until the time which is appointed of God that the dead shall come forth, and be reunited,

both soul and body, and be brought to stand before God, and be judged according to their works.

22. Yea, this bringeth about the restoration of those things of which has been spoken by the mouths of the prophets.

23. The soul shall be restored to the body, and the body to the soul; yea, and every limb and joint shall be restored to its body; yea, even a hair of the head shall not be lost; but all things shall be restored to their proper and perfect frame.

24. And now, my son, this is the restoration of which has been spoken by the mouths of the prophets—

25. And then shall the righteous shine forth in the kingdom of God.

26. But behold, an awful death cometh upon the wicked; for they die as to things pertaining to things of righteousness; for they are unclean, and no unclean thing can inherit the kingdom of God; but they are cast out, and consigned to partake of the fruits of their labors or their works, which have been evil; and they drink the dregs of a bitter cup.

16. This verse has proven problematic in the past. On the surface, it would appear that Alma is suggesting that the first resurrection consists of the rising of all people who lived and died from the days of Adam to the meridian of time—righteous and wicked alike—at the time of Christ's resurrection. We know from Abinadi (see Mosiah 15:21–22) and from modern revelation (see D&C 76:50–80) that only the celestial and the terrestrial bodies come forth in the first resurrection. Alma finally clarifies his meaning in verse 20 when he states that "the souls and the bodies are reunited, of the righteous, at the resurrection of Christ." (See also Joseph Fielding Smith, *Doctrines of Salvation* 2:300; *Answers to Gospel Questions* 1:35–36.)

17–18. Though individuals have been—since A.D. 34—raised from the dead with celestial bodies, the final judgment and assignment to kingdoms of glory will take place after the thousand years of Christ's reign on earth.

22. The resurrection is the preeminent example of the doctrine of restoration, spoken of later by Alma (see Alma 41).

23. See commentary on Alma 11:43.

25. Then shall the righteous shine forth] "Here, then, is eternal life," Joseph Smith explained, "to know the only wise and true God; and you have got to learn how to be Gods yourselves, and to be kings and priests to God, the same as all Gods have done before you, namely, by going from one small degree to another, and from a small capacity to a great one; from grace to grace, from exaltation to exaltation, until you attain to the resurrection of the dead, and are able to dwell in everlasting burnings, and to sit in glory, as do those who sit enthroned in everlasting power" (*Teachings*, pp. 346–47).

26. They die as to things pertaining to things of righteousness] That is, they suffer the second spiritual death (see Alma 12:16, 32; 42:9; Helaman 14:16–18).

26. They are unclean] All will repent and become clean before the resurrection of the body, except the sons of perdition. These "remain filthy still" (2 Nephi 9:16; Mormon 9:14; D&C 88:35, 102).

26. They drink the dregs of a bitter cup] That is, they face the full effects of the justice of the Almighty God (Mosiah 3:26), a justice which could have been mitigated by their own repentance through the divine grace of the Holy One of Israel.

The Resurrection Restores Order to All Things

Alma 41:1–2

1. And now, my son, I have somewhat to say concerning the restoration of which has been spoken; for behold, some have wrested the scriptures, and have gone far astray because of this thing. And I perceive that thy mind has been worried also concerning this thing. But behold, I will explain it unto thee.

2. I say unto thee, my son, that the plan of restoration is requisite with the justice of God; for it is requisite that all things should be restored to their proper order. Behold, it is requisite and just, according to the power and resurrection of Christ, that the soul of man should be restored to its body, and that every part of the body should be restored to itself.

1. Burdened with sin, Corianton feigned considerable offense at the idea that a merciful God would punish the sinner. He tended to excuse his actions by wresting the scriptures. In this and the following chapter, Alma, with great power and inspiration, explains the law of restoration and the perfect balance that must exist between mercy and justice, both of which refute the idea that either salvation or the blessings of the gospel can be enjoyed by those entangled in sin and resistant to spiritual enticements to free themselves from it.

1. Wrested] To wrest the scriptures is to twist or distort them. It is a form of literary torture that wrenches from holy writ the justification needed for whatever course or purpose its tormentors desire. See also Alma 13:20; 2 Peter 1:20; D&C 10:63.

2. All things . . . restored to their proper order] The resurrection is a perfect manifestation of a larger law—the law of restoration. It illustrates beautifully the justice and order upon which the kingdom of heaven is founded. In the resurrection each person is called forth by that law to which he has chosen to give allegiance. Thus, those choosing to live a celestial law will be called forth in a celestial resurrection; those who choose to live a terrestrial standard will come forth in a terrestrial resurrection; the adherents of a telestial standard will come forth in a telestial resurrection; and the sons of perdition will come forth in a resurrection of their own. The order of resurrection is from most righteous to most wicked—Christ is the first fruits of them that slept, and the sons of perdition will be the last. In the morning of the first resurrection, celestial spirits will be inseparably united with celestial bodies; in the afternoon of the first resurrection, terrestrial spirits will be eternally united with terrestrial bodies; in the morning of the second resurrection, or the resurrection of the unjust, telestial spirits will be endlessly bound with telestial bodies; and finally, those who even in the resurrection are filthy still, the sons of perdition, will be called forth.

"Ye who are quickened by a portion of the celestial glory shall then receive of the same, even a fulness. And they who are quickened by a portion of the terrestrial glory shall then receive of the same, even a fulness. And also they who are quickened by a portion of the telestial glory shall then receive of the same, even a fulness. And they who remain shall also be quickened; nevertheless, they shall return again to their own place, to enjoy that which they are willing to receive, because they were not willing to enjoy that which they might have received." (D&C 88:29–32.)

We Will Be Judged by Our Works and Our Desires

Alma 41:3–7

3. And it is requisite with the justice of God that men should be judged according to their works; and if their works were good in this life, and the desires of their hearts were good, that they should also, at the last day, be restored unto that which is good.

4. And if their works are evil they shall be restored unto them for evil. Therefore, all things shall be restored to their proper order, every thing to its natural frame—mortality raised to immortality, corruption to incorruption—raised to endless happiness to inherit the kingdom of God, or to endless misery to inherit the kingdom of the devil, the one on one hand, the other on the other—

5. The one raised to happiness according to his desires of happiness, or good according to his desires of good; and the other to evil according to his desires of evil; for as he has desired to do evil all the day long even so shall he have his reward of evil when the night cometh.

6. And so it is on the other hand. If he hath repented of his

sins, and desired righteousness until the end of his days, even so he shall be rewarded unto righteousness.

7. These are they that are redeemed of the Lord; yea, these are they that are taken out, that are delivered from that endless night of darkness; and thus they stand or fall; for behold, they are their own judges, whether to do good or do evil.

3. How perfect the wisdom of God! Both heart and soul will be weighed in the balance on Judgment Day. It is the combination of (1) works accomplished in the stewardships given and (2) the desires of the heart that give the true weight of the soul. We will each be judged according to what we did in the circumstances that were ours, and to what we would have done if we had been allowed control over those circumstances. Such are the seeds we planted, and such will be the harvest we will reap. See also the commentary on Alma 29:5.

3. The desires of their hearts] Thanks be to God that we will be judged not alone for our works but also according to the desires of our hearts (see D&C 137:9). Elder Dallin H. Oaks has written: "Just as we will be accountable for our evil desires, we will also be rewarded for our righteous ones. Our Father in Heaven will receive a truly righteous desire as a substitute for actions that are genuinely impossible. My father-in-law was fond of expressing his version of this principle. When someone wanted to do something for him but was prevented by circumstances, he would say: 'Thank you. I will take the good will for the deed.'

"This is the principle that blessed Abraham for his willingness to sacrifice his son Isaac. The Lord stopped him at the last instant (see Genesis 22:11–12), but his willingness to follow the Lord's command 'was accounted unto him for righteousness' (D&C 132:36).

"This principle means that when we have done all that we can, our *desires* will carry us the rest of the way. It also means that if our desires are right, we can be forgiven for the unintended errors or mistakes we will inevitably make as we try to carry those desires into effect. What a comfort for our feelings of inadequacy!" (*Pure in Heart*, p. 59.)

4–6. The law of restoration is simply a manifestation of the law of the harvest. Good seeds produce good fruit, while evil seeds produce evil fruit. All will harvest as they have sown (see Galatians 6:7–8).

7. Redeemed of the Lord] That is, redeemed to the extent that they pass through death into paradise and eventually inherit a celestial glory.

7. That endless night of darkness] See commentary on Alma 34:33.

7. They are their own judges] In the ultimate sense, Christ-Jehovah is the keeper of the gate and the judge of all men and women (2 Nephi 9:41; John 5:22). In addition, priesthood leaders—as exemplified by the Twelve who will judge the whole house of Israel—stand as judges of those persons who lived and labored during their ministry and under their direction (see Matthew 19:28; 1 Nephi 12:9; Mormon 3:18–19; D&C 29:12; Bruce R. McConkie, *Millennial Messiah,* p. 520). In one sense, however, each of us becomes his or her own judge, since we make those decisions which determine the kind of life we will live here and thus where and with whom we will dwell hereafter. Truly, as Samuel warned, "whosoever perisheth, perisheth unto himself; and whosoever doeth iniquity, doeth it unto himself; for behold, ye are free; ye are permitted to act for yourselves" (Helaman 14:30). Because in that day of judgment the works of man will be evident, because there will be nothing hidden, and because we will have a perfect knowledge of our uncleanness as well as of our happiness, it will not be necessary for a designated person to consider our case and adjudicate our life. We will be what we have become. Our natures will have been prepared for that kingdom of glory which is most appropriate to the decisions we have made in mortality.

Salvation Is Available to All Through Obedience

Alma 41:8–11

8. Now, the decrees of God are unalterable; therefore, the way is prepared that whosoever will may walk therein and be saved.

9. And now behold, my son, do not risk one more offense against your God upon those points of doctrine, which ye have hitherto risked to commit sin.

10. Do not suppose, because it has been spoken concerning restoration, that ye shall be restored from sin to happiness.

Behold, I say unto you, wickedness never was happiness.

11. And now, my son, all men that are in a state of nature, or I would say, in a carnal state, are in the gall of bitterness and in the bonds of iniquity; they are without God in the world, and they have gone contrary to the nature of God; therefore, they are in a state contrary to the nature of happiness.

8. The decrees of God are unalterable] "There is a law, irrevocably decreed in heaven before the foundations of this world, upon which all blessings are predicated—and when we obtain any blessing from God, it is by obedience to that law upon which it is predicated" (D&C 130:20–21). Again the Lord declares: "All who will have a blessing at my hands shall abide the law which was appointed for that blessing, and the conditions thereof, as were instituted from before the foundation of the world" (D&C 132:5).

8. Whosoever will may walk therein and be saved] Salvation is available to all who choose the path of faith and obedience. None are excluded from walking that path. Those who die without the opportunity to walk that path in this life, and yet would have done so had the opportunity come, will be granted that blessing in the world to come. Thus came the word of the Lord to the Prophet Joseph Smith: "All who have died without a knowledge of this gospel, who would have received it if they had been permitted to tarry, shall be heirs of the celestial kingdom of God; also all that shall die henceforth without a knowledge of it, who would have received it with all their hearts, shall be heirs of that kingdom; for I, the Lord, will judge all men according to their works, according to the desires of their hearts" (D&C 137:7–9).

It is occasionally taught that some were born into this life without the capacity to obtain the fulness of the Father. The idea suggests that God is without the capacity to save all of his creations, and that he has given commandments to some which they cannot keep. Such suggestions are neither flattering to God nor in accord with scriptural writ. Indeed, the third Article of Faith states: "We believe that through the Atonement of Christ, all mankind may be saved [meaning exalted], by obedience to the laws and ordinances of the Gospel." Again, Nephi asked: "Hath he commanded any that they should not partake of his salvation? Behold I say unto you, Nay; but he hath given it free for all men; and he hath commanded his people that they should persuade all men to repentance. Behold, hath the Lord commanded any that they should not partake of his goodness? Behold I say unto you, Nay; but all men are privileged the one like unto the other, and none are forbidden." (2 Nephi 26:27–28.) If the command to accept the gospel is to all, the promise of its blessings must likewise be to all.

9–10. It appears quite evident from these verses that Corianton had been espousing a doctrine of salvation solely by the mercy or grace of God, and that he was much offended with the idea that he would be punished for his transgressions. Any doctrine that does not make sin abhorrent is not of God. The idea that salvation can be obtained independent of personal righteousness was first espoused by Lucifer when he sought the throne of God in the premortal councils. As repentance is to precede baptism, so righteousness is to precede the receipt of the gift of the Holy Ghost.

10. Wickedness never was happiness] How can one find happiness in doing that which cannot, absolutely cannot, bring happiness? Those who follow the ways of the world may prosper by the world's standards, but while doing so they will not know that peace of soul that comes through hearkening to the light within us, the light that bids us to do good. They may "have joy in their works for a season, and by and by the end cometh, and they are hewn down and cast into the fire, from whence there is no return" (3 Nephi 27:11). That is to say, "where God and Christ dwell they cannot come, worlds without end" (D&C 76:112).

11. All men that are in a state of nature] That is, all natural men, all who live without God or godliness in the world, all who live lives independent of the revealed witness of the truth and the sanctifying powers of the Spirit. See *Commentary* 2:151–54; see also Robert L. Millet, *Life in Christ*, chapter 3.

11. The gall of bitterness] See Mosiah 27:29; Alma 36:18.

Deeds of the Flesh Are Harvested in the Resurrection

Alma 41:12–15

12. And now behold, is the meaning of the word restoration to take a thing of a natural state and place it in an unnatural state, or to place it in a state opposite to its nature?

13. O, my son, this is not the case; but the meaning of the word restoration is to bring back again evil for evil, or carnal for carnal, or devilish for devilish—good for that which is good; righteous for that which is righteous; just for that which is just; merciful for that which is merciful.

14. Therefore, my son, see that you are merciful unto your brethren; deal justly, judge righteously, and do good continually; and if ye do all these things then shall ye receive your reward; yea, ye shall have mercy restored unto you again; ye shall have justice restored unto you again; ye shall have a righteous judgment restored unto you again; and ye shall have good rewarded unto you again.

15. For that which ye do send out shall return unto you again, and be restored; therefore, the word restoration more fully condemneth the sinner, and justifieth him not at all.

12–15. A person cannot be separated from his deeds. We are what we do and, apart from sins properly repented of, we will be judged for what we have done. All are rewarded according to their deeds in the flesh.

14. Ye shall have justice restored unto you] In the words of Alma, if we are merciful, just, and righteous, we shall have justice rewarded unto us. That is, we will receive the reward of the righteous, we will be saved in the kingdom of God. Most of the time we speak of justice as that which comes eventually to the wicked. It is also that which comes to the faithful. (See also 2 Nephi 9:46.)

Salvation Comes Because of the Fall

Alma 42:1–11

1. And now, my son, I perceive there is somewhat more which doth worry your mind, which ye cannot understand—which is concerning the justice of God in the punishment of the sinner; for ye do try to suppose that it is injustice that the sinner should be consigned to a state of misery.

2. Now behold, my son, I will explain this thing unto thee. For behold, after the Lord God sent our first parents forth from the garden of Eden, to till the ground, from whence they were taken—yea, he drew out the man, and he placed at the east end of the garden of Eden, cherubim, and a flaming sword which turned every way, to keep the tree of life—

3. Now, we see that the man had become as God, knowing good and evil; and lest he should put forth his hand, and take also of the tree of life, and eat and live forever, the Lord God placed cherubim and the flaming sword, that he should not partake of the fruit—

4. And thus we see, that there was a time granted unto man to repent, yea, a probationary time, a time to repent and serve God.

5. For behold, if Adam had put forth his hand immediately, and partaken of the tree of life, he would have lived forever, according to the word of God, having no space for repentance; yea, and also the word of God would have been void, and the great plan of salvation would have been frustrated.

6. But behold, it was appointed unto man to die—therefore, as they were cut off from the tree of life they should be cut off from the face of the earth—and man became lost forever, yea, they became fallen man.

7. And now, ye see by this that our first parents were cut off both temporally and spiritually from the presence of the Lord; and thus we see they became subjects to follow after their own will.

8. Now behold, it was not expedient that man should be reclaimed from this temporal death, for that would destroy the great plan of happiness.

9. Therefore, as the soul could never die, and the fall had brought upon all mankind a spiritual death as well as a temporal, that is, they were cut off from the presence of the Lord, it was expedient that mankind should be reclaimed from this spiritual death.

10. Therefore, as they had become carnal, sensual, and devilish, by nature, this probationary

state became a state for them to prepare; it became a preparatory state.

11. And now remember, my son, if it were not for the plan of redemption, (laying it aside) as soon as they were dead their souls were miserable, being cut off from the presence of the Lord.

2–11. The revelations of the Restoration give Latter-day Saints a perspective of the Creation, the Fall, and the Atonement that differs from the theologies of the world as the night differs from the day. By the light of the Restoration, condemnation gives way to praise as we speak of father Adam, and the coldness of death gives way to the promise of an eternal union as we speak of the importance of families. The fall of Adam, we learn, was necessary for the exaltation of Adam and all his posterity. Death, we discover, is but a requisite for resurrection and eternal glory, and the plan of salvation is aptly described as "the great plan of happiness." Had there been no fall, there could have been no atonement. The fall of Adam brought temporal and spiritual death into the world, and it is from these deaths that man and all forms of life are ransomed through the atonement of Christ. Salvation comes because of the Fall and the Atonement.

"Properly understood, it becomes apparent that the fall of Adam is one of the greatest blessings ever given of God to mankind. It is the way and the means whereby the spirit children of the Father go forth from their celestial home to gain mortal and then immortal bodies. And it provides the way for the experiences, tests, and trials that prepare the faithful for eternal life. Is it any wonder, then, that Michael himself—who stood next to the Lord Jehovah in power, might, and dominion, when they both dwelt in the presence of the Father—is it any wonder that Michael was the one chosen to come here as Adam to make such glorious blessings available to the billions of his descendants who should be born on earth?" (Bruce R. McConkie, *New Witness*, p. 87.)

1. See commentary on Alma 41:1, 9–10.

2. First parents] See *Commentary* 1:196–97.

2. The ground, from whence they were taken] See commentary on Mosiah 2:25–26.

2. Drew out the man] The Bible language is "drove out the man" (Genesis 3:24). The expression affirms Adam's reluctance to leave the glory and security of the garden and his unfitness to remain there in his fallen state.

2. Cherubim] *Cherubim* is the (Hebrew) plural of *cherub*, though it is used in the scriptures as a singular noun. "In the celestial hierarchy, cherubs are represented as spirits next in order to seraphs" (Webster's Dictionary, 1828). Regarded as chief among their duties is that of guarding the holy place, or the place where God dwells.

2. The tree of life] In the allegorical representations of Eden it is from the tree of life that the nourishment of immortality is obtained. Thus the cherubim were called upon to guard the fruits of the tree from Adam and Eve in their fallen state. See also commentary on 1 Nephi 11:2–11.

3. Man had become as God] Having partaken of the tree of the knowledge of good and evil—that is, having obtained the capacity to distinguish between opposites, and being able now to understand the difference between good and evil—Adam had, on this matter, become as God. Thereafter, through the righteous exercise of agency, Adam could pursue a course that would eventually endow him with a fulness of the Father. "As to the fall," Elder Bruce R. McConkie wrote, "the scriptures set forth that there were in the Garden of Eden two trees. One was the tree of life, which figuratively refers to eternal life; the other was the tree of knowledge of good and evil, which figuratively refers to how and why and in what manner mortality and all that appertains to it came into being. . . . Eve partook without full understanding; Adam partook knowing that unless he did so, he and Eve could not have children and fulfill the commandment they had received to multiply and replenish the earth." (*New Witness*, p. 86.) Elsewhere Elder McConkie wrote: "The account is speaking figuratively. What is meant by partaking of the fruit of the tree of the knowledge of good and evil is that our first parents complied with whatever laws were involved so that their bodies would change from their state of paradisiacal immortality to a state of natural mortality." ("Christ and the Creation," *Ensign*, June 1982, p. 15.)

3. And live forever] The thought would be more complete were it to read "and live forever *in his sins.*" It is not endless life that the Lord sought to prevent by placing the cherubim and a flaming sword to guard the tree of life; rather, it was endless life in an unrepentant state. Thus God in his mercy granted Adam "a probationary time, a time to repent and serve God."

4. A probationary time] Mortal life, a period wherein we could prove ourselves, whether or not we would do all things whatsoever the Lord our God would command us (see Abraham 3:25). See also 2 Nephi 2:21; Alma 12:24; 42:10.

5. The word of God would have been void] See Alma 12:26.

5. The great plan of salvation would have been frustrated] God has all the attributes of godliness in their perfection. It is not within his nature to do that which is less than godly. He cannot create that which is unwholesome or evil. That which he creates is without corruption or sin of any kind. Thus it was requisite with the plan of salvation that Adam fall, that he introduce mortality and corruption, that he, through the Fall, create a condition in which men might know opposition and knowingly and deliberately seek God. Had Adam not partaken of the forbidden fruit, had he not transgressed, had he not introduced death and corruption into a world where it had not existed in any form, had he not thereby imposed upon his posterity both a temporal and a spiritual death, the plan of salvation would have been of none effect. Had there been no fall, there could be no atonement; and if there were no atonement, there would be no Savior; and if there were no Savior, there could be no plan of salvation.

6. It was appointed unto man to die] Jacob declared, "Death hath passed upon all men, to fulfill the merciful plan of the great Creator" (2 Nephi 9:6). All must die in order to gain the victory over mortality. Death is a prerequisite to resurrection and eternal glory.

6. Lost forever . . . fallen man] All are lost, all are fallen, save there be an atonement! "Wherefore, all mankind were in a lost and in a fallen state," Lehi explained, "and ever would be save they should rely on this Redeemer" (1 Nephi 10:6). All are hardened and lost (see Alma 34:9). All of Adam's posterity are subject to both temporal and spiritual deaths. Hence the need for one who is God's Son to redeem them. Hence the true and proper doctrine of salvation by the grace of God.

7. Cut off both temporally and spiritually] Having been driven from the garden of Eden, Adam and Eve now commence their mortal probation. The intimacy they once enjoyed with God is now lost to them; they have left "father and mother" and are now to "cleave" unto each other (see Genesis 2:24). They face the surety of death and the struggle to overcome the temptations of the flesh, that they might be worthy of the directions of the Spirit. In temporal death their spirits and bodies will separate, the body returning to the dust whence it was taken and the spirit being consigned to the world of disembodied souls. Spiritual death is their separation from the divine presence, alienation from the author of righteousness.

7. They became subjects to follow after their own will] The fallen man seeks to do his own will, the redeemed man the will of the Father. The carnal man seeks to satiate the flesh, the spiritual man to receive and abide by the things of the Spirit. Being dead as to divine experience, the sensual and devilish man knows and revels only in that which is temporary and fleeting, while the new creature in Christ seeks to gain the mind of Christ and to do always those things which bring the approbation of heaven.

8. It was not expedient that man should be reclaimed from this temporal death] The "man" to whom reference is made in this verse is the man Adam. It was not expedient that he be allowed to partake of the fruit of the tree of life and thus void the Fall and frustrate the plan of salvation. Hence the angel with a flaming sword was placed at Eden's gate to prevent Adam and Eve from returning in their fallen state to eat of the tree of life.

9. The soul could never die] The soul, meaning here the spirit of man, cannot change its form or be destroyed. Such notions as human spirits taking the bodies of animals in another life, or the annihilation of wicked spirits on the Day of Judgment, or the recycling of the wicked, are wholly false.

10. They had become carnal, sensual, and devilish, by nature] See commentary on Mosiah 3:19 and on Alma 26:21–22.

10. Probationary state] See Alma 12:22–34.

11. Laying it aside] That is, supposing there were no plan of redemption, supposing (hypothetically) that Christ had not come into the world and placed immortality and eternal life within the reach of Adam and Eve's posterity.

11. Their souls were miserable] That is, as Jacob taught, their spirits would have become subject to the father of lies and be damned evermore (2 Nephi 9:7–9). See *Commentary* 1:236–40.

Justice and Mercy Find Perfect Union in Christ

Alma 42:12–15

12. And now, there was no means to reclaim men from this fallen state, which man had brought upon himself because of his own disobedience;

13. Therefore, according to justice, the plan of redemption could not be brought about, only on conditions of repentance of men in this probationary state, yea, this preparatory state; for except it were for these conditions, mercy could not take effect except it should destroy the work of justice. Now the work of justice could not be destroyed; if so, God would cease to be God.

14. And thus we see that all mankind were fallen, and they were in the grasp of justice; yea, the justice of God, which consigned them forever to be cut off from his presence.

15. And now, the plan of mercy could not be brought about except an atonement should be made; therefore God himself atoneth for the sins of the world, to bring about the plan of mercy, to appease the demands of justice, that God might be a perfect, just God, and a merciful God also.

12. This fallen state, which man had brought upon

himself] Adam brought the fallen condition, mortality, through partaking of the forbidden fruit. All men and women are subject to this condition. All. Jehovah spoke to Adam: "Inasmuch as thy children are conceived in sin, even so when they begin to grow up, sin conceiveth in their hearts, and they taste the bitter, that they may know to prize the good" (Moses 6:55). Robert L. Millet has written: "No, of course we do not believe, with Calvin, in the moral depravity of men and women. No, we do not believe, with Luther, that man, because of his carnality and depravity, does not even have the power to choose good over evil. And we do not believe that children are born in sin, that they inherit the so-called sin of Adam either through sexual union or by birth. Rather, children are *conceived* in sin: meaning first, that they are conceived into a world of sin, and second, that conception is the vehicle by which the effects of the Fall (not the original transgression, which God has forgiven) are transmitted to Adam's posterity. To say that we are not punished for the transgression is not to say that we are not subject to and affected by it. . . . Adam's fallen nature is passed on to his children and thereby from generation to generation. Thus sin is implanted in man's nature at conception, just as death is implanted at the same time. Both of these—death and sin—are present only in seed form at conception, and therefore a child is neither dead nor sinful when born. Death and sin do, however, come to pass as a result of man's nature as he grows up. Sin comes naturally, just as does death." (*Life in Christ*, pp. 24–25.)

This is what we call the fall of man. Adam, and thus all of us as his children, were freed from whatever "original guilt" might once have been as a result of Adam's transgression (see Moses 6:53–54). But what of our own fall? Gerald N. Lund has written: "If we know good from evil and then sin (which, according to Paul, all men do), then we must talk about a second fall. This is not the fall of Adam. This is *one's own personal fall*. This fall, which our own, not Adam's, transgression brings about, requires redemption as surely as mankind needed redemption from the consequences of Adam's fall. We'll term this the 'fall of me.' . . . Now, since we have no one to blame for this except ourselves, our redemption becomes conditional upon our actions. This is what Lehi meant [2 Nephi 2:7] when he said that the sacrifice that the Messiah offered to satisfy the ends of the law is viable only for those with a broken heart and a contrite spirit." (*Jesus Christ, Key to the Plan of Salvation*, p. 95.)

13. God could not be God save he possessed in his nature all the attributes of godliness. God, for instance, cannot be God and not possess that attribute of justice in its perfection. If, for the sake of argument, he lacked the attribute of justice, he would, by definition, cease to be God. Thus, Alma reasons, he cannot both save his children and be unjust or ignore the law of justice. The redemptive labor assures that he will be just, and the law of justice assures that men will not be saved in an unrepentant state. Thus, Alma most appropriately states that: "The plan of redemption could not be brought about, only on conditions of repentance of men in this probationary state." In so stating, he responds perfectly to the erroneous idea that men can be saved solely by the grace or mercy of God, without repentance and efforts to live a worthy life. Such a doctrine isolates one of the attributes of Deity (that of grace or mercy) at the expense of others, and thus robs our Eternal Father of the very nature of godliness.

13. God would cease to be God] "God cannot and will not cease to be God. His title, his status, and his exalted position are forever fixed and immutable. Nor need the Saints of God spend a particle of a second worrying and fretting about the Almighty falling from grace. Joseph Smith explained in the Lectures on Faith (lecture 4) that for the Saints to do so is to err in doctrine as to the true nature of God and thus fall short of that dynamic faith which leads to life and salvation. Alma's hypothetical case is just that—purely hypothetical. He is arguing toward the impossible, the absurd, to emphasize the logical certainty of the principle that mercy cannot rob justice. It is as if Alma had said: 'It is as ridiculous to suppose that mercy can rob justice and that men and women can break the laws of God with impunity, as it is to suppose that God can cease to be God.' In fact, Alma concludes, 'God ceaseth not to be God, and mercy claimeth the penitent, and mercy cometh because of the atonement.' (Alma 42:23)." (Robert L. Millet, *Life in Christ*, p. 78.)

14–15. Justice was not compromised, mercy was not slighted, the demands of the law were met as the Son of God made himself an offering for all.

14. The justice of God] Justice is not just an abstract principle, not merely some eternal ideal, some mystical regulation in a law-driven universe. Justice is an attribute of Deity, a condition and requirement of God. It is the justice *of God* which rewards righteousness. It is the justice *of God* which punishes sin.

15. God himself] The great, the last, the eternal sacrifice was "not a sacrifice of man" (Alma 34:10) but of a God. Jesus Christ, the God of the Old Testament, the God of the New Testament, the literal Son of the Eternal Father, the maker of heaven and earth, offered himself up as atonement to answer the ends of the Fall and satisfy the demands of justice. Elder Boyd K. Packer testified: "Know this: Truth, glorious truth, proclaims there is . . . a Mediator. 'For there is one God, and one mediator between God and men, the man Christ Jesus' (1 Timothy 2:5). Through him mercy can be fully extended to each of us without offending the eternal law of justice. This truth is the very root of Christian doctrine. You may know much about the gospel as it branches out from there, but if you only know the branches and those branches do not touch that root, if they have been cut free from that truth, there will be no life nor substance nor redemption in them." (CR, April 1977, p. 80.)

Repentance Requires Suffering

Alma 42:16–26

16. Now, repentance could not come unto men except there were a punishment, which also was eternal as the life of the soul should be, affixed opposite to the plan of happiness, which was as eternal also as the life of the soul.

17. Now, how could a man repent except he should sin? How could he sin if there was no law? How could there be a law save there was a punishment?

18. Now, there was a punishment affixed, and a just law given, which brought remorse of conscience unto man.

19. Now, if there was no law given—if a man murdered he should die—would he be afraid he would die if he should murder?

20. And also, if there was no law given against sin men would not be afraid to sin.

21. And if there was no law given, if men sinned what could justice do, or mercy either, for they would have no claim upon the creature?

22. But there is a law given, and a punishment affixed, and a repentance granted; which repentance, mercy claimeth; otherwise, justice claimeth the creature and executeth the law, and the law inflicteth the punishment; if not so, the works of justice would be destroyed, and God would cease to be God.

23. But God ceaseth not to be God, and mercy claimeth the penitent, and mercy cometh because of the atonement; and the atonement bringeth to pass the resurrection of the dead; and the resurrection of the dead bringeth back men into the presence of God; and thus they are restored into his presence, to be judged according to their works, according to the law and justice.

24. For behold, justice exerciseth all his demands, and also mercy claimeth all which is her own; and thus, none but the truly penitent are saved.

25. What, do ye suppose that mercy can rob justice? I say unto you, Nay; not one whit. If so, God would cease to be God.

26. And thus God bringeth about his great and eternal purposes, which were prepared from the foundation of the world. And thus cometh about the salvation and the redemption of men, and also their destruction and misery.

16–26. With a plainness unmatched elsewhere in scripture,

Alma explains why there is no true repentance without punishment. His instruction is most relevant for our day, in which inconstant theology and cheap grace abound in the media ministries. It is generally forgotten that discipline and discipleship are branches of the same tree, and that both involve bringing a person to a condition of order and obedience. Wise parents quickly learn that discipline is a manifestation of love, and yet many of the same parents would suppose that heavenly parents would not do likewise. Alma's chain of thought is quite simple: if there are laws, there must be punishments for the violation of the laws; and thus, if God has given laws, there must in like manner be punishments affixed. Repentance is the process by which we make retribution for the violation of God's laws.

16. Repentance could not come . . . except there were a punishment] Having quoted this phrase, President Spencer W. Kimball instructed the priesthood leaders of the Church: "Ponder on that for a moment. Have you realized that? There can be no forgiveness without real and total repentance, and there can be no repentance without punishment. This is as eternal as is the soul. . . . Please remember these things when somebody comes before you who has broken the laws of God. It is so easy to let our sympathies carry us out of proportion; and when a man has committed sin, he must suffer. It is an absolute requirement—not by the bishop—but it is a requirement by nature and by the very part of a man." (CR, April 1975, p. 115.)

16. Opposite to the plan of happiness] By its very nature, the gospel blesses or curses. If there is a plan or path of happiness, of necessity there must be a path of unhappiness; if there is a course that brings joy and rejoicing, of necessity there must be a course that brings bitterness and sorrow. If there are commandments, the obedience to which brings blessings, it follows that to violate those commandments must bring punishments.

"The voice of warning shall be unto all people, by the mouths of my disciples, whom I have chosen in these last days," the Lord declared. "And they shall go forth and none shall stay them, for I the Lord have commanded them. Behold, this is mine authority, and the authority of my servants. . . . And verily I say unto you, that they who go forth, bearing these tidings unto the inhabitants of the earth, to them is power given to seal both on earth and in heaven, the unbelieving and rebellious; yea, verily, to seal them up unto the day when the wrath of God shall be poured out upon the wicked without measure—unto the day when the Lord shall come to recompense unto every man according to his work, and measure to every man according to the measure which he has measured to his fellow man." (D&C 1:4–10.)

17. There is no repentance without punishment. To suppose that the Atonement excuses one from the labors of remorse, the pain of healing, or the responsibility to make appropriate restitution where possible is to deny the justice of God. Pain helps lessons stick and makes them the more valuable. Blessings withheld may teach more than blessings granted.

18. Remorse of conscience] Thanks be to God for our consciences, those moral monitors which strive with us, which lead and teach and direct and point toward the good and the godly. Conscience is a manifestation of the Light of Christ or the Spirit of Jesus Christ, through which, if we heed its divine influence, we shall be led to the greater light of the Holy Ghost (see Moroni 7:16–19; D&C 84:45–48; Joseph F. Smith, *Gospel Doctrine*, pp. 67–68; Bruce R. McConkie, *New Witness*, p. 260). When we fail to hearken to this light—when we act against our values and what we know to be right—we suffer remorse of conscience.

23. The atonement bringeth to pass the resurrection of the dead] The atonement of Christ saves us from physical death through the resurrection, and—if we will—from spiritual death through repentance and forgiveness.

24. None but the truly penitent are saved] This is what Lehi meant when he taught that only those who have a broken heart and a contrite spirit can be saved (2 Nephi 2:7). Only those who are meek and lowly of heart—a condition caused by godly sorrow for sin and unconditional surrender to the will of the Lord—are acceptable to the Most High (see Moroni 7:44).

Sin Cannot Be Excused

Alma 42:27–30

27. Therefore, O my son, whosoever will come may come and partake of the waters of life freely; and whosoever will not come the same is not compelled to come; but in the last day it shall be restored unto him according to his deeds.

28. If he has desired to do evil, and has not repented in his days, behold, evil shall be done unto him, according to the restoration of God.

29. And now, my son, I desire that ye should let these things trouble you no more, and only let your sins trouble you, with that trouble which shall bring you down unto repentance.

30. O my son, I desire that ye should deny the justice of God no more. Do not endeavor to excuse yourself in the least point because of your sins, by denying the justice of God; but do you let the justice of God, and his mercy, and his long-suffering have full sway in your heart; and let it bring you down to the dust in humility.

27–30. Reasons abound to excuse untoward behavior, and there appears to be no shortage of theological justifications for sinful acts. Nevertheless, eternal principles do not yield to excuses. It is an absolute verity that no unclean thing can enter into the presence of God. It is an undeviating principle that covenants are to be kept with exactness and honor.

27. Partake of the waters of life freely] See commentary on Alma 41:8. See also 2 Nephi 26:25–28.

27. Restored . . . according to his deeds] See Alma 41:14.

28. In his days] His probationary estate—mortality.

29. There is an appropriate guilt, a proper remorse of conscience, that men and women must enjoy if they are to remain on that strait and narrow path that leads ultimately to eternal life. There is a fine line between the devil's dissonance (which is evil and demoralizing) and divine discontent (which is of God and is a source for gradual and constant improvement). True Saints pray constantly about their feelings. They ask the Father in the name of the Son to educate their desires, to shape their affections, to fine-tune their feelings to the end that they feel what they ought to feel. No one wants to feel any more guilt than is appropriate. But no one seeking salvation would want to feel any less than is necessary. "Now I rejoice," Paul wrote to the Corinthian Saints, "not that ye were made sorry, but that ye sorrowed to repentance." And then the Apostle added: "For godly sorrow worketh repentance to salvation," while "the sorrow of the world worketh death." (2 Corinthians 7:10–11; compare Mormon 2:13.)

29. These things] This seems to be a reference to the specific doctrinal difficulties with which Corianton had wrestled (see Alma 40:1; 41:1; 42:1).

Corianton Recalled to the Ministry

Alma 42:31

31. And now, O my son, ye are called of God to preach the word unto this people. And now, my son, go thy way, declare the word with truth and soberness, that thou mayest bring souls unto repentance, that the great plan of mercy may have claim upon them. And may God grant unto you even according to my words. Amen.

31. Go thy way] Corianton's sins were grievous. And yet we have every reason to believe that Alma's preaching touched the soul of his errant son, that Corianton "crossed himself" (see Alma

39:9), repented, and returned to the ministry. We read of Corianton's labors a year or so later: "Thus ended the nineteenth year of the reign of the judges over the people of Nephi. Yea, and there was continual peace among them, and exceedingly great prosperity in the church because of their heed and diligence which they gave unto the word of God, which was declared unto them by Helaman, and Shiblon, and Corianton, and Ammon and his brethren, yea, and by all those who had been ordained by the holy order of God." (Alma 49:29–30.)

Elder Orson F. Whitney held out this hope for the parents of wandering or wayward children: "You parents of the wilful and the wayward: Don't give them up. Don't cast them off. They are not utterly lost. The shepherd will find his sheep. They were his before they were yours—long before he entrusted them to your care; and you cannot begin to love them as he loves them. They have but strayed in ignorance from the Path of Right, and God is merciful to ignorance. Only the fulness of knowledge brings the fulness of accountability. Our Heavenly Father is far more merciful, infinitely more charitable, than even the best of his servants, and the Everlasting Gospel is mightier in power to save than our narrow finite minds can comprehend." (CR, April 1929, p. 110.) In that same spirit President J. Reuben Clark Jr. observed: "I feel that [the Lord] will give that punishment which is the very least that our transgression will justify. . . . I believe that when it comes to making the rewards for our good conduct, he will give the maximum that is possible to give." (From "As Ye Sow . . . ," address delivered at Brigham Young University, 3 May 1955.)

This story (Alma chapters 39–42) points up a deeply significant principle—the value of teaching doctrine. One perusing these chapters might be prone to ask: "The boy has a moral problem; why preach to him? Why spend so much time discussing the spirit world, resurrection, judgment, the law of restoration, and the mercy and justice of God?" Elder Bruce R. McConkie explained: "The foundation upon which we build our whole Church system is one of testimony and faith and conversion. It is our theology; it is the doctrine God has given us in this day; it is the restored and revealed principles of eternal truth—these are the things that give us the ability to operate our programs and build houses of salvation." (Address at a Regional Representatives Seminar, 3 April 1981, typescript pp. 9–10; cited in Mark L. McConkie, ed., *Doctrines of the Restoration,* pp. 226–27.) Or, as Elder Boyd K. Packer testified: "True doctrine, understood, changes attitudes and behavior. The study of the doctrines of the gospel will improve behavior quicker than a study of behavior will improve behavior. Preoccupation with unworthy behavior can lead to unworthy behavior. That is why we stress so forcefully the study of the doctrines of the gospel." (CR, October 1986, p. 20.)

31. Declare the word with truth and soberness] What is meant by the charge to teach the gospel "with truth?" Our word *true* is derived from the Old English *treowe*, which meant "faithful," "trustworthy," or "loyal." Thus, to teach the gospel with truth is to be faithful to the message; it is to be a trustworthy servant; it is not to take thought as to what people want to hear or to be concerned with what might give offense; it is to deliver the message as the message has been given to us in the scriptures and by the power of the Holy Ghost.

War and the Saints of God

Alma 43–62

Among the questions that naturally arise from a reading of Alma chapters 43–62 are the following: Given the constraints of space on Mormon's abridgment of the large plates, why would he devote so much time to a discussion of war? Given that the Book of Mormon has been written for our day, that Mormon and the other prophet-writers saw our day and prepared this sacred volume in a way that would help us address the problems and challenges of the last days, what lessons do we learn from the twenty chapters on warfare? Though the list below is by no means exhaustive, we might consider the following important lessons.

1. *The Christian's attitude toward war.* "War is basically selfish," President David O. Mckay stated. "Its roots feed in the soil of envy, hatred, desire for domination. Its fruit, therefore, is always bitter. They who cultivate and propagate it spread death and destruction and are enemies of the human race. War originates in the hearts of men who seek to despoil, to conquer, or to destroy the individuals or groups of individuals. Self-exaltation is a motivating factor; force, the means of attainment. War is rebellious action against moral order. . . . War impels you to hate your enemies. The Prince of Peace says, love your enemies. War says, curse them that curse you. The Prince of Peace says, pray for them that curse you. War says, injure and kill them that hate you. The risen Lord says, do good to them that hate you.

"We see that war is incompatible with Christ's teachings. The gospel of Jesus Christ is the gospel of peace. War is its antithesis and produces hate. It is vain to attempt to reconcile war with true Christianity. . . . There are, however, two conditions which may justify a truly Christian man to enter—mind you, I say enter, not begin—a war: (1) an attempt to dominate and deprive another of his free agency; and (2) loyalty to his country. Possibly there is a third, viz., defense of a weak nation that is being unjustly crushed by a strong, ruthless one. . . .

"To deprive an intelligent human being of his free agency is to commit the crime of the ages. So fundamental in man's eternal progress is his inherent right to choose that the Lord would defend it even at the price of war. Without freedom of thought, freedom of choice, freedom of action within lawful bounds, man cannot progress." (CR, April 1942, pp. 70–74.)

It is in that spirit that the Nephite military leaders approached war. "And now the design of the Nephites was to support their lands, and their houses, and their wives, and their children, that they might preserve them from the hands of their enemies; and also that they might preserve their rights and their privileges, yea, and also their liberty, that they might worship God according to their desires. For they knew that if they should fall into the hands of the Lamanites, that whosoever should worship God in spirit and in truth, the true and the living God, the Lamanites would destroy." (Alma 43:9–10.)

Though in many cases the Lamanites did fight with great human strength, motivated by their desire for domination, "the Nephites were inspired by a better cause, for they were not fighting for monarchy nor power but they were fighting for their homes and their liberties, their wives and their children, and their all, yea, for their rights of worship and their church. And *they were doing that which they felt was their duty which they owed to their God*; for the Lord had said unto them, and also unto their fathers, that: *Inasmuch as ye are not guilty of the first offense, neither the second, ye shall not suffer yourselves to be slain by the hands of your enemies.* And again, the Lord has said that: Ye shall defend your families even unto bloodshed." (Alma 43:44–47, italics added.) In regard to the fact that the Nephites had been instructed never to begin a war, Mormon wrote: "Now the Nephites were taught to defend themselves against their enemies, even to the shedding of blood if it were necessary; yea, and *they were also taught never to give an offense, yea, and never to raise the sword except it were against an enemy, except it were to preserve their lives.* And this was their faith, that by so doing God would prosper them in the land." (Alma 48:14–15, italics added; compare 3 Nephi 3:20–21; D&C 98:23–36.)

2. *The importance of righteous military leaders.* The Nephite military leaders were not bloodthirsty. They hated war and hated the thought of shedding the blood of their brethren. They utilized clever strategy regularly, not only to win the war more rapidly but

also to save lives on both sides (see Alma 43:29–30). Later in the story Mormon points out that "it was the custom among all the Nephites to appoint for their chief captains, (save it were in their times of wickedness) some one that had the spirit of revelation and also prophecy" (3 Nephi 3:19). And what more beautiful tribute could be paid to Captain Moroni than the following by Mormon: "Moroni was a strong and a mighty man; he was a man of a perfect understanding; yea, a man that did not delight in bloodshed; a man whose soul did joy in the liberty and the freedom of his country, and his brethren from bondage and slavery; yea, a man whose heart did swell with thanksgiving to his God, for the many privileges and blessings which he bestowed upon his people; a man who did labor exceedingly for the welfare and safety of his people. Yea, and he was a man who was firm in the faith of Christ, and he has sworn with an oath to defend his people, his rights, and his country, and his religion, even to the loss of his blood." To sum up: "Yea, verily, verily I say unto you, if all men had been, and were, and ever would be, like unto Moroni, behold, the very powers of hell would have been shaken forever; yea, the devil would never have power over the hearts of the children of men." (Alma 48:11–13, 17.)

3. *Our attitude toward constituted government.* In our day the Lord has instructed us that Latter-day Saints in the United States are to be subject to the powers that be until Christ reigns as King of kings (D&C 58:21–22; 134:1, 5). Though some of Moroni's actions might be offensive to the more pacifistic of this modern age, he acted in harmony with what he felt was his and others' duty to God, even to the point of compelling dissenters to take up arms in support of the government during war (see Alma 51:15–16). At those times when he sensed that moral support for government or the cause of liberty was fading, Moroni single-handedly sought to foster enthusiasm and engender support for the government by reminding the people of their promises to God. This was the essence of the "Title of Liberty" episode. That incident was more than a large pep rally, more than an emotional appeal; it was a covenant renewal ceremony in which this mighty prophet-leader called upon the people to remember their duty to God, duty to church, duty to country, and duty to one another as Christians.

For the Nephites, righteousness was at the heart of good government; a government was only as good as its people and its leaders. They were convinced that they could enjoy the blessings and protection of the Almighty only in a state of faithfulness and fidelity to their covenants. Thus the people "cast their garments at the feet of Moroni, saying: We covenant with our God, that we shall be destroyed, even as our brethren in the land northward [the Jaredites], if we shall fall into transgression; yea, he may cast us at the feet of our enemies, even as we have cast our garments at thy feet to be trodden under foot, if we shall fall into transgression" (Alma 46:22). Similarly, in the exchange of letters between Moroni and the chief judge Pahoran, even though Moroni is unaware of Pahoran's plight (the judgment seat having been taken over by the king-men), we see the nobility of soul and fearlessness of Moroni in his attitude toward upholding the Nephite government and destroying all influences which would seek to rob men and women of their inalienable rights (see Alma 59–61).

In what might be termed an oath of office for the chief judgeship, we see again the depth of commitment manifest by those chosen to serve the people. "And it came to pass that in the same year that the people of Nephi had peace restored unto them [ca. 67 B.C.], that Nephihah, the second chief judge, died, having filled the judgment-seat with perfect uprightness before God. . . . Behold, it came to pass that the son of Nephihah [Pahoran] was appointed to fill the judgment-seat, in the stead of his father; yea, he was appointed chief judge and governor over the people, with an oath and sacred ordinance to judge righteously, and to keep the peace and the freedom of the people, and to grant unto them their sacred privileges to worship the Lord their God, yea, to support and maintain the cause of God all his days, and to bring the wicked to justice according to their crime." (Alma 50:37, 39.)

4. *The power and influence of a righteous home.* Because righteousness was central to the maintenance of the government, proper training in the home, in the family setting, was absolutely necessary. This is illustrated beautifully in the lives of Helaman's two thousand stripling warriors. These were young men of unusual capacity, persons whose performance on the battlefield could be described as no less than miraculous. In the words of Mormon: "And they entered into a covenant to fight for the liberty of the Nephites [their fathers, the Anti-Nephi-Lehies, had covenanted not to take up weapons of war], yea, to protect the land unto the laying down of their lives; yea, even they covenanted that they never would give up their liberty, but they would fight in all cases to protect the Nephites and themselves from bondage. Now behold, there were two thousand of these young men, who entered into this covenant and took their weapons of war to defend their country. And now behold, as they never had hitherto been a disadvantage to the Nephites, they became now at this period of time also a great support; for they took their weapons of war, and they would that Helaman should be their leader. And they were all young men, and *they were exceedingly valiant for courage, and also for strength and activity; but behold, this was not all—*

they were men who were true at all times in whatsoever thing they were entrusted. Yea, they were men of truth and soberness, for they had been taught to keep the commandments of God and to walk uprightly before him." (Alma 53:17–21, italics added.)

Helaman later explained the source of their commitment: "Now they never had fought," he wrote to Moroni, "yet they did not fear death; and they did think more upon the liberty of their fathers than they did upon their lives; yea, *they had been taught by their mothers, that if they did not doubt, God would deliver them. And they rehearsed unto me the words of their mothers, saying: We do not doubt our mothers knew it.*" (Alma 56:47–48, italics added.) Truly the righteous home is the basis of morality and decency, the essential element in the preservation of a society.

5. *A person's external circumstances need not determine his attitude or his faithfulness.* One of the vital messages of the Book of Mormon is that one can remain untainted from the sins of the world, no matter what the extent of the degradation of the day. In the days of Alma, in the midst of gross wickedness there was an element of consummate righteousness (see Alma chapters 1 and 4). Similarly, during a period which might be called the worst of times, in about 30 B.C., God raised up two young men, Nephi and Lehi (sons of Helaman), whose unswerving devotion to truth wrought a mighty change among thousands of people who listened to their words and witnessed their spiritual power.

It was during the period of wars that Alma was taken from the midst of the people, presumably translated and taken from the earth without tasting death. Having prophesied concerning the eventual demise of the Nephite nation and then blessed all his sons, Alma "blessed the earth for the righteous' sake." Further, "he blessed the church, yea, all those who should stand fast in the faith from that time henceforth. And when Alma had done this he departed out of the land of Zarahemla, as if to go into the land of Melek. And it came to pass that he was never heard of more; as to his death or burial we know not of. Behold, this we know, that he was a righteous man; and the saying went abroad in the church that he was taken up by the Spirit, or buried by the hand of the Lord, even as Moses. But behold, the scriptures saith the Lord took Moses unto himself [see Deuteronomy 34:1–6; Joseph Fielding Smith, *Doctrines of Salvation* 2:107, 109–11; Bruce R. McConkie, *Mormon Doctrine*, p. 515]; and we suppose that he has also received Alma in the spirit, unto himself; therefore, for this cause we know nothing concerning his death and burial." (Alma 45:8–19.) In short, one can live a life of transcendent faithfulness in the midst of harshness and wickedness.

Oddly enough, Mormon writes of a time during the days of

Nephite wars when, because of the steadiness of the members of the Church, "they did prosper exceedingly, and they became exceedingly rich; yea, and they did multiply and wax strong in the land. And thus we see how merciful and just are all the dealings of the Lord, to the fulfilling of all his words unto the children of men. . . . Behold, *there never was a happier time among the people of Nephi, since the days of Nephi,* than in the days of Moroni, yea, even at this time, in the twenty and first year of the reign of the judges." (Alma 50:18–19, 23, italics added.) Indeed, the Nephite record gives a profound lesson about how one responds to his or her circumstances. Note this language at the end of the wars: "And thus ended the thirty and first year of the reign of the judges over the people of Nephi; and thus they had had wars, and bloodsheds, and famine, and affliction, for the space of many years. And there had been murders, and contentions, and dissensions, and all manner of iniquity among the people of Nephi; nevertheless for the righteous' sake, yea, because of the prayers of the righteous, they were spared. But behold, *because of the exceedingly great length of the war between the Nephites and the Lamanties many had become hardened, . . . and many were softened because of their afflictions, insomuch that they did humble themselves before God, even in the depth of humility.*" (Alma 62:39–41, italics added.)

6. *Why God allows the righteous to be slain.* War is ugly. Its effects are poignant and painful. Its reach is devastating. It rushes into premature death a great many of the sons and daughters of God. Captain Moroni, supposing foul play on the part of Pahoran, wrote: "Do ye suppose that, because so many of your brethren have been killed it is because of their wickedness? I say unto you, if ye have supposed this ye have supposed in vain; for I say unto you, there are many who have fallen by the sword; and behold it is to your condemnation [referring to the unrighteous]; for *the Lord suffereth the righteous to be slain that his justice and judgment may come upon the wicked*; therefore ye need not suppose that the righteous are lost because they are slain; but behold, they do enter into the rest of the Lord their God." (Alma 60:12–13, italics added; compare Mosiah 17:10; Alma 14:11; 46:39.)

7. *A prophetic pattern of what is to come.* Though it is not pleasant to entertain such a thought, it may be that the chapters on warfare have been preserved to prepare us for things to come. In the Preface to the Doctrines and Covenants, the Savior said: "I . . . will that all men shall know that the day speedily cometh; the hour is not yet, but is nigh at hand, when peace shall be taken from the earth, and the devil shall have power over his own dominion" (D&C 1:35). In the prophecy on wars which was given some fourteen months later, we learn that the war between the

States would prove to be the beginning of the end, so far as peace is concerned; indeed, "the time will come that war will be poured out upon all nations" (D&C 87:2; see also *Commentary* 2:6–7).

We have in the Book of Mormon a superlative collection of stories, lessons, precepts, and warnings which, if pondered and studied, will help to prepare us as Latter-day Saints for perilous times that surely shall be. The decades preceding Christ's first coming may serve as a pattern or type of the years preceding his second coming. President Ezra Taft Benson has explained: "In the Book of Mormon we find a pattern for preparing for the Second Coming. A major portion of the book centers on the few decades just prior to Christ's coming to America. By careful study of that time period, we can determine why some were destroyed in the terrible judgments that preceded His coming and what brought others to stand at the temple in the land of Bountiful and thrust their hands into the wounds of His hands and feet. From the Book of Mormon we learn how disciples of Christ live in times of war." (*A Witness and a Warning*, pp. 20–21.)

Hagoth Leads Many Nephites to the Isles of the Sea

Alma 63:1–17

1. And it came to pass in the commencement of the thirty and sixth year of the reign of the judges over the people of Nephi, that Shiblon took possession of those sacred things which had been delivered unto Helaman by Alma.

2. And he was a just man, and he did walk uprightly before God; and he did observe to do good continually, to keep the commandments of the Lord his God; and also did his brother.

3. And it came to pass that Moroni died also. And thus ended the thirty and sixth year of the reign of the judges.

4. And it came to pass that in the thirty and seventh year of the reign of the judges, there was a large company of men, even to the amount of five thousand and four hundred men, with their wives and their children, departed out of the land of Zarahemla into the land which was northward.

5. And it came to pass that Hagoth, he being an exceedingly curious man, therefore he went forth and built him an exceedingly large ship, on the borders of the land Bountiful, by the land Desolation, and launched it forth into the west sea, by the narrow neck which led into the land northward.

6. And behold, there were many of the Nephites who did enter therein and did sail forth with much provisions, and also many women and children; and they took their course northward. And thus ended the thirty and

seventh year.

7. And in the thirty and eighth year, this man built other ships. And the first ship did also return, and many more people did enter into it; and they also took much provisions, and set out again to the land northward.

8. And it came to pass that they were never heard of more. And we suppose that they were drowned in the depths of the sea. And it came to pass that one other ship also did sail forth; and whither she did go we know not.

9. And it came to pass that in this year there were many people who went forth into the land northward. And thus ended the thirty and eighth year.

10. And it came to pass in the thirty and ninth year of the reign of the judges, Shiblon died also, and Corianton had gone forth to the land northward in a ship, to carry forth provisions unto the people who had gone forth into that land.

11. Therefore it became expedient for Shiblon to confer those sacred things, before his death, upon the son of Helaman, who was called Helaman, being called after the name of his father.

12. Now behold, all those engravings which were in the possession of Helaman were written and sent forth among the children of men throughout all the land, save it were those parts which had been commanded by Alma should not go forth.

13. Nevertheless, these things were to be kept sacred, and handed down from one generation to another; therefore, in this year, they had been conferred upon Helaman, before the death of Shiblon.

14. And it came to pass also in this year that there were some dissenters who had gone forth unto the Lamanites; and they were stirred up again to anger against the Nephites.

15. And also in this same year they came down with a numerous army to war against the people of Moronihah, or against the army of Moronihah, in the which they were beaten and driven back again to their own lands, suffering great loss.

16. And thus ended the thirty and ninth year of the reign of the judges over the people of Nephi.

17. And thus ended the account of Alma, and Helaman his son, and also Shiblon, who was his son.

---

1. Helaman had died (see Alma 62:52).

2. And also did his brother] This appears to be a reference to Corianton, who apparently took his father's counsel to heart, repented, returned to the ministry (Alma 42:31), and proved true and faithful thereafter.

3. Moroni died at a rather young age, approximately forty-four years old (see Alma 43:17).

4–9. In the Church it is generally held that Hagoth was the father of the Polynesians, that his expeditions to the isles of the sea were a part of the foreordained plan whereby the descendants of father Lehi, as children of Abraham, might be spread to all nations and thus fulfill God's covenant with the father of the faithful (Abraham 2:8–11). In speaking to the Saints in Samoa, President Spencer W. Kimball said: "I thought to read to you a sacred scripture which pertains especially to you, the islanders of the Pacific. It is in the sixty-third chapter of Alma. [He reads Alma 63:4, 7–10.] And so it seems to me rather clear that your ancestors moved northward and crossed a part of the South Pacific. You did not bring your records with you, but you brought much food and provisions. And so we have a great congregation of people in the South Seas who came from the Nephites, and who came from the land southward and went to the land northward, which could have been Hawaii. And then the further settlement could have been a move southward again to all of these islands and even to New Zealand. The Lord knows what he is doing when he sends his people from one place to another. That was the scattering of Israel. Some of them remained in America and went from Alaska to the southern point. And others of you came this direction." (Samoa Area Conference Report, February 1976, p. 15.)

To another group of Saints in the South Seas, President Kimball observed: "President Joseph F. Smith, the president of the Church, reported, 'You brothers and sisters from New Zealand, I want you to know that you are from the people of Hagoth.' For New Zealand Saints, that was that. A prophet of the Lord had spoken. . . . It is reasonable to conclude that Hagoth and his associates were about nineteen centuries on the islands, from about 55 B.C. to 1854 before the gospel began to reach them. They had lost all the plain and precious things which the Savior brought to the earth, for they were likely on the islands when the Christ was born in Jerusalem." (Temple View Area Conference Report, February 1976, p. 3.)

8. We suppose that they were drowned in the depths of the sea] This is one of the subtle testimonies of the truthfulness of this record. Had Joseph Smith simply been creating the Book of Mormon, fabricating it (rather than translating it), he probably would not have inserted such ideas into the narrative. Here we see that Mormon, a powerful prophet-editor, was simply unaware of what became of Hagoth and his followers. Living almost five centuries after their departure from the promised land, Mormon could have inquired as to their whereabouts, but presumably he had not done so, or if he had, he had not learned by revelation what became of those people.

12. See Alma 37:27–32.

The Book of

Helaman

Though but a brief segment of the entire record, the book of Helaman is packed full of timeless and timely messages. In that book we read with sadness of the rise of secret combinations and the Gadianton bands, and we have reaffirmed in our minds and hearts that Satan, that insane insomniac who is the king of Babylon, is alive and well on planet earth. At the same time we glory in the call and ministry of Nephi and Lehi, sons of Helaman, two spiritual giants raised up in a wicked day to declare repentance and lead the believing souls to peace and salvation. We thrill with the messianic prophecies of Samuel the Lamanite and treasure up his marvelous words concerning our deliverance from death and sin through the mortal ministry of Christ the Lord.

Kishkumen Murders Pahoran

Helaman 1:1–13

1. And now behold, it came to pass in the commencement of the fortieth year of the reign of the judges over the people of Nephi, there began to be a serious difficulty among the people of the Nephites.

2. For behold, Pahoran had died, and gone the way of all the earth; therefore there began to be a serious contention concerning who should have the judgment-seat among the brethren, who were the sons of Pahoran.

3. Now these are their names who did contend for the judgment-seat, who did also cause the people to contend: Pahoran, Paanchi, and Pacumeni.

4. Now these are not all the sons of Pahoran (for he had many), but these are they who did contend for the judgment-seat; therefore, they did cause three divisions among the people.

5. Nevertheless, it came to pass that Pahoran was appointed by the voice of the people to be chief judge and a governor over the people of Nephi.

6. And it came to pass that Pacumeni, when he saw that he

could not obtain the judgment-seat, he did unite with the voice of the people.

7. But behold, Paanchi, and that part of the people that were desirous that he should be their governor, was exceedingly wroth; therefore, he was about to flatter away those people to rise up in rebellion against their brethren.

8. And it came to pass as he was about to do this, behold, he was taken, and was tried according to the voice of the people, and condemned unto death; for he had raised up in rebellion and sought to destroy the liberty of the people.

9. Now when those people who were desirous that he should be their governor saw that he was condemned unto death, therefore they were angry, and behold, they sent forth one Kishkumen, even to the judgment-seat of Pahoran, and murdered Pahoran as he sat upon the judgment-seat.

10. And he was pursued by the servants of Pahoran; but behold, so speedy was the flight of Kishkumen that no man could overtake him.

11. And he went unto those that sent him, and they all entered into a covenant, yea, swearing by their everlasting Maker, that they would tell no man that Kishkumen had murdered Pahoran.

12. Therefore, Kishkumen was not known among the people of Nephi, for he was in disguise at the time that he murdered Pahoran. And Kishkumen and his band, who had covenanted with him, did mingle themselves among the people, in a manner that they all could not be found; but as many as were found were condemned unto death.

13. And now behold, Pacumeni was appointed, according to the voice of the people, to be a chief judge and a governor over the people, to reign in the stead of his brother Pahoran; and it was according to his right. And all this was done in the fortieth year of the reign of the judges; and it had an end.

1–7. At the death of the chief judge, Pahoran I, three of his sons vie for the right to succeed their father in the office of chief judge. This creates three "divisions" among the people, a problem that is settled by a vote of the people. Pahoran II is elected by "the voice of the people" to be the chief judge and governor. Pacumeni submits to the will of the people and supports and unites with Pahoran, but the third brother, Paanchi, rebels against the vote and fans the flames of emotion among his followers, who in turn instigate a rebellion against the people.

5. The voice of the people] This refers to a democratic vote of the people wherein the outcome is determined by the consent of the majority. This principle of elections by the "voice of the people" in the Book of Mormon was based on King Mosiah II's decision to allow the people to vote for judges to rule over them; he taught that the "voice of the people" will rarely desire that which is "contrary to that which is right" (see Mosiah 29:25–27).

8. Tried according to the voice of the people, and con-

demned unto death] Paanchi is tried for a capital offense, not because he disagreed with the outcome of the election or because he sought to become the chief judge, but rather that he "raised up in rebellion and sought to destroy the liberty of the people." His crime is one of sedition and treason. He is to be judged according to the laws established by Mosiah II. The exact nature of the "voice of the people" that found him guilty and condemned him to death is not given in the text, but based on other uses of the phrase it is either a democratic process, such as a jury of peers, or possibly a theo-democratic council of judges, as is perhaps implied by the record of the trial of Nehor (see Alma 1:10–15).

9–12. Followers of Paanchi, angry that he would not only not become their chief judge but that he also was condemned to die for his crimes, employ Kishkumen to murder the newly appointed chief judge, Pahoran II. After Kishkumen murders Pahoran, these followers of Paanchi enter into a "covenant" bound by secret oaths to tell no one of their complicity in the murder. A number of those accomplices to the murder are executed, yet many hide themselves by mingling among the people. This remnant of dissidents becomes the genesis of the "secret combinations" that would continually plague the people of Nephi and would ultimately bring about their destruction as a nation.

13. Pacumeni was appointed . . . chief judge . . . according to his right] The "voice of the people" had selected Pahoran and rejected Paanchi. With the death of Pahoran, it became the right of Pacumeni to assume the chief judgeship as a result of a new vote of the people.

Moronihah Defeats the Lamanites

Helaman 1:14–34

14. And it came to pass in the forty and first year of the reign of the judges, that the Lamanites had gathered together an innumerable army of men, and armed them with swords, and with cimeters and with bows, and with arrows, and with head-plates, and with breastplates, and with all manner of shields of every kind.

15. And they came down again that they might pitch battle against the Nephites. And they were led by a man whose name was Coriantumr; and he was a descendant of Zarahemla; and he was a dissenter from among the Nephites; and he was a large and a mighty man.

16. Therefore, the king of the Lamanites, whose name was Tubaloth, who was the son of Ammoron, supposing that Coriantumr, being a mighty man, could stand against the Nephites, with his strength and also with his great wisdom, insomuch that by sending him forth he should gain

power over the Nephites—

17. Therefore he did stir them up to anger, and he did gather together his armies, and he did appoint Coriantumr to be their leader, and did cause that they should march down to the land of Zarahemla to battle against the Nephites.

18. And it came to pass that because of so much contention and so much difficulty in the government, that they had not kept sufficient guards in the land of Zarahemla; for they had supposed that the Lamanites durst not come into the heart of their lands to attack that great city Zarahemla.

19. But it came to pass that Coriantumr did march forth at the head of his numerous host, and came upon the inhabitants of the city, and their march was with such exceedingly great speed that there was no time for the Nephites to gather together their armies.

20. Therefore Coriantumr did cut down the watch by the entrance of the city, and did march forth with his whole army into the city, and they did slay every one who did oppose them, insomuch that they did take possession of the whole city.

21. And it came to pass that Pacumeni, who was the chief judge, did flee before Coriantumr, even to the walls of the city. And it came to pass that Coriantumr did smite him against the wall, insomuch that he died. And thus ended the days of Pacumeni.

22. And now when Coriantumr saw that he was in possession of the city of Zarahemla, and saw that the Nephites had fled before them, and were slain, and were taken, and were cast into prison,

and that he had obtained the possession of the strongest hold in all the land, his heart took courage insomuch that he was about to go forth against all the land.

23. And now he did not tarry in the land of Zarahemla, but he did march forth with a large army, even towards the city of Bountiful; for it was his determination to go forth and cut his way through with the sword, that he might obtain the north parts of the land.

24. And, supposing that their greatest strength was in the center of the land, therefore he did march forth, giving them no time to assemble themselves together save it were in small bodies; and in this manner they did fall upon them and cut them down to the earth.

25. But behold, this march of Coriantumr through the center of the land gave Moronihah great advantage over them, notwithstanding the greatness of the number of the Nephites who were slain.

26. For behold, Moronihah had supposed that the Lamanites durst not come into the center of the land, but that they would attack the cities round about in the borders as they had hitherto done; therefore Moronihah had caused that their strong armies should maintain those parts round about by the borders.

27. But behold, the Lamanites were not frightened according to his desire, but they had come into the center of the land, and had taken the capital city which was the city of Zarahemla, and were marching through the most capital parts of the land, slaying the people with a great slaughter,

both men, women, and children, taking possession of many cities and of many strongholds.

28. But when Moronihah had discovered this, he immediately sent forth Lehi with an army round about to head them before they should come to the land Bountiful.

29. And thus he did; and he did head them before they came to the land Bountiful, and gave unto them battle, insomuch that they began to retreat back towards the land of Zarahemla.

30. And it came to pass that Moronihah did head them in their retreat, and did give unto them battle, insomuch that it became an exceedingly bloody battle; yea, many were slain, and among the number who were slain Coriantumr was also found.

31. And now, behold, the Lamanites could not retreat either way, neither on the north, nor on the south, nor on the east, nor on the west, for they were surrounded on every hand by the Nephites.

32. And thus had Coriantumr plunged the Lamanites into the midst of the Nephites, insomuch that they were in the power of the Nephites, and he himself was slain, and the Lamanites did yield themselves into the hands of the Nephites.

33. And it came to pass that Moronihah took possession of the city of Zarahemla again, and caused that the Lamanites who had been taken prisoners should depart out of the land in peace.

34. And thus ended the forty and first year of the reign of the judges.

14–24. The Lamanites, under the direction of Coriantumr, attack the Nephites and manage to occupy the city of Zarahemla. Pacumeni, the chief judge, in his attempt to flee before the invading Lamanite armies, is killed by Coriantumr himself. The Lamanites kill or imprison many inhabitants of Zarahemla and begin a march toward the city of Bountiful.

18. Because of so much contention and so much difficulty in the government] Because of the controversy and contention surrounding the selection of the chief judge and the subsequent rebellion, and the confusion, fear, and difficulties associated with the murder of Pahoran, the Nephites are unprepared to defend themselves against an outside attack from the Lamanites. Dissension and conflict from within creates a vulnerability to attack from without. "A house divided against itself cannot stand." This important principle not only has application to governmental or national security but is also significant in the institutional Church and in our individual homes. Contention and dissension are a tool of the adversary (see 3 Nephi 11:28–29) that weakens the institution and makes it vulnerable to "attacks" from destructive outside influences. (See Marvin J. Ashton, CR, April 1978, pp. 9–12.)

25–34. The invasion of the Lamanites is repelled by Moronihah, the leader of the Nephite armies and the righteous son of Captain Moroni (see Alma 62:43). Coriantumr is slain in the battle and the Nephites regain control of the city of Zarahemla.

33. Prisoners should depart out of the land in peace] In contrast to the treatment of prisoners and innocent victims of war by the Lamanites (see Helaman 1:22), Moronihah allows the Lamanite prisoners of war to depart in peace. Those righteous military leaders who are disciples of Christ and are filled with the Spirit of the Lord treat even their enemies with kindness and compassion (see Alma 44:5–7). Even in most difficult circumstances, such as war, the Lord expects his disciples to "love your enemies, . . . do good to them that hate you" (Matthew 5:44; 3 Nephi 12:44).

The Demise of Kishkumen and the Rise of the Gadianton Band

Helaman 2:1–14

1. And it came to pass in the forty and second year of the reign of the judges, after Moronihah had established again peace between the Nephites and the Lamanites, behold there was no one to fill the judgment-seat; therefore there began to be a contention again among the people concerning who should fill the judgment-seat.

2. And it came to pass that Helaman, who was the son of Helaman, was appointed to fill the judgment-seat, by the voice of the people.

3. But behold, Kishkumen, who had murdered Pahoran, did lay wait to destroy Helaman also; and he was upheld by his band, who had entered into a covenant that no one should know his wickedness.

4. For there was one Gadianton, who was exceedingly expert in many words, and also in his craft, to carry on the secret work of murder and of robbery;

therefore he became the leader of the band of Kishkumen.

5. Therefore he did flatter them, and also Kishkumen, that if they would place him in the judgment-seat he would grant unto those who belonged to his band that they should be placed in power and authority among the people; therefore Kishkumen sought to destroy Helaman.

6. And it came to pass as he went forth towards the judgment-seat to destroy Helaman, behold one of the servants of Helaman, having been out by night, and having obtained, through disguise, a knowledge of those plans which had been laid by this band to destroy Helaman—

7. And it came to pass that he met Kishkumen, and he gave unto him a sign; therefore Kishkumen made known unto him the object of his desire, desiring that he would conduct him to the judgment-seat that he might murder Helaman.

8. And when the servant of Helaman had known all the heart of Kishkumen, and how that it was his object to murder, and also that it was the object of all those who belonged to his band to murder, and to rob, and to gain power, (and this was their secret plan, and their combination) the servant of Helaman said unto Kishkumen: Let us go forth unto the judgment-seat.

9. Now this did please Kishkumen exceedingly, for he did suppose that he should accomplish his design; but behold, the servant of Helaman, as they were going forth unto the judgment-seat, did stab Kishkumen even to the heart, that he fell dead without a groan. And he ran and told Helaman all the things which he had seen, and heard, and done.

10. And it came to pass that Helaman did send forth to take this band of robbers and secret murderers, that they might be executed according to the law.

11. But behold, when Gadianton had found that Kishkumen did not return he feared lest that he should be destroyed; therefore he caused that his band should follow him. And they took their flight out of the land, by a secret way, into the wilderness; and thus when Helaman sent forth to take them they could nowhere be found.

12. And more of this Gadianton shall be spoken hereafter. And thus ended the forty and second year of the reign of the judges over the people of Nephi.

13. And behold, in the end of this book ye shall see that this Gadianton did prove the overthrow, yea, almost the entire destruction of the people of Nephi.

14. Behold I do not mean the end of the book of Helaman, but I mean the end of the book of Nephi, from which I have taken all the account which I have written.

1–14. Helaman II, son of Helaman, is appointed as chief judge by the voice of the people to succeed Pacumeni, who has been killed by Coriantumr. In his quest for power and to set himself up as leader, Kishkumen seeks to murder the new chief judge. His plans are thwarted by a servant of Helaman, who has learned of the secret designs of Kishkumen and his followers; Kishkumen is stabbed in the heart by that servant. The chief judge then orders that "this band of robbers and secret murderers" be captured so that they can be brought to justice. Gadianton, who has become the leader of this "secret combination," and his followers escape justice by fleeing into the wilderness.

4. Expert in many words, and also in his craft] Mormon describes Gadianton, the leader of the band formed by Kishkumen, as "exceedingly expert in many words, and also in his craft." It is significant that these traits are similar to those found in such anti-Christs as Sherem (see Jacob 7:4), Nehor (see Alma 1:3–6), and Korihor (see Alma 30:12–18). Gadianton's use of many words and flattery to bring about his evil designs, as in the cases of the anti-Christs, was acquired through the tutelage of Satan. Gadianton was "expert in his craft" because he had been taught and influenced "according to the power of the devil" (Jacob 7:4).

8. His object . . . to murder, and to rob, and to gain power] Mormon tells us that it was the design or "secret plan" of the Gadianton band to murder, rob, and gain power. Power was the ultimate objective. Robbery and murder are merely means to that end.

13. This Gadianton did prove the overthrow, yea, almost the entire destruction of the people of Nephi] This editorial statement of Mormon foreshadows the numerous references and examples of the "secret plans and combinations" that follow. Mormon is instructing his readers concerning this underlying and recurring theme in the sad story of the demise of the Nephite nation that follows.

Nephite Migration to the Land Northward

Helaman 3:1–12

1. And now it came to pass in the forty and third year of the reign of the judges, there was no contention among the people of Nephi save it were a little pride which was in the church, which did cause some little dissensions among the people, which affairs were settled in the ending of the forty and third year.

2. And there was no contention among the people in the forty and fourth year; neither was there much contention in the forty and fifth year.

3. And it came to pass in the forty and sixth, yea, there was much contention and many dissensions; in the which there were an exceedingly great many who departed out of the land of Zarahemla, and went forth unto the land northward to inherit the land.

4. And they did travel to an exceedingly great distance,

insomuch that they came to large bodies of water and many rivers.

5. Yea, and even they did spread forth into all parts of the land, into whatever parts it had not been rendered desolate and without timber, because of the many inhabitants who had before inherited the land.

6. And now no part of the land was desolate, save it were for timber; but because of the greatness of the destruction of the people who had before inhabited the land it was called desolate.

7. And there being but little timber upon the face of the land, nevertheless the people who went forth became exceedingly expert in the working of cement; therefore they did build houses of cement, in the which they did dwell.

8. And it came to pass that they did multiply and spread, and did go forth from the land

southward to the land northward, and did spread insomuch that they began to cover the face of the whole earth, from the sea south to the sea north, from the sea west to the sea east.

9. And the people who were in the land northward did dwell in tents, and in houses of cement, and they did suffer whatsoever tree should spring up upon the face of the land that it should grow up, that in time they might have timber to build their houses, yea, their cities, and their temples, and their synagogues, and their sanctuaries, and all manner of their buildings.

10. And it came to pass as timber was exceedingly scarce in the land northward, they did send forth much by the way of shipping.

11. And thus they did enable the people in the land northward that they might build many cities, both of wood and of cement.

12. And it came to pass that there were many of the people of Ammon, who were Lamanites by birth, did also go forth into this land.

1–12. Because of the dissension and contention in the land, many people migrated to the land northward. The Book of Mormon does not identify where they went to in that land, other than to record that it was "an exceedingly great distance" from Zarahemla and near "large bodies of water." Other information concerning the desolation of the area and the former inhabitants is found in Mosiah 8:8 and Mosiah 21:26–27 (see *Commentary* 2:273–74).

7. Became exceedingly expert in the working of cement] Because of the desolation of forests and the dearth of building lumber, the people resorted to the use of cement for construction and also imported lumber from the land southward (see verse 10). While this is not significant doctrinally, it does give an additional external evidence of the truthfulness of the book, since Joseph Smith could not have been aware, as a result of his own intellect and learning, of this important item that has since been substantiated by modern scientific findings. For an in-depth discussion of the role of cement in ancient construction see Hugh W. Nibley, *Since Cumorah*, p. 254; *An Approach to the Book of Mormon*, pp. 347–48; and the research findings of Matthew G. Wells and John W. Welch in "Concrete Evidence for the Book of Mormon," in *Insights* [a newsletter and research update published by the Foundation for Ancient Research and Mormon Studies, Provo, UT], May 1991, p. 2.

Nephites Keep Many Historical Records

Helaman 3:13–16

13. And now there are many records kept of the proceedings of this people, by many of this people, which are particular and very large, concerning them.

14. But behold, a hundredth part of the proceedings of this people, yea, the account of the Lamanites and of the Nephites, and their wars, and contentions, and dissensions, and their preaching, and their prophecies, and their shipping and their building of ships, and their building of temples, and of synagogues and their sanctuaries, and their righteousness, and their wickedness, and their murders, and their robbings, and their plundering, and all manner of abominations and whoredoms, cannot be contained in this work.

15. But behold, there are many books and many records of every kind, and they have been kept chiefly by the Nephites.

16. And they have been handed down from one generation to another by the Nephites, even until they have fallen into transgression and have been murdered, plundered, and hunted, and driven forth, and slain, and scattered upon the face of the earth, and mixed with the Lamanites until they are no more called the Nephites, becoming wicked, and wild, and ferocious, yea, even becoming Lamanites.

13–16. Mormon interjects the comment that many records have been kept concerning specifically these people who migrated northward and the Nephite nation generally. The doctrinal significance of these verses consists not so much in their informing the reader of the many historical records that deal with virtually every aspect of Nephite culture as in their reminding us that the primary purpose of the Book of Mormon is not one of history. Mormon's statement is that his record or abridgment does not contain a "hundredth part" of all the history. He is not apologizing, but is again stating that his objective and his charge as an abridger and record-keeper is of a spiritual and not a secular nature. (See Jacob 3:13; Words of Mormon 1:5; Alma 13:31; 3 Nephi 5:8–9; see also *Commentary* 2:31, 121–22.)

Peace and Prosperity During the Reign of Helaman II

Helaman 3:17–28

17. And now I return again to mine account; therefore, what I have spoken had passed after there had been great contentions, and disturbances, and wars, and dissensions, among the people of

Nephi.

18. The forty and sixth year of the reign of the judges ended;

19. And it came to pass that there was still great contention in the land, yea, even in the forty and seventh year, and also in the forty and eighth year.

20. Nevertheless Helaman did fill the judgment-seat with justice and equity; yea, he did observe to keep the statutes, and the judgments, and the commandments of God; and he did do that which was right in the sight of God continually; and he did walk after the ways of his father, insomuch that he did prosper in the land.

21. And it came to pass that he had two sons. He gave unto the eldest the name of Nephi, and unto the youngest, the name of Lehi. And they began to grow up unto the Lord.

22. And it came to pass that the wars and contentions began to cease, in a small degree, among the people of the Nephites, in the latter end of the forty and eighth year of the reign of the judges over the people of Nephi.

23. And it came to pass in the forty and ninth year of the reign of the judges, there was continual peace established in the land, all save it were the secret combinations which Gadianton the robber had established in the more settled parts of the land, which at that time were not known unto those who were at the head of government; therefore they were not destroyed out of the land.

24. And it came to pass that in this same year there was exceedingly great prosperity in the church, insomuch that there were thousands who did join themselves unto the church and were baptized unto repentance.

25. And so great was the prosperity of the church, and so many the blessings which were poured out upon the people, that even the high priests and the teachers were themselves astonished beyond measure.

26. And it came to pass that the work of the Lord did prosper unto the baptizing and uniting to the church of God, many souls, yea, even tens of thousands.

27. Thus we may see that the Lord is merciful unto all who will, in the sincerity of their hearts, call upon his holy name.

28. Yea, thus we see that the gate of heaven is open unto all, even to those who will believe on the name of Jesus Christ, who is the Son of God.

17–28. During the reign of Helaman II, a righteous and equitable ruler, the wars and contentions cease and there is great peace and prosperity among the people. During this time of prosperity the Church is blessed in that tens of thousands are baptized "unto repentance." This growth of the Church is so remarkable that even the teachers and leaders of the Church are "astonished beyond measure." This statement mirrors similar statements of modern Church leaders concerning the current astonishing growth of the Church. Perhaps this period of time is just the Nephite fulfillment of the Lord's revelation to Habakkuk—one that may have multiple fulfillments, not only in ancient Israel but also among the Nephites, the modern Church, and in years yet to come—wherein God said, "I will work a work in your days, which ye will not believe, though it be told you" (Habakkuk 1:5).

24. There was exceedingly great prosperity in the church] Frequently the first reaction to the word *prosperity* in the Book of Mormon is the concept of temporal blessings, or the "good things of the earth." Undoubtedly, such prosperity can be linked to some degree with righteousness (see Dean L. Larsen, *Ensign*, May 1991, pp. 10–12). The context of this prosperity, however, makes it clearly spiritual in nature and linked to the blessings of the Church membership resulting from faithfulness. It is important that we not think of prosperity only in terms of material gain.

27–28. Speaking of the growth of the Church and the blessings of prosperity that were abundantly poured out upon those who were "baptized unto repentance," Mormon uses his "thus we see" instructional method to teach an important doctrinal concept. He tells the reader that the Lord is mindful of and merciful to all who call upon his holy name in sincere and faithful prayer. There is no other condition. God is no "respecter of persons" (see Acts 10:34–35). Therefore the invitation to come unto the Lord, be transformed by his gospel, and partake of the blessings of heaven is available to all (see 2 Nephi 26:33; see also *Commentary* 1:311–12).

Pride in Church Members Leads to Persecution and Affliction

Helaman 3:29–37

29. Yea, we see that whosoever will may lay hold upon the word of God, which is quick and powerful, which shall divide asunder all the cunning and the snares and the wiles of the devil, and lead the man of Christ in a strait and narrow course across that everlasting gulf of misery which is prepared to engulf the wicked—

30. And land their souls, yea, their immortal souls, at the right hand of God in the kingdom of heaven, to sit down with Abraham, and Isaac, and with Jacob, and with all our holy fathers, to go no more out.

31. And in this year there was continual rejoicing in the land of Zarahemla, and in all the regions round about, even in all the land which was possessed by the Nephites.

32. And it came to pass that there was peace and exceedingly great joy in the remainder of the forty and ninth year; yea, and also there was continual peace and great joy in the fiftieth year of the reign of the judges.

33. And in the fifty and first year of the reign of the judges there was peace also, save it were the pride which began to enter into the church—not into the church of God, but into the hearts

of the people who professed to belong to the church of God—

34. And they were lifted up in pride, even to the persecution of many of their brethren. Now this was a great evil, which did cause the more humble part of the people to suffer great persecutions, and to wade through much affliction.

35. Nevertheless they did fast and pray oft, and did wax stronger and stronger in their humility, and firmer and firmer in the faith of Christ, unto the filling their souls with joy and consolation, yea, even to the purifying and the sanctification of their hearts, which sanctification cometh because of their yielding their hearts unto God.

36. And it came to pass that the fifty and second year ended in peace also, save it were the exceedingly great pride which had gotten into the hearts of the people; and it was because of their exceedingly great riches and their prosperity in the land; and it did grow upon them from day to day.

37. And it came to pass in the fifty and third year of the reign of the judges, Helaman died, and his eldest son Nephi began to reign in his stead. And it came to pass that he did fill the judgment-seat with justice and equity; yea, he did keep the commandments of God, and did walk in the ways of his father.

29–37. The period of peace, prosperity, and "continual rejoicing in the land" (verse 31) described previously was soon shattered by the onset of pride in the hearts of many members of the Church. Puffed up in their pride, they persecuted the more humble Saints.

29. Whosoever will may lay hold] The word of God is available and open to all; the only prerequisite to receiving it is a sincere search and earnest prayer.

29. The word of God, which is quick and powerful] The scriptures, words of the living prophets, and the inspiration of the Holy Ghost constitute the word of God. These means can illuminate the "cunning and the snares and the wiles of the devil" and direct the "man of Christ" in the path that leads to exaltation. For Paul's explanation of the instructional and spiritual value of the word of God see 2 Timothy 3:15–17; see also 1 Nephi 15:24; 2 Nephi 32:3; commentary on Alma 31:5.

34. Lifted up in pride, even to the persecution of many of their brethren] Pride and persecution of others are sins in and of themselves, but Mormon describes the pride-resultant persecution as a "great evil" because it was Saint-against-Saint persecution. It was coming from those who knew the gospel and had been enlightened and prospered by it. Their knowledge increased their accountability (see D&C 82:3) and made their pride-induced persecution of their fellow Church members an even greater evil that would produce a great condemnation.

35. Filling their souls with joy and consolation] Because of the persecution of the prideful members of the Church, humble followers of Christ were being forced to "wade through much affliction." As a result of the pain and affliction, these Saints fasted and prayed much, which resulted in greater faith in Christ, which in turn filled their souls with joy and consolation. Even amidst affliction, firm faith in Christ—nurtured and strengthened through fasting and prayer—brings "the peaceable things of the kingdom" (see D&C 36:2; 42:61). It is this peace and joy the Savior promised to give to those who faithfully seek it (see John 14:27).

35. Sanctification cometh because of their yielding their hearts unto God] To "yield [our] hearts unto God" is to inquire diligently to know the mind and will of the Almighty; to give way to and follow the impressions of the Spirit; to have no will but God's will; to have an eye single to the glory of God (see D&C 20:31; 88:67–68; 3 Nephi 27:19–21). Sanctification comes by the power of the Holy Ghost only to those who "overcome by faith" in Jesus Christ (see D&C 76:53)—which is yielding our hearts to him. (For a more in-depth discussion of sanctification as a fruit of firm faith in Christ and yielding ourselves in obedience to his laws, see Joseph Fielding McConkie and Robert L. Millet, *The Holy Ghost*, pp. 104–11; Robert L. Millet, *By Grace Are We Saved*, pp. 51–60.)

Nephite Dissenters Stir Up Lamanites to War Against the Nephites

Helaman 4:1–10

1. And it came to pass in the fifty and fourth year there were many dissensions in the church, and there was also a contention among the people, insomuch that there was much bloodshed.

2. And the rebellious part were slain and driven out of the land, and they did go unto the king of the Lamanites.

3. And it came to pass that they did endeavor to stir up the Lamanites to war against the Nephites; but behold, the Lamanites were exceedingly afraid, insomuch that they would not hearken to the words of those dissenters.

4. But it came to pass in the fifty and sixth year of the reign of the judges, there were dissenters who went up from the Nephites unto the Lamanites; and they succeeded with those others in stirring them up to anger against the Nephites; and they were all that year preparing for war.

5. And in the fifty and seventh year they did come down against the Nephites to battle, and they did commence the work of death; yea, insomuch that in the fifty and eighth year of the reign of the judges they succeeded in obtaining possession of the land of Zarahemla; yea, and also all the lands, even unto the land which was near the land Bountiful.

6. And the Nephites and the armies of Moronihah were driven even into the land of Bountiful;

7. And there they did fortify against the Lamanites, from the west sea, even unto the east; it being a day's journey for a Nephite, on the line which they had fortified and stationed their armies to defend their north country.

8. And thus those dissenters of the Nephites, with the help of a numerous army of the Lamanites, had obtained all the possession of the Nephites which was in the land southward. And all this was done in the fifty and eighth and ninth years of the reign of the judges.

9. And it came to pass in the sixtieth year of the reign of the judges, Moronihah did succeed with his armies in obtaining many parts of the land; yea, they regained many cities which had fallen into the hands of the Lamanites.

10. And it came to pass in the sixty and first year of the reign of the judges they succeeded in regaining even the half of all their possessions.

1–10. Commencing with dissension from within the Church, there arose rebellion in the land that led to civil strife and bloodshed. The rebellious who were driven from the land went into an alliance with the Lamanites by stirring them up to anger against the Nephites. Weakened by internal strife, the Nephites were driven from Zarahemla by the Lamanites, and bloody war raged in the land. This episode serves as an additional witness that strife and dissension from within, whether it be in church or state, weakens the institution and makes it vulnerable to attacks from without (see Helaman 1:18).

Source of Nephite Destruction Is the Wickedness of the Church

Helaman 4:11–13

11. Now this great loss of the Nephites, and the great slaughter which was among them, would not have happened had it not been for their wickedness and their abomination which was among them; yea, and it was among those also who professed to belong to the church of God.

12. And it was because of the pride of their hearts, because of their exceeding riches, yea, it was because of their oppression to the poor, withholding their food from the hungry, withholding their clothing from the naked, and smiting their humble brethren upon the cheek, making a mock of that which was sacred, denying the spirit of prophecy and of revelation, murdering, plundering, lying, stealing, committing adultery, rising up in great contentions, and deserting away into

the land of Nephi, among the Lamanites—

13. And because of this their great wickedness, and their boastings in their own strength, they were left in their own strength;

therefore they did not prosper, but were afflicted and smitten, and driven before the Lamanites, until they had lost possession of almost all their lands.

11–13. The "great slaughter" of the Nephites could have been averted, we are told by Mormon, had they remained faithful (see Mosiah 27:13; *Commentary* 2:306). Mormon attributes much of the wickedness and abominations of the nation to "those also who professed to belong to the church of God." Because of their wickedness they had cut themselves off from the protection the Lord extends to the righteous (see D&C 35:14) and were left to their own strength. With no claim upon the promises of the Lord, they were smitten and driven until they "had lost possession of almost all of their lands." It is significant that Mormon identifies specific things that comprised the wickedness and abominations of the Nephite Church members. This itemization is doctrinally important not merely as a historical account but also as a warning to the latter-day Church.

1. *Pride of their hearts because of their exceeding riches.* It is significant that Mormon lists pride first on his list, because pride, which is enmity toward God and one's fellowmen, is that which leads to all other transgressions. It is, as President Ezra Taft Benson declared, "the universal sin" which causes men to "let go of the iron rod." Mormon identifies riches as the source of the pride of the Nephites. Riches, in and of themselves, did not create damning pride among the Nephites, but the enmity that results from the "love of money" (see 1 Timothy 6:10) is what leads to a disregard for God and others, resulting thereafter in self-indulgence and wickedness. It should be remembered, however, that there are other sources of pride as well. Whatever the source, pride is a "damning sin in the true sense of the word. It limits or stops progression" and "adversely affects all of our relationships." (CR, April 1989, pp. 3–7.)

2. *Oppression of the poor.* The proud rich look down upon those less fortunate and label them as lazy and unworthy. Their elevated sense of self-importance causes them to unrighteously judge, mock, withhold support from, and even persecute the less fortunate. Since pride is competitive in nature, the oppression of the poor by the proud rich becomes the object of the game. The Lord has repeatedly rebuked those who would pridefully withhold their means from the poor and persecute them with their haughty attitudes (see 2 Nephi 9:30; Mosiah 4:16–26; Alma 5:55; D&C 56:16–18).

3. *Making a mock of that which is sacred.* Since pride is a sin of elevating oneself above God and the will of God, it is no wonder that the proud mock the things of God. This mockery not only includes the making light of sacred doctrines, practices, and covenants (see 1 Nephi 19:7; Jacob 6:8) but also manifests itself in the mockery of other people, who are also "sacred things" in that they are literally sons and daughters of the Living God (see Alma 5:30, 54).

4. *Denying the spirit of prophecy and revelation.* The pride-induced denial of the spirit of prophecy and revelation may be very blatant and open, but often it comes in more subtle, disguised forms. Speaking of the proud, President Benson illustrated some of these means: "We pit our will against God's. When we direct our pride toward God, it is done in the spirit of 'my will and not thine be done.' . . . The proud cannot accept the authority of God giving direction to their lives (see Helaman 12:6). They pit their perceptions of truth against God's great knowledge, their abilities versus God's priesthood power, their accomplishments against His mighty works. . . . The proud wish God would agree with them. They aren't interested in changing their opinions to agree with God's." (CR, April 1989, p. 4.)

5. *Murdering, plundering, lying, stealing, committing adultery.* "Selfishness is one of the more common faces of pride," declared President Benson (CR, April 1989, p. 5). The selfish proud, with enmity toward their fellowmen, see nothing wrong with resorting to selfish means to fulfill their desires and attain their ends. Prideful selfishness inevitably leads to other transgressions against one's fellowmen. Elder Neal A. Maxwell declared: "Selfishness is much more than an ordinary problem because it activates all the cardinal sins! It is the detonator in the breaking of the Ten Commandments.

"By focusing on oneself, it is naturally easier to bear false witness if it serves one's purpose. It is easier to ignore one's parents instead of honoring them. It is easier to steal, because what one wants prevails. It is easier to covet, since the selfish conclude that nothing should be denied them.

"It is easier to commit sexual sins, because to please oneself is the name of that deadly game in which others are often cruelly used. The Sabbath day is easily neglected, since one day soon becomes just like another. If selfish, it is easier to lie, because the truth is conveniently subordinated.

"The selfish individual thus seeks to please not God, but himself. He will even break a covenant in order to fix an appetite." (CR, October 1990, p. 15.)

6. *Rising up in great contentions.* The scriptures teach that anoth-

er form of wickedness that results from pride is contention. "Only by pride cometh contention" (Proverbs 13:10; see also Proverbs 28:25). Contentions result from the prideful power struggle that comes from pitting ourselves—our possessions or our intellect—against others. The proud are easily offended, hold grudges, withhold forgiveness, and will not receive counsel or correction. All of these internal traits become a fertile seedbed for the external manifestation of contention. The Savior warned of the evil of contention (see 3 Nephi 11:28–29), because it repels the Spirit of the Lord and opens the door to other "fiery darts" of the adversary. "Contention does not usually begin as strife between countries," Elder Russell M. Nelson declared. "More often, it starts with an individual, for we can contend within ourselves over simple matters of right and wrong. From there, contention can infect neighbors and nations like a spreading sore. . . . The work of the adversary may be likened to loading guns in opposition to the work of God. Salvos containing germs of contention are aimed and fired at strategic targets essential to that holy work. These vital targets include—in addition to the individual—the family, leaders of the Church, and divine doctrine." (CR, April 1989, pp. 85–86.)

7. *Boastings in their own strength.* A proud person puffs himself and his strength up as he puts down his dependence on the Lord. Pride inevitably leads to boasting, which inevitably leads to a loss of the strength of the Lord and causes the proud person to be left alone, relying solely on his own puny mortal strength (see D&C 3:4, 13). "One of the most common of all sins among worldly people," Elder Marvin J. Ashton has taught, "is relying on and then boasting in the arm of flesh. This is a most serious evil. It is a sin born of pride, a sin that creates a frame of mind which keeps men from turning to the Lord and accepting his saving grace. When a man knowingly or unknowingly engages in self-exultation because of his riches, his political power, his worldly learning, his physical prowess, his business ability, or even his works of righteousness, he is not in tune with the Spirit of the Lord. . . . The many admonitions in the scriptures to avoid boasting send the message that we should realize the source of all our blessings. Everything is given by God. All talent, creativity, ability, insight, and strength comes from him. In our own strength we can do nothing. . . . When we seek the praise of man more than the praise of God, it will become easy to fall." (CR, April 1990, pp. 84–85.)

Because of Transgression the Nephites Become Weak

Helaman 4:14–26

14. But behold, Moronihah did preach many things unto the people because of their iniquity, and also Nephi and Lehi, who were the sons of Helaman, did preach many things unto the people, yea, and did prophesy many things unto them concerning their iniquities, and what should come unto them if they did not repent of their sins.

15. And it came to pass that they did repent, and inasmuch as they did repent they did begin to prosper.

16. For when Moronihah saw that they did repent he did venture to lead them forth from place to place, and from city to city, even until they had regained the one-half of their property and the one-half of all their lands.

17. And thus ended the sixty and first year of the reign of the judges.

18. And it came to pass in the sixty and second year of the reign of the judges, that Moronihah could obtain no more possessions over the Lamanites.

19. Therefore they did abandon their design to obtain the remainder of their lands, for so numerous were the Lamanites that it became impossible for the Nephites to obtain more power over them; therefore Moronihah did employ all his armies in maintaining those parts which he had taken.

20. And it came to pass, because of the greatness of the number of the Lamanites the Nephites were in great fear, lest they should be overpowered, and trodden down, and slain, and destroyed.

21. Yea, they began to remember the prophecies of Alma, and also the words of Mosiah; and they saw that they had been a stiffnecked people, and that they had set at naught the commandments of God.

22. And that they had altered and trampled under their feet the laws of Mosiah, or that which the Lord commanded him to give unto the people; and they saw that their laws had become corrupted, and that they had become a wicked people, insomuch that they were wicked even like unto the Lamanites.

23. And because of their iniquity the church had begun to dwindle; and they began to disbelieve in the spirit of prophecy and in the spirit of revelation; and the judgments of God did stare them in the face.

24. And they saw that they had become weak, like unto their brethren, the Lamanites, and that the Spirit of the Lord did no more preserve them; yea, it had withdrawn from them because the Spirit of the Lord doth not dwell in unholy temples—

25. Therefore the Lord did cease to preserve them by his miraculous and matchless power, for they had fallen into a state of unbelief and awful wickedness; and they saw that the Lamanites were exceedingly more numerous than they, and except they should cleave unto the Lord their God they must unavoidably perish.

26. For behold, they saw that the strength of the Lamanites was as great as their strength, even man for man. And thus had they fallen into this great transgression; yea, thus had they become weak, because of their transgression, in the space of not many years.

14–26. Through the preaching of Nephi and Lehi, some of the Nephites repent of their sins and again begin to prosper as the Lord promised. As a whole, however, the Church dwindles because of the loss of spiritual strength resulting from individual and collective unrighteousness. Without the Spirit of the Lord sustaining them, they become "weak like unto the Lamanites" and fail in their own attempts to repel the onslaught of that enemy.

14. Did prophesy many things unto them concerning their iniquities, and what should come unto them if they did not repent] Nephi and Lehi, sons of Helaman, are fulfilling their role as prophets. They are not merely predicting impending doom upon the Nephites but rather are speaking forthrightly concerning conditions they observed and, as prophets, are declaring repentance. A prophet is a "forthteller" and "preacher of righteousness." It is clear from this passage and numerous others that to prophesy concerning iniquity is to (1) proclaim the mind and will of God by teaching the requirement of true gospel living; and (2) plainly teach the consequences of sin (see Alma 37:32–34).

15. As they did repent they did begin to prosper] This is a literal fulfillment of the words of the Lord through his prophets that "inasmuch as ye keep my commandments ye shall prosper" (see 1 Nephi 2:20; see also 2 Nephi 1:9, 20, 31; Mosiah 1:7; Alma 37:13; Helaman 12:1).

23. Because of their iniquity . . . they began to disbelieve in the spirit of prophecy and in the spirit of revelation] Some people rationalize their apostasy and their life of sin by saying that they do not believe in prophecy and revelation. It is significant to note from this verse that iniquity led the people to deny the spiritual workings of the Lord, not the other way around. Wickedness destroys faith in the Lord and brings a loss of spiritual knowledge and a denial of such things as prophecy and revelation.

24. They had become weak] Because of their wickedness, the Spirit of the Lord was withdrawn, the Lord no longer protected them, and they were left in a weakened condition. This is as much a physical reality as it is spiritual. Just as righteousness and faithfulness to covenants brings a "renewing" of the body (see D&C 84:33), so wickedness can have a very real effect on the physical body that can sap strength and produce sicknesses and intense suffering (see Alma 15:3, 5; 1 Corinthians 11:27–30; see also Elder Boyd K. Packer's discussion of this concept in CR, October 1977, pp. 89–90).

Corruption of the Nephite Government

Helaman 5:1–3

1. And it came to pass that in this same year, behold, Nephi delivered up the judgment-seat to a man whose name was Cezoram.

2. For as their laws and their governments were established by the voice of the people, and they who chose evil were more numerous than they who chose good, therefore they were ripening for destruction, for the laws had become corrupted.

3. Yea, and this was not all; they were a stiffnecked people, insomuch that they could not be governed by the law nor justice, save it were to their destruction.

1–3. The government of the Nephites was "ripening for destruction" because the majority of the people were evil, were choosing evil leaders, and were corrupting good laws and framing evil ones. They had reached the point of which King Mosiah had warned: "And if the time comes that the voice of the people doth choose iniquity, then is the time that the judgments of God will come upon you" (Mosiah 29:27).

3. They could not be governed by the law nor justice, save it were to their destruction] The people had become so wicked that the voice of the people chose only that which was evil. As a result they turned from just laws and righteous principles and would not be governed by such. The voice of the people desired that they be governed by those principles that the righteous leaders knew would surely lead to physical captivity, destruction, and ultimately spiritual death.

Nephi and Lehi Devote Themselves to Preaching

Helaman 5:4–20

4. And it came to pass that Nephi had become weary because of their iniquity; and he yielded up the judgment-seat, and took it upon him to preach the word of God all the remainder of his days, and his brother Lehi also, all the remainder of his days;

5. For they remembered the words which their father Helaman spake unto them. And these are the words which he spake:

6. Behold, my sons, I desire that ye should remember to keep the commandments of God; and I would that ye should declare unto the people these words. Behold, I have given unto you the names of our first parents who came out of the land of Jerusalem; and this I have done that when you remember your names ye may remember them; and when ye remember them ye may remember their works; and when ye remember their works ye may know how

that it is said, and also written, that they were good.

7. Therefore, my sons, I would that ye should do that which is good, that it may be said of you, and also written, even as it has been said and written of them.

8. And now my sons, behold I have somewhat more to desire of you, which desire is, that ye may not do these things that ye may boast, but that ye may do these things to lay up for yourselves a treasure in heaven, yea, which is eternal, and which fadeth not away; yea, that ye may have that precious gift of eternal life, which we have reason to suppose hath been given to our fathers.

9. O remember, remember, my sons, the words which king Benjamin spake unto his people; yea, remember that there is no other way nor means whereby man can be saved, only through the atoning blood of Jesus Christ, who shall come; yea, remember that he cometh to redeem the world.

10. And remember also the words which Amulek spake unto Zeezrom, in the city of Ammonihah; for he said unto him that the Lord surely should come to redeem his people, but that he should not come to redeem them in their sins, but to redeem them from their sins.

11. And he hath power given unto him from the Father to redeem them from their sins because of repentance; therefore he hath sent his angels to declare the tidings of the conditions of repentance, which bringeth unto the power of the Redeemer, unto the salvation of their souls.

12. And now, my sons, remember, remember that it is upon the rock of our Redeemer, who is Christ, the Son of God, that ye must build your foundation; that when the devil shall send forth his mighty winds, yea, his shafts in the whirlwind, yea, when all his hail and his mighty storm shall beat upon you, it shall have no power over you to drag you down to the gulf of misery and endless wo, because of the rock upon which ye are built, which is a sure foundation, a foundation whereon if men build they cannot fall.

13. And it came to pass that these were the words which Helaman taught to his sons; yea, he did teach them many things which are not written, and also many things which are written.

14. And they did remember his words; and therefore they went forth, keeping the commandments of God, to teach the word of God among all the people of Nephi, beginning at the city Bountiful;

15. And from thenceforth to the city of Gid; and from the city of Gid to the city of Mulek;

16. And even from one city to another, until they had gone forth among all the people of Nephi who were in the land southward; and from thence into the land of Zarahemla, among the Lamanites.

17. And it came to pass that they did preach with great power, insomuch that they did confound many of those dissenters who had gone over from the Nephites, insomuch that they came forth and did confess their sins and were baptized unto repentance, and immediately returned to the Nephites to endeavor to repair unto them the wrongs which they had done.

18. And it came to pass that Nephi and Lehi did preach unto the Lamanites with such great power and authority, for they had power and authority given unto

them that they might speak, and they also had what they should speak given unto them—

19. Therefore they did speak unto the great astonishment of the Lamanites, to the convincing them, insomuch that there were eight thousand of the Lamanites who were in the land of Zarahemla and round about baptized unto repentance, and were convinced of the wickedness of the traditions of their fathers.

20. And it came to pass that Nephi and Lehi did proceed from thence to go to the land of Nephi.

4–20. Recognizing that his work as a public servant in the governmental arena was futile because of the wickedness of the citizenry, Nephi gave up the judgment-seat and, along with his brother Lehi, devoted himself full-time to the preaching of the gospel. In this he followed the pattern of his great-grandfather Alma (see Alma 4:15–20) in doing what was of most worth (see D&C 15:6). It is the preaching of the words of Christ that changes hearts, lives, and even governments (see Alma 31:5). It is not laws or alliances but living the gospel of the Prince of Peace that ensures lasting peace and prosperity.

5. Their father Helaman had died (see Helaman 3:37). What follows are his words (verses 6–12), presumably recorded by them just before or following his death, words which were preserved on the large plates kept by the prophets and copied by Mormon onto his own plates as a part of his abridgment.

6. A name can serve as a powerful motivation to righteousness, something which is ever with the one who bears it, something that is a constant reminder.

8. Lay up for yourselves a treasure in heaven] The "treasure in heaven" is the kingdom in heaven (Matthew 13:44); the Church of the Firstborn (D&C 76:54); or in other words, eternal life. Laying up for ourselves a treasure in heaven means living the principles and keeping the commandments that enable one to receive that "treasure" through the grace of Jesus Christ (see Matthew 6:20; 3 Nephi 13:20; D&C 6:27).

8. That precious gift of eternal life] "And if you keep my commandments and endure to the end you shall have eternal life, which gift if the greatest of all the gifts of God" (D&C 14:7; see also 6:13).

9. There is no other way nor means whereby man can be saved] "There is a name that is above every name that is named, whether on earth or in heaven, save only the name of the almighty Elohim. There is a name that brings joy to the desolate heart, a name that speaks peace to the sorrowing soul. There is a name that falls in hushed and hallowed tones from the lips of Saints and angels, a name that leads true believers on both sides of the veil to glory and honor everlasting. It is the name of the one sent of God to bring salvation, the name of the one who paid an infinite price to ransom us from Satan's grasp. It is the blessed name of Jesus Christ." (Robert L. Millet and Joseph Fielding McConkie, *In His Holy Name*, p. 16.) See Mosiah 3:18; 5:12; see also commentary on Alma 5:38–42.

10. He should not come to redeem them in their sins, but to redeem them from their sins] The plan of salvation called for a Savior to redeem fallen mankind from their condition of sinfulness on condition of faith in Christ, repentance, baptism, reception of the Holy Ghost, and continued obedience to gospel principles and ordinances. Redeeming one *in* sin would go counter to the plan of salvation and would destroy agency and accountability (see Alma 11:34, 37). In the premortal councils of heaven, by stating that he would save them all Lucifer essentially proposed the redemption of all men and women in their sins. "If you undertake to save all," said Brigham Young, "you must save them in unrighteousness and corruption" (*JD* 13:282). Elder Orson Pratt also taught the difference between the Father's plan to save his children from sin and Lucifer's design to save all mankind in their sins. "There must be an agency wherever intelligence exists, and without agency no intelligent beings could exist; and . . . Satan sought to destroy this . . . and to redeem them all in their sins" (*JD* 21:288). This distinction seems important in light of the philosophies of anti-Christs in the Book of Mormon (and in modern days) who claim "that all mankind should be saved at the last day, and that they need not fear nor tremble . . . for the Lord . . . had also redeemed all men; and, in the end, all men should have eternal life" (Alma 1:4; see also 2 Nephi 28:8).

11. He hath power given unto him from the Father] The power given to the Savior to "redeem them from their sins because of repentance" was in the seed of immortality that Jesus had by virtue of being the Only Begotten of the Father in the flesh. His divine nature and his life of sinlessness empowered him to bring about the Atonement. This power is an essential difference between Christ and man. This power was absolutely necessary in order for the infinite and eternal sacrifice to be made. It could not be a sacrifice of a man, but rather must be the sacrifice of a God. Abinadi explained that "God himself shall come down among the children of men, and shall redeem his people" (Mosiah 15:1–3).

11. The tidings of the conditions of repentance] Angels and prophets have declared the "good tidings of great joy" (Luke 2:10; see also Isaiah 61:1; Mosiah 3:3; 15:14). Those good tidings are founded in the mission of the Savior, the plan of mercy that makes repentance possible (see D&C 76:40–42; 3 Nephi 11:32–40).

11. Which bringeth unto the power of the Redeemer, unto the salvation of their souls] This passage may be better understood if one word, which is implicit in the scripture, were explicitly inserted. "Which bringeth unto [them] the power of the Redeemer. . . . " Amulek taught that as a result of the people's "faith unto repentance" the Atonement and the mercy of Christ "can satisfy the demands of justice, and encircles them in the arms of safety" (Alma 34:15–16). Our faith and repentance brings to us that power which redeems—even the power of the Redeemer.

12. The rock of our Redeemer] Christ is the only sure foundation upon which man must build his life in order to withstand the powers of the adversary. Helaman reminds his sons, and us, that if we are solidly built upon Christ we cannot fall. Numerous scriptural passages refer to this concept with various images and symbols: Christ as a sure foundation, a cornerstone, a nail in the sure place (see Isaiah 22:23; Matthew 7:24–27; 1 Corinthians 3:11–15). Jesus Christ, as the chief cornerstone, is the foundation stone upon which the plan of salvation, the whole gospel structure, rests. There is safety from Satan and his minions only in Christ. There is security only in his word and through his infinite and eternal power. (For a more detailed discussion of how the Saints need to build their lives upon Christ, the sure foundation, and enjoy the blessings that come therefrom, see Robert L. Millet, *Life in Christ*, pp. 106–13.)

17. They did preach with great power] See Alma 17:2–3; Alma 31:5.

18. They also had what they should speak given unto them] As agents of the Lord they sought to be in tune so that they could speak the words of their Principal. They were led and guided by the power of the Holy Ghost, and as such had the very words divinely provided for them. Always and forever the counsel of the Master to his servants is, "Treasure up in your minds continually the words of life, and it shall be given you in the very hour that portion that shall be meted unto every man" (D&C 84:85). "Lift up your voices unto this people," Christ commanded in a modern revelation; "speak the thoughts that I shall put into your hearts, and you shall not be confounded before men; for it shall be given you in the very hour, yea, in the very moment, what ye shall say" (D&C 100:5–6).

Miracles Attend the Ministry of Nephi and Lehi

Helaman 5:21–52

21. And it came to pass that they were taken by an army of the Lamanites and cast into prison; yea, even in that same prison in which Ammon and his brethren were cast by the servants of Limhi.

22. And after they had been cast into prison many days without food, behold, they went forth into the prison to take them that they might slay them.

23. And it came to pass that Nephi and Lehi were encircled about as if by fire, even insomuch that they durst not lay their hands upon them for fear lest they should be burned. Nevertheless, Nephi and Lehi were not burned; and they were as standing in the midst of fire and were not burned.

24. And when they saw that they were encircled about with a pillar of fire, and that it burned them not, their hearts did take courage.

25. For they saw that the Lamanites durst not lay their hands upon them; neither durst they come near unto them, but stood as if they were struck dumb with amazement.

26. And it came to pass that Nephi and Lehi did stand forth and began to speak unto them, saying: Fear not, for behold, it is God that has shown unto you this marvelous thing, in the which is shown unto you that ye cannot lay your hands on us to slay us.

27. And behold, when they had said these words, the earth shook exceedingly, and the walls of the prison did shake as if they were about to tumble to the earth; but behold, they did not fall. And behold, they that were in the prison were Lamanites and Nephites who were dissenters.

28. And it came to pass that they were overshadowed with a cloud of darkness, and an awful solemn fear came upon them.

29. And it came to pass that there came a voice as if it were above the cloud of darkness, saying: Repent ye, repent ye, and seek no more to destroy my servants whom I have sent unto you to declare good tidings.

30. And it came to pass when they heard this voice, and beheld that it was not a voice of thunder, neither was it a voice of a great tumultuous noise, but behold, it was a still voice of perfect mildness, as if it had been a whisper, and it did pierce even to the very soul—

31. And notwithstanding the mildness of the voice, behold the earth shook exceedingly, and the walls of the prison trembled again, as if it were about to tumble to the earth; and behold the cloud of darkness, which had overshadowed them, did not disperse—

32. And behold the voice came again, saying: Repent ye, repent ye, for the kingdom of heaven is at hand; and seek no more to destroy my servants. And it came to pass that the earth shook again, and the walls trembled.

33. And also again the third time the voice came, and did speak unto them marvelous words which cannot be uttered by man; and the walls did tremble again, and the earth shook as if it were about to divide asunder.

34. And it came to pass that the Lamanites could not flee because of the cloud of darkness which did overshadow them; yea, and also they were immovable because of the fear which did come upon them.

35. Now there was one among them who was a Nephite by birth, who had once belonged to the church of God but had dissented from them.

36. And it came to pass that he turned him about, and behold, he saw through the cloud of darkness the faces of Nephi and Lehi; and behold, they did shine exceedingly, even as the faces of angels. And he beheld that they did lift their eyes to heaven; and they were in the attitude as if talking or lifting their voices to some being whom they beheld.

37. And it came to pass that this man did cry unto the multitude, that they might turn and look. And behold, there was power given unto them that they did turn and look; and they did behold the faces of Nephi and Lehi.

38. And they said unto the man: Behold, what do all these things mean, and who is it with whom these men do converse?

39. Now the man's name was Aminadab. And Aminadab said unto them: They do converse with the angels of God.

40. And it came to pass that the Lamanites said unto him: What shall we do, that this cloud of darkness may be removed from overshadowing us?

41. And Aminadab said unto them: You must repent, and cry unto the voice, even until ye shall have faith in Christ, who was taught unto you by Alma, and Amulek, and Zeezrom; and when ye shall do this, the cloud of darkness shall be removed from overshadowing you.

42. And it came to pass that they all did begin to cry unto the voice of him who had shaken the earth; yea, they did cry even until the cloud of darkness was dispersed.

43. And it came to pass that when they cast their eyes about, and saw that the cloud of darkness was dispersed from overshadowing them, behold, they saw that they were encircled about, yea every soul, by a pillar of fire.

44. And Nephi and Lehi were in the midst of them; yea, they were encircled about; yea, they were as if in the midst of a flaming fire, yet it did harm them not, neither did it take hold upon the walls of the prison; and they were filled with that joy which is unspeakable and full of glory.

45. And behold, the Holy Spirit of God did come down from heaven, and did enter into their hearts, and they were filled as if with fire, and they could speak forth marvelous words.

46. And it came to pass that there came a voice unto them, yea, a pleasant voice, as if it were a whisper, saying:

47. Peace, peace be unto you, because of your faith in my Well Beloved, who was from the foundation of the world.

48. And now, when they heard this they cast up their eyes as if to behold from whence the voice came; and behold, they saw the heavens open; and angels came down out of heaven and ministered unto them.

49. And there were about three hundred souls who saw and heard these things; and they were bidden to go forth and marvel not, neither should they doubt.

50. And it came to pass that they did go forth, and did minister unto the people, declaring throughout all the regions round about all the things which they had heard and seen, insomuch that the more part of the Lamanites were convinced of them, because of the greatness of the evidences which they had received.

51. And as many as were convinced did lay down their weapons of war, and also their hatred and the tradition of their fathers.

52. And it came to pass that they did yield up unto the Nephites the lands of their possession.

21–52. As with all faithful servants of the Lord, Nephi and Lehi spoke with such power and authority that people were astonished and thousands upon thousands were converted and "baptized unto repentance." Despite their great success they were imprisoned, as were other prophets before them (see Alma 14:17–24; 21:13–14). Because of their faith and righteousness they even turned a prison into a temple—a site of miraculous manifestations and occurrences, a site of a grand spiritual rebirth for many Lamanites (see 3 Nephi 9:20).

21. That same prison] See Mosiah 7:6–8.

23. Encircled about as if by fire] This pentecostal occasion came to pass largely because of the faith and power of Nephi and Lehi, because two men paid the price to prepare themselves to teach and minister with power and authority of God. This particular experience could refer to a general protective influence of the Spirit (compare Daniel 3:19–27) or, more likely, to the presence of heavenly beings (see verse 39) in the prison with Lehi and Nephi (compare 3 Nephi 17:24).

24. A pillar of fire] This is a manifestation of the glory and power of the Almighty. See Exodus 24:17; D&C 137:2–3.

30. A still voice of perfect mildness] The Lord will not shout to gain our attention. He whispers. The Spirit speaks in perfect mildness but penetrates to the heart and very core of the soul (see 1 Kings 19:11–12; 3 Nephi 11:3; D&C 8:2–3).

33. Marvelous words which cannot be uttered by man] We presume that Mormon had access to these words but wisely chose or was directed by the Spirit to keep them from hearts and minds unprepared to receive them (compare 3 Nephi 26:8–12).

36. They did shine exceedingly, even as the faces of angels] Compare this experience with that of Moses (Exodus 34:29–35), Abinadi (Mosiah 13:5), and Stephen (Acts 6:15).

41. Cry unto the voice, even until ye shall have faith in Christ] Several hundred people observed the miraculous events surrounding the imprisonment of Lehi and Nephi. Aminadab, a

Nephite dissenter, became a spiritual as well as a physical witness of these events and as a consequence preached to the others. Under the influence of the Spirit, Aminadab urged the others to pray to the voice they had heard until they could obtain a faith in Christ. Faith comes as a gift of God only when the initial desire is nurtured and nourished (see Alma 32:27). "Faith is a gift of God," wrote Elder Orson Pratt. "In what manner does He impart this gift to the mind by the immediate operation of the Holy Spirit independent of any other means? Does He bestow it unsought for and irrespective of the preparation of the mind? Does He confer it independent of the agency of man? To say that man obtains this gift without preparing himself, or without the exercise of any agency, is to deprive him of all responsibility in regard to whether he has faith or not." (In *The True Faith,* p. 8.)

41. Christ, who was taught unto you by Alma, and Amulek, and Zeezrom] Theirs must have been a marvelous ministry, their testimonies of the Christ of immeasurable impact, inasmuch as these witnesses had been borne some fifty years earlier.

44. They were filled with that joy which is unspeakable and full of glory] This is a gift of the spirit that comes from being pure and righteous and from "knowing the peaceable things of the kingdom" (D&C 36:2). Spiritual outpourings that come as one comes to know, understand, and experience the Atonement always include "unspeakable" joy (see Mosiah 4:20; Alma 19:14; Alma 28:8, 14; Alma 36:20; 3 Nephi 17:18).

45. They were filled as if with fire] The reception of the Holy Ghost is the baptism of fire spoken of in the scriptures (see Matthew 3:11; 2 Nephi 31:13, 17; Moses 6:66; see also *Commentary* 1:364). They were baptized with fire, but, in the words of the Savior, "they knew it not" (3 Nephi 9:20).

45. They could speak forth marvelous words] Being filled with the Spirit of the Lord, men, women, and even babes can speak forth marvelous words, praises, and prophecies (see Alma 32:23; 3 Nephi 26:14; Joel 2:28–29). It is one of the gifts or fruits of the Spirit (see D&C 46:10–26) such as are reserved for and bestowed upon those who are in tune with the Spirit.

47. Peace be unto you] The promise given by the voice of the Lord to the people who believed on the words of Lehi and Nephi is the same for all dispensations. Peace to the soul—"not as the world giveth" (John 14:27)—comes as a gift of grace through unshaken faith in Christ's holy name and through "relying wholly upon the merits of him who is mighty to save" (2 Nephi 31:19).

47. Because of your faith in my Well Beloved] Here we have the voice or words of Elohim, the Eternal Father. Whether he spoke them himself, or whether they were spoken by the Son by divine investiture of authority (see *Commentary* 2:227–29), we cannot tell from the passage.

48. Angels came down out of heaven and ministered unto them] "There never has been a gospel dispensation without the ministering of angels. A people who cannot claim the ministering of angels cannot claim an everlasting gospel. . . . Without the ministering of angels and other forms of revelation, our theology would be like a body without a spirit." (Robert L. Millet and Joseph Fielding McConkie, *The Life Beyond*, p. 71.) Joseph Smith explained that "there are no angels who minister to this earth but those who do belong or have belonged to it" (D&C 130:5). Thus President Joseph F. Smith observed: "When messengers are sent to minister to the inhabitants of this earth, they are not strangers, but from the ranks of our kindred, friends, and fellow-beings and fellow-servants. The ancient prophets who died were those who came to visit their fellow creatures upon the earth. They came to Abraham, to Isaac, and to Jacob; it was such beings—holy beings if you please—who waited upon the Savior and administered to him on the Mount. . . .

"In like manner our fathers and mothers, brothers, sisters and friends who have passed away from this earth, having been faithful, and worthy to enjoy these rights and privileges, may have a mission given them to visit their relatives and friends upon the earth again, bringing from the divine Presence messages of love, of warning, of reproof and instruction, to those whom they had learned to love in the flesh." (*Gospel Doctrine*, pp. 435–37.)

Converted Lamanites Exhort the Nephites to Faith and Repentance

Helaman 6:1–14

1. And it came to pass that when the sixty and second year of the reign of the judges had ended, all these things had happened and the Lamanites had become, the more part of them, a righteous people, insomuch that their righteousness did exceed that of the Nephites, because of their firmness and their steadiness in the faith.

2. For behold, there were many of the Nephites who had become hardened and impenitent and grossly wicked, insomuch that they did reject the word of God and all the preaching and prophesying which did come among them.

3. Nevertheless, the people of the church did have great joy because of the conversion of the Lamanites, yea, because of the church of God, which had been

established among them. And they did fellowship one with another, and did rejoice one with another, and did have great joy.

4. And it came to pass that many of the Lamanites did come down into the land of Zarahemla, and did declare unto the people of the Nephites the manner of their conversion, and did exhort them to faith and repentance.

5. Yea, and many did preach with exceedingly great power and authority, unto the bringing down many of them into the depths of humility, to be the humble followers of God and the Lamb.

6. And it came to pass that many of the Lamanites did go into the land northward; and also Nephi and Lehi went into the land northward, to preach unto the people. And thus ended the sixty and third year.

7. And behold, there was peace in all the land, insomuch that the Nephites did go into whatsoever part of the land they would, whether among the Nephites or the Lamanites.

8. And it came to pass that the Lamanites did also go whithersoever they would, whether it were among the Lamanites or among the Nephites; and thus they did have free intercourse one with another, to buy and to sell, and to get gain, according to their desire.

9. And it came to pass that they became exceedingly rich, both the Lamanites and the Nephites; and they did have an exceeding plenty of gold, and of silver, and of all manner of precious metals, both in the land south and in the land north.

10. Now the land south was called Lehi, and the land north was called Mulek, which was after the son of Zedekiah; for the Lord did bring Mulek into the land north, and Lehi, into the land south.

11. And behold, there was all manner of gold in both these lands, and of silver, and of precious ore of every kind; and there were also curious workmen, who did work all kinds of ore and did refine it; and thus they did become rich.

12. They did raise grain in abundance, both in the north and in the south; and they did flourish exceedingly, both in the north and in the south. And they did multiply and wax exceedingly strong in the land. And they did raise many flocks and herds, yea, many fatlings.

13. Behold their women did toil and spin, and did make all manner of cloth, of fine-twined linen and cloth of every kind, to clothe their nakedness. And thus the sixty and fourth year did pass away in peace.

14. And in the sixty and fifth year they did also have great joy and peace, yea, much preaching and many prophecies concerning that which was to come. And thus passed away the sixty and fifth year.

4 5. There is a spirit of tragic irony in these verses. The Lamanites have received the gospel through the Nephites, but many of the Nephites have fallen into apostasy. It must have been an unusual experience for many of the more zealous Lamanite converts to labor among the Nephites and encourage them to return to the faith of their fathers. There is a similarly ironic episode in the history of the restored Church, one which tugs at the heartstrings much as this missionary movement must have done.

John Taylor had been converted to the gospel and baptized in Canada in May of 1836 through the inspired preaching of Elder Parley P. Pratt. B. H. Roberts writes of a difficult time in the history of the Church: "In March of the following year [1837], Elder Taylor visited Kirtland, and there met the Prophet Joseph Smith, who entertained him at his house and gave him many items of information pertaining to the work of the Lord in this dispensation. At that time there was a bitter spirit of apostasy rife in Kirtland. A number in the quorum of the Twelve were disaffected towards the Prophet, and the Church seemed on the point of disintegration. Among others, Parley P. Pratt was floundering in darkness, and coming to Elder Taylor told him of some things wherein he considered the Prophet Joseph in error. To his remarks Elder Taylor replied:

"'I am surprised to hear you speak so, Brother Parley. Before you left Canada you bore a strong testimony to Joseph Smith being a prophet of God, and to the truth of the work he has inaugurated; and you said you knew these things by revelation, and the gift of the Holy Ghost. You gave to me a strict charge to the effect that though you or an angel from heaven was to declare anything else I was not to believe it. Now Brother Parley, it is not man that I am following, but the Lord. The principles you taught me led me to Him, and I now have the same testimony that you then rejoiced in. If the work was true six months ago, it is true today; if Joseph Smith was then a prophet, he is now a prophet.'

"To the honor of Parley, be it said, he sought no further to lead Elder Taylor astray; nor did he use much argument in the first place. 'He with many others,' says Elder Taylor, 'were passing under a dark cloud; he soon made all right with the Prophet Joseph, and was restored to full fellowship.'" (B. H. Roberts, *The Life of John Taylor*, pp. 39–40.)

7–9. This is a most unusual time in Nephite–Lamanite history, a short-lived but glorious era in which Nephites and Lamanites dwell safely together under the protective hand of righteousness.

10. See Omni 1:14–15; Helaman 8:21.

Wickedness Resumes with the Rise and Growth of Secret Combinations

Helaman 6:15–41

15. And it came to pass that in the sixty and sixth year of the reign of the judges, behold, Cezoram was murdered by an unknown hand as he sat upon the judgment-seat. And it came to pass that in the same year, that his son, who had been appointed by the people in his stead, was also murdered. And thus ended the sixty and sixth year.

16. And in the commencement of the sixty and seventh year the people began to grow exceedingly wicked again.

17. For behold, the Lord had blessed them so long with the riches of the world that they had not been stirred up to anger, to wars, nor to bloodshed; therefore they began to set their hearts upon their riches; yea, they began to seek to get gain that they might be lifted up one above another; therefore they began to commit secret murders, and to rob and to plunder, that they might get gain.

18. And now behold, those murderers and plunderers were a band who had been formed by Kishkumen and Gadianton. And now it had come to pass that there were many, even among the Nephites, of Gadianton's band. But behold, they were more numerous among the more wicked part of the Lamanites. And they were called Gadianton's robbers and murderers.

19. And it was they who did murder the chief judge Cezoram, and his son, while in the judgment-seat; and behold, they were not found.

20. And now it came to pass that when the Lamanites found that there were robbers among them they were exceedingly sorrowful; and they did use every means in their power to destroy them off the face of the earth.

21. But behold, Satan did stir up the hearts of the more part of the Nephites, insomuch that they did unite with those bands of robbers, and did enter into their covenants and their oaths, that they would protect and preserve one another in whatsoever difficult circumstances they should be placed, that they should not suffer for their murders, and their plunderings, and their stealings.

22. And it came to pass that they did have their signs, yea, their secret signs, and their secret words; and this that they might distinguish a brother who had entered into the covenant, that whatsoever wickedness his brother should do he should not be injured by his brother, nor by those who did belong to his band, who had taken this covenant.

23. And thus they might murder, and plunder, and steal, and commit whoredoms and all manner of wickedness, contrary to the laws of their country and also the laws of their God.

24. And whosoever of those who belonged to their band should reveal unto the world of their wickedness and their abominations, should be tried, not according to the laws of their country, but according to the laws of their wickedness, which had

been given by Gadianton and Kishkumen.

25. Now behold, it is these secret oaths and covenants which Alma commanded his son should not go forth unto the world, lest they should be a means of bringing down the people unto destruction.

26. Now behold, those secret oaths and covenants did not come forth unto Gadianton from the records which were delivered unto Helaman; but behold, they were put into the heart of Gadianton by that same being who did entice our first parents to partake of the forbidden fruit—

27. Yea, that same being who did plot with Cain, that if he would murder his brother Abel it should not be known unto the world. And he did plot with Cain and his followers from that time forth.

28. And also it is that same being who put it into the hearts of the people to build a tower sufficiently high that they might get to heaven. And it was that same being who led on the people who came from that tower into this land; who spread the works of darkness and abominations over all the face of the land, until he dragged the people down to an entire destruction, and to an everlasting hell.

29. Yea, it is that same being who put it into the heart of Gadianton to still carry on the work of darkness, and of secret murder; and he has brought it forth from the beginning of man even down to this time.

30. And behold, it is he who is the author of all sin. And behold, he doth carry on his works of darkness and secret murder, and doth hand down their plots, and

their oaths, and their covenants, and their plans of awful wickedness, from generation to generation according as he can get hold upon the hearts of the children of men.

31. And now behold, he had got great hold upon the hearts of the Nephites; yea, insomuch that they had become exceedingly wicked; yea, the more part of them had turned out of the way of righteousness, and did trample under their feet the commandments of God, and did turn unto their own ways, and did build up unto themselves idols of their gold and their silver.

32. And it came to pass that all these iniquities did come unto them in the space of not many years, insomuch that a more part of it had come unto them in the sixty and seventh year of the reign of the judges over the people of Nephi.

33. And they did grow in their iniquities in the sixty and eighth year also, to the great sorrow and lamentation of the righteous.

34. And thus we see that the Nephites did begin to dwindle in unbelief, and grow in wickedness and abominations, while the Lamanites began to grow exceedingly in the knowledge of their God; yea, they did begin to keep his statutes and commandments, and to walk in truth and uprightness before him.

35. And thus we see that the Spirit of the Lord began to withdraw from the Nephites, because of the wickedness and the hardness of their hearts.

36. And thus we see that the Lord began to pour out his Spirit upon the Lamanites, because of their easiness and willingness to believe in his words.

37. And it came to pass that the Lamanites did hunt the band of robbers of Gadianton; and they did preach the word of God among the more wicked part of them, insomuch that this band of robbers was utterly destroyed from among the Lamanites.

38. And it came to pass on the other hand, that the Nephites did build them up and support them, beginning at the more wicked part of them, until they had overspread all the land of the Nephites, and had seduced the more part of the righteous until they had come down to believe in their works and partake of their spoils, and to join with them in their secret murders and combinations.

39. And thus they did obtain the sole management of the government, insomuch that they did trample under their feet and smite and rend and turn their backs upon the poor and the meek, and the humble followers of God.

40. And thus we see that they were in an awful state, and ripening for an everlasting destruction.

41. And it came to pass that thus ended the sixty and eighth year of the reign of the judges over the people of Nephi.

15–41. What a painful reality it is that Satan never sleeps! At this period of Book of Mormon history righteousness is allowed to have a foothold for only five years before wickedness is given an organized thrust through the bands of Gadianton; the hordes of hell are unleashed again upon the Nephites and Lamanites. The chief judge and his son are murdered (verses 15, 19) by the secret combinations; the government is taken over by the wicked; both Nephites and Lamanites join hands with demons in human form to spread death and desolation; and the secret oaths and covenants and signs of old, those silent and subtle means of communication had by the ungodly from the days of the first Master Mahan (see Moses 5:31), are revealed and spread among the people.

17. What went wrong? Why would the people turn again to evil? How could they fall so quickly into decay and perversion? Herein is the key: The lust for riches. The unbridled quest for power and money. Pride. How sickening is the cycle and how nauseating is man's obsession with himself and his worldly possessions!

20–21. The Nephites, now sinning against greater light and thus heirs to the greater condemnation, fall deeper into the pit of despair than their Lamanite brethren. Hardened more surely than those brethren, the Nephites begin to uphold that which the Lamanites seek to dispel.

25–26. Alma had recommended that Helaman teach his people an eternal hatred of sin and, more specifically, make known generally the wickedness and God-ordained destruction of the Jaredites. On the other hand, he had forbidden Helaman to make known the secret signs and covenants and oaths of the secret combinations described on the twenty-four gold plates. (See Alma 37:21–32.) Helaman had been true to his word. How, then, had such things come to be known by the wicked among the Nephites and Lamanites? Simply stated, Satan delivered an independent revelation—he put such ideas and information into the hearts and minds of the ungodly (see 3 Nephi 3:9; 6:28).

27. That same being who did plot with Cain] The story of the origin and rise of secret combinations on earth was once contained in the record of Old Testament times. Such plain and precious truths concerning the nature of the gospel anciently; the particulars of the plan of salvation and the then future ministry of Jesus Christ as prophesied among the ancients; and the manner in which Cain plotted with Satan to become Master Mahan, master of the great secret, that he could murder and get gain—these matters were deleted from the Bible records before that book was compiled. They were known among the Nephites through that scriptural record we know as the brass plates. These truths were restored by revelation to Joseph Smith the Seer through his inspired translation of the Bible. (See Moses 5.)

28. See Genesis 11:1–4; Ether 1:3.

30. He who is the author of all sin] "Wherefore, because that Satan rebelled against me, and sought to destroy the agency of man, which I, the Lord God, had given him, and also, that I should give unto him mine own power; by the power of mine Only Begotten, I caused that he should be cast down; and *he became Satan, yea, even the devil, the father of all lies*, to deceive and to blind men, and to lead them captive at his will, even as many as would not hearken unto my voice" (Moses 4:3–4, italics added; compare John 8:44).

31. Trample under their feet the commandments of God] That is, they set at naught, count as worthless, the commandments of God (see 1 Nephi 19:7).

31. Build up unto themselves idols of their gold and their silver] See commentary on Alma 31:1.

34–36. Mormon uses his "and thus we see" statements here to summarize the hardness of the Nephites—the loss of spiritual strength—and, on the other hand, the spiritual growth of the Lamanites because of their openness to counsel and divine direction.

Nephi Laments the Wickedness of His People

Helaman 7:1–9

1. Behold, now it came to pass in the sixty and ninth year of the reign of the judges over the people of the Nephites, that Nephi, the son of Helaman, returned to the land of Zarahemla from the land northward.

2. For he had been forth among the people who were in the land northward, and did preach the word of God unto them, and did prophesy many things unto them;

3. And they did reject all his words, insomuch that he could not stay among them, but returned again unto the land of his nativity.

4. And seeing the people in a state of such awful wickedness, and those Gadianton robbers filling the judgment-seats—having usurped the power and authority of the land; laying aside the commandments of God, and not in the least aright before him; doing no justice unto the children of men;

5. Condemning the righteous because of their righteousness; letting the guilty and the wicked go unpunished because of their money; and moreover to be held in office at the head of government, to rule and do according to their wills, that they might get gain and glory of the world, and, moreover, that they might the more easily commit adultery, and steal, and kill, and do according to their own wills—

6. Now this great iniquity had come upon the Nephites, in the space of not many years; and when Nephi saw it, his heart was swollen with sorrow within his breast; and he did exclaim in the agony of his soul:

7. Oh, that I could have had my days in the days when my father Nephi first came out of the land of Jerusalem, that I could have joyed with him in the promised land; then were his people easy to be entreated, firm to keep the commandments of God, and slow to be led to do iniquity; and they were quick to hearken unto the words of the Lord—

8. Yea, if my days could have been in those days, then would my soul have had joy in the righteousness of my brethren.

9. But behold, I am consigned that these are my days, and that my soul shall be filled with sorrow because of this the wickedness of my brethren.

5. Condemning the righteous because of their righteousness] Wickedness and righteousness have no tolerance for each other. Like light and darkness, they cannot share the same space at the same time. If light is to shine, darkness must flee; if darkness is to reign, the light must give way. Each seeks the victory over the other. Thus it is that the truly pure, honest, and righteous cannot avoid the bile, spleen, and gall of the wicked. To be above reproach is to assure that you will be reproached. Nephi, son of Lehi, warned that in the last days men would "revile against that which is good," saying that it was of "no worth." The adversary, he warned, would "rage in the hearts of the children of men, and stir them up to anger against that which is good." (2 Nephi 28:16, 20.)

Nephi Declares Repentance

Helaman 7:10–19

10. And behold, now it came to pass that it was upon a tower, which was in the garden of Nephi, which was by the highway which led to the chief market, which was in the city of Zarahemla; therefore, Nephi had bowed himself upon the tower which was in his garden, which tower was also near unto the garden gate by which led the highway.

11. And it came to pass that there were certain men passing by and saw Nephi as he was pouring out his soul unto God upon the tower; and they ran and told the people what they had seen, and the people came together in multitudes that they might know the cause of so great mourning for the wickedness of the people.

12. And now, when Nephi arose he beheld the multitudes of people who had gathered together.

13. And it came to pass that he opened his mouth and said unto them: Behold, why have ye gathered yourselves together? That I may tell you of your iniquities?

14. Yea, because I have got upon my tower that I might pour out my soul unto my God, because of the exceeding sorrow of my heart, which is because of your iniquities!

15. And because of my mourning and lamentation ye have gathered yourselves together, and do marvel; yea, and ye have great need to marvel; yea, ye ought to marvel because ye are given away that the devil has got so great hold upon your hearts.

16. Yea, how could you have given away to the enticing of him who is seeking to hurl away your souls down to everlasting misery and endless wo?

17. O repent ye, repent ye! Why will ye die? Turn ye, turn ye unto the Lord your God. Why has he forsaken you?

18. It is because you have hardened your hearts; yea, ye will not hearken unto the voice of the good shepherd; yea, ye have provoked him to anger against you.

19. And behold, instead of gathering you, except ye will repent, behold, he shall scatter you forth that ye shall become meat for dogs and wild beasts.

11. He was pouring out his soul] There are some prayers, some pleadings to God, in which the supplicant truly bends and stretches his soul. Even Jesus, the greatest of all, came to a time of personal and cosmic crisis when "being in an agony he prayed more earnestly" (Luke 22:44). Here Nephi is pained over the sins and iniquities of his day and raises his voice high that it reaches the heavens.

15. Ye are given away] That is, you have surrendered your will, delivered your agency to him who has sought the agency of man since premortal times.

16. Everlasting misery and endless wo] Hell, the abode of the wicked in the postmortal spirit world. See commentary on Alma 40:13–14.

17. Why will ye die] Jacob likewise pleaded with his people: "While [the Lord's] arm of mercy is extended towards you in the light of the day, harden not your hearts. Yea, today, if ye will hear his voice, harden not your hearts; for why will ye die? For behold, after ye have been nourished by the good word of God all the day long, will ye bring forth evil fruit, that ye must be hewn down and cast into the fire?" (Jacob 6:5–7; see also Ezekiel 18:20–32.)

17. Why has he forsaken you?] God forsakes man in the sense that he removes his Holy Spirit and thus leaves him to himself, spiritually unattended.

19. To illustrate the doctrines of gathering and scattering, Nephi used as a type the assembling of those who came to hear him. The faithful of all dispensations have gathered to be taught the gospel and also to facilitate the observance of their covenants. When they have rebelled against those teachings and broken their vows, their lands of promise have been taken from them and they have been driven, scattered, and often destroyed. Nephi applies that principle to his immediate audience—as they have gathered to hear him, so they must repent; and if they fail to do so they will be scattered, he prophesies, and become "meat for dogs and wild beasts."

The Promises of God unto the Lamanites

Helaman 7:20–29

20. O, how could you have forgotten your God in the very day that he had delivered you?

21. But behold, it is to get gain, to be praised of men, yea, and that ye might get gold and silver. And ye have set your hearts upon the riches and the vain things of this world, for the which ye do murder, and plunder, and steal, and bear false witness against your neighbor, and do all manner of iniquity.

22. And for this cause wo shall come unto you except ye shall repent. For if ye will not repent, behold, this great city, and also all those great cities which are round

about, which are in the land of our possession, shall be taken away that ye shall have no place in them; for behold, the Lord will not grant unto you strength, as he has hitherto done, to withstand against your enemies.

23. For behold, thus saith the Lord: I will not show unto the wicked of my strength, to one more than the other, save it be unto those who repent of their sins, and hearken unto my words. Now therefore, I would that ye should behold, my brethren, that it shall be better for the Lamanites than for you except ye shall repent.

24. For behold, they are more righteous than you, for they have not sinned against that great knowledge which ye have received; therefore the Lord will be merciful unto them; yea, he will lengthen out their days and increase their seed, even when thou shalt be utterly destroyed except thou shalt repent.

25. Yea, wo be unto you because of that great abomination which has come among you; and ye have united yourselves unto it, yea, to that secret band which was established by Gadianton!

26. Yea, wo shall come unto you because of that pride which ye have suffered to enter your hearts, which has lifted you up beyond that which is good because of your exceedingly great riches!

27. Yea, wo be unto you because of your wickedness and abominations!

28. And except ye repent ye shall perish; yea, even your lands shall be taken from you, and ye shall be destroyed from off the face of the earth.

29. Behold now, I do not say that these things shall be, of myself, because it is not of myself that I know these things; but behold, I know that these things are true because the Lord God has made them known unto me, therefore I testify that they shall be.

21–23. The Lord's people have always been a covenant people. Covenants, by their nature, eschew that which is self-centered while creating an interdependency between the covenant parties. Their salvation is to be found in the grace of Christ and the unity of the Saints. When attention is shifted from the covenant to "get[ting] gain," obtaining the "praise of men," and acquiring "gold and silver," of necessity the covenant is sacrificed upon the altar of vanity, and the god of this world becomes the object of worship. Whereas previously the surrendering of self in the honoring of the covenant constantly brought a renewal of strength, now the insatiable appetite for self-aggrandizement not only robs the covenant breaker of strength but also destroys both his character and his soul. Such had become the plight of many within the nation of the Nephites.

24. They are more righteous than you] The Nephites had feasted upon the good things of the gospel while the Lamanites had tasted but a meager ration, and yet the latter were more faithful: this to their glory and to the shame of the Nephites. The divine word proclaims: "For of him unto whom much is given much is required; and he who sins against the greater light shall receive the greater condemnation" (D&C 82:3). See also Luke 12:48; Helaman 15:11–15.

24. He will lengthen out their days] The children of Israel under Moses, like the seed of Lehi, witnessed many miracles in their behalf. God declared: "Therefore shall ye keep all the commandments which I command you this day, that ye may be strong, and go in and possess the land, whither ye go to posses it; and that ye may prolong your days in the land, which the Lord sware unto your fathers to give unto them and to their seed, a land that floweth with milk and honey" (Deuteronomy 11:8–9). As obedience and possession go hand in hand, so the proverb declares: "The fear of the Lord is the beginning of wisdom: and the knowledge of the holy is understanding. For by me thy days shall be multiplied, and the years of thy life shall be increased." (Proverbs 9:10–11.)

God is not without a purpose in choosing a people as his own and giving them a particular land of inheritance. They are to stand as a witness of his goodness and of his holiness. Should they choose to rebel against that purpose, they cannot expect to be strong nor to abide long upon that land he has given them. "Hear, O my son, and receive my sayings; and the years of thy life shall be many" (Proverbs 4:10).

24. Increase their seed] Righteous posterity has ever been the crowning blessing of the faithful. Because of his faithfulness Abraham received promises concerning his seed that were to continue both in the world and out of the world. Indeed, he was promised that they would be "as innumerable as the stars," or if you were to count the "sand upon the seashore ye could not number them" (D&C 132:30). For those who enter into the new and everlasting covenant of marriage, "this promise is yours also, because ye are of Abraham" (D&C 132:31).

29. Following the prophetic pattern Nephi places a seal upon the testimony of his words, declaring revelation as their source and that what he has spoken is true. This is the pattern that should always be followed in declaring repentance or in teaching the gospel; that is, we are first to declare the message and then seal the testimony of the message with the testimony of its verity as revelation and as truth.

Corrupt Judges Incite the People Against Nephi

Helaman 8:1–10

1. And now it came to pass that when Nephi had said these words, behold, there were men who were judges, who also belonged to the secret band of Gadianton, and they were angry, and they cried out against him, saying unto the people: Why do ye not seize upon this man and bring him forth, that he may be condemned according to the crime which he has done?

2. Why seest thou this man, and hearest him revile against this people and against our law?

3. For behold, Nephi had spoken unto them concerning the corruptness of their law; yea, many things did Nephi speak which cannot be written; and nothing did he speak which was contrary to the commandments of God.

4. And those judges were angry with him because he spake plainly unto them concerning their secret works of darkness; nevertheless, they durst not lay their own hands upon him, for they feared the people lest they should cry out against them.

5. Therefore they did cry unto the people, saying: Why do you suffer this man to revile against us? For behold he doth condemn all this people, even unto destruction; yea, and also that these our great cities shall be taken from us, that we shall have no place in them.

6. And now we know that this is impossible, for behold, we are powerful, and our cities great, therefore our enemies can have no power over us.

7. And it came to pass that thus they did stir up the people to anger against Nephi, and raised contentions among them; for there were some who did cry out: Let this man alone, for he is a good man, and those things which he saith will surely come to pass except we repent;

8. Yea, behold, all the judgments will come upon us which he has testified unto us; for we know that he has testified aright unto us concerning our iniquities. And behold they are many, and he knoweth as well all things which shall befall us as he knoweth of our iniquities;

9. Yea, and behold, if he had not been a prophet he could not have testified concerning those things.

10. And it came to pass that those people who sought to destroy Nephi were compelled because of their fear, that they did not lay their hands on him; therefore he began again to speak unto them, seeing that he had gained favor in the eyes of some, insomuch that the remainder of them did fear.

3. Nothing did he speak which was contrary to the commandments of God] Nephi spoke the truth. He acted within the bounds and parameters of his prophetic calling, and he did only what he was commanded to do by his Principal. He did no wrong in the sight of God and reasonable men. But he preached against falsehood, hypocrisy, and pride and thereby incited the rabble of the unrighteous.

5–6. Those whose wickedness was exposed by Nephi responded with the ferociousness of a trapped animal. They could not lay hands on him for fear of the people, so they sought to turn the people against him. Of Nephi's warning of impending destruction they said, "this is impossible," "we are powerful," "our cities great," "our enemies can have no power over us." Yet they trembled at the testimony of a lone man. Truth is more powerful than great cities, and wickedness more destructive than alien armies.

Validity draws the fire. Jacob's older sons mocked the dreams of their younger brother Joseph, saying they were foolishness; yet they could not rest until they had sold him into bondage. Joseph Smith was a youth of no social standing and no hint of eminence; yet men of high standing excited the public mind against him. Why the opposition against that which has been declared foolish? Again, validity draws the fire.

Moses Testified That the Messiah Would Be God's Son

Helaman 8:11–15

11. Therefore he was constrained to speak more unto them saying: Behold, my brethren, have ye not read that God gave power unto one man, even Moses, to smite upon the waters of the Red Sea, and they parted hither and thither, insomuch that the Israelites, who were our fathers, came through upon dry ground, and the waters closed upon the armies of the Egyptians and swallowed them up?

12. And now behold, if God gave unto this man such power, then why should ye dispute among yourselves, and say that he hath given unto me no power whereby I may know concerning the judgments that shall come upon you except ye repent?

13. But, behold, ye not only deny my words, but ye also deny all the words which have been spoken by our fathers, and also the words which were spoken by this man, Moses, who had such great power given unto him, yea, the words which he hath spoken concerning the coming of the Messiah.

14. Yea, did he not bear record that the Son of God should come? And as he lifted up the brazen serpent in the wilderness, even so shall he be lifted up who should come.

15. And as many as should look upon that serpent should live, even so as many as should look upon the Son of God with faith, having a contrite spirit, might live, even unto that life which is eternal.

11–15. Chief among the plain and precious things taken from the Old Testament was the testimony that the Messiah would be the Son of God. Alma declared this doctrine to be the seed that grows up into the tree of everlasting life. In so doing he cited the testimony of three Old Testament prophets—Zenos, Zenock, and

Moses. He then quoted Zenos and Zenock to that effect. His quotation from Moses, however, though a Messianic prophecy, does not specifically state that the Messiah would be the "Son of God." (See Alma 33.) In the present instance, Nephi refers to the same text that Alma quoted and also declares that it described the Messiah as God's Son.

It would be difficult to overstate the importance of the doctrine of Christ's divine sonship. Alma, as noted, referred to it as the tree of everlasting life, meaning that all the doctrines of the kingdom are fruits plucked from this tree and are of necessity rooted in this doctrine. The Atonement, the Resurrection, and the personal nature of God serve as classic examples. Of his own life, Christ said: "No man taketh it from me, but I lay it down of myself. I have power to lay it down, and I have power to take it again." (John 10:18.) That is to say: "Because my mother is a mortal woman I have inherited blood, or the ability to die, from her; and because God is my Father I have inherited immortality, or the ability to live, from him." Thus Christ, because he is the Only Begotten of the Father in the flesh, is the only man who ever walked the face of this earth who had the capacity to both live and die—to lay down his life and to take it again. He became the first fruits of the resurrection, his body and spirit joining in an inseparable union. All who became heirs of mortality as a result of the fall of Adam become heirs of immortality through the death and resurrection of Christ. Every spirit that has been clothed with a body will have claim upon that body in the worlds to come. Like our Father, in whose image and likeness we are, we will be personal beings, and like him will have body, parts, and passions. Such are the fruits of divine sonship.

12. Why should ye dispute . . . and say that he hath given unto me no power] In this sermon Nephi seeks to establish himself as a servant of God in the prophetic tradition. If the people believed that God granted miraculous power to Moses and the ancient prophets, why should they think the Almighty unable to do so in their own time? If Moses could prophesy of the Messiah, why could not he, Nephi, prophesy impending judgment if the people would not repent?

13. To deny the words of modern prophets is, at the same time, to deny the words of the ancient prophets. To reject the spirit of revelation in one age is to reject it in all ages. So it is with all the fruits of the gospel—to deny their power and effect among the ancients is to deny their power in our day. If an acorn brought forth the mighty oak in ancient days, it can do no less in our day. If the seed of faith opened the heavens and brought forth miracles among the Saints of former days, it must of necessity produce the same effects today.

14–15. This is a classic Old Testament type for Christ. "As Moses lifted up the serpent in the wilderness, even so must the Son of man be lifted up" (John 3:14). See *Commentary* 1:136. See also Alma 33:19–22.

All Prophets Testify of Christ

Helaman 8:16–24

16. And now behold, Moses did not only testify of these things, but also all the holy prophets, from his days even to the days of Abraham.

17. Yea, and behold, Abraham saw of his coming, and was filled with gladness and did rejoice.

18. Yea, and behold I say unto you, that Abraham not only knew of these things, but there were many before the days of Abraham who were called by the order of God; yea, even after the order of his Son; and this that it should be shown unto the people, a great many thousand years before his coming, that even redemption should come unto them.

19. And now I would that ye should know, that even since the days of Abraham there have been many prophets that have testified these things; yea, behold, the prophet Zenos did testify boldly; for the which he was slain.

20. And behold, also Zenock, and also Ezias, and also Isaiah, and Jeremiah, (Jeremiah being that same prophet who testified of the destruction of Jerusalem) and now we know that Jerusalem was destroyed according to the words of Jeremiah. O then why not the Son of God come, according to his prophecy?

21. And now will you dispute that Jerusalem was destroyed? Will ye say that the sons of Zedekiah were not slain, all except it were Mulek? Yea, and do ye not behold that the seed of Zedekiah are with us, and they were driven out of the land of Jerusalem? But behold, this is not all—

22. Our father Lehi was driven out of Jerusalem because he testified of these things. Nephi also testified of these things, and also almost all of our fathers, even down to this time; yea, they have testified of the coming of Christ, and have looked forward, and have rejoiced in his day which is to come.

23. And behold, he is God, and he is with them, and he did manifest himself unto them, that they were redeemed by him; and they gave unto him glory, because of that which is to come.

24. And now, seeing ye know these things and cannot deny them except ye shall lie, therefore in this ye have sinned, for ye have rejected all these things, notwithstanding so many evidences which ye have received; yea, even ye have received all things, both things in heaven, and all things which are in the earth, as a witness that they are true.

16–24. The reality of God and Christ as his Son are the two greatest revelations of all eternity. John the Revelator said that "the testimony of Jesus is the spirit of prophecy" (Revelation 19:10). That is to say, no one can have that spirit without that knowledge. Adam testified of Christ; Enoch, Noah, and Abraham did likewise, as did all their faithful followers. Never has there been a prophet of God in any age who was not a special witness of Christ. Never has there been a prophet who did not know that the Messiah would be the literal son of God. All the prophets who have prophesied since the world began have testified of these things (see Jacob 7:11; Mosiah 13:33).

Awaiting the crucified Christ in the world of spirits was an innumerable host of the dead "who had been faithful in the testimony of Jesus while they lived in mortality; and who had offered sacrifice in the similitude of the great sacrifice of the Son of God, and had suffered tribulation in their Redeemer's name. All these had departed the mortal life, firm in the hope of a glorious resurrection, through the grace of God the Father and his Only Begotten Son, Jesus Christ." (D&C 138:12–13.)

17. Abraham saw of his coming] To the perfidious Pharisees, Christ testified, "Your father Abraham rejoiced to see my day: and he saw it, and was glad" (John 8:56). The biblical antecedent to this account is found only in the Joseph Smith Translation, where we read: "It came to pass, that Abram looked forth and saw the days of the Son of Man, and was glad, and his soul found rest, and he believed in the Lord; and the Lord counted it unto him for righteousness" (JST, Genesis 15:12).

18. Order of God . . . after the order of his Son] Book of Mormon prophets referred to that which we call the Melchizedek Priesthood as the "holy order," the "order of God," or the "order of his Son." From modern revelation we know that in ancient times the priesthood was called the Holy Priesthood, after the Order of the Son of God (see D&C 107:3). See commentary on Alma 5:44.

18. A great many thousand years before his coming] The atonement of Jesus Christ is truly endless and eternal. It is infinite. It is timeless, stretching from the period before the world was until the days when mortal time shall be no more. Adam and his children repented of their sins in the name of, and by virtue of the blood shed by, Jesus Christ, precious blood which would not be spilt till four thousand years later.

19. Zenos did testify boldly; for the which he was slain] Judging from the contents of the Book of Mormon, Zenos and Isaiah were the two dominant voices among the prophets recorded on the brass plates. Both died as martyrs. The present text seems to suggest that Zenos, who was fearless in testimony, was slain for teaching the doctrines of redemption through Christ and of his divine sonship.

20. Zenock] An ancient Hebrew prophet, some of whose teachings were recorded in the brass plates. We know nothing of him personally. See also 1 Nephi 19:10; Alma 33:15–16.

20. Ezias] This is the lone Book of Mormon reference to Ezias. We are left to wonder whether perhaps this man is the same as the one called Esaias, a contemporary of Abraham, one who is twice mentioned in the revelations given to Joseph Smith (see D&C 76:100; 84:12–13).

21. All the sons of Zedekiah were put to death except Mulek, a person whom some scholars believe to have been a child at the time of Jerusalem's destruction. The band of Israelites we know as the Mulekites, presumably of the tribe of Judah, left Jerusalem, were led by the Lord to the Americas, and arrived on that continent at about the same time as the Lehites. See 2 Kings 25:7; Omni 1:14–15; Helaman 6:10.

22. Lehi . . . testified of these things] See 1 Nephi 1:18–19.

23. He is God] "My soul delighteth in proving unto my people that save Christ should come all men must perish," Nephi wrote. "For if there be no Christ there be no God; and if there be no God we are not, for there could have been no creation. But *there is a God, and he is Christ,* and he cometh in the fulness of his own time." (2 Nephi 11:6–7, italics added.) Elder Bruce R. McConkie wrote: "*Christ-Messiah is God!* Such is the plain and pure pronouncement of all the prophets of all the ages. In our desire to avoid the false and absurd conclusions contained in the creeds of Christendom, we are wont to shy away from this pure and unadorned verity; we go to great lengths to use language that shows there is both a Father and a Son, that they are separate Persons and are not somehow mystically intertwined as an essence or spirit that is everywhere present. Such an approach is perhaps essential in reasoning with the Gentiles of sectarianism; it helps to overthrow the fallacies formulated in their creeds. But having so done, *if we are to envision our Lord's true status and glory, we must come back to the pronouncement of pronouncements, the doctrine of doctrines, the message of messages, which is that Christ is God. And if it were not so, he could not save us."* (*Promised Messiah,* p. 98, italics added.)

24. Heaven and . . . earth . . . witness that they are true] "The earth rolls up her wings, and the sun giveth his light by day, and the moon giveth her light by night, and the stars also give their light, as they roll upon their wings in their glory, in the midst of the power of God. Unto what shall I liken these kingdoms, that ye may understand? Behold, all these are kingdoms, and any man who hath seen any or the least of these hath seen God moving in his majesty and power." (D&C 88:45–47; compare Alma 30:44.) "All things have their likeness," the Lord said, "and

all things are created and made to bear record of me, both things
which are temporal, and things which are spiritual; things which
are in the heavens above, and things which are on the earth, and
things which are in the earth, and things which are under the
earth, both above and beneath: all things bear record of me"
(Moses 6:63).

Nephi Sustains His Testimony with a Prophecy

Helaman 8:25–28

25. But behold, ye have rejected the truth, and rebelled against your holy God; and even at this time, instead of laying up for yourselves treasures in heaven, where nothing doth corrupt, and where nothing can come which is unclean, ye are heaping up for yourselves wrath against the day of judgment.

26. Yea, even at this time ye are ripening, because of your murders and your fornication and wickedness, for everlasting destruction; yea, and except ye repent it will come unto you soon.

27. Yea, behold it is now even at your doors; yea, go ye in unto the judgment-seat, and search; and behold, your judge is murdered, and he lieth in his blood; and he hath been murdered by his brother, who seeketh to sit in the judgment-seat.

28. And behold, they both belong to your secret band, whose author is Gadianton and the evil one who seeketh to destroy the souls of men.

25. Laying up . . . treasures in heaven] It is a good doctrine
that our works follow us in the worlds to come (see D&C 59:2).
Valiant servants in the cause of God are promised that they "[lay]
up in store" blessings for the world to come (D&C 4:2–4). Indeed,
by such service, James said, the faithful servant could "hide a
multitude of sins" (James 5:20). "Lay not up for yourselves treasures upon earth, where moth and rust doth corrupt, and where
thieves break through and steal: but lay up for yourselves treasures in heaven, . . . for where your treasure is, there will your
heart be also" (Matthew 6:19–21; see also 3 Nephi 13:19–21; compare Luke 12:13–21).

25. Nothing can come which is unclean] See 3 Nephi
27:19.

**25. Ye are heaping up for yourselves wrath against the
day of judgment]** That is, You are denying God, who shall,
unless you repent, deny you at the time of judgment. Those who
become vessels of wrath in this life shall surely inherit the wrath
of an offended God at the time of the final divine decree.

27–28. Patience is a requisite to witnessing the fulfillment of most prophecy. Not so in the present case. Nephi surprises his hearers by telling them that the chief judge, Seezoram, had been murdered by his brother, Seantum, who coveted his office. Runners are then sent to verify the prophecy.

The Place of Signs and Wonders in God's Plan

Helaman 9:1–41

1. Behold, now it came to pass that when Nephi had spoken these words, certain men who were among them ran to the judgment-seat; yea, even there were five who went, and they said among themselves, as they went:

2. Behold, now we will know of a surety whether this man be a prophet and God hath commanded him to prophesy such marvelous things unto us. Behold, we do not believe that he hath; yea, we do not believe that he is a prophet; nevertheless, if this thing which he has said concerning the chief judge be true, that he be dead, then will we believe that the other words which he has spoken are true.

3. And it came to pass that they ran in their might, and came in unto the judgment-seat; and behold, the chief judge had fallen to the earth, and did lie in his blood.

4. And now behold, when they saw this they were astonished exceedingly, insomuch that they fell to the earth; for they had not believed the words which Nephi had spoken concerning the chief judge.

5. But now, when they saw they believed, and fear came upon them lest all the judgments which Nephi had spoken should come upon the people; therefore they did quake, and had fallen to the earth.

6. Now, immediately when the judge had been murdered—he being stabbed by his brother by a garb of secrecy, and he fled, and the servants ran and told the people, raising the cry of murder among them;

7. And behold the people did gather themselves together unto the place of the judgment-seat—and behold, to their astonishment they saw those five men who had fallen to the earth.

8. And now behold, the people knew nothing concerning the multitude who had gathered together at the garden of Nephi; therefore they said among themselves: These men are they who have murdered the judge, and God has smitten them that they could not flee from us.

9. And it came to pass that they laid hold on them, and bound them and cast them into prison. And there was a proclamation sent abroad that the judge was slain, and that the murderers had been taken and were cast into prison.

10. And it came to pass that on the morrow the people did assemble themselves together to mourn and to fast, at the burial of the great chief judge who had been slain.

11. And thus also those judges

who were at the garden of Nephi, and heard his words, were also gathered together at the burial.

12. And it came to pass that they inquired among the people, saying: Where are the five who were sent to inquire concerning the chief judge whether he was dead? And they answered and said: Concerning this five whom ye say ye have sent, we know not; but there are five who are the murderers, whom we have cast into prison.

13. And it came to pass that the judges desired that they should be brought; and they were brought, and behold they were the five who were sent; and behold the judges inquired of them to know concerning the matter, and they told them all that they had done, saying:

14. We ran and came to the place of the judgment-seat, and when we saw all things even as Nephi had testified, we were astonished insomuch that we fell to the earth; and when we were recovered from our astonishment, behold they cast us into prison.

15. Now, as for the murder of this man, we know not who has done it; and only this much we know, we ran and came according as ye desired, and behold he was dead, according to the words of Nephi.

16. And now it came to pass that the judges did expound the matter unto the people, and did cry out against Nephi, saying: Behold, we know that this Nephi must have agreed with some one to slay the judge, and then he might declare it unto us, that he might convert us unto his faith, that he might raise himself to be a great man, chosen of God, and a prophet.

17. And now behold, we will detect this man, and he shall confess his fault and make known unto us the true murderer of this judge.

18. And it came to pass that the five were liberated on the day of the burial. Nevertheless, they did rebuke the judges in the words which they had spoken against Nephi, and did contend with them one by one, insomuch that they did confound them.

19. Nevertheless, they caused that Nephi should be taken and bound and brought before the multitude, and they began to question him in divers ways that they might cross him, that they might accuse him to death—

20. Saying unto him: Thou art confederate; who is this man that hath done this murder? Now tell us, and acknowledge thy fault; saying, Behold here is money; and also we will grant unto thee thy life if thou wilt tell us, and acknowledge the agreement which thou hast made with him.

21. But Nephi said unto them: O ye fools, ye uncircumcised of heart, ye blind, and ye stiffnecked people, do ye know how long the Lord your God will suffer you that ye shall go on in this your way of sin?

22. O ye ought to begin to howl and mourn, because of the great destruction which at this time doth await you, except ye shall repent.

23. Behold ye say that I have agreed with a man that he should murder Seezoram, our chief judge. But behold, I say unto you, that this is because I have testified unto you that ye might know concerning this thing; yea, even for a witness unto you, that I did know of the wickedness and

abominations which are among you.

24. And because I have done this, ye say that I have agreed with a man that he should do this thing; yea, because I showed unto you this sign ye are angry with me, and seek to destroy my life.

25. And now behold, I will show unto you another sign, and see if ye will in this thing seek to destroy me.

26. Behold I say unto you: Go to the house of Seantum, who is the brother of Seezoram, and say unto him—

27. Has Nephi, the pretended prophet, who doth prophesy so much evil concerning this people, agreed with thee, in the which ye have murdered Seezoram, who is your brother?

28. And behold, he shall say unto you, Nay.

29. And ye shall say unto him: Have ye murdered your brother?

30. And he shall stand with fear, and wist not what to say. And behold, he shall deny unto you; and he shall make as if he were astonished; nevertheless, he shall declare unto you that he is innocent.

31. But behold, ye shall examine him, and ye shall find blood upon the skirts of his cloak.

32. And when ye have seen this, ye shall say: From whence cometh this blood? Do we not know that it is the blood of your brother?

33. And then shall he tremble, and shall look pale, even as if death had come upon him.

34. And then shall ye say: Because of this fear and this paleness which has come upon your face, behold, we know that thou art guilty.

35. And then shall greater fear come upon him; and then shall he confess unto you, and deny no more that he has done this murder.

36. And then shall he say unto you, that I, Nephi, know nothing concerning the matter save it were given unto me by the power of God. And then shall ye know that I am an honest man, and that I am sent unto you from God.

37. And it came to pass that they went and did, even according as Nephi had said unto them. And behold, the words which he had said were true; for according to the words he did deny; and also according to the words he did confess.

38. And he was brought to prove that he himself was the very murderer, insomuch that the five were set at liberty, and also was Nephi.

39. And there were some of the Nephites who believed on the words of Nephi; and there were some also, who believed because of the testimony of the five, for they had been converted while they were in prison.

40. And now there were some among the people, who said that Nephi was a prophet.

41. And there were others who said: Behold, he is a god, for except he was a god he could not know of all things. For behold, he has told us the thoughts of our hearts, and also has told us things; and even he has brought unto our knowledge the true murderer of our chief judge.

1–41. Signs are the language of God, angels, and prophets.

Their purpose may be to communicate the approbation of heaven, as in the promise that signs will follow them that believe (D&C 84:65–73; Mark 16:17–18), or to dramatize divine displeasure, as with the plagues of Egypt (Exodus 4:8 ff). In the scriptural sense, a "sign" is something by which another thing is shown or represented, and this often in a miraculous manner. Numerous words share a close kinship with it and thus constitute commentary on its meaning. They include *signal, signature, signify,* and *ensign.* Companion words include *token, mark,* and *wonder.* Signs and wonders are a word-combination that appear frequently in the scriptures.

The word *wonder* appears about thirty-five times in the Old Testament, and in more than half of these instances it is used as a synonym for the word *sign* (see Deuteronomy 28:45-46; Ezekiel 12:6, 11). As used by Isaiah in reference to the great "marvellous work and a wonder" of the last days, the word *wonder* carries with it the idea of a "miraculous" event (see Isaiah 29:14). Indeed, the Book of Mormon has been given to our dispensation as a "sign" and "wonder" to attest the verity of the restoration of the gospel (see 3 Nephi 21:1–7; Ether 4:17). All gospel dispensations are associated with signs or confirmatory evidence of their genuineness.

As the Book of Mormon was given as a sign or wonder attesting to all honest truth-seekers the authenticity of the Restoration, so Joseph Smith, in harmony with the scriptural pattern, was given a sign to confirm the verity of all that Moroni told him. The sign was that when it became known that the Lord had entrusted him with this ancient record, the workers of iniquity would seek his overthrow. "They will circulate falsehoods to destroy your reputation," Moroni said, "and also will seek to take your life; but remember this, if you are faithful, and shall hereafter continue to keep the commandments of the Lord, you shall be preserved to bring these things forth; for in due time he will again give you a commandment to come and take them. When they are interpreted the Lord will give the holy priesthood to some, and they shall begin to proclaim this gospel and baptize by water, and after that they shall have power to give the Holy Ghost by the laying on of their hands. *Then will persecution rage more and more; for the iniquities of men shall be revealed, and those who are not built upon the Rock will seek to overthrow this church; but it will increase the more opposed, and spread farther and farther,* increasing in knowledge till they shall be sanctified and receive an inheritance where the glory of God will rest upon them." (*Messenger and Advocate* 2:199, italics added.)

All revelation is itself a miracle, for revelation is not the child of natural causes. It is an eternal verity that God can be known only by revelation, and thus it naturally follows that all we know about our Eternal Father comes to us, as did the Book of Mormon, in the form of a sign or wonder. So it is with the establishment of all dispensations and the call of all prophets. Each has its attendant signs. With Moses it was first the burning bush; then the rod that became a serpent; following that, the hand that turned leprous and was healed again (see Exodus 3 and 4). Gideon thought it not improper to test his call to save Israel by requiring the Lord to dampen his fleece during the night while leaving the surrounding ground dry, and then asked to have the process reversed the following night (Judges 6:36–40). So familiar was this principle that Hezekiah, when Isaiah promised him an extension of his life, asked, "What shall be the sign that the Lord will heal me?" Isaiah responded by asking the king if he would choose to have the shadow on the dial go forward ten degrees or back ten degrees. Hezekiah chose to have the shadow go backward, and so it was done. (See 2 Kings 20:8–11.)

As a host of signs have been given us by which we are to know the time of Christ's return, so the ancients were given many signs by which they were to have known the time of his birth. These signs included such things as the shepherds being told they would find the Christ Child wrapped in swaddling clothes and lying in a manger (Luke 2:12), as well as the marvel of a new star in the heavens which the wise men from the East followed, that they might bring gifts to their newborn king (Matthew 2:1–10). Samuel, the Lamanite prophet, was the instrument for bringing forth marvelous prophecies among the Nephites, identifying the time of Christ's birth and the signs incident to that birth and to his crucifixion (see Helaman 14).

Let it suffice to say that prophets establishing the legitimacy of their prophetic office and the message they have been commissioned to bring, as Nephi does in the instance of this chapter, are an inseparable part of the very system by which the heavens communicate with mortals. Signs are and ever have been tokens of divine authority and power.

41. Excessive religious zeal is as dangerous to the salvation of men as stubborn unbelief. Any virtue overdone becomes a vice. To honor and reverence the Lord's anointed is a requisite of salvation; to deify them is to falsify their nature and to pervert the message with which they are entrusted. It is to make of them the object of worship in place of the God who gave us life. This most damning and dangerous practice also finds expression in the deifying of the words of the prophets. The Pharisees of Jesus' day had done this with the law of Moses. Their reverence was for the law rather than for the Lawgiver. They bowed the knee to the law while crucifying him of whom it testified. In our day there are those who do much the same thing, wherein they make all man-

ner of claims for the Bible which it does not make for itself,
including the idea that it is complete, final, inerrant and infallible.
The effect of such verbal shrines and theological pilgrimages is to
divert worship from the only true and living God to salvation in a
book, rather than in the injunction of the Master who said,
"Follow me" (Matthew 4:19).

Nephi Granted the Sealing Power

Helaman 10:1–10

1. And it came to pass that there arose a division among the people, insomuch that they divided hither and thither and went their ways, leaving Nephi alone, as he was standing in the midst of them.

2. And it came to pass that Nephi went his way towards his own house, pondering upon the things which the Lord had shown unto him.

3. And it came to pass as he was thus pondering—being much cast down because of the wickedness of the people of the Nephites, their secret works of darkness, and their murderings, and their plunderings, and all manner of iniquities—and it came to pass as he was thus pondering in his heart, behold, a voice came unto him saying:

4. Blessed art thou, Nephi, for those things which thou hast done; for I have beheld how thou hast with unwearyingness declared the word, which I have given unto thee, unto this people. And thou hast not feared them, and hast not sought thine own life, but hast sought my will, and to keep my commandments.

5. And now, because thou hast done this with such unwearyingness, behold, I will bless thee forever; and I will make thee mighty in word and in deed, in faith and in works; yea, even that all things shall be done unto thee according to thy word, for thou shalt not ask that which is contrary to my will.

6. Behold, thou art Nephi, and I am God. Behold, I declare it unto thee in the presence of mine angels, that ye shall have power over this people, and shall smite the earth with famine, and with pestilence, and destruction, according to the wickedness of this people.

7. Behold, I give unto you power, that whatsoever ye shall seal on earth shall be sealed in heaven; and whatsoever ye shall loose on earth shall be loosed in heaven; and thus shall ye have power among this people.

8. And thus, if ye shall say unto this temple it shall be rent in twain, it shall be done.

9. And if ye shall say unto this mountain, Be thou cast down and become smooth, it shall be done.

10. And behold, if ye shall say that God shall smite this people, it shall come to pass.

2. Pondering] To ponder is to give serious reflection and thought to something; it is to weigh that which is ponderous in our minds. Such an attitude of spiritual searching has consistently proven to be the seedbed of revelation. See 1 Nephi 11:1; D&C 76:19; 138:11; Joseph Smith—History 1:11–12.

4. Nephi is to be greatly blessed because he has been a fearless and tireless teacher of the gospel. He has taught with that power known only to those who are entirely true to the message they have been commissioned to bear. As the Lord praises Nephi for his devoted discipleship, so has he cause to rebuke others. "With some I am not well pleased, for they will not open their mouths, but they hide the talent which I have given unto them, because of the fear of man. Wo unto such, for mine anger is kindled against them. And it shall come to pass, if they are not more faithful unto me, it shall be taken away, even that which they have." (D&C 60:2–3.)

4. Hast not sought thine own life] Those who have an eye single to the glory of God seek, like their Master, to do only those things which please the Father (see John 8:29). They strive to know the will of God and then proceed to do it. They have no secret or private agenda, no desire to "do their own thing," no yearning for personal applause or self-aggrandizement.

5. I will bless thee forever] Even the timeless waves of eternity will not be able to wear away the blessings that God will place on the head of his faithful servant.

5. Mighty in word and in deed] Nephi's words were to be God's words. Nephi's works were to be God's works. Thus he would be mighty in word and deed, a mortal type and representative of the Almighty.

5. All things shall be done unto thee according to thy word] So complete is the trust that God has in Nephi, so perfect is the assurance that he would not do or say anything contrary to the divine will, that Nephi is granted the promise that all that he asks, all that he says, and all that he does in the name of the Lord will be honored. What Nephi prays for he will get, because his hands are clean and his heart pure. His prayers and his deepest yearnings are directed and motivated by the Holy Spirit. "He that asketh in the Spirit asketh according to the will of God; wherefore it is done even as he asketh" (D&C 46:30). Further: "And if ye are purified and cleansed from all sin, ye shall ask whatsoever you will in the name of Jesus and it shall be done. But know this, it shall be given you what you shall ask." (D&C 50:29–30.) This latter scriptural passage seems to have at least two possible meanings: first, those who pray in the Spirit have it given to them— revealed to them—what they should pray for; second, those who so live as to come under the influence of this marvelous grace and Christian discipline—these are they who receive what they pray for. Like Nephi, their hearts cry out only for the right things.

John the Beloved explained: "If our heart condemn us not,
then have we confidence toward God. And whatsoever we ask,
we receive of him, because we keep his commandments, and do
those things that are pleasing in his sight." (1 John 3:21–22.) Enos
likewise wrote: "And it came to pass that after I had prayed and
labored with all diligence, the Lord said unto me: I will grant unto
thee according to thy desires, because of thy faith" (Enos 1:12).

6. The keys of the sealing power spoken of in verse seven are
the same as those held by the prophet Elijah. It was by the
authority of these keys that he sealed the heavens for three and a
half years, and by that same authority broke that seal and brought
forth rain (see 1 Kings 17:1; 18:1, 45). Thus it was within his
power to cause a famine to come upon his land. The authority to
bring forth blessings is also the authority to withhold blessings.
The power to bless is also the power to curse. Of his servants in
this day, the Lord has said that those who "go forth, bearing these
tidings unto the inhabitants of the earth, to them is power given
to seal both on earth and in heaven, the unbelieving and rebellious; yea, verily, to seal them up unto the day when the wrath of
God shall be poured out upon the wicked without measure" (D&C
1:8–9). It was Elijah who conferred these keys upon Peter, James,
and John on the Mount of Transfiguration (see Matthew 17:3;
Teachings, p. 158) and who also conferred them upon Joseph
Smith and Oliver Cowdery (D&C 110:13–16).

**7. Whatsoever ye shall seal on earth shall be sealed in
heaven]** Such was the promise granted Peter by the Savior. "I will
give unto thee the keys of the kingdom of heaven: and whatsoever thou shalt bind on earth shall be bound in heaven: and whatsoever thou shalt loose on earth shall be loosed in heaven"
(Matthew 16:19). These keys were subsequently given to each
member of the Twelve (see John 20:23) and the same keys were
restored to Joseph Smith, to whom the Lord said: "I have conferred upon you the keys and power of the priesthood, wherein I
restore all things, and make known unto you all things in due
time. And verily, verily, I say unto you, that whatsoever you seal
on earth shall be sealed in heaven; and whatsoever you bind on
earth, in my name and by my word, saith the Lord, it shall be
eternally bound in the heavens; and whosesoever sins you remit
on earth shall be remitted eternally in the heavens; and whosesoever sins you retain on earth shall be retained in heaven. And
again, verily I say, whomsoever you bless I will bless, and whomsoever you curse I will curse, saith the Lord; for I, the Lord, am
thy God." (D&C 132:45–47.)

It is unlikely that this is the first time that the keys of the
priesthood were granted to a Nephite prophet-leader; more likely,

this is simply the first mention of it. We would suppose that Lehi, as a leader of the Nephite dispensation, was given the keys of the kingdom. Nephi and Jacob and Mosiah and Alma and Mormon and Moroni—many of the Nephite prophets—surely had the directing power, the right of presidency, the keys of the kingdom, bestowed upon them. The fact that temples were established among the Nephites early in their history (see 2 Nephi 5:16) suggests that sealings and marriages and ordinances of the Melchizedek Priesthood were a part of their religious life.

Nephi Led by the Spirit from Congregation to Congregation

Helaman 10:11–19

11. And now behold, I command you, that ye shall go and declare unto this people, that thus saith the Lord God, who is the Almighty: Except ye repent ye shall be smitten, even unto destruction.

12. And behold, now it came to pass that when the Lord had spoken these words unto Nephi, he did stop and did not go unto his own house, but did return unto the multitudes who were scattered about upon the face of the land, and began to declare unto them the word of the Lord which had been spoken unto him, concerning their destruction if they did not repent.

13. Now behold, notwithstanding that great miracle which Nephi had done in telling them concerning the death of the chief judge, they did harden their hearts and did not hearken unto the words of the Lord.

14. Therefore Nephi did declare unto them the word of the Lord, saying: Except ye repent, thus saith the Lord, ye shall be smitten even unto destruction.

15. And it came to pass that when Nephi had declared unto them the word, behold, they did still harden their hearts and would not hearken unto his words; therefore they did revile against him, and did seek to lay their hands upon him that they might cast him into prison.

16. But behold, the power of God was with him, and they could not take him to cast him into prison, for he was taken by the Spirit and conveyed away out of the midst of them.

17. And it came to pass that thus he did go forth in the Spirit, from multitude to multitude, declaring the word of God, even until he had declared it unto them all, or sent it forth among all the people.

18. And it came to pass that they would not hearken unto his words; and there began to be contentions, insomuch that they were divided against themselves and began to slay one another with the sword.

19. And thus ended the seventy and first year of the reign of the judges over the people of Nephi.

13. "Faith cometh not by signs, but signs follow those that believe" (D&C 63:9).

16–17. Nephi, the son of Lehi, attested to having been ministered to by angels and added: "Upon the wings of his Spirit hath my body been carried away upon exceedingly high mountains. And mine eyes have beheld great things, yea, even too great for man; therefore I was bidden that I should not write them." (2 Nephi 4:25.) Moses, we are told, was caught up in a like manner "into an exceedingly high mountain," where he conversed with God face to face (see Moses 1:1–2). Ezekiel shared similar experiences, having been transported from captivity in Babylon to the temple mount in Jerusalem (see Ezekiel 40:2). The Savior himself was carried by the Spirit to and from the wilderness of Judea to the pinnacle of the temple in Jerusalem and also to "an exceeding high mountain" (JST, Matthew 4:5, 8). Philip was transported by the Spirit of the Lord in order to fill missionary appointments (Acts 8:39). John the Revelator also testified that an angel of the Lord "carried me away in the spirit to a great and high mountain, and shewed me that great city, the holy Jerusalem, descending out of heaven" (Revelation 21:10).

Nephi Seals the Heavens That There Might Be Famine

Helaman 11:1–23

1. And now it came to pass in the seventy and second year of the reign of the judges that the contentions did increase, insomuch that there were wars throughout all the land among all the people of Nephi.

2. And it was this secret band of robbers who did carry on this work of destruction and wickedness. And this war did last all that year; and in the seventy and third year it did also last.

3. And it came to pass that in this year Nephi did cry unto the Lord, saying:

4. O Lord, do not suffer that this people shall be destroyed by the sword; but O Lord, rather let there be a famine in the land, to stir them up in remembrance of

the Lord their God, and perhaps they will repent and turn unto thee.

5. And so it was done, according to the words of Nephi. And there was a great famine upon the land, among all the people of Nephi. And thus in the seventy and fourth year the famine did continue, and the work of destruction did cease by the sword but became sore by famine.

6. And this work of destruction did also continue in the seventy and fifth year. For the earth was smitten that it was dry, and did not yield forth grain in the season of grain; and the whole earth was smitten, even among the Lamanites as well as among the Nephites, so that they were

smitten that they did perish by thousands in the more wicked parts of the land.

7. And it came to pass that the people saw that they were about to perish by famine, and they began to remember the Lord their God; and they began to remember the words of Nephi.

8. And the people began to plead with their chief judges and their leaders, that they would say unto Nephi: Behold, we know that thou art a man of God, and therefore cry unto the Lord our God that he turn away from us this famine, lest all the words which thou hast spoken concerning our destruction be fulfilled.

9. And it came to pass that the judges did say unto Nephi, according to the words which had been desired. And it came to pass that when Nephi saw that the people had repented and did humble themselves in sackcloth, he cried again unto the Lord, saying:

10. O Lord, behold this people repenteth; and they have swept away the band of Gadianton from amongst them insomuch that they have become extinct, and they have concealed their secret plans in the earth.

11. Now, O Lord, because of this their humility wilt thou turn away thine anger, and let thine anger be appeased in the destruction of those wicked men whom thou hast already destroyed.

12. O Lord, wilt thou turn away thine anger, yea, thy fierce anger, and cause that this famine may cease in this land.

13. O Lord, wilt thou hearken unto me, and cause that it may be done according to my words, and send forth rain upon the face of the earth, that she may bring forth her fruit, and her grain in the season of grain.

14. O Lord, thou didst hearken unto my words when I said, Let there be a famine, that the pestilence of the sword might cease; and I know that thou wilt, even at this time, hearken unto my words, for thou saidst that: If this people repent I will spare them.

15. Yea, O Lord, and thou seest that they have repented, because of the famine and the pestilence and destruction which has come unto them.

16. And now, O Lord, wilt thou turn away thine anger, and try again if they will serve thee? And if so, O Lord, thou canst bless them according to thy words which thou hast said.

17. And it came to pass that in the seventy and sixth year the Lord did turn away his anger from the people, and caused that rain should fall upon the earth, insomuch that it did bring forth her fruit in the season of her fruit. And it came to pass that it did bring forth her grain in the season of her grain.

18. And behold, the people did rejoice and glorify God, and the whole face of the land was filled with rejoicing; and they did no more seek to destroy Nephi, but they did esteem him as a great prophet, and a man of God, having great power and authority given unto him from God.

19. And behold, Lehi, his brother, was not a whit behind him as to things pertaining to righteousness.

20. And thus it did come to pass that the people of Nephi began to prosper again in the land, and began to build up their waste places, and began to multiply and

spread, even until they did cover the whole face of the land, both on the northward and on the southward, from the sea west to the sea east.

21. And it came to pass that the seventy and sixth year did end in peace. And the seventy and seventh year began in peace; and the church did spread throughout the face of all the land; and the more part of the people, both the Nephites and the Lamanites, did belong to the church; and they did have exceedingly great peace in the land; and thus ended the seventy and seventh year.

22. And also they had peace in the seventy and eighth year, save it were a few contentions concerning the points of doctrine which had been laid down by the prophets.

23. And in the seventy and ninth year there began to be much strife. But it came to pass that Nephi and Lehi, and many of their brethren who knew concerning the true points of doctrine, having many revelations daily, therefore they did preach unto the people, insomuch that they did put an end to their strife in that same year.

1–23. Famine is one of heaven's most eloquent sermons. When virtually all else has failed to get the attention of the rebellious and turn them to God, famines have succeeded. Famines can strip men of every sense of self-sufficiency and turn their eyes and ears to the voice of heaven. (See Isaiah 51:19; Jeremiah 14:13–18; Amos 4:6.) In this story it seems that Nephi felt that the people simply did not see the connection between devastating war and their sinful ways.

By way of warning to the Saints of the last days, the Savior said: "Behold I speak for mine elect's sake; for nation shall rise against nation, and kingdom against kingdom; there shall be famines, and pestilences, and earthquakes, in divers places" (Joseph Smith—Matthew 1:29). The Lord inquired: "How oft have I called upon you by the mouth of my servants, and by the ministering of angels, and by mine own voice, and by the voice of thunderings, and by the voice of lightnings, and by the voice of tempests, and by the voice of earthquakes, and great hailstorms, and by the voice of famines and pestilences of every kind, and by the great sound of a trump, and by the voice of judgment, and by the voice of mercy all the day long, and by the voice of glory and honor and the riches of eternal life, and would have saved you with an everlasting salvation, but ye would not!" (D&C 43:25.) Again to the rebellious in this day the Lord has said: "There are none to deliver you; for ye obeyed not my voice when I called to you out of the heavens; ye believed not my servants, and when they were sent unto you ye received them not. Wherefore, they sealed up the testimony and bound up the law, and ye were delivered over unto darkness." (D&C 133:71–72.)

19. Our account, Mormon's abridgment, is one that stresses the life and labors of Nephi. His brother, Lehi, was of the same spiritual calibre—he walked in the light of the Spirit, sought out the will of the Lord and did it, and enjoyed the powers and gifts of heaven.

23. There is a definite relationship between knowing the "true points of doctrine" and "having many revelations daily." Knowledge alone is not a barometer of righteousness, but certain knowledge, when learned and lived, points one toward that redemption which is in Christ and the abundant life that is available to the true disciple. In addition, those who know the doctrines of salvation teach the doctrines of salvation. There is strength in their testimony and power in their words. "Those who preach by the power of the Holy Ghost," Elder Bruce R. McConkie has written, "use the scriptures as their basic source of knowledge and doctrine. They begin with what the Lord has before revealed to other inspired men. But it is the practice of the Lord to give added knowledge to those upon whose hearts the true meanings and intents of the scriptures have been impressed. Many great doctrinal revelations come to those who preach from the scriptures. When they are in tune with the Infinite, the Lord lets them know, first, the full and complete meaning of the scriptures they are expounding, and then he ofttimes expands their views so that new truths flood in upon them, and they learn added things that those who do not follow such a course can never know." (*Promised Messiah*, pp. 515–16.)

The Wickedness of Gadianton Revived

Helaman 11:24–38

24. And it came to pass that in the eightieth year of the reign of the judges over the people of Nephi, there were a certain number of the dissenters from the people of Nephi, who had some years before gone over unto the Lamanites, and taken upon themselves the name of Lamanites, and also a certain number who were real descendants of the Lamanites, being stirred up to anger by them, or by those dissenters, therefore they commenced a war with their brethren.

25. And they did commit murder and plunder; and then they would retreat back into the mountains, and into the wilderness and secret places, hiding themselves that they could not be discovered, receiving daily an addition to their numbers, inasmuch as there were dissenters that went forth unto them.

26. And thus in time, yea, even in the space of not many years, they became an exceedingly great band of robbers; and they did search out all the secret plans of

Gadianton; and thus they became robbers of Gadianton.

27. Now behold, these robbers did make great havoc, yea, even great destruction among the people of Nephi, and also among the people of the Lamanites.

28. And it came to pass that it was expedient that there should be a stop put to this work of destruction; therefore they sent an army of strong men into the wilderness and upon the mountains to search out this band of robbers, and to destroy them.

29. But behold, it came to pass that in that same year they were driven back even into their own lands. And thus ended the eightieth year of the reign of the judges over the people of Nephi.

30. And it came to pass in the commencement of the eighty and first year they did go forth again against this band of robbers, and did destroy many; and they were also visited with much destruction.

31. And they were again obliged to return out of the wilderness and out of the mountains unto their own lands, because of the exceeding greatness of the numbers of those robbers who infested the mountains and the wilderness.

32. And it came to pass that thus ended this year. And the rob-

bers did still increase and wax strong, insomuch that they did defy the whole armies of the Nephites, and also of the Lamanites; and they did cause great fear to come unto the people upon all the face of the land.

33. Yea, for they did visit many parts of the land, and did do great destruction unto them; yea, did kill many, and did carry away others captive into the wilderness, yea, and more especially their women and their children.

34. Now this great evil, which came unto the people because of their iniquity, did stir them up again in remembrance of the Lord their God.

35. And thus ended the eighty and first year of the reign of the judges.

36. And in the eighty and second year they began again to forget the Lord their God. And in the eighty and third year they began to wax strong in iniquity. And in the eighty and fourth year they did not mend their ways.

37. And it came to pass in the eighty and fifth year they did wax stronger and stronger in their pride, and in their wickedness; and thus they were ripening again for destruction.

38. And thus ended the eighty and fifth year.

24–38. Joseph Smith taught that gospel dispensations were always opposed by counter-dispensations. It is not the lot of faith, righteousness, and all attendant principles to go unopposed. As the light of day is followed by the dark of night, so the light of the gospel will be opposed by the prince of darkness. As the Saints gather in holy places to receive holy instruction, so the wicked assemble in their dark chambers to swear oaths and design their secret plans.

Man's Disobedient Nature

Helaman 12:1–6

1. And thus we can behold how false, and also the unsteadiness of the hearts of the children of men; yea, we can see that the Lord in his great infinite goodness doth bless and prosper those who put their trust in him.

2. Yea, and we may see at the very time when he doth prosper his people, yea, in the increase of their fields, their flocks and their herds, and in gold, and in silver, and in all manner of precious things of every kind and art; sparing their lives, and delivering them out of the hands of their enemies; softening the hearts of their enemies that they should not declare wars against them; yea, and in fine, doing all things for the welfare and happiness of his people; yea, then is the time that they do harden their hearts, and do forget the Lord their God, and do trample under their feet the Holy One—yea, and this because of their ease, and their exceedingly great prosperity.

3. And thus we see that except the Lord doth chasten his people with many afflictions, yea, except he doth visit them with death and with terror, and with famine and with all manner of pestilence, they will not remember him.

4. O how foolish, and how vain, and how evil, and devilish, and how quick to do iniquity, and how slow to do good, are the children of men; yea, how quick to hearken unto the words of the evil one, and to set their hearts upon the vain things of the world!

5. Yea, how quick to be lifted up in pride; yea, how quick to boast, and do all manner of that which is iniquity; and how slow are they to remember the Lord their God, and to give ear unto his counsels, yea, how slow to walk in wisdom's paths!

6. Behold, they do not desire that the Lord their God, who hath created them, should rule and reign over them; notwithstanding his great goodness and his mercy towards them, they do set at naught his counsels, and they will not that he should be their guide.

1. Unsteadiness of the hearts of the children of men] Mormon here begins a series of personal musings on the pathetic and pitiful plight of fallen man. With so many of the lessons of the immediately preceding events (Helaman 1–11) before him, he bemoans the fact that man, in roller-coaster fashion, is so very prone to wax and wane in his devotion to God and his commitment to the good. Book of Mormon prophets described spiritual maturity and stability as being "steadfast" or "steady" (see *Commentary* 2:162). Conversely, unsteadiness is to be as the reed driven with the winds of social clamor and to be as unpredictable as spring weather—running both hot and cold.

1. Put their trust in him] "Trust in the Lord with all thine heart," the proverb admonishes, "and lean not unto thine own understanding. In all thy ways acknowledge him, and he shall direct thy paths." (Proverbs 3:5–6.) Two of the most significant questions a member of the Church of Jesus Christ can ask are: In whom do I trust? On whom do I rely? That is, in the spirit of unnatural, unproductive, overmuch self-reliance am I more prone to trust in my own unaided efforts or am I willing to place my whole allegiance in Christ the Lord? True Saints rely wholly, they rely alone, upon the merits of Christ, the author and finisher of our faith (see 2 Nephi 31:19; Moroni 6:4).

2–6. How strange it is that though we rejoice in the richness of the fruits of the tree of everlasting life we often forget quickly him who planted the tree. Frequently it follows that the richer the harvest and the greater the variety of fruits, the more quickly we forget and the more susceptible we become to such plights as pride and vanity. Our hearts become so hard, our ears and eyes so dull, that in order to get our attention the Lord must shout at us with such afflictions as death, terror, famine, and pestilences of all kinds. Many become like the wayward children of Adam, of whom it is said that they "loved Satan more than God." The text does not suggest that they had no love for God, only that they loved Satan more. They became intoxicated with wine made of the grapes of carnality, sensuality, and devilishness. (See Moses 5:13.)

2. Then is the time that they do harden their hearts] Too often, the Savior indicated, the people of the covenant are "slow to hearken unto the voice of the Lord their God; therefore, the Lord their God is slow to hearken unto their prayers, to answer them in the day of their trouble. In the day of their peace they esteemed lightly my counsel; but, in the day of their trouble, of necessity they feel after me." (D&C 101:7–8; compare Jeremiah 22:21.)

2. Trample under their feet the Holy One] "The things which some men esteem to be of great worth, both to the body and soul, others set at naught and trample under their feet. Yea, even the very God of Israel do men trample under their feet; I say, trample under their feet but I would speak in other words—they set him at naught, and hearken not to the voice of his counsels." (1 Nephi 19:7; see also Alma 5:53.)

3–5. Mormon here ponders and laments over the fact that people are by nature slow to embrace righteousness but eager to sin. Indeed, one of the things the God of Israel hates is "feet that be swift in running to mischief" (Proverbs 6:18).

6. Through Isaiah the Lord Jehovah spoke anciently: "I have spread out my hands all the day unto a rebellious people, which walketh in a way that was not good, after their own thoughts" (Isaiah 65:2). In our day that same Lord has declared: "They seek not the Lord to establish his righteousness, but every man walk-eth in his own way, and after the image of his own god, whose image is in the likeness of the world, and whose substance is that of an idol, which waxeth old and shall perish in Babylon, even Babylon the great, which shall fall" (D&C 1:16).

The Power of God's Word

Helaman 12:7–26

7. O how great is the nothing-ness of the children of men; yea, even they are less than the dust of the earth.

8. For behold, the dust of the earth moveth hither and thither, to the dividing asunder, at the command of our great and ever-lasting God.

9. Yea, behold at his voice do the hills and the mountains trem-ble and quake.

10. And by the power of his voice they are broken up, and become smooth, yea, even like unto a valley.

11. Yea, by the power of his voice doth the whole earth shake;

12. Yea, by the power of his voice, do the foundations rock, even to the very center.

13. Yea, and if he say unto the earth—Move—it is moved.

14. Yea, if he say unto the earth—Thou shalt go back, that it lengthen out the day for many hours—it is done;

15. And thus, according to his word the earth goeth back, and it appeareth unto man that the sun standeth still; yea, and behold, this is so; for surely it is the earth that moveth and not the sun.

16. And behold, also, if he say unto the waters of the great deep—Be thou dried up—it is done.

17. Behold, if he say unto this mountain—Be thou raised up, and come over and fall upon that city, that it be buried up—behold it is done.

18. And behold, if a man hide up a treasure in the earth, and the Lord shall say—Let it be accursed, because of the iniquity of him who hath hid it up—behold, it shall be accursed.

19. And if the Lord shall say—Be thou accursed, that no man shall find thee from this time henceforth and forever—behold, no man getteth it henceforth and forever.

20. And behold, if the Lord shall say unto a man—Because of thine iniquities, thou shalt be accursed forever—it shall be done.

21. And if the Lord shall say—Because of thine iniquities thou shalt be cut off from my pres-ence—he will cause that it shall be so.

22. And wo unto him to whom he shall say this, for it shall be unto him that will do iniquity, and he cannot be saved; there-fore, for this cause, that men might be saved, hath repentance been declared.

23. Therefore, blessed are they who will repent and hearken unto the voice of the Lord their God; for these are they that shall be saved.

24. And may God grant, in his great fulness, that men might be brought unto repentance and

good works, that they might be
restored unto grace for grace,
according to their works.

25. And I would that all men
might be saved. But we read that
in the great and last day there are
some who shall be cast out, yea,
who shall be cast off from the
presence of the Lord;

26. Yea, who shall be consigned
to a state of endless misery, fulfilling the words which say: They
that have done good shall
have everlasting life; and they
that have done evil shall have
everlasting damnation. And thus
it is. Amen.

7–26. God, who is the creator of all things, has dominion and
power over them. When God speaks, all that is of God hears and
responds. "For I am the Lord thy God; I dwell in heaven; the earth
is my footstool; I stretch my hand over the sea, and it obeys my
voice; I cause the wind and the fire to be my chariot; I say to the
mountains—Depart hence—and behold, they are taken away by a
whirlwind, in an instance, suddenly" (Abraham 2:7).

The priesthood of God—which, when granted to man, is the
authority to speak and act in the stead of Deity—has from the earliest of times been understood to embrace the power to do the
kinds of things listed in these verses by Mormon. The Lord told
Enoch: "Every one being ordained after this order and calling
should have power, by faith, to break mountains, to divide the
seas, to dry up waters, to turn them out of their course; to put at
defiance the armies of nations, to divide the earth, to break every
band, to stand in the presence of God; to do all things according to
his will, according to his command, subdue principalities and
powers; and this by the will of the Son of God which was from
before the foundation of the world" (JST, Genesis 14:30–31).

"So great was the faith of Enoch that he led the people of God,
and their enemies came to battle against them; and he spake the
word of the Lord, and the earth trembled, and the mountains fled,
even according to his command; and the rivers of water were
turned out of their course; and the roar of the lions was heard out
of the wilderness; and all nations feared greatly, so powerful was
the word of Enoch, and so great was the power of the language
which God had given him" (Moses 7:13).

7–8. Having had the vastness of God's creations revealed to
him, having obtained some sense of God's glory and power, Moses
declared: "Man is nothing, which thing I never had supposed." As
mortal men, we have every claim upon the virtue of humility.
Nevertheless, when Satan sought to have Moses worship him,
Moses, as a result of the same experience in which he had learned
of his own nothingness, responded with the incredulous question,
"Who are thou?" and then added, "I am a son of God, in the
similitude of his Only Begotten." (Moses 1:10, 13.)

In one sense, then, we come to see ourselves as less than the dust of the earth as we, like the people of Benjamin, view ourselves in our carnal and unredeemed state, as we realize our absolute need for the Redeemer (see Mosiah 4:1–2). Here Mormon explains another way in which the children of men are less than the dust of the earth—the inanimate dust of the earth obeys when God speaks, whereas the highest of the animate creation, man, so often fails to hearken to and obey the word of the Lord. See commentary on Mosiah 4:5.

9–13. One of the great prophecies that attends the transition of this earth from its present telestial state to the Edenic or paradisiacal state of the Millennium is that of the mountains being made low and the valleys being brought up (see Isaiah 40:4; JST, Luke 3:10). "It shall be a voice as the voice of many waters, and as the voice of a great thunder, which shall break down the mountains, and the valleys shall not be found. He shall command the great deep, and it shall be driven back into the north countries, and the islands shall become one land; and the land of Jerusalem and the land of Zion shall be turned back into their own place, and the earth shall be like as it was in the days before it was divided." (D&C 133:22–24.)

14–15. Reference is here made to the biblical account that shows Joshua commanding the sun and the moon to stand still so that his army might complete their rout of the Amorites (Joshua 10:12–14). Here a corrective note is added to that account, which supposed the sun to rotate around a stationery earth. (See also Isaiah 38:7–8; 2 Kings 20:8–11.) These verses provide a subtle but certain assurance that the prophet-editor Mormon, like many of the ancient spiritual leaders, was anything but primitive in his understanding concerning God, man, and the universe.

17. This is precisely what would later happen to the city of Moronihah (see 3 Nephi 8:10).

18–19. See Helaman 13:18–23.

24. Grace for grace] "With divine assistance people are in a position to receive additional attributes and powers of the Spirit through repentance and subsequent faithfulness: they may receive what the scriptures speak of as 'grace for grace.' . . . To receive 'grace for grace' is to receive of the Father as we give to others. In this, as in all other enterprises in this life, Jesus Christ is our exemplar and our pattern." (Robert L. Millet, *By Grace Are We Saved*, p. 39; see also D&C 93:12–20.)

25. I would that all men might be saved] Such a blessing is available. It is indeed possible. No person came into this life incapable of gaining salvation. "We believe that through the Atonement of Christ, all mankind may be saved, by obedience to the laws and ordinances of the Gospel" (Articles of Faith 1:3).

Nephi's prayer was very similar to Mormon's: "And I pray the Father in the name of Christ that many of us, if not all, may be saved in his kingdom at that great and last day" (2 Nephi 33:12). At the same time, spiritual casualties are inevitable. The Prophet Joseph Smith explained: "The contention in heaven was—Jesus said there would be certain souls that would not be saved; and the devil said he could save them all" (*Teachings*, p. 357).

25. Who shall be cast off from the presence of the Lord] This is a broad classification, ranging from those who inherit the terrestrial and telestial kingdoms to the sons of perdition, those who inherit a kingdom of no glory and remain filthy forevermore. All these are cut off from the presence of the Father and, as revelation states concerning the candidates for the telestial glory, "they shall be servants of the Most High; but where God and Christ dwell they cannot come, worlds without end" (D&C 76:112).

26. Mormon is employing language—concerning the resurrection of life and the resurrection of damnation—reminiscent of that used in the Gospel of John (5:28–29). Either Jesus and Mormon were drawing upon the words of an earlier prophet or Mormon learned the same doctrine through an independent revelation from that same Lord.

26. Everlasting damnation] The phrase "everlasting life" describes more than a life that does not end; it is descriptive of the kind and quality of life enjoyed by the obedient and faithful, the life of exalted and glorified beings. Conversely, "everlasting damnation" is not properly understood to mean an endless stint in hell, but rather is descriptive of the kind of punishment—God's punishment—which will be meted out to the defiant (see D&C 19:4–12).

Samuel Predicts the Destruction of the Nephites

Helaman 13:1–9

1. And now it came to pass in the eighty and sixth year, the Nephites did still remain in wickedness, yea in great wickedness, while the Lamanites did observe strictly to keep the commandments of God, according to the law of Moses.

2. And it came to pass that in this year there was one Samuel, a Lamanite, came into the land of Zarahemla, and began to preach unto the people. And it came to pass that he did preach, many days, repentance unto the people, and they did cast him out, and he was about to return to his own land.

3. But behold, the voice of the Lord came unto him, that he should return again, and prophesy unto the people whatsoever things should come into his heart.

4. And it came to pass that they would not suffer that he should enter into the city; there-

fore he went and got upon the wall thereof, and stretched forth his hand and cried with a loud voice, and prophesied unto the people whatsoever things the Lord put into his heart.

5. And he said unto them: Behold, I, Samuel, a Lamanite, do speak the words of the Lord which he doth put into my heart; and behold he hath put it into my heart to say unto this people that the sword of justice hangeth over this people; and four hundred years pass not away save the sword of justice falleth upon this people.

6. Yea, heavy destruction awaiteth this people, and it surely cometh unto this people, and nothing can save this people save it be repentance and faith on the Lord Jesus Christ, who surely shall come into the world, and shall suffer many things and shall be slain for his people.

7. And behold, an angel of the Lord hath declared it unto me, and he did bring glad tidings to my soul. And behold, I was sent unto you to declare it unto you also, that ye might have glad tidings; but behold ye would not receive me.

8. Therefore, thus saith the Lord: Because of the hardness of the hearts of the people of the Nephites, except they repent I will take away my word from them, and I will withdraw my Spirit from them, and I will suffer them no longer, and I will turn the hearts of their brethren against them.

9. And four hundred years shall not pass away before I will cause that they shall be smitten; yea, I will visit them with the sword and with famine and with pestilence.

2. Samuel, a Lamanite] With Samuel the Lamanite, the Book of Mormon story takes a peculiar twist. So far as righteousness and wickedness were concerned, the Nephites and Lamanites had exchanged places. The Nephites were puffed up with pride, were full of vain boastings, envyings, strifes, and malice. They would persecute any who dared challenge their behavior and involved themselves in all manner of iniquity, not stopping short of murder. Indeed, they cast out, stoned, and killed the servants of God who were sent among them. At the same time they reverenced false teachers and prophets who flattered them in their vileness. In contrast, most of the Lamanites walked circumspectly before God, faithfully honoring their covenants. As the preceding verse notes, the Lamanites were strict to observe the law of Moses.

3. Whatsoever things should come into his heart] This phrase is an appropriate description of the spirit of revelation. The Lord told Oliver Cowdery that he would be told things in his mind and in his heart (D&C 8:2), while Joseph Smith and Sidney Rigdon were directed by the Lord to lift up their voices and "speak the thoughts that I shall put into your hearts." With this direction came the promise that they would not be confounded (see D&C 100:5). Such was the nature of the revelation Joseph Smith had that led him to the Sacred Grove. Describing the feelings that he experienced when he read James 1:5, he said: "Never did any passage of scripture come with more power *to the heart of man* than this did at this time to mine. It seemed to enter with great force into every feeling of my heart. I reflected on it again and again." (Joseph Smith—History 1:12, italics added.)

5. Nearly all the events prophesied by Samuel, as terrible and heartrending as they were, found fulfillment before the inspired historians of the Book of Mormon sealed up the record. The fact that such a great length of time would pass before all these judgments came upon them attests to God's great patience and longsuffering.

5. The sword of justice falleth upon this people] Alma, in speaking to his oldest son, Helaman, said: "I have somewhat to prophesy unto thee; but what I prophesy unto thee ye shall not make known; yea, what I prophesy unto thee shall not be made known, even until the prophecy is fulfilled; therefore write the words which I shall say. And these are the words: Behold, I perceive that this very people, the Nephites, according to the spirit of revelation which is in me, in four hundred years from the time that Jesus Christ shall manifest himself unto them, shall dwindle in unbelief. Yea, and then shall they see wars and pestilences, yea, famines and bloodshed, even until the people of Nephi shall become extinct." (Alma 45:9–11.)

6. As faith must be in Christ, so the remission of sins must be in him also. There is no other system by which a remission of sins can come.

6. Be slain for his people] The temple ritual symbolism of the shedding of the blood of the lamb without blemish was well known to the faithful of ancient times (see Moses 5:7; D&C 138:13–14).

7. An angel] Alma had prophesied some seventy-five years earlier that angels would declare the glad tidings of Christ's birth to just and holy men in the New World (see Alma 13:26).

7. Glad tidings] See Luke 2:10; Mosiah 3:3; Alma 13:22–23.

8. The wickedness and iniquities of the Nephites would cause the Spirit of the Lord to withdraw from them. With the loss of that Spirit would come the loss of his word, for that word can only be understood by the Spirit which they had so grievously offended.

9. The sword . . . famine . . . pestilence] War, famine, and pestilence—each represents a sermon from heaven delivered to gain the attention of those who have refused the whisperings of the Spirit and the voice of prophets.

Because of the Righteous the Wicked
Are Temporarily Spared

Helaman 13:10–14

10. Yea, I will visit them in my fierce anger, and there shall be those of the fourth generation who shall live, of your enemies, to behold your utter destruction; and this shall surely come except ye repent, saith the Lord; and those of the fourth generation shall visit your destruction.

11. But if ye will repent and return unto the Lord your God I will turn away mine anger, saith the Lord; yea, thus saith the Lord, blessed are they who will repent and turn unto me, but wo unto him that repenteth not.

12. Yea, wo unto this great city of Zarahemla; for behold, it is because of those who are righteous that it is saved; yea, wo unto this great city, for I perceive, saith the Lord, that there are many, yea, even the more part of this great city, that will harden their hearts against me, saith the Lord.

13. But blessed are they who will repent, for them will I spare. But behold, if it were not for the righteous who are in this great city, behold, I would cause that fire should come down out of heaven and destroy it.

14. But behold, it is for the righteous' sake that it is spared. But behold, the time cometh, saith the Lord, that when ye shall cast out the righteous from among you, then shall ye be ripe for destruction; yea, wo be unto this great city, because of the wickedness and abominations which are in her.

10–14. There are no private sins. All sin has the effect of weakening the fabric of society. Because of this, it is inevitable that the righteous will suffer because of the transgressions of others. Nevertheless the Lord goes to great lengths to protect and spare the righteous. The present verses undoubtedly recall to the reader's mind the account of Abraham bartering with the Lord over Sodom. "Wilt thou also destroy the righteous with the wicked," Abraham asked? "Peradventure there be fifty righteous within the city: wilt thou also destroy and not spare the place for the fifty righteous that are therein? That be far from thee to do after this manner, to slay the righteous with the wicked: and that the righteous should be as the wicked, that be far from thee: Shall not the Judge of all the earth do right?" So the Lord consented not to destroy Sodom if fifty righteous people could be found therein. Abraham asked again, What if there be but forty-five? And the Lord consented—if there were forty-five he would spare the city. What if there be but forty? Once more the Lord consented not to destroy the city. And what if there be but thirty? twen-

ty? or ten? Abraham asked, each in their turn. And to each the
Lord consented—he would spare the city if there were only ten
righteous people within it. As sin, be it public or private, weakens
the fabric of society, so all that is wholesome and good reaches out
to bless and even preserve it. (See Genesis 18:23–32; see also
Alma 10:22; 3 Nephi 9:11.)

The Earth Is Cursed to the Nephites

Helaman 13:15–23

15. Yea, and wo be unto the
city of Gideon, for the wickedness
and abominations which are in
her.

16. Yea, and wo be unto all the
cities which are in the land round
about, which are possessed by the
Nephites, because of the wickedness and abominations which are
in them.

17. And behold, a curse shall
come upon the land, saith the
Lord of Hosts, because of the people's sake who are upon the land,
yea, because of their wickedness
and their abominations.

18. And it shall come to pass,
saith the Lord of Hosts, yea, our
great and true God, that whoso
shall hide up treasures in the
earth shall find them again no
more, because of the great curse
of the land, save he be a righteous
man and shall hide it up unto the
Lord.

19. For I will, saith the Lord,
that they shall hide up their treasures unto me; and cursed be they
who hide not up their treasures
unto me; for none hideth up their
treasures unto me save it be the
righteous; and he that hideth not
up his treasures unto me, cursed
is he, and also the treasure, and
none shall redeem it because of
the curse of the land.

20. And the day shall come that
they shall hide up their treasures,
because they have set their hearts
upon riches; and because they
have set their hearts upon their
riches, and will hide up their treasures when they shall flee before
their enemies; because they will
not hide them up unto me, cursed
be they and also their treasures;
and in that day shall they be smitten, saith the Lord.

21. Behold ye, the people of this
great city, and hearken unto my
words; yea, hearken unto the
words which the Lord saith; for
behold, he saith that ye are cursed
because of your riches, and also
are your riches cursed because ye
have set your hearts upon them,
and have not hearkened unto the
words of him who gave them
unto you.

22. Ye do not remember the
Lord your God in the things with
which he hath blessed you, but ye
do always remember your riches,
not to thank the Lord your God
for them; yea, your hearts are not
drawn out unto the Lord, but
they do swell with great pride,
unto boasting, and unto great
swelling, envyings, strifes, malice,
persecutions, and murders, and all
manner of iniquities.

23. For this cause hath the Lord
God caused that a curse should
come upon the land, and also
upon your riches, and this
because of your iniquities.

15–23. Because the Nephites had become worshippers of worldly things and had made gold, silver, and other precious things the god to whom they bowed and to whom they rendered their praise and their offerings of homage, the true and living God threatened that a curse would come upon the land, causing their riches to vanish and their buried treasures to disappear, never to be found again (compare Mormon 1:18). On the other hand, the righteous, those who chose to serve the God of heaven, could safely hide up their treasures that had been consecrated for the benefit of his kingdom; they would be protected and could be brought forth when necessary.

21. Hearken unto my words . . . the words which the Lord saith] Samuel spoke by the power of the Holy Ghost and thus with what Nephi called "the tongue of angels." He spoke "the words of Christ" (2 Nephi 32:2–3). That is, he spoke what Christ wanted spoken, what the Master himself would have said had he been personally present. Samuel's was a divine investiture of authority; he, as the agent of God, spoke in behalf of his Principal. "What I the Lord have spoken, I have spoken," Christ declared in this dispensation, "and I excuse not myself; and though the heavens and the earth pass away, my word shall not pass away, but shall all be fulfilled, whether by mine own voice or by the voice of my servants, it is the same" (D&C 1:38). At the time of the organization of the restored Church, Christ spoke similarly: "Wherefore, meaning the church, thou shalt give heed unto all his [Joseph Smith's] words and commandments which he shall give unto you as he receiveth them, walking in all holiness before me; for his word ye shall receive, as if from mine own mouth, in all patience and faith" (D&C 21:4–5).

The World Reverences Dead Prophets While Rejecting Living Prophets

Helaman 13:24–29

24. Yea, wo unto this people, because of this time which has arrived, that ye do cast out the prophets, and do mock them, and cast stones at them, and do slay them, and do all manner of iniquity unto them, even as they did of old time.

25. And now when ye talk, ye say: If our days had been in the days of our fathers of old, we would not have slain the prophets; we would not have stoned them, and cast them out.

26. Behold ye are worse than they; for as the Lord liveth, if a prophet come among you and declareth unto you the word of the Lord, which testifieth of your sins and iniquities, ye are angry

with him, and cast him out and seek all manner of ways to destroy him; yea, you will say that he is a false prophet, and that he is a sinner, and of the devil, because he testifieth that your deeds are evil.

27. But behold, if a man shall come among you and shall say: Do this, and there is no iniquity; do that and ye shall not suffer; yea, he will say: Walk after the pride of your own hearts; yea, walk after the pride of your eyes, and do whatsoever your heart desireth—and if a man shall come among you and say this, ye will receive him, and say that he is a prophet.

28. Yea, ye will lift him up, and ye will give unto him of your substance; ye will give unto him of your gold, and of your silver, and ye will clothe him with costly apparel; and because he speaketh flattering words unto you, and he saith that all is well, then ye will not find fault with him.

29. O ye wicked and ye perverse generation; ye hardened and ye stiffnecked people, how long will ye suppose that the Lord will suffer you? Yea, how long will ye suffer yourselves to be led by foolish and blind guides? Yea, how long will ye choose darkness rather than light?

24–29. The world loves and honors its own, and living prophets have never been received by it. Christ promised the meridian Apostles that they would be hated of all nations for his name's sake and that they would be delivered up and killed (Joseph Smith—Matthew 1:7). Only when death has silenced the voice of a prophet does the world erect shrines in his honor. Similarly, it has been observed that many who eulogize George Washington or Abraham Lincoln would have been bitter opponents of these men had they lived in their day. Most who profess to reverence or worship Christ today do so very selectively, ignoring that which would have brought them into conflict with him had they been contemporaries.

To those who were about to crucify him, the Christ said: "Woe unto you, scribes and Pharisees, hypocrites! because ye build the tombs of the prophets, and garnish the sepulchres of the righteous, and say, If we had been in the days of our fathers, we would not have been partakers with them in the blood of the prophets. Wherefore ye be witnesses unto yourselves, that ye are the children of them which killed the prophets. Fill ye up then the measure of your fathers. Ye serpents, ye generation of vipers, how can ye escape the damnation of hell?" (Matthew 23:29–33.) Surely it cannot be without significance that the citizenry of hell includes those who rejected the prophet or prophets of their own age in the pretense of loyalty to prophets then dead (see D&C 76:99–101). For a discussion on why people reject prophets and how the prophets' claims should be evaluated, see Joseph Fielding McConkie and Robert L. Millet, *Sustaining and Defending the Faith,* chapter 5; see also Spencer W. Kimball, "Listen to the Prophets," *Ensign*, May 1978, p. 77.

24. Ye do cast out the prophets] We note with some interest that those in America—at the time of the destructions following the death of Christ—who had cast out the prophets and rejected their words were the ones destroyed. The "more righteous" among them, those who were spared and abode the day, were those who gave heed to the words of the oracles of God (see 2 Nephi 26:3; 3 Nephi 9:10; 10:12).

25. In the days of our fathers of old] See JST, Matthew 23:26–29.

26–27. False prophets say what the people want to hear. Their counsel is colored by their constituency, their warnings watered down by the demands of the audience. Paul warned of a day when wicked people would "not endure sound doctrine; but after their own lusts shall they heap to themselves" the kind of teachers and preachers and prophets who tickle the ears, false witnesses who crave acceptance and popularity more than righteousness (2 Timothy 4:3–4).

26. He is a sinner] "Cursed are all those that shall lift up the heel against mine anointed, saith the Lord, and cry they have sinned when they have not sinned before me, saith the Lord, but have done that which was meet in mine eyes, and which I commanded them. But those who cry transgression do it because they are the servants of sin and are the children of disobedience themselves." (D&C 121:16–17.)

28. He saith that all is well] See *Commentary* 1:338–39.

29. Led by foolish and blind guides] Each person is responsible for his or her own spiritual welfare. Though the Lord expects us to be loving and caring to others and especially to encourage those who are weak in the faith, no one of us can be blessed or blamed on the basis of someone else's faithfulness or waywardness. Nor will he who is the embodiment of truth and justice and judgment be patient everlastingly with those who trust their lives to "blind guides," to those who wander in the morass of uncertainty, who proceed with great confidence down the wide road to destruction, all in the name of discipleship.

A Day of Lamentation to Come to the Wicked

Helaman 13:30–39

30. Yea, behold, the anger of the Lord is already kindled against you; behold, he hath cursed the land because of your iniquity.

31. And behold, the time cometh that he curseth your rich-

es, that they become slippery, that ye cannot hold them; and in the days of your poverty ye cannot retain them.

32. And in the days of your poverty ye shall cry unto the Lord; and in vain shall ye cry, for your desolation is already come upon you, and your destruction is made sure; and then shall ye weep and howl in that day, saith the Lord of Hosts. And then shall ye lament, and say:

33. O that I had repented, and had not killed the prophets, and stoned them, and cast them out. Yea, in that day ye shall say: O that we had remembered the Lord our God in the day that he gave us our riches, and then they would not have become slippery that we should lose them; for behold, our riches are gone from us.

34. Behold, we lay a tool here and on the morrow it is gone; and behold, our swords are taken from us in the day we have sought them for battle.

35. Yea, we have hid up our treasures and they have slipped away from us, because of the curse of the land.

36. O that we had repented in

the day that the word of the Lord came unto us; for behold the land is cursed, and all things are become slippery, and we cannot hold them.

37. Behold, we are surrounded by demons, yea, we are encircled about by the angels of him who hath sought to destroy our souls. Behold, our iniquities are great. O Lord, canst thou not turn away thine anger from us? And this shall be your language in those days.

38. But behold, your days of probation are past; ye have procrastinated the day of your salvation until it is everlastingly too late, and your destruction is made sure; yea, for ye have sought all the days of your lives for that which ye could not obtain; and ye have sought for happiness in doing iniquity, which thing is contrary to the nature of that righteousness which is in our great and Eternal Head.

39. O ye people of the land, that ye would hear my words! And I pray that the anger of the Lord be turned away from you, and that ye would repent and be saved.

30–39. As the day will come when every corruptible thing upon the earth will be destroyed, so the day will come when every individual must account for that which he chose to do, as well as for that which he chose to leave undone. Those who chose to forget the Lord their God will have a bright recollection restored to them of all their forgetfulness.

31. Your riches . . . become slippery] James, the brother of our Lord, wrote: "Go to now, ye rich men, weep and howl for your miseries that shall come upon you. Your riches are corrupted, and your garments are motheaten. Your gold and silver is cankered; and the rust of them shall be a witness against you, and shall eat your flesh as it were fire. Ye have heaped treasure together for the last days." (James 5:1–3.) The Lord has said in our day: "Wo unto you rich men, that will not give your substance to the poor, for your riches will canker your souls; and this shall be your lamentation in the day of visitation, and of judgment, and of indignation: The harvest is past, the summer is ended, and my soul is not saved!" (D&C 56:16.)

32. Your destruction is made sure] After a person refuses to have faith in Christ and rejects Christ's offer to make him free from sin; after he spurns the ordinances of salvation and thus forsakes the only channel by which the powers of godliness might be enjoyed in his life; after he lives in such a way as to offend and grieve the Holy Spirit, the only true source of light and comfort in a troubled and sin-tangled world; after a person fails to humble himself before God, fails to partake of the bread of life and the living waters, fails to receive and abide by the word of the Almighty —after making these negative responses and remaining unrepentant, that person will find his calling and destruction made sure (compare *Teachings*, p. 150). His is the plight of the hopeless, the destiny of the doomed, the abode of the damned. Having chosen darkness, deceit, and degradation in this life, he will be rewarded with or have restored to him hereafter circumstances consistent with that choice. Where God and Christ and the faithful dwell such souls cannot come, worlds without end (see D&C 76:112).

37. We are surrounded by demons] See Mormon 2:10.

38. Your days of probation are past] See commentary on Alma 34:33. This life is a probationary estate, a time of testing, trying, and proving. Those who keep this their "second estate shall have glory added upon their heads for ever and ever" (Abraham 3:26). Those who use their mortal probation unwisely, having had what God judges to be a complete and fair chance to accept the gospel and the covenants of salvation, will not have that chance restored to them in the spirit world. Though they may accept the gospel there, to their everlasting benefit, they will have forfeited the chance for exaltation. Assuming they lead honorable lives in mortality, their promise is that of terrestrial glory (see D&C 76:73–75). Joseph Smith declared the doctrine poetically as follows:

> These are they that are hon'rable men of the earth;
> Who were blinded and dup'd by the cunning of men;
> They receiv'd not the truth of the Savior at first;
> But did, when they heard it in prison, again.
>
> Not valiant for truth, they obtain'd not the crown,
> But are of that glory that's typ'd by the moon:
> They are they, that come into the presence of Christ,
> But not to the fulness of God, on his throne.
> (In Lyndon W. Cook, *The Revelations of the Prophet Joseph Smith* [Salt Lake City: Deseret Book Co., 1985], p. 164.)

38. Procrastinated the day of your salvation until it is everlastingly too late] All tests must end. Mortality must end. The day of probation must end. There is that point at which every chance has been given and when the day of darkness has come—that day in which no labor can be performed. For those who have failed to repent before that dreadful day it may be said that they "have procrastinated the day of [their] salvation until it is everlastingly too late, and [their] destruction is made sure" (see Alma 34:32–35).

38. That which ye could not obtain] It is impossible to find happiness in doing evil. It cannot be done. It is a hopeless exercise to attempt it.

Signs Promised to Announce the Birth of Christ

Helaman 14:1–7

1. And now it came to pass that Samuel, the Lamanite, did prophesy a great many more things which cannot be written.

2. And behold, he said unto them: Behold, I give unto you a sign; for five years more cometh, and behold, then cometh the Son of God to redeem all those who shall believe on his name.

3. And behold, this will I give unto you for a sign at the time of his coming; for behold, there shall be great lights in heaven, insomuch that in the night before he cometh there shall be no darkness, insomuch that it shall appear unto man as if it was day.

4. Therefore, there shall be one day and a night and a day, as if it were one day and there were no night; and this shall be unto you for a sign; for ye shall know of the rising of the sun and also of its setting; therefore they shall know of a surety that there shall be two days and a night; nevertheless the night shall not be darkened; and it shall be the night before he is born.

5. And behold, there shall a new star arise, such an one as ye never have beheld; and this also shall be a sign unto you.

6. And behold this is not all, there shall be many signs and wonders in heaven.

7. And it shall come to pass that ye shall all be amazed, and wonder, insomuch that ye shall fall to the earth.

2–7. All things testify of Christ. At his birth the heavens resounded forth in magnificent splendor with all manner of signs and wonders. Here Samuel foretells a day without night following it, and a new star, along with the other signs and wonders, all of which would attest to the birth of the Prince of Light. How appropriate and typical—with the coming of the Light of Life into the world there would be no darkness!

2. This testimony of Samuel is perfect. It gives expression to three saving doctrines: first, that the promised Messiah is to be God's Son; second, that he is the Redeemer for all mankind; and third, that redemption comes only to those who take upon them his name. Each expression is an indispensable doctrine of salvation; each is a doctrine taught in great plainness in the Book of Mormon; and each is a doctrine whose true meaning has been lost to our modern world.

2. I give unto you a sign] See commentary on Helaman 9.

2. The Son of God] See commentary on 1 Nephi 11:18 and Alma 33.

2. To redeem] Redemption is made from the effects of Adam's fall. Adam's posterity are subject to both physical and spiritual death. The atonement of Christ brings an unconditional and universal victory over the physical death. All things that are subject to death are to be pardoned from its effects and granted an inseparable union of body and spirit. Victory over spiritual death, which is synonymous with exaltation or eternal life, becomes ours when we take upon ourselves the name of Christ and endure in faith to the end of our mortal probation.

2. Believe on his name] See verse 13.

5. There shall a new star arise] Our Lord's birth into mortality was accompanied by the appearance of "a new star" in the heavens. It is apparent that another prophet, or perhaps even a number of prophets in the Old World, had also prophesied of this sign, for when the wise men arrived in Jerusalem seeking the "Messiah of the Jews" they said, "We have seen his star in the east, and have come to worship him" (JST, Matthew 3:2). The statement seems to assume that the Jews of Jerusalem were aware that a new star would bear record of the holy birth, as at least the leaders were that the birth itself would take place in Bethlehem (Micah 5:2). After the wise men had been questioned by Herod, "the star, which they saw in the east, went before them, till it came and stood over where the young child was. When they saw the star, they rejoiced with exceeding great joy." (Matthew 2:9–10.)

There is no Old Testament prophecy on this aspect of the Savior's birth that is comparable to that of Samuel the Lamanite. The nearest allusion is found in the prophecy of Balaam, who, speaking of the Messiah himself, said: "There shall come a Star out of Jacob, and a Sceptre shall rise out of Israel" (Numbers 24:17). This prophecy obviously refers to the first coming of Christ but does not announce itself as indicating a sign of his birth. The only other related passage is in the book of Revelation, where Christ refers to himself as "the bright and morning star" (Revelation 22:16). The appearance of a star, or of a phenomenon of light accompanying the birth of one destined to a significant role in history, is a common motif in the literature of the ancient

Near East. Such legends are but the dim reflection of the lost prophecy of the star that was to announce the Messiah's birth.

Biblical prophecies contain a number of symbolic references to people as stars or planets. The seven stars represent angels or messengers of the seven churches of the book of Revelation (see Revelation 1:16, 20). Eleven stars stand for the brothers of Joseph, who did obeisance to him in his dream (see Genesis 37:9). At the battle between Barak and Sisera the stars are viewed as fighting against Sisera (see Judges 5:20), indicating that the heavens favored the Israelites. Stars also denoted rulers of earth (see Daniel 8:10; Revelation 6:13). When the "foundations of the earth" were laid and it had been announced that the spirit children of God could come and obtain bodies, "the morning stars sang together, and all the sons of God shouted for joy" (Job 38:4, 7). Those spirits that were cast out of heaven for rebellion against Christ in the pre-existent council are called stars (see Revelation 12:4), and, of course, before his fall Lucifer was a "bright morning star" (New English Bible, Isaiah 14:12). The innumerable stars are used as an indication of the extent of Abraham's posterity (see Genesis 15:5).

Believing on the Son of God

Helaman 14:8–13

8. And it shall come to pass that whosoever shall believe on the Son of God, the same shall have everlasting life.

9. And behold, thus hath the Lord commanded me, by his angel, that I should come and tell this thing unto you; yea, he hath commanded that I should prophesy these things unto you; yea, he hath said unto me: Cry unto this people, repent and prepare the way of the Lord.

10. And now, because I am a Lamanite, and have spoken unto you the words which the Lord hath commanded me, and because it was hard against you, ye are angry with me and do seek to destroy me, and have cast me out from among you.

11. And ye shall hear my words, for, for this intent have I come up upon the walls of this city, that ye might hear and know of the judgments of God which do await you because of your iniquities, and also that ye might know the conditions of repentance;

12. And also that ye might know of the coming of Jesus Christ, the Son of God, the Father of heaven and of earth, the Creator of all things from the beginning; and that ye might know of the signs of his coming, to the intent that ye might believe on his name.

13. And if ye believe on his name ye will repent of all your sins, that thereby ye may have a remission of them through his merits.

8. Believe on the Son of God] Elder Bruce R. McConkie wrote: "Belief brings salvation and belief brings damnation. Men are saved or damned, depending upon what they believe. If they believe in Christ and his saving truths, they are heirs of salvation. If they believe in a false system of salvation, they will be damned. It is one thing to worship the living Lord and quite another to worship dead deities that have been graven by art and man's device." (*New Witness*, p. 23.) It is one thing to accept Christ as our Savior and quite another to accept him as our Lord and Master. The former is to profess the acceptance of the blessings of salvation, the latter to assume the burdens of discipleship, of submitting ourselves to his guidance and Lordship. In the present text, salvation is inextricably woven into the acceptance of the doctrine of Christ's divine sonship.

11–12. Samuel here sets forth at least four dimensions to his prophetic call, four reasons why he has been sent to prophesy to the Nephites: (1) that the wicked Nephites might know of the judgments of God which should surely come upon the unrepentant; (2) that the Nephites might know the "conditions of repentance"; (3) that Samuel might testify of the divine sonship of Jesus Christ; and (4) that the Nephites might know of the signs of the Lord's coming to the earth.

12. Jesus Christ . . . Father of heaven and of earth] Christ is the Father of the faithful—the Father of all who are born again and take upon themselves his name. He is the Father in the sense that through his atoning sacrifice we are born into a newness of life and are born again in the resurrection as immortal and eternal beings. He is also the Father in the sense that he did the labor of creation—all things having been created by him. See *Commentary* 2:168–76, 225–30.

12. The Creator of all things from the beginning] Christ is "the light and the Redeemer of the world; the Spirit of truth, who came into the world, because the world was made by him, and in him was the life of men and the light of men. The worlds were made by him; men were made by him; all things were made by him, and through him, and of him." (D&C 93:9–10.) "By him, and through him, and of him, the worlds are and were created, and the inhabitants thereof are begotten sons and daughters unto God" (D&C 76:24).

13. Believe on his name] The thoughtful student of scripture must be aware that it is one thing to believe in Christ and quite another to "believe on his name." To believe in the name of Christ is here announced as embracing repentance from all our sins; whereas one may profess to believe in Christ and yet not have abandoned sin. There are certain prerequisites to believing on the name of Christ: First, the acceptance of Christ and the willingness to be a witness of him at all times and in all things and in all places (see Mosiah 18:9). Second, the acceptance of the gospel of Jesus Christ. This precludes the right to pick and choose, to sort out the doctrines that could bring inconvenience and social embarrassment. Third, the acceptance of those who have been commissioned to represent the Lord; that is, to sustain and uphold his anointed servants. And fourth, to sustain and be loyal to that Church upon which he has placed his name and within which is found the authority to perform the ordinances of salvation.

13. A remission of them through his merits] Strictly speaking, we do not gain a remission of sins through our own labors. Though we are required to have faith in Christ and come unto him through denying ourselves of all ungodliness, we are made clean through Christ's merits, through his works, through his atoning sacrifice. See commentary on Alma 22:14; see also 2 Nephi 2:3; 31:19; Moroni 6:4; D&C 45:3–5.

Christ Raises Man from Death

Helaman 14:14–19

14. And behold, again, another sign I give unto you, yea, a sign of his death.

15. For behold, he surely must die that salvation may come; yea, it behooveth him and becometh expedient that he dieth, to bring to pass the resurrection of the dead, that thereby men may be brought into the presence of the Lord.

16. Yea, behold, this death bringeth to pass the resurrection, and redeemeth all mankind from the first death—that spiritual death; for all mankind, by the fall of Adam being cut off from the presence of the Lord, are considered as dead, both as to things temporal and to things spiritual.

17. But behold, the resurrection of Christ redeemeth mankind, yea, even all mankind, and bringeth them back into the presence of the Lord.

18. Yea, and it bringeth to pass the condition of repentance, that whosoever repenteth the same is not hewn down and cast into the fire; but whosoever repenteth not is hewn down and cast into the fire; and there cometh upon them again a spiritual death, yea, a second death, for they are cut off again as to things pertaining to righteousness.

19. Therefore repent ye, repent ye, lest by knowing these things and not doing them ye shall suffer yourselves to come under condemnation, and ye are brought down unto this second death.

14–19. These verses are without peer in the Bible. The New Testament tells the story of *how* Christ suffered and died in the working out of an infinite and eternal sacrifice. Yet it is to such discourses as the one here delivered by Samuel that we must turn to learn *why* that suffering and death were necessary. Christ died that salvation might come. He died to bring to pass the resurrection of the dead. He died that all men might be redeemed from the effects of Adam's fall. He died that all men might enjoy the eternal union of body and spirit and that there might be a way whereby they could again attain—this time forever—the presence of that God who gave them life.

15. He surely must die that salvation may come] Our Lord's death was absolutely necessary. There was no other way. It was essential that he suffer and bleed and die. We are not saved because Jesus was a great speaker. We are not saved because his words are like manna to the starving soul. We are not saved because of his goodness and kindness, even his perfection. All of these things stand as guides, as illustrations of the kind of things we ought to do and be; Jesus was our exemplar. As Paul said, however, "If in this life only we have hope in Christ, we are of all men most miserable" (1 Corinthians 15:19). Our hope in Christ indeed stretches beyond this vale of tears, not alone because of his immaculate life but also because of the regeneration and redemption which come to us as a result of his death.

15–17. In a sense all men and women are redeemed by Christ from spiritual death—the separation from God—at least temporarily. One of the blessings of the Atonement is that following their resurrection all persons shall stand before the Holy One of Israel to be judged of the deeds done in the mortal body. Those who have sought to live in accordance with gospel law and thus have been quickened by a portion of the celestial glory shall receive a fulness of the same and thus be fitted and equipped to be with God everlastingly. Those, however, who have lived a terrestrial or telestial law, and thus are quickened by a portion of those respective glories, shall be quickened by a fulness of the same. These shall then be denied the presence of the Father forevermore. Even the sons of perdition, at least those who received a mortal body, shall stand before God and be judged. They shall be cast out into outer darkness to a kingdom of no glory (see D&C 88:29–32).

18. It bringeth to pass the condition of repentance] That is, Christ's death, the supreme illustration of mercy, makes repentance and forgiveness possible. "And thus mercy can satisfy the demands of justice, and encircles them in the arms of safety" (Alma 34:16).

18. A spiritual death, yea, a second death] To experience spiritual death in mortality is to be cut off from the presence of God or to be alienated from things of the Spirit, from things of righteousness (see Alma 12:16; 40:26; 42:9). Those who refuse to repent and comply with gospel law in this life shall be subject in life to come to what the scriptures call the second death, meaning the second spiritual death. Those who suffer this death are denied access to God the Father forever.

Signs That Will Announce Christ's Death

Helaman 14:20–29

20. But behold, as I said unto you concerning another sign, a sign of his death, behold, in that day that he shall suffer death the sun shall be darkened and refuse to give his light unto you; and also the moon and the stars; and there shall be no light upon the face of this land, even from the time that he shall suffer death, for the space of three days, to the time that he shall rise again from the dead.

21. Yea, at the time that he shall yield up the ghost there shall be thunderings and lightnings for the space of many hours, and the earth shall shake and tremble; and the rocks which are upon the face of this earth, which are both above the earth and beneath, which ye know at this time are solid, or the more part of it is one solid mass, shall be broken up;

22. Yea, they shall be rent in twain, and shall ever after be found in seams and in cracks, and in broken fragments upon the face of the whole earth, yea, both above the earth and beneath.

23. And behold, there shall be great tempests, and there shall be many mountains laid low, like unto a valley, and there shall be many places which are now called valleys which shall become mountains, whose height is great.

24. And many highways shall be broken up, and many cities shall become desolate.

25. And many graves shall be opened, and shall yield up many of their dead; and many saints shall appear unto many.

26. And behold, thus hath the angel spoken unto me; for he said unto me that there should be thunderings and lightnings for the space of many hours.

27. And he said unto me that while the thunder and the lightning lasted, and the tempest, that these things should be, and that darkness should cover the face of the whole earth for the space of three days.

28. And the angel said unto me that many shall see greater things than these, to the intent that they might believe that these signs and these wonders should come to pass upon all the face of this land, to the intent that there should be no cause for unbelief among the children of men—

29. And this to the intent that whosoever will believe might be saved, and that whosoever will not believe, a righteous judgment might come upon them; and also if they are condemned they bring upon themselves their own condemnation.

20–29. As the heavens rejoiced with signs and wonders to attest the birth of God's Son, so they lamented his death. From the time he gave up the ghost until the time that he rose again, the New World mourned in darkness. Thus for the space of three days there was no light on the face of the land. For a space of three hours thunder and lightning voiced anguish for Christ's suffering, while the earth shook and trembled. Rocks above and beneath the earth were rent, while mountains became valleys and valleys became mountains. See 3 Nephi 8.

25. Many graves shall be opened] This occurrence requires a brief comment. The rise of many Saints from the graves was not, strictly speaking, a sign of his death, but rather took place at the time of the Lord's resurrection. Following the resurrection of Christ, who was the first to break the bands of death, came the resurrection of "many" of the faithful Saints who had lived and died since the days of Adam. These, we are told, would "appear unto many," to whom they became apostles or special witnesses of the Resurrection. It stands to reason that these messengers of glory would choose first to visit their own progeny (see *Teachings,* pp. 295–96). The resurrection is the perfect and undeniable evidence that Jesus is indeed the Son of God and that he has, in reality, broken the bands of death.

A similar event took place in the Old World. Matthew tells us that at Jesus' death "the veil of the temple was rent in twain from the top to the bottom; and the earth did quake, and the rocks rent; and the graves were opened; and many bodies of the saints which slept arose, and came out of the graves after his resurrection, and went into the holy city, and appeared unto many" (Matthew 27:51–53). Following his resurrection, they came forth and made their calls on those worthy of their presence in the Holy City.

Some have been troubled by the question why both the Bible and the Book of Mormon say that *many* of the graves were opened and *many* of the Saints came forth, rather than saying that *all* the Saints were resurrected at this time. The answer to this question must involve the teaching of the gospel in the spirit world. While his body lay in the tomb, Christ visited the faithful spirits in prison, meaning those in the spirit world (see D&C 45:17; 138:50), and issued calls from among their number for them to commence the teaching of the gospel in the world of the spirits (see D&C 138:30–31). Thus it may be that among the righteous all received a call to labor as messengers of the Lord, some in the world of the spirits and the others among mortals. Those laboring among the spirits presumably were resurrected upon the completion of their mission in the spirit world.

27. Compare the prophecy of Zenos as in 1 Nephi 19:10.

Agency Is Granted to All

Helaman 14:30–31

30. And now remember, remember, my brethren, that whosoever perisheth, perisheth unto himself; and whosoever doeth iniquity, doeth it unto himself; for behold, ye are free; ye are permitted to act for yourselves; for behold, God hath given unto you a knowledge and he hath made you free.

31. He hath given unto you that ye might know good from evil, and he hath given unto you that ye might choose life or death; and ye can do good and be restored unto that which is good, or have that which is good restored unto you; or ye can do evil, and have that which is evil restored unto you.

30. Whosoever doeth iniquity, doeth it unto himself] All accountable souls are responsible for their own actions. Ultimately, everyone will stand exalted or condemned by their own choices. We may harm others with evil, but none more than ourselves. Again, we can bless others through our righteousness, but none more than ourselves. We are our choices, and thus, in the words of Alma, we are our own judges (see Alma 41:7).

30. For behold, ye are free] This freedom is not something inherent in man. It comes through the Atonement. Lehi taught: "The Messiah cometh in the fulness of time, that he may redeem the children of men from the fall. And *because that they are redeemed from the fall they have become free forever*, knowing good from evil; to act for themselves and not to be acted upon." (2 Nephi 2:26, italics added.) "Stand fast therefore in the liberty wherewith Christ hath made us free" (Galatians 5:1).

30. Ye are permitted to act for yourselves] This phrase is an expression of the doctrine of agency, though the word itself is not used in the Book of Mormon. No doubt the concept of agency, which is the ability and freedom to choose good or evil, is among the plain and precious things taken from the scriptural records that constitute our modern Bible. Agency is the gift of God freely granted to all people. Were there no agency, no power resting within man to choose, there could be no good nor evil, and justice and mercy would be unknown even to God.

31. For agency to exist, laws and opposites must exist, and a knowledge of the laws and a power of choice must be enjoyed by the agent, as with Samuel's hearers. All such people are free to choose who or what they will worship as their God.

31. He hath given unto you that ye might know good from evil] See Moroni 7:16; D&C 84:46–47.

31. Ye can do good and be restored unto that which is good] See Alma's discussion of the law of restoration, Alma 41.

God Chastens Those He Loves

Helaman 15:1–4

1. And now, my beloved brethren, behold, I declare unto you that except ye shall repent your houses shall be left unto you desolate.

2. Yea, except ye repent, your women shall have great cause to mourn in the day that they shall give suck; for ye shall attempt to flee and there shall be no place for refuge; yea, and wo unto them which are with child, for they shall be heavy and cannot flee; therefore, they shall be trodden down and shall be left to perish.

3. Yea, wo unto this people who are called the people of Nephi except they shall repent, when they shall see all these signs and wonders which shall be showed unto them; for behold, they have been a chosen people of the Lord; yea, the people of Nephi hath he loved, and also hath he chastened them; yea, in the days of their iniquities hath he chastened them because he loveth them.

4. But behold my brethren, the Lamanites hath he hated because their deeds have been evil continually, and this because of the iniquity of the tradition of their fathers. But behold, salvation hath come unto them through the preaching of the Nephites; and for this intent hath the Lord prolonged their days.

1–2. This is a warning similar to the one delivered by the Savior to the people in the Old World just prior to his death (see Joseph Smith—Matthew 1:2, 16).

3. Have been a chosen people] The fact that a people were once chosen of the Lord does not necessarily mean that they will always retain that designation. All blessings and birthrights can be forfeited. To be chosen is to have been called or designated as the Lord's servant. Those so grouped together during their mortal probation have more abundant opportunities than others to make and keep the covenants of salvation and to act as an ensign to the nations. Should they prove unworthy of that status, the Lord can release them from it just as he would any unworthy office holder in the Church. (See D&C 121:16–21.)

3. Chastened them because he loveth them] "As many as I love, I rebuke and chasten: be zealous therefore, and repent" (Revelation 3:19). As the circumstance dictates, chastening may include rebukes for misconduct or subjection to trials and afflictions.

4. The Lamanites hath he hated] This is strong language. One would assume that Samuel did not mean to convey the thought that God actually hated the Lamanites, at least not in the sense that mortal men hate one another. Rather, because of their rebellion, because they rejected the light and spurned the association with God through the Spirit that they might have enjoyed, they alienated themselves from the love of the Father. It is not that God does not love them, but that he simply is unable to bless them as he would those who choose the right. "If you keep not my commandments," a modern revelation attests, "the love of the Father shall not continue with you, therefore you shall walk in darkness" (D&C 95:12). In the same vein, John the Beloved wrote: "Whoso keepeth [God's] word, in him verily is the love of God perfected: hereby know we that we are in him. . . . Love not the world, neither the things that are in the world. If any man love the world, the love of the Father is not in him." (1 John 2:5, 15.)

4. The Lord prolonged their days] See commentary on Helaman 7:24.

Converted Lamanites Are True to the Faith

Helaman 15:5–10

5. And I would that ye should behold that the more part of them are in the path of their duty, and they do walk circumspectly before God, and they do observe to keep his commandments and his statutes and his judgments according to the law of Moses.

6. Yea, I say unto you, that the more part of them are doing this, and they are striving with unwearied diligence that they may bring the remainder of their brethren to the knowledge of the truth; therefore there are many who do add to their numbers daily.

7. And behold, ye do know of yourselves, for ye have witnessed it, that as many of them as are brought to the knowledge of the truth, and to know of the wicked and abominable traditions of their fathers, and are led to believe the holy scriptures, yea, the prophecies of the holy prophets, which are written, which leadeth them to faith on the Lord, and unto repentance, which faith and repentance bringeth a change of heart unto them—

8. Therefore, as many as have come to this, ye know of yourselves are firm and steadfast in the faith, and in the thing wherewith they have been made free.

9. And ye know also that they have buried their weapons of war, and they fear to take them up lest by any means they should sin; yea, ye can see that they fear to sin—for behold they will suffer themselves that they be trodden down and slain by their enemies, and will not lift their swords

against them, and this because of their faith in Christ.

10. And now, because of their steadfastness when they do believe in that thing which they do believe, for because of their firmness when they are once enlightened, behold, the Lord shall bless them and prolong their days, notwithstanding their iniquity—

6. Those who are truly converted feel a compulsion to share the blessings of the gospel with others, especially and particularly with those of their own family.

7. Faith comes by hearing the word of God as that word is preached or written by servants of God, a word always attended by the spirit of prophecy and revelation (see Romans 10:17; *Teachings*, p. 148). The scriptures have the power to motivate one to righteousness, to change one's heart, to serve a significant role in one's spiritual rebirth (see 2 Timothy 3:16; Alma 37:8).

7. Led to believe the holy scriptures] The conversion of the Lamanites was not social but spiritual. It was rooted in the spirit and testimony of the scriptures. Because it was well rooted, it would yield great blessings, even to generations yet unborn (see verses 11–17). President Ezra Taft Benson has warned that "social, ethical, cultural, or educational converts will not survive under the heat of the day unless their taproots go down to the fulness of the gospel which the Book of Mormon contains" (*A Witness and a Warning*, p. 6).

8. Firm and steadfast] See 2 Nephi 31:20; Mosiah 5:15. To be firm and steadfast is to be constant, consistent, and vigilant in one's faith and approach to living the gospel.

9–10. See commentary on Alma 23 and 24.

Latter-day Lamanites Blessed by the Faith of Their Fathers

Helaman 15:11–17

11. Yea, even if they should dwindle in unbelief the Lord shall prolong their days, until the time shall come which hath been spoken of by our fathers, and also by the prophet Zenos, and many other prophets, concerning the restoration of our brethren, the Lamanites, again to the knowledge of the truth—

12. Yea, I say unto you, that in the latter times the promises of the Lord have been extended to our brethren, the Lamanites; and notwithstanding the many afflictions which they shall have, and notwithstanding they shall be driven to and fro upon the face of the earth, and be hunted, and shall be smitten and scattered abroad, having no place for refuge, the Lord shall be merciful unto them.

13. And this is according to the

prophecy, that they shall again be brought to the true knowledge, which is the knowledge of their Redeemer, and their great and true shepherd, and be numbered among his sheep.

14. Therefore I say unto you, it shall be better for them than for you except ye repent.

15. For behold, had the mighty works been shown unto them which have been shown unto you, yea, unto them who have dwindled in unbelief because of the traditions of their fathers, ye can see of yourselves that they never would again have dwindled in unbelief.

16. Therefore, saith the Lord: I will not utterly destroy them, but I will cause that in the day of my wisdom they shall return again unto me, saith the Lord.

17. And now behold, saith the Lord, concerning the people of the Nephites: If they will not repent, and observe to do my will, I will utterly destroy them, saith the Lord, because of their unbelief notwithstanding the many mighty works which I have done among them; and as surely as the Lord liveth shall these things be, saith the Lord.

11–17. In that day when the Lamanites would again despise the Holy One of Israel, they, like their counterparts in the Old World, would be destined to become a hiss and a byword, a people who wander and perish in the flesh. Yet Zenos foresaw a day when Israel would no longer harden their hearts and would again be gathered to the covenant of salvation (see 1 Nephi 19:11–19). Also, according to the prophets the gospel was destined to come again to the Lamanites in the last days, notwithstanding that in the interim they would become "a dark, a filthy, and a loathsome people. . . . led about by Satan, even as chaff is driven before the wind, or as a vessel is tossed about upon the waves, without sail or anchor, or without anything wherewith to steer her; and even as she is, so are they. And behold, the Lord hath reserved their blessings, which they might have received in the land, for the Gentiles who shall possess the land. But behold, it shall come to pass that they shall be driven and scattered by the Gentiles; and after they have been driven and scattered by the Gentiles, behold, then will the Lord remember the covenant which he made unto Abraham and unto all the house of Israel. And also the Lord will remember the prayers of the righteous, which have been put up unto him for them." (Mormon 5:15–21.)

13. Be numbered among his sheep] On the matter of the latter-day gathering the Book of Mormon is both plain and repetitious. The gathering is always to the waters of baptism, where a covenant is made to take upon oneself the name of Christ. It always embraces "being numbered among his sheep," or being an active member of his Church.

16. This is the promise that the Lamanites will gather to the fold in the last days.

17. It is here prophesied that the Nephites will be utterly destroyed because of their wickedness.

The Conclusion of Samuel's Ministry Among the Nephites

Helaman 16:1–8

1. And now, it came to pass that there were many who heard the words of Samuel, the Lamanite, which he spake upon the walls of the city. And as many as believed on his word went forth and sought for Nephi; and when they had come forth and found him they confessed unto him their sins and denied not, desiring that they might be baptized unto the Lord.

2. But as many as there were who did not believe in the words of Samuel were angry with him; and they cast stones at him upon the wall, and also many shot arrows at him as he stood upon the wall; but the Spirit of the Lord was with him, insomuch that they could not hit him with their stones neither with their arrows.

3. Now when they saw that they could not hit him, there were many more who did believe on his words, insomuch that they went away unto Nephi to be baptized.

4. For behold, Nephi was baptizing, and prophesying, and preaching, crying repentance unto the people, showing signs and wonders, working miracles among the people, that they might know that the Christ must shortly come—

5. Telling them of things which must shortly come, that they might know and remember at the time of their coming that they had been made known unto them beforehand, to the intent that they might believe; therefore as many as believed on the words of Samuel went forth unto him to be baptized, for they came repenting and confessing their sins.

6. But the more part of them did not believe in the words of Samuel; therefore when they saw that they could not hit him with their stones and their arrows, they cried unto their captains, saying: Take this fellow and bind him, for behold he hath a devil; and because of the power of the devil which is in him we cannot hit him with our stones and our arrows; therefore take him and bind him, and away with him.

7. And as they went forth to lay their hands on him, behold, he did cast himself down from the wall, and did flee out of their lands, yea, even unto his own country, and began to preach and to prophesy among his own people.

8. And behold, he was never heard of more among the Nephites; and thus were the affairs of the people.

1. Confessed unto him their sins] "By this ye may know if a man repenteth of his sins—behold, he will confess them and forsake them" (D&C 58:43). Confession of sin involves two dimensions: disclosure of the deed(s), and covenant and commitment to Christ through the appointed priesthood leader (see Brent L. Top, *Though Your Sins Be As Scarlet,* chapter 4).

1. And denied not] To "deny not" is to be candid in the confession of sin and weakness. It is to be open and pliable to counsel, direction, and the promptings of the Spirit.

2. As the Spirit of the Lord brings peace and joy, so the spirit of the adversary is associated with anger and bitterness. Truth can give reasoned response to error, while wickedness acknowledges the weakness of its position by seeking the blood of those it makes its adversaries.

4. Nephi, the son of Helaman, was a man of great spiritual power. Signs, wonders, miracles, and prophecy were all common to his ministry. Nephi was presumably the local priesthood leader, and it would appear that those touched by the power of Samuel's message were sent to Nephi to receive the ordinances of salvation. This would be similar to a situation in which a nonmember attended a stake conference in which a visiting General Authority was present. If the investigator were to be moved by the message of the authority, he or she would be encouraged to be further taught by the missionaries and then to receive baptism at the hands of local legal administrators.

6–8. A very early testimony of God's protective hand was provided by Nephi, son of Lehi. "I, Nephi, will show unto you that the tender mercies of the Lord are over all those whom he hath chosen, because of their faith, to make them mighty even unto the power of deliverance" (1 Nephi 1:20). Such a promise is always contingent upon the will of the Omniscient One in individual cases.

Trusting in Human Reason Alone Leads to Destruction

Helaman 16:9–25

9. And thus ended the eighty and sixth year of the reign of the judges over the people of Nephi.

10. And thus ended also the eighty and seventh year of the reign of the judges, the more part of the people remaining in their pride and wickedness, and the lesser part walking more circumspectly before God.

11. And these were the conditions also, in the eighty and eighth year of the reign of the judges.

12. And there was but little alteration in the affairs of the people, save it were the people began to be more hardened in iniquity, and do more and more of that which was contrary to the commandments of God, in the eighty and ninth year of the reign of the judges.

13. But it came to pass in the

ninetieth year of the reign of the judges, there were great signs given unto the people, and wonders; and the words of the prophets began to be fulfilled.

14. And angels did appear unto men, wise men, and did declare unto them glad tidings of great joy; thus in this year the scriptures began to be fulfilled.

15. Nevertheless, the people began to harden their hearts, all save it were the most believing part of them, both of the Nephites and also of the Lamanites, and began to depend upon their own strength and upon their own wisdom, saying:

16. Some things they may have guessed right, among so many; but behold, we know that all these great and marvelous works cannot come to pass, of which has been spoken.

17. And they began to reason and to contend among themselves, saying:

18. That it is not reasonable that such a being as a Christ shall come; if so, and he be the Son of God, the Father of heaven and of earth, as it has been spoken, why will he not show himself unto us as well as unto them who shall be at Jerusalem?

19. Yea, why will he not show himself in this land as well as in the land of Jerusalem?

20. But behold, we know that this is a wicked tradition, which has been handed down unto us by our fathers, to cause us that we should believe in some great and marvelous thing which should

come to pass, but not among us, but in a land which is far distant, a land which we know not; therefore they can keep us in ignorance, for we cannot witness with our own eyes that they are true.

21. And they will, by the cunning and the mysterious arts of the evil one, work some great mystery which we cannot understand, which will keep us down to be servants to their words, and also servants unto them, for we depend upon them to teach us the word; and thus will they keep us in ignorance if we will yield ourselves unto them, all the days of our lives.

22. And many more things did the people imagine up in their hearts, which were foolish and vain; and they were much disturbed, for Satan did stir them up to do iniquity continually; yea, he did go about spreading rumors and contentions upon all the face of the land, that he might harden the hearts of the people against that which was good and against that which should come.

23. And notwithstanding the signs and the wonders which were wrought among the people of the Lord, and the many miracles which they did, Satan did get great hold upon the hearts of the people upon all the face of the land.

24. And thus ended the ninetieth year of the reign of the judges over the people of Nephi.

25. And thus ended the book of Helaman, according to the record of Helaman and his sons.

10. The lesser part walking more circumspectly before God] "Enter ye in at the strait gate," the Master implored; "for wide is the gate, and broad is the way, which leadeth to destruction, and many there be who go in thereat; because strait is the gate, and narrow is the way, which leadeth unto life, and *few there be that find it*" (3 Nephi 14:13–14, italics added).

12–14. How interesting it is that two people can sit side by side in the temple and one see angels while the other is offended by the ritual. So it is in the society of which we are all a part—some find reason and opportunity to harden themselves in iniquity, while others, who breathe the same air and struggle with the same problems, find occasion to do great good and have the attendant opportunity to entertain angels.

15–18. The gospel cannot answer the demands of human reason as imposed upon it by unbelievers. Surely, for instance, the doctrine of resurrection defies such reason. No scientific experience or theory can sustain the testimony of Job that after skin worms had destroyed his body, in the flesh he would see God (see Job 19:25). Nor is it "reasonable" to suppose that Christ could return in the clouds of heaven, bring great hosts with him, and call forth the righteous from the graves and the holy upon the earth to come forth to meet him in the air. Earth-bound principles do not reach to heaven. God's knowledge, wisdom, and power far exceed man's. (See Isaiah 55:8–9.)

19. This shows the relationship between rebellion and misunderstanding. Indeed, the prophecies were direct and forthright to the effect that Jesus Christ would show himself to the Nephites. Mormon described a people who "because of their unbelief . . . could not understand the word of God" (Mosiah 26:3).

20–21. Compare the rationalizations of Laman and Lemuel in 1 Nephi 16:38.

22. Satan . . . did go about spreading rumors and contentions] There is a quiet dignity about one who has been born of God, while on the other hand there is an overwhelming urge among the impure to sow discord and kindle discontent.

End of Volume III

Bibliography

Ballard, M. Russell. "Small and Simple Things." *Ensign*. Salt Lake City: The Church of Jesus Christ of Latter-day Saints, May 1990, pp. 5–8.

Ballard, Melvin J. "The Three Degrees of Glory." Sermon delivered on September 22, 1922, at Ogden, Utah.

Benson, Ezra Taft. *Come Unto Christ*. Salt Lake City: Deseret Book Co., 1983.

————. "A Mighty Change of Heart." *Ensign*. Salt Lake City: The Church of Jesus Christ of Latter-day Saints, October 1989, pp. 2–5.

————. "What I Hope You Will Teach Your Children About the Temple." *Ensign*. Salt Lake City: The Church of Jesus Christ of Latter-day Saints, August 1985, pp. 6–10.

————. *A Witness and a Warning*. Salt Lake City: Deseret Book Co., 1988.

Cannon, George Q. *Gospel Truth*. Salt Lake City: Deseret Book Co., 1987.

Clarke, Adam. *Clarke's New Testament Commentary*. 6 vols. Nashville: Abingdon, 1977.

Conference Report. Salt Lake City: The Church of Jesus Christ of Latter-day Saints, April 1929; April 1957; April 1970; October 1973; Samoa Area Conference, February 1976; Temple View Area Conference, February 1976; April 1977; October 1977; April 1978; October 1986; April 1989; October 1989; April 1990; October 1990.

Hafen, Bruce. *The Broken Heart*. Salt Lake City: Deseret Book Co., 1989.

Hymns of The Church of Jesus Christ of Latter-day Saints. Salt Lake City: Corporation of the President of The Church of Jesus Christ of Latter-day Saints, 1985.

Improvement Era. Salt Lake City: The Church of Jesus Christ of Latter-day Saints, vol. 20, 1917.

International Standard Bible Encyclopedia, ed. Geoffrey W. Bromiley. 4 vols. Grand Rapids: W. B. Eerdmans, 1979.

The Interpreter's Bible, ed. George Arthur Buttrick. 12 vols. New York: Abingdon-Cokesbury Press, 1951–57.

Journal of Discourses. 26 vols. Liverpool: F. D. Richards and Sons, 1851–86.

Juvenile Instructor. Salt Lake City: The Church of Jesus Christ of Latter-day Saints, vol. xxvii, 1892.

Kimball, Spencer W. "Listen to the Prophets." *Ensign.* Salt Lake City: The Church of Jesus Christ of Latter-day Saints, May 1978, pp. 76–78.

Larsen, Dean L. "Beware Lest Thou Forget the Lord." *Ensign.* Salt Lake City: The Church of Jesus Christ of Latter-day Saints, May 1991, pp. 10–12.

Lewis, C. S. *Mere Christianity.* New York: Macmillan, 1952.

Lund, Gerald N. *Jesus Christ, Key to the Plan of Salvation.* Salt Lake City: Deseret Book Co., 1991.

Maxwell, Neal A. *Even As I Am.* Salt Lake City: Deseret Book Co., 1982.

McConkie, Bruce R. "Christ and the Creation." *Ensign.* Salt Lake City: The Church of Jesus Christ of Latter-day Saints, June 1982, pp. 9–15.

———. *Doctrinal New Testament Commentary.* 3 vols. Salt Lake City: Bookcraft, 1965–73.

———. "The Doctrinal Restoration." *The Joseph Smith Translation: The Restoration of Plain and Precious Things,* eds. Monte S. Nyman and Robert L. Millet. Provo, Utah: Religious Studies Center, Brigham Young University, 1985.

———. *The Millennial Messiah.* Salt Lake City: Deseret Book Co., 1982.

———. *Mormon Doctrine,* 2nd. ed. Salt Lake City: Bookcraft, 1966.

———. *The Mortal Messiah.* 4 vols. Salt Lake City: Deseret Book Co., 1979–81.

———. *A New Witness for the Articles of Faith.* Salt Lake City: Deseret Book Co., 1985.

———. "The Parable of the Unwise Builder." Regional Representatives Seminar, April 3, 1981; cited by Mark L. McConkie, ed., in *Doctrines of the Restoration* (Salt Lake City: Bookcraft, 1989).

———. *The Promised Messiah.* Salt Lake City: Deseret Book Co., 1978.

McConkie, Joseph Fielding and Robert L. Millet. *Doctrinal Commentary on the Book of Mormon.* 4 vols. Salt Lake City: Bookcraft, 1987–92.

———. and Robert L. Millet. *The Holy Ghost.* Salt Lake City: Bookcraft, 1989.

———. and Robert L. Millet. *Sustaining and Defending the Faith.* Salt Lake City: Bookcraft, 1985.

Messenger and Advocate. Kirtland, Ohio: The Church of Jesus Christ of Latter-day Saints, 1834–35.

Millet, Robert L. *An Eye Single to the Glory of God*. Salt Lake City: Deseret Book Co., 1991.

———. *By Grace Are We Saved*. Salt Lake City: Bookcraft, 1989.

———. *Life In Christ*. Salt Lake City: Bookcraft, 1990.

———. and Joseph Fielding McConkie. *In His Holy Name*. Salt Lake City: Bookcraft, 1988.

———. and Joseph Fielding McConkie, *The Life Beyond*. Salt Lake City: Bookcraft, 1986.

The New English Bible, 2nd ed. Oxford: Oxford University Press, 1970.

Nibley, Hugh W. *An Approach to the Book of Mormon*. Salt Lake City: Deseret Book Co., 1964.

———. *Since Cumorah*. Salt Lake City: Deseret Book Co., 1967.

Oaks, Dallin H. *Pure in Heart*. Salt Lake City: Bookcraft, 1988.

Origen. *Contra Celsum*. 5 vols. Paris: Editions du Cerf, 1967–76.

Packer, Boyd K. "Follow the Brethren." *1965 Brigham Young University Speeches of the Year*. Provo, Utah: Brigham Young University Publications, 1965.

Pratt, Orson. "The True Faith," *A Series of Pamphlets*. Liverpool, England: Franklin D. Richards, 1852.

Roberts, B. H. *The Life of John Taylor*. Salt Lake City: Bookcraft, 1963.

Smith, George Albert. *Sharing the Gospel with Others*. Salt Lake City: Deseret Book Co., 1948.

Smith, Joseph F. *Gospel Doctrine*. Salt Lake City: Deseret Book Co., 1971.

———. Editorial on the Resurrection. *Improvement Era*. Salt Lake City: The Church of Jesus Christ of Latter-day Saints, June 1904; cited in *Teachings of the Prophet Joseph Smith* (Salt Lake City: Deseret Book Co., 1976).

Smith, Joseph Fielding. *Answers to Gospel Questions*. 5 vols. Salt Lake City: Deseret Book Co., 1957–66.

———. *Doctrines of Salvation*. 3 vols. Comp. Bruce R. McConkie. Salt Lake City: Bookcraft, 1954–56.

Smith, Joseph, Jr. *History of The Church of Jesus Christ of Latter-day Saints*, ed. B. H. Roberts. 7 vols. Salt Lake City: The Church of Jesus Christ of Latter-day Saints, 1932–51.

———. *Lectures on Faith*. Salt Lake City: Deseret Book Co., 1985.

———. *Teachings of the Prophet Joseph Smith*. Comp. Joseph Fielding Smith. Salt Lake City: Deseret Book Co., 1976.

Smith, Lucy Mack, *History of Joseph Smith by His Mother*. Salt Lake City: Bookcraft, 1958.

A Sure Foundation: Answers to Difficult Gospel Questions. Salt Lake City: Deseret Book Co., 1988.

Times and Seasons. 6 vols. Nauvoo, Illinois: The Church of Jesus Christ of Latter-day Saints, 1839–46.

Top, Brent L. *Though Your Sins Be As Scarlet*. Salt Lake City: Book-
    craft, 1989.
Wells, Matthew G. and John W. Welch. "Concrete Evidence for
    the Book of Mormon." *Insights*. Provo, Utah: Foundation for
    Ancient Research and Mormon Studies, May 1991.

Subject Index

yielding to God, 344
Heaven, treasures in, 353, 378, 403
Heavenly Father, 30, 65, 79, 103
    literal father of Christ, 51, 241–43
    love of, 11, 418
    Man of Holiness, 141
    name of, 37
    presence of, 413
    See also Elohim; God
Hedonism, 213
Helam, land of, 151
Helaman (son of Alma), 266–72,
    276–78, 288, 292
Helaman (son of Helaman), 337, 341,
    353, 355
    stripling warriors of, 324
Hell, 7, 17, 27, 42, 86, 179, 214,
    299–300, 369, 404
Hezekiah, 383
High priests, 26, 96
History, 26
Holy Ghost, 51, 56, 80, 84, 88, 122,
    235, 247
    baptism of fire and, 99, 359
    Comforter, 23, 40, 117, 136, 220
    companionship of, 181, 268
    contending against, 258
    conversion through, 156
    gift of, 84, 86, 90, 99, 105, 353,
        362
    grieving of, 407
    guidance of, 318, 355
    inspiration of, 343
    joy in presence of, 188
    knowledge through, 285
    prayers motivated by, 385
    sanctifier, 99
    sin against, 148, 289–91
    sins burned out by, 53
    speaking by power of, 9, 40, 75,
        125, 144, 165, 194, 215, 355,
        403
    still voice of perfect mildness, 358
    teaching by power of, 24, 287
    withdrawal of, 53, 257
Home, 324, 325, 335
Home teachers, 273
Hope, 159–60, 235, 245
Humanism, 4, 204
Humility, 7, 20, 21, 26, 28, 32, 33, 49,
    56, 106, 114, 222–25, 255
Hunger, 11
Hyde, Orson, 40–41

Hypocrisy, 35, 72, 229, 237, 254, 372

— I —

Idleness, 165, 229, 287
Idolatry, 215, 260, 395, 403
Immortality, 23, 88, 89, 184
Independence, Missouri, temple in,
    249
Inspiration, 154, 238, 253, 343
    See also Holy Ghost
Interpreters, 278
Isaac, 94, 305
Isabel (harlot), 288
Isaiah, 158, 180, 376, 382, 383,
    394–95
Islands of the sea, 328–29
Israel, children of, 91, 93, 229, 371
    gathering of, 369, 420
    lost tribes of, 184
    scattering of, 329

— J —

Jackson County, Missouri, temple at,
    249
Jacob (Old Testament patriarch), 94
Jacob (son of Lehi), 313
    keys held by, 387
    on arousing faculties, 234
    on Christ, 243
    on death, 88
    on guilt, 30–31
    on repentance, 369
    on returning to God in sins, 256,
        258
    on wasting probation, 255
James, on hiding multitude of sins,
    378
    on prayer, 221
    on riches, 406
    on service, 98
Jaredites, 277–78, 324, 365–66
    record of, 277–78, 366
Jeremiah, 140
Jershon, land of, 189
Jerusalem (Old World city), 51, 388
    temple at, 120
Jerusalem (Lamanite city), 151
Jesus Christ, 33, 87, 189, 391
    advancement from grace to grace,
        96, 234
    all things testify of, 377–78, 408

on liberty, 187
warning of, 351
Mosiah, sons of, 1, 59, 124, 149, 165,
    182–83, 192, 194
Mothers, 268, 324
Mount of Transfiguration, 386
Mountains, 388
Mourning, 192
Mulek, 377
Mulekites, 377
    on lineage of Judah, 21
Muloki, 146
Murder, 5, 14, 33, 148, 167–68, 277,
    289–90, 333, 337, 365, 399
Music, 26–27, 177
Mysteries of God, 82–85, 91, 295
Mysteries of the kingdom, 97, 107,
    232

— N —

Names, 165, 353
Natural man, 66, 84, 181, 203–4, 247,
    269, 308
Nehor, 4–5, 14, 111, 113–14, 151–52,
    204, 333
Nehors, desolation of, 119
Nelson, Russell M., on contention, 348
Nephi (son of Lehi), 165, 217–18, 272,
    281
    keys held by, 387
    on being past feeling, 236
    on last days, 367–68
    on priestcraft, 3
    on redemption from sins, 76
    on robe of righteousness, 31
    on salvation by grace, 158
    on salvation free to all, 307
    on speaking plainly, 39
    on worldliness, 11–12
    visions of, 197, 242, 267
    warning of, 4
Nephi (son of Helaman), 10, 365, 331,
    350, 351, 358–59, 422
    prayer of, 397–98
    prophecies of, 378–79
    sealing power granted to, 384–86
    testimony sealed, 371
Nephihah (chief judge), 23, 272, 324
Nephites, apostasy of, 361, 370
    Church among, 57, 163
    covenant people in promised land,
    185–86

destruction of, prophesied, 421
funeral custom of, 192
laws of, 202
loss of spiritual strength, 366
of lineage of Joseph, 21
priesthood among, 101, 117
records of, 65, 340
scriptures among, 41, 109, 157,
    240, 272
temples among, 387
weights and measures of, 73
wickedness of, 399
worship among, 121
Neum, 240, 272
New and everlasting covenant of
    marriage, 40, 94, 371
New Testament, 412
New Zealand, 329
Nihilism, 205, 213
Noah (Old Testament prophet),
    foreordination of, 94
    testified of Christ, 376
Noah (Nephite king), 65, 174
    priests of, 110, 150, 174, 295

— O —

Oaks, Dallin H., on clean hands and
    pure hearts, 31
    on desires, 196, 305
Oaths, 69, 323, 324
Obedience, 88, 102, 141, 185, 194,
    200, 230, 307, 317, 353
    absolute, required by God, 262
    blind, 203
Oneness, 10
Oppression, of the poor, 346
Order, 40, 41, 47
Ordinances, 40, 47, 60, 91, 95, 102,
    157, 194, 199, 217, 227, 249,
    353, 412, 422
    administered by Church, 3, 160,
    163, 192
    among Nephites, 387
    centered on Atonement, 294
    form of worship, 225
    in name of Christ, 142
    paradise entered through, 299–300
    sacred, 84
    spurning of, 407
    temple, 37
    types of Christ, 102, 250
Ordinations, 40, 47, 96–98, 116

Scripture Index

NEW TESTAMENT

3:2 (JST)	33, 409	9:62	130
3:10	43	10:20	45
3:11	99, 359	12:13–21	378
3:25 (JST)	86	12:41–44 (JST)	105
4:3–4	113	12:48	65, 371
4:5	113, 388	13:1–5	15
4:6	113	16:29–31	152
4:8	388	20:1	161
4:17	33	22:44	369
4:19	384	23:29	298
4:23	26, 161	23:30	86, 298
5:16	292	23:31–43	298
5:44	336		
6:19	378	**John**	
6:20	353, 378	1:42 (JST)	278
6:21	378	3:3	82
6:25–34	221	3:14	242, 283, 375
6:38 (JST)	293		
7:9–11	84	3:15	242
7:24–27	355	5:22	79, 306
7:29	287	5:28–29	398
9:5 (JST)	115	5:30	103
10:7	33	5:43	37
11:28–30	244	6:47–50	35
12:25–27 (JST)	291	6:53	35
12:39	213	6:54 (JST)	35, 177
12:43–45	300	6:55–56	35
13:5–6	238	7:17	234
13:10–13	84	7:18	287
13:15	236	8:29	385
13:44	353	8:44	38, 366
14:22–32	283	8:56	376
16:19	386	9:1–3	115
16:25–26 (JST)	292	10:10	283
17:3	386	10:14	36
19:16–22	159	10:17	52
19:28	306	10:18	52, 374
20:1–16	298	10:25	37
23:26–29 (JST)	405	12:28	37
23:29–33	404	14:6	286
25:40	11	14:26	24
27:51–53	415	14:27	56, 344, 359
Mark		15:1, 5	122
6:1–5	59	17:17	141, 169
16:17–18	382	17:18–19	169
		20:23	386
Luke			
1:20, 62–63	211	**Acts**	
2:10	354, 400	3:4	283
2:12	383	3:19–21	290
2:17	105	4:12	36, 285
3:5–7 (JST)	105	5:3–4	82
3:9	43	5:11	213
3:10	397	5:29–31	107
3:16	99	6:15	358
5:23 (JST)	115	8:39	388

BOOK OF MORMON

DOCTRINE AND COVENANTS

PEARL OF GREAT PRICE